Reports of Cases in the Court of Chancery From 1660 to 1673

English Law Reports of the Early Modern Period

Volume One: *Equity Cases in the Court of Exchequer, 1660–1714*, Edited by W. H. Bryson, 2007. [This volume can be cited as Eq. Cases Exch.]

Volume Two: *Robert Paynell's Exchequer Reports (1627–1631),* Edited by W. H. Bryson, 2009. [This volume can be cited as Paynell Exch.]

Volume Three: *Robert Paynell's King's Bench Reports (1625–1627),* Edited by W. H. Bryson, 2010. [This volume can be cited as Paynell K.B.]

Volume Four: *Reports of Cases in the Court of Exchequer in the Time of King George I (1714–1727),* Edited by W. H. Bryson, 2013. [This volume can be cited as Exch. Cases *temp.* Geo. I.]

Volume Five: *Reports of Cases in the Court of Exchequer in the Time of King Charles II,* Edited by W. H. Bryson, 2017. [This volume can be cited as Exch. Cases *temp.* Char. II.]

Volume Six: *Reports of Cases in the Court of Chancery in the Time of King George I,* Edited by W. H. Bryson, 2019. [This volume can be cited as Chan. Cases *temp.* Geo. I.]

Volume Seven: *Paul Jodrell's Chancery Reports (1737 to 1751),* Edited by W. H. Bryson, 2020. [This volume can be cited as Jodrell.]

Volume Eight: *Reports of Cases in the Court of Chancery in the Time of Queen Anne,* Edited by W. H. Bryson, 2021. [This volume can be cited as Chan. Cases *temp.* Anne.]

Medieval and Renaissance
Texts and Studies

Volume 583

Center for Law Reporting

Volume 9

Reports of Cases in the Court of Chancery from 1660 to 1673

EDITED BY

W. H. BRYSON

Arizona Center
for Medieval &
Renaissance Studies
Tempe, Arizona
2022

Arizona Center
for Medieval &
Renaissance Studies

Published by ACMRS (Arizona Center for Medieval and Renaissance Studies)
Tempe, Arizona

ISBN 978-0-86698-643-4

Library of Congress Cataloging-in-Publication Data

Names: England and Wales. Court of Chancery, issuing body. | Bryson, William Hamilton, 1941- editor.
Title: Reports of cases in the Court of Chancery from 1660 to 1673 / edited by W. H. Bryson.
Description: Tempe, Arizona : Arizona Center for Medieval and Renaissance Studies, [2022]. | Series: Medieval and renaissance texts and studies ; volume 583 | Summary: "A comprehensive collection of all known Chancery reports in this time period"-- Provided by publisher.
Identifiers: LCCN 2022037028 | ISBN 9780866986434 (cloth)
Subjects: LCSH: Law reports, digests, etc.--England. | Equity--England--Cases. | LCGFT: Court decisions and opinions.
Classification: LCC KD232.5 .B794 2022 | DDC 346.42/00409033--dc23/eng/20221101
LC record available at https://lccn.loc.gov/2022037028

∞
This book is set in Adobe Caslon Pro.
Printed in the United States of America.

Introduction

The Chancery reports included in this collection date from the judicial tenures in that court of Sir Edward Hyde, earl of Clarendon (1609-1674), Sir Orlando Bridgeman (1606-1674), and Sir Anthony Ashley Cooper, earl of Shaftesbury (1621-1683).

Sir Edward Hyde is primarily remembered as a politician and historian of England during the Interregnum and the Restoration of the Stuarts in the middle third of the seventeenth century. Also, there was the completely unforeseen quirk of history that made him *post mortem* the grandfather of two queens regnant of England, Mary II and Anne.

He was, in his younger years, a successful lawyer, and, then, after the Restoration in 1660, he was made the Lord Chancellor and earl of Clarendon. Thus, he sat as an equity judge in the Court of Chancery from 1660 until his political downfall in 1667. He lived in exile in France from 1667 until his death in 1674. He was a thoroughly competent and well respected judge.

Bridgeman had an excellent legal mind. Before becoming Lord Keeper of the Great Seal, he was the Chief Justice of the Court of Common Pleas. He sat in the Court of Chancery from 1667 to 1672.

When the earl of Clarendon was the Lord Chancellor, from 1660 to 1667, he regularly had as judicial assistants judges from the high courts of common law to sit with him in his Court of Chancery, and the Chief Justice of the Court of Common Pleas, Sir Orlando Bridgeman, frequently sat next to him in that capacity. Later, Bridgeman also regularly requested the common law judges to assist him in the Court of Chancery. It is interesting to note that one of the best common law judges, when he became an equity judge, felt the need to have assistant judges. This shows that equity and common law were not and are not rivals as to the substantive law.

Bridgeman was succeeded in the Court of Chancery by the Earl of Shaftesbury on 17 November 1672. Shaftesbury had been admitted to Lincoln's Inn, but he was never called to the bar; in fact, he was the last Lord Chancellor not to have been a practicing lawyer. He was, however, Chancellor of Exchequer from 1661 to 1672, but it is not known whether he ever sat as a judge in the Court of Exchequer. He was the son-in-law of the famous Chancery judge, Lord Coventry, his first wife being Margaret Coventry. Shaftesbury was removed from his position as Lord Chancellor for political reasons on 9 November 1673, to be succeeded by Sir Heneage Finch, later earl of Nottingham (1621-1682).

As was the long standing and, indeed, medieval custom, of the Court of Chancery, Lord Clarendon regularly called to his assistance the justices of the common law courts. Sir Matthew Hale (1609-1676), who was at this point of his distinguished career Chief Baron of the Court of Exchequer, frequently sat in the Court of Chancery at this time, and some of this more famous judge's opinions are published here along with the Chancellor's.

Lord Nottingham (1621-1682) reported in his *Prolegomena of Chancery and Equity* many Chancery cases from 1660 until his appointment to the Chancery bench in 1673. They are included here, and are thus added to the canon of Chancery reports. We give thanks Mr. David Yale and to the Cambridge University Press for permission to re-publish them here. Also added to the canon are the Chancery reports found in Lincoln's Inn MS. Hill 125. We thank the Masters of the Bench of Lincoln's Inn for their kind permission to print them here.

Table of Cases Reported

[These references are to case numbers, not page numbers.]

Reports of Cases in the Court of Chancery From 1660 to 1673

1

Copplestone v. Foxwell

(Ch. 1660)

The question in this case was whether the conveyance in issue was a mortgage or not.

1 Chancery Cases 1, 22 E.R. 664

Chief Justice Foster in the absence of the Chancellor.

The plaintiff made an absolute conveyance in fee to the defendant by a lease and release of lands worth £1000 [sic] *per annum* in consideration of £1000. The plaintiff, at the making of the conveyance, had but the reversion in fee expectant on an old life, which shortly after died. The plaintiff then made livery to the defendant.

The bill was that the said conveyance was a mortgage and that he might be admitted to redeem. The proof was that the defendant had said several times after the conveyance that he knew not how long he should enjoy the said lands, and had said also that he would take his money again with damages. This was strongly urged by the plaintiff's counsel to be a mortgage.

Churchill, of the defendant's counsel, insisted that it is a maxim that none can come to redeem a mortgage when the mortgagee cannot compel the payment of the mortgage money, for the remedy ought to be reciprocal. And, in this case, the defendant has no remedy to enforce the payment of this money. And moreover, he insisted that, if it were a mortgage, it must be so *a principio*, either by a condition in the deed itself or by another collateral deed made at the same time, for the condition ought to be made and conceived at the same time with the conveyance. And, in the principal case, it was not said that it was a mortgage at first, but by agreement subsequent. And, then, he said that was a nude agreement and no manner of execution of it.

The matter, by consent, was referred to be determined in an amicable way.

Note it is a general rule that a nude or naked agreement, *i.e.* without consideration, is not good in law or equity; *contra*, if the consideration be only unequal.

2 Freeman 150, 22 E.R. 1122

The plaintiff made an absolute conveyance to the defendant by a lease and release of lands worth £100 *per annum* in consideration of £1000. The plaintiff, at the making of the conveyance, had but the reversion in fee, expectant on an old life, which shortly after died. The plaintiff then made a livery to the defendant.

The bill was that the said conveyance was made as a mortgage and the plaintiff was to be admitted to redeem. The proof was that the defendant had said several times after the mortgage that he knew not how long he should enjoy the lands and that, if the plaintiff would pay him his money and damages, he should have his land again. And this was strongly urged by the plaintiff's counsel to be a mortgage.

Churchill, of the defendant's counsel, insisted that none can come to redeem a mortgage where the mortgagee cannot compel the payment of the mortgage money, for the remedy ought to be reciprocal. And, in this case, the defendant has not any remedy for his money and, moreover, that, if it were a mortgage, it must be so *a principio*, either by a condition in the deed itself or by some collateral deed or agreement made at the same time, as a defeasance at law cannot be after the estate executed, and, in this case, it appears not that it was a mortgage at first, but a nude subsequent agreement, of which there was no execution.

The matter was compromised by consent.

[Reg. Lib. 1659 A, f. 413.]

2

Venables v. Foyle

(Ch. 1660–1661)

A court of equity, where justice requires, can discharge a final decree, grant a bill of interpleader, or grant a decree quia timet.

All process of contempt in the normal course in equity to a serjeant at arms must be issued before an injunction for possession can be issued.

1 Chancery Cases 2, 22 E.R. 664

Katharine Venables, being a tenant to Winchester College of the rectory of Andover and indebted £700 to the defendant, agreed with him that he should pay £400 to the College for her and that he should surrender her lease and take a new one in his name. And it was also agreed that she should for the first year of the new lease hold the premises and pay the College their rent and, if she did at the first year's end pay the defendant his £1100 with damages, the defendant should assign to the plaintiff. The first year effluxed, and the plaintiff neither paid the defendant his money nor the College their rent. And, at three years' end, she permitted the defendant to enter upon the premises and to enjoy them.

Thereupon, the defendant exhibited a bill to have the plaintiff (then defendant) redeem or be foreclosed of the redemption. She answered, and her intent thereby appeared to be that the plaintiff should satisfy himself by receipt of the profits and not to pay him. Hereupon, the then plaintiff (now defendant) assigned the said lease to Nicholas Venables, the plaintiff Katharine's son, in consideration of an account made up between them two of what was really due to the defendant on the mortgage. This assignment recited the said suit by Foyle to have Katharine redeem and that his interest was a mortgage forfeited, and Nicholas Venables covenanted to indemnify Foyle against Katharine.

This being the case, Katharine exhibited her bill for to be relieved against Nicholas Venables and Foyle, setting forth the estate to Foyle to be (as it was) a mortgage, and sought to be admitted to the redemption against them both.

Nicholas Venables pleaded several outlawries against her so that she could not proceed against him.

Foyle answered fairly that he had assigned to Nicholas Venables upon his paying him what was due and not more.

This case proceeded to a hearing against Foyle only, and, in verity, the case was no more but that a mortgagee assigns his mortgage over for his due debt.

But it was much insisted by the plaintiff's counsel that there was a breach of trust in Foyle.

And it was decreed that Foyle should account for all the profits both before and after the assignment and pay the overplus above his own debt with damages to the plaintiff and convey and procure all claiming under him to convey to the plaintiff free from encumbrances done by him and them.

Afterwards, Foyle, not being able to perform this decree, exhibited a bill against Katharine and Nicholas Venables setting forth a fraud and practice between them and that he was willing to account unto the time of his assignment and to comply with the decree as far as he was able, and prayed Nicholas Venables might come to an account from the time of the assignment and recovery.

Nicholas Venables exhibited a bill against his mother, claiming the original lease by a title paramount to hers.

And, at the hearing of the said causes about a year and half after, it appeared that Nicholas Venables had a title to the lease paramount to his mother. And Foyle was upon the hearing of the matter discharged of the decree against him, for equity will take all proper methods to redress or prevent a mischief and, therefore, on the appearing of this new matter, it was very just to discharge Foyle from the former decree. And, for the same reason, it is that bills of interpleader and suits *quia timet* are allowed.

2 Freeman 151, 22 E.R. 1123

Trinity [term] 1660, 12 Car. II. Lord Chancellor, Judge Foster.

The defendant, being a mortgagee of a lease belonging to Winchester College, exhibited his bill formerly against the plaintiff to redeem or be foreclosed. The plaintiff (then the defendant), by her answer, said that she was not willing to redeem but that the plaintiff Foyle would satisfy himself by perception of the profits. Thereupon, an account was made up between the plaintiff and the defendant as to what was due to the defendant, after which, for the whole debt, the defendant Foyle assigns to Nicholas Venables, her son, reciting the said suit to redeem and that his title was a mortgage forfeited.

Now, Katherine [Venables] exhibits her bill against them both for a redemption.

Nicholas Venables pleads several outlawries.

Foyle answered fairly that he had assigned over to Nicholas Venables for what was his due and no more.

This cause proceeded to hearing against Foyle only, and, in verity, the case was no more but that a mortgagee assigns over for his due debt.

The plaintiff's counsel insisted that it was a breach of trust and it was agreed that Foyle should account for all the profits, both before and after the assignment, and pay the overplus above his own debt with damages to the plaintiff, and convey, and procure all under him to convey to the plaintiff free from encumbrances.

Afterwards, Foyle, not able to perform the decree, exhibited his bill against Katherine Venables and Nicholas Venables, setting forth a fraud and practice between them, that he was willing to account to the time of the assignment, and that Nicholas Venables might account for what he received afterwards and reconvey.

Nicholas Venables exhibited his bill against Katherine, his mother, claiming the original lease by a title paramount to hers.

And, at the hearing of these two last causes about a year and half after, it appearing that Nicholas Venables had a title to the lease paramount to his mother, Foyle was upon this matter discharged of the decree against him.

Nelson 60, 21 E.R. 789

Mrs. Venables, being tenant to Winchester College of the rectory of Andover and indebted to the defendant Foyle in £700, agreed with him that he should pay £400 more to the College and that she would surrender her lease and take a new one in his name. And it was also agreed that she should for the first year of the said lease hold the premises and pay the College rent and that, if she, in that year, did pay Mr. Foyle £1100 and interest, then he should assign the new lease to her.

The £400 was paid, and the new lease taken in Mr. Foyle's name. The first year expired, and Mrs. Venables neither paid the money to Mr. Foyle nor the rent to the College. But, at the end of three years, she permitted him to enter upon part of the rectory and tithes and to enjoy the same.

Afterwards, he exhibited his bill against her either to pay the money or be foreclosed of the equity of redemption.

She put in her answer, by which it appeared that her intent was that the plaintiff should satisfy himself by the perception of the profits and not to pay him in specie.

Thereupon, Mr. Foyle, the plaintiff, upon an account stated of what was really due to him and in consideration of the payment thereof by her son, Nicholas Venables, did assign the said lease to him. In which deed of assignment, the suit between him and Mrs. Venables was recited and that his interest in the lease was only a forfeited mortgage. And the assignee, Nicholas Venables, covenanted to indemnify Mr. Foyle against his mother etc.

This being the case, she now exhibited her bill against her son and Mr. Foyle to be relieved, setting forth that the estate to him was but a mortgage and, therefore, that, upon payment of the money, she ought to redeem against both.

Nicholas, the son, pleaded several outlawries, so she could not proceed against him.

And Mr. Foyle answered that he had assigned his interest to the son upon payment of what was really due to him and no more, so that the case was thus, *viz.* a mortgage being forfeited, the mortgagee assigns his interest to another upon payment of the money, though it was insisted for the plaintiff that this was a breach of trust in Mr. Foyle.

And the court was of opinion that Mr. Foyle should account for all the profits, both before and after his assignment to Venables, the son, and pay himself in the first place and the surplus to the plaintiff and that he should convey and procure all persons claiming under him to convey the lease to the plaintiff free from encumbrances done or committed by him or them.

Afterwards, Mr. Foyle, being not able to perform this decree, exhibited another bill against Mrs. Venables and her son, Nicholas, setting forth a fraud and practice between them and that he was willing to account to the time of the assignment, but not afterwards, and to comply with the decree as far as he was able, and he prayed that Nicholas might be compelled to account from the time of the assignment to him and to convey etc.

Then Nicholas exhibited another bill against his mother, claiming the original lease by a title paramount to her.

And it appearing that he had such a title, Mr. Foyle was discharged against him.

1 Chancery Reports 178, 21 E.R. 542

The plaintiff moves for a writ of assistance to be put into possession, according to a decree and injunction which had been served, but disobeyed.

The defendant insists that the plaintiff ought to prosecute the defendant with all process of contempt to enforce the defendant to yield obedience to the decree before any injunction or writ of assistance can regularly be awarded for possession, by the rules of this court, and that there has been no other process than a [writ of] attachment issued against the defendant for the breach of the injunction or non-performance of the decree.

It was referred to the Six Clerks. The Six Clerks certified that they do find that, by a rule in the Lord Bacon's time, all process of contempt ought to issue against the person to a serjeant at arms before an injunction should issue for the possession and that they had seen precedents in Queen Elizabeth's time and the beginning of King James's, agreeing with the said rule. But they did not conceive that the said rule did bind the prerogative of this court, but that, if the court saw just cause upon a motion, upon an attachment only, to grant an injunction, and that there are divers precedents to that purpose, and that, by the late Rules, the course has been upon an affidavit of personal service of the decree and an attachment upon a motion to grant an injunction and, upon a contempt thereof, a commission was granted to put and keep the party in possession.

This court upon reading precedents in the Lord Coventry's time and of affidavits, whereby it appears that possession has been demanded and refused to be delivered according to the injunction, which was served and disobeyed, ordered that a commission or a writ of assistance be awarded to put and keep the plaintiff or his agents in possession, *nisi causa*.

The defendant insisted that, though he be prosecuted to a serjeant at arms, that, by the course of the court, after a serjeant at arms, an injunction for possession must be first granted and served and the party in contempt for not obeying thereof, before a writ of assistance is to issue, especially against tenants of the premises who were not parties to the suit and that there is no injunction for possession since the serjeant at arms. But, in the end, this court discharged the writ of assistance and injunction formerly granted as irregular, and the plaintiff is to issue out all process of contempt in course to a serjeant at arms before an injunction is to issue.

[Reg. Lib. 12 Car. II, f. 670.]

3

Barnard v. Whitechapel Paupers

(Ch. 1660)

Where a devisee has elected to receive a legacy of land subject to a charge by paying the charge, he or she cannot later contest the devise.

Lincoln's Inn MS. Hill 125, f. 22v, pl. 2

1 September 1660.

Upon exceptions to the decree upon the Statute 43 Eliz.,[1] the case was [thus]. A husband and wife purchased lands to them and to the heirs of the husband. The husband, by his will in writing, devised the same lands to the wife for her life, paying *inde* to the poor etc. 40s. *per annum*. And he dies. The wife entered and paid the 40s. for one or two years, and, then, she refused.

The [Charity] Commissioners decreed the wife to continue the payment.

The wife excepted to the decree because the devise [was] void and she was not bound for the payment.

The decree was confirmed by the Chancellor [LORD CLARENDON] by the opinion of BRIDGEMAN, the Chief Baron, first, the payment of the 40s. *per annum*, which is an annual rent or charge, made an election in the wife to take by the devise as by the first purchase.

Second, the commissioners gave costs to the prosecutor on the behalf of the charitable use. And an exception was taken to it because the Statute does not give them power to award costs, but to the Chancellor upon an appeal.

As to this point, the court will advise.

4

Tilly v. Egerton

(Ch. 1660)

When a mortgage is redeemed, the money paid goes to the heir, not to the administrator, of the creditor-mortgagee.

2 Freeman 125, 22 E.R. 1102

27 October, 12 Car. II [1660]. Lord Chancellor, Justice Bridgeman.

Nicholas Tilley, the plaintiff's brother, being seised in fee of a messuage etc. in the County of Southampton, by a deed in 1642, mortgaged to Egerton in fee for security of £150 with interest. Afterwards, in the presence of Egerton, the plaintiff purchased the premises of Nicholas Tilley, and paid him part of the purchase money in hand, and gave him security for the residue. Afterwards, in 1651, the plaintiff did agree with Egerton for the redemption and purchase of the premises and that, in satisfaction thereof, the plaintiff should pay £6 for ten years and then £120 at the ten years' end, the premises were to be conveyed to the plaintiff and the deeds were to be delivered up to him. And, upon the said agreement, the deed of mortgage and other deeds were to be delivered up by the consent of the plaintiff and John Egerton to John Collier, an attorney, to draw

[1] Stat. 43 Eliz. I, c. 4, s. 1 (*SR*, IV, 968–969).

the agreement into writing to the end it might be sealed by the plaintiff and John Egerton. But, before that could be done, John Egerton, in 1653, died, leaving the defendant Egerton his heir. And Julian Egerton, his wife, the other defendant, took out letters of administration. The heir and administratrix contested in their answers who should have the money, the bill being for an interpleader.

And it was decreed for the heir.

Vide St. John, executor of Grobham, against Wareham, the same point was decreed 16 March 11 Car. I [1635].[1]

Lord Nottingham, *Prolegomena*, p. 291

27 October 1660, 12 Car. II, by Clarendon, Chancellor, assisted by Bridgeman, Chief Justice.

Where the plaintiff, having purchased of the mortgagor his equity, agreed with the mortgagee to pay £6 *per annum* for ten years for the redemption, it was decreed to pay the money to the heir of the mortgagee, and not to his executors, because no defect of assets appeared.

1 Chancery Reports 181, 21 E.R. 543

Nicholas Tilly, the plaintiff's brother, being seised in fee of lands, by a deed in 1642, mortgaged the premises to John Egerton in fee for £150 with interest, payable in 1643, and £6 upon that day annually, until 1649, and the 28th of March 1649, for the payment of £108, by Nicholas Tilly, his executors, administrators, or assigns. Afterwards, in the presence of John Egerton, the plaintiff purchased the fee simple of the premises of Nicholas Tilly, and paid him part of the purchase money in hand, and gave him security for the residue. And, in 1652, the plaintiff agreed with the said John Egerton for the redemption and the purchase of the premises of him. And, in satisfaction thereof, the plaintiff was to pay him £6 for ten years from Lady Day then next and £120 at the ten years' end, and, at the ten years' end, the premises were to be conveyed to the plaintiff, and the deeds to be delivered up. And, upon the said agreement, the deed of mortgage and other writings were by consent to be delivered up to one Collier to draw the agreement. And, before the agreement was drawn, the said John Egerton, in 1653, died, leaving Vincent Egerton, his brother and heir, and the defendant, Julian, his relict. And Julian took administration. And after John Egerton's death, the said Vincent and Julian contested who should have the £6 *per annum*, Vincent claiming it as heir and Julian as administratrix, and each threatened the plaintiff to recover the same from him again; so that, ever since John Egerton's death, the plaintiff is in arrear of it. Vincent died, leaving the defendant William, his son and heir, between whom and Julian, the same dispute grew, so that to whom the

[1] *St. John v. Wareham* (Ch. 1635), 73 Selden Soc. 202, 3 Swanston 631, 36 E.R. 1001, 15 Viner Abr. 455, n.

£6 *per annum* and arrears this court should adjudge it to belong and the growing payments and the £120 at the ten years end and the premises then to be conveyed is the bill.

The defendant insists that Julian exhibited her bill against the said Vincent Egerton and Nicholas Tilly to have the mortgage money paid to her as administratrix to John Egerton, but failed therein. The defendant Julian claims the mortgage money by the plaintiff's agreement with John Egerton, as his administratrix, to enable her to pay his debts, he not leaving assets sufficient.

This court, with the assistance of the judges, decreed the plaintiff shall have the redemption of the mortgaged premises. And, forasmuch as the defect of assets of the mortgagee was not proved, this court was of opinion that the heir of the mortgagee ought to have the money to be paid for the redemption of the premises, and decreed the arrears of the £6 *per annum* and the growing payments for the ten years and the £120 at the ten years' end shall be paid by the plaintiff to the defendant William Egerton.

But note the point is now settled that, in all cases, the mortgage money is to be paid to the executor or administrator.

3 Chancery Reports 63, 21 E.R. 729

27 October, 22 Car. II [sic]. Lord Chancellor, Lord Chief Justice Bridgeman.

Nicholas Tilley, the defendant's father, being seised in fee of a messuage etc. in the County of Southampton, by a deed, in 1642, mortgaged it to Egerton in fee, for the security of £150 with interest. Afterwards, in the presence of Egerton, the plaintiff purchased the premises of Nicholas Tilley, and paid him part of the purchase money in hand, and gave security for the residue. And, in 1651, the plaintiff did agree with Egerton for the redemption and purchase of the premises and that, in satisfaction thereof, the plaintiff should pay him £6 for ten years and then £120 at the ten years' end, the premises to be conveyed to the plaintiff, and the deeds to be delivered up to him. And, upon the said agreement, the deed of mortgage and other the writings concerning the premises were delivered up by the mutual consent of the plaintiff and John Egerton to Joseph Collier, an attorney, to draw the agreement into writing to the end it might be sealed by the plaintiff and John Egerton. But, before the agreement was drawn into writing, John Egerton, 1653, died, leaving the defendant his heir. And Julian, his wife, the other defendant, took forth letters of administration. The heir and administratrix contested by their answer whose should be the money, the bill being for an interpleader.

And it was decreed for the heir.

Vide St. John, executor to Grobham, against Warehall and others, touching the same point, decreed 16 March, 11 Car. II [1659].

73 Selden Soc. 203

27th October, 12 Car. II.

The plaintiff, having purchased from the mortgagor in fee his equity and agreed with the mortgagee to pay £6 *per annum* for ten years, upon a suit for this redemption after the death of the mortgagee, was decreed to pay that money to that heir of the mortgagee and not to his administratrix, because no want of assets was proved, though alleged.

This precedent, though made by the earl of Clarendon with advice of Bridgeman, Chief Justice, I [Lord Nottingham] could not approve. And I well remember the bar was unsatisfied when the decree was made, for the original proviso mentioning neither heirs nor executors, if the money had been paid at the day and the mortgagee had been then dead, the heir could not have had the money. Then, for equity to give the heir that money after the forfeiture, which he could not have had before the forfeiture, was somewhat strange and arbitrary, especially when the mortgagee himself had agreed to take a certain sum, which should be ten years in paying, and so turned it into a chattel in equity.

[Other copies of this report: 3 Swanston 631, 36 E.R. 1002.]
[Other reports of this case: 1 Eq. Cas. Abr. 326, 21 E.R. 1079.]
[Reg. Lib. 1660 B, f. 170.]

5

Wells v. Wells

(Ch. 1660)

A review of a judgment in the Court of Delegates lies in the sound judicial discretion of the Lord Chancellor.

Lincoln's Inn MS. Hill 125, f. 23, pl. 1

In vacation December 1660. Upon a petition [. . .] the Chancellor at his house.

A sentence was given against a will. And, upon an appeal to the Judges Delegate, the sentence was repealed, and a sentence was given for the will. A petition was [filed] to r[everse] by a commission of review, which was referred to the Chancellor. And the case was debated before him. And it was agreed that such a commission is not demandable *in ratione juris* but in favor. And the circumstances of equity were debated *pro et contra*.

Et tandem the Chancellor, who inclined against at first, denied the commission because the petitioner had rested quiet eleven months after the sentence. And [there is] no remedy for costs and nothing appeared but that it was desired for vexation.

6

Holworthy v. Anonymous

(Ch. 1660)

Goods mortgaged to a merchant to sell do not belong to the merchant, and thus are not covered by an insurance policy on the merchant's goods.

After an appeal from the Court of Policies and Assurance, the appellate court can enter a final judgment for the successful party on the appeal.

In a case of insurance without an account, the custom is to give the whole money insured without regard to the value of the lost goods in the case of a total loss.

Lincoln's Inn MS. Hill 125, f. 26

7 December 12 Car. II.

Upon opening the matter etc., this cause being an appeal from a sentence given in the Court of Policies and Assurance etc., in this cause, these points were resolved and adjudged.

First, the appellant insured on oils and merchandises lost or not lost from Ms. to Ma. valued and without account. At Ms., he bought a cask to put his oils in, and he shipped the cask. One Salle Cosces [?], having lemons at Ms., where the ship was, and wanting moneys, pawned or, as the merchants' word is, hypothecated the lemons to Holworthy, the appellant, who was to carry the lemons to Ma. and there sell them and pay himself and the surplusage to Sally Cosces, who received the moneys from Holworthy for the lemons, which Holworthy had provided and laid on board at London to have sent to Ma. and were within the policy. Salle Cosces being a German, the ship with the lemons was taken at sea and lost on the account that Sally Cosces was an enemy.

The first question [was] if the lemons thus hypothecated were within the assurance. And the court, in April 1657, resolved that they were not, for they were not the plaintiff's and possibly the court might go on the ground that they were lost on Salle Cosces' account, who was taken for an enemy, and the insurers would have had little good by the remuneration of the plaintiff in such a case.

Second, then, the question was whether the cask, being an empty cask and provided only in order to fill oils in them, were merchandises within the policy. And that being to be determined by the custom of merchants was referred to a jury of merchants, four [?] to be returned etc. And it was tried for the appellant that they were merchandises etc.

Then the defendants insisted that the appeal in this case lies only for the insurer where a sentence is given against him, because the clause of the Statute[1] is that the money decreed shall be paid before the appeal or security etc. But the court allowed the appeal, and that was at first [?] also on the demurrer [?].

[1] Stat. 43 Eliz. I, c. 12, s. 3 (*SR*, IV, 979).

Then, the defendants moved that, though the court might hold the plea, yet, in this case, at the suit of the insured when he is dismissed, yet they could not go any farther than either to affirm or reverse the sentence, which the court did, but the appellant prayed also a sentence for the money insured, being £1200 by several defendants insured, which sentence the insurers' court ought to have given.

But the court referred the consideration of two judges, WYNDHAM and ATKYNS, who heard arguments therein and certified, and the court concurred, the court ought to give a judgment for the plaintiff for that, though the words of the Statute are to reverse or affirm, yet it is a consequence necessary that this court give judgment for the plaintiff, else the plaintiff should begin again continually and, as in [an action of] formedon in the Common Bench abated, the King's Bench proceeds; if, on error, the writ be affirmed.

Then the defendants insisted that the insured ought not to have judgment for £1200, the cask being but worth £20, as it was agreed, and the Statute is the plaintiff shall recover according to equity.

But the appellant prayed a decree for the whole £1200.

This point was also referred to a trial by merchants whether, in a case of insurance without an account, the custom be to give the whole money insured without regard to the value in case of a total loss.

And the merchants gave a verdict for the plaintiff, the appellant, [. . .] they found the whole sum insured in damages.

And now on the debate, the Lord Chancellor [LORD CLARENDON], assisted with Justice TYRREL, concurred. And the appellant at last had judgment for the £1200.

7

Adrian v. Ent

(Ch. 1660)

Where a commission of review is granted to a decree of the Court of Delegates, the decree of that court will be stayed.

Lincoln's Inn MS. Hill 125, f. 23, pl. 2

A sentence was given against a will below and for a former will, and that [was] reversed in the [Court of] Delegates, and a later will [was] set up. A commission of review was obtained by the petitioner in the former will, and an inhibition [was sent] to the Delegates. Dr. Ent sues for an account of the commission of review with the inhibition stayed or suppressed. The proceeding here is the question.

8

Boreman v. Yate

(Ch. 1660–1667)

A court of equity can appoint commissioners to settle boundaries.

In this case, the marriage settlement in issue was valid and enforceable.

Lincoln's Inn MS. Hill 125, f. 23v

25 December 12 Car. II [1660].

John Yate, having issue, the defendant Yate, married a second wife, Elizabeth. And he, being a tenant in tail expectant in remainder after the death of Thomas, his father, with a remainder to the heirs of John himself, did covenant in consideration of the marriage and a £1000 portion to levy a fine to the intent that Elizabeth, his wife, should after his death and the death of Thomas, his father, receive £180 *per annum* out of the premises and the heirs male of the body of John by Elizabeth £150 more during the life of Elizabeth and £300 *per annum* after her death and a clause of distress for each rent. No use of the land [was] limited to whom the land should go, but it was left to the construction of the law. The fine was accordingly levied. Thomas, being the tenant for life in possession, had a power to make leases; so also had John as tenant in tail before the fine was levied by a former conveyance. There were divers leases made by Thomas in being. And, after the death of John, the father, Thomas, the grandfather, and John, the grandchild, defendant, suffered a recovery to uses for a jointure and other purposes on the marriage of the defendant, John. Elizabeth, the wife of John, the father, conveys her interest in the £150 *per annum* to Bowman, which was a voluntary conveyance. The plaintiff Bowman, as assignee of Elizabeth, and Yate, the son of Elizabeth by John, exhibited their bill for relief. And they ground their equity because the deeds were lost, (But that appeared otherwise), secondly, on the father's promise to make good the rents in value and title (but that, being verbal, no hold was taken of it), third, the bounds were confounded with other lands of the defendants, and fourth, there was no distress to be had in regard of the prior leases. There was also a covenant for farther assurance. But that would help little in this case because, though the assurance was good, there was no remedy sufficient and the wife's assurance was good.

On the first hearing, the court directed a commission to distinguish the lands and certify the value, reserving the considering of the equity. The commissioners certify the lands and the value of the lands out of lease to be £72 *per annum*, which were subject to distress, and the rest of the lands were in lease by former leases by the grandfather and so not subject to distress but the whole lands when they came in possession would be £302 *per annum*, the rent being £300 *per annum*.

The commission being returned and the cause coming thereon to be heard, the case for the wife's rent differed from that of the heir for the rent limited to the wife was a good rent in law. And, therefore, the cases distinctly considered by the court, the point as to the wife being no other than that the land was not of value to answer the rent and it is not reason[able] that the provision made for her food and maintenance should expect a remedy by distress until all the leases were expired and it is not likely she should ever have distress until then and then not sufficient for the arrears. Therefore, the court declared that she ought in equity to have the profits of the land itself to be transferred to her to make good the rent and her equity is with her interest well transferred to the assignee, though he paid no consideration for it, for the defendant is not at all concerned in that, the first grant being on a valuable consideration.

But the case, as to the second son was of more difficultly as was conceived because that the limitation to him was void in law for he was male, but not heir male, for the eldest son, the defendant, was the heir, so as the plaintiff could not take as heir male of the body of his father by Elizabeth and, if such an assurance so ill penned and invalid in law should be made good in equity, it were of ill consequence, and, then, it were better to have an ill than a good assurance. And the scope of the deed is to pass an estate by way of a use, as is apparent by the clause of distress. And, as to the wife, it does so. And, as to the heir male, it did intend so to do and, therefore, to make it good by way of a trust or as an agreement is to make it what was not one by the parties meant to be made and make some [. . .] in the deed etc.

The court declared that, though it was void as a limitation, yet here appeared a clear intention that the heir male by this second marriage should have a rent of £300 *per annum* after the mother's death and £150 *per annum* while she lived. And, in truth, there is no use of the land itself limited by the deed saving that in the clause whereby John, the father, has power limited to make leases; the rents are limited to be reserved to him and his heirs. And, though it be not a good rent in law which is limited nor good by way of a trust, yet it is good by way of agreement and intention and though, in a limitation of a use, as this case is, none can take who is not heir as well as male where the heir male is to take as a purchaser, yet it must needs be otherwise understood in the case of an agreement for a settlement to be made as if John, the father, had contracted to make a settlement on his heirs male by the second wife it must be understood in such a sense necessarily as that the sons of that marriage should be benefitted though the first son live.

Therefore, the court declared the heir also relievable in this case. And the court entering into consideration how to relieve both plaintiffs when the profits of the land would not satisfy either, the solicitors informed that Bowman and the plaintiff, the heir, were agreed among themselves as touching the proportioning of their rents.

[It was] decreed the profits of the land to the plaintiffs so far as to satisfy and the defendant to account of arrears of profits received by him.

1 Chancery Cases 145, 22 E.R. 734

Seymor Boreman and Francis Yeat, plaintiffs, against John Yeat, Esq., defendant.

The bill was grounded upon an agreement made upon the marriage of John Yeat, the father of the plaintiff Francis, with Frances, his mother, and a tripartite deed 15 Car. I [1639–40] in pursuance thereof, whereby John, the father, became seised in tail, and, after the death of Thomas's father, covenants to levy a fine to the intent Elizabeth, mother of Frances, his second wife, after the death of Thomas and himself, and her assigns should have during her life out of the premises £150 *per annum* if John should have heirs male of his body that should so long live, and to the heirs male of the body of John by the said Elizabeth, another £150 *per annum* during the life of the said Elizabeth and that the heirs male of the body of John and Elizabeth have £300 *per annum* out of the premises with a clause of distress and a covenant to make further assurance. A fine was levied accordingly August 1663.

John, the father, died in the life of Thomas, his father. Elizabeth sold her right to the £150 limited to herself after the death of Thomas to the plaintiff Boreman. And, in October, before the bill, Thomas died, whereby the plaintiffs became entitled to the several rents, the lands descending to the defendant as heir to his grandfather, being the eldest son of John by a former marriage. And he had all the deeds, and refused to pay the rents, pretending the lands were not sufficient, and the limitation in law was defective. And the lands lying intermixed with others and the boundaries confused, the plaintiffs could not distrain, and so they prayed relief here. And they charged also that the defendant's father agreed that, if the lands were too small in value or defective in title, he would make both good. To have that done and to discover the buttals and boundaries and to have the rents arrear and growing rents paid was the scope of the bill.

The defendant, by answer, insisted that the plaintiff's proper remedy was at law and that Boreman had not a good title, because he had not any attornment, for aught appeared, or any good conveyance from Elizabeth, and justified the detainer of the deeds.

On the first hearing, 25 January 12 Car. II [1661], [the court] ordered a commission to go to set out the lands, and Boreman's title to be determined on the return of the commission. The commissioners certified that they had set out the lands, the present rents whereof were but £70 *per annum*, and that the lands charged were £300 *per annum*. And then the cause came again to be heard before the Lord Chancellor and the two Chief Justices, 12 January 1660[/61]. And, as to Boreman's title as assignee to Elizabeth, by which he claimed the arrears from Thomas Yeat's death, during Elizabeth's life, the matter stood upon was that he did not prove he had paid any purchase money.

The court conceived that was not material, he claiming under Elizabeth, who was entitled by the marriage agreement, and so capable of relief.

And the next point was as to the other plaintiffs to £100 *per annum* during Elizabeth's life, and £300 after to him and the heirs male of his body. Whereupon, the court declared that, though the limitation of these rents were defective in law, so as the plaintiff could have no remedy at law, yet, by the true meaning of the marriage agreement, the plaintiff Francis is well described to take the rent, and both the plaintiffs were well entitled and ought to have relief so far forth as the lands and rents reserved on the leases, and the lands, as they shall come out of the lease, shall be of a value to make good the same and that Boreman ought to be first paid. And they decreed the same accordingly and the defendant to account for the mesne profits etc. and for the future the rents reserved. And the lands out of which the rents and profits are issuing at the highest yearly value, not exceeding £200 *per annum*, after the leases expire, should be liable to the payment of those rents to the plaintiff Boreman during Elizabeth's life and, after, £300 *per annum* to the plaintiff Francis, according to the true meaning of the deed.

Nelson 121, 21 E.R. 805

20 January 1666[/67], between Seymour Boreman and Yate.

Thomas Yate [was] the father, John Yate, the son, and Francis, the grandson. The bill was grounded on an agreement upon the marriage of John Yate, with Frances, his first wife, by a tripartite indenture, 15 Car. I [1639–40], by which Thomas was made tenant for life, remainder in tail to John, who had issue by that marriage, the defendant, his eldest son. The said John did afterwards upon the marriage with Elizabeth, his second wife and mother of Francis, the plaintiff, covenant to levy a fine to the intent that Elizabeth might after the death of Thomas and the said John have and receive £150 *per annum* out of the lands for her life, and, if he should have heirs male, then those heirs male should have another £150 out of the lands during the life of Elizabeth, and, after her decease, the heirs male of his body and of Elizabeth should have £300 *per annum* with a clause of distress and a covenant to make further assurance.

John died in the lifetime of Thomas, his father; then Elizabeth sold her right to the £150 to the plaintiff Boreman; then Thomas died, and the lands descended to the defendant as heir to the grandfather, being the eldest son of John by the first marriage, and he had all the deeds, and refused to pay the rents, pretending the lands were not sufficient and that the limitation was defective in law and that the lands lay intermixed with others and the boundaries [were] confused, so that the plaintiff could not distrain. Therefore, he prayed relief and to discover and set forth the boundaries and the rents arrear and that the same might be decreed etc.

The defendant, in his answer, set forth that the proper remedy was at law and that Boreman had not a good title, because the grantee for life did not attorn and so the conveyance of the rent to him from Elizabeth was not good.

On the first hearing, a commission was directed to settle the boundaries, and the commissioners certified that it was done and that the present rent was but £70 *per annum*.

On the second hearing, the point was that, though the limitation of £150 *per annum* was defective in law, for Francis being not named in the limitation, that being to the heirs male, and he was not the heir male, for John, his father, had a son by another marriage, the now defendant, yet the court was of opinion that, by the true meaning of the marriage agreement, the plaintiff Francis is a person well described to take the rent, and yet to be relieved, and the rent to be paid to the plaintiff during the life of Elizabeth.

2 Merivale 347, 35 E.R. 971

In the Case of Seymour v. Boreman, a son of the second marriage claimed to take under the appellation of 'heir male of the body of the father and mother' while there was a son of the first marriage living.

Though the intention was perfectly clear, yet the Lord Keeper [Lord Clarendon] said the limitation was defective at law and the plaintiff could have no remedy there but that, according to the true meaning of the marriage agreement, he was well described to take the rent.

It was, therefore, by virtue of the contract, that the court was there enabled to put upon the word 'heirs' a sense which, legally and strictly, it did not bear.

9

Peasley v. Burgess

(Ch. 1660–1661)

A judgment creditor cannot garnish a judgment in favor of his own debtor.

Lincoln's Inn MS. Hill 125, f. 25v

In Christmas vacation 12 Car. II.

Peasly had a judgment against Burgesse at common law for a £100 debt. Burgesse had a decree against Plucknet for a £700 debt. £200 was in court here. Burgess had nothing to satisfy Peasly except the £200, the which, if it was in the hands of Burgesse, would be liable to the debt of Peasly by a [writ of] *fieri facias*. But, as long as the money remained here, the plaintiff had no means of satisfaction as he had used his utmost endeavor and he had purchased a *fieri facias* and [a writ of] *capias ad satisfaciendum*.

The court was moved, but would not deliver the money to the plaintiff, by which he exhibited a bill upon the matter aforesaid. But the court dismissed it though the precedent of Rosse and Hodges [was] urged where the court in such a case ordered money that Hodges obtained by a decree against Rosse to be brought into court to the intent that it will be employed in satisfaction of an account taken, who had a decree against Hodges, and another between Larkin and Westwood, 11 Car.

10

Perrott v. Ashfield

(Ch. 1660–1661)

The issue in this case was the validity of a marriage settlement.

Lincoln's Inn MS. Hill 125, f. 28

Perrott v. the Ashfields, Sir John Underhill, and several others.

The case was [thus]. Sir Marmaduke Dorrell, *inter alia*, was possessed of the fifth part of Cole Farm for twenty-one years, which expired *anno* 1641. And he was also possessed of the manor of Lilstock etc. for divers years. [In] a treaty of a marriage to be had between him and Anne Clapham, he did agree to settle on her £600 *per annum* for her life, £500 *per annum* whereof was settled thus, *viz.* he procured Sir Samson Dorrell, his son, who was tenant in tail of the manors of Fulmer and Missenden to cut off the entail and make himself tenant in fee thereof and then to make a lease for ninety years thereof, or such a term, to some friends of the said Anne determinable on her death and then re-demise the same to Sir Samson for a lesser term rendering £500 *per annum*. Then, Sir Marmaduke settles the leases.[1]

11

Bretton v. Bretton

(Ch. 1660–1661)

A devise to younger children, according to the intent of the testator in this case, did not include an heir, even though he was younger than his sisters.

3 Chancery Reports 1, 21 E.R. 710

Money was bequeathed to younger children where there were divers daughters and one son, who was the heir at law and had a fair inheritance and yet was by birth a younger child.

It was decreed that he was not a younger child within the devise, and should not take by it, he being heir at law.

[1] This report ends here.

2 Freeman 158, 22 E.R. 1128

Money was bequeathed to younger children where there were divers daughters and one son, who was the heir at law and had a fair inheritance, yet was by birth a younger child.

It was decreed that he was not a younger child within the devise and should not take by it, being heir at law.

The like case was adjudged so by the Master of the Rolls, *inter* Mead and Cane *et al.*, 16 July 1663.[1]

Nelson 63, 21 E.R. 790

The testator bequeathed money to younger children. And, afterwards, he died, and left several daughters and one son, who was heir at law and who had a fair inheritance from his father, and he was by birth younger than the daughters, who claimed a share of the money by virtue of the devise.

But it was decreed that he was not to be comprehended under the name of a younger child within the intent and meaning of the will, and, therefore, should not take by it as such, he being heir at law, as aforesaid.

[Other reports of this case: 1 Eq. Cas. Abr. 202, 21 E.R. 990.]

12

Williams v. Dutton

(Ch. 1660–1661)

There is a court of law for some matters within the County Palatine of Chester.

1 Chancery Reports 183, 21 E.R. 544

This court, with the assistance of the judges, allowed the jurisdiction of the County Palatine of Chester.

[Reg. Lib. 12 Car. II, f. 109.]

13

Witchcot v. Souch

(Ch. 1660–1661)

A court of equity can vary the terms of a trust in order to effectuate the intent of the settlor.

---

[1] *Mead v. Cave* (Ch. 1663), see below, Case No. 111.

1 Chancery Reports 183, 21 E.R. 544

The time for the sale of lands by trustees being elapsed, so that the trustees have no power to execute the trust, this court, with the assistance of the judges, were of opinion that, by the elapse of time, no advantage ought to be taken, but decreed the trustees to proceed with the sale notwithstanding.

[Reg. Lib. 12 Car. II, f. 112.]

14
Micklethwait v. Boatman

(Ch. 1660–1661)

A court of equity has the power to disallow interest for rents and profits.

1 Chancery Reports 184, 21 E.R. 544

This court would not allow interest for rents and profits.

[Reg. Lib. 12 Car. II, f. 179.]

15
Saunders v. Hord

(Ch. 1660–1661)

The Statute of Limitations bars stale redemptions of mortgages.

1 Chancery Reports 184, 21 E.R. 544

The plaintiff seeks a redemption of a mortgage as heir and administrator of the mortgagor. The defendant demurs for that he ought not to be troubled or questioned for any matters in the bill in regard of the antiquity of the transactions, they being not privy or parties, the matters being acted in 38 Eliz. [1595–96], and he pleaded that the plaintiff has not made any entry in twenty years, and is barred by the Statute 21 Jac.,[1] the plaintiff claiming as heir to his said father. And he pleaded also a fine and recovery suffered by the said father in 3 and 15 Jac. [1605–06 and 1617–18].

This court allowed both the plea and demurrer.

[Reg. Lib. 12 Car. II, f. 332.]

[1] Stat. 21 Jac. I, c. 16 (*SR*, IV, 1222–1223).

16

Pollard v. Lady Grenville

(Ch. 1660–1662)

In this case, a lease that was void at common law was held to be a valid execution of a power of appointment where the supposed lessor had received the profits of the transaction.

1 Chancery Reports 184, 21 E.R. 544

One George Cuttiford, in 1631, became bound in a bond of £200 for the payment of £104, which money was employed for the use of the defendant Dame Greenvil during her widowhood. And she, in December 1637, in pursuance of a power reserved to her by the deed of settlement of her estate before her marriage with Sir Richard Greenvil to make leases for three lives or twenty-one years of any part of her said estate, she, in consideration of several debts, as also of the said bond of £200, demised to the said Cuttiford, his executors, etc. the premises for twenty-one years, to commence from and after the 25th of March then next ensuing, for saving harmless the said Cuttiford, his heirs, etc. from the said bond.

The defendant, Dame Greenvil, insisted that the power reserved to her was only to make a lease or leases in possession and the lease made by her to Cuttiford was to commence from a time to come, so that the same was void in law, and, if the lease were good, yet she received the profits during coverture, and so is not accountable for them.

This court was assisted with the judges. And, it appearing that the debt now in question was taken up and employed for the use of the defendant Dame Greenvil, who created the trust for the payment of her debts and she, by virtue of the power reserved to her before marriage, received the profits of the premises and, although the lease granted to Cuttiford may not in strictness of law be a good lease, yet this court was satisfied that the same does amount to a good declaration of her power in equity to make a lease for twenty-one years in being and that her reception of the profits was under that power and subject to the trust. And [the court] decreed that the said debt in question be paid to the plaintiff, and, in respect the principal debt and damages does surmount the penalty of the bond, it was also decreed that the defendant should pay £200.

1 Chancery Cases 10, 22 E.R. 668

The Lord Chancellor, the Master of the Rolls, Chief Justice Hyde, Justice Twysden.

The plaintiff lent the Lady Greenvil £100, and one Culliford, as her chief agent and friend, became bound for the same. And the lady having a power to make a lease in possession for twenty-one years of her estate, makes a lease to

Culliford for twenty-one years to secure him from the debt aforesaid and several other debts he was engaged for the said Lady. But the lease was made to commence from a time to come, which was void in law in respect her power was but as aforesaid. And Culliford had the possession for some time, but was afterwards ousted by force by the lady's husband. But her husband not long afterwards dying, she enjoyed it for the remainder of the term.

And Culliford being dead and leaving no assets, the plaintiff, therefore, preferred his bill here for the debt aforesaid.

But, for that it appeared to the court that the money was employed for his use who created the trust for the payment of debts and she having received the profits for thirteen years and for that the lease was not good in strictness of law, yet the court was satisfied that the same did amount to a good declaration of her power in equity to make the lease for twenty-one years in being and that the receipts of the profits was also under that power and subject to the trust. And, although the defendant did set forth by an answer that Culliford, at the time of his death, was indebted to her, yet the defendant was decreed to pay the debt.

Lincoln's Inn MS. Hill 125, f. 31v

George Cutteford became bound to Jope in £200 for money for the Lady. And she, having before her marriage with Sir Richard Grenville, conveyed her lands, *unde* Okehampton Park was parcel, to Grills and others with a power to lease for twenty-one years any part etc. in possession, as was by the plaintiff pretended. She, [in] 1637, reciting this and other debts for securing Cutteford of and from the said obligations and payment of the moneys, makes a lease to Cutteford for twenty-one years from Michaelmas following. Cutteford, sometime, entered and took the profits. But it appeared that, afterward, the Lady took the profits. The lease, in time, expired [in] 1658. Sir Richard died; the Lady survived.

The plaintiff, executor of Jope, exhibits his bill for the payment of the debt. And [it was] decreed accordingly, notwithstanding that, by the Lady's counsel, it was insisted on that, first, the lease was void to Cutteford, for it appeared by the lease the power was to lease in possession and this lease commenced *in futuro*.

Chancellor [Lord Clarendon]: I regarded not that she took the profits.

Second, the creditor was not a party to the deed and could not take advantage of it nor have a title by it. And Cutteford nor the defendant Grace, his wife, are not plaintiffs nor have paid anything thereon.

Third, the Lady was married all the while. And, if Sir Richard Grenville were alive, he could not be charged. And how can the wife be charged after the husband's death for a receipt during the marriage whereas he could not have been charged in equity in his lifetime. It is *casus* [. . .].

Fourth, the court decreed the Lady to pay, and yet [there was] no account against the executrix of Cutteford, who, for aught appeared, might have received sufficient [assets].

Query *in omnibus*. I conceive that the reason was because that the Lady having reserved the disposition of her estate to herself during the marriage, the court did look on her as acting and obliging herself as if she had been sole.

[Reg. Lib. 12 Car. II, f. 429.]
[Related cases: Earl of Suffolk v. Grenville (Ch. 1631), Chancery Repts. *tempore* Coventry 155.]

17

Russell v. Bodvil

(Ch. 1660–1661)

A writ of sequestration lies to enforce a final decree in equity.

1 Chancery Reports 186, 21 E.R. 545

The plaintiff moves for a commission to the sheriff to put the plaintiff and his sequestrators in possession.

The defendants insist that the commission desired is to execute orders for alimony, for which there is now no jurisdiction in this court and there is now no law in being to support any such decree. And, if there were, there is no decree signed and enrolled. And a sequestration, injunction, and commission are not grantable but on a decree signed and enrolled, and they are not to extend to an agent of a sequestrator, nor the commission to the Sheriff is awardable before one first to the justices.

This court, being assisted with the judges on this point, whether the Act for Judicial Proceedings[1] did revive and maintain the decree made for alimony in this cause or not, His Lordship [Lord Clarendon], after the hearing of the learned arguments on both sides, declared that, inasmuch as the decree made in this cause does depend on His Lordship's judgment, His Lordship referred it to several of the judges upon the arguments.

The plaintiff moved for a writ of assistance to put the plaintiff's sequestrators in possession of the lands decreed, the said decree being certified to be a good decree.

His Lordship declared that he does conceive the decree to be in force, and leaves the plaintiff to proceed thereupon as upon other decrees.

The defendant stood out all process to a serjeant at arms, whereon a sequestration issued and an injunction to commissioners. This court ordered a commission to the sheriff to put the plaintiff's sequestration into possession.

[Reg. Lib. 12 Car. II, f. 38.]

---

[1] Stat. 12 Car. II, c. 3 (*SR*, V, 180–181).

18

Underhill v. Whitchot

(Ch. 1660–1661)

Possession of land can be awarded by a court of equity for contempt of a final decree.

1 Chancery Reports 188, 21 E.R. 545

The defendant being in contempt for not performing a decree to an attachment, an injunction for possession was awarded.

[Reg. Lib. 12 Car. II, f. 460.]

19

Plumpton v. Plumpton

(Ch. 1660–1661)

In this case, the plaintiff was entitled to receive her legacy in full even though other siblings were born after the death of the testator.

1 Chancery Reports 188, 21 E.R. 545

Henry, the plaintiff's late grandfather, deceased, being seised in fee of lands and of a personal estate in 1638, made his will, and his eldest son, Andrew Plumpton, the defendant, executor, whereby he devised to two of the children of Henry Plumpton, his younger son, the plaintiff's father, either already begotten or which hereafter shall be lawfully begotten on the body of Christian, his then wife, £100 apiece to each of them to be paid unto them at their several ages of twenty-one or days of marriage, which should first happen, and, after[wards], he died. And, at the time of the said will, the plaintiff was the eldest daughter of the said Henry Plumpton, the younger, in the will named, and is of the age of twenty-one, and so is entitled to have the said £100 and damages as aforesaid.

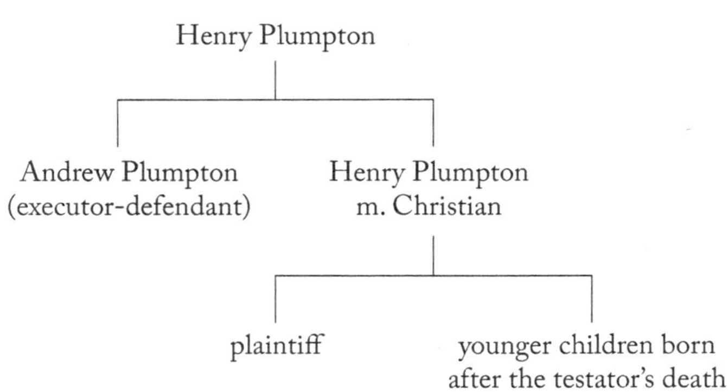

The defendant insists that the said legacy belongs to the plaintiff's younger sisters, who were born since the testator's death, and insists that, if the testator had intended £100, part of the said £200 legacy, to the plaintiff, he would have named her in the will, in regard she was the daughter of the said Henry and Christian and born before the making of the said will. And, therefore, he supposes the intent of the testator was to leave the disposing thereof to the said defendant to the end he might dispose thereof at his discretion to such of the children of the said Henry and Christian, his wife, as were most deserving and that, by the words of the said will, the children that were afterwards begotten between Henry and Christian should be equally concerned with the plaintiff, who has a brother and sister since born of the said Christian, who may claim the same of this defendant, they having as much right and interest in the same as the plaintiff. And the defendant conceived he is equally obliged to pay them the said legacy.

This court declared that the plaintiff is a person, by the will, capable to take and demand the said legacy of £100, and decreed the said £100, part of the said £200 legacy, so given by the said will as aforesaid to be paid by the defendant to the plaintiff, the plaintiff being of age and in a capacity to claim the same. And this court further declared the said £100 legacy does wholly belong to the plaintiff by the said will and that, by the words of the said will, none of the other children of the said Henry and Christian can claim the said legacy of £100 so given to the said plaintiff.

[Reg. Lib. 12 Car. II, f. 186.]

20

Philips v. Hele

(Ch. 1660–1661)

In this case, it was the intention of the testator to devise an equity of redemption to the plaintiff.

1 Chancery Reports 190, 21 E.R. 546

John Philips, being seised in fee simple of the premises, did by a deed in December 1654, for £160, mortgage the same to Elizabeth Knowling with a proviso that, if the said John Philips, his heirs, or assigns should pay to her, her executors, or assigns in three years after the said deed the said £60 with interest, then the deed to be void. And in December 1655, the said John Philips, in respect of the disobedience of his daughter Joan, the defendant, and for the continuance of his lands in his own name and blood, did by a will devise the said premises for the plaintiff in these words, *viz.*, 'all the rest of my goods, chattels, and lands, I bequeath to Ralph Philips, the younger, to discharge all things charged in my will, whom I make my whole and sole executor', which will was published in the presence of the defendant Joan. So the plaintiff, as devisee of the said John Philips of the said lands, exhibited this bill for the redemption of the premises.

But the defendant, William Hele, in the right of the said Joan, his wife, claiming the inheritance of the premises and the equity of redemption as heir of the said John Philips and a verdict at law being found for the plaintiff on a *devisavit vel non devisavit*, the defendant insists that the right of the premises and of the redemption was in the heir at law notwithstanding the devise was only in the case of a defect of a personal estate to satisfy all the testator's debts and legacies, because the devise does not import a fee simple estate, but only for the life of the devisee.

This court ordered a case to be made and to be referred to Baron Turner, who certified and declared his opinion that, according to the devise, the lands ought to continue with the plaintiff and his heirs both in law and equity and that without any kind of trust whatsoever and that the plaintiff has a right to redeem the mortgage, and not the heir, which this court decreed accordingly.

[Reg. Lib. 12 Car. II, f. 182.]

21

Bingham v. Hussey

(Ch. 1660–1661)

A marriage settlement that creates a vested right cannot be altered by a later deed.

1 Chancery Reports 192, 21 E.R. 547

Thomas Hussey settles by deed 22 Car. I [1646–47] on Delaline Hussey, his son, in consideration of a £600 portion with the wife of Delaline, and covenanted to levy a fine. And, afterwards, in 1655, the defendant procured him to make another settlement contrary to the former, and left out the limitation to the heirs male, and levied by a fine thereof.

This court, upon the proofs of the first agreement, decreed the latter deed and fine to be void and set aside and the premises to be enjoyed according to the first deed as if a fine had been levied.

[Reg. Lib. 12 Car. II, f. 170.]

22

Lady Howard v. Earl of Suffolk

(Ch. 1660–1661)

A decree in an English court of equity is in personam only, and does not bind the defendant's personal property.

1 Chancery Reports 192, 21 E.R. 547

The earl of Suffolk, being by a decree to pay the Lady Howard the arrears of an annuity and having some furniture and other movables at Bruges in Flanders, commenced suits in those parts, and arrested and seised the same there, which is expressly against the laws, rights, usages, and customs of England, which suits and process by means of a letter from the king of England were transmitted thence hither to be determined here. And the proceedings in Flanders appeared to be grounded only on the decree here.

That court taking the matter into consideration, declared and pronounced that, by the laws, rights, and course of justice in England, the said decree made against the earl of Suffolk, notwithstanding any contempt thereof, does not charge or bind his goods or movables, but his person only, nor could they be attached or seized by the decree. And [the court] discharged the arrest and seizure, and ordered this his judgment to be put into Latin and exemplified under the great seal of England.

[Reg. Lib. 12 Car. II, f. 372.]

23

Cornell v. Sykes

(Ch. 1660–1661)

In this case, the laches of the plaintiff was excused by the disability of her coverture.

1 Chancery Reports 193, 21 E.R. 547

Alice Cornel, the plaintiff's mother, whose heir the plaintiff is, being seised to her and her heirs, according to the custom of the manor, of copyhold lands, she and her husband and Paul Cornel, in the year 1635, mortgaged the premises by a surrender to Dr. Mountford for £30. And, for the non-payment thereof, the premises were forfeited, and the said Dr. Mountford took possession and disposed of the premises to Joan, his wife, for life, the reversion to the defendant Mary and her heirs. And the said Alice Cornel later died, her husband being living and leaving the plaintiff, her son and heir. She not being able to redeem during her marriage and since the premises are conveyed to one Holland, so the bill is for the plaintiff to redeem.

The defendant insisted that the plaintiff ought not to redeem, being so long since, and that the said defendant Mary had conveyed away the premises to the defendant Holland.

This court being satisfied that, in regard of the impediment in the plaintiff's mother to redeem during her marriage, the plaintiff ought to redeem, and decreed accordingly.

[Reg. Lib. 12 Car. II, f. 465.]

24

Davenport v. Longueville

(Ch. 1660–1661)

In this case, the court of equity refused to relieve a debtor against a penal bond.

1 Chancery Reports 196, 21 E.R. 548

This cause is on a case stated, *viz.* that, in 1639, the defendants, Sir Edward Longuevile and John Pollard, became bound with Sir Peter Temple and for his debt to the plaintiff in a bond of £500 for the payment of £250, which bond the plaintiff sued, and, in 1646, got a judgment against the defendant Pollard. And, in Trinity [term] 1658, he got another judgment against Sir Peter Temple on the same bond, and, in the same term, he got a judgment against the defendant, Sir Edward Longuevile. And the plaintiff extended their lands. And, in 1647, Pollard paid the plaintiff £100, and, in 1652, Sir Edward Longuevile, being under an arrest, secured to the plaintiff £500. And it was then agreed, and the plaintiff covenanted by articles between him and the said Sir Edward Longuevile that the said Sir Edward paying the said £500 and the other damages and costs sustained by reason of the said judgments against Sir Peter Temple and Pollard and the execution done thereupon being satisfied, that he would assign to the said Sir Edward the said judgments and extents thereon. In November 1652, a treaty was between the plaintiff and Sir Peter Temple and Pollard when the plaintiff owned he had received the £100 from Pollard and that the £500 was secured by the said Sir Edward Longuevile as aforesaid and that there was £60 more secured to the plaintiff in discharge of the said judgments. Whereupon, a writing, relating to the discharge of all the said judgments, was sealed and delivered by the plaintiff. And, afterwards, the plaintiff assigned the said judgments to the defendant, Thomas Longuevile, in trust for the said Sir Edward, and covenants that he neither had or would hinder, stay, impeach, release, discharge, determine, bar, or avoid them or either of them, and he enters into a bond of £500 for the performance of the said covenants. And Longuevile brings an [action of] ejectment in the plaintiff's name on the extent had against Pollard's lands. Whereupon, Pollard brought an *audita querela* against the plaintiff, and declared upon the aforesaid writing sealed by the plaintiff. And the plaintiff pleaded *non est factum*; whereupon, a verdict passed for Pollard. And, afterwards, he put the said £500 bond in suit against the plaintiff. To be relieved against which and to set aside the said release of the said judgments is the bill. This court thought not fit to relieve the plaintiff, but dismissed the bill.

The plaintiff, afterwards, exhibits his bill of review to reverse the said dismission.

And the plaintiff insisted for error that the bill is to be relieved against the £500 bond, which is for the performance of covenants, and the damnification thereupon is considerable, yet the whole penalty thereof will be recovered against the plaintiff; whereas, by the course of this court, the defendant ought to have no more than he is really damnified and shall recover upon an action of covenant at law besides what the said defendant shall make appear to be damnified he has an equity to be reimbursed for the same out of the estates of Sir Peter Temple and Pollard, as if such a note by the said Davenport had never been made.

The defendant insisted that the defendant, Sir Edward Longuevile, does swear that he is damnified above the penalty of the said bond £400 at least, and, the defendant being so damnified, this court does not in such cases direct any trial, but dismisses the plaintiff's bill.

This court conceived the said decree of dismission to be just and no error therein, and decreed the said dismission do stand confirmed, and dismissed the bill of review.

[Reg. Lib. 12 Car. II, f. 389.]
[Related cases: Longvil v. Damport (U.B. 1658), 2 Siderfin 63, 82 E.R. 1259.]

25

Weld v. Lenthall

(Ch. 1661)

A judgment by confession that is an abuse by a jailer is void and unenforceable.

Lincoln's Inn MS. Hill 125, f. 30v

5 February 1660[/61]. Sir Humphrey Weld v. Sir John Lenthall.

Canfield was in the custody of Sir John Lenthall, Marshall of the King's Bench, in execution for £2000 at the suit of Anne Moseley. Canfield was very poor, and maintained much at the charity of Sir Humphrey Weld. And he gave a warrant to Sir John Lenthall to acknowledge a judgment of £4000 or £5000, the intent whereof was to secure Sir John Lenthall for any escape of Canfield.

(Note this was a device to evade the Statute of 23 Hen. VI,[1] which avoids bonds taken for ease etc. Query if a judgment be not within the equity of that law.)

[1] Stat. 23 Hen. VI, c. 9 (*SR*, II, 334–336).

Afterwards, Moseley sues Sir John Lenthall on a pretense of an escape. Weld desires Sir John Lenthall that he might, at Weld's costs, defend the suit, whereto Sir John Lenthall assented, saying 'God forbid else'. Weld retained an attorney to assist in the business with [. . .], Sir John Lenthall's attorney, and paid them their fees and the charges of the suit. And then a plea was administered of fresh suit and reprisal. And an issue [was] joined thereon. The plaintiff proceeded not to trial in Trinity term nor Michaelmas term, but his attorney, one Lensay [?], was often demanded whether he, the said Moseley would go to trial, who held the defendant in suspense. But, after Michaelmas term, he said he would not, for now they had taken a better cause, for Sir John Lenthall had entered a judgment by force of the warrant of attorney. And he assigned the benefit of it to Moseley.

Canfield being still in the prison to this day, Weld exhibits his bill on the pretense that the escape was by contrivance and the escape [was] voluntary. The case on the proof was *ut supra*. [There was] no express proof of a combination but *ut supra* and that Sir John Lenthall was spoken to by Mr. Weld to restrain Canfield and that he would no longer stand [as] his surety. Whereupon, Sir John Lenthall said that then he must be in the common jail. And he was accordingly put into the common jail. But two hours after, when Weld was gone, he put him out of the common jail into the rules again. And some of the servants of Sir John Lenthall persuaded him that he might go abroad. The action of escape was brought within five days after the escape, for Canfield went abroad.

The decree [was] that the judgment be discharged. The court proceeded without making the *cestui que trust* or Damport, for whom Moseley was trustee, and defendant in the cause but not served *ad audiendum judicium*.

26

Summer v. Summer

(Ch. 1661)

Neither the heir of a trustee nor his wife have any interest in the lands held in trust by the trustee.

Lincoln's Inn MS. Hill 125, f. 29v, pl. 1

6 February 1660[/61].

The plaintiff conveyed his lands to John Summer in fee on trust. John died, he being married at the time of the conveyance. The plaintiff exhibited his bill against the heir of the said John and against his wife, who claimed dower.

The trust being proved, [there was] a decree by the Chancellor [Lord Clarendon] and the Master of the Rolls, Sir Harbottle Grimston, who [held] against the heir and the wife.

27

Whitingham v. Bate

(Ch. 1661)

A bona fide purchaser for value will not be required to make discovery of his title.

Lincoln's Inn MS. Hill 125, f. 30

6 February 1660[/61]. By the Master of the Rolls.

Cranwell, being seised etc., mortgages to Hatch and after[wards] to Stanton and then to Piers. And he was indebted to the plaintiff by a judgment. Bate, having notice of the judgment, buys in the several mortgages. And the heir joined in several assurances to him.

Whitingham exhibits his bill to be let in for his judgment and to discover the title of Bate, who pleaded that he was a purchaser for a valuable consideration. And he demanded judgment if he should answer farther. The plea was allowed. The plaintiff replied in effect that the pretended purchase was but on trust and fraud.

The case appeared at the hearing *ut supra*. And, because there was no more but the mortgage money and damages paid and £5 only to the heir and no farther consideration to the heir, it was but a subtlety and devise to shift the hand in order to open a countenance of a purchase.

And, therefore, [it was] decreed for the plaintiff, paying what Bate had really paid and charges of defense of the title at law to the land, touching which it was said some suits have been.

The court proceeded though the heir was not brought to a hearing. But he had answered and confessed the consideration [?] to Bate, and so had no interest.

28

Adderley v. Boughton

(Ch. 1661)

A mortgagee-creditor does not bear the loss of interest that occurred by a civil disturbance.

Lincoln's Inn MS. Hill 125, f. 29v, pl. 2

7 February 1660[/61].

[In] 1639, a mortgage was made to the defendant, Sir William Boughton, who, for non-payment, entered [in] 1644, and he held the lands until 1647. And then they were sequestered for the supposed delinquency of Aderley. The defendant endeavored to remove the sequestration. And, then, it was alleged that they were detained by the committees of Parliament for the like delinquency of the defendant.

This was alleged but not proved. Yet, in the debate *de bene esse* admitted by the court and counsel, the question was whether the plaintiff, heir of the mortgagor, should bear the loss of the profits taken for the delinquency of the one or the other.

The court decreed that the defendant having a debt not answered in law and being a defendant, that he should bear the loss neither of the one nor the other. But, as touching the moderation of interest, the court advised. Note they were both delinquents.

But, the Chancellor [Lord Clarendon] said that, if the defendant had been *rectus in curia* according to those times and had not endeavored the reversal of the sequestration, it should have been put on his account the losses of the profits. And, in that case, the Chancellor said that he did not regard the reason offered that it, the first fault, was in the mortgagor in the non-payment of his money.

29

Power v. Wallop

(Ch. 1661)

A forfeiture of a copyhold for the copyholder's making a lease of the copyhold can be waived or avoided by estoppel.

Lincoln's Inn MS. Hill 125, f. 32, pl. 1

Hilary [term] 12 Car. II.

The plaintiff, being a copyholder for life in the time of the Troubles, demised her tenement without license.

The court seemed willing to relieve, but doubted if it could be done in a case of a willful forfeiture, and directed precedents to be found.

Gray's Inn MS. 34, p. 413, pl. 1

Trinity term, 13 Car. II.

By Justice Wyndham: Making a lease for years of a copyhold by a copyholder is not a total destruction of the copyhold, but, after the lease, it is copyhold again.

Bridgeman, Chief Justice of the Common Bench, [held] *contra*, for a copyholder has but an estate at will, and, when he makes a greater estate, he destroys his own, and works a disseisin to the lord. [It is] *contra* of waste.

[It was held] by both and the Chancellor [Lord Clarendon], if a lord enter for a forfeiture committed by making a lease for years, the tenant is not relievable in Chancery, but there may be circumstances which make it relievable. And this case being that the bailiff of the manor undertaking for a license, the party, in trust thereof, did lease etc. It was relieved and decreed that the lord should admit her to her estate again notwithstanding that forfeiture.

Note this [Robert] Wallop [1601–1667], who was then lord, was one of the king's judges and in the Tower [of London] for it and, afterwards, attainted etc. *Vide* Statute 13 Car. II, c. 15,[1] a proviso for this and Mrs. Power is in the said Act to hold her said copyhold according to that decree in Chancery.

30

Oke v. Oke

(Ch. 1661)

A trustee's widow has no rights in the lands that her late husband held as a trustee.

Lincoln's Inn MS. Hill 125, f. 32, pl. 2

11 February 1660[/61].

The plaintiff, John Oke, tenant for life of himself and his son [?] of a copyhold, surrendered it to Hanniball, his brother, on an agreement that, when Hanniball was satisfied of certain moneys, he should re-surrender to John. The money being paid to Hanniball, he demanded the possession to John, the father, but, being requested to re-surrender, he did not do it, but he married the defendant Avece Oke, and he died.

Avece being entitled to her widow's estate, John exhibited a bill against Avice, and though she had a new estate derived from the custom which is paramount and John, the father's. estate was surrendered etc., yet [it was] decreed she should surrender.

31

Pile v. Pile

(Ch. 1661–1662)

In this case, it was the testator's intent that the legacies were in addition to the legatees' portions.

1 Chancery Reports 199, 21 E.R. 549

The testator gives £3000 apiece to daughters by a marriage settlement. And, afterwards, he cuts off the entail of his estate. And, by his will, he gives the same daughters £3000 apiece. The plaintiff, the heir, insists that the marriage settlement and will make but one settlement and the £3000 in both is but one £3000.

---

[1] Stat. 13 Car. II, c. 15 (*SR*, I, 317–319).

This court, with the assistance of the judges, it appearing by proof that the testator declared after the marriage settlement that he would add to his daughters' portions, were of opinion, and declared he cut off the entail on purpose to add to the portions and that the said £3000 in the marriage settlement and the said £3000 in the will made £6000 apiece, and they could not expound the deeds and will otherwise, and so dismissed the plaintiff's bill.

[Other reports of this case: 1 Eq. Cas. Abr. 204, 21 E.R. 991.]
[Reg. Lib. 13 Car. II, f. 61.]

32

Mompesson v. Drew

(Ch. 1661–1662)

There cannot be an entail of a chattel.

1 Chancery Reports 200, 21 E.R. 549

Sir Thomas Drew, being to renew a lease with the Dean and Chapter of Exeter, by his deed 9 Car. I [1633–34], whereunto the former lessees and trustees were parties, covenanted and declared that the said trustees and such persons in whose name such estate was or should be received, should stand seised or possessed thereof for the said Sir Thomas and his Lady during their lives and, after their decease, to William, his son, and Elizabeth, his wife, for their lives, and, after[wards], to the heirs male of the body of the said William and, for default thereof, to such person or persons as the said Sir Thomas should by will or any other writing nominate or appoint. William died without issue.

This court declared that the said remainder, for default of heirs male of William, to such persons as Sir Thomas should appoint in the said deed of 9 Car. I, was a void remainder in law and that there can be no entail of a chattel and the limitation to the said William and the heirs male of his body does vest the entire trust of the remaining term and the disposition thereof in equity in and upon him, so that the premises do in right belong to his executrix.

[Reg. Lib. 13 Car. II, f. 346.]

33

Wake v. Calley

(Ch. 1661–1662)

In this case, the bond creditors and the debtor's heir agreed out of court for the payment of the penalty of the bond where the debt was long overdue and unpaid.

1 Chancery Reports 201, 21 E.R. 550

A bond of £1600 penalty was entered into 19 Jac. [1621–22] to perform covenants in an indenture, the covenantors to pay £77 *per annum* until £1100 be paid. But the covenants not being performed, the plaintiff sues the bond against the heir of the obligor.

This court declared that the £1100 and interest thereupon ought to be paid and, by the consent of the parties, ordered and decreed that the £1600, the penalty of the said bond, be paid by the said defendant to the plaintiff in full of all the principal and interest and £40 costs.

[Reg. Lib. 13 Car. II, f. 395.]

34

Tibbots v. Hurst

(Ch. 1661–1662)

A surrender of a copyhold to the use of a decedent's will cannot defeat the decedent's creditors.

1 Chancery Reports 202, 21 E.R. 550

Barnabas Hurst, husband of the defendant, Katherine, senior, died indebted to the plaintiff in £30 and to others. And, intending to pay all his debts, in November 1659, he surrendered his messuage called the Woolsac to the use of his will. And, the same day, he made his will, whereby he devised the said messuage to the said Katherine, his wife, and he gave to the defendant, Katherine, junior, his daughter, £30 to be paid within a year after the other defendant Katherine's, her mother's, marriage, and £20 more at her mother's death. And he made the said Katherine, his wife, his executrix, and she to pay all debts which he owed. And he died, leaving Katherine, junior, his sole daughter and heir.

And the defendant Katherine, the executrix, intending to preserve the said messuage to herself for life and, afterwards, to Katherine, junior, she pretends that she is not liable to pay her testator's debts farther than she has assets of his personal estate. And, combining with the other defendant, Katherine, junior, who claims the said copyhold premises by descent, as heir to her father, at least after her mother's death, the executrix does refuse to sell the premises to pay the testator's debts, insisting that she is not empowered by the will in express words and that, both before and after the said will and surrender, the testator declared his intent was that his wife, by a sale of the premises, should raise money for the payment of his debts.

The defendant, Katherine, junior, says that she claims the premises as heir to her father from his death, and hopes to enjoy the same accordingly if her father did not legally dispose thereof.

This court referred the case to the judges to certify what estate the said relict or infant has in the said copyhold messuage and lands (as the will is) and whether the said relict may sell the same.

The judges are of opinion that the defendant Katherine, the elder, by the said will, has an estate of fee simple in the messuage and tenement, and may dispose thereof accordingly.

This court, thereupon, decreed the defendant, Katherine, the elder, shall sell for the best price the said messuage for the payment of the plaintiff's debts and also the other just debts of the testator and the purchaser is to enjoy against her and the defendant Katherine, junior, the infant, and her heirs. The infant, when she come of age, shall join in or confirm the sale.

[Reg. Lib. 13 Car. II, ff. 429, 629.]

35

Wood v. Caley

(Ch. 1661–1662)

In this case, the bequest in issue vested in the legatee, and was payable to her administrator.

1 Chancery Reports 204, 21 E.R. 550

William Bourne, by his will, gave Anne Wood, the plaintiff's daughter and his grandchild, all his debts, credits, and cattle to be employed for the infant's best benefit, and the executor to sell the same and, with the money, to purchase lands therewith for the use of the said Anne and her heirs and, if she died before sixteen or without issue, then, her heir should within one year after her decease pay unto the defendant Caley and to Dorothy Biwood £10 apiece. And he made Thomas Caley, the defendant's father, executor. The said Anne died without issue before any lands were purchased by the executor, though he had sold and the money [was] lying by him, and, after that, he refused to purchase. And the administration of Anne being granted to the plaintiff, he was thereby entitled to the goods of the testator Bourne, which were given to the said Anne. But the said executor of Bourne insisted that they belonged to him as executor of Bourne, the infant being dead and the money not bestowed in land.

This court decreed the defendant, the executor of Bourne, to come to an account with the plaintiff for the testator's personal estate and to pay it to the plaintiff with interest.

[Reg. Lib. 13 Car. II, f. 430.]

36

Craddock v. Marsh

(Ch. 1661–1662)

The redemption of a mortgage can be lost by the laches of the mortgagor.

1 Chancery Reports 205, 21 E.R. 551

The plaintiff moved this court that the Statute of Limitations[1] may not be made use of at law in bar to any action that shall be brought touching the matter in question in case the time limited by the said Statute elapsed since the plaintiff's bill was exhibited into this court, this being the point in controversy.

The defendant insisted that, upon hearing this cause, upon precedents produced by the plaintiff touching this point before Mr. Justice Hyde, 28 July 1660, who, not being satisfied therewith, declared he saw no cause to give the plaintiff relief and that, if any person shall bring a bill into this court and, upon a hearing of the cause, the same shall be dismissed, it is as much as if he had not brought any bill at all, and so, by the course of the court, he ought not to be relieved in this court.

As to this point, this court, with the judges, declared and ordered that, since, upon the hearing of this cause, the court then saw no cause to relieve the plaintiff, that the plaintiff's bill be dismissed out of this court and that the said defendant shall not be debarred from pleading any plea to any action at law hereafter to be brought by the plaintiff against the defendant for the matters in question.

[Reg. Lib. 13 Car. II, f. 346.]

37

Clapham v. Bowyer

(Ch. 1661–1662)

The redemption of a mortgage can be lost by the laches of the mortgagor.

1 Chancery Reports 206, 21 E.R. 551

A mortgage not being relieved after twenty years forfeiture and the estate descending to an heir and he sells the same, all this was pleaded, and [it was] held good.

[Reg. Lib. 13 Car. II, f. 337.]

[1] Stat. 21 Jac. I, c. 16 (*SR*, IV, 1222–1223).

38

Emerson v. Dallison

(Ch. 1661)

The Act of Indemnity of 1660 did not pardon court costs.

Dickens 7, 21 E.R. 168

6 March 1660[/61].

Costs under an order to expunge scandal out of a bill and tax costs were taxed at £100. Upon exceptions, they were reduced to £50. A bill of indemnity[1] having passed, the plaintiff applied to be discharged from the payment.

Lord Clarendon, Chancellor, assisted by the judges, determined he was not exempted by the Act from the payment.

1 Chancery Reports 194, 21 E.R. 547

The plaintiff having inserted into his bill scandal against the defendant, Mr. Raworth, which was referred to a Master to tax costs of such scandal, and the said Master taxed £100 costs for the defendant, Mr. Raworth, in respect thereof, His Lordship [Lord Clarendon], with the judges, declared that the said scandal was very great, yet, nevertheless, ordered that the said costs be reduced to £50 to be paid by the said plaintiff unto the said Raworth and also £5 more to be paid by Mr. Welcome, whose hand was set to the bill.

And the plaintiff insisted that the costs were pardoned by the Act of Indemnity. But His Lordship [Lord Clarendon], with the judges, were of opinion they were not.

[Reg. Lib. 1660 A, f. 30.]

39

Dawson v. Montagu

(Ch. 1661)

A purchaser of land that was held in trust who knows of the trust is not a bona fide purchaser for value even if he does not know that the trust was itself upon a trust, and he will not have any relief in a court of equity.

Lord Nottingham, *Prolegomena*, p. 255

Easter [term], 13 Car. II.

A *cestui que trust* conveys to J.S. in trust for himself, and so creates a trust on a trust. J.S., the second trustee, sells the land to J.D., who has no notice of the

[1] Stat. 12 Car. II, c. 11 (*SR*, V, 226–234).

first original trust, but was content to be charged with the second trust, and, [for the rest, prayed relief]. He shall never be relieved in Chancery, nor compel the first trustee to convey to him, for a purchaser of land without notice of a trust shall keep the land discharged. But a purchaser of a trust, as J.D. here, without notice of a precedent trust, purchases at his peril, for a court of equity will never direct the execution of a trust against conscience.

40

Thinne v. Thinne

(Ch. 1661–1664)

A grant of a manor passes reputed manors.

1 Levinz 27, 83 E.R. 280

Easter term, 1661.

An action of *assumpsit* on a feigned issue was directed out of Chancery for trying whether certain lands did pass by a common recovery and if the entail of them were thereby barred. And, on the evidence, the case was thus. A man seised of the manor of Lavington and of divers other lands there, which, in truth, were not parcel of the manor, but were purchased by the lord of the manor divers years before and, after the purchase, reputed parcel. And being so seised, with the intent to make a tenant to the *praecipe*, he bargains and sells the manor and all lands, parcel or reputed parcel, to A., against whom a *praecipe* was brought and a common recovery as suffered by the name of the said manor with a voucher of the lord. And if this recovery should bar the entail as to the lands that were not parcel was the question.

It was agreed that they passed by the bargain by the name of the reputed parcel. But it was insisted that they did not pass by the recovery of the manor, for, though, by a recovery of the manor, a manor in reputation, though it be not in truth a manor, shall pass, as Sir Moyle Finch's Case, 6 Co.,[1] is, because, otherwise, the recovery should be void. But, here, where there is a manor in fact to answer the name of a manor in the recovery, other lands which are not parcel, but in reputation, shall not pass. And, though the lands have been used with the manor now fourscore years and reputed parcel, yet they shall not pass by the recovery of the manor with its appurtenances, as it is so, for the word 'appurtenances' shall not pass a thing that is not parcel, and there may be a difference between a fine and a *praecipe* for a common recovery where the demand ought to be of certain things by certain names.

And Justice Twysden said that he had seen the opinion of all the justices at one time that the fine in Sir Moyle Finch's Case did not pass the reputed manors

[1] *Avery v. Crat* (1606), 6 Coke Rep. 63, 77 E.R. 348.

but that Sir Edward Coke, after he came to be Chief Justice, caused it to be adjudged as he reports it. And he said it was well he did so, for it would concern the settlements of very many estates. And, therefore, this case here was found specially.

And, afterwards, in Michaelmas term, 15 Car. II [1663], it was argued at the bar by *Jones*, of the one side, and *Winnington*, of the other. And the judges were then of divers opinions. And in Easter term, 16 Car. II [1664], it was argued again by *Finch*, of the one part, and Serjeant *Glynne*, of the other. And the court took time until the end of the term to deliver their opinion, and then all agreed.

And Hyde, Chief Justice, delivered the opinion for all of them that the lands reputed parcel passed by the recovery as well as the other lands and so they did in a conveyance in the case of the king, for he had made grants of the manor of St. James, which is not a manor but in reputation. And common recoveries are common assurances, and the indenture of bargain and sale which made the tenants to the *praecipe* and declared the intent was to suffer a recovery, not only of the manor, but also of all lands, parcel or reputed parcel thereof. And these lands have been reputed parcel for eighty years. And they made no difference between a fine and a recovery of a manor, where it is nothing but a manor in reputation, nor where it is a manor indeed, and other lands, besides the manor, not parcel, but so reputed both shall pass by the fine or recovery, the indenture showing the intent to pass the manor and all lands reputed parcel.

1 Keble 26, 83 E.R. 790

16 May 1661.

The court conceived that parcel of a manor in reputation only will not pass by the general words 'of the manor *cum pertinentiis*' in a recovery suffered by a tenant in tail; *a fortiori*, where the issue was out of the Chancery to find whether this parcel was docked by the recovery, which does only mention the manor in general '*cum pertinentiis*'. But it is otherwise if the grantor himself were seised in fee. Yet [they] directed it to be specially found, because desired by Serjeant *Maynard* for the plaintiff.

And Foster, Chief Justice, said that whatever his own opinion were, he would never deny a special verdict desired by any serjeant.

And it was said by Wyndham a tenancy escheat can never again be parcel of the manor, nor can any man have the same lands in fee and yet hold them of two manors, though the land may be parcel of one and the services of another manor, which the others agreed.

1 Keble 591, 83 E.R. 1129

Michaelmas term, 15 Car. II, 1663.

Upon an issue out of Chancery whether an entail were cut off of the manor in question and of Near Mead and Leverton Lees, the special verdict find these lands no parcel of the manor, but demised by copy as parcel in the time of Edward VI, and, ever since, in reputation, the manor and both the closes are in one man's possession. And whether, by eighty years' possession, this will pass *per nomen manerii* in a common recovery is the question.

Jones, for the plaintiff, conceived it did, though, without an act of Parliament, lands can neither be made a manor nor parcel [thereof]. But the name of the manor is only such a description of the thing that may make it known to the vicinage, as Sir Moil Finch's Case, which differs not from ours, being only of a manor in reputation in a fine. The objection that the demand is satisfied by the manor without these lands will make no difference, for we must look to the intention of the parties, which cannot be satisfied without these lands pass also as parcel. Expressly in this point is the case, 1 Cr. 308, Sir George Symond's Case,[1] there being only a reputation but for five years and, in a fine, which differs not from a recovery. Also the contrary would be very inconvenient to purchasers, who, by often changing, have made many parts of a manor separate and no parcels.

Winnington, for the defendant: The recovery is only '*de manerio cum pertinentiis*', although the bargain and sale be precedent, which [phrase] signifies nothing, being only to make a tenant to the *praecipe*, [they] have ample words to pass the manor. And these parcels by particular names as lands, Pl. Com. 168,[2] they cannot be parcel of other lands, but may pass by general reputation with this difference, when there is nothing but what is in reputation that passes. But here is a real manor that passes by the recovery. And, therefore, other lands that are only parcel in reputation shall not pass like an estoppel, which cannot pass part so and part by way of an interest. 2 Co., Sir R. Heyward's Case.[3] Nor can any conveyance go to two intents or two several ways, which double intent must be here to make the grant good. Hub. 171.[4] A mistake of the place or thing does only cause an abridgment of the grant, but does not make it void in all. So, Dyer 376, on a mistake of person; so Ognell's Case, on a mistake of an inferior termor.[5] Also this is rather a question of fact, the issue being whether the tail were [barred] by a recovery, and not whether they were parcel or not.

---

[1] *Symonds v. Green* (Ch. 1633), Croke Car. 308, 79 E.R. 868, Chancery Repts. *tempore* Coventry 206.

[2] *Hill v. Grange* (1556), 1 Plowden 164, 75 E.R. 253, also 2 Dyer 130, 73 E.R. 284.

[3] *Heyward's Case* (Wards 1595), 2 Coke Rep. 35, 76 E.R. 489, also 2 Anderson 202, 123 E.R. 621, Popham 95, 79 E.R. 1205.

[4] *Stukeley v. Butler* (1615), Hobart 168, 80 E.R. 316, also Moore K.B. 880, 72 E.R. 970.

[5] *Windham v. Windham* (1581), 3 Dyer 376, 73 E.R. 843, also 1 Anderson 58, 123 E.R. 352; *Ognel v. Underhill* (1587), 4 Coke Rep. 48, 76 E.R. 1000, also 4 Leonard 115, 74 E.R. 766, 1 Anderson 178, 123 E.R. 417.

KELYNG conceived the question proper, and so found, leaving it to the judgment of the court whether, by such reputation, it will pass as parcel. He also held strongly that the closes pass as parcel by this reputation.

WYNDHAM held this case is different from Sir Moil Finch's and from the other of a fine, in that a *praecipe* must demand things according to truth. But he doubted it as a considerable point.

TWYSDEN, held accordingly. And the remainder of the tenancy for life, although really a parcel of the manor, will not pass, as, in a fine, it will by such general words. And Sir Moil Finch's Case was only carried by Cooke, when Chief Justice, against the resolution of all the judges, and, therefore, it is not to be extended, although Sir Moil Finch's Case be not to be questioned, for the many estates that depend on it.

Adjornatur.

1 Keble 691, 83 E.R. 1188

Tuesday, 3 May 1664.

Finch, for the plaintiff: The tail is docked by the recovery of this reputative parcel. And, although it has been otherways adjudged, 3 Cr., Mallet's Case, 524,[1] yet Sir Moil Finch's Case, which was later judged, was *contra*, that it was docked. And, first, a manor in reputation will pass by the king's grant. But I agree reputation of a manor is not sufficient to hold a court baron if the king bring a *quo warranto*, as Staverton's Case, in Yelverton, p. 190.[2] But it is sufficient for a customary court to grant customary estates.

To the objection that, though a reputed manor may be recovered, yet, in this case, where there is somewhat to be recovered in the recovery upon which it may work, that which is but parcel in reputation shall not pass, I answer, that the reason is the same in both cases, for a common recovery is but a common assurance and, if what is parcel in reputation shall not pass in a common recovery, it shall not pass in an ordinary conveyance, which would be very mischievous. 1 Cr. 308 is a judgment in this point.

Glynne, for the defendant: Admit, if a fine or recovery be had of a reputed manor, it does pass, notwithstanding Mallet's Case to the contrary. And so is the law, ruled in Sir Moil Finch's Case. But, when there is a manor to pass, I agree you shall not bring in anything by reputation, because the party had well expressed himself. And his meaning shall not be extended beyond the words. If a man devise his lands and, in truth, he has nothing but tithes, those tithes shall pass; but, if he has both lands and tithes, the tithes shall not pass. Stiles 261, pl. 294.[3] So, if a remainder be limited to the son of J.S. and he has no true son but by

1 *Mallet v. Mallet* (1596), Croke Eliz. 524, 78 E.R. 772.

2 *Rex v. Staverton* (1610), Yelverton 190, 80 E.R. 126.

3 *Ritch v. Sanders* (1651), Style 261, 278, 82 E.R. 695, 709, 1 Eagle & Younge 407.

reputation, 3 Cr. 509, pl. 34, the remainder shall go to him;[1] but, if he had other sons, the reputed son shall not take, Moor 10, pl. [*blank*]. And agreeable hereto was the resolution in Hill against Grange, Pl. Com.

The court inclined for the plaintiff. *Sed adjornatur.*

1 Keble 716, 83 E.R. 1203

Saturday, 14 May 1664.

Hyde, Chief Justice, delivered the opinion of the court, that this Moor Meadow and Lanerton Lezo, which, since 4 & 5 Ph. & Mary, have been reputed and demised by copy as parcel of the manor of Buckland, but *revera* were no parcel, yet they pass by the bargain and sale and recovery of the manor had against the tenant in tail, because the bargain and sale which leads the recovery shows that the intent was to pass all lands, parcel or reputed so, and the recovery, being pursuant thereto and having sufficient lands, will pass this, the rather being a common assurance. Judgment [was] for the plaintiff.

2 Modern 235, 86 E.R. 1046

Easter [term], 16 Car. II [1664], in the King's Bench.

In a special verdict, the case was that Sir Thomas Thinn, being seised of the manor of Buckland in tail and of twenty acres of land called and known by a particular name, which twenty acres of land were in the time of Edward VI reputed parcel of the same manor and always used with it, sold the said manor and all the lands reputed parcel thereof with the appurtenances, of which he did suffer a common recovery. And it was adjudged upon great consideration that, though the recovery did not mention the twenty acres particularly, yet it did dock the entail thereof, because the indenture which leads the uses of the recovery was of the lands reputed parcel thereof or enjoyed with it and that the shortness in the recovery was well supplied by the deed, in which case the court were guided by the resolution in Sir George Symonds' Case.

1 Siderfin 190, 82 E.R. 1050

Easter term, 16 Car. II [1664]. Sir Henry Frederick Thin *versus* Sir James Thin.

It was found by a special verdict that Sir Thomas Thin was seised of the manors of Buckland and Laverton and of the Moore Meades, which latter are the lands in question, in tail. And he, being so seised, suffered a common recovery of the said manors with the appurtenances. And the jury found that the Moore Meades were not parcel of the manors nor any of them, but that, in the time of Edward VI, they were demised by copy as a parcel of the manor etc., *praetextu quorum*, they were reputed parcel of the manors. And the question was whether

[1] *Blodwell v. Edwards* (1596), Croke Eliz. 509, 78 E.R. 758, also Moore K.B. 430, 72 E.R. 675, Noy 35, 74 E.R. 1005.

it was a real manor and other lands that were reputed parcel of the manor and a common recovery was suffered of the manor with the appurtenances if the lands that were reputed parcel of the manor passed by this common recovery. And, after several arguments, it was adjudged for the plaintiff, *scil.* that Moore Meades, which were only parcel in reputation, passed by this common recovery, because it appeared by the verdict that it was the intent and meaning of the parties that it will pass, because the indenture of uses are [*blank*] 'or reputed as parcel thereof or occupied and enjoyed therewith', so that it is within the words. But another reason [is] because the constant practice and received opinion after Sir Moyle Finch's Case, Co. 6, has been that that which was parcel only in reputation passes.

But Twysden, Justice, said that Sir Moyle Finch's Case, reported by Lord Coke differed from the judgment then given. And Serjeant Finch, who was then concerned, went to Lord Coke and said that he was dissatisfied and would have it in judgment again. But Lord Coke dissuaded him. And, then, almost all of the justices gave to Serjeant Finch under their hands that the manor of [*blank*] there mentioned did not pass. But, inasmuch as the constant practice has been otherwise in settlements after this time, they thought that it will be dangerous to question it.

Note that Serjeant *Glynne*, who argued for the defendant, took exception to the verdict, *scil.* that it was insufficient, because, here, there is not any reputation expressly found, but the contrary, because it is found expressly that they are not parcel of the manor and, then, it is found that they were demised as parcel *praetextu quorum* they were reputed so that it was not expressly found that they were reputed parcel of the manor, but *praetextu quorum* is similar to the case where the jury finds a request and a denial in [an action of] trover etc. But, *per curiam*, the verdict is a good verdict, and the reputation was well found though the last words were omitted.

1 Ventris 51, 86 E.R. 37

Upon a special issue directed out of Chancery, the case was thus. One was seised in tail of the manor of B. and of two closes, which in reality were not part, but reputed part, thereof. And he suffered a recovery only of the manor with the appurtenances. And whether the recovery was a bar as to the two closes was the question.

And, in the 16th year of this king [1664], it was resolved by all the court, and Hyde, Chief Justice, delivered the opinion of the court that the lands reputed parcel of the manor should pass by reason of the deed of covenants to lead the uses which explained the intent.

Dyer 223; 1 Cro., Sir George Symond's Case; Hob. 177; Dyer 376; Long Quinto, Edw. IV, 303; 6 Co., Sir Moyle Finch's Case; Modern Rep. 250.[1]

[Entered: Hilary term 12 & 13 Car. II, rot. 448.]
[Related cases: Nott v. Thinn (Ch. 1673), Reports *tempore* Finch 70, 23 E.R. 37; Coventry v. Hall (Ch. 1683), Chancery Reports *tempore* North 74.]

41

Apprice v. Flower

(Ch. 1661)

Remainders and limitations of a trust of a term to persons before they are in being and also subsequent limitations and remainders are void as creating perpetuities contrary to the rules of law.

Pollexfen 27, 86 E.R. 501

24 May, 13 Car. II, upon a case stated after it had been solemnly argued.

John Flower, the elder, possessed of several terms in lands, by deed, granted them to John Selfe and others on these trusts: to himself for life and, after his death, as to part thereof, to the use of Elenor Flower for life and, after, to Jeffery Flower for life and, after, to his eldest son on the body of Mary Compton to be begotten for life, remainder to their second son for life, and so to their next and other sons, one after the other according to their ages, until the ends of the terms if any of them should so long live, and, if Jeffery Flower die without issue male of his body, then to John Flower, son of John Flower, the elder, and John, his son, for the residue of the term and, as to the residue of the lands, from the death of John Flower, the elder, to Jeffery Flower and Mary Compton for their lives and, after, to their next heir male for life, and so from heir male to heir male of their bodies to be begotten, one after the other, as they should be in age etc. until the end of the terms if any of them so long live, and, if Jeffery die without issue male or if all his sons die before the end of the terms, then to the use of their daughters, and, for default of issue, to the executors of Jeffery.

John Flower, the elder, made his will and Elenor, his wife, his executrix, who, after his decease, proved it. And, then, she made her will and the said Jeffery her executor, who, after her death, proved her will and survived John Flower, his brother, and John, his son, and Mary Compton, whom he married. And, afterwards, he married Eleonor Bowman, by whom he had issue, Thomas and

[1] *Symonds v. Green* (Ch. 1633), *ut supra*; *Swinnerton v. Miller* (1617), Hobart 177, 80 E.R. 324; *Windham v. Windham* (1581), *ut supra*; YB Mich. 5 Edw. IV, Long Quinto, f. 103 (1465); *Avery v. Crat* (1606), 6 Coke Rep. 63, 77 E.R. 348; *Addison v. Otway* (1677), 1 Modern 250, 86 E.R. 861, also 2 Modern 233, 86 E.R. 1044, 3 Keble 771, 84 E.R. 1003, 2 Ventris 31, 86 E.R. 291, 1 Freeman 227, 240, 89 E.R. 162, 171.

Eleonor, to whom, by his will, he gave all his personal estate to be equally divided between them. And he made them his executors, and died. And they proved his will.

The question [was] whether the trusts of the terms belong to Thomas Flower, son and heir of Jeffery Flower, or to Thomas and Eleonor Flower, executors of Jeffery, equally to be divided between them.

After a case stated and consideration had thereof and of several arguments had thereon, by the Lord Chancellor [Lord Clarendon] and two judges, they all agreed in opinion that the trusts of the terms limited to the first and other sons of Jeffery before they were in being and all the subsequent limitations and remainders were void, and tended to create a perpetuity contrary to the rules of law, and that the whole trusts of the terms vested in Jeffery in respect of the void limitations or remainders or as executor of Eleonor Flower, executrix of John Flower, the elder, who created the trust, and that the trust of the whole estate and terms did belong to Thomas and Eleonor, executors of Jeffery, equally to be divided between them. And he decreed the same accordingly.

1 Chancery Reports 175, 21 E.R. 542

This is on a case stated, *viz.* that John Flower, the elder, being possessed by several leases and assignments for several terms of years of the premises, made his will, and Eleanor, his wife, executrix, who proved the same. And she made her will, and Jeffery, son of the said John and Eleanor, her executor. And the said Jeffery made his will, and the plaintiff Eleanor and the defendant John Flower, his only children, his executors, and died. And, by his said will, he bequeathed unto them all his personal estate to be divided between them. And the said John Flower, the elder, by deed 4 August 38 Eliz. [1596], in consideration of a marriage between the said Jeffery and Mary Compton, assigned the premises and terms therein unto Anthony Self and others to the use of the said John Flower, the elder, for life, and the trustees, whereof the said Anthony Self was the survivor, their executors, and assigns should after the said John's decease stand possessed of the north part of the premises to the use of the said Eleanor Flower for her life and, after[wards], to Jeffery for life, and, after[wards], to his eldest son of the body of Mary Compton for life, and, after[wards], to the second son of the said Jeffery and Mary, and, after[wards], to the next son for life, and so from son to son of the said Jeffery, the one after the other, for life, until the end of the said terms, and, if the said Jeffery should die without any son or issue male of his body, either by the said Mary or otherwise, or if all his sons should die before the end of the said terms, then, he limits the same to John Flower, son of the said John, the elder, and John, his son and that the said trustees should stand possessed of the residue of the premises after the death of the said John Flower, the elder, to the use of the said Jeffery for life and, after[wards] to the said Mary for life and, after[wards], to the eldest son of the said Jeffery and Mary for life and, after[wards], to the next heir male of Jeffery and Mary for life and so from one heir male to the other heir male of the said Jeffery, one after the other, for life until the end of the said terms, and, if the said Jeffery should die without any son or issue male by the said Mary or other wife or if all his sons should die before the end of the said terms, then, to the use of his, the said Jeffery's and Mary's daughter and daughters and, for default thereof, to the use of the executors and assigns of the said Jeffery. And the said Jeffery survived John, the elder, and Eleanor, his wife, and the said John Flower, his brother and nephew, and also Mary Compton. And, after[wars], he married Ellen Bowman, by whom he had issue, the plaintiff Eleanor and the defendant Thomas, his only children. And the defendant Thomas Flower entered upon the premises in 1650, and has enjoyed them ever since.

This court, with the assistance of the judges, having advisedly considered of the case, are clearly of opinion that the remainders or limitations of the trust of the said term to the first and other son of the said Jeffery before they were in being and also the subsequent limitations and remainders were utterly void and tended to raise and create a perpetuity contrary to the rules of law and the whole trusts of the said terms vested in the said Jeffery, either as executor of the said John, the elder, that created the same or, immediately, in respect of the said void remainders or limitations and also that the trust of the said whole estate and terms does belong to the plaintiff Eleanor and the defendant Thomas Flower, executors of the said Jeffery, equally to be divided between them. And [the court] decreed the lands, according to the said trust, to go accordingly.

[Reg. Lib. 12 Car. II, f. 485.]

42

Pearse v. Reeve

(Ch. 1661)

A remainder of a trust of a term to a person after the default of issue of another person is void.

Lord Nottingham, *Prolegomena*, p. 229

Easter [term], 13 Car. II.

A trust of a term was limited to Robert Reeves, the younger, for so many years as he should live, then to Elizabeth, his wife, for so many years as she should live, then to the children of Robert and Elizabeth for so many years as they should live, and, if they die within the term without issue of their bodies or, having issue, so that issue die within the term, then to William Ironmonger. Robert and Elizabeth die without issue. William Ironmonger devises to his grandchildren, the Pearses.

[It was] resolved by Hyde, Twysden, and Brown, to whom this was referred, that the limitation to William Ironmonger was void in law and equity as being a possibility upon a possibility; second, the limitation to the children of R. Reeves in this manner, being a perfect entailing of a term and a foreign possibility to expect a dying without issue within the term, is also void; third, such a tendency would not be good in a devise. And, accordingly, the bill of Pearse against Reeves was dismissed.

Pollexfen 29, 86 E.R. 501

Robert Reeve, possessed of a term in lands, by deed, assigns the same to William Iremonger and others upon these trusts: that Robert Reeve, the younger, should receive the profits during his life, paying £44 *per annum* to Robert Reeve, the elder, and Alice, his wife, during their lives, and, after his death, Elizabeth, his wife, to receive the profits for her life, and, after both their deaths, the trustees to permit their children to receive the profits during their lives and, if Robert Reeve and Elizabeth die within the terms without issue or, having issue, if that issue die within the term, then the premises for the residue of the term to be to the use of William Iremonger and his assigns.

Robert Reeve, the elder, and Alice, his wife, died. And Elizabeth, the wife of Robert Reeve, the younger, died without issue. And William Iremonger, surviving his trustees, in the lifetime of Robert Reeve, the younger, by his will, devised the premises and all his estate therein to William Pearse and others charged with £20 *per annum* to William Pearse. And, then, William Iremonger and Robert Reeve, the younger, died, Robert Reeve having no issue by Elizabeth, his wife.

The first question [was] whether the limitations of the trust to William Iremonger in remainder be good in law or not.

The second question [was] whether the devise *supra* of William Iremonger be good in equity.

By order 22 February 13 Car. II [1661], this case was sent to Mr. Justice Hyde, Mr. Justice Twysden, and Mr. Justice Browne, by the Lord Chancellor [Lord Clarendon], who were desired to consider thereof and to give their opinions thereon, who, under the case and under their hands, gave this as their opinion.

[As to the first point,] the limitation of the trust to William Iremonger in remainder is void in law:

First, because Robert Reeve and Elizabeth had no children in being at the time of the executing of the trust and so it is a possibility upon a possibility, which cannot be by the rules of law;

Second, the limiting of the term to Robert Reeve, the younger, and to his wife and their children, as in the trust, is a perfect entailing of the term, and it is a foreign possibility to expect such a dying without issue within the term as in the trust and that such a limitation of a term is therefore void;

Third, though we do not hold it fit to call in question the judgment in Matthew Manning's Case,[1] yet we do not think it safe to stretch the law against the ordinary rules of law further than in that case it is done. And, therefore, if the devisor, by his will, does limit the remainder of it to his children or to the issue of his body whereby his intention appears to limit it in a kind of perpetuity to his issue or to his children, we hold such limitation to be void.

As to the second point in the case, we hold the limitation of the trust to the grandchildren to be void in equity, because, in this case, *aequitas sequitur legem*.

43

Jones v. Bradshaw

(Ch. 1661)

Where a decedent, before his death, ordered that his money that was in the hands of another be paid to a third party, that money is not assets of his estate.

2 Freeman 153, 22 E.R. 1124

Easter [term], 1661. Sir Samuel Jones and William Jones, executors of Sir William Jones v. Bradshaw.

Mary Cotton bequeathed £500 to one Dormer, and made Sir William Jones her executor, and died. Sir William Jones sold lands of his to Sir Samuel Jones, and left £500 of the purchase money in Sir Samuel Jones's hands, who gave a bond for the £500 to Sir William Jones. Sir William made his will and the plaintiffs his executors, and died. They inventoried the £500 as part of Sir William's estate.

Afterwards, Dormer obtains a decree against the plaintiffs for the £500 upon this, that the £500 was left in Sir Samuel Jones's hands with the intent and upon trust that he should pay it to Dormer, the court then declaring it was not assets of Sir William Jones's estate though inventoried as such.

Afterwards, the defendant, Bradshaw, brought [an action of] debt against the plaintiffs in this cause on a bond of their testator, Sir William Jones, they not having other assets and this £500 being so decreed as above. But that the decree and payment thereupon was not to be given in evidence or pleadable at law in that action.

Thereupon, the executor plaintiffs exhibit their bill here against Bradshaw, setting forth their case to the effect *supra*. The question was whether the plaintiffs should have an allowance for the payment of the said £500 against the now defendant.

And it was decreed that they should and that the matter should go to an account.

---

[1] *Clark v. Manning* (1609), 8 Coke Rep. 94, 77 E.R. 618.

And *Sir John Maynard* said that, if a man sell his land and leave £500 of the purchase money in the purchaser's hands and then give or appoint this money to be paid to a stranger and after makes his will, this stranger shall have the money, and it shall not be assets.

Vide Hob. 265.[1]

Nelson 74, 21 E.R. 793

Sir Samuel Jones and William Jones, executors of Sir William Jones, *versus* Bradshaw.

Mary Cotton bequeathed £500 to one Dormer, and made Sir William Jones her executor, and died. Sir William, the executor, sold lands to Sir Samuel Jones, and left £500 of the purchase money in his hands, who gave a bond for it to Sir William Jones in his own name.

Afterwards, Sir William Jones made the plaintiffs his executors, and died. They inventoried this £500 as part of Sir William's estate. And Mr. Dormer, the legatee, having exhibited a bill against them, obtained a decree for the £500, suggesting that it was left in the purchaser's hands with an intent and upon trust that he should pay it to Dormer.

And the court declared it was not assets of Sir William Jones's estate.

Then Bradshaw, the now defendant, brought an action of debt against the now plaintiffs, as executors of Sir William Jones, upon a bond of their testator. And they having not assets after the payment of the £500 to Dormer and that decree and payment not being pleadable to the action or to be given in evidence at law, they exhibited their bill against Bradshaw, setting forth the case as before mentioned.

And the question was whether the plaintiffs should have allowance for the payment of the £500 against the now defendant.

And it was decreed they should and that the matter should go to an account.

And it was the opinion of *Sir John Maynard* that, if a man should sell his lands and leave part of the purchase money in the hands of the vendee and then gives or appoints money to be paid to a stranger, he shall have it, and it shall not be assets.

Vide Hob. Rep. 265.

3 Chancery Reports 2, 21 E.R. 710

Easter Term, 13 Car. II [1661]. Sir Samuel Jones and William Jones, executors to Sir William Jones *contra* Bradshaw.

Mary Cotton bequeathed £500 to one Dormer, and made the testator her executor and died. And he sold lands of his to the plaintiff, Sir Samuel Jones, and

[1] *Edwards v. Graves* (1619), Hobart 265, 80 E.R. 410.

left £500 of the purchase money in Sir Samuel's hands, who gave a bond to the testator in his own name for it.

The testator made his will, and made the plaintiffs executors, and died. They inventoried the £500 as part of the testator's estate. Afterwards, Dormer obtained a decree against the plaintiff for £500 upon this equity, that £500 was left in Sir Samuel's hands with interest and upon trust that he should pay it to Dormer, the court declaring that it was not assets of Sir William Jones's estate. Afterwards, the defendant Bradshaw brought an action against the plaintiffs on a bond of their testator.

And the plaintiffs not having assets in respect of the £500 upon Dormer's decree and that decree and payment upon it not being pleadable or to be given in evidence at law, thereupon, the plaintiffs exhibit their bill here against the defendant, setting forth the case *ut supra*.

And the question was whether the plaintiffs should have an allowance for the payment of the £500 against the now defendant.

And it was decreed they should and that the matter should go to an account and the £500 so paid to be allowed the plaintiffs on account.

And *Sir John Maynard* said that, if a man should sell his land and leave part of the purchase money in the purchaser's hands and gives or appoints this money to be paid to a stranger and, after[wards], makes his will, the stranger shall have the money, and it shall not be assets.

Vide Hob. 265.

2 Vernon 57, 23 E.R. 646

An executor had paid money pursuant to a decree of this court. And, upon a *plene administravit*, they would not permit him to give that payment in evidence at law. The court decreed that it should be allowed, and referred the matter to an account in this court.

[Other reports of this case: 2 Eq. Cas. Abr. 464, 22 E.R. 396.]
[Reg. Lib. 161 A, f. 402.]

44

Collwell v. Child

(Ch. 1661–1667)

An arbitral award of only part of the submission to arbitration is void and will be set aside.

An impossible or repugnant award will be set aside.

1 Chancery Cases 86, 22 E.R. 707

Colwel against Sir William Child, a Master of this court. In court, the Master of the Rolls in the absence of the Chancellor.

All of the parties to a suit here consent to refer the whole matter to Serjeant Maynard finally to be heard and determined. And old Child, the now defendant's father, signified his consent by subscribing a paper for that purpose, so as the award was made by a certain day limited in this paper. That elapsed, and, then, the court in the presence of all parties but old Child, who was then absent, by the assent of his solicitor referred it back to Serjeant Maynard. But it was not inserted in the order that he should finally determine. Upon this, Serjeant Maynard made an award, which was afterwards decreed unless cause shown. Old Child showed for cause that he did not consent. And his solicitor made an oath he did not consent that Serjeant Maynard should finally determine.

Yet the award was decreed. Hereupon, a bill of review was brought, and error was assigned. And, upon the hearing of this bill of review, it was insisted that the matter of old Child's dissent was *dehors* and not contained in the decree. And it was said the court could not take notice of that, inasmuch as there did not appear any dissent in the decree itself.

The first error assigned was that the assent of the solicitor shall not bind the party.

Against which, it was objected that solicitors are here as attorneys at law. And, if an attorney confess judgment, the party is bound by it, and that, usually, solicitors are looked upon here as attorneys at law, as, for instance, in a Master's report made in the presence of solicitors.

But it was answered and resolved by the court that, although solicitors' assent to interlocutories may bind, yet it cannot bind to a reference finally to determine. And it was said and admitted that an attorney's assent to an award shall bind his client. And this error was declared by the court to be a good cause of reversal. And it was declared it should not lie upon the plaintiff to show old Child's dissent, for it appears upon the decree that it was the solicitor's assent. And, if the decree want a sufficient foundation, it is error, and the plaintiff shall not be put to show a negative.

And the plaintiff's counsel cited a case between Brooks and Dickens, about 1652, where an award was set aside for that the party did not actually assent to the reference, and yet he attended the reference in the business.

[Second], for that the award was but for a parcel of the matter in controversy, and not of the whole matter, whereof the reference was to determine. And this error was allowed.

[Third], for that the decree was impossible, for, by the award (decreed), old Child was to pay a sum of money 24 January 1654 or surrender an estate and the decree was dated after the said 24 January 1654 and so it was impossible. And this was allowed to be error.

[Fourth], for that the award was repugnant, for it awarded old Child to deliver up an obligation of £800 in satisfaction of £400 of £1000 which he was to pay and to vacate a suit in satisfaction of £600 residue of the said £1000, although there was not any residue after the £400 and £600 were satisfied. And this was ruled to be for error also.

And so the decree was reversed.

Then, it was moved that the solicitor, who assented and who was now solicitor in this present cause, should pay costs to the defendant Dr. Child.

But it was resolved he should not, for that the assent he gave was in court and the court knew such assent would not bind the party and it was the folly of the other party to proceed on that assent.

1 Chancery Reports 195, 21 E.R. 548

This case is on a bill of review. The bill sets forth that the former causes being heard in 1653, the court proposed a reference of the matter to arbitration, and the defendant Dr. Child, and the solicitor for the testator, William Child, submitted thereunto, whereupon the court ordered the differences should be referred to Serjeant Maynard in case the testator then living at Worcester should in writing under his hand and seal signify his consent to be bound by the said Serjeant Maynard's award without an appeal, which the testator did do if the award were made within a fortnight after the end of that Hilary term, which reference became fruitless.

And, in Trinity [term], 1654, the court again renewed the said arbitration, provided the award was made within three weeks after the end of that term, which was consented unto by the said Dr. Child and the solicitor for the said testator then present in court. And it was ordered accordingly. And an award was made in pursuance of both the said orders, and it was confirmed by a decree signed and enrolled, which decree the plaintiff insists is erroneous, for that the consent of the solicitor is not binding in such case, having no power from the party to consent thereunto.

The defendant, Dr. Child, insists that the said testator's solicitor attended the Serjeant with counsel and took a copy of the award as soon as the same was published, and, in all the time before the said award was decreed, the said solicitor or counsel never mentioned any dissent of the said testator at all.

The plaintiff insisted that the said second reference was intended to report and certify and finally to end and that the said testator's solicitor was forced into the said reference, being then accused to be an incendiary between the father and son.

This court, upon these and other errors, reversed the said decree.

2 Freeman 154, 22 E.R. 1125

Collwell v. Sir William Child, Master in Chancery. Master of the Rolls.

All of the parties to the suit were content to refer the whole matter to Serjeant Maynard finally to hear and determine. And old Child, the now defendant's father, signified his consent by subscribing a paper to that purpose, so as the award was made by a certain day limited by that paper. That time elapsed, and, then, the court, in the presence and by the consent of all parties but old Child, who was then absent, and by the assent of his solicitor, referred the matters back to Serjeant Maynard. But it was inserted in the order that he should finally determine.

Upon this, Serjeant Maynard made an award which was afterwards decreed *nisi causa*. Old Child showed for cause that he did not consent, and his solicitor made an oath that he did not consent that Serjeant Maynard should finally determine.

Yet, the award was decreed.

Thereupon, a bill of review was brought, and error was assigned. And upon the hearing of this bill of review, it was insisted that the matter was *dehors* and not contained in the decree. And it was said that the court could not take notice of that, inasmuch as nothing of the dissent appeared in the decree.

Then, it was insisted that the assent of a solicitor to an award of a final determination shall not bind the party. To which, it was objected that solicitors here are like attorneys at law who may confess judgment etc. And, to prove that solicitors are so considered, they instanced in Masters' reports made by solicitors' assent.

To which, it was answered and resolved by the court, that, though solicitors' consents shall bind their clients in interlocutory orders, yet they shall not bind in orders of award for final determination.

Second, it was resolved that it shall not come on the plaintiff's side to show the dissent of old Child, but on the defendant's [to show his assent], for, by the decree, it appears that the award was made by the assent of the solicitor, and, if the decree want a sufficient foundation, it is error, and the plaintiff shall not be bound to prove a negative. And a case was cited between Brookes and Dickers, 1652, where an award was set aside for that the party did not actually assent to the reference, although he attended the reference in the business. The award was but of part of the matters in controversy, and the submission was of the whole matters and that was allowed to be error.

Third, the award was but of part of the matters in controversy, and the submission was of the whole matters. And that was allowed to be error.

Fourth, the decree was impossible because old Child was awarded to pay a sum of money 24 January 1664[/65], whereas the decree was dated after 1664, and so it was impossible. And this error was allowed.

Fifth, that the award was repugnant, *viz.* it appearing that old Child was to pay so much in satisfaction of £1000 in controversy and that he should also pay another sum in satisfaction of the residue of the £1000, whereas it appeared there was no residue. And this error was allowed, and the decree was reversed.

Then, it was moved that the solicitor should pay costs for his pretended assent, but it was resolved that he should not, for the assent was in court, and, being an act of the court, the solicitor shall be indemnified.

Nota: If there be error in one part of a decree not dependent but distinct from the other, the court will reverse but for part. So, at law, a *scire facias* [can be] to reverse a patent for part.

[Other reports of this case: 1 Eq. Cas. Abr. 49, 50, 21 E.R. 865, 866.]
[Reg. Lib. 1660, f. 590.]

45

Lady Griffin v. Boynton

(Ch. 1661)

A lost deed or will can be proved by a copy and established by a court of equity.

Nelson 82, 21 E.R. 795

Easter [term], 13 Car. II [1661].

The plaintiff having only a copy of a deed of feoffment under which she claimed the land, the original being lost, and the defendant having a counterpart, the plaintiff desired by her bill that the copy might be compared with the counterpart, and, if it agreed, that the same might be allowed in pleading as a good deed, sealed and delivered, which was accordingly granted. And it was referred to a Master to settle the same.

So, where a plaintiff claimed lands by a will, which was proved, but the original was taken out of the Prerogative Office so that the plaintiff could have no remedy at law, and, therefore, he prayed the aid of this court. And it was decreed that the copy of the probate of the will out of the Register's book in the Prerogative Office should be admitted in evidence at law at any trial which should be had concerning the title of the said lands as the true original will. This was decreed in the same year, *viz*. 13 Car. II, *inter* Lord Gorges *versus* Foster.

46

Martin v. Gobe

(Ch. 1661)

The question in this case was whether, upon a foreclosure of a mortgage, the land goes to the heir or to the executor of the creditor-mortgagee.

73 Selden Soc. 203

17th July, 13 Car. II, *anno* 1661, between Martin and Hall, executors of Andrews, plaintiffs, and Gobe and Bridget, his wife, daughter and heir of Andrews, defendants.

The earl of Carlisle mortgaged the manor of D. to Andrews in fee for £1000 payable to him and his executors, and he covenants to pay the money, and, in default of payment, to make further assurance to Andrews and his heirs. And he gives a bond to perform covenants. The mortgage is forfeited. Then Andrews makes his will, gives his only daughter and heir but £20, his wife his household stuff, his executors the residue of all his personal estate, and dies.

The heir, to whom the forfeited mortgage descends, exhibits a bill against the earl of Carlisle to redeem or be foreclosed. And she obtains such a decree. The executors, who were no parties to that suit, exhibit a new bill against the earl of Carlisle and the heir to have this money, as being due to them by the very original defeasance of the mortgage and secured by the covenants and bonds, which belong to them to put in suit.

But this last bill was dismissed, and the first decree, which gave the money to the heir or the land unredeemable, was well approved by CLARENDON, C., and the Master of the Rolls [GRIMSTON]. They went upon these grounds. The executors wanted no assets; the heir had no other provision, but was disinherited; the gift of the personal estate would not carry a fee simple mortgage to executors.

This precedent I [Lord Nottingham] could not approve, though I were of counsel with the heir in obtaining the decree and dismission, for the decree was obtained by the precedent of Tilly's Case[1] and when there was no executor to contest it. The dismission of the executors was obtained because the court was already engaged in a former decree. But the reasons of it are not very strong, for assets or not assets is not the measure of justice to executors, but a pretense for favor to the heir, who either ought to have the money, though there be no assets, or not to have it, though there be assets. Disherison of the heir is an argument of compassion, not of right. And the gift of the personal estate by the will cannot make the case of the executors the worse, whose title was good without that bequest, for a stronger case for executors can never happen, the defeasance of the mortgage, the covenant, and the bonds all speaking for the executors.

[Other copies of this report: 3 Swanston 632, 36 E.R. 1002.]

Lord Nottingham, *Prolegomena*, p. 290

17 July 1661, 13 Car. II, by Clarendon, Chancellor, and the Master of the Rolls, between Martin and Hall, executors of Andrews, plaintiffs, and Gobe and Bridget, his wife, heir of Andrews, defendants.

[1] *Tilly v. Egerton* (Ch. 1660), see above, Case No. 4.

The earl of Carlisle mortgages the manor of D. to Andrews in fee for £1000 payable to him and his executors, and he covenants to pay the money and, in default of payment, to make further assurance to Andrews and his heirs. And he gives a bond to perform covenants. The mortgage is forfeited. Then Andrews makes his will, and gives his only daughter and heir but £20, his wife his household stuff, his executors the residue of all his personal estate, and dies.

The heir, to whom the forfeited mortgage descends, exhibits a bill against the earl of Carlisle to redeem or be foreclosed, and obtains such a decree. The executors, who were no parties to that suit, exhibit a bill against the earl of Carlisle and the heir to have the money, as being secured by covenants and bonds which belong to executors to put in suit.

But this last bill was dismissed and the first decree, which gave the money to the heir or the land [to be] irredeemable, was well approved, for there being no want of assets to the executors and no provision for the heir by the will, it was against equity to disinherit her of what descends. And, besides, the testator, having given nothing to the executors but the residue of his personal estate, which did not pass a fee simple mortgage, could not intend a disinherison.

2 Vernon 67, 23 E.R. 652

The heir of the mortgagee had foreclosed the mortgagor, the executor of the mortgagee being no party. And, afterwards, upon a bill by the executor against the heir of the mortgagee and against the mortgagor, the land was decreed to the executor.

[Earlier proceedings in this case: *sub nom.* Earl of Carlisle v. Gobe (Ch. 1660), 118 Selden Soc. 736, 3 Chancery Reports 94, 21 E.R. 739, Nelson 52, 21 E.R. 787, 2 Freeman 148, 22 E.R. 1121, 2 Eq. Cas. Abr. 173, 22 E.R. 148.]
[Order of 1 March 1660: Public Record Office C.33/213, f. 220v.]

47

Davies v. Beversham

(Ch. 1661–1663)

Where a purchaser of land dies and devises the land before the conveyance be executed, the land passes in equity to the devisee.

1 Chancery Cases 39, 22 E.R. 683

The Lord Chancellor, Master of the Rolls. Davie v. Beardsham.

Davie agrees for the purchase of certain copyhold lands which were surrendered out of court to his use. But, before admittance, he dies, having other copyholds and having made his will after the said contract. And he thereby devised to the plaintiff, who was then and at his death, his visible heir, all his copyholds after his death. His wife, being *priviment enceinte* at his death, is delivered of the defendant's wife, who then becomes the heir of the devisor. The plaintiff, taking it for granted that the copyholds so contracted for did not pass by the will, suffered the heir to be admitted thereunto, and held the same of the heir for twenty years, and paid her rent for that time, and had agreed so to do as long as he should hold them.

Afterwards, differences arising between the heir and him about other matters, the plaintiff exhibited his bill (*inter alia*) to have those copyhold lands decreed him.

And it was declared upon the hearing by the court that it was clear the said copyholds so agreed for did pass the will to the plaintiff, for that the purchaser had an equity to recover the land and the vendor stood trusted for the purchaser and as he should appoint until a conveyance be executed. And the case of the Lady Fohaine, about 1657, was cited, where it was ruled that, if, upon articles for a purchase, the purchaser dies and devises the land before the conveyance be executed, the land passes in equity.

But, in the principal case, inasmuch as the plaintiff had admitted the title to be in the heir and paid her rent and agreed so to do, the court would not decree it but declared, if the plaintiff had come in time, it was proper to be decreed.

2 Freeman 157, 22 E.R. 1127

Michaelmas [term], 13 Car. II.

Henry Davies agrees for the purchase of certain copyholds which were surrendered out of court to his use. But, before admittance, he dies, having other copyholds. And having made his will after the said contract, he devised to the plaintiff, who was then his visible heir, all his copyholds. His wife, after his death, being then *priviment enceinte* was delivered of the defendant's wife, who then became heir to the devisor. The plaintiff, admitting that the copyhold contracted for did not pass by the will, takes a lease of it from the heir for twenty years, and agrees to hold it longer at the rent.

Afterwards, differences arising, the plaintiff sues for the copyhold so contracted for as passing by the devise *supra*.

And it was declared by the court that the copyhold did pass by the will to the plaintiff, for that the purchaser had an equity to recover the lands and the vendor stood seised in trust for the purchaser. And the case of the Lady Falcomb, 1651, was cited, wherein it was ruled that, if, upon articles for a purchase, the purchaser dies and devises the land before the conveyance be executed, the lands do pass in equity.

But, in the principal case, because the plaintiff had admitted the title to be in the defendant and paid rent and agreed so to do, the court would not decree, but declared, if the plaintiff had come in time, it had been proper for a decree.

Nelson 76, 21 E.R. 793

Michaelmas [term], 13 Car. II [1661]. Daire v. Beversham.

Henry Daire agreed for the purchase of copyhold lands, which were surrendered out of court to his use. But he died before admittance, having other copyhold lands and also having made his will after the said agreement. And he, thereby, devised to the plaintiff and his heirs all his copyhold lands, he being at that time his heir at law. But his wife being with child, she was afterwards delivered of a daughter, now the wife of the defendant Beversham.

The plaintiff taking it for law that the copyhold land, for which Henry Daire had contracted and to which he never was admitted, did not pass by his will, he suffered the daughter to be admitted. And she held the same for twenty years, and the plaintiff paid rent for that time, and agreed so to do as long as he should hold the lands.

Afterwards, differences arising between him and her, the plaintiff exhibited his bill to have these copyhold lands decreed to him.

And, upon hearing the cause, it was declared by the court, that it was clear the copyhold lands, for which the testator had agreed and which were surrendered to him out of court, did pass by his will, though he died before admittance, for that the purchaser had an equity by the contract to recover the same and the vendor stood entrusted for him until a legal conveyance was executed. And he cited the Lady Foliamb's Case in 1651, wherein it was ruled that, if articles are signed for a purchase and then the purchaser devises the lands and dies before any other conveyance is executed, the lands do pass in equity.

But, in the principal case, no decree was made, because the plaintiff had admitted the title to be in the defendant as heir at law, and he paid his rent for many years. But [it was] declared, if he had come in time, it was proper for a decree.

3 Chancery Reports 4, 21 E.R. 711

Michaelmas [term], 13 Car. II [1661]. The Lord Chancellor and the Master of the Rolls.

Henry Davie agrees for the purchase of certain copyhold lands, which were surrendered out of court to his wife. But, before admittance, he dies, having other copyholds. And, having made his will after the said contract, [he], thereby, devised to the plaintiff, who was then and at his death his visible heir, all his copyhold after his death. His wife, being *privement enceinte*, after his death, is delivered of the plaintiff's wife, who then becomes the heir to the devisor. The plaintiff, taking it for granted that the copyholds so contracted for did not pass by the will, suffered the heir to be admitted thereunto. And he held the same of the heir for twenty years, and paid her the rent for that time, and had agreed so to do, so long as he should hold them.

But, afterwards, differences arising between the heir and him about other matters, the plaintiff exhibited his bill (*inter alia*) to have these copyholds decreed to him.

And, upon the hearing, it was declared by the court that it was clear the said copyholds so agreed for did pass by the will to the plaintiff, for that the purchaser had by the contract only an equity to recover the land and the vendor stood trusted for the purchaser and as he should appoint until a conveyance be executed. And the Case of the Lady Fohamb, in 1651, was cited, where it was ruled that, if, upon articles for a purchase, the purchaser dies and devises the lands before the conveyance be executed, the lands do pass in equity.

But, in the principal case, inasmuch as the plaintiff had admitted the title to be in the heir and paid her rent and agreed so to do, the court would not decree, but declared, if the plaintiff had come in time, it was proper to decree.

[Other reports of this case: 1 Eq. Cas. Abr. 174, 21 E.R. 968.]

48

Needler v. Wright

(Ch. 1661–1662)

In this case, the court held the conveyance in issue to be valid, and not voluntary or fraudulent.

Nelson 57, 21 E.R. 788

Needler *versus* Barbara and Robert Wright. Lord Clarendon, assisted by the Lord Chief Justice Hyde.

Charles Wright, being seised in fee of an estate expectant upon the determination of the life of Dorothy Wright, did in 1636 for a valuable consideration demise the same to one Blemell for fifty-one years to commence after the death of the said Dorothy, rendering rent, etc. Blemell surrendered the said lease. And, afterwards, the said Charles Wright, in consideration of £25, demised the premises to one Lawrence for sixty-one years to commence as aforesaid, and covenanted that he was seised in fee, that he had power to make leases, and that he would make any further assurance. And he confessed judgment for the performance of covenants, and also made an oath that he was seised in fee etc.

The interest of this lease, by several mesne assignments, came to the plaintiff Needler. And, Dorothy Wright being dead, the plaintiff assigned the lease to another in trust to attend the inheritance. And, by a fine and recovery and also by deed enrolled, he purchased the reversion and inheritance of the premises. And, being in possession, he laid out £1000 and upwards in building, and enjoyed the same until the death of Charles Wright. After whose death, Barbara and Robert Wright claim the lands by virtue of an old dormant entail precedent to any of the said estates, Barbara claiming only an estate for life and Robert the inheritance by virtue of a deed and fine by which it was entailed on him.

The plaintiff exhibited his bill to have the validity of this deed examined, alleging it to be voluntary.

And, thereupon, a trial at law was directed, whether fraudulent or not.

And no fraud being proved, a verdict passed for the defendant.

And, thereupon, the court would give no relief nor the defendant any costs.

49

Bulstrode's Case

(Ch. 1661)

A mortgagor can have relief against a statute of a mortgagee that has been extended.

Lincoln's Inn MS. Hill 125, f. 32v, pl. 1

Michaelmas [term] 13 Car. II.

Bowstred conveyed his lands in fee absolutely, but he had covenants of reconveyance in case he paid £1000, which was not paid at the day. Afterwards, the mortgagee (for such he was in effect) acknowledged a statute for a just debt. Bulstrod paid his money. And, then, he exhibits his bill to be relieved against the statute.

Objection: The conusee has a legal interest and comes in for a good and valuable consideration. And it was agreed that, if he had been a purchaser or a second mortgagee without notice, that Bulstrod could have had no relief to set aside the purchaser or second mortgagee without satisfaction. But, in the case of a statute or [confessed] judgment, it was otherwise. And Bulstrod was relieved.

Note there is a particular contract for the land in the one case; in the other, there is not, but *concedit quod de terris suis etc. debitum tenetur.* But, in equity, these lands are none of his [. . .] if Bulstrod had notice of the extent when he paid his money, for he might have paid him [. . .]. The court took no such difference.

50

Hamby v. Read

(Ch. 1661–1665)

In this case, a settlement of land was construed and enforced by a court of equity.
An original bill does not lie to explain the intent of a final decree.

Lincoln's Inn MS. Hill 125, f. 32v, pl. 2

Michaelmas [term], 13 Car. II.

The father of the plaintiff had settled upon Read, the father of the defendant, now an infant, and Ogle, cousins of Read, the manor of Wrangle and other lands to the value of £600, and he died, the plaintiff being his son and heir of two years of age.

Sir John Mounson in the behalf of the plaintiff, then being an infant, questioned the assurances made by the father of the plaintiff upon Read and Ogle, upon which, for the prevention of suits, articles of agreement were made between Sir John Mounson of one part in the behalf of the plaintiff and Read and Ogle of the other part, by which Sir John Mounson etc. covenanted that the plaintiff, at his full age, with one William Hamby to whom it was supposed by a former settlement a remainder in tail was limited will be assured of the lands to Read of that which was conveyed to him and to Ogle of that which was conveyed to him, and, upon request, Read covenanted to assure the manor of Wrangle upon the plaintiff and, if this was not done of £110 *per annum* to supply such value from other land there. Olge covenanted to convey Maulton Manor to the plaintiff at fifteen years' value, and Read was to pay £110 *per annum* in the interim, which was paid for some years. The infant did not disturb the settlement of his father but, afterwards, at full age [. . .] upon the settlement according to the covenant of Sir John Mounson and for William also that he will join. And he prays for an assurance or enjoyment of Wrangle. But Read, the covenantor, was dead, his heir being an infant under age.

The bill was [brought] by the plaintiff alone (without Sir John Mounson, the covenantee) against the heir and executor of Read, who answered. And, upon oyer of the articles, [it was] decreed that the plaintiff enjoy Wrangle against the infant defendant and that he will make an assurance at his full age and the executor pay the profits £110 *per annum* received by the father and the infant after his death. There was no default that William had not [. . .] it no request [?] to him proved, but the plaintiff, before [he] benefit from the decree, was to procure Sir John Mounson to release and William to join in the assurance. The purchase [was] also decreed of Maulton.

1 Chancery Cases 44, 22 E.R. 686

18 February. Reed v. Hanby.

The bill was to explain a decree, wherein the case was one [was] seised of the manor of Wrangle, worth near about £110 *per annum*, and another of a farm in Wrangle held of the same manor, worth £250 *per annum*. And the fee of both came after into one person's hands, he having articled to settle the manor of Wrangle, worth £110 *per annum* with the improvements. It was, on the articles, decreed his heir should convey the manor of Wrangle with all the improvements to the plaintiff in the first suit and, if the manor was not worth £110 *per annum*, it should be made up out of the other lands. By this decree and unity of possession of the manor and farm, the plaintiff claimed all the manor and farm.

And the bill, being to explain the decree, charged the farm to be worth £250 *per annum* and the manor £110 *per annum*, and, therefore, desired to have the decree explained, whether the decree intended all or only the manor, according to the articles.

The demurrer was for that it was an original bill, and sought to alter or change the decree.

For the plaintiff, it was insisted that the plaintiff was without any possibility of help but by this bill, for that, it being to be relieved upon a fact not in issue nor appearing in the former cause, a bill of review would not lie for it and that the defendant, by having demurred, had admitted the bill to be true. And, then, the case was that the lands claimed without the decree were worth £400 *per annum*, whereas the articles on which the decree was founded were but for £110 *per annum*. And, therefore, it was strongly urged that they ought to answer.

For the defendant, it was replied that no original bill ought to explain a decree upon any matter precedent to the decree. And the consequence of that was alleged to be dangerous, for it would be introductive of a means to blemish and hinder the execution of a decree. And, as to the hardship of the decree or the intent of it, it was insisted that that would be fit for determination upon an execution for non-performance, where the defendant might set forth what he had to say for his excuse, and then it would be proper for the court to declare what was the intent of the decree and that the justice or the injustice of the decree might then be determined.

And of this opinion, the court seemed to be. But the plaintiff's counsel insisting that the defendant would be bound in a prosecution on the decree by the letter of it and could not then put any interpretation on it against the letter of it, they therefore prayed leave of the court to set forth the special matter on examination, which the court would not give an order for.

And as to the plaintiff's objection that the demurrer admitted the bill and so ought to have an answer, because the manor and lands were of the value *ut supra*, it was answered by the defendant's counsel *allegari non debuit quod probatum non relevat*.

And the demurrer was allowed.

Then the plaintiff's counsel prayed the signing and enrolling of the dismission on the demurrer might be stayed until the plaintiff was examined on interrogatories for breach of the decree etc.

But the court denied it.

2 Freeman 179, 22 E.R. 1144

18 February, 15 Car. II [1663]. Lord Chancellor, Baron Turner.

One, seised of the manor of Wrangle worth £110 *per annum* and of a farm in Wrangle worth £250 *per annum*, articles to sell the manor and, if that the manor were not worth £110 *per annum*, he would make it up with the farm lands. The plaintiff got a decree upon these articles, which was so penned that the whole farm was by general words included.

The defendant exhibited a bill to have the decree explained, on which the defendant demurred.

It was insisted that no bill of review did lie because nothing could appear to the court on the body of this decree to alter it.

On the other side, it was insisted that it ought not to be by an original bill because it would tend to overthrow all decrees and hinder their execution and diminish their force, and that the way must be to set forth the matter on interrogatories upon the writ of execution.

To which, it was answered by the plaintiff's counsel that the defendant in the first decree could not set forth any such matter in the interrogatories, but only answer to the contempts, admitting the words of the decree. Also, the plaintiff insisted that the demurrer confessed the matter of the bill.

But the court allowed the demurrer good [and] dismissed the plaintiff's bill but without prejudice to his setting forth what he could on the prosecution of the said decree to excuse himself.

Lord Nottingham, *Prolegomena*, p. 298

Hilary [term] 16 Car. II.

Hanby had a decree against Reed to convey the manor of Wrangell in Lincolnshire according to articles. Reed exhibits a new bill, pretending that Blackacre in Wrangell was not within the articles, nor intended to be comprised within the decree.

And, on a demurrer, the bill was dismissed, as being against all the forms of the court: first, because no man can exhibit a bill to pray an explanation of a former decree, but, when he is served with the decree and attached for disobedience, if he can set forth anything special to excuse himself, let him; second, else these inconveniences will follow: (i) the intention of the court will be put in issue, *quod absurdum est*; (ii) no man hereafter will either perform a decree or bring a bill of review until he has first tried a bill of explanation; (iii) and yet the bill of explanation suspends not the former decree nor hinders any process upon it.

Lord Nottingham, *Prolegomena*, p. 300

Hilary [term] 16 Car. II.

Hanby had a decree against Read to convey the manor of Wrangell in Lincolnshire according to articles. Read exhibits a bill, pretending that Blackacre in Wrangell was not within the articles, nor intended to be comprised within the decree.

And, on a demurrer, the bill was dismissed, for a bill to explain a decree must not be received. But the defendant, when he appears on the attachment for disobedience to the decree, must set forth the special matter, and, if that excuses, it is well and good. Otherwise, by this new bill, the intention of the court would be put in issue, which is absurd. And yet, this new bill neither suspends the former decree nor hinders process of contempt upon it. But, if this bill be admitted, then, it would be a good ground for a motion to stay process on the decree, which course would be new and dangerous, for then every man, before he perform a decree or bring a bill of review, would resort to bill of explanation.

[Other reports of this case: 2 Eq. Cas. Abr. 77, 21 E.R. 67.]
[Reg. Lib. 1663 B, f. 397.]

51

Barnes's Case

(Ch. 1661)

A court of equity can grant relief against a false return of a writ that was filed by a sheriff.

Lincoln's Inn MS. Hill 125, f. 35, pl. 2

27 September 13 Car. II.

A *scire facias* was sued on an old judgment. A *scire feci* [was] returned against Barnes, who, in truth, was a purchaser of lands from the creditor before the judgment in the original action; yet, on the return of the *scire feci*, judgment [was] given against him at law, he having no notice, in truth, though the sheriff's return was otherwise.

And, on a bill, [he was] relieved because [there was] no notice proved. And a trial [was] directed if his lands were extendible on the first judgment or not.

52

Emmanuel College v. Ackland

(Ch. 1661)

A decree in favor of an advowson cannot be frustrated by an institution and induction of a rector to fill a vacancy in the church.

Lincoln's Inn MS. Hill 125, f. 35v

The College had a decree against Ewins for the advowson of North Cadbury 2 Car. [1626 × 1627]. The church falling void, Dr. Ducke presented Mr. Ackland, who was instituted and inducted. And after that he had been above a year in possession as the incumbent, the College took out a subpoena against Mr. Ackland in the nature of a *scire facias* to execute the decree and to cause him to resign. And the Lord Chancellor ordered it.

After, the defendant, having leave by order to set forth what he would for his excuse of the contempt, alleged *ut supra*. It was debated [whether] the decree was for the advowson, not for the parsonage. And the incumbent came not in by the patron only, but by the institution, and he had been in [for] a year. And there was no reason to dismiss [?] the church after such a plenarty, and no reason that the plaintiff, who had the title in equity, should be in a better case than if he had a title in law, which is bound to six months. And, if they had discovered in a writ of right, yet, if the church fall void and the tenant present and his incumbent [be] in by six months, he shall never be removed. And the precedent would be of dangerous consequence to the peace of the church, for, if a mortgagor or a *cestui que trust* obtain a decree and will not execute it but stand upon his decree, he may by this means always disturb the church *toties quoties* it falls void letting a plenarty be had and then, after many years, remove the incumbent this way by a subpoena. And it may be in time a means to introduce simony, for he may set up an incumbent and, if he will not compound with him, oust him.

Justice WYNDHAM, who heard the matter, ordered against Mr. Ackland on the matter as also because he concurred that the order had already settled it. But, if not, he said that the plenarty, though for ten years, altered not the case.

53

Anonymous

(Ch. 1661)

A mortgagor of two mortgages shall redeem both or none.

Lincoln's Inn MS. Hill 125, f. 36

Michaelmas [term] 13 Car. II. Rolls.

A mortgagor of two mortgages shall redeem both or none. [It was] decreed the contrary in Trinity or Michaelmas [term] last between Loid and [blank]. [It was] decreed in court and affirmed before the Lord Chancellor [LORD CLARENDON] on appeal from the decretal order.

Note they were both old mortgages.

54

Manley v. Manley

(Ch. 1661)

Where the ownership of land is in litigation, a purchaser of the land takes it subject to the outcome of the litigation.

Lincoln's Inn MS. Hill 125, f. 33v

9 November 1661, 13 Car. II.

The case [was thus]. Sir Richard Manley, father of the plaintiff, by articles on a marriage and in consideration of a marriage portion that he received, covenanted to settle all his lands on the plaintiffs. Part was settled. He, afterwards, agreed particularly to settle on the plaintiffs a house. And, by a former decree, the same was to be accordingly done. And a decree [was] made for enjoyment against Sir Richard and all claiming by, from, or under him since the bill. But it fell out that Sir Richard, six days before the former bill [was] exhibited, *viz.* 4 November, did by bargain and sale in consideration of £300 (so mentioned in the deed) convey the house to George Cox, one of the defendants, a kinsman of Sir Richard Manley's second wife, and, 4 February following, George Cox, for £286 (as was mentioned in the deed and proved to be paid by one witness, *viz.* George Cox himself) conveyed to Thomas Manley.

The bill is exhibited against the defendant, who conveyed the title to himself under Thomas Manley to put the decree in execution.

Ob[jection] first: If the plaintiff have a right, he has an ordinary remedy to serve the decree. And, if the defendant be bound by the decree and come in *pendente lite*, there needs no new bill. A new bill is irregular.

Response: If the plaintiff should proceed in the ordinary course, he cannot so well examine if the plaintiff, who comes in by fraud to defraud the decree, should be bound thereby and does thereby properly bring this bill to sift and examine the matter, for, in truth, the defendant claims under a title paramount to the decree *prima facie.*

Curia regarded yet not this objection, but overruled it.

The great question was if the defendant's interest should be bound by the decree. And [it was] adjudged he should, not because he came under Cox, whose conveyance was very suspicious, being made so shortly before the bill and acknowledged but the same day the bill was exhibited, but because there was no manner of proof of payment of the £300. And it was very unlikely that, if Cox had purchased for £300 [on] 4 November, that, in February following, he would have sold for £286 to Thomas Manly. And it was proved Cox was procured to sell at Sir Richard Manly's request. So, as the purchase of Cox was taken to be in trust for Sir Richard and, consequently, Thomas Manly, in effect, came in *pendente lite.*

Reporter: Query; he himself seems no clear purchaser.

55

Wheldale v. Brazenose College

(Ch. 1661)

A court of equity can order an accounting and the payment of debts.

Lincoln's Inn MS. Hill 125, f. 34v

Wheldale, executor of Dr. Ratcliffe v. Brazen Nose College.

The College, [in] 1643, being greatly indebted, *viz.* £1500 to Buchers etc., the bishop of Lincoln, the visitor, sent a visitation before the commissioners. The fellows complained of the Doctor [Ratcliffe] for that he held a lease of the College lands contrary to their statutes. The bill pretends that the Doctor and fellows came to an agreement that the Doctor should yield up his leases to be sold, the money to pay the College debts, and the College having divers debts due, the Doctor should be reimbursed out of those debts.

The defendants, on oath, denied the agreement.

The proof was positive by Dr. Chaworth and various by others.

The Doctor [Ratcliffe], by his will, 1648, gave several legacies out of this £1500, *viz.* £500 to the College, £400 for an almshouse to Steeple Aston (the administration whereof belonging to Brazennose College) and other great sums out of his estate to the College, £150 to the plaintiffs, his executors. And they sued for the £150 out of the debts.

The defendants insisted on the weakness of the proofs against their oaths, second, that the Doctor has since paid debts of his own to the College in 1644, 1645, [and] 1646, which he would have recouped, especially it appearing under his hand that he was present and subscribed an account [in] 1644, when the debts of the College, out of which he was to be paid, were paid in to the College, third, he was a benefactor, but it is hard the now fellows should pay etc. And an agreement by parol cannot bind the College, especially an agreement made between the Principal and fellows, the head and members.

But the court decreed an account and payment out of the debts.

56

Shoreditch v. Garret

(Ch. 1661)

A court of equity has a general jurisdiction over cases of fraud.

Lincoln's Inn MS. Hill 125, f. 34 [bis]

Michaelmas [term] 13 Car. II.

Michael Shoreditch, the grandfather, mortgaged to Ed. Say. And that was paid, but [there was] no reconveyance. The mortgagor died. Richard, his son, by persuasion of his mother's friends (she being sick and afterwards died) and Ed. Say entailed the lands to Richard for life, the remainder to the now plaintiff in tail, which was done to assure them to the plaintiff in case his father should marry. After[wards], Richard did mortgage to Garret, who exhibited a bill to have the money or lands and to discover encumbrances. The son appeared. One of the Six Clerks was assigned his guardian, but, after[wards], Richard, his father, who set forth the said assurance.

On [the] hearing, the court respited their judgment as to the assurance, but decreed against a lease for sixty years set forth also by the father. The cause was revived against the son and, without a trial, the assurance [was] decreed fraudulent. And this chiefly [was] assigned for error, because it was done without a trial or verdict, it being a cause of inheritance.

TWYSDEN and WYNDHAM, justices, inclined, and said it was their opinion it might be, being that they had conusance of fraud before the Statute 27 Eliz.,[1] but respited their opinions, and ordered an answer notwithstanding the demurrer to the bill of review, but saving the advantage until the hearing.

57

Forrester v. Barker

(Ch. 1661)

In this case, the court enforced a contract in favor of third-party beneficiaries thereof, who were the creditors of a decedent's estate.

Lincoln's Inn MS. Hill 125, f. 34v [bis]

Michaelmas [term] 13 Car. II, at the Rolls.

The heirs, male and female [. . .], consented about the inheritance of Rowland Barker, debtor to Forrester. Margaret, the defendant, as guardian to her child, articles with the heirs etc. in the behalf of her son, an infant heir male, and in the behalf of herself, the substance whereof was that she should pay all the debts of Rowland, except some which the others undertook and to discharge Margaret of those others.

The creditors are plaintiffs to enforce Margaret to make payment to them [. . .] within Margaret's share. But she refused to pay farther than she had assets and then her son, the heir of Rowland, was liable. And she insisted that the plaintiffs were no parties to the articles and the scope was to serve one another only, not for the benefit of the creditors.

Curia: The articles [are] to pay, and [the court] decreed [?] the debt.

[1] Stat. 27 Eliz. I, c. 4 (*SR*, IV, 709–711).

58

Thurbon v. Courthip

(Ch. 1661)

In this case, the testator's timing of the payment of legacies did not create a conditional gift, but it was only a direction as to when the payments were to be made.

Lincoln's Inn MS. Hill 125, f. 35, pl. 1

15 November 1661, at the Rolls.

[It was] decreed that legacies payable at several times yet must be paid in expectation and the legacies to his sister's children were appointed in the negative not to be paid until all the rest were satisfied and paid; yet they shall come in for their proportion.

Reporter: Query; the estate falling short, they can never be paid.

But the court held it not a condition to the legacy, but to go only to the time of payment.

59

Hollowell v. Abney

(Ch. 1661–1663)

Notice to an agent is notice to the principal.

1 Chancery Cases 38, 22 E.R. 682

26 November [1663]. Merry against Abney, the father, and Abney, the son, and Kendal. All which were heard on Abney, the son's, plea, about Trinity [term] 12 Car. II [1661], and the same cause was heard this day. Chief Justice Foster, the Master of the Rolls.

Kendal contracted with the plaintiff to sell him certain lands in Leicestershire. Afterwards, Abney, the father, who lived near the lands, in behalf of Abney, the son, a merchant in London, purchased those lands of Kendal, and had a conveyance from Kendal to Abney, the son, and his heirs.

The plaintiff's bill was to be relieved upon his contract with Kendal and against the conveyance to Abney. And he charged notice of his contract to both the Abneys. Abney, the son, pleads himself to be a purchaser *bona fide* without any notice of Kendal's contract with the plaintiff and without any trust for his father.

The court declared that notice to the father in this case was notice to the son, and should affect the son, who was the purchaser, so that notice of a dormant encumbrance to a party that purchased for another shall affect the very purchaser.

And accordingly was this cause decreed, it appearing at the hearing that Abney, the father, had notice of Merry's contract before he purchased for his son.

2 Freeman 151, 22 E.R. 1123

26 November 1663, 15 Car. II. Judge Foster and the Master of the Rolls. Merry v. Abney.

Kendall contracted with the plaintiff to sell him certain lands in Leicestershire, after which, Abney, the father, living near those lands, in the behalf of Abney, the son, a merchant in London, purchased those lands of Kendall, and had a conveyance from Kendall to Abney, the son, and his heirs.

The plaintiff's bill was to be relieved upon this contract with Kendall and against the conveyance. And he charged notice of this contract to both the Abneys.

Abney, the son, pleaded himself a purchaser *bona fide* upon a valuable consideration without notice of Kendall's contract with the plaintiff and without any trust for his father.

Curia: Notice to the father, who transacted, is notice to the son, and shall affect him; so notice of a dormant encumbrance to one who purchases for another is notice to the purchaser. And, accordingly, this case was decreed at the hearing, *viz.* that they should convey to Merry, the plaintiff, it appearing at the hearing that Abney, the father, had notice of Merry's contract before he purchased for his son.

Nelson 59, 21 E.R. 789

Hollowell, Kirk, and Merry *versus* Abney, Abney, and Kendall.

Kendall contracted with Merry to sell him certain lands in Leicestershire. Afterwards, Abney, the father, who lived near the lands, purchased the same of Kendall, in behalf of Abney, his son, a merchant in London, and had a conveyance from Kendall to Abney, the son, and his heirs.

The plaintiff Merry exhibited his bill to be relieved upon his contract with Kendall and against the conveyance to Abney, and charged notice of this contract to both the Abneys.

Abney, the son, pleaded that he was a purchaser *bona fide* for a valuable consideration without any notice of Kendall's contract with Merry and without any trust for his father.

The court declared that, in this case, notice to the father was notice to the son, and should affect him, though a purchaser, for notice of a dormant encumbrance to a party who purchases for another shall affect the purchaser himself, and decreed that Abney should convey to Merry, the plaintiff, it appearing that his father had notice of the contract before he purchased for his son.

[Other reports of this case: 1 Eq. Cas. Abr. 330, 21 E.R. 1081.]

60
Davis v. Wakefield
(Ch. 1661)

If a plaintiff sue simultaneously in the Court of Chancery and the Court of Exchequer for the same matter, he will be required to elect to proceed on only one suit.

3 Chancery Reports 2, 21 E.R. 710

27 November, Michaelmas [term], 13 Car. II [1661]. Master of the Rolls.

A bill was exhibited in Chancery, and a plea was allowed to it. The plaintiff declines that, and brings a new bill in the Exchequer for the same matter.

It was ordered that the plaintiff elect in which court he will proceed. If he elect in the Exchequer, the bill in Chancery is dismissed; if, in Chancery, an injunction is awarded to stay his proceedings in the Exchequer, *nisi causa*.

61
Shelley v. Lord Earsfield
(Ch. 1661–1662)

In this case concerning the distribution of decedent's estate, the matter was certified on a stated case to common law judges, and they certified how it should be done.

1 Chancery Reports 206, 21 E.R. 551

This is on a case stated and the judges' resolutions thereon. The case is *viz.* that Sir Thomas Earsfield, on the 19th August 1633, being seised in fee of divers manors in Kent and Sussex, for 5s. paid, sells all his manors and lands to Sir Robert Napper, Sir Thomas Middleton, Sir Richard Napper, and Thomas Middleton, Esq., for six months.

Sir Thomas Earsfield, on the 20 August 1653, releases to them and their heirs to the uses following:

First, to the use of Sir Thomas for life without impeachment of waste;

Second, to the heirs of Sir Thomas lawfully begotten and, for want of such issue, etc.;

Third, the remainder of all (except one messuage or tenement in the occupation of John Hill) to the said Lady Christian Earsfield for life, as for Hill's tenement, to the use of Ashton Earsfield, brother of the said Sir Thomas, for ninety-nine years if he live so long;

Fourth, the remainder of all the premises limited to Danie Christian for life, then to the use of Ashton Earsfield for ninety-nine years if he so long live, and, after the determination of the several estates limited, to Ashton Earsfield;

Fifth, to Robert Napper, Sir Thomas Middleton, Sir Richard Napper, and Thomas Middleton, and their heirs during the life of Ashton Earsfield;

Sixth, remainder to the first son of Ashton and the heirs male of his body and so to every other son of the said Ashton;

Seventh, remainder to the use of John Earsfield, son of Sir Thomas Earsfield, late of Hollington, deceased, and the heirs male of his body with remainders over, provided nevertheless, that, after the death of the said Sir Thomas and Dame Christian, all the said recited manors and lands shall stand charged with the payment of £100 *per annum* to Bridget Shelly etc. during the life of the said Bridget and also with the payment of £50 *per annum* to Grace White for her life, provided that, if either of them be not paid in twenty days, then the said Bridget and Grace to distrain until payment, and to this farther use, that, if the said Ashton Earsfleid should die without issue male of his body, then the said lands shall stand charged with the payment of £4000 to the said Bridget Shelley and her children, *viz.* £2000 to the said Bridget to be disposed of as the said Bridget should appoint and £2000 residue to such eldest son of the said Bridget as shall be living at the death of the said Ashton Earsfield without issue male of his body.

[There was] the like proviso of £1000 to the said Grace White and her children, but, if she die without children, that then the said £1000 is to be paid to the eldest son of the said Bridget which shall be living at Grace's death. And, therefore, the said Grace is to give security to repay the said £1000 to the said Bridget's children in case Grace die without issue.

The said several sums of £4000 and £1000 were to be paid within three years after the death of the said Ashton, and, in the meantime, Bridget and Grace and their children were to have the ordinary interest of the said several sums paid to them out of the said lands with a power of revocation in the said deed to the said Sir Thomas to alter any of the uses or wholly to make void the deed.

Sir Thomas died in 1653. Ashton Earsfield died 18 June 1654 without issue male. Dame Christian died 4 March 1659.

Sir Thomas had three sisters, *viz.* Timothea Brown, Bridget Shelley, and Grace White. William Shelley, the eldest son of the said Bridget, survived Ashton Earsfield, and made Bridget, his mother, his executrix, and he died before Dame Christian.

Timothy Shelley was the eldest son of Bridget at the death of Dame Christian. The defendant, John Earsfield, within a fortnight after the death of Dame Christian, entered into all the lands.

The estate is now let at £662 *per annum*, but it was formerly reputed worth £800 *per annum*. But Abbot's Marsh, being near the sea, is subject to great charges.

One-third part of the said lands is claimed by Ambrose Brown, son of the said Timothea, who was one of the sisters and co-heirs of the said Sir Thomas Earsfield.

The lands of £662 *per annum* are claimed by Elizabeth and Mary Goring, daughter of Sir Thomas Earsfield, father of the said Sir Thomas by his first wife, as co-heirs of Herbert Earsfield, eldest son of Sir Thomas, the father.

The rent of Hill's Farm, let at £58 *per annum* for ten years yet to come, is only reserved to Sir Thomas, his executors, etc. during the term, and the word 'heirs' is omitted. And the title thereof is questioned by Brown and White, as if the said farm were not well conveyed to the defendant John Earsfield.

The mansion house called Denn Place and the farm houses were much out of repair at the death of the Lady Earsfield, and the repairs thereof will cost £500.

The points in question are:

First, whether the £5000 be charged on the estate either in law or equity;

Second, if it be, then, when the payment of the interest of the said £5000 must begin, whether from the death of Ashton Earsfield or the Lady Earsfield, and how the £5000 must be paid;

Third, whether the annuities of the said £100 *per annum* and £50 *per annum*, appointed to Bridget Shelley and Grace White, shall continue after the payment of the interest money begins for the said £5000;

Fourth, who shall be at the charge of the repairs of the said mansion and farm houses, all being very ruinous at the death of the said Lady;

Fifth, who shall be at the charges of the suits concerning Hill's Farm, which is withheld from the defendant Earsfield, and concerning Worth, let at £166 *per annum*, claimed by Mr. Goring, and the rents thereof detained from the said defendant;

Sixth, how the interest of the said £5000 shall be paid whilst the rents of Hill's Farm and Worth are claimed as aforesaid, the same being near one-half of the lands limited to the defendant Earsfield;

Seventh, to whom the £2000 claimed by the suit as executrix to William Shelley ought to be paid, whether to the executrix of the said William Shelley, who was the eldest son of the said Bridget at the death of Ashton, or to Timothy Shelley, who was the eldest son at the death of the said Lady Earsfield.

The defendant Earsfield is but sixteen years old.

The court, taking these questions to be of great weight, ordered the case to be delivered to the judges for their opinions therein, both for law and equity.

The judges, having considered the case and points, have certified, *viz.*

> We have taken this case and the several questions thereupon into consideration, and are of opinion.
>
> First, that the £5000 is well charged upon the estate in equity;
>
> Second, that the £5000 ought not to be paid until the death of the Lady Earsfield, and, therefore, no interest is to be paid for it but from her death, from which time it becomes due;
>
> Third, that the annuities of £100 and £50 *per annum* have no dependence or relation to the payment of the £5000, and, therefore, ought still

to continue to be paid during the respective lives of the said Bridget and Grace without any abatement of the £5000 or of the interest for the same;

Fourth, that there ought not to be any allowance or abatement out of the £5000 or annuities or interest towards the repairs of the houses, but the same are to be done at the charges of the present owner;

Fifth, that the defendant Earsfield, who is solely concerned in the suits, is to bear the charges of such as he shall commence, or as shall be brought concerning the said lands;

Sixth, that the whole interest of the £5000 ought to be paid from the time that it was due, notwithstanding any claim made to part of the lands upon which it stands charged;

Seventh, that the £2000 appointed to be paid to the eldest son of Bridget that should be living at the death of Ashton without issue male ought to be paid to Bridget as executrix to William Shelley, her eldest son then living;

Eighth, that the limitation in the deed to the use of the heirs of Sir Thomas Earsfield lawfully begotten and to be begotten and for want of such issue etc., is a good limitation to create an estate tail in Sir Thomas Earsfield and the heirs of his body.

/s/ *Foster*, *Bridgeman*, and *Hale*

This court confirmed the judges' certificate.

[Reg. Lib. 13 Car. II, f. 571.]

62

Hurdret v. Calladon

(Ch. 1661–1662)

Where a suit in equity is dismissed for lack of equitable jurisdiction, the equity court can order the defendant not to plead the Statute of Limitations at common law where the suit in equity was timely filed.

1 Chancery Reports 214, 21 E.R. 553

The bill is to have an account from the defendant of money and goods, for which the defendant insists the plaintiff has a remedy at law.

The plaintiff insists that, by reason of the efflux of time, the defendant would plead the Statute of Limitations,[1] which, at the time of the bill exhibited into this court, the defendant could not do, the plaintiff being then within the time of the said Statute and the plaintiff cannot go to law without the direction of this court, that the Statute shall not be given in evidence.

[1] Stat. 21 Jac. I, c. 16 (*SR*, IV, 1222–1223).

This court ordered precedents to be searched for where the court has ordered that no advantage should be taken of the Statute of Limitations of personal actions in cases where the suit had been begun here and the time had been effluxed pending the suit.

This court, upon precedents and rehearing the cause, dismissed the plaintiff's bill.

[Reg. Lib. 13 Car. II, f. 446.]

63

Norton v. Bonest

(Ch. 1661–1662)

A written trust agreement cannot be defeated by evidence of an intention to the contrary that was voluntary and ambulatory.

1 Chancery Reports 215, 21 E.R. 554

The bill is to be relieved for £700 and the proceeds thereof lent by Thomas Bonest, the testator, to Robert Hanscombe upon a mortgage of lands by a lease of ninety-nine years, which the said testator took the security in the defendant Thomas Bonest's name, and, afterwards, by his will, devised several legacies. And he devised all the rest and gave his personal estate to the plaintiff, whom he made executor. And the said mortgage was taken in the defendant's name in trust for the testator. And the plaintiff insists that the said Bonest ought to assign the trust to the plaintiff.

But the defendant insists that the testator intended that, in case the said money on the mortgage were not paid in in his lifetime, that the defendant Bonest should have it and that the testator took no declaration or other writing of the trust from the defendant or desired any.

The Master of the Rolls [Grimston] would not relieve the plaintiff, but he dismissed the bill. But the Lord Chancellor [Lord Clarendon] assisted with the Lord Chief Justice of England [Foster] declared that, notwithstanding the intention of the testator, yet there is no more declared than an intention, which is voluntary and ambulatory. And [it was] never put into action. And the estate in law, which the defendant claims, being settled on a trust, the same trust is not discharged by any words of an intention, but that the estate remains upon the first foundation, which was the trust, which is devisable by the will, which, being made above three years after the declaration of any intention under which the testator claims and the testator having by the said will given the defendant another estate and devised all his estate not before given unto the plaintiff and the defendant not proving that the testator renewed his intention after the will made, therefore, this court is of opinion that the trust is devised to the plaintiff by the will and that there is just cause to relieve the plaintiff. And he decreed the defendant to assign the said trust to the plaintiff.

[Reg. Lib. 13 Car. II, f. 478.]

64

Meynel and Sterling v. Cooper

(Ch. 1661–1662)

Where a debtor is a litigant in and has the privilege of the Court of Chancery, his creditors cannot have him arrested and imprisoned in another court. If he be so imprisoned, a writ of privilege will issue, and any action of escape will be enjoined. However, the creditors can sue for their debts.

1 Chancery Reports 217, 21 E.R. 554

Richard Conquest, being arrested and imprisoned at the suit of one Cooper upon mesne process, and, after[wards], made an escape, who, upon a fresh pursuit, being retaken, is in custody again. But the said Conquest making it appear to this court that he had a cause depending here and he, attending the same, was arrested and detained contrary to the ancient privilege of this court, whereupon this court ordered the bailiff Cohome, who last took him, to be committed to the Fleet [Prison] for refusing to discharge him; this court ordered the said Meynel and Sterling, Sheriffs of Middlesex, to discharge the said Conquest out of custody.

The sheriffs acquainting the court the case is as aforesaid and that the said Cooper threatens to bring an action of escape against the sheriffs, this court again ordered the said Cohome to be committed a close prisoner and that the sheriffs should forthwith discharge the said Conquest out of custody and that a writ of privilege be awarded in that behalf. Whereupon, the sheriffs discharged the said Conquest out of custody. Yet the said Cooper brought his action against the sheriffs for the escape, and will enforce the sheriffs to pay the debt, and so, consequently, invalidate and overthrow the ancient and undoubted privilege of this court.

The court ordered the said action against the sheriffs touching the arrest for setting at liberty the said Conquest to be discharged, unless the said Cooper show cause.

The said Cooper offered several reasons for cause. But this court disallowed the same, and confirmed the first order and that the said action be discharged and all proceedings at law against the sheriffs be stayed.

But the said Cooper insisted that his debt is great and, if the said Conquest be under the protection of this court, Cooper is like to lose it.

This court declared Cooper may, notwithstanding the former orders, proceed against Conquest in order to the satisfaction of his debt, as he should see cause.

[Reg. Lib. 13 Car. II, ff. 677, 694.]

65

Rowel v. Walley

(Ch. 1661–1662)

Where an equity of redemption comes to a life tenant and the land is redeemed, the life tenant will pay one-third of the debt and the remainderman will pay two-thirds.

1 Chancery Reports 218, 21 E.R. 555

The bill is that the plaintiff Hannah, being the widow of Anthony Sharp, predecessor to her husband Simon Geering, who left her a considerable estate, and, on their marriage, settled a messuage and lands in Kent, called Great Walton, on her for a jointure, and, afterwards, the said Simon prevailed with the said plaintiff Hannah to sell a lease, whereof she was possessed as administratrix to the said Anthony Sharp, her former husband, of the value of £40 *per annum*. And he also prevailed with her to join in a mortgage of the aforesaid jointured land for £300 to Henry Walley, father of the said defendant. And, *in anno* 1650, the said Simon and the plaintiff Hannah, for £300, did by a deed bargain and sell to the said Henry Walley the said jointure lands to him, his heirs, and assigns forever, in which deed, the said Simon covenanted that he and the plaintiff Hannah would make better assurance by a fine. And, in the said deed, was a proviso that, if the said Simon Geering and the plaintiff Hannah or either of them or their heirs, executors, etc. did pay to the said Henry Walley, his executors, etc. £348 at the time therein mentioned, then, the said fine was to enure to the said Simon Geering and the plaintiff Hannah and the longest liver of them, and, after[wards], to the right heirs of the said Simon forever. And, in Michaelmas term 1650, a fine was levied. And the monies not being paid according to the proviso and Simon wanting more money, the said Simon and Hannah, by a deed of confirmation, in April 1653, for £146 more, besides the £348, confirmed the said mortgaged premises to the said Henry Walley and his heirs on redemption. But, before the redemption, the said Simon Geering died, and the said Hannah ordered the tenant of the premises to attorn to Walley until a satisfaction of his demands. And, afterwards, the plaintiff Rowel intermarried with the said Hannah. And, afterwards, the said Henry Walley, by a will, devised the said premises to the defendant James Walley and his heirs. So, to redeem the said premises and to secure the said Hannah's jointure is the scope of the bill.

The defendant James Walley insists he is willing to assign and convey the premises as this court shall direct, without whose direction, he cannot safely do any act, the other defendant Thomas Geering, the son and heir of the said Simon Geering, the mortgagor, being an infant.

This court, thereupon and hearing the answer of the defendant Thomas Geering, by his guardian, whereby the settlement upon the plaintiff Hannah is owned to be as aforesaid, was satisfied that the estate of the defendant Walley in the premises is but a mortgage and that the plaintiff Hannah ought in equity to enjoy the premises during her life, notwithstanding the fine by her passed as aforesaid.

But this court being tender of the prejudice of the infant by a redemption of the premises before he came of age, a question arose in what manner a redemption should be made and by whom, whether by the said Hannah or the said infant, and by whom the said mortgage money should be paid.

This court conceived it most just that the said plaintiff Hannah and the said infant should proportionably pay what was due upon the said mortgage at the time of the death of the said Simon Gearing, the mortgagor, rating the said estate for life of her, the said Hannah, in the premises at one-third and the reversion in fee of the said infant at two-thirds from the time of the said Simon's death.

[Reg. Lib. 13 Car. II, f. 909.]

66

Bowen v. Edwards

(Ch. 1661–1662)

In this case, a suit for a redemption of a mortgage was not barred by the plaintiff's laches.

1 Chancery Reports 221, 21 E.R. 555

The plaintiff's suit is to have a redemption of lands. And, the defendant insists on the antiquity of the said mortgage and that, by reason of long leases in being at the time of the mortgage, the defendant could not receive any benefit of the premises until the leases expired.

The Lord Chancellor [Lord Clarendon], at this hearing, being 17 November 1660, dismissed the bill.

But the plaintiff praying a re-hearing on the merits of this cause and offering precedents where relief has been frequently given upon mortgages more ancient, this court granted a re-hearing upon the penalty of treble costs if the plaintiff is not relieved.

The case [was] *viz.* that the plaintiff, being seised in fee of the premises worth £200 *per annum* in 1637, mortgaged the same to the defendant's father for

£250, and the plaintiff agreed, and, accordingly, sealed a deed for the absolute purchase of the premises to the defendant's father if the £250 were not paid at the end of seven years.

The defendant insists that the plaintiff, being possessed of the premises in reversion, after the expiration of certain leases for years from the Crown, did by deed with a fine and recovery thereupon and dated 24 January 1637, sell the said premises to the defendant's father in fee, who never in his lifetime received any profits, the leases expiring after his death, which came to the defendant. And he hopes, accordingly, to enjoy it, being an absolute estate without any defeasance.

The Master of the Rolls [GRIMSTON], being assisted with Mr. Justice HYDE, on the pleading of the first order and a bill which was exhibited by the defendant's father against the plaintiff to have the lands or money, which makes it appear a mortgage, and of several precedents where relief has been given in cases of like nature, decreed a redemption paying principal and damages.

[Reg. Lib. 13 Car. II, f. 180.]

67

Goring, ex dem. Alford v. Bickerstaff

(Ch. 1662)

The grant of a term to several persons in remainder, one after the other, if such persons be all in being and particularly named, does not create an entail of a chattel or create a perpetuity.

Lincoln's Inn MS. Hill 125, f. 36v

Henry Goring etc., plaintiffs v. Charles Bickerstaff and Elizabeth, his wife, John Everfield, the Lady Anne Alford, and John Alford.

The plaintiff's bill was to have the direction of the court to whom they were to perform a trust reposed in them by John Alford, deceased, all the defendants claiming the benefit thereof by several titles.

The case [was thus]. John Alford conveyed to the use of himself for his life, reminder to his first nine [?] sons in tail, remainder to Sir Edward Alford, his brother, for life, the remainder to his sons etc. in tail with remainders over, provided John might lease for twenty-one years. [On] 3 January 24 Car. [1649], John Alford made a lease to the plaintiffs in trust for John for his life, after[wards], to his wife for her life on certain trusts, and, after the death of Frances, then, during the residue of the term to permit such persons to receive the profits as John should appoint and nominate and for default of such nomination and after the death of such person or persons.

1 Chancery Cases 4, 22 E.R. 665

20 January [1662]. Henry Goring, baronet, and others, plaintiffs, against Charles Bickerstaff and Elizabeth, his wife, John Everfield, by his guardian Dame Anne Alford, widow, and John Alford, by Dame Anne, his mother and guardian, defendants. Upon an appeal from a decree made by the Master of the Rolls by the defendant Dame Anne only. The Lord Chancellor, Chief Justice Foster, Justice Wyndham, Chief Baron Hale.

John Alford, deceased, being seised of the manor of Hams etc., by indenture dated 1 April, 14 Car. I [1638] and a fine thereupon, settles the same to the use of himself for life, the remainder, as to part, to the use of Frances, his wife, for life, for her jointure, remainder to his first and to his fourth son in tail, remainder to Sir Edward Alford, his brother, for life, remainder to Sir Edward and to his first and all other his sons, reversion to his own right heirs, under a proviso that it should be lawful for the said John and Sir Edward, when they should be solely seised of the premises or any part thereof, by virtue of any of the limitations, at their pleasures, to make leases of the same or any part thereof for one and twenty years under what rent they pleased.

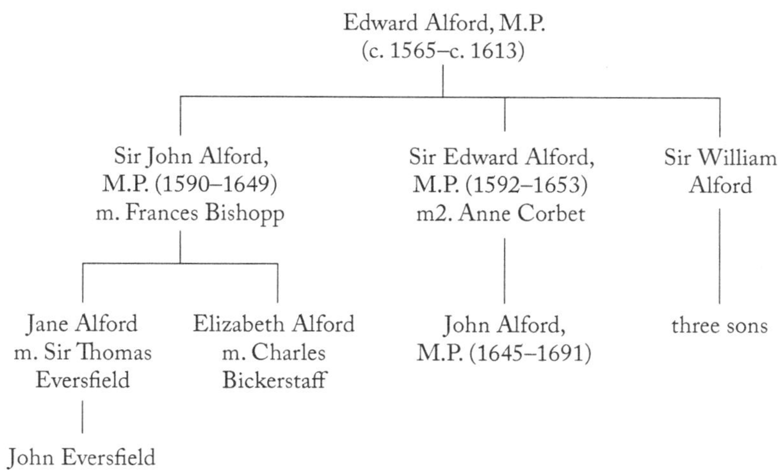

7 July 1643, John Alford made his will, and, thereby, he gave his daughter Jane, the defendant Everfield's mother, £600, to his daughter, Elizabeth, now wife of the defendant Bickerstaff, £500 to make her portion £3000, and devised to her all his messuages in White Friars in London, Pickhatch and Goswell Street in Middlesex, and in Wigonholt in Sussex to her and to the heirs of her body, the reversion to Sir Edward Alford and his heirs, provided that, if Sir Edward paid Elizabeth £2500 at her marriage or at twenty-one years of age, which of them should first happen, the estate to her to cease, and the premises to remain to Sir

Edward and his heirs. And, of his said will, he made Frances, his own wife, executrix.

And, afterwards, pursuant to his power by the indenture of 1 April 14 Car. I [1638], he, by an indenture of the first of January 1648, did demise to the plaintiffs the greatest part of the manor of Hams etc. from Michaelmas then last past for twenty-one years under 10s. yearly rent upon trust that they should permit the said John Alford, during his life, to take and receive the rents, issues, etc. of the said manor, and upon further trust that, after his death, Frances, his wife, should receive the rents, profits, etc. in satisfaction of her jointure so far as the premises, by any former assurance, were liable thereunto and to permit her, during her life, if the term so long continued, to receive out of the residue of the rents of the premises £120 *per annum* and certain firewood and faggots and that the plaintiffs should pay the said Jane Everfield £50 *per annum* during the life of her husband, and should permit the said Frances, his wife, during her life, if the term so long continued, to receive the residue of the rents during the residue of the term of twenty-one years if she should so long live to the intent she should pay thereout so much money towards the legacies of his will as his personal estate should be wanting to pay and to pay the residue to such person as the said John Alford should by his will appoint and, for want of such nomination, to receive the same to her own use and upon further trust that the plaintiffs, after the death of Frances, during the residue of the term of twenty-one years, should permit such person and persons as the said John Alford, by any writing by him signed and sealed in the presence of two credible witnesses or his last will, should nominate. And, for want of such nomination or after the death of the nominee, the heir of the said John Alford [was] to take and receive all and singular the rents of the premises.

The said John Alford, by deed the same first of January 1648, signed and sealed in the presence of four credible witnesses, thereby reciting the said demise and trust, did nominate and appoint the eldest son of William Alford, his brother, to have out of the residue of the premises £50 *per annum* during the said term and, his two younger sons £60 apiece and the said Sir Edward Alford to receive the residue of the rents and profits by the trust of the said demise limited to be paid to the said Frances, and, after her death, to take and receive the residue of the rents and profits during the residue of the said term to his own use.

It appeared by one witness that John Alford, three or four days before his death, which was before the trust and the declaration of trust, did acquaint that witness that he had settled the estate in Hams well, as he thought he could, and that this brother, Sir Edward Alford, was by an agreement between them to have all his estate there after his death and that he thereout appointed some allowance to his daughter Everfield and declared that his daughter Elizabeth, now wife of the defendant Bickerstaff, was not to have anything out of his estate there, for that he had otherwise provided for her. John Alford, the night of the same day the demise and declaration bore date, died without issue male, leaving the daughters his heirs. Sir Edward Alford died intestate September 1653. The defendant Dame Anne, his relict, had taken out administration. Jane, the mother of the defendant John Everfield and whose heir he was, died in the life of Frances, her mother. Frances having proved John Alford her husband's will, died in 1659, having made the defendant, Elizabeth Bickerstaff executrix. The defendant Dame Anne, as administratrix of Sir Edward Alford, defendant, John Alford, as first son and heir of Sir Edward Alford, defendant, Bickerstaff and his wife, in her right, she being one of the co-heirs of John Alford and executrix of Frances, who was the executrix of John Alford, and John Everfield, as heir to Jane, co-heir with Elizabeth Bickerstaff, claimed the benefit of the trust during the residue of the twenty-one years after Frances's death.

So the plaintiffs being trustees, *ut supra*, the defendants all claiming the benefit of the trust under several titles, the bill was to have the defendants interplead and to desire the direction of the court to whom the trust belonged.

Upon the first hearing by the Master of the Rolls, 2 November, 13 Car. II [1661], inasmuch as the power reserved to John Alford by the lease is that, after the death of Frances, the trustees should permit and suffer such person and persons as he should nominate and, after the death of the nominee, his own right heirs to receive the profits etc., the court was of opinion that John Alford had no power to nominate any person to receive the rents etc. but during the life of the nominee, and no longer, for, after the nominee's death, the heirs at law are nominated by the original deed to receive etc. And, when, after, by deed poll, Sir Edward Alford is appointed to receive the rents, that must be intended if he so long live, for the deed poll recites the lease and is in pursuance of the trust therein, and that John Alford's intention in the original lease was plain, that, after the death of the nominee, his own heirs should have the residue of the trust and, both the deeds being executed at one time, are to be taken as one assurance. And, if he had meant the heirs, executors, or administrators of Sir Edward should have the remaining part after Sir Edward, he would have named them as well as Sir Edward. And for that the interest of the term was always in the plaintiff, and never any real or legal interest in Sir Edward but as nominee to receive the profits, he being dead, the trust to him ceases, and nothing passes to his heirs or executors, but it remains to Elizabeth, the surviving daughter, heir and executrix to John Alford. And the testimony of that one witness can be intended to relate to no other settlement but the first by deed and fine and not the trust of the lease, which was not in being when the said John Alford had the discourse with that witness, but was made the day of his death and that the residue of the term of twenty-one years does belong to the heir at law of John Alford, who, in a doubtful case, ought to be preferred, especially when it is so consonant to John Alford's intention and the defendant Bickerstaff is also his executrix and daughter. And both, therefore, order and decree the same accordingly and that the rents, in arrear and for the future, be paid to the defendant Bickerstaff during the coverture between them and, after, to the defendant Elizabeth Bickerstaff during the residue of the term.

And, upon the appeal, the question was upon the whole case whether John Alford had a power to dispose of the trust of the whole term of twenty-one years after the death of Frances and how far he had a power to dispose of it and whether there were not a restriction by the limitation of the first deed to the heirs after the death of the nominee that did disable his disposition thereof farther, except to his heirs, and whether John Alford had disposed the whole term or not and which of the parties ought to have the remainder of the trust.

The counsel of the defendant Bickerstaff now offered farther that John Alford had no power after two distinct limitations to two several persons to limit it to a third after the death of the second, because it would make an executory devise upon an executory devise to tend to the entailing of a chattel and creating a perpetuity and that the limitation of John Alford was out of the power and trust, and not of any interest in the remainder of the term.

They did all agree in one uniform opinion that the limitation of a term to several persons in remainder one after another, if those persons were in being and particularly named, could in no wise tend to the entail of a chattel or the creation of a perpetuity. But the limiting of it to a person not in being did and that, where any person had the trust of a possibility in remainder of a term, he had a good power to declare and make a disposition of the trust of such possibility but that the limitation of such remainder in possibility of a chattel real to the heir of the person limiting was a void limitation and the estate in interest did again revert to John Alford, who made that limitation. And he, having, by the deed poll the same day of the lease, which was made pursuant to the power of the first settlement, limited to Sir Edward Alford the whole remaining term after the death of Frances without any other limitation or restriction, which he might easily have done if he so intended, the same was a good limitation of it to Sir Edward, his executors, and administrators. And, if the power in John Alford had been defective, his interest ought to come in aid and supply it to make good such limitation, for, otherwise, there would be no disposition at all of the remaining term and the legacies of £50 and £60 to William Alford's children would be avoided and the interest in the remaining term might be pretended to be in the trustees and they claim the estate discharged of the trust, there being nothing to oppose the power or intention of John Alford in limiting the whole remainder of the term to Sir Edward but the implicated, misplaced, and mistaken expression of the lease.

The whole court was clear of opinion that the former decree was grounded upon a mistaken foundation and that, taking both deeds together, no other equitable or reasonable interpretation can be made thereof, but that according to the power, interest, and intention of John Alford, who, it appears by one witness, never intended the estate to whom it was decreed by the former decree, the whole remaining term in the said lease and trust therein after the death of Frances, for the residue was well limited and appointed to Sir Edward Alford, his executors, and administrators and that the defendant Dame Anne is well entitled thereunto. And both order and decree that the former order and decree be discharged and that the plaintiffs shall come to an account for and pay the said Dame Anne the rents and profits of the said manor, which are in arrear and to grow due until the expiration of the remainder of the said term of twenty-one years, and convey to her for the residue of the term if so required. And, in so doing, they shall be protected and saved harmless by the authority of this court.

Vide Moor's Rep. 809, Totton *contra* Mollineaux; 1 Co. Rep. 156; 3 Cro. 577; 10 Co. 47, 48, 52. And *quaere*, why the trust of a possibility in the remainder of a term is disposable over and the possibility in interest in the reversion of a term is not assignable; *vide* 8 Co. Rep. 96, Mat. Manning's Case.[1]

2 Freeman 163, 22 E.R. 1132

Chancellor, Chief Justice Foster, Chief Justice Bridgeman, and Chief Baron Hale. Sir Henry Goring *et al.*, plaintiffs; Charles Bickerstaffe, Elizabeth, his wife, John Eversfield, *per guardianum suum*, Dame Anne Alford, widow, and John Alford, by the said Dame Anne, his guardian, defendants.

Sir John Alford deceased, being seised of the manor of Hams etc., by indenture, 9 April, 14 Car. I [1638], and a fine thereupon, settled the same to the use of himself for life, the remainder, as to part, to the use of Frances, his wife, for life, for her jointure, the remainder to his first and fourth son in tail, remainder to Sir Edward Alford, his brother, for life, remainder to Sir Edward Alford's first and all others of his sons in tail, remainder to his own right heirs, under a proviso that it should be lawful for Sir John and Sir Edward, when they should be solely seised of the premises, or any of them, at their pleasure, to make leases of the same or any part thereof for twenty-one years under what rent they pleased.

7 July 1643, Sir John Alford made his will, whereby he gave his daughter Jane, the defendant Eversfield's mother, £600, and to his daughter Elizabeth, now the wife of the defendant Bickerstaffe, £500, to make her portion £3000, and devised to her all his messuages in White Friars, London, Pitch Hatch and Huswell Street in Middlesex, and in Wiggen Hold in Sussex, *habendum* to her and the heirs of her body, remainder to Sir Edward Alford and his heirs, provided that, if Sir Edward paid Elizabeth £2500 at her marriage or twenty-one years, which should be first, the estate to her was to cease, and the premises were to remain to Sir Edward and his heirs. And, of his said will, he made Frances, his own wife, executor.

---

[1] *Tatton v. Molineux* (1610), Moore K.B. 809, 72 E.R. 920, also Pollexfen 24, 86 E.R. 500; *Lloyd, ex dem. Roberts v. Wilkinson* (1598), 1 Coke Rep. 148, 76 E.R 337, also Moore K.B. 478, 72 E.R. 707; *Mayor of London v. Alford* (1640), Croke Car. 576, 79 E.R. 1095, also W. Jones 452, 82 E.R. 238; *Lampet v. Starkey* (1612), 10 Coke Rep. 46b, 77 E.R. 994, also 2 Brownlow & Goldesborough 172, 123 E.R. 880; *Clark v. Manning* (1609), 8 Coke Rep. 94, 77 E.R. 618.

And, afterwards, pursuant to this power, by indenture 14 April, Car. I, and by indenture 3 January 1648, he did demise to the plaintiffs the greatest part of the manor of Hams etc. from Michaelmas then last past for twenty-one years, rendering 10s., in trust that they should permit the said Sir John Alford, during his life, to take and receive the rents and issues of the said manor, and, upon farther trust, that, after his decease, Frances, his wife, should receive the profits of the said manor in satisfaction of her jointure, so far as the premises by any former assurances were any way liable thereunto, and to permit her, during her life, to receive out of the residue of the premises £120 *per annum* during the life of her husband if the term so long continued, and should permit his said wife if the term so long continued, to receive the residue of the rents during the residue of the term of twenty-one years if she should so long live to the intent she should pay thereout so much money towards the legacies as his personal estate should be wanting in and to pay the residue to such persons as the said Sir John Alford should appoint by his will and, for want of such appointment, to retain the same to her own use and, upon farther trust, that the plaintiffs, after the death of Frances, during the residue of the term of twenty-one years, should permit such person and persons as the said Sir John Alford should in his lifetime by any writing by him sealed in the presence of any two credible witnesses or by his last will appoint, and, for want of such nomination and after the death of such nominee, the heirs of the said Sir John Alford to have and receive all and singular the rents of the premises.

The said Sir John Alford, by a deed poll the same 3d of January 1648[/49], signed and sealed in the presence of four credible witnesses, thereby reciting the said demise and trust, did nominate the eldest son of Sir William Alford, his brother, to have out of the residue of the premises £50 *per annum* and his two youngest sons £60 apiece. And the said Sir Edward Alford was to receive the rest of the profits by the trust of the said demise limited to be paid by the said Frances, and, after her death, to receive the residue of the profits during the residue of the term to his own use.

It appeared by one witness that Sir John Alford, three or four days before his death, which was before the trust and the declaration of trust, did acquaint that witness that he had settled that estate in Hams well, as he thought, and that his brother Sir Edward Alford was by agreement to have all his estate after his death and that he thereout appointed some allowance to his daughter Eversfield, and he declared that the defendant Elizabeth, now wife of the defendant Bickerstaffe, was not to have anything out of his estate there, for that he had otherwise provided for her. Sir John Alford, the night of the same day wherein the declaration bears date, died without issue male, leaving the two daughters his heirs. Sir Edward Alford died intestate 1653; the defendant Dame Anne, his relict, had take out administration. Jane, the mother of the defendant Jane Eversfield and whose heir she was, died in the life of Frances, her mother; Frances, having proved the said will of her husband, died in 1659, having made Elizabeth Bickerstaffe her executrix. The defendant Dame Anne, administratrix of Sir Edward Alford, the defendant John Alford, as first son and heir of Sir Edward Alford, the defendant Bickerstaffe and his wife, as executrix to Jane, who was executrix of Sir John Alford, and John Eversfield, as coheir with Elizabeth to Sir John Alford, all claimed the benefit of the trust, during the residue of twenty-one years after Frances's death.

The bill was that the defendants should interplead and to have the direction of the court to whom the trust belonged.

Upon the hearing by the Master of the Rolls [Grimston], 28 November, Car. II, inasmuch as the power reserved to Sir John Alford by the lease is that, after the death of Frances, the trustees should permit such persons as he should nominate, and, after the death of the nominee, his own right heirs to receive the rents etc., the court was of opinion that Sir John Alford has thereby no power to nominate any person to receive the rents etc. but during the life of the nominee and no longer, for, after the death of the nominee, the heirs at law are nominated by the original deed to receive etc. And, when, after the deed poll, Sir Edward is nominated to receive the rents, that must be intended if he live so long, for the deed poll recites the deed and is in pursuance of the trusts therein, and that Sir John Alford's intention in the original lease is certain, that, after the death of the nominee, his own heirs should have the residue of the trust, and both the deeds, being executed together, are to be taken but as one assurance, and, if he had intended that the heirs, executors, or administrators of Sir Edward should have the remaining part after Sir Edward's death, he would have named them as well as Sir Edward, and, for that the interest of the term was always in the plaintiff, and not in Sir Edward, but only as nominee to the profits, he being dead, the trust to him ceases, and nothing passes to the heir or administratrix, but it remains to Elizabeth, the surviving daughter, heir, and executrix of Sir John Alford. And the testimony of Elizabeth can be intended to relate to no other settlement but the first, by deed and fine, and not to the second, raising the trust in the lease, which was not then in being, made after the discourse the day of his death. And the residue of the trust of the term does remain to the heirs at law of Sir John Alford, who, in a doubtful case, ought to be preferred, especially when it is so consonant to the intention of John Alford, and the defendant Elizabeth also, his executrix. And he does, therefore, order and decree the same accordingly and that the rent arrear and for the future be paid her etc.

And, upon the appeal, the question was upon the whole case, whether Sir John Alford had a power to dispose of the residue of the term of twenty-one years after the death of Frances or whether he were not restrained by the limitation of the trust to the heirs after the death of the nominee.

It was offered by the counsel of the appellant that Sir John Alford, after two limitations to two persons, had not power to limit to a third after the death of the second, because it is an executory devise upon an executory devise and tends to the entailing of a chattel and the making of a perpetuity. And this limitation of John Alford, they said, was out of the power of the trust, and not out of the interest of the term.

The court did all agree in one uniform opinion, that the limitation of a term to several persons in remainder, one after another, if those persons were in being and particularly named, could not tend to a perpetuity, otherwise, if the persons were not in being, and that a man might declare the trust of a possibility in remainder, but that the limitation of a trust of such possibility to the heir of the limitor was a void limitation and the trust was in the limitor, though of a chattel real. And he, having by the deed poll the same day, limited the lease, which was made pursuant to the power of the first settlement, to Sir Edward Alford, the whole remaining term after the death of Frances without any other limitation or restriction, which he might have done, the same was a good limitation of it to Sir Edward Alford, his executors, and administrators. And, if the power of Sir John Alford had been defective, his interest ought to come in aid to make good the legacies of £50 and £60 *per annum* and of the remaining term, and, otherwise, the trustees might come in and claim the lease discharged of all trusts. And, there being nothing to oppose the limitation of the trusts, but the implicated and mistaken expressions of the deed, the whole court resolved that the former decree was grounded upon a mistaken foundation and that, taking both deeds together, they ought to be interpreted that the power, interest, and limitation of Sir John Alford was to Sir Edward Alford, being explained by the said one witness, and that Sir Edward Alford, his executors, and assigns ought to have the term after the death of Frances. And Dame Anne was, therefore, entitled thereunto as administratrix of Sir Edward Alford. And, therefore, it was ordered and decreed accordingly and that the former order and decree be discharged and that the plaintiffs shall come to an account for and pay the said Dame Anne the rents and profits and convey to her if required etc.

Mo. 890, Hatton, Cox, and Molineux; 1 Co. 156; 1 Cro. 577; 10 Co. 47; 8 Co. 42. And *quaere*, why the trust of a possibility of a term is declarable when the remainder of a possibility is not assignable. 8 Co. 96.

Lord Nottingham, *Prolegomena*, p. 227

30 January, 13 Car. II.

January 3, 1648[/49], John Alford demises to Sir Henry Goring for twenty-one years in trust for himself for life, remainder to Frances, his wife, for life, remainder to such as he, by deed or will, shall appoint and, in default of such appointment and after the death of such nominee, the remainder to the right heirs for the said John Alford. And, afterwards, by a deed poll bearing date the same day, he limits to William Alford's eldest son £50 [*per annum*] etc. and the whole, after the death of Frances, to Sir Edward Alford during the term. And, the same day also, he dies. And, in this case, three points were resolved:

First, that the limitation of a term to several persons in remainder one after another if they be all in being and alive together is good, and does, in no sort, tend to the perpetuity of a chattel, especially where each remainder is but for life, and so all the candles are, as it were, lighted together, but, otherwise, [it] might be if a remainder was limited to a person not *in esse*;

Second, the limitation of this trust of the possibility of the remainder of a term to the right heirs of John Alford, the person limiting, was void as a limitation, and the estate did again revest in John Alford, as his old interest, and not by virtue of the new limitation;

Third, if the limitation made by John Alford to Sir Edward Alford was not good by virtue of his power, which allows no nominee to take longer than during his life, yet here, though the power be not pursued or be defective, the interest of John Alford ought to come in aid and supply of that power to strengthen and make good such limitation, which proceeding from the intention and interest of the owner cannot be controlled by the doubtful penning of the power.

And the decree of the Master of the Rolls [Grimston] to the contrary was reversed by the Lord Chancellor [Lord Clarendon] assisted by the three chiefs, Foster, Bridgeman, and Hale.

O. Bridgeman 584, 124 E.R. 758

Hilary term, 13 & 14 Car. II [1662].

The 30th of January, the Lord Chief Justice [Foster], Lord Chief Baron [Hale], and myself [Bridgeman], were called as assistants by My Lord Chancellor [Lord Clarendon] to hear a cause formerly heard before the Master of the Rolls.

The case was this in effect. John Alford, seised of the manor of Hamsey, settles it (or so much of it as was now in question) upon himself for life and, after, to the use of Frances, his wife, for life, (remainder to his first and other sons, but he died without issue), remainder to his brother, Sir Edward Alford, for life, remainder to his first son in tail, and so to the second and third and other sons of Sir Edward in tail, with remainders over. And John Alford reserves unto himself a power to make leases for twenty-one years.

January 3, 1648, John Alford, reciting his power, makes a lease to Sir Henry Goring and others for twenty-one years upon trust to permit him, the said John Alford, during his life, to receive the profits to his own use and, after his death, they should permit Frances, his wife, during her life, to receive the profits to her own use. And some other uses were therein expressed, and upon further trust that the trustees, after the death of Frances, during the residue of the said term of twenty-one years, should permit such person or persons as the said John Alford should at any time during his life by writing by him signed and sealed or by his last will in writing to such purpose nominate and appoint, and, for want of such nomination and appointment and after the death of such person or persons so nominated and appointed, the heirs of the said John Alford [were] to take and receive all and singular the rents, issues, and profits of the premises.

And, by a deed poll of the same date, reciting that, by another indenture between etc. of the same date, he had by a trust therein limited and appointed his wife to pay certain rents to such persons as by his last will etc. he should appoint and, by a like trust in the said indenture expressed he had limited the trustees to permit such person and persons as he should by any writing etc. or last will etc. to such purpose nominate and appoint to take and receive all the rents and profits of the said manor after the death of the said Frances. And during the term granted and limited by the said indenture, the said John Alford, in pursuance of the intent of the said indenture, did by the said indenture nominate and appoint the eldest son of William Alford, a younger son of his, to have out of the said residue £50 *per annum* during the said term and his two younger sons to have £60 apiece, and Sir Edward Alford, his brother, to receive the residue of the said residue of the said rents and profits limited to be paid by the said Frances Alford, and also to take and receive after the death of the said Frances the residue of all and singular the rents and profits of the said manor during the residue of the said term then to come to his own use, according to the true intent and meaning of the trust of the said indenture.

John Alford dies the same night, January 3, 1648, leaving two daughters, his heirs, Jane Ersfield and Elizabeth, now married to Bickerstaff. Sir Edward Alford died intestate September 1653, leaving John, his son and heir. Jane Ersfield also dies, John Ersfield being her son and heir. The Lady Alford takes administration of the estate of Sir Edward.

Frances Alford was by the will of John Alford made *anno* 1643, before the lease made by John Alford, made his executrix. And she proved the will, and, having survived Sir Edward and her daughter, Jane Ersfield, in 1659, makes her will, and Elizabeth Bickerstaff, her daughter, executrix.

Sir Henry Goring and the other trustees exhibited their bill, setting forth the whole matter and the several pretensions, and they pray an interpleader and the direction of the court to whom they shall pay the profits.

The Master of the Rolls [Grimston] decrees it to Elizabeth Bickerstaff. And the reasons appear in the decree. First, he conceived that, by the indenture, John Alford had reserved to himself a power to nominate one who should take for life only and no more, because he limited it after the death of such person so nominated and appointed to his right heir to receive the profits, and that by the deed poll. Though he did appoint Sir Edward to receive the same generally during the residue of the term, yet it was to be intended for his life, for he nominated not his heirs or executors. And it refers to the other deed, for he mentions that 'in pursuance of the intent of the indenture' he did limit etc. And the close of the indenture is 'according to the true meaning of the indenture'. And the interest of the term being in others and he having no power but to limit for the life of Sir Edward, it shall go to the surviving heir of John Alford, who is also his executrix, being executrix of the executrix. And he conceived the heirs took (as purchasers, as I apprehend), and, in a doubtful case [they] ought to be favored.

Upon the rehearing, we [Foster, Hale, and Bridgeman] agreed, first, that admitting anything vested in the heirs of John, be it by a possibility or a trust, it survived to Elizabeth, for, though John Ersfield, the son of Jane, was a co-heir at the time of the death of Frances, when it was to take effect, yet, by the death of John Alford, Jane being then a co-heir with Elizabeth, it vested in her and Elizabeth together, be it a possibility or an interest, whatsoever you will call it, and so survived to Elizabeth.

But, secondly, we held (and indeed that point and the grounds whereupon the Master of the Rolls decreed it were in a manner waived by the counsel), that the word 'heirs' could not vest any estate in the heir (it being a chattel) but such as would result to John Alford himself, And, being words of limitation and no heir in being and parties *antenati*, they cannot take as heirs. It has been often adjudged a devise of a term to a man and his heirs (or heirs male of his body, with remainders over), vested in the first devisee. And in Busby Mansell's Case,[1] which concerned Sir John Aubrey, it was after solemn argument adjudged in the Exchequer, that one having a term, devised the profits of the land to his wife for so many years as she should live, remainder to his son for life, remainder to the heirs male of the body of his son, that it was adjudged a void remainder, and it was said, if a term be assigned in trust for another and the heirs male of his body with a remainder over, it vests in his executors.

And, thirdly, we held that, upon consideration of both the deeds, John Alford left himself a power upon the indenture to appoint the trust during the team, and not only for the life of the person appointed, for the first words are 'during the term to receive the profits', and the words 'after the death of the person so nominated' are but by implication, and, indeed, to be understood as the fault of the clerk 'for want of appointment', or 'after the estate appointed (if appointed but for life) be determined', 'then to his right heirs'.

And the latter deed, which makes no recital, but supposing a power to limit it during the whole term and limiting it to Sir Edward during the term, makes it clear, as also his appointing of the rents to others during the term.

But, fourthly, admitting he had reserved to himself a special power to limit it but for life, yet the rest of the trust returned back to him in interest, and, by virtue thereof, he had power to dispose of the trust during the whole term. And, though it was objected that, though the residue of the term, after the death of the party nominated, should result back to John Alford, yet that was but as a possibility, as, if a termor for years grant it for life, there remains to him but a possibility which he cannot grant over, yet it was not regarded, for there is a residue of a trust resulting to him in natural equity. The trustees cannot have it, and it is against no rule of law that he should dispose of it. And, admitting he had recited his power and expressed that he had made the appointment by virtue of his

[1] *Busby Mansell's Case*, cited at O. Bridgeman 56, 124 E.R. 465.

power, the law will draw it out of his general power or interest, *ut res valeat.* See Clere's Case, 6 Co. 18; and Spark's Case, Tr. 43 Eliz.,[1] a grant to one for life, remainder to his executors, his administrators shall have it, and, therefore, it is in his power to dispose it.

But the great doubt of the case was this (which was not insisted on at the Rolls), that, upon the lease for years, John Alford having limited the trust to himself for life, remainder to his wife for life, he could limit none over. And it was said to be the opinion of the judges that Manning's Case, 8 Co. 95,[2] was not to be enlarged. And, therefore, a devise of a term to A. for life, remainder to B. for life, remainder to C. for life, they held to be void as to C.; and it shall be so in a trust if so in a devise.

But the Chief Baron [Hale] and myself [Bridgeman], the Chief Justice not gainsaying it, held that such a devise was good, for, as the Chief Baron said, the candles are lighted all at once and they are all persons *in esse* and [there is] no danger of perpetuities. But whether a devise in such a case to A. for life, remainder to B. for life, remainder to C. for life, remainder to the first son of C. and the heirs male of his body, there being no son *in esse,* we did not touch, though I think that is not good, because there must be an estate vested. And, by the rule of Manning's Case, in an executory devise, the last devise must be supposed first. And, by that construction, the devise to the son not *in esse* cannot be vested and lodged so as to raise up the others upon it.

But, in our case, being a trust, we clearly held the trust might be limited of a term to A. for life, remainder to B. for life, remainder to C. for life, with other remainders over to persons *in esse,* for the trustee cannot have anything to his own use and they are to pursue the directions of the trustor and he may discharge any trust for himself.

And I [Bridgeman] held that, in the case of a trust, the trust of the term might be limited over to persons not *in esse* and the frequent practice had been accordingly. And I, after[wards], asked the Chief Baron's opinion, and he clearly agreed with me in it. And I laid this for a ground, that, where it shall not be a perpetuity, if a freehold were limited in use, it shall not be void in the like limitation of a trust of a term and that such limitations of terms shall not be avoided but where they tend to create perpetuities. It was said, if a term be granted in trust for A. and the heirs of his body and after in trust for B. and the heirs of his body, that A. dying without issue, it has been decreed his executors or administrators shall have it, and not he in the remainder, for that it shall follow the rule of law in like cases upon a devise. But I think there was but one such case. And I doubt of it, for

[1] *Parker v. Clere* (1599), 6 Coke Rep. 17, 77 E.R. 279, also Moore K.B. 567, 72 E.R. 763, Croke Eliz. 877, 78 E.R. 1102, Croke Jac. 31, 79 E.R. 24; *Spark v. Spark* (1599–1602), Croke Eliz. 658, 666, 840, 78 E.R. 897, 904, 1066, Moore K.B. 666, 72 E.R. 826, Yelverton 9, 80 E.R. 7.

[2] *Clark v. Manning* (1609), 8 Coke Rep. 94, 77 E.R. 618.

there is no danger of a perpetuity. A., the *cestui que trust*, might have compelled the trustees to have executed an estate, as it was adjudged in Hampden's Case, who was a devisee of a term to him and the heirs of his body with a remainder over. And, therefore, there is no inconvenience, and the trustees may pursue the intention of the trustor without prejudice in law. See Hambden's Case.

In the principal case, the decree was reversed, and [it was] decreed for the Lady Alford, and not for the son who had the freehold, for it appeared to be a term in gross and nothing appeared of an intention in any of the persons, either John Alford or Sir Edward Alford, that it should wait upon the freehold.

In this case, *Maynard* said that, about 7 Car., My Lord Coventry adjudged that a devise to A. for life, remainder to B. for life, remainder to C. for life, was good to C., and the case was said to be between Poody and Barker.

And a case was cited to be decreed about a year since, by the advice of three judges, between Flower and Aprice,[1] of a trust of a term with several remainders to one, two, and other sons, which was agreed to be naught as tending to a perpetuity. Query the case.

8 May 1638, 14 Car., A., possessed of a term for years, devised it to his wife for eighteen years, and, after, to B., his eldest son for life, and, after, to the eldest issue of B. for life and died, and, after the eighteen years, B. entered, and was possessed, and, after[wards], he had issue a son, and after[wards] makes a feoffment in fee, and dies. This shall not destroy the son's estate, he being born before the feoffment. And so it was resolved and certified by Jones, Croke, and Berkeley. And the Lord Keeper's opinion was accordingly between Cotton and Heath, reported by Rolls.[2]

Pollexfen 31, 86 E.R. 502

The case was touching a limitation of a term in lands, upon which the Lord Chancellor [Lord Clarendon] had delivered his opinion. But he granted a re-hearing, at which the Lord Chief Justice Foster, the Lord Chief Justice Bridgeman, and the Lord Chief Baron Hale assisted. The Lord Chancellor [LORD CLARENDON] altered his opinion formerly delivered, all which being very long and on several deeds is here omitted to be expressed. But, by the order on this hearing, it appears that the Lord Chancellor and the judges did deliver this general opinion.

The limitation of a term to several persons in remainder, one after the other, if such persons be all in being and particularly named, can in no wise tend to the entail of a chattel or creating of a perpetuity, but the limiting of it to a person not in being does. And, where a person has such a trust of a possibility in the remainder of a term limited after persons all in being, he has good power to declare and make a disposition of the trust of such a possibility. But the limitation of a

1 *Apprice v. Flower* (Ch. 1661), see above, Case No. 41.

2 *Cotton v. Heath* (Ch. 1638), Chancery Repts. *tempore* Coventry 287, 1 Eq. Cas. Abr. 191, 21 E.R. 981.

remainder in possibility of a chattel real to the heir of a person limiting the same is a void limitation, and the estate, in point of interest, does revert and fix in the person that made such void limitation.

And, according to this opinion, this case was decreed.

[Reg. Lib. 1661 A, ff. 192, 416.]

68

Bennet v. Box

(Ch. 1662–1664)

The question in this case was whether the trust property of a deceased beneficiary was an asset of his estate that could be reached by his creditors.

Lincoln's Inn MS. Hill 125, f. 37, pl. 2

Bennet and Box and Bennet v. Stonehouse.

Allen bound him[self] and his heirs to John Bennet by a bond in £600, at which time, Allen and Hammond were seised of certain lands to them and their heirs in trust for Allen, who died. The defendants, heirs of Allen, had a decree for executing the trust in this court, and the land was accordingly conveyed.

The plaintiffs, executors of John Bennet, the obligee, exhibit their bill to make this land liable as assets in equity. They having first put the bond in suit at law, where one of the defendants pleaded *riens per discent*, the other co-heir pleaded *riens etc. propter* a little house.

The question before Justice Hide May 6 was on a demurrer if the lands should be assets in equity. And, because of the consequence of the case, a decree [was made] that a case should be made and he would take the advice of the other justices etc.

Lord Nottingham, *Prolegomena*, p. 246

In the Case of Bennet and Box, a man, who had purchased land to him and his heirs in the name of J.S., his trustee, did afterwards become bound in an obligation, and he died. And, then, J.S. died. The heir of the purchaser exhibits a bill against the heir of the trustee for a conveyance. The creditor brings [an action of] debt against the heir of the purchaser on the obligation, who pleads nothing by descent. Then comes the creditor into Chancery, and exhibits [his] bill against the heirs of the obligor and the trustee, and prays that, when the estate in trust shall be declared to be executed, it may likewise be decreed to be assets.

But, on a reference to all the judges of England, it was resolved by them, and so decreed by Clarendon, Chancellor, it shall not be assets.

The reasons on which the judges went were these. First, at common law, a use was not assets in equity. Second, a Statute was made 19 Hen. VII, chap. 15,[1] to subject lands in use to the execution of a judgment. Therefore, without a statute, it could not be. Third, when a trustee executes an estate to the heir, he is not in by course of descent; therefore, equity cannot make him liable, as, if the heir sell the assets descended, equity will not make the money liable. And it has been ruled that, if the heir of the mortgagor and mortgagee join in a sale and the heir has the surplus of the money, this surplus shall not be assets in equity. Fourth, otherwise, a mischief would ensue, for the heir would be in a worse condition where assets descend in equity than when he has assets at law, for assets at law may be aliened before the writ brought; assets in equity cannot be aliened.

Yet the practicers in Chancery are much dissatisfied with this resolution, for they think it but reasonable that equity should advance the payment of debts and suppress fraud; else a man may borrow money to buy land and, by taking the conveyance in trust, no assets shall descend to his heir. And why should not the descent of a trust in fee to the heir be assets in equity as well as the trust of a term be assets to the executors, which is every day's experience? Even the common law itself takes notice of assets in equity. Therefore, money recovered by an executor by a decree in Chancery is assets in equity on *plene administravit* pleaded. Sir Francis Moore 858, Harcourt and Wrenham's Case.[2] And the Statute 43 Eliz., ch. 4, of charitable uses,[3] relieves breaches of trust, if the offenders have assets at law or equity. And, if lands be conveyed in trust to be sold for the payment of debts, this is not assets in law but equity, as the book is. Dyer 264.[4] By this construction which the judges make, a debt in equity shall fare better than a debt in law, for an estate in equity shall be liable to a debt in equity, but not to a debt in law. Now, as at common law, when an heir enters for condition broken, he is *quasi* by descent, because the condition descends; so, in equity, he ought to be in *quasi* by descent, when he enters upon the execution of a trust, for the trust did descend. If an heir aliens and repurchases, this is assets in equity. If the ancestor aliens to trustees and the heir repurchases, why should not this be assets in equity since it depends merely on circumstances *utrum* the repurchase be *bona fide* or no? It is not fit the Chancery should regard it as a mischief that the heir cannot alien assets in equity, for it is no harm to creditors that it should be so. But, in truth, it is not so, for a man may alien the trust, though he cannot alien the land, and it has been heretofore debated in Chancery, if a trustee and the heir join in an alienation before a subpoena be brought, whether this do not discharge the heir in equity as much as an alienation before an original [writ], which very debate admits that, without such alienation, the heir would be liable in equity.

---

1 Stat. 19 Hen. VII, c. 15 (*SR*, II, 660).

2 *Harecourt v. Wrenham* (1614), Moore K.B. 858, 72 E.R 953.

3 Stat. 43 Eliz. I, c. 4 (*SR*, IV, 968–970).

4 *Anonymous* (1567), 3 Dyer 264, 73 E.R. 588.

1 Chancery Cases 12, 22 E.R. 669

Sir Thomas Bennet and Sir William Brownlow, knights, plaintiffs, against Mary Box, relict of Henry Box and daughter of Ralph Allen, Walter Stonehouse, son and heir of Elizabeth Stonehouse, another of the daughters of Ralph Allen, George Burdet, son and heir of Martha Burdet, another of the daughters of Ralph Allen.

Anno 15 Jac. [1617–18], Ralph Allen purchased lands in his own name and in the name of Edward Hammond in trust for Ralph Allen and his heirs, and Hammond was to take nothing thereby. But the trust is not expressed in the conveyance. William Allen, Senior, did borrow £600 of John Bennet. And the said William Allen, Ralph Allen, and William Allen, Junior, son and heir of the said Ralph Allen (William Allen, Senior, being first bound in the bond), 1630, did become bound unto the said John Bennet, since deceased, for the payment of the said £600 by bond of £1000, wherein they bound themselves and their heirs, under whom the plaintiffs are well entitled to the debt in question.

And one witness deposes that Ralph Allen was a good husband, not one that contracted any debts of his own, and he believes he and William Allen, Junior, were only sureties for William Allen, Senior.

Ralph Allen dies, and Hammond survives, and after[wards] dies. Then, William Allen, son and heir of Ralph Allen, dies without issue. And the now defendants, as heirs at law, bring their bill against the heirs of Hammond, who had the estate in law, to have the lands conveyed in performance of the trust, which is decreed to them accordingly, and the lands are conveyed unto them as heirs at law of Ralph Allen. The now the plaintiffs bring their action of debt at law against Henry Box, since deceased, and the now defendants, as heirs of Ralph Allen. The defendants thereunto pleaded *riens per descent praeter* a third part of a messuage, worth £6 13s. 4d. *per annum*.

January 1662, the now plaintiffs bring their bill in this court against the defendants and Henry Box, the defendant's late husband, who had the lands decreed and conveyed unto them as heirs of Ralph Allen to have them decreed, as heirs, to pay the just debts of Allen or to have the said lands made liable to pay the said debt as assets in equity.

The defendants, Box and Stonehouse, pleaded that the said action still depended, which is a double vexation. And they demur, and demand judgment whether they, as heirs, shall be charged in equity without any trust or agreement further than the law charges them.

On the hearing thereof, a case was stated on the bill, plea, and demurrer. And, afterwards, Henry Box died. And, before any bill of revivor against the defendants, it was ordered, May 12, 1653, that the defendants do answer the plaintiffs' bill, but the benefit of the plea was to be considered at the hearing.

The defendants deny that they have entered into or received any of the profits of the said lands, the same being ever since 7 Car. extended for the debts of Ralph

Allen and, ever since, held by Sir John Banks and his executors, and, formerly, before the extents were let at £500 *per annum*, and, after, at £300 *per annum*, and, now, but at about £400 *per annum*, and whereout above £60 is deducted for the charges of the sea banks, and the rest will not pay the interest of the principal debt, as the extendors allege.

An original [writ] was filed by the plaintiffs against Henry Box and the other defendants on the bond in question in the Common Pleas, bearing *teste* 16 February 1659[/60].

The defendant Walter Stonehouse did for £400 bargain and sell his third part of the reversion in fee of the lands in question to Henry Box, deceased, by a deed bearing date 3 October 1660, and the said Henry paid then to the said Walter the £400 purchase money for the same. And the defendants, as they swear by their answer, had not then or in some months after any notice of the said original, and no notice [was] proved.

And one witness deposes he believes there was no notice, for, he being conversant in all Mr. Box's affairs, if there had been any notice, he should have heard of it, as he verily believes.

The defendant George Burdet, after the other defendants were ordered to answer, put in his answer, and, thereby, he insisted on the same matter the other defendants did by their plea and demurrer. And he was on June the 9th last past served with process *ad audiendum judicium* upon 21 June following, but he appeared not at the hearing or any for him.

The first question was whether the said lands, as this case is, shall or ought to be decreed as assets in equity;

Secondly, or whether the plaintiffs ought to have any decree in this case against the defendants.

Chief Justice Hyde, Chief Baron Hale, and Justice Wyndham, were of opinion, on hearing counsel on both sides, that the lands in the said case and the bill mentioned (as the case is stated) are not nor ought to be decreed as assets in equity and that the plaintiffs ought not to have any decree against the defendants.

Afterwards, in Hilary vacation 1664, the bill was dismissed upon the judges' certificate.

And the like was 14 November 1660 or 1661, in a case wherein Clark was plaintiff against Sir Thomas Fanshawe.

2 Freeman 184, 22 E.R. 1149

Sir Thomas Bennett and Sir William Brown v. Box *et al.*

This case concerns assets in equity, by which it appears that the ancestor's encumbrances on it were so great the revenue on it would not pay the interest.

For which reason, it was resolved, [it was] no assets in equity.

[Other reports of this case: 2 Eq. Cas. Abr. 465, 22 E.R. 396.]
[Reg. Lib. 1664 B, ff. 271, 400.]

69

Lee v. Hale

(Ch. 1662)

Where a testator devises a moiety of his estate and then makes other legacies and then a devise of the residuum, the first devisee take a full moiety of the entire estate and the other devisees and creditors will be paid out of the second moiety.

1 Chancery Cases 16, 22 E.R. 671

31 January.

First, [it was] ruled that a devise of the moiety of the personal estate to the wife and then of divers legacies and, after, of the residue to another, that the wife shall have a full moiety if the other moiety be sufficient to pay the debts and that the debts shall go out of the other moiety, Dyer 164,[1] against which it was objected that the husband could not bequeath any part until the debts be paid and that, therefore, the debts ought to be first deducted out of the whole goods.

But that objection was overruled, the other moiety left being sufficient for the debts in his case.

Second, it was ruled that, by the bequest of a moiety of the personal estate, where the testator had monies, bonds, and a lease for years, a moiety of the lease passed, against which, it was objected that that was not usually reckoned personal estate.

2 Freeman 157, 22 E.R. 1127

31 January, 14 Car. II, 1661[/62]. Chancellor, Master of the Rolls, Judge Hyde.

There was a devise of the moiety of the personal estate to the wife and then of divers legacies and then of the residue to another. It was resolved the wife shall have a full moiety if the other moiety be sufficient to pay the debts and that the debts shall go wholly out of the other moiety, Dy. 164, against which, it was objected that the husband should not bequeath any part until the debts be paid and that, therefore, the debts ought to be first deducted out of the whole.

But that objection was overruled, the other moiety being sufficient for the debts in this case.

[Also it was] ruled that, by the bequest of a moiety of the personal estate, where the testator had money, bonds, and a lease for years, a moiety of the lease for years passed, although it was objected that that was not usually reckoned personal estate.

[Other reports of this case: 1 Eq. Cas. Abr. 199, 21 E.R. 988.]
[Reg. Lib. 1661 B, f. 446.]

---

[1] *Anonymous* (1558), 2 Dyer 164, 73 E.R. 357.

70

Gilbert v. Faules

(Ch. 1662)

A plaintiff cannot voluntarily dismiss his own case after a judgment has been decreed.

1 Chancery Cases 40, 22 E.R. 684

12 and 17 February, 14 Car. II [1662]. The Lord Chancellor, the Master of the Rolls. Guilbert v. Hawles.

The bill was exhibited to be relieved against an action for rent. And, at the hearing of the cause, it was decreed to account and that the plaintiff should pay what was due to the defendant on the account. The account was stated by a Master. Then, the plaintiff moved to dismiss his bill, paying what costs the court would assess, which was opposed, for that the judgment of the court being given, the plaintiff ought not to abuse the court and depart from it. And the Case of Wingfield and Thomas was cited, whereby, upon an obligation, the plaintiff here was decreed to pay principal, damages, and use, and, afterwards, the plaintiff there would have dismissed his bill, but it was denied.

Churchill insisted that *quilibet potest renunciare juri pro se introducto.*

The Master of the Rolls [Grimston] directed it to be moved before the Chancellor. And, 17 February, it being moved before him, it was denied.

And the said Chancellor [Lord Clarendon] and Judge Browne, in 17 Car. II [1665–66], between Cheatly and Packington, gave the same rule in the like case.

2 Freeman 158, 22 E.R. 1128

12 and 17 February, 14 Car. II [1662].

A bill was exhibited to be relieved against an action for rent. And, at the hearing of the cause, it was decreed to an account. The account was stated by the Master. Then, the plaintiff moved to dismiss his bill, paying what costs the court would assess, which was opposed, for that the judgment of the court being given, the plaintiff ought not to abuse the court and depart from it. And the Case of Wingfield and Thomas was cited where, upon an obligation, the plaintiff here was decreed to pay the principal, damages, and costs, and, after[wards], the plaintiff there would have dismissed his bill, but it was denied.

Churchill: Quilibet potest renunciare juri pro se introducto.

The Master of the Rolls [Grimston] directed it to be moved before the Lord Chancellor. And, the 17 February, it being moved before him, it was denied.

And the Lord Chancellor [Lord Clarendon] and Judge Browne, in 17 Car. II [1665–66], between Cheatly and Packington, gave the same rule in the like case.

71

Turberville's Case

(Ch. 1662)

Where a vendor of land dies before receiving the purchase money, the purchase money will be paid to the vendor's heir, and not to his executor or administrator.

Lincoln's Inn MS. Hill 125, f. 37

5 May 1662, 14 Car. II, by the Master of the Rolls in court.

Turberville, the father, by parol, agrees to sell and convey land to the plaintiff in fee, and £5 was paid in part. And possession was delivered, but no conveyance [was] made. The vendor died.

A bill was exhibited against the heir and executor. And the question was between the heir and the executor who should have the residue of the purchase money. The heir claimed it because he was to part with the land and it was not secured to the party in his life. The executor said he had a remedy for it by an action at law, which the court could not in justice take from him. And, if he had security for it, it is agreed he should retain it. And the promise is a security on which he might recover at law. But so, it was objected, had the heir a remedy at law for the land.

Curia decreed the money to the heir not being secured by a bond etc. and no debts appearing.

72

Edgeworth v. Davies

(Ch. 1662)

The Court of Chancery has jurisdiction over trusts of land lying in the County Palatine of Chester.

Lincoln's Inn MS. Hill 125, f. 37v, pl. 1

1 July 14 Car. II.

[It was] ruled on a demurrer and precedents that a suit in Chancery here lies for a trust of lands in the County Palatine of Cheshire by the Chancellor [Lord Clarendon] and Justice Brown.

1 Chancery Cases 40, 22 E.R. 684

1 July, 14 Car. II.

The bill was exhibited to have an account of the profits of land which the defendant had received on trust for the plaintiff during his minority and for monies received upon bonds belonging to the plaintiff and for writings etc.

The defendant pleaded that the lands lay in Cheshire and that the defendant lived in Cheshire, in the County Palatine of Cheshire and Lancashire, and, therefore, not within the jurisdiction of this court.

This plea having been formerly argued before judges in the absence of the Chancellor, they ordered precedents to be produced, which were as follows. Hern against Smith, 12 Eliz., for that the lands lay within the Duchy, was overruled; Sherborn against Vaughan, 13 May, 14 Car., the bill was to be relieved on trust; the defendant pleaded the jurisdiction of the duchy; this was *ex parte.* But, in My Lord Coventry's time, Hales against Daniel, 24 October Car. I, *ad idem*;[1] in which case, the thing being for a personal estate, the court overruled the plea of the County Palatine, and, in the same cause, Mr. Page, to whom it was referred to certify, reported upon the view of precedents that the jurisdiction of the counties palatine was allowable between parties dwelling in the same county and for lands there and for matters local.

And, in the argument of the principal case, was cited the Case of Sir John Egerton and the earl of Darby.[2]

And upon long debate in the principal case, the plea was overruled but without costs.

2 Freeman 159, 22 E.R. 1129

1 July, 14 Car. II [1662].

A bill was exhibited to have an account of the profits of land, which the defendant had received on a trust for the plaintiff during his minority, and for money received upon bonds for the plaintiff and for writings etc.

The defendant pleaded that the lands lay in Cheshire within the County Palatine of Chester and in Lancashire within the Duchy and that the defendant lived within the County Palatine of Chester and not within the jurisdiction of this court.

This case having been formerly argued before the judges, in the absence of the Chancellor, they caused precedents to be searched. And now precedents were produced, as Herne v. Smith, 12 Eliz. [1569–70], for that lands lay within the Duchy, was overruled; Smith v. Delves, 7 November 2 Jac. [1604];[3] a bill being for evidences, the defendant pleads that the lands concerned lie in Cheshire and that he lived there and so it was not within the jurisdiction of this court, but of the County Palatine, but, upon argument, the suit not being for the lands, but for the writings, the plea was overruled; Sherborne v. Vaughan, 13 May, 14 Car.

---

[1] *Sherbourne v. Houghton* (Ch. 1638–1639), Nelson 37, 21 E.R 783, Chancery Repts. *tempore* Coventry 293; *Hulse v. Daniell* (Ch. 1629), 118 Selden Soc. 597, Chancery Repts. *tempore* Coventry 115.

[2] *Egerton v. Earl of Derby* (1614), E. Coke, *Fourth Institute* (1644), p. 213, also 12 Coke Rep. 114, 77 E.R. 1390, 1 Eq. Cas. Abr. 137, 21 E.R. 940.

[3] *Smith v. Delves* (Ch. 1604), 117 Selden Soc. 338.

1 [1638], the bill was to be relieved on a trust; the defendant pleaded the jurisdiction of the Duchy; this was *ex parte*; but, in My Lord Coventry's time, Hales v. Daniell, 24 October 5 Car. 1 [1629], *ad idem*, in which case, the bill being for a personal thing, that court overruled the plea of County Palatine. And in the same case, Mr. Page, to whom it was referred to certify, reported upon a view of precedents that the jurisdiction of the County Palatine was allowable between parties dwelling in the same county and for lands there and for matters local.

And, in the argument of the principal case, I[1] cited the case of Sir John Egerton and the Earl of Darby, 4 Inst.

And, upon long debate in the principal case, the plea was overruled, but without costs. Hob. 77, Owen v. Holt.[2]

Nelson 66, 21 E.R. 791

Lord Chancellor Hyde and Mr. Justice Brown.

The bill was exhibited to have an account of the profits of lands, which the defendant had received upon a trust for the plaintiff during his minority, and for money received upon bond, and for writings.

The defendant pleaded that the lands lay in Cheshire within the County Palatine of Chester and in Leicestershire and Lancashire within the Duchy of Lancaster and that he lived in the County Palatine of Chester, and not within the jurisdiction of this court.

This plea having been formerly argued before the judges in the absence of the Lord Chancellor, they order precedents to be produced, which was done as follows: Farne *versus* Smith, 12 Eliz. [1569–70]. [There was] a plea that lands lay within the Duchy of Lancaster, and [it was] overruled. Smith *versus* Delves, 7 November *Anno* 2 Jac. I [1604]. The bill being to produce writings and evidences, the defendant pleaded that the lands which those writings concerned lay in Cheshire and that the parties lived there, and [it was] concluded that the matter was not within the jurisdiction of this court, but, the suit being not for the land itself, but for the writings, the plea was held idle and overruled. Sherborn *versus* Haughton, 3 May, 14 Car. I [1638]. The bill was to be relieved upon a trust. The defendant pleaded the jurisdiction of the Duchy. [The defendant was] ordered to answer. Hales *versus* Daniel, 24 October 5 Car. I [1629]. The bill being to discover a personal estate and the defendant pleading the jurisdiction of the County Palatine, it was referred by My Lord Coventry to Mr. Page to search for precedents and make his report to the court, who certified that the jurisdiction of the counties palatine was allowed between parties dwelling within the same and for lands there and for all local matters.

[1] Probably Anthony Keck rather than Richard Freeman.

[2] *Owen v. Holt*, Hobart 77, 80 E.R. 227.

And, in the argument of the principal case, the *Fourth Institute* was cited, Sir John Egerton *versus* Earl of Derby; and Hob. 77, Owen *versus* Hall.

And, after a long debate, the plea was overruled, but without costs.

[Other reports of this case: 1 Eq. Cas. Abr. 137, 21 E.R. 940.]
[Reg. Lib. 1661 A, f. 746.]

73

Anonymous

(Ch. 1662)

Where two separate claims are joined in a single suit, the defendant cannot demur to only one count.

Lincoln's Inn MS. Hill 125, f. 37v, pl. 2

The same day [1 July 1662], by the Chancellor *assistante* Justice Browne.

Two plaintiffs join in suit for two distinct matters, the one not concerned in the other matter. [It was] adjudged the defendants' demurrer [was] good for this cause. It is not lawful for one to maintain the other, which, if this should be, they might do.

The like [was] ruled between [*blank*], where the father and children, plaintiffs, the father suing for an account, the children for legacies.

74

Clerke v. Lord Angier

(Ch. 1662)

A husband can sue without making his wife a co-plaintiff for a legacy to her after the marriage if it is for a rent, but she must be a co-plaintiff if it is for a bond.

1 Chancery Cases 41, 22 E.R. 684

3 July, 14 Car. II [1662].

A legacy being given to a married woman, who was married when the legacy was given, the husband of the wife, without her, exhibits a bill for it. Because the wife was no party, the defendant demurred, for, of things merely in action belonging to the wife, as a bond etc., she ought to join in the suit. But otherwise it is of a rent running in the wife's right after marriage. If the husband alone should sue the bond and be nonsuited or dismissed, that will not conclude the case. But, if he die before judgment or decree, the wife cannot revive the suit.

2 Freeman 160, 22 E.R. 1130

3 July, 14 Car. II [1662]. Chancellor, Baron Turner.

A legacy being given to a wife while she was married, the husband of the wife, without her, exhibits a bill for it. Because the wife was no party, the defendant demurred, for, of things merely in action belonging to a wife, as a bond, etc., she ought to join in the suit. But otherwise it is of a rent accruing in the wife's right after marriage. And, if the husband alone should sue or be dismissed, that will not conclude the wife. And, if he die before judgment or decree, the wife cannot revive the suit.

Nelson 78, 21 E.R. 794

Clerke v. Lord Anglesey.

A legacy was devised to a wife, then under coverture. And the husband, alone, without his wife, exhibited a bill to recover it. And, because she was not a party, the defendant demurred.

And [it was] ruled good, for, of things merely in action belonging to a wife, as a bond, she ought to be joined. But it is otherwise in case of rent accruing to the husband in the right of his wife after marriage.

[Other reports of this case: 1 Eq. Cas. Abr. 64, 21 E.R. 878.]

75

Anonymous

(Ch. 1662)

Where a suit for discovery of a deed does not pray for further relief, the plaintiff need not swear that he does not have the deed already.

1 Chancery Cases 11, 22 E.R. 669

After Trinity term, 14 Car. II.

The bill was barely to discover a deed. The defendant demurred, because the plaintiff had not made an oath according to the course of the court that he had not the deed.

Serjeant *Glynne*, for the plaintiff, insisted that the oath was not required by the course of the court in this case. And he took this difference, that, when the bill alleges the want of a deed and seeks to be relieved upon the matter of that deed by a decree, there, such an oath is necessary, but, where the bill seeks no decree, but barely to have the defendant discover whether he has such a deed or not or to have the deed produced at a trial, in that case, the plaintiff ought not to be put to his oath, for it is not to be presumed the plaintiff would exhibit a bill in either of the latter cases if he had the deed.

This difference was well approved of by the Lord Chancellor [LORD CLARENDON], and, thereupon, the demurrer was overruled.

2 Freeman 160, 22 E.R. 1130

After Trinity term, 1662.

The bill was barely to discover a deed. The defendant demurred, for that the plaintiff had not made an oath according to the course of the court that he had not the deed.

Serjeant *Glynne*, for the plaintiff: In this case, an oath is not required, and he took this difference that, when the bill alleges the want of a deed and seeks relief upon the matter of that deed by a decree, there, such an oath is necessary. But when the bill seeks no relief, but barely desires that the defendant would discover whether he has such a deed or not or to have it produced at a trial, in that case, the plaintiff ought not to be put to his oath, for it is not presumed the plaintiff would exhibit a bill in either of the latter cases if he had the deed.

This was approved by the Lord Chancellor [LORD CLARENDON], and, therefore, the plea was overruled.

Nelson 78, 21 E.R. 794

Trinity [term], 14 Car. II [1662].

The bill was only for the discovery of a deed, to which the defendant demurred, because the plaintiff had not made an oath according to the course of the court that he had not the deed.

But Serjeant *Glynne* insisted for the plaintiff that the course of the court did not require such an oath in this case because the bill is barely for a discovery, and not to be relieved as to the deed, for, where the bill alleges the want of a deed and seeks relief upon the matter contained in the deed, in such a case, it is necessary that the plaintiff should make an oath that he has it not. But, where the plaintiff, by his bill, seeks only for a discovery of a deed and no decree upon the matter therein contained but that he may produce it at a trial or the like, in such case, he ought not to be put to his oath, for it is not to be presumed he would exhibit a bill if he had the deed to produce.

And this difference was now allowed, and the demurrer was overruled.

3 Chancery Reports 5, 21 E.R. 711

After Trinity [term] 14 Car. II.

The bill was barely for the discovery of a deed. The defendant demurred, for that the plaintiff had not made an oath, according to the course of the court that he had not the deed.

Serjeant *Glynne*, for the plaintiff, insisted that the oath was not required by the course of the court in this case. And he took this difference, that, when the bill alleges the want of a deed and seeks to be relieved upon the matter of that deed by a decree, there, such an oath is necessary, but, where the bill seeks no decree, but barely to have the defendant discover whether he has such a deed or no or to have the deed produced at a trial, in this case, the plaintiff ought not to be put to his oath, for it is not to be presumed the plaintiff would exhibit a bill in either of the latter cases if he had the deed.

Note this difference was well approved by the Lord Chancellor [Lord Clarendon], and, thereupon, the demurrer was overruled.

76

Spiller v. Herbert

(Ch. 1662)

Where the testimony of a single witness to the terms of a contract is supported by other circumstantial evidence, it will be allowed as sufficient proof.

A decree against a life tenant will bind tenants in remainder.

Lincoln's Inn MS. Hill 125, f. 37v, pl. 3

15 October 1662.

Sir Henry Spiller and Philip, earl of Pembroke, made an agreement for a marriage between James Herbert [d. 1677], the infant, and Jane [Spiller], child and heir apparent of Sir [Henry] Spiller, the earl to settle £2000 *per annum* and Sir Henry Spiller the like value *cum pertinentiis* the manors of Haddenham and Kenson, The marriage proceeded.

The earl exhibited his bill against Sir Henry Spiller, offering performance of his part and praying that Sir Henry Spiller might, on his part, perform etc. The agreement was decreed. And, then, the earl settled his lands. Sir Henry Spiller died, and the earl, James Herbert, did exhibit a second bill founded on the first against the plaintiff Spiller, on whom, before the marriage agreement, Sir Henry Spiller had settled the manor of Haddenham and Kenson to the use of Sir Henry Spiller for life, remainder to Spiller for life, with remainders to his first, second, and other sons in tail, with divers remainders over. But Haddenham was with a power of revocation, but Kenson [was] without such a power. Which conveyances were set forth by Spiller in his answer to the second bill, but not by Sir Henry Spiller in his answer to the first, who only set forth that he was seised, but not of what estate.

And, at the hearing, [it was] decreed for Haddenham, but reserved to a trial at law for Kenson, whether, as to Kenson, the conveyance was fraudulent, and until then, possession [was] settled with James Herbert, according to the agreement.

Now, Spiller brings a bill of review on both decrees against James Herbert and his wife. The errors assigned were on the first decree that it was grounded on the testimony of a single witness, Mr. Stephens.

But, on reading the decree, it did appear that, indeed, Stephens was the only witness to the particulars of the agreement, but his testimony [was] supported by divers other witnesses of circumstances and confessions and, therefore, as to that, on demurrer, the decree was affirmed.

As to the second decree, it was also affirmed, because the conveyance in itself was fraudulent and no conveyance as to purchasers on a valuable consideration, as this was, especially because, if Sir Henry Spiller had made a conveyance, according to the decree, Spiller's conveyance had been void in law. And it was his fault it was not executed.

And the Lord Chancellor [Lord Clarendon] and Justice Tyrell both agreed that such a decree against Sir Henry Spiller should bind them in the remainder.

Note, else Spiller and Herbert might have gone to new process of the agreement, *et videtur.*

77

Churchill v. Grove

(Ch. 1662–1663)

Where a conusee of a confessed judgment extends it against a purchaser, he must prove express notice of the judgment in the purchaser or else he will not be relieved against the purchaser.

Lincoln's Inn MS. Hill 125, f. 38v

Eodem die [15 October 1662].

The case, in effect, [was thus]. Crooke, indebted by statute to Grove, mortgaged the manor of Dibden to Churchill for years. Grove extends that and other manors. And, being put to divers suits in Chancery etc., he came to an agreement that, for £3500, part of his debt, Crooke should convey the manor of Dibden on the extent to friends in trust for Grove in fee, after which contract, before the conveyance, Grove had notice of the mortgage, but proceeded in the purchase.

Then, afterwards, Churchill exhibited his bill against Crook only, and had a decree after several orders to hold the mortgage free from [any] equity of redemption, And now, he exhibits a bill to bring Grove to account, suggesting him satisfied.

Grove answers this bill, and offers to pay the plaintiff what was due on account, deducting what the plaintiff Churchill had received, for Crook had secured him to satisfy Churchill. But he demurred if he should account. Churchill's bill was to have the lands by reason of his decree and an account.

But Mr. Grove's demurrer was allowed.

1 Chancery Cases 35, 22 E.R. 681

14 November [1663].

The plaintiff, having a judgment and a mortgage, exhibited his bill against the mortgagor and the conusee of a statute by the mortgagor to have a discovery of what is due on the statute, that being precedent to the plaintiff's securities, and, upon payment, to have the same set aside.

The conusee pleaded that, he having extended his statute and the conusor and he stated accounts and the sum of £3000 being due to him, he, in consideration thereof, had an absolute conveyance of part of the extended lands. And he showed what lands were conveyed to him by the conusor and that, thereupon, he assigned the residue of the extended lands to the conusor and that so he was a purchaser without notice of the plaintiff's title for a valuable consideration.

It was also pleaded that the conusor was in execution on the plaintiff's judgment and so the plaintiff could not extend the lands nor the lands be liable during the life of the conusor.

On the plaintiff's part, it was to the first point insisted that it did not appear that the defendant was a purchaser, there being no new money paid upon the executing of the conveyance, but coming in for the consideration of money due on the statute was no purchase. And it was common equity for him that had the subsequent judgment to be relieved against the precedent statute on payment of what was due, and there was, for ought appeared, no more there, and the account made up between the conusor and conusee on the pretended purchase ought not to affect the plaintiff, and, therefore, the defendant's purchase, being subsequent to the plaintiff's security, ought not to be aided by the statute, and, the plaintiff's judgment being of record, the defendant was bound to take notice thereof at his peril, and, in this case, the defendant ought not to protect his pretended subsequent purchase by his precedent statute, but he ought, upon payment of the statute, to yield possession to the plaintiff.

But this was strongly opposed by the defendant's counsel, who insisted that the defendant was a purchaser and that, though no new money was advanced on the purchase, yet he assigned over and parted with part of the extended lands in consideration thereof, which was as valuable as money and that it was the constant justice of this court, that, if a purchaser *bona fide* did buy in an older encumbrance, statute, or judgment, and there were a judgment or statute mesne between that and his purchase, of which he had no notice at his purchase, that he should protect his purchase with the older encumbrance so brought in. And it was insisted that, though the judgments were on record and a purchaser is bound to take notice thereof at law, yet, in equity, where the conusee of a judgment comes to be helped to extend his judgment against a purchaser, he must prove express notice of the judgment in the purchaser or else shall never be relieved against the purchaser.

And, upon this point, the plea was allowed.

And, as to the other point, that the conusor being in execution upon the judgment and so the land not to be charged during his life, it was strongly insisted that was no good exception in equity, for that the bill was to discover encumbrances, which the plaintiff could not have after the conusor's death. And it was positively affirmed that it had been ruled here that a bill will lie, notwithstanding the debtor was in execution upon the judgment. But this point was not much debated.

Howbeit, the court inclined in opinion that this part of the plea was not good.

2 Freeman 176, 22 E.R. 1142

14 November, 15 Car. II [1663]. Lord Chancellor, Baron Turner.

The plaintiff, having a judgment and a mortgage, exhibits his bill against one that had a precedent statute and against the mortgagor to discover what was due upon the statute and, upon payment, to set the statute aside.

The conusee pleaded that he, having extended the recognizance, came to an account with the mortgagor, and, there being £3000 due, he purchased part of the extended lands for the same, and assigned the other part to the mortgagor and this was without notice of the plaintiff's title, and he was a purchaser for a valuable consideration. And he also pleaded that the plaintiff had taken the conusor of the judgment in execution thereon and, therefore, the lands could not be liable during his life.

On the plaintiff's part, as to the first point, it was insisted that it did not appear that the defendant was a purchaser, there being no new money paid on the executing of the conveyance, but that, coming in for the money formerly due, it was no purchase, that it was common in equity for him that had the subsequent judgment to be relieved against him that had the precedent statute upon payment of what was due, that, therefore, the defendant's pretended purchase being subsequent to the plaintiff's judgments ought not to affect him, that the plaintiff's judgments were on record, so everyone ought to take notice of them at his peril.

The defendant's counsel insisted that it was a purchase, that the defendant had parted with part of the extended lands which were as valuable as money, that it was the constant justice of this court that, if a purchaser *bona fide* did buy in any older statute or judgment and there was a judgment *mesne* between that and his title by purchase, of which he had no notice at his purchase, that he should protect his purchase by the older encumbrances so bought in, and that, though, at law, a purchaser must at his peril take notice of a judgment because it affects the land, yet, when one prays the relief of this court to have the benefit of a judgment, he shall never have that relief against a purchaser *bona fide* unless he can prove express notice in the purchaser of the said judgment when he purchased.

And, upon this point, the plea was allowed.

But, as for the other point, that the plaintiff had taken the conusor of the judgment in execution, it was confidently affirmed and not denied that it was no plea, because the land would become chargeable after the death of him in execution, and that, therefore, the defendant ought to answer and discover.

Nelson 89, 21 E.R. 797

The mortgagor confessed a judgment to the plaintiff, and had likewise acknowledged a statute to the defendant, which was precedent either to the mortgage or judgment. Thereupon, the plaintiff, who was the judgment creditor, exhibited his bill against the mortgagor and the conusee of the statute to have a discovery of what was due on the statute and that, upon payment of the money, it might be set aside.

The conusee pleaded that he had extended the land. And, there being £3000 really due to him, the conusee, in consideration of so much money received, had made an absolute conveyance of part of the extended lands to him and that, his debt being satisfied by that conveyance, he had assigned the rest of the extended lands, to the conusor, and so he became a purchaser of the lands for a valuable consideration without any notice of the plaintiff's title. He also pleaded that the conusor was in execution at the plaintiff's judgment and, therefore, he could not extend his lands, neither were they liable to his debt during the life of the conusor.

And, upon arguing this plea, it was insisted on the part of the plaintiff as to the first point that it did not appear the defendant was a purchaser, there being no money paid upon executing the conveyance, the consideration whereof was the money due on the statute and that was no purchase and that it was common equity for him who had any subsequent judgment to be relieved against any precedent statute upon payment of what was justly due and that, therefore, the account made up between the conusor and conusee on the pretended purchase ought not to affect the plaintiff, so that, the defendant's purchase being subsequent to the plaintiff's security, ought not to be aided by the statute. And, the plaintiff's judgment being on record, the defendant was bound to take notice of it at his peril, and, therefore, ought, upon payment of the statute, to yield the possession to the plaintiff.

But, on the other side, it was insisted that the defendant was a purchaser and that, though no money was advanced on the purchase, yet the consideration of his assigning some part of the extended lands to the conusor was as good and valuable as money [and] that it was the constant justice of this court that, if a purchaser *bona fide* bought in another statute or judgment and there were intermediate judgments between that and the purchase, of which he had no notice, that, in such case, the precedent statute or judgment should protect the purchaser against all those intermediate judgments [and] that, though the plaintiff's judgment was on record and a purchaser [was] bound to take notice thereof, because it charges the land at law, yet, in equity, where the conusee of a statute or judgment comes for the assistance of this court to extend his judgment against a purchaser, he must prove that the purchaser had express notice of the judgment; otherwise, he shall not be relieved.

And, upon this point, the plea was allowed to be good.

As to the other point, that the conusor being in execution on the judgment at the suit of the plaintiff and so the lands [were] not to be extended during his life, it was argued that was no good exception in equity, for that the bill was to discover encumbrances and the plaintiff could have no such discovery after the conusor's death, and, therefore, he ought to have it now. And it has been ruled here that such a bill will lie, notwithstanding the debtor is in execution at the suit of the plaintiff.

But yet the court inclined that this part of the plea was likewise good.

[Reg. Lib. 1663 A, f. 145.]

78

Anonymous v. Perrot

(Ch. 1662)

An administrator of a decedent's estate must allege in his complaint who granted his letters of administration.

Lincoln's Inn MS. Hill 125, f. 39, pl. 1

Eodem die [15 October 1662].

An administrator brought a bill, and named himself administrator and [alleged] that administration was duly committed to him, but he did not show by whom or in what diocese so that the defendant could inform himself of the truth.

Ideo, the demurrer to it for this reason [was] allowed, even though the plaintiff now offered to produce the letters of administration.

79

Clopton v. Clopton

(Ch. 1662)

A purchaser for value of entailed lands will not be defeated of his title where his predecessor in title, a tenant in tail, sold but did not execute a proper fine and recovery.

Lincoln's Inn MS. Hill 125, f. 39, pl. 2

24 October 14 Car. II.

William Clopton [1538–1592], seised of divers manors and being a recusant convict, 3 December 13 Eliz. [1570], for a competent sum of money, did bargain and sell the manors to Woodhouse etc., who, 6 December 13 Eliz. [1570], bargained them again to William Clopton, and therein, the consideration was not mentioned for money, but, as it was averred, [it] was *revera* for a small sum of money paid privately and was done to the intent to make it good or bad as Clopton should please for his advantage.

William Clopton, the same year, entailed all the premises, and, [had] issue R., who had issue, the plaintiff's mother and Jane, late countess of Totnes, inheritable to the entail after the death of William and R. Jane purchased the estate of her sister, and conveyed to the defendant's father, who, for £2000 and marriage, settled the lands, under which settlement, the defendant claims.

The plaintiff sued at law, for the alienation of his mother was without a fine or recovery and nothing opposed his title to avoid it but the deed to Woodhouse, who was but a trustee at most. And the defendant, to bar the plaintiff's title at law, set up Woodhouse's title, who himself claimed no title, nor did the defendant offer to derive any title from him.

Therefore, the bill was now that Woodhouse's deed and title, being but a trust for the plaintiff, might not be given in evidence against the plaintiff, who was a *cestui que trust*.

But because the defendant is in under a valuable consideration, the court dismissed the bill. *Nota*.

80

Wise v. Prestwood

(Ch. 1662)

Where land is devised to pay the decedent's debts, if it is not sufficient, then the decedent's debts will paid out of his personal estate.

Lincoln's Inn MS. Hill 125, f. 39v

26 October, 14 Car. II.

Thomas Prestwood, seised in fee, mortgaged to Kellond for 300 years. And, lying sick, he made a lease for 1000 years to Kellond etc. on trust declared by the same deed to be in consideration and on trust to pay the debts he did or should owe. And he died. Dr. John Wise took administration. The plaintiffs, being heirs, exhibited their bill against Kellond to redeem and pay the debts and then to have the leases assigned to them. And they prayed against the wife, administratrix, that the personal estate in her hands might be employed for the payment of the debts in his ease.

Pending that suit, the administratrix exhibits a bill in court against Kellond to redeem and pay the debts. And, the same term, she has a decree and the leases assigned to her.

The cause of Wise, the heir, coming to be heard, he had a decree against the widow, first, if there be debts and the ancestor make a lease in trust to pay debts and leave a personal estate to his administrator, Mr. Attorney General [*Palmer*] and Serjeant *Glynne* insisted that, in that case, the heir shall not have a decree against the executor or administrator to employ the personal estate in aid of the heir, though it be true the creditor is free to charge them. Mr. Attorney [General] vouched the Lady St. John's Case in accord [. . .] etc. But, if, by a will, he gives his personal estate away, it is free.

Thereupon, the defendant Labird, to prove the intent of the testator to be that the personal estate should not be liable to pay the debts unless that the lease and profits were not sufficient, he read one witness to it, which, with the defendant's answer, sufficed, as the defendant pretended.

But the court decreed *in toto* for the plaintiff and the personal estate to come in aid of the heir etc.

81

Collicott v. Hill

(Ch. 1662)

A contract that was the result of surprise is not the act of the contracting parties, and is not valid and enforceable.

In this case, the seller intended to convey with a special warranty and not with a general warranty of seisin.

In this case, the court of equity ordered the defendant, after a final judgment at common law, to release his judgment and to pay costs.

1 Chancery Cases 15, 22 E.R. 671

The case was to this purpose. Dr. Coldcot, having purchased church lands in fee under the title of the Usurper [Oliver Cromwell] during the Rebellion, sold the same in fee to the defendant's testator, and covenanted that he was lawfully seised etc. The church being restored and the estate voided, the covenantee sued the covenant, and recovered damages to the value of the purchase money.

To be relieved in this was the scope of the bill, which did suggest a surprise upon the plaintiff in getting him into that covenant and that it was declared by Dr. Coldcot when he sealed and the defendant's testator that it was intended Dr. Coldcot should not undertake any further than against himself.

Upon the hearing, it was proved that the matter of the covenant, upon which the judgment was had against the plaintiff, was controverted in the paper draught and put out by the plaintiff's counsel and in again by the defendant's counsel with the alteration only that, whereas the covenant was that the plaintiff was lawfully seised etc., the plaintiff's counsel put out 'lawfully', which signified nothing, for to covenant one is seised is intended lawfully.

But some proof being that it was declared upon sealing that the plaintiff should undertake for his own act only, it was decreed that the defendant should acknowledge satisfaction on the judgment and pay costs.

And a like case to this between Farrer and Farrer was heard and decreed after the same manner about six months before.

2 Freeman 173, 22 E.R. 1139

Michaelmas [term], 14 Car. II [1662]. Lord Chancellor, Master of the Rolls.

Dr. Collicott, having purchased the fee of church lands, sold them with a general covenant. The church is restored; the lands are evicted. The vendee brings [an action of] covenant, and recovers the value of the lands.

The plaintiff, in his bill, suggests that the said covenant was gotten by surprise and that it was agreed only that he should covenant against his own acts, which appearing upon proof, the court ordered the defendant to acknowledge satisfaction on the judgment.

The like [case was] between Ferrar and Ferrar about six months before.

[Other reports of this case: 1 Eq. Cas. Abr. 27, 21 E.R. 849.]
[Reg. Lib. 1662 A, f. 196.]

82

Anonymous

(Ch. 1662)

A widow does not have dower rights in lands held by her husband as a trustee.

A widow will have dower rights where she can prove that the purpose of a trust was to defraud her of her dower.

Lord Nottingham, *Prolegomena*, p. 329

Michaelmas [term], 14 Car. II, *per* Clarendon, Chancellor.

A bill was exhibited to be relieved against dower, because the husband was only seised in trust for the plaintiff, to whom he conveyed.

[It was] resolved: first, if the fact be so, the plaintiff shall be relieved; but, second, if the fact can be no otherwise proved than by a confession of the husband or recitals in a deed, the truth shall be tried; else, this may be a trick to defeat dower.

So the parties compromised in court for £20.

83

Meynell v. Garraway

(Ch. 1662–1663)

In this case, the defendant was a bona fide purchaser of value without notice of a second mortgage, and he took the land free of the second mortgage.

Nelson 63, 21 E.R. 790

Lord Clarendon assisted by Sir Orlando Bridgeman.

One Wingate, in the year 1652, mortgaged a lease to one, and, in the next year, *viz.* 1653, he mortgaged the same lease to Meynell, the plaintiff. And both the mortgages being forfeited, the defendant Mr. Garraway, *anno* 1656, purchased the inheritance. And having notice of the first mortgage, he discharged the same out of the purchase money. But, before he had discharged that mortgage and had got it assigned in trust to attend the inheritance, he had notice of the second mortgage. And the money being demanded of him and he refusing to pay it, Meynell exhibited his bill to discover whether Garraway was a purchaser *bona fide* for a valuable consideration and that he might satisfy this second mortgage upon assigning the interest to him.

And it being referred to a trial at law, whether a valuable consideration was really paid as also whether the purchaser had notice of the last mortgage before he bought the inheritance and when he had such notice and there being a verdict that he had notice before the first mortgagee had executed the assignment but that he had paid Wingate for the inheritance before he had notice of the second mortgage, the plaintiff's bill was dismissed.

84

Whorwood v. Whorwood

(Ch. 1662–1663)

Decrees for alimony made by the Court of Chancery during the interregnum, when there were no ecclesiastical courts, are valid and enforceable.

1 Chancery Reports 223, 21 E.R. 556

The plaintiff insisted for error that there is no foundation whereon to justify the said decree or proceedings thereon, for that there is no confirmation thereof by the Act of Judicial Proceedings,[1] and that there are several votes in the Commons' House of Parliament for that purpose.

---

[1] Stat. 12 Car. II, c. 3 (*SR*, V, 180–181).

This court referred it to the judges on these two points, *viz.* whether the decrees for alimony made in the late times are confirmed by the said Act and whether, in this case, bills of review do lie for the reversal of the same.

The judges certified in Michaelmas term 1662 that decrees for alimony made in the Court of Chancery in the late times are confirmed by the Act for Confirmation of Judicial Proceedings and that a bill of review does not lie for want of authority in that court to make decrees in cases of alimony, but it lies for other defects not remedied or provided for by that Act. And all the judges of England agreed to the same opinion, though not subscribed.

[Reg. Lib. 14 Car. II, f. 1016.]

85

Cropley v. Marquess of Newcastle

(Ch. 1662–1663)

In this case, the court found that the plaintiff was a bona fide purchaser for value of the land in issue.

1 Chancery Reports 225, 21 E.R. 557

Edward Cropley, deceased, the plaintiff's father and testator, in 1640, did lend to the defendant £1200 on a bond. The plaintiff, as executor to his said father, is entitled to the said bond. And the defendant being beyond the sea and having authorized Edward Butler to manage his affairs and to pay his debts and for that purpose to sell his estate, the defendant importuned the plaintiff to purchase the capital messuage in Clerkenwell and the manor of Flabrough now in question, assuring the plaintiff it would be a great kindness to the defendant, the marquess, and enable him to pay his debts and provide for his children. And he told the plaintiff that he should have a good title, for that the marquess, before the troublesome times, had settled the premises on himself for life, remainder to his brother, Sir Charles Cavendish, the said Robert Butler, James Whitehead, and John Rolston and their heirs upon trust to sell. But the plaintiff desired to have the marquess's approbation of the said sale, whereupon the said Butler told the plaintiff that the marquess, since his departure, wrote several letters to him and Viscount Mansfield, the eldest son of the said marquess, to expedite the sale, and had by letters also the marquess's approbation and allowance of the plaintiff's purchase of the premises. And, upon the said Butler's offer, that the said Cropley, Viscount Mansfield, and Henry, now Viscount Mansfield, the marquess's second son, should join with the trustees in the conveyance, he was encouraged to proceed in the purchase of Flabrough, and he agreed to give £7400 for the same. And, as to the manner of the conveyance and title, the plaintiff relied on the said Butler, who was unwilling to produce the deeds of settlement on the trustees, lest he should thereby discover the posture and condition of the marquess's estate. By a deed in 1654 enrolled, whereby the said Charles, viscount Mansfield, since deceased, and Henry, now viscount Mansfield, then eldest and second son of the said marquess, and all the trustees were parties, the said manor was conveyed to the plaintiff and his heirs forever. And the plaintiff paid the said £7400, *viz.* £5600 in ready money and £1800 was allowed the plaintiff for his debt. And, afterwards, the said Butler pressed the plaintiff to buy the house in Clerkenwell, and he wrote to the marquess touching the same. The marquess, by the name of John Forrest, which name he then used, wrote an answer to Butler, and thanked him for what he had done, and ordered him to sell the said house, whereupon, the plaintiff, by a deed of 30 January 1654 enrolled, for the consideration of £1400 paid to the said sons and trustees, had the same messuage conveyed to trustees for the plaintiff and his heirs. But the said marquess, being returned again into England, says he gave no authority or consent to the said sales and that the trustees had only the power to sell the reversion after his death, and he will not confirm the said purchases, pretending he has an estate for life in the premises, which neither his sons nor the trustees had a power to sell, and he claims the premises for his life.

The defendant, the marquess, insists he did not intend his trustees to sell any other estate than they were entrusted with and that the reversion itself was a bargain great enough for the money agreed for.

Now the point in controversy is whether the defendant, the marquess, did consent to or allow of the said respective sales as to his own estate for life, reserved to him by the said indenture tripartite, or whether the plaintiff's said respective purchases should only relate to the reversion in fee after the marquess's death.

This court, with the assistance of the judges, on the reading a paper of advice under the hands of the marquess's learned counsel in 1649 and letters from the marquess, were all clear of opinion that the defendant, the marquess, did consent to the absolute sale of the inheritance of the manor of Flabrough and the house in Clerkenwell and that the plaintiff is a fair purchaser thereof for a full consideration which came and was applied to the marquess's use and benefit. And the said Charles, viscount Mansfield, having covenanted for enjoying Flabrough against the marquess was a farther evidence of the intention of the parties. And [the court] decreed that the plaintiff and his heirs shall enjoy the said manor of Flabrough and the house in Clerkenwell against the marquess and all claiming under him, and the marquess to make assurance of his estate in the premises to the plaintiff and his heirs etc.

[Reg. Lib. 14 Car. II, f. 923.]

86

Eyre v. Jackson

(Ch. 1662–1664)

Neither interest nor court costs are payable to a successful plaintiff on a bill of review.

1 Chancery Reports 229, 21 E.R. 558

The bill is a bill of review to reverse a decree, whereby the now plaintiffs were decreed to give the now defendant satisfaction for his losses, the now plaintiffs having plundered the said defendant in the late times of his goods, household stuff, and of debt books, bonds, and specialties, so as he could not make proofs to ground an action at law, and the now plaintiffs were decreed to pay the now defendant £400, besides the goods and money which the said now defendant received back from the plaintiffs, and the same to be in satisfaction of the defendant's damages, losses, and costs, and he to prosecute which of the now plaintiffs he pleases upon the said decree, and the now plaintiffs to prosecute each other to pay their proportions.

The now plaintiffs insist that the decree is erroneous and ought to be reversed, for that it is contrary to the rules and practice of this court to deprive the courts of law of the determination there determinable or to assess damages for a trespass, which ought to be ascertained by a jury at law and not otherwise, and the plaintiffs have paid the said £400 above eight years before the bill was exhibited to their prejudice. So the plaintiffs insist that the decree ought to be reversed and they restored to all they have lost and been damnified by the said erroneous decree.

The defendant pleaded and demurred, and he insisted that the now plaintiffs were decreed to pay £400, and they paid the same, and rested satisfied therewith eight years. And he also pleaded the Act of Oblivion[1] in bar of the plaintiffs' demand, which was reserved until the hearing. And, on the hearing of the said decree, it was reversed.

But, as to the point of restitution, His Lordship [Lord Clarendon] would advise whether the Act of Oblivion ought to bar the now plaintiffs from being restored to what they have lost by the said decree.

This court, with the judges, declared that the now plaintiffs, notwithstanding the Act of Oblivion, ought to be restored to all they have lost or been damnified by the same decree, and reversed the decree, and ordered the defendant to re-pay the £400 with damages and costs.

But the defendant insisted that, by the rules of the common law, where a judgment is reversed and restitution awarded, the courts of law give neither damages nor costs and that this court does usually guide itself by the rules at law.

[1] Stat. 12 Car. II, c. 11 (*SR*, V, 226–234).

This court desired to see precedents where damages and costs had been given in cases of this nature, and, finding no precedents could be produced, this court would not charge the defendant with damages or costs.

2 Freeman 181, 22 E.R. 1146

23 May, 16 Car. II [1664]. Jackson v. Eyre.

The defendant had a decree for money. The plaintiff, by a bill of review, reversed this decree, and the money was decreed to the plaintiff.

Curia: On a search of precedents, the defendant shall not pay damage for this money.

Nelson 83, 21 E.R. 795

Jackson v. Digry.

Upon a motion, the question was upon a bill of review, by which money was decreed back from the defendant to the plaintiff, which he had gotten from him by a former decree, whether the party should pay damages or not. Upon a former motion in this case, the court directed to search precedents, and none were found where any damages or costs were given on a bill of review. And this was compared to cases where judgments have been reversed upon a writ of error, *viz.* that the party shall be restored to all that he had lost *per judicium praedictum*, but no damages or costs.

And so it was decreed.

3 Chancery Reports 15, 21 E.R. 714

23 May, 16 Car. II [1664]. Jackson v. Eyre.

Upon a motion, the question was whether on a bill of review, whereby money was decreed back from the defendant to the plaintiff, which the defendant had formerly gotten from the plaintiff by a former decree, the plaintiff should pay damages for that money. And this having been formerly moved, directions were given to search for precedents, whether damages had been given on a bill of review. And no precedents were now produced. And it was confidently affirmed there was no precedent of any damages or costs given on a bill of review. And [he] compared it to a judgment in a writ of error, where the judgment is that the party shall recover *quicquid amisit per judicium praedictum*, but no damages or costs. And, in this case, it was ruled there should be none.

[Other reports of this case: 2 Eq. Cas. Abr. 174, 22 E.R. 149.]
[Reg. Lib. 14 Car. II, ff. 751, 875, 910.]

87

Martin v. Perryman

(Ch. 1662–1663)

A court of equity can order a partition, even where the interests of persons under a disability and secured creditors are involved.

1 Chancery Reports 235, 21 E.R. 559

This court decreed a partition, notwithstanding married women and infants and some encumbrances were in this case concerned.

[Reg. Lib. 14 Car. II, f. 966.]

88

Anonymous

(Ch. 1662)

Where a mortgagor's heir re-enters upon the mortgaged land and then releases the equity of redemption, he must pay to the mortgagee the mesne profits that he, the heir, received.

Lincoln's Inn MS. Hill 125, f. 40v, pl. 1

The mortgagee enters for the non-payment. The mortgagor's heir re-enters and keeps possession. The mortgagee exhibits his bill to have his money with damages or to be freed of the equity of redemption and, in such case, to have the mesne profits since the entry.

[It was] decreed accordingly. And an election being made by the defendant to quit the equity of redemption, he was ordered afterwards to pay the mesne profits.

89

Marquess of Antrim v. Duke of Buckingham

(Ch. 1662–1663)

Where an unmarried woman reserves to herself a power of appointment, this power cannot be exercised after she marries.

Lincoln's Inn MS. Hill 125, f. 40v, pl. 2

Michaelmas [term] 14 Car. II.

The duchess of Buckingham, seised in fee of a reversion expectant on an estate for life, did while she was unmarried convey etc. to the use of herself for life, the remainder to the now duke, her son, in tail with a power to herself to lease for twenty-one years or three lives in possession. She, after[wards] married the plaintiff. And then she and the plaintiff, her husband, made a lease of etc. to Cox for twenty-one years, the first tenant for life being living at the time of the lease, but since dead. The lease was in trust with the profits etc. to pay the debts of the duchess.

The marquess, being the mortgagee for divers debts of the duchess and having paid drivers other of her debts, did now exhibit this bill to have the profits applied to pay the debts.

Cox, by an answer, confessed the trust. The duke denied it, and, by an answer, he insisted that the lease was not pursuant to the power in two respects, first, because the lease was made of a reversions, whereas the power was to lease in possession, secondly, because, by her second marriage with the plaintiff, she is now disabled to execute the power.

Bridgeman, Chief Justice of the Common Bench, [and] Hale, Chief Baron, assist at the hearing of the cause. Hale held the case considerable, and suspended his opinion until a case made to be argued.

Bridgeman, for the first point, inclined that the power was well executed, notwithstanding that the first tenant for life was living, for, when a reversion is conveyed so with a power to lease in possession, the possession must be intended of such a possession as may be of the thing intended to be leased by the possession of a reversion.

But he said he was very clear as to the second point, that the lease was void. The difference is between a power in gross. Such a power is not suspended or disabled by a revocation, as a devise to sell may be executed by a married woman. But, where it arises out of an interest and is annexed to an interest and charges the interest of the married woman, she cannot execute such a power. And he vouched Thorowgood's Case, *quod vide.*

The Chancellor [Lord Clarendon] dismissed the bill *in toto. Quod mirum.*

Vide Daniel and Ubly's Case;[1] a wife who had a power and an interest married, and executed it well enough. And the counsel of the defendant told me that they doubted etc.

1 Chancery Cases 17, 22 E.R. 672

January [1663].

The Lady Antrim, mother of the defendant, being a *feme sole* and seised of a reversion after one life, settles the lands to the use of herself for life, remainder in tail, with a power for her, being *sole*, to make leases for three lives in possession. The woman marries. And, then, she and her husband make leases for twenty-one years (in the life of the tenant for life) to commence from the date for the payment of debts etc., as was alleged.

---

1 *Daniel v. Upley* (1626), Paynell K.B. 61, 135.

The first question was if this lease by the husband and wife was good.

BRIDGEMAN: The power is not pursued, for, by the marriage, she has put herself in the power of her husband, and it is the deed of her husband, and not hers. And he took a diversity between a naked power and a power which flows from an interest, for, when a bare power is given to a woman by a will to sell lands, although she marry, she may sell, and she may sell the lands to her husband, because it was not created by herself out of any interest of her own. But where a woman upon a settlement of her own estate reserves a power which flows from an interest, that power ought to be executed by the *feme sole*, and, if by the husband and wife, it is not good. And yet he said such a power ought to be taken liberally, though, formerly, they were taken strictly.

The second question was if this lease was a lease in possession, inasmuch as it commences at the time of the date, for it was said, although an estate for life were before it, yet it was in possession in relation to the estate of the reversion.

BRIDGEMAN doubted whether the lease was void in that point. But he was clear it was in the other point.

HALE said both points are worth a trial and argument at law.

The Chancellor [LORD CLARENDON] concurred with BRIDGEMAN. And the bill was dismissed.

2 Freeman 168, 22 E.R. 1135

January 1662[/63]. The Lord Chancellor, Chief Justice Bridgeman, Chief Baron Hale.

The Lady Margaret of Antrim, mother of the defendant, being a *feme sole* seised of a reversion after one life, conveys the land to the use of herself for life, the remainder to [*blank*] in tail, with a power for her, being unmarried, to make leases for three lives or twenty-one years in possession. The woman marries, and, then, she and her husband lease for twenty-one years in the life of the tenant for life to commence from the date for the payment of debts etc. [The question was] if this lease by the husband and wife were good.

BRIDGEMAN: This power is not pursued, for, by marrying, she has put herself under the power of her husband. And there is a difference between a nude power and a power which flows from an interest, for, when a bare power is given to a woman by a will to sell lands, although she marry, yet she may sell, and may sell to her husband. But, when she reserves a power out of an interest of her own, *contra*, but such a power ought to be expounded benignly at this day, though formerly it was taken strictly.

The second point, being whether the lease from that date were good, was not resolved.

Afterwards, HALE and the Chancellor [LORD CLARENDON], concurring with BRIDGEMAN, the bill was dismissed.

O. Bridgeman 617, 124 E.R. 777

The plaintiff's suit being to have a lease made good in equity, which was made by Catherine, late duchess of Buckingham, for the payment of certain debts alleged to have been contracted by the said duchess, who, as the plaintiff's bill sets forth, being seised in fee of several manors, lands, and tenements, and being indebted to several persons by indenture dated in June 1633 and a fine, to raise money for payment of her debts and for other considerations, did settle the premises to the use of herself for life without waste, the remainder to the defendant, the duke of Buckingham, her son, in tail male, with a remainder over, with a proviso and a power reserved, that it should be lawful for her, during her life, by any deed or deeds indented, to grant the premises or any part thereof for twenty-one years in possession or two or three lives in possession, whereupon the then yearly rent or more should be reserved and payable during the term to her and such persons to whom the immediate reversion or remainder should belong. And, afterwards, she intermarried with the plaintiff. And, in October 1649, after the intermarriage, the plaintiff and the duchess leased the premises for twenty-one years to Richard, earl of W., Oliver, lord B. of L., and James Stewart, esquire, their executors, and assigns, in trust for the said countess, but principally to raise money to pay her debts, for which the plaintiffs, Archibald Steward and John Traylman, stood bound, which trust, although not expressed in the lease, was declared by writing under the hands and seals of the lessees. And shortly after the making of the said lease, the said duchess and also James Steward, one of the trustees, died. And, in September 1660, the surviving trustees, with the plaintiff's consent and for her benefit, assigned their interest in the premises to the defendants, Cox and Robert Castle, who refused to execute their trust and who permit the defendant, the duke of Buckingham, to take the profits of the premises, by means whereof, the plaintiff cannot be reimbursed the money he has really paid in discharge of part of the said debt, but is likely to be charged with all the debts contracted by the duchess out of his own estate, so as to have the said lease made good in equity and to compel the said defendant, the duke, to suffer the other defendants to take the profits during the lease to pay the said debts, according to the intention of the duchess, and that the said duke may account for the profits received by him or his agents is the prayer of the bill.

Whereunto, it was insisted by the counsel for the defendant, the duke of Buckingham, that the said duke, having put in an answer and plea, sets forth by way of answer that it does not appear that the lease aforesaid was made in trust to raise money to discharge the debts of the duchess, who, he believes, was not indebted at the making of the settlement, or, if she were, it concerned not him, there being no provision by the settlement to raise money to pay her debts by any lease to be afterwards made. And, therefore, if the said lease had been made upon such trust as is pretended by the plaintiff, it was not pursuant to the power reserved on the settlement. And, for plea, he says that the duchess, at the time of the settlement made, was seised of the premises not in possession, but in reversion expectant upon the death of Cicely, countess of Rutland, who was living at the time of the lease, and was seised of the premises for the term of her life, and, afterwards, while the said countess was so seised, the duchess was disabled to make any lease for years in possession. And, therefore, the lease in question was unwarrantably made, and so had been if the duchess had been unmarried at the time of the making thereof. And it was not pursuant to the power in the settlement.

The court, hereupon and upon debate of the matter, saw no cause of equity to give the plaintiff any relief, and does, therefore, order that the matter of the plaintiff's bill be from thenceforth clearly and absolutely dismissed out of this court with costs.

3 Salkeld 276, 91 E.R. 822

The Lady Antrim, being a single woman, settled her estate for life, remainder to her in tail, with a power to make leases (being *sole*) for three lives, etc. Afterwards, she married, and then she and her husband made a lease etc. for the payment of debts.

And, *per curiam*, this is void, being not pursuant to the power, for the lease of the husband and wife is the lease of the husband and the difference is between a naked power and a power which arises from an interest, for, if a woman has only a naked or bare power, as by a will, to sell lands, she may sell, though she marry, because this is not a power created out of any interest. But, where a power is reserved upon a settlement, she must execute it pursuant to that power when it was at first reserved.

1 Siderfin 101, 82 E.R. 995

Note the Lord Chancellor [LORD CLARENDON] called to himself BRIDGEMAN, Chief Justice of the Common Bench, and HALE, Chief Baron of the Exchequer, to hear a case that was to this effect. The father of the present duke of Buckingham made a jointure to his duchess with a power that she may make leases for twenty-one years in possession. And he died. His duchess, the mother of the present duke, took for her second husband the Lord Antrim. And he and his wife, who was the duchess, made leases for twenty-one years to commence *in presenti*. But some of them were of lands that were in lease before and, thus, the lands were not in possession.

And two questions were moved:

First, whether the power that the duchess had to make leases be well executed by her and her husband. Yes: Godbolt 327, pl. 419.[1]

[1] *Anonymous* (1623), Godbolt 327, 78 E.R. 192.

Second, whether he, by force of this power could make leases of lands that are not in possession. No: Cr. Jac. 319, pl. 2; Mo. 494.[1]

[Other reports of this case: 1 Eq. Cas. Abr. 343, 21 E.R. 1090.]
[Lib. Reg. 1662 B, f. 377.]

90

Denny v. Filmer

(Ch. 1663–1683)

No error in a decree can be assigned as error unless it is expressly alleged in the bill of review.

After an appearance by the defendant, if all of the processes of contempt are not strictly followed, this is not a sufficient error to justify a reversal on a bill of review.

A second bill of review does not lie after a first bill of review has been dismissed.

Lord Nottingham, *Prolegomena*, p. 296

20 January, 14 Car. II, Hilary [term], Sir William Denny *contra* Filmer.

In a bill of review, the error assigned was that the original bill did not set forth any such title on which any such decree could be made. And, at the bar, it was thus explained, *viz.* that the bill made a title to no more than a third part and the defendant was decreed to convey the whole.

[It was] resolved that no error can be assigned in the decree which is not expressly alleged in the bill of review, for an obscure intimation of it will not suffice nor the general conclusion which prays that, for this and other errors appearing in the record, the decree may be reversed, *idque licet* error be apparent when it is opened, wherein the forms of this court differ from the courts at law, for, there, an advantage may be taken of any error espied either at bar or bench. Here, nothing can be insisted on not particularly alleged, but this court will keep their own forms.

Lord Nottingham, *Prolegomena*, p. 292

20 January, Hilary [term] 14 Car. II.

Filmer exhibits a bill against Sir William Denny [to compel him] to execute a conveyance according to trusts. Sir William Denny, on an affidavit made, gets time to appear, but never answers, and, after a *non est inventus* returned by a serjeant at arms, the bill is decreed *pro confesso*. And this matter, amongst others, was assigned for error on a review, for, by the printed rules and the course of the

---

[1] *Shecomb v. Hawkins* (1612), Croke Jac. 318, 79 E.R. 273, also Yelverton 222, 80 E.R. 145, 1 Brownlow & Goldesborough 148, 123 E.R. 721; *Bullen v. Bullen* (1594), Moore K.B. 361, 72 E.R. 630.

court, after a serjeant at arms, there ought to have been a sequestration [for a year], then an injunction for the possession, then the bringing of the party to the bar, and, on denial to answer *in facie curiae*, then and not until then, to decree the bill *pro confesso*. And it was said the practice was so in David Jenkins's Case, and, long before that, in 15 Jac. in Magdalene College Case, where the Master and Fellows refused to answer and departed from their plea and demurrer.

But yet [it was] resolved by the Chancellor [LORD CLARENDON] and BRIDGEMAN, Chief Justice, to be no error, for, though a decree thus may be against the ordinary rules, yet *factum valet*, for the contempt committed was after a personal appearance, for an affidavit amounts to it. So it is *quasi* a departure in despite of the court. And, in this case, a sequestration was vain, for Filmer was in possession and sued only for a conveyance. And an injunction was needless, because it was but a consequence of the sequestration, so that there was no remedy left in this case but a decree. And the Lord BRIDGEMAN said that there was a difference in all courts between rules for process and fundamental rules of law and equity relating to the judgments themselves. The first are not so binding.

2 Freeman 172, 22 E.R. 1138

20 January, 14 Car. II [1663].

Error [was alleged] upon a bill of review for that the decree was that the bill should be taken *pro confesso*. The error was that the defendant was not brought in by process of contempt and, thereon, had a day assigned to answer, on which the defendant demurred for that it appeared by the decree that he appeared by his clerk on the process of contempt and prayed farther time to answer by his counsel.

Curia: Let the defendant answer, saving the benefit of his demurrer until hearing. And, afterwards, it was heard.

And because of the defendant's appearances *ut supra* and because, afterwards, he stood out all process of contempt and would not answer, [it was] resolved the decree was well grounded.

Nelson 64, 21 E.R. 790

Lord Chancellor Hyde and Lord Chief Justice Bridgeman.

A bill of review [was brought] to reverse a decree, and the error assigned was that the decree was founded upon a bill taken *pro confesso* when the defendants to that bill were not brought in upon any contempt.

There was a demurrer to this bill of review. And, in arguing the same, it was insisted that the decree was regular, for, though the defendants were not brought in upon any process of contempt, yet they appeared by their clerk upon service of a subpoena and, afterwards, moved the court for a longer time to put in their answer than of course they could have, which time was granted. And this was compared to a judgment at law by a default, where, after the defendant has once appeared and, afterwards, makes default, judgment shall be entered against him.

But, on the other side, it was insisted, that the decree was erroneous and not warranted by any precedent, because the defendants were not brought into court upon any process of contempt, neither was any day assigned to answer before the bill was taken *pro confesso*. And this was alleged to be the constant course and rule of the court.

Thereupon, it was ordered, that the defendants should answer by a certain day and the benefit of this demurrer should be saved to them until the hearing the cause, which was afterwards heard by SIR HARBOTTLE GRIMSTON, Master of the Rolls, who, upon long debate, was of opinion that the decree was erroneous. But he appointed precedents to be searched.

And, afterwards, the cause coming to be heard by My Lord Chancellor [LORD CLARENDON], assisted by the Chief Justice BRIDGEMAN, they were of opinion that, because the defendants appeared to the subpoena to answer and craved a farther day and had it and still stood out all contempts and could not be taken, that the decree was well grounded. And he ordered the bill of review to be dismissed.

1 Vernon 135, 23 E.R. 369

Eodem die [6 February 1683]. Dunny v. Filmore.

A bill having been taken *pro confesso*, a bill of review was brought. And a demurrer, having been put in to it, was allowed. And, now, a new bill of review being brought, the defendant demurred and, for cause, showed that a bill of review lies not after a bill of review.

And the demurrer was allowed.

2 Chancery Cases 133, 22 E.R. 881

1683.

A decree passed where the bill was never answered, but the bill was taken *pro confesso*, though the party defendant never answered, but only appeared by his clerk, and the bill was never read in court as it ought to have been.

A bill of review was brought. And, on demurrer, it was dismissed.

Now, the heir brought another bill of review. And, though there was manifest error, not only in the form of the court, but in the right, *viz.* two heirs having title as heirs, one of them plaintiff had a decree for the whole, who had title but to a moiety.

Yet My Lord NORTH dismissed the bill, and said there was no remedy but in Parliament. And he cited Mordant or Morgan's Case, where a bill was grounded on a deed, whereto two witnesses were examined, but the deed was not produced, and, the witnesses not agreeing, the bill was dismissed, and a bill of review was brought and dismissed, and after[wards] the deed was found, and [there was] an affidavit of it etc., and then a bill of review was exhibited, but dismissed *quia* of the former bill, which, said the Lord Keeper [NORTH], was a hard case.

To which it was answered that it differs from the present case, for, there, the cause was heard on the merits, but, here, there is not so much as an answer.

Lord Keeper [NORTH] dismissed the bill.

1 Vernon 417, 23 E.R. 558

Upon a bill of review, the court had decreed the whole estate to the plaintiff. And, though it appeared even upon the face of the decree that the plaintiff had a title but to one moiety only, yet it was there resolved that no bill of review would lie upon a bill of review. And the defendant was left without a remedy.

[Other reports of this case: 1 Eq. Cas. Abr. 81, 21 E.R. 894.]

91

Parker v. Plummer

(Ch. 1663)

Specific performance of a contract for a leasehold will be enforced against the successor of the seller.

1 Chancery Cases 42, 22 E.R. 685

27 January, 14 Car. II [1663]. Upon an appeal from a decree at the Rolls. Parker v. Palmer.

Parker sold a lease which he had from the dean and chapter for three lives to Palmer etc. And it was agreed Palmer should pay £4320 for it. After[wards], the defendant agreed with the plaintiff that, if he would abate him £420, he would re-convey the lease whenever the king and dean and chapter were restored. The plaintiff, thereupon, abated the £420.

And the king and church being now restored, the plaintiff exhibited his bill for the lease, which the Master the Rolls [GRIMSTON] decreed to him.

Note that this was decreed against the son of the purchaser, the father being dead.

The question was whether he came in by a settlement or as an occupant.

Upon an appeal to this decree, it was affirmed by the Lord Chancellor [LORD CLARENDON] and BRIDGEMAN.

And, in this case, it was objected that this court ought not to decree that, for it was but in the nature of a wager and the consideration was unequal and penal and that an action [at common law] more properly lay and that it was at the discretion of the court to decree an agreement or not when it ought to be performed *ex debito justitiae*. Yet it was decreed *ut supra*.

2 Freeman 167, 22 E.R. 1134

27 January, 14 Car. II [1663]. Upon an Appeal from a decree at the Rolls.

Parker sold a lease, which he had for three lives from the dean and chapter, to Plummer. And it was agreed Plummer should pay £4320 for it. After[wards], the defendant agreed with the plaintiff that, if he would abate him £420, he would reconvey the lease whenever the king and dean and chapter were restored. The plaintiff, thereupon, abated the £420. And, King Charles being now restored, the plaintiff exhibits his bill for the lease, which the Master of the Rolls [GRIMSTON] decreed to him.

Note this was decreed against the son of the purchaser, the father being dead. *Quaere*, whether he came in by a settlement or as occupant.

Upon an appeal, this decree was affirmed by the Lord Chancellor [LORD CLARENDON] and Justice BRIDGEMAN.

In this case, it was objected that this court ought not to decree it, for it was in the nature of a wager and the consideration was unequal and penal and that an action more properly lay and that it was in the discretion of the court to decree agreements or not, which was where they ought to be performed *ex debito justitiae*. Yet it was decreed *ut supra*.

[Other reports of this case: 1 Eq. Cas. Abr. 17, 21 E.R. 839.]
[Reg. Lib. 1662 B, f. 274.]

92

Fuller v. Lance

(Ch. 1663)

Participants in an assignment for the benefit of creditors who do not join in later bankruptcy proceedings will be excluded from a share of the bankruptcy proceeds.

1 Chancery Cases 18, 22 E.R. 672

Fuller, being a goldsmith in London and being disabled, agreed with most of his creditors to assign over all his estate upon an oath to several persons in trust for the payment of his debts as far as his estate would pay, he having such allowance for himself and family as was agreed upon. And most of the creditors signed the said agreement. But some of the persons that signed, finding that Fuller had done some act of violation of the agreement, took out a commission of bankruptcy against the said Fuller, and seized all the estate they could come by, and pretended that some of the creditors aforesaid that signed the agreement and that they were not privy to the suing out of the commission, had notice in due time, though they had neglected the same and that it was seven months from the date of the commission before the commissioners assigned.

And Fuller and other the persons concerned in the first agreement and excluded by the commission of bankruptcy, being not comprised, as aforesaid, preferred their bill against the assignees of the commission of bankruptcy to have the agreement performed or, at least, to be admitted to an equal dividend with them.

But this court would give no relief therein; and the rather, for that it was made to appear that Fuller had made a sale of some of the goods he assigned to the creditors. But [the court] dismissed the bill.

93

Hall v. Higham

(Ch. 1663)

Where a debtor is given relief in a court of equity against a penalty, he must pay the creditor the contracted for principal, interest, and any court costs at common law and in equity.

3 Chancery Reports 5, 21 E.R. 711

Hilary [term] 14 Car. II [1663].

The plaintiff's bill is to be relieved against the penalty of a bond.

And it is ordered he shall pay interest and costs, which will extend unto the defendant's costs at law as well as in Chancery.

Vide the report, Trinity [term] 1663.

94

Hill v. Reynolds

(Ch. 1663)

A court of equity can cure a procedural error committed by a pauper who could not afford to pay the fees of the court.

Lincoln's Inn MS. Hill 125, f. 41v, pl. 2

Hilary [term] 15 Car. II.

The defendant, [being] in contempt, [was] brought to the bar, and [it was] ordered the bill to be taken *pro confesso* unless he answered by a day. He not answering, the bill was decreed, and the decree [was] enrolled and, after[wards], possession [was] obtained accordingly.

The truth was that the defendant was poor and in person and did in order to obey the court draw and engross his answer and tendered it to the plaintiff's clerk in court, who would not file it because the defendant could not pay the fees or would not. And so, for the want of an answer, the decree passed. The defendant did move against the decree. And it was referred to the Six Clerks if it were regularly enrolled, who certified it was.

Yet, after[wards], on further reference of this special matter, the Lord Chancellor [Lord Clarendon], as this case is, set aside the decree, and ordered that the enrollment and the docket thereof be vacated. And, after[wards], he ordered the possession to be restored *cum exitibus*.

95

Savile v. Darcy

(Ch. 1663)

An appellant in a bill of review can put up an appeal bond in lieu of performing the decree.

1 Chancery Cases 42, 22 E.R. 685

A decree was obtained for a great sum of money. A bill of review was brought, and new matter was assigned. The rule of court was pleaded that the defendant ought first to pay the money before the bill should be brought into court.

Let him give good security for the money, and we will dispense with the rule. The like case was between Baston and Biron, by order of the House of Peers, about 1662.[1]

2 Freeman 172, 22 E.R. 1139

A decree [was made] for a great sum of money. A bill of review was brought, and new matter was assigned. The rule of court was pleaded that the defendant ought first to pay the money before the bill be brought.

Curia: Let him give good security for the money, and we will dispense with the rule, And the like [case was] between Baston and Byron, by order of the House of Peers, about 1662.

[Other reports of this case: 1 Eq. Cas. Abr. 82, 21 E.R. 894.]

96

Adrian v. Ent

(Ch. 1663)

The question in this case was whether a London citizen can devise a deceased child's share to a third person.

[1] *Byron v. Balston* (Ch. 1664), see below, Case No. 142.

Lincoln's Inn MS. Hill 125, f. 42

Adrian and Dr. Ent's [Case was] certified in this case by the Recorder of London, and [it was] decreed accordingly. A citizen and freeman of London, having only one child, devises the child's part to Dr. Ent in the case of the child's death within age. And the child dying, Dr. Ent, under the title of the devisee, recovered the child's part against the executor of the child. But, if there had been another child, such a devise of the father is not good against the other child.

The defendants, in the life of the child, had laid out divers great sums of money amounting to more than the finding money and divers sums for a child's funeral and physic. (The finding money is such use of money for the child's portion as the custom of the City allows.)

The question before the Master was whether the same should be allowed on the account between the plaintiff, legatee of the father, and the executor of the daughter. The Mayor and the Court of Aldermen, at the procurement of the executor, did certify that, in such a case of expense for physic and direction, the executor was allowable beyond the finding money out of the principal. And they, a second time, certify on perusal of the particulars of the accounts [what] they ought to be allowed by the custom.

And, thereupon, the Master did give an allowance. But, an exception being taken thereto, the Chancellor [Lord Clarendon] disallowed a great part thereof; though it should be good against the child, it shall not bind the legatee.

Yet ob[serve] that the legatee could claim no more than the child.

2 Ventris 341, 86 E.R. 475

By the custom of London, if a man die leaving three sons, his estate shall be equally divided amongst them. And, if either of them die within age, his part shall survive to the other. The father taking notice of this custom, devised that, if any of his sons die within age, his part should not survive, but that it should go to J.S.

It was resolved that the father could not thus give the child's portion, because it was but a possibility and a thing not vested in himself.

Lord Nottingham, *Prolegomena*, p. 321

The father devises to three sons their orphanage part, and, if they all die before twenty-one, that J.S. shall have it. They all three die. The administrator of the survivor claims it.

[It was] resolved on a certificate of Wilde, then Recorder, that the father can devise this possibility, and [it was] so decreed.

97

Thyn v. Foster

(Ch. 1663)

Where a person who has a power to assign dies without exercising the power, his or her administrator will be considered to be the assignee of the power.

Lord Nottingham, *Prolegomena*, p. 268

Easter [term] 15 Car. II, by the advice of Hale, Chief Baron.

Lady Katherine Thyn having recovered a manor for dower, she, as lady for the time, granted a copyhold to Foster for three lives. Foster declares this to be in trust for her and her assigns. Whereupon, after the lady's death, a question arose whether her administrator could have the benefit of this trust thus declared, as assignee in law, the lady having made no actual assignment.

[It was] ruled he should, for it is not material how Foster declared the trust, but how My Lady intended it.

Lord Nottingham, *Prolegomena*, p. 275

Easter [term] 15 Car. II.

A copyhold was granted for life in trust for Lady Katherine Thyn and her assigns. She dies without making any actual assignee.

It was decreed that the administrator should be *quasi* an assignee in equity to have the benefit of this trust.

Which yet is not so in law, for the law will never carry anything to an assignee in law, where there may be an assignee in fact. Hobart 9, 10, Pease and Stileman's Case; 1 Inst. 210.[1]

98

Roberts v. Wilks

(Ch. 1663)

The question in this case was whether a suit in another court for the same matter will be stayed by an injunction to the party by the court that had priority of suit.

2 Freeman 161, 22 E.R. 1130

Easter [term] 15 Car. II, 1663.

The plaintiff here exhibited his bill first, to which the defendant put in an insufficient answer and so detained the plaintiff here. And, then, he [the defendant] exhibited a bill in the Exchequer in the nature of a cross-suit, and posted

[1] *Pease v. Stileman*, Hobart 9, 80 E.R. 160; E. Coke, *First Institute* (1628), f. 210.

on that cause there, wherefore the plaintiff moved for an injunction to stay proceedings on that bill in the Exchequer.

3 Chancery Reports 9, 21 E.R. 712

Easter [term] 15 Car. II [1663].

The plaintiff exhibited his bill, to which, the defendant put in an insufficient answer, and so delayed the plaintiff. And, then, he exhibited a bill in the Exchequer in the nature of a cross-suit, and posted on that cause there, wherefore the plaintiff here moved for an injunction to stay proceedings on the bill in the Exchequer.

[Reg. Lib. 1662 B, f. 683.]

99

Lady Dacres v. Chute

(Ch. 1663)

A husband and wife cannot make a contract with each other.

A defendant can amend his or her answer with leave of court before a replication has been filed.

1 Chancery Cases 21, 22 E.R. 673

Dorothea, dame Darcy against Chaloner Chute, Henry Haughton, and others. The Lord Chancellor, the Master of the Rolls.

The plaintiff, being a widow and seised of a jointure worth £700 *per annum*, Mr. Chute, the father, made a suit to marry her. And she agreeing to it, he, before the marriage, agreed with her by a deed in writing that it should be lawful for her or such as she should appoint during the marriage to receive and dispose of the rents of her jointure as she pleased. The deed was put in Haughton's hands, he being the plaintiff's agent formerly.

Then, the plaintiff and Mr. Chute married, he having first agreed with trustees of hers to settle her a jointure. And they lived together ten years, during all which time, Haughton received the rents of the lady's said jointure of £700 *per annum* and constantly, with the approbation of the plaintiff, accounted for and paid the same to Mr. Chute, her husband. And the plaintiff all that time never appointed Haughton to receive the rents for her, nor claimed any benefit by the agreement left in Haughton's hands.

But, at the ten years' end, Mr. Chute dying, having made the defendant, his son, executor, the plaintiff exhibited her bill to have an account from Haughton, and charged £1000 to be resting in his hands unaccounted for, that was received in Mr. Chute, her husband's, lifetime, and she made title to the same by the said agreement made by Mr. Chute with herself before marriage.

And, upon the hearing, a case being cited and urged by the defendant's counsel, the court declared the aforesaid agreement before marriage with the plaintiff herself was immediately by the marriage extinguished. The court would not relieve the plaintiff thereupon, but ordered the defendant Haughton to account before a Master for what he received after Mr. Chute's death.

2 Freeman 148, 22 E.R. 1120

Easter [term] 15 Car. II, 1663. Lady Dorothea Dacres, plaintiff; Charles Chute and Henry Houghton, defendants.

The plaintiff being a widow and having a £700 *per annum* jointure, the defendant Chute's father made suit to marry her. But, before the marriage, it was agreed by a writing between them that it should be lawful for her or such as she should appoint during the coverture to receive and dispose of the rents and her jointure as she pleased. Houghton, the defendant, was employed by her to collect the rents. And he paid them to Mr. Chute by the plaintiff's approbation. Mr. Chute, after ten years, dies, and left the defendant Chute, his son, his executor, against whom and the said Houghton, she exhibited her bill, suggesting £1000 to be in Houghton's hands, parcel of the said rent.

Whereupon it was decreed by the Lord Chancellor [LORD CLARENDON] and the Master of the Rolls [GRIMSTON] that the said agreement, being so made between the said Mr. Chute and the plaintiff, was extinguished by the marriage, upon urging the foregoing precedent.[1]

3 Chancery Reports 6, 21 E.R. 711

Easter [term] 15 Car. II [1663]. Lord Chancellor, Master of the Rolls.

The plaintiff being a widow, seised of a jointure of £700 *per annum*, and Chute, the defendant's father, made suit to marry her. And she consenting, he, before the marriage, agreed with her by a deed in writing that it should be lawful for her or such as she should appoint during the marriage to receive and dispose of the rents of her jointure as she pleased. This deed was put into Houghton's hands, he being formerly the plaintiff's agent.

Then, the plaintiff and Mr. Chute married, he having first agreed with trustees of hers to settle her a jointure. And they lived together ten years, during all which time, Houghton received the rents of the said jointure of £700 a year, and, constantly, with the approbation of the plaintiff, accounted for and paid the same to Mr. Chute, her husband. And the plaintiff, in all that time, never appointed Houghton to receive the rents for her, nor ever claimed any benefit by the agreement left in Houghton's hands.

---

[1] *Pitt v. Pelham* (Ch. 1667–1672), 1 Chancery Reports 283, 21 E.R. 574, Lincoln's Inn MS. Misc. 500, f. 24, 1 Chancery Cases 176, 22 E.R. 750, 2 Freeman 134, 22 E.R. 1110, Lord Nottingham, *Prolegomena*, p. 240, T. Jones 25, 84 E.R. 1130, 1 Levinz 304, 83 E.R. 419, 1 Eq. Cas. Abr. 265, 21 E.R. 1034, Lincoln's Inn MS. Misc. 500, f. 121.

But, at the ten years' end, Mr. Chute dying, having made the defendant, his son, his executor, the plaintiff exhibited her bill to have an account from Houghton, and charged £1000 to be resting in his hands unaccounted for that was received in Mr. Chute's, her husband's, lifetime. And she made a title to the same by the said agreement before marriage, made by Mr. Chute with herself.

And upon the hearing, the cause *inter* the Earl of Suffolk and Greenvill[1] being cited and urged in the argument of the defendant's counsel, the court declared the aforesaid agreement before the marriage was immediately extinguished by the marriage and that the plaintiff could not be relieved thereupon, but ordered Houghton to account before a Master for what he had received after Mr. Chute's death.

1 Chancery Cases 29, 22 E.R. 677

23 October [1663]. The Lord Chancellor, the Master of the Rolls.

The defendant having mistaken herself in her answer, as was alleged, having therein sworn something which was found by her afterwards to be otherwise, it was alleged by her counsel and an affidavit was made by herself too for that purpose, that those matters untruly set forth were added in the margin of the draught after she had perused it, and so she was thereby surprised. And it was alleged that no replication was filed *prout* the certificate, and an affidavit of notice of this motion to the other side was read.

But the plaintiff making no defense, it was, *ex parte* on the defendant's motion, ordered that she be at liberty to amend her answer in the said matters mistaken. And it was said that a like liberty had been given to a defendant to amend his answer before a replication in a case between Chettle and Chettle in the Lord Coventry's time.[2]

2 Freeman 173, 22 E.R. 1139

23 October, 15 Car. II [1663]. Chute v. Lady Dacres.

It was alleged that the defendant was mistaken in her answer and desired she might amend, the matter being inserted by counsel after her perusal, which was admitted by the court, no replication being filed, as it was in the Lord Coventry's time *inter* Chettle v. Chettle.

[Other reports of this case: 1 Eq. Cas. Abr. 29, 63, 21 E.R. 850, 877.]
[Reg. Lib. 1663 A, ff. 7, 596, 683, 750.]

---

1 *Earl of Suffolk v. Grenville* (Ch. 1631), Chancery Repts. *tempore* Coventry 155.

2 *Chettle v. Chettle* (1633), Tothill 13, 21 E.R. 108.

100

Hide v. Petit

Bedingfield v. Zouch

(Ch. 1663–1673)

An order of a court of equity can be enforced by a writ of sequestration.
A submission to arbitration is revokable by any party thereto.

Lincoln's Inn MS. Hill 125, f. 41v, pl. 1

Two causes were put off until the Chancellor etc. Now [it was] resolved that [writs of] sequestration lay in the Chancery, both of land in [. . .] and of other land, and of personal estate also. [. . .] Hilary [term] 15 Car. II [1663], the same day, the same resolution between Bedingfield and Zouch.

[There was a] decree [upon a] bill *pro confesso* by the advice of Bridgeman also upon an extremity of the contempt even though the defendant was not brought to the bar by [a writ of] *habeas corpus*, but he had appeared and prayed a commission, and afterwards, he sat out all process.

2 Freeman 168, 22 E.R. 1135

In the vacation before Trinity [term] 15 Car. II [1663]. Chancellor, Baron Turner.

[It was] resolved that all decrees in Chancery, as well for personal as for real things, shall be executed by [a writ of] sequestration.

And both these causes were brought into Parliament, and dismissed thence.

1 Chancery Cases 91, 22 E.R. 709

25 October [1667]. Hide v. Petit.

There having been a decree in this case for a personal duty and a sequestration awarded against the defendant's real and personal estate by the late Lord Chancellor, assisted by Baron Turner, it was now moved by the defendant's counsel against this sequestration and insisted that this court did not anciently grant a sequestration but sparingly and that only of the thing in demand and that the sequestration in this case took more than all the executions at law and that sequestrations had been extended so far of late as to sequester things in action, which no execution at common law can reach, and the consequence of which would be destructive to trade and commerce. And, besides, when any purchaser is brought into this court upon the process of sequestration, upon sequestration that this purchase is subsequent to the sequestration or for other reason bound thereby, whereas, in any persons so brought in are really purchasers or have other good titles, which neither are nor ought to be bound thereby, those persons so brought in are looked upon as contemnors and delinquents and forced to answer interrogatories blindfold, without having a copy of them or liberty to show them to counsel, by which means, persons coming into this court to defend their interest are often, through their own unskillfulness, concluded in their just rights, even against right, to the great dishonor of the court and of justice.

But to maintain the sequestration, it was insisted by *Fountaine* that they were very ancient in this court, and he cited a case, 17 Jac. [1619–20], Zacheverel against Zacheverel,[1] where a sequestration was awarded both against lands and goods and the thing decreed was a personal duty.

And the sequestration was awarded by the court assisted with the judges upon a view of four precedents. Russel against Read;[2] the defendant being in the Fleet [Prison], the money decreed was sequestered, it being in the Fleet; this in the Lord Coventry's time. And 18 February 1662[/63], assisted with Baron Turner in this principal case, and the Case of Bedingfield and Zouch; that a sequestration should be the usual process of this court. And the course of the court is the law of the land. And an executor might bring an action here before the Statute[3] gave it.

And it was urged, if you should take away sequestrations, the justice of the court would be illusory and that, after a suitor had been at great charges in obtaining a decree, if the defendant would lie in prison, there would be no remedy for the plaintiff to come by the fruit of his decree and the remedy by imprisonment would be ineffectual, for, if he go abroad, no escape lies. Upon a judgment in a court baron, a [writ of] *levari facias* goes, which takes all the profits of the lands. And a statute before a mayor takes all. And, therefore, it is not unreasonable that so great a court as this should have an effectual means of bringing suitors to the fruit of their suit, which, without a sequestration, cannot be done.

And, as to sequestering things in action, there is no such thing sequestered in this case. And, as to the danger of bringing persons that came in for their interest as delinquents by means of sequestration and their being deprived of counsel to answer, that is the case of every decree and contempt where there is no sequestration. And it is the course there as well as in the course of sequestrations.

The court will see precedents. And, after[wards], at another time, [the court] declared it was satisfied the sequestration in the principal case was well awarded and that sequestrations were a necessary process of this court.

2 Freeman 125, 22 E.R. 1101

Michaelmas [term] 1667. Lord Keeper, Baron Turner.

1 Perhaps *Sacheverel v. Sacheverel* (Ch. 1621), Tothill 38, 21 E.R. 116.

2 *Russel v. Read* (1635 × 1636), Tothill 102, 21 E.R. 136; Eq. Cases Exch. 264; T. E. Tomlins, *Law Dictionary*, vol. 2, *sub tit.* 'sequestration'; R. North, *Lives of . . . Baron Guilford* (1826), vol. 1, p. 420.

3 Perhaps Stat. 17 Car. II, c. 8, s. 2 (*SR*, V, 580).

Fountaine, in maintenance of the jurisdiction of Chancery to grant sequestrations on the real and personal estate for the breach of a decree for a personal duty, urged Sacheverill v. Sacheverill in King James's time.

The contrary side admitted it well in case the defendant had gone beyond the sea; so, if he will absolutely lie in prison.

Lord Keeper [Bridgeman] hinted that a court baron, in a judgment in deceit, did sequester the profits of the real estate by a judgment in debt. The mayor of the staple may do it. Therefore, it is reasonable the High Court of Chancery may do it.

Fountaine alleged that it always had been done, and so was the law of the court, which is consequently the law of the nation. The common law did not attach the bodies for personal duties; yet attachments or subpoenas had been always allowed as the process in Chancery. And, in Chancery, there has been an account against executors time out of mind, though not by the common law or statute law at this day. But *Fountaine* would not defend the sequestration of choses in action or on a copyhold estate, which was in question, being on a motion to discharge such a sequestration for a personal duty. Serjeant *Fountaine* said, he knew several bills to be relieved against general securities by statutes by giving securities on particular lands.

Lincoln's Inn MS. Misc. 500, f. 107, pl. 3

25 October 1670. Hide v. Petit.

This case has pended in this court twenty-four years upon merchant's accounts between the plaintiff and one Freeman, to whom the defendant is administrator. And a decree was made by the late Lord Chancellor [Lord Clarendon] for the plaintiff that was afterwards reversed in the House of Peers and sent back for the judgment of the Lord Keeper, who, upon a hearing of the cause found it to be an intricate and perplexed thing and much to depend upon the usage and science of merchant's accounts.

And, on account of this, in open court, the plaintiff and the defendant signed an order by consent to stand to the award of John and William Jolliff, two merchants nominated by the Lord Keeper, to whom it was referred to examine all the accounts *ab origine*, who examined the accounts of London and Venice and awarded that the defendant will pay to the plaintiff £456 18s., which they thought to be due to the plaintiff, but there being other accounts between the said parties concerning the same cause and in difference between them, the arbitrators did not make any award of them, pretending that they were difficult and intricate.

And the plaintiff who for some time had a sequestration of the dependant's real estate and received the rents and profits of it. And the arbitrators did not consider it nor make any allowance for them.

But, before any award was made, the defendant revoked the submission and authority given to the arbitrators.

And, in this case, there were two questions: first, whether such submissions by consent entered in court and signed with the hand of the party could be revoked; second, if it could not be, whether the award is good, inasmuch as it does not determine all of the things submitted.

And the Lord keeper [BRIDGEMAN] called to his assistance Raynsford, one of the justices of the King's Bench, and WYNDHAM, one of the barons of the Exchequer, who were both of the opinion and thus declared this that, first, the submission in question and the authority given to the arbitrators is revokable both in a court of equity are in a court of common law and that the court here cannot decree this award to be performed, the authority of the arbitrators being revoked, because it is of the nature and essence of all authorities to be revokable and nothing except legislative authority can make them otherwise. And consent of the parties will not alter the law, as consent to detain distress against sureties and pledges or to sell a distress will not alter the law, which is otherwise established, and that such a submission is revokable a precedent in this court between Norton and Rawly, 16 July 16 Car. II,[1] was cited, and the order was read, by which it is thus resolved.

But they both held that this revocation was a contempt to the court and, for this, the revoker could be imprisoned by this court.

As to the second, they held that the award is not good because, though upon consideration of the London and Venice accounts, the arbitrators could see a reason to give to the plaintiff £456 18s., yet, if they had examined the other accounts with which they did not intermeddle, they could have found cause to diminish this sum or possibly to give money to the defendant. And the consent of parties will not be drawn beyond their intentions in the submission. Also it is not reasonable that the plaintiff will take the profits of the defendant's lands without making allowance or deduction for them, which the arbitrators have not done.

And thus the award was not regarded, but the cause stood in court as it was before the submission.

And *Maynard*, King's Serjeant, for the plaintiff, prayed for a [writ of] attachment against the defendant for his contempt to the court in revoking the submission. And a day was given to show cause why it should not be granted.

1 Chancery Cases 185, 22 E.R. 754

25 October [1670]. The Lord Keeper, the Master of the Rolls, Justice Rainsford, Justice Wyndham.

The parties in court signed an order by consent to refer their matters to arbitrators finally to determine and their award to be final and stand ratified by a decree without any appeal. One of the parties, after that he had attended the

[1] *Norton v. Rowley* (Ch. 1664), see below, Case No. 162.

reference and found they inclined to order him to pay the other party a sum of money, countermands the submission.

And the first question was whether this submission was revocable.

Of which, the Lord Keeper [Bridgeman], at first, seemed to doubt. But, on argument and producing a precedent in point, Norton against Rowland, 8 July 1664 and 10th of the same July, the judges were both of opinion that there could be no submission to an award in law or equity but what was revocable and that nothing under a legislative power can make such a submission irrevocable which, in its nature, is revocable. But it was an abuse to the court, as it was conceived, to revoke it, for which the court might justly lay the party by the heels. And so, in this cause, an attachment was awarded against him *nisi causa*.

In this case, it was observed that, whereas, formerly, the course was upon submission to award an attachment against the party failing, yet, of late, the courts of law do refuse to grant attachments in such cases, but leave the party to his action, the rule being evidence of his submission.

In the principal case, the arbitrators had determined some matters, and had left others undetermined, and submitted those other matters to the court. And whether this was, therefore, such an award, being but part of the matters referred, as was fit for the court to decree was the question. And though, at law, an award may be good, though but for part of the matters referred, unless the submission be conditional to make an award on the premises, yet equity, as it was insisted, ought not to decree such an award, unless it be of all matters referred.

And so were both the judges of that opinion, for it is not a determination pursuant to the reference, and so the award was set aside.

2 Freeman 133, 22 E.R. 1109

25 October 1670. Lord Keeper, Justice Rainsford, Baron Wyndham.

This cause had been many years depending in court. It was decreed upon an appeal to Parliament by Petit [to be] sent back to be reheard. Upon the hearing, again, it was referred to an account before a Master. Upon hearing exceptions to the Master's report, an order was made by the consent of both parties to stand to the award of A. and B. Jolleis, two eminent merchants. They, several times, attended the Jolleis. Petit perceiving that the Jolleis would condemn him by their award in £400, before the arbitrators had drawn up their award, Petit, by a deed under hand and seal, revokes the authority given to the arbitrators, and retracts the submission. However, the arbitrators make their award.

And, upon debate, it was held that the award ought not to be decreed in regard of the said revocation. But the court awarded a [writ of] attachment against Petit unless he showed cause. And the judges went on this reason: first, that an authority in its nature is revocable by law, though referred by an order of court, and a case was cited between Norton and Rolls in the very point, where the award was to have been made by Sir Mundford Brampston; second, this award could not be decreed, because some matters referred were not determined by the award and so were not final, and cases were cited, Ward v. Sawer; Child v. Colwell;[1] and 13 Car., Mayer's Case, where, by an order of court, the submission and award were to be final without an appeal or exception, that yet the court did allow exceptions to the award as against a Master's report, and the words 'without appeal or exception' are but *formula clericorum*.

But the court gave no opinion in the point.

Lord Nottingham, *Prolegomena*, p. 308

Hide obtained a decree against Petit as administrator of Freeman for £800, which some merchants, on a reference from the court, had reported due, and had a sequestration. The decree was afterwards set aside in Parliament, and the matter left to an ordinary proceeding on an account. There, both parties agreed to refer it to other merchants, and subscribed their names to the Register's book to testify their consent to the order of reference.

The arbitrators first certify their opinion that it was fit Petit should pay Hide £400.

But the court, disliking that, referred it to the arbitrators to give a positive judgment or award.

Petit, disliking that reference, revokes his submission. And, then, the arbitrators award £400. But, in that award, it appeared they considered of other matters not in the bill nor the answer, and had not considered of the profits received by Hide under the sequestration to deduct them.

Whereupon two points arose: first, whether such a submission was revocable after a consent subscribed that it should be final; second, if not, whether such an award as this should be decreed.

[It was] resolved by BRIDGEMAN, Keeper, Justice RAINSFORD, and Baron WYNDHAM: first, that the subscription may be revoked, for consent does not alter the law. Nothing but an act of Parliament can do that. Therefore, if a lord and tenant agree that a distress shall be sold, yet it may not be.

Lord Nottingham, *Prolegomena*, p. 273

11 April 1673.

If the factor keep no books or such as he does keep be kept in great disorder and confusion, there, all things shall be presumed in favor of the principal who charges him. And, in this case, the administrator of a factor was called to account for matters transacted in 1627, *viz.* forty-six years since and twenty years after the death of the factor. But an abstract of the accounts, sent by the factor in 1629, not excepted to until March 1630, and the exception answered in April 1630 without further reply, were allowed as conclusive in all points not excepted to, and the rest was referred to an examination.

[1] *Collwell v. Child* (Ch. 1661–1667), see above, Case No. 44.

[Other reports of this case: 1 Eq. Cas. Abr. 49, 21 E.R. 866.]
[Reg. Lib. 1667 A, f. 189, 1670 A, f. 12.]

101

Godscall v. Walker

(Ch. 1663)

A court of equity will give relief to an infant who was the victim of fraud.

2 Freeman 169, 22 E.R. 1136

11 May, 15 Car. II [1663].

A judgment was gotten against an infant by practice.

It was ordered that it be referred to a Master to examine how much money the infant received.

Note the guardian was a party to the practice.

Nelson 84, 21 E.R. 796

Godscall v. Walker and Wall.

The bill was to be relieved against several judgments in debt obtained from Sir John Godscall, an infant, by practice between the defendant Walker, a goldsmith, and Wall, an attorney, and the guardian of the infant.

And it was referred to a Master to examine the real consideration either in money or goods, for which the said judgments were had, and to make his report, that farther order might be taken therein.

3 Chancery Reports 10, 21 E.R. 713

11 May, 15 Car. II [1663]. Godscall v. Walker and Wall.

The bill was to be relieved against several judgments in debt from Sir John Godscall, an infant. And, by a practice between the defendants, Walker and Gouldsmith, and Wall, the attorney, and the infant's guardian, [they] drew into examination the reality of the debt, for which the judgments were and how the same arose.

And [it was] decreed that it be referred to a Master to examine the real consideration in money or wares, for which the said judgments were had. And, thereupon, the court declared further order should be taken.

[Reg. Lib. 1662 A, ff. 524, 675.]

102

Binion v. Stone

(Ch. 1663)

Where a purchaser of land pays the full purchase price and directs the seller to convey to his five year old son, the son will be considered to hold only as a trustee for his father, the purchaser.

2 Freeman 169, 22 E.R. 1135

13 May 1663. Lord Chancellor, Chief Baron Hale, Justice Wyndham.

Sir George Binion bought a house for £2000 in the name of his son, then five years of age. Sir George's estate being ordered to be sold for delinquency, the trustees for the sale sold it to Stone, to whom, for £500, Sir George's son and his wife conveyed, making an oath they were not seised, in trust for Sir George. Sir George seeks relief against Stone as for a trust.

And, in regard the estate was sold as Sir George's and that the son was but five years old at the purchase, the court presumed it a trust, for which Sir George was relievable.

Nelson 68, 21 E.R. 791

Sir George Binion purchased a house for £2000 in the name of his son, an infant of five years old, and the same was conveyed to his son by a deed enrolled.

All the estate of Sir George being exposed to sale by the Parliament for his delinquency, this house was sold as part of his estate to one Stone, who, after Sir George's son came of age, gave him and his mother £500 to make a farther conveyance of the house to him, which they did, having both made oath that they were not trustees for Sir George.

Sir George, afterwards, exhibits his bill to be relieved against Stone, and suggests a trust in his wife and his son for himself. And it was insisted that it should be presumed as such a trust in respect of the infancy of the son when the purchase was made by the father and that the money was paid by him and that the sale of the house was in his right and for his delinquency.

And so the Lord Chancellor [Lord Clarendon] inclined to decree it.

But an offer being made to repay Stone the £500, time was given to the parties to consider of it, and, if they did not agree, the court declared they would advise with some judges about it, for Hale and Wyndham held it to be a trust upon which Sir George might be relieved. And, thereupon, Stone accepting the £500, he was decreed to reconvey.

3 Chancery Reports 9, 21 E.R. 712

23 May, 15 Car. II [1663].

A house being purchased by a deed enrolled in Chancery and £2000 paid by Sir George Benion in the name of his son, then an infant of five years old, Sir George's estate being all exposed to sale by the Parliament for delinquency, this house was sold as part of it by the trustees for sale of delinquent estates to one who sold it to Stone. Stone, afterwards, gave £500 to Sir George's son, being then of age and Sir George's wife to convey the house to him, which they did for that consideration. And, first, they made an oath before a magistrate that they were not trustees for Sir George.

Sir George exhibits his bill to be relieved against Stone, and suggests a trust in his son and wife for him. And it was then insisted that, in respect of the infancy of the son upon the purchase made and the father's payment of the purchase money and the sale of the house for delinquency as Sir George's, it should be presumed a trust for the father.

My Lord Chancellor [LORD CLARENDON] inclined to decree it on this point.

But Sir George's counsel offering Stone the £500 again, time was given to the parties to consider thereof, and, if they did not agree, the court declared they would advise with some judges and deliver their opinion, for HALE and WYNDHAM declared it a trust, for which Sir George was relievable. But Stone accepting the offer of £500, it was decreed he should convey on the payment of it.

103

Humfries v. Griffith

(Ch. 1663)

The Welsh courts of great sessions do not have equity jurisdiction.

2 Freeman 169, 22 E.R. 1136

May, 15 Car. II [1663]. Lord Chancellor; Master of the Rolls.

An appeal was taken from a decree in the Grand Sessions of Montgomery. The decree was that an infant should convey.

Curia: We will reverse the decree, but will not so far countenance the jurisdiction of that court as to express it to be for the infancy of the defendant.

[Reg. Lib. 1662 A, f. 579.]

104

Viscountess Cranborne v. Delahay

(Ch. 1663)

A decree made on a point of right cannot to be reviewed as to a dilatory plea, which might have been pleaded in abatement.

2 Freeman 169, 22 E.R. 1136

21 May, 15 Car. II [1663]. Lord Chancellor, Justice Wyndham.

A bill was exhibited to reverse a decree in May 1655, where the duchess of Hamilton, the defendant's late wife, was plaintiff against the Lord Cranborne, the now plaintiff's late husband, and other defendants.[1] The errors assigned were that the duchess was, in truth, a married woman at the time of the decree had, as it appears by the now defendant's answer in this court in another cause. So there was no cause in court, the cause being abated by her marriage, wherein she was the plaintiff.

The deed of the earl of Darlington, under which she claimed, being a deed of feoffment of the Friary of Guildford, was void, for the estate thereof was in trustees at that time and no livery of seisin was ever made on that deed. And, therefore, it ought not to be supported in equity to the disherison of the plaintiff, Viscountess Cranborne, coheir at law with the said duchess to the said earl of Darlington.

To this, the defendant demurred, and, for cause, showed that, for ought appeared, the decree was well grounded and that the first error was not a matter appearing in the body of the said decree but *dehors*, and yet it was alleged as error and not as new matter, and that the now plaintiff could not take advantage thereof, neither could any ever take advantage of it but the defendant, who had not excepted to it. And it was but a matter of abatement and not in point of right. And, after a decree in point of right, it ought not to be admitted.

As to the first, it was resolved that a decree made in point of right ought not to be reviewed on the point of a dilatory plea, which might have been pleaded in abatement.

To the second, because the earl of Darlington was seised of a trust, that the deed, though in the nature of a feoffment, should pass the trust without livery and seisin, for the trust might have been declared by parol; *a fortiori* in this case.

Then, it was much insisted by the plaintiff's counsel that the defendants should be put to answer.

[1] *Duchess of Hamilton v. Countess of Dirlton* (1654), 1 Chancery Reports 165, 21 E.R. 539.

But it was resolved that they should not answer because, by possibility, no other matter can come before the court than what is in the demurrer. And so the demurrer was allowed.

Nelson 85, 21 E.R. 796

A bill of review [was brought] to reverse a decree made in May 1655, in which cause the duchess of Hamilton, the defendant's late wife, when unmarried, was plaintiff and the now plaintiff, the Lord Cranborne, and his lady were defendants. The errors assigned were, first, that the duchess was a married woman at the time of the decree made, for it appeared by Delmahoy's answer in this court to another bill that, after the bill [was] exhibited by the duchess and before the hearing of that cause, she and the defendant intermarried, and so there was no cause in court for the foundation of such a decree, it being abated by the marriage.

The second error [was] that, the duchess's father being seised in fee of a trust estate in the priory of Guildford and of other lands in England, he conveyed the same to the duchess and her heirs by a deed in the nature of a feoffment, which was not executed by livery and seisin and, therefore, was void at law and not to be supported in a court of equity to disinherit the now plaintiff, who, together with the duchess, were daughters and co-heirs of their said father.

To this bill, the defendant demurred, and, for cause, showed that it did not appear by the bill but that the decree was well grounded, for the first error assigned was not matter appearing in the body of the decree, but quite out of it and *dehors*, neither was it proper for any other person than the defendant to take advantage of it. Besides, it was only matter in abatement, and did not concern the right. And, after a decree was made in point of right, any matter that might be pleaded in abatement was not such an error as to ground a bill of review.

And the court was of that opinion.

As to the second error assigned, since the father was seised of a trust, the deed, though it was in the nature of a feoffment, might pass that trust, though not executed by livery. And it was sufficient to declare the same, which, as the law then stood, might be declared by parol.

It was then insisted that the defendant might answer the bill.

And, after a long debate, the court declared that, since the cause was now as entirely before them as it could be upon an answer, there being no other matter possible to be discovered or set forth, it was not fit for the defendant to answer. And so the demurrer was allowed.

Dickens 8, 21 E.R. 169

If a woman, pending the suit, marries, and the cause proceeds, and a decree is made, this is not sufficient to reverse the decree.

And so it was held by the Lord Chancellor [LORD CLARENDON], assisted by the judges, on a plea to a bill of review on that ground, who said that marriage was a matter of abatement only, not of right, and was matter of fact out of the decree.

1 Chancery Reports 231, 21 E.R. 558

Lady Cramborne *contra* Dalmahoy and Dr. [sic] Hamilton's wife.

The bill is to review and reverse a decree made the 3d of May 1655 in a cause wherein Elizabeth, duchess of Hamilton, was plaintiff against Elizabeth, countess of Dirlton, and the countess of Cramborne, now plaintiff, defendants, to settle the trust of Gilford Park and other lands, and the equity of redemption of Wauborough and other lands, all in the County of Surrey, and directing the reversion of all the premises after the death of the said countess of Dirlton to be conveyed by the defendants therein named to the said duchess, her heirs, and assigns.

The now plaintiff insists that the decree is erroneous, and ought to be reversed, for that, at the making thereof, there was no bill or cause in court depending, for that the duchess of Hamilton, who was the plaintiff in the said decree, sued as an unmarried woman, and, after her bill in 1653, which was before the decree, she married the now defendant Mr. Dalmahoy, whereby the bill of the duchess and all proceedings abated and became void. And no bill of [revivor] was brought, and the said duchess continued married until after the decree. And the decree was contrary to law and justice, it appearing that the deed, made by the earl of Dirlton, whereupon the decree was grounded, was in the nature of a feoffment, but never executed by a livery, appeared to be voluntary to disinherit the now plaintiff. And, if it could not operate at law, it ought to have no force or countenance in equity, being made but the day before he died.

To which bill, the defendant pleaded and demurred, and insisted that the decree ought not to be reversed or that the error that the duchess was married is only matter of abatement, and not to the right and appears not in the body of the decree, but is a matter of fact out of the decree, and that the plaintiff has assigned for error and not for new matter, and, were it so, she might have had advantage thereof before the hearing, and ought not now to be admitted to it which no advantage could be taken thereof but by an abatement.

And the other error assigned is no error, but the cause was adjudged upon the deeds and proofs of the earl of Dirlton's intentions.

This court, with the assistance of the judges, held the plea and demurrer good, and dismissed the plaintiff's bill of review.

[Reg. Lib. 1662 A, f. 519.]

105

Heath v. Hanley

(Ch. 1663)

An implied trust is not within or barred by the Statute of Limitations.

1 Chancery Cases 20, 22 E.R. 673

21 May [1663]. Sir Edward Heath against Henly and Whitwick. The Lord Chancellor, the Master of the Rolls.

The plaintiff was son and executor of the late Chief Justice Heath,[1] who was made Chief Justice at Oxford during the difference between the king and Parliament, but he never sat as Chief Justice in Westminster Hall. And the bill was to have an account of monies received by the defendants, being prothonotaries of the King's Bench, which was alleged to belong to the said Chief Justice, and which monies they, by their office, ought to receive for the Chief Justice by an implied trust, *virtute officii*.

The defendant pleaded the Statute of Limitations, 21 Jac., 16.[2]

Upon the arguing of this plea, it was insisted by the plaintiff's counsel that this trust was not within the said Statute.

And it was answered of the other part that a guardian was within the Statute, and he was trusted.

[It was] ordered that the defendants should answer.

2 Freeman 156, 22 E.R. 1127

21 May, 15 Car. II.

The plaintiff was son and executor to the last Chief Justice Heath, so made at Oxford during the difference between king and Parliament, but he never sat as Chief Justice in Westminster Hall. The bill was to have an account of money received by the defendants as prothonotaries of the King's Bench, which was all to belong to the Chief Justice, which monies they, by their office, ought to receive for the Chief Justice by an implied trust *virtute officii*.

The defendants pleaded the Statute of Limitations, 21 Jac., 16.

[The plaintiff] insisted that the trust was not within the Statute of Limitations.

[It was] answered on the other part that a guardian etc. was within the Statute, and he was trustee, etc.

[It was] ordered that the defendants should answer.

---

[1] P. E. Kopperman, 'Heath, Sir Robert (1575–1649)', *Oxford Dictionary of National Biography*, vol. 26, pp. 182–185.

[2] Stat. 21 Jac. I, c. 16 (*SR*, IV, 1222–1223).

Nelson 75, 21 E.R. 793

21 May, 15 Car. II [1663].

The plaintiff was son and heir and also executor of the late Chief Justice Heath, who was made Chief Justice at Oxford during the time of the civil wars, but never sat as Chief Justice in Westminster Hall. And the bill was to have an account of money received by the defendants as prothonotaries of the King's Bench and which, by virtue of their office, they ought to receive for the use of the said Chief Justice.

The defendants pleaded the Statute of Limitations, 21 Jac., cap. 6.

And, upon arguing this plea, it was insisted by the plaintiff's counsel that, this being an implied trust *virtute officii*, it was not within the said Statute, though a guardian is, and he is a trustee.

And, therefore, it was ordered that the defendants should answer.

3 Chancery Reports 8, 21 E.R. 712

21 May, 15 Car. II [1663]. Sir Edward Heath *contra* Henley and Whitwick. Lord Chancellor and Justice Wyndham.

The plaintiff was son and executor of the late Chief Justice Heath, who was made Chief Justice at Oxford during the difference between the king and the Parliament, but he never sat as Chief Justice in Westminster Hall.

And the bill was to have an account of money received by the defendants, being Prothonotaries of the King's Bench, which was alleged to belong to the said Chief Justice and which monies they, by their office, ought to receive for the Chief Justice by an implied trust *virtute officii*.

The defendants pleaded the Statute of Limitations, 21 Jac. And, upon the arguing thereof, it was insisted by the plaintiff's counsel that this trust was not within the said Statute. And it was answered on the other side that a guardian was within the Statute and he was a trustee.

But the defendants were ordered to answer.

[Other reports of this case: 1 Eq. Cas. Abr. 303, 21 E.R. 1062.]
[Reg. Lib. 1663 A, f. 992.]

106

Randall v. Richford

(Ch. 1663–1664)

A witness who seeks to correct his own deposition will not be allowed to do so.

1 Chancery Cases 25, 22 E.R. 676

2 June [1663].

A witness alleged he had mistaken himself at a commission. The commission being returned, he came to London, and made an oath that he was surprised. A special commission issued to re-examine the witnesses, which was done accordingly.

But this special commission was superseded by a motion by the advice of the Master of the Rolls with the Six Clerks as contrary to the course of the court.

2 Freeman 178, 22 E.R. 1144

28 January, 15 Car. II [1664].

A witness alleged he had mistaken himself at a commission. The commission being returned, he came to London, and made an oath that he was surprised. A special commission issued to re-examine this witness, which was done accordingly.

But this special commission was suppressed by a motion by advice with the Master of the Rolls with the Six Clerks as contrary to the course of the court.

Nelson 92, 21 E.R. 798

Randall v. Richards.

A witness, having committed a mistake in his examination before commissioners, applied himself to them to rectify it, who told him that the commission was returned to London. And he, coming there, made an oath of it and that he was surprised by a hasty examination. But, the commission not being opened, it was returned back to the commissioners with a special commission to open it and permit the witness to rectify his mistake.

And, afterwards, the special commission being executed and returned, a motion was made to suppress the depositions, because [they were] unduly taken and that no such special commission ought to have been.

Whereupon, it was referred to the Master of the Rolls [Grimston] to examine into it, who called to his assistance the Six Clerks. And they were all of opinion that no such commission had ever been or ought to be now granted. So the depositions and the special commission were suppressed.

[Other reports of this case: 1 Eq. Cas. Abr. 102, 21 E.R. 911, 2 Eq. Cas. Abr. 417, 22 E.R. 354.]

[Reg. Lib. 1663 B, f. 139.]

107

Bellasis v. Erwin

(Ch. 1663)

A condition of marriage with consent is not enforceable unless there be a gift over to a third party.

1 Chancery Cases 22, 22 E.R. 674

4 June [1663]. Sir Henry Bellasis and his wife against Sir William Ermine.

The suit was for a portion of £8000 given to the plaintiff's wife.

The defendant pleaded it was given her, provided she did marry with the consent of A. and, if not, she should have but £100 *per annum* and that she married without the consent of A.

[It was] ordered that the plea stand overruled. And the court all declared this proviso was but *in terrorem* to make the person careful and that it would not defeat the portion.

But it was said, in the case of her marriage without the consent of A., if the party that gave the portion had limited it to another, there, it had been otherwise. And, in this case, the wife was not unequally married, for the plaintiff is the heir apparent at law of the Lord Bellasis.

2 Freeman 171, 22 E.R. 1137

4 June, 15 Car. II [1663]. Sir Henry Bellasis *et uxor* v. Sir William Erwin. Lord Chancellor, Chief Baron Hale, Justice Hyde.

A suit was brought for a portion of £8000. The defendant pleaded it was given her provided she married with the consent of A., and, if not, then to have but £100 *per annum*.

Curia: This is but *in terrorem*, but, it would be otherwise if the portion had been limited to a third person.

[Other reports of this case: 1 Eq. Cas. Abr. 110, 21 E.R. 918.]
[Reg. Lib. 1662 A, f. 729.]

108

Crisp v. Bluck

(Ch. 1663–1674)

A debtor will be relieved in a court of equity for any amount of money due above the penalty of a bond plus interest and court costs.

Every judgment whensoever entered, if entered before the essoin day of the subsequent term, is accounted to be a judgment as of the first day of the term before.

1 Chancery Cases 23, 22 E.R. 674

26 June [1663]. Crispe and others, executors of Sir Nicholas Crispe, against Blake.

In 1642, Sir Nicholas Crispe and four others became bound to the defendant's testator in £1600 for the payment of £1000 and interest at six months' end. Interest was paid until 1644. In Michaelmas 1662, the defendant got a judgment against Sir Nicholas Crispe and one other of the obligors for £1600, being the penalty. Afterwards, there was paid by them, against whom the judgment was, and the other obligors at several times to above £1600.

And so the bill was to have the judgment vacated and the bond delivered up, paying so much as would make up the penalty of the judgment and interest for the same since the judgment.

It was insisted on by the plaintiffs' counsel that, when the judgment was had on the bond, it remained no longer a debt on the bond, nor was interest due on the judgment; so, what was paid after must be taken as paid on the judgment. And, if they had brought that £1600 into a court at law (and offered to pay it before execution), the court at law would have accepted it. And, therefore, being willing to make up what was paid already, the full of the judgment and damages since the judgment, [the plaintiff] ought to be relieved against the judgment.

On the defendant's part, it was insisted that there was more money due for interest on the bond and that that was paid as well by those obligors against whom there was no judgment as by those against whom the judgment was. And what was paid by those against whom there was no judgment, their part of what was paid in by the course of the court was to be taken as interest, there being more interest due on the bond than the money paid. And there is no equity in this case to hinder the defendant from the recovering of what he can at law, there being much more in conscience due. And, if what is justly due be to be received by any course of law, no equity ought to hinder it, so as he do not receive more than principal, interest, and costs, which the defendant offers to take on account.

It was replied by the plaintiff's counsel that one satisfaction by any of the obligors shall be a discharge at law for the rest and a release to one obligor is a discharge to all the rest. And, when a man takes a security by a penalty, he sets up his rest there, and makes himself judge of what he would have, and ought not to have more.

And, after a long debate, where the Case of Whitchcot and Underhill[1] was cited, it was ordered that the plaintiffs do pay so much with what was paid as will make up the penalty of the judgment and damages at £6 *per centum* for the penalty and costs here and at law, and, thereupon, the bond was to be delivered up, and the judgment vacated, but with this proviso, that, if the £250 paid in November 1662 were paid before the judgment was entered into and the judgment

[1] *Underhill v. Whitchot* (Ch. 1660–1661), see above, Case No. 18.

entered after of that term, that that must be taken as paid as interest, because the defendant received it on the bond, the judgment then not being entered, which a Master is to examine, and, if he find it, to allow the same as paid on the bond for interest, and the Master to take the account.

So note that a judgment on a bond, on which there is more due than the penalty for principal and interest, is worse security than the bond only. This seems very hard and unreasonable, and the equity hereof may well be questioned.

Lord Nottingham, *Prolegomena*, p. 304

Michaelmas [term] 21 Car. II. Bluck v. Crisp.

Mr. [Matthew] Bluck, one of the Six Clerks, obtained a judgment against Sir Nicholas Crisp, one of the late farmers, on a bond, in which the rest of the farmers were also bound. And, then, he exhibited a bill against Sir Nicholas Crisp, the heir and executor, to discover assets.

And [it was] resolved it could be [done] without making the other farmers parties, for they cannot be parties of a suit in aid of a judgment against one.

Sic nota equity may assist the execution of an inequitable suit after judgment, as here, but not the commencement of such a suit as in the case next before.[1] *Quaere rationem* of the diversity, *quia videtur nulla*.

2 Chancery Reports 88, 21 E.R. 624

1673–1674. Crisp v. Bluck.

This case comes to be heard upon a bill of review and an appeal from a decree made by the Lord Chancellor Shaftesbury. The plaintiff's original bill being to be relieved against a bond of £1600 penalty for the payment of £1000 and interest entered into by the plaintiff's father, the testator, and others to William Bluck, the younger, in 1642. The defendant commenced the suit on the said bond in 1662, and had a judgment thereupon against the plaintiff's father only. And the principal and interest due on the said bond far surmounting the penalty when the judgment was obtained and the defendant being twenty years kept out of his money, but having received several sums in part since the action at law was brought, it was decreed that whatever monies were received before the judgment was actually entered should be taken in discharge of the interest of the said £1000 original debt and that the defendant should be satisfied after the judgment was entered the whole money thereupon recovered with damages from the time the judgment was actually entered, deducting what he had received since the actual entry of the judgment and allowing his costs at law and moderate costs in this court. And it was found that the judgment was not actually entered until the vacation after Michaelmas term 1662, and so only £250 paid in November 1662 was accounted interest of the original debt, and not towards the money recovered

1 *Whitmore v. Crisp* (Ch. 1671), Lord Nottingham, *Prolegomena*, p. 303.

by the judgment. And the account was so settled and decreed, and the money was paid accordingly.

Yet, for a reversal of the said decree, the now plaintiff, for error, assigns that the same tends to the invalidating of the course of the Court of King's Bench, it being by the decree admitted that the said judgment was entered in the vacation after Michaelmas term 1662, and not before. Whereas, it is evident by the records of the King's Bench the said judgment was entered on record in Michaelmas term 1662, and, by construction of law, is supposed and presumed to be recorded the first day of that term, against which record, no evidence or averment ought to be admitted. And all monies paid after the first day of that term ought in equity to be applied towards the satisfaction of the judgment, and so the £250 paid in November 1662 in part of a debt in question ought not to go to satisfy the interest, but in part to discharge the principal.

The Lord Chancellor SHAFTESBURY was of the opinion that no notice could be taken of any actual entry of any judgment at law, but that every judgment whensoever entered, if before the essoin day of the subsequent term, ought to be accounted a judgment of the first day of the term before, and allowed. And he held the said error to be good, and decreed the £250 paid in November 1662 should go and be applied as part of the satisfaction of the £1600 and damages due on the judgment, and what other monies were paid by any other of the obligors, their heirs, executors, administrators, or assigns since the 20th of October 1662, if not paid on another account, shall be applied in further satisfaction of the said judgment, first, to discharge the interest and, then, to sink the principal, and, as to so much, he did reverse the said decree.

And the defendant appealed from this said decree to the Lord Keeper FINCH, and insisted that, by his answer to the original bill, [it was] said, when the £250 was paid, the judgment was not entered, and, presently, after hearing the original cause, the late Lord Keeper Bridgeman, calling to his assistance the Master of the Rolls [GRIMSTON], who declared that the defendant should not account for any money as received on the judgment until the said judgment, which was his security, was really and actually entered, if the plaintiff insisted as before, which was overruled. And the plaintiff then brought a bill of review, to which the defendant pleaded and demurred, and, thereupon, the Lord Bridgeman declared the decree to be just as to the £250. And the decree made by the Lord Shaftesbury is to unravel the account settled and to charge the defendant with £4000, when, by the original bill or bills of review, they do not charge him with above the penalty of the said judgment.

This court now declared that the examination of the time of the actual entry of the judgment in this case did not impeach the judgment, but was only to guide the conscience of the court in the application of the payment of the money. And, therefore, as this case is, the whole money having been decreed and settled as aforesaid, the examination of the time of the actual entry of the said judgment tended not to the invalidating thereof, but only to inform the court when and how it came to be recorded, which, in cases of originals filed to prevent the Statutes of Limitation[1] and other cases of like nature, are usually examined in courts of law, the court saw no cause to relieve the plaintiffs on their bill of review, and dismissed their bill of review.

Reports *tempore* Finch 89, 23 E.R. 48

John Crisp and Thomas Crisp, Esq., by a bill of review, plaintiffs; Matthew Bluck, Esq. defendant.

A bill of review to reverse a decree, wherein the case appeared to be thus, *viz.* Sir Nicholas Crisp, the plaintiff's father, and several others were bound in a bond of £1600 penalty to the defendant Bluck for the payment of £100, which coming due at Michaelmas 1662 and not being paid, the bond was put in suit. And judgment was obtained against Sir Nicholas Crisp alone for the principal and interest, amounting at that time to more than the penalty of the bond. After this action brought by the said Bluck, he received several sums of money in part. And, in a former suit between these parties, it was decreed that what money the obligee had received before the judgment was entered should go in discharge of the interest of the £1000 original debt and that, after the judgment was actually entered, then the obligee should be satisfied and paid the whole money recovered with damages from the time the judgment was entered, deducting what he had received since the judgment was entered.

Now, this judgment being entered in Michaelmas term 1662 and £250 being received by the obligee in November following, this was, by the Master, accounted interest of the original debt, and not towards the money recovered by the judgment. And the error assigned was that the judgment being entered in Michaelmas term, that must relate to the first day of the term; therefore, what money was paid after that first day ought to be applied towards satisfaction of the judgment, which the LORD SHAFTESBURY decreed accordingly, and that what other money was paid by any other of the obligors on the bond in question or by their heirs etc. since 20 October 1662 should be applied in farther satisfaction of the said judgment, first, to discharge the interest and then to sink the principal.

Upon an appeal to the Lord Keeper BRIDGEMAN, so much of the said decree, by which it was ordered that what money was paid after the first day of Michaelmas term should be applied towards satisfaction of the judgment was reversed and that the defendant should not account for any money received on the judgment until it was actually entered, which last decree upon this bill of review before the LORD NOTTINGHAM, was confirmed, the same having been settled, examined, and decreed by so many decrees. And, therefore, he dismissed this bill of review.

[1] Stat. 21 Jac. I, c. 16 (*SR*, IV, 1222–1223).

73 Selden Soc. 34

March, 26 Car. II, 1673/74.

Bluck, in 1642, lends the farmers of the customs £1000, and takes a penal bond of £1600, and, in Michaelmas [term] 1662, he obtains judgment upon this bond against Sir Nicholas Crisp. And, at divers times, he receives £1200. Bluck exhibits a bill against the heir of Crisp to discover assets. Crisp exhibits a cross-bill against Bluck to discover what had been received.

It was ordered that Bluck should confess by answer £1200 received and Crisp should confess by answer £400 assets more, and so proceed to a hearing. At the hearing, the Master of the Rolls [GRIMSTON] decreed that what was paid before the actual entry of the judgment should be accounted as paid for interest [and] what was paid since the actual entry should go in satisfaction of the judgment. Whereupon the case fell out to be that, upon 14 November 1662, Bluck was paid £250 and the judgment, though of Michaelmas 1662, yet was not actually entered until the midst of January following. So the question grew whether this £250 should be accounted interest or principal.

The LORD BRIDGEMAN referred it to the Master of the Rolls to explain his own order, who declared it interest, and the LORD BRIDGEMAN, upon an appeal, confirmed it.

Crisp brings a bill of review, which was heard by the EARL OF SHAFTESBURY, assisted with WYNDHAM and ATKYNS, and they reversed the decree because, in law, the judgment relates to the first day of the term, *viz.*, to the 20th of October, being the essoin day, and it is against the dignity of the proceedings of law to examine the time of the actual entry when the time of the legal entry of judgment is certain and known. And they cited 3 Car. Cro. 102, Sandford and Cooper's Case,[1] where a statute acknowledged 22 January was executed and the execution defeated by a judgment of Hilary term which related to the 20th of January, being the essoin day, and not to the 23rd of January which was the *quarto die post*. So they ruled the £250 to be principal.

But before enrolment, *viz.*, after an enrolment by surprise set aside, I [LORD NOTTINGHAM] was petitioned to rehear the cause. And, upon debate, I dismissed the bill of review, and confirmed the former proceedings, although the consequence of that dismission were to make Crisp pay more at last than the penalty of the judgment, for I observed that, if Crisp had never paid anything, he could not have been compelled to pay more than the £1600, yet, when he pays part and leaves the whole judgment at law still in force, he has by this necessitated himself to fly into equity, and, by consequence, to submit to the standing rules of legal equity, *viz.*, to pay the whole principal and interest due on the bond or be dismissed. And the court, seeing this, probably made the first decree by mediation

[1] *Sandford v. Cooper* (1628), Croke Car. 102, 79 E.R. 690, also Hutton 95, 23 E.R. 1125.

without which the money received after judgment could not regularly have been decreed principal. And it is as probable the mediation had not prevailed if the word 'actual entry' had not been consented to. Therefore, actual entry ought to signify something more than legal entry, and the actual entry is sometimes considerable in law, for, if an original writ be filed in the middle of a term and part of the term be within the Statute of Limitations[1] and part without, the time of the filing is enquirable, and the benefit of the Statute shall not be lost to the defendant by relation, as was ruled Hilary 1649, Cale and Simson's Case. So here, the relation shall not take away the advantage of legal equity, and it was the folly of Crisp to pay without a legal discharge of so much of the £1600. Nor could any *audita querela* help him in this case or, if it could, he should have brought it.

Yet I reproved Bluck for so rigorous an exaction of a debt he would for twenty years together in the time of the farmers' distress have been glad to have taken 2s. 6d. in the pound for. But now being tied up to rules, I could not break them in this case.

[Other copies of this report: British Library MS. Stowe 406, f. 71.]
[Reg. Lib. 25 Car. II A, f. 357.]

109

Parry v. Brown

(Ch. 1663)

Where a person has a power to lease and the lease is greater than the power, the lease is enforceable to the extent of the power.

1 Chancery Cases 23, 22 E.R. 674

26 June [1663]. Pawcy v. Bowen.

It was resolved that, where a person has a power to lease for ten years and he leases for twenty years, that the lease for twenty years shall be good for ten years of the twenty in equity. And it was said to have been so settled several times in this court.

2 Freeman 171, 22 E.R. 1137

26 May [sic] 1663.

[It was] resolved that, where a person has power to lease for ten years and he leases for twenty, it is good in equity for ten. And so has it been frequently resolved in this court.

[1] Stat. 21 Jac. I, c. 16 (*SR*, IV, 1222–1223).

Nelson 87, 21 E.R. 796

Parry v. Bowen.

[It was] resolved that, where a person has the power to lease for ten years only and he makes a lease for twenty years, that such lease shall be good in equity for ten years. And so it has been settled several times in this court.

3 Chancery Reports 11, 21 E.R. 713

26 June, 15 Car. II [1663]. Parry v. Bowen.

[It was] resolved that, where a person has a power to lease for ten years and he leases for twenty years, that the lease shall be good for ten years in equity. And it was said to be so settled several times in this court.

[Other reports of this case: 1 Eq. Cas. Abr. 342, 21 E.R. 1089.]

110

Inglet v. Vaughan

(Ch. 1663)

Upon an arrest for not performing a final decree, the commissioners have the discretion to allow the judgment-debtor to give bail or not, but, if bail is refused, they must bring him into court forthwith.

1 Chancery Reports 261, 21 E.R. 567

One Horwel having arrested the defendant upon a commission of rebellion at the plaintiff's suit for the breach of a decree and imprisoned him for six weeks in the said Horwel's house and other places and refused to take bail for the defendant's appearance to answer the contempt, and the defendant had by order of this court entered his appearance upon the said arrest by his clerk in court. It was referred to the Six Clerks to certify whether, upon a commission of rebellion for the breach of a decree, a bill ought to be taken or not, who certified that commissioners on a commission of rebellion may either take or refuse bail at their discretion, but, in case they refuse, then, they ought to bring the party up to the court without delay and [show] that bail was offered.

This court, on the reading of a precedent in the like nature made in the Lord Ellesmere's time, ordered that the said Horwel stand committed to the Fleet [Prison] for his abuse and to pay to the defendant his costs and charges sustained by his imprisonment, to be taxed by a Master.

Dickens 7, 21 E.R. 168

A question arose upon a commission of rebellion for not performing a decree, whether bail ought to be taken. Upon a reference, it was held to be in the discretion of the commissioners, but, if they refused, they ought to bring the party into court without delay.

[Reg. Lib. 15 Car. II A, f. 476.]

111

Mead v. Cave

(Ch. 1663)

A devise to younger children, according to the intent of the testator in this case, did not include an heir, even though he was younger than his sisters.

1 Chancery Reports 224, 21 E.R. 556

Charnel Petty, grandfather of the plaintiff and the defendant, Charnel Mead, by his will, devised lands to trustees that they should out of the profits thereof pay unto the younger children of his daughter Mead, the plaintiff's mother, £400 equally to be divided. And the said plaintiff's mother had six children, so that five of them are within the intent of the will to have £80 apiece. But the defendant, Charnel Mead, insisted that the £80 apiece does not belong to the plaintiffs, for that they are elder in seniority of years than he, the defendant, Charnel Mead, the sixth child, being a younger child than any of them, and that he ought to have the said money, whereas, younger children, in this case, are to be taken as distinguished from the heir at law and not from the elder children in age and that it was the intent of the testator it should be so appears by this, that the defendant Charnel Mead was his father's eldest son and was to inherit a fair estate by descent from him after his death.

This court was clear of opinion that the plaintiffs were within the said trust and that the defendant Charnel Mead ought to be excluded by the intentions of the testator, and decreed the plaintiffs £80 apiece and the defendant Charnel Mead to be totally excluded.

[Reg. Lib. 14 Car. II, f. 915.]

112

Kildway v. Aldwickle

(Ch. 1663)

A defendant in the Mayor's Court of London can remove his case into the Court of Chancery where he cannot summons his witnesses into the London court.

Lord Nottingham, *Prolegomena*, p. 299

16 July, 15 Car. II.

On a bill exhibited in the Mayor's Court in London, it is usual for the defendants to exhibit a bill in Chancery, setting forth the general equity of their case and suggesting that their witnesses live out of the Mayor's Court's jurisdiction etc. and then pray a *certiorari* to remove the cause in the Mayor's Court, which is usually granted. And this latter is usually called a *certiorari* bill. Second, the *certiorari* is made returnable within fourteen days after the receipt, and the plaintiff must give a bond to examine witnesses within the fourteen days to prove the suggestions of his bill. Third, if the plaintiffs neglect to examine in that time, the defendant, on a certificate from the Examiner, may move for a [writ of] *procedendo*. Fourth, if the plaintiff examine in time, then, the examinations are to be referred to a Master, and, if he certifies the suggestions proved, then, the cause is to be retained, and to proceed in the ordinary course. Fifth, but these examinations are not to be used at the hearing. Sixth, if the Master certify the suggestions are not proved, a [writ of] *procedendo* is to be awarded. Seventh, but, if the defendant put in an answer to the *certiorari* bill, then, he admits the bill, and bars himself of a *procedendo*.

[This was] so certified by the Six Clerks. But, there, the defendant had also called for a replication. And, in Banks and Dethick's Case, Michaelmas [term] 24 Car. II [1672], the defendant, having answered, gave notice of a motion, but did not move for a *procedendo*.[1]

113

Smith v. Oxenden

(Ch. 1663)

Where an agent for an exporter does not pay foreign import duties that were due, he does not have to account for them to his principal.

1 Chancery Cases 25, 22 E.R. 675

The case was the East India Company sued their factor for an account of £12,000 in gold he carried hence into the East India. He, upon his account, demanded (according to the usual custom) allowance for so much paid for customs to the king in India. It was insisted that he never paid the customs there for the gold. So, whether the factor or the principal merchant should have the benefit of the customs was the question.

---

[1] *Dethick v. Banks* (Ch. 1673–1674), 2 Chancery Reports 92, 21 E.R. 625, Repts. *tempore* Finch 16, 23 E.R. 9, 73 Selden Soc. 18, 19.

And this was referred to merchants. And two merchants certified that, by the course of merchants, the factor should retain the benefit of the non-payment of the customs, for that, if the principal's freight, by his non-payment of the customs, had been lost, he must have answered for it to the employer, and so run the hazard wholly. And, in this case, the factor, by the law in East India, had it been discovered that he had concealed the gold and not entered it into the custom books, was to have lost his life as a felon. Two other merchants certified that the employer was to have the benefit of the non-payment of the customs.

And, upon these certificates, it was decreed that the factor should have the benefit of the customs, for it was a duty to be paid, and the employer could make no title to it against him that was in possession and he that has possession has right against all but him that has the very right.

Vide Borr against Vandale.[1]

2 Freeman 173, 22 E.R. 1139

Trinity [term], 15 Car. II [1663].

The East India Company sued their factor for an account of £1200 in gold. He accounted for so much of it paid to the Emperor of East India for custom. The company insisted that none was paid, admitting which, it was referred to merchants, who ought to have the benefit in case the factor defrauded the Emperor of India of the custom.

And it was certified by the merchants that the factor ought to have it, for, if the gold had been seized for non-payment of customs, the factor had been chargeable, wherefore he shall have the benefit.

Vide casum proximum.[2]

[Other reports of this case: 1 Eq. Cas. Abr. 369, 21 E.R. 1109.]
[Reg. Lib. 1662 B, f. 939.]
[Related cases: Love v. Oxenden (Ch. 1671), Lord Nottingham, *Prolegomena*, p. 271.]

114

Gerrard v. Fitton

(Ch. 1663–1664)

A court of equity can cancel a forged deed.

Lincoln's Inn MS. Misc. 497, p. 147, pl. 4

Trinity term, 15 Car. II.

---

[1] *Borre v. Varde* (Ch. 1663), see below, Case No. 119.

[2] *Borre v. Varde* (Ch. 1663), see below, Case No. 119.

The last day of this term, it was moved that a decree made in a cause between Charles, lord Gerrard, and Alexander Fitton might be made absolute. The decree passed on the behalf of the lord Gerrard, who made his title by a will and that a deed by which Fitton claimed being found forged in a trial at law should be damned unless Fitton should within a year recover the lands at law by force of the deed, which, for that time, he is to have the use of, now, in another trial at Chester, the verdict passing against Fitton and the time being expired, the decree was made absolute, *viz.* that the deed should be damned.

[Other copies of this report: Lincoln's Inn MS. Hill 83, p. 134, pl. 2.]

1 Siderfin 170, 82 E.R. 1038

Hilary term, 15 & 16 Car. II.

A deed that was found by a verdict to be forged concerning an estate of £1200 *per annum* in Cheshire was by an order brought into the Chancery. And a time of one year was given to Phitton to justify the deed by a new trial where he pleased. And, because within the year, he had a new trial at Chester and it was found against him, it was now moved that the deed, the year being past, will be cancelled and condemned. And it was done accordingly.

[Later proceedings in this case: Earl of Macclesfield v. Fitton (Ch. 1683–1684), Chancery Repts. *tempore* North 134.]

115

Sheldon v. Weldman

(Ch. 1663–1664)

The Statute of Limitations does not apply to trusts.

The Statute of Limitations applies to suits in equity for matters that are also remediable at common law.

1 Chancery Cases 26, 22 E.R. 676

11 October [1663]. Chief Justice Hyde.

The bill was to have an account of money delivered by the plaintiff's father, whose executor the plaintiff was, to the defendant to compound for the plaintiff's father's estate (sequestered for delinquency) at Goldsmiths' Hall.

The defendant pleaded the Statute of Limitation of accounts, 21 Jac., 16.[1]

Upon arguing his plea, it was insisted by the plaintiff's counsel that an account for monies delivered upon a trust was not within this Statute and that it had been so ruled.

---

[1] Stat. 21 Jac. I, c. 16 (*SR*, IV, 1222–1223).

And, thereupon, the plea was overruled, and the defendant ordered to answer.

And in Trinity vacation, 16 Car. II [1664], the case being heard by the Lord Chancellor [Lord Clarendon], Justice Twysden, and Wyndham, the two judges and the Lord Chancellor declared and were of opinion that the Statute of Limitations did not bar this suit, because it was on a trust that the defendant had the money for which the account was sought. But, for another reason, the bill was dismissed.

2 Freeman 156, 22 E.R. 1126

11 October, 13 Car. II, 1661 [sic]. Judge Hyde. Sheldon v. Wildeman.

A bill was exhibited to have money delivered by the plaintiff's father to the defendant to compound for the plaintiff's father's estate then sequestered for deducting money at Goldsmiths' Hall. The plaintiff was executor to his father.

The defendant pleaded the Statute of Limitations, 21 Jac., 16.

Upon arguing this plea, it was insisted by the plaintiff's counsel that an account for money delivered on a trust was not within the Statute. And it was so resolved.

And, thereupon, the defendant was ordered to answer, and the plea was overruled.

In Trinity vacation, 16 Car. II, the cause was heard by the Lord Chancellor [Lord Clarendon], Judge Wyndham, and Twysden. And they were all of opinion that the Statute of Limitations did not bar the suit because it was a trust. But the bill was dismissed for another reason.

Lord Nottingham, *Prolegomena*, p. 325

5 July, 16 Car. II, by the Chancellor and Twysden and Wyndham. Sheldon v. Wiseman.

[It was] resolved: first, if a suit in Chancery be grounded on a mere trust, the Statute of Limitations is no bar; second, if a suit in Chancery be for a matter remediable at common law, which is barred by the Statute of Limitations, the suit in equity is barred also; third, if money be delivered on an account, which is to be continuing, or of long agitation as to merchandize, or, as in the principal case, to the purchasing of the plaintiff's estate at Drury House, there, no account lies until the employment be finished or countermanded or a request to account [be made]. Therefore, the time of limitation is to be computed from thence, and cannot incur[1] before.

[Other reports of this case: 1 Eq. Cas. Abr. 304, 21 E.R. 1063.]

[1] Sic in MS. for accrue.

116

Scroope v. Scroope

(Ch. 1663)

If a father purchases land in the name of himself and his son jointly and then dies, though the father paid all the purchase money, it is an advancement of the son by the father.

1 Chancery Cases 27, 22 E.R. 677

15 October [1663]. Gervas Scroope, an infant, against Sir Adrian Scroope. Chief Justice Hyde.

A bill was exhibited to be relieved touching the manor of Gidley in Lincolnshire. And it sets forth that Gervas Scroope, deceased, father of the defendant and grandfather of the plaintiff, was seised in fee thereof, and devised the same to the plaintiff and his heirs and that the defendant, having gotten all the writings, laid claim to the same, and got into possession thereof, and did pretend that the said manor was purchased heretofore in the name of the said Sir Gervas and him and to their heirs, and that so Sir Gervas had no power, being a joint tenant, to devise the same, whereas his, the said defendant's name, was used in the said conveyance in trust for the said Gervas, and the purchase was made, and the money paid by Sir Gervas, and that so the defendant's title was but as a trustee for Sir Gervas, and, consequently, for the plaintiff, to whom Sir Gervas had devised the same.

The defendant pleaded that the premises were, the 19th of June, 13 Car. I [1637], by a good conveyance in law well executed for £4600 really and *bona fide* paid, conveyed by J.S. to Sir Gervas Scroope and the defendant and their heirs, the defendant being the son and heir apparent of Sir Gervas, and that the said £4600 was raised by Sir Gervas by the sale of the lands, which were the ancient inheritance of the family and which, if they had not been sold, had descended on the defendant. And he averred that all the courts of the said manor that were kept in Sir Gervas's life were kept in as well the defendant's name as in Sir Gervas's name and that the said conveyance to Sir Gervas and him was really and *bona fide* without any trust for Sir Gervas or any other and that, Sir Gervas being dead, the defendant claimed the premises by survivorship. And he demanded judgment.

The plaintiff did not attend, but was alleged to be out of town, and prayed it might stand for another day.

But the court, directing the plea to be opened, which was done and afterwards read, declared it clearly to be a good plea unless the plaintiff could prove an express trust. And, if he could have done that, he ought to have replied. But, not having replied, the plea must be taken to be true and that, albeit the purchase was made by the father in his own and his son's name, it should *prima facie* be intended an advancement for the son, and not presumed a trust unless declared so, and that it was anciently the way to join the son in a purchase to avoid wardship.

And the Case of Crisp against Prat, 1 Cro. 550, and Sir Sidney Mountague's Case, there, were in the debate of this case urged.[1]

And the court declared to the defendant's counsel, this being the case, that nothing could be said against the plea, and so allowed it. 17 November 1663, the plea was re-heard, and, upon argument on both sides, was allowed with double costs.

2 Freeman 171, 22 E.R. 1138

October, 15 Car. II [1663]. Judge Hyde. Sir Gervase Scroope v. Sir Adrian Scroope.

A bill was exhibited to be relieved for the manor of Gedney. The plaintiff claimed by the devise of Sir Gervase Scroope, grandfather of the plaintiff, father of the defendant. The defendant pleads that Sir Gervase bought the manor in the name of Sir Gervase and the defendant, that the money for the purchase was raised by the sale of lands of inheritance, which would have come to the defendant if not sold, and the courts were held in both their names, and he was never seised in trust for Gervase, and, now, he claimed the whole by survivorship.

Curia: This is a good plea unless it can be proved an express trust, which could not be done but by a replication, and, there being no replication, the plea shall be taken as true, for, *per curiam*, the purchase shall be intended an advancement for the son. 3 Cro. 550, and Sir Sidney Montague's Case there, and Crisp v. Pratt.

This plea was reheard the 17th of November 1663. And, on argument on both sides, [it was] allowed.

Lord Nottingham, *Prolegomena*, p. 240

If a father purchases land in the name of himself and his son jointly and then dies, though the father paid all the money, yet the law shall not imply a trust for the father in the son without other circumstances, but rather [it is] an advancement of the son by the father.

[It was] so ruled in the Case of Sir Adrian Scroop, who was a joint purchaser with Lord Gervas Scroop, his father, by LORD CLARENDON.

[Reg. Lib. 1663 B, f. 135.]

[1] *Crisp v. Pratt* (1639), 1 Croke Car. 549, 79 E.R. 1072, also March 34, 82 E.R. 399, W. Jones 437, 82 E.R. 230; *Lady Gorge's Case* (1634), Croke Car. 550, 79 E.R. 1073.

117

Nanny v. Martin

(Ch. 1663–1665)

Where a husband and wife have a decree for money in the right of the wife, and, then, the husband dies, the wife shall have the money and not the executor of the husband.

1 Chancery Cases 27, 22 E.R. 676

15 October [1663]. The Lord Chancellor, Chief Justice Hyde.

A husband and wife have a decree for money in the right of the wife, and, then, the husband dies. A question is moved who shall have the benefit of the decree, whether the wife or the executor of the husband.

And this case being referred to Chief Justice Hyde, he had given his opinion that the benefit of the decree belongs to the wife and that it was so in a judgment at law.

And an exception being taken to that certificate of the judge, he refused to hear the matter of the exception, but left it to the Chancellor. But he declared his opinion was still the same. And 18 January 1663[/64], at the seal, the Lord Chancellor [Lord Clarendon] would not refer it back, but confirmed the judge's certificate.

2 Freeman 172, 22 E.R. 1138

15 October, 15 Car. II [1663]. Judge Hyde.

A husband and wife have a decree for money in the right of the wife. The husband dies.

Curia: The wife shall have the benefit of the decree as if it had been a judgment at law. And the Lord Chancellor [Lord Clarendon] afterwards, 18 January 1665, declared he was of the same opinion in this case, and confirmed Judge Hyde's certificate.

1 Chancery Reports 233, 21 E.R. 559

The case was that Hugh Nanney, deceased, and Sarah, his wife, exhibited their bill into this court against the defendant, John Martin, for a legacy of £300 and other monies devised unto the plaintiff Sarah before marriage by the will of Martin Cornick, her father, deceased. 2 December 13 Car. II [1661], it was decreed that the plaintiff be paid the £300 and other monies payable by the said John Martin.

This decree was enrolled. And, afterwards, the plaintiff, Hugh Nanney, died intestate. Anne Nanney took administration of the goods of the said Hugh Nanney, and, by virtue thereof, she claims the said £300 and other monies decreed unto the said Hugh Nanney and Sarah, his wife, in the lifetime of the said Hugh Nanney. Whether the money so decreed do belong unto the administratrix of the said Hugh Nanney or to the complainant Sarah is the question. This court referred it to a judge to certify.

The judge gave his opinion *viz.*:

> First, I conceive that a decree in Chancery for money on any other personal thing, being a judgment in equity, is of the like nature with and ought to be governed by the same rules as a judgment for a debt or damages at common law, and, consequently, that the interest or benefit of this decree and the money due thereby ought to go and be unto such of the said parties as should have right thereto in case it were a judgment for a debt or damages at common law;
>
> Secondly, if a judgment be had by a husband and wife at common law in an action brought by them both for a debt due unto the wife before marriage and the husband dies after the judgment and before execution sued, I conceive that the debt due on this judgment belongs to the wife and she shall sue execution upon the judgment, and not the executor or administrator of the husband, all which I humbly submit to the judgment of this honorable court.
>
> /s/ *Robert Hyde*

This court confirmed the judge's certificate.

[Other reports of this case: 1 Eq. Cas. Abr. 68, 21 E.R. 881.]
[Reg. Lib. 1663 B, f. 821, 14 Car. II, ff. 334, 535, 15 Car. II, f. 232.]

118

Manning v. Burges

(Ch. 1663)

A redemption of a mortgage will be ordered upon a tender of the money due to the creditor, and no interest is payable after the date of the tender.

1 Chancery Cases 29, 22 E.R. 678

26 October [1663]. At the Rolls. The Master of the Rolls.

A mortgage was forfeited. The mortgagor, afterwards, meeting the mortgagee, said 'I have monies, now I will come and redeem the mortgage'. The mortgagee said to him he would hold the mortgaged premises as long as he could and, then, when he could hold them no longer, 'let the Devil take them if he would'. And, afterwards, the mortgagor went to the mortgagee's house with money more than sufficient to redeem the mortgage, and tendered it there. But it did not appear that the mortgagee was within or that the tender was made to him.

And it was decreed a redemption, and the defendant to have no interest from the time of the tender, because of his willfulness.

A like case was between Peckham and Legay about a year since.

2 Freeman 174, 22 E.R. 1140

26 October, 15 Car. II [1663]. Master of the Rolls.

If a mortgage be forfeited and the mortgagor tender the money to the mortgagee and then prefer his bill to redeem, the mortgagee shall have no interest from the time of the tender.

[Other reports of this case: 1 Eq. Cas. Abr. 286, 318, 21 E.R. 1050.]
[Reg. Lib. 1663 B, f. 235.]

119

Borre v. Varde

(Ch. 1663)

An agent must account to his principal as to any customs duties due to the king of England whether they were paid or not.

Lincoln's Inn MS. Hill 125, f. 42v, pl. 2

Michaelmas [term] 15 Car. II. Borre v. Vandevalde.

The bill was for the defendants to interplead. Lewellin was severally indebted to the defendants. And some claimed property in the goods. Borre, sued by them all, having goods of Llewellin in his hands. He prayed he might not be doubly charged or trebly charged, but all the defendants might interplead, who ought to have the goods etc. Vandervalde and the rest all answered. Barre did reply to Vandevalde and not to the rest. And the cause proceeded to examination betwixt them, and [was] brought now to a hearing by Vandevalde, all the other defendants being served with process.

But the court would not proceed because [there was] no replication to the other defendants and one defendant cannot bring another to a hearing on a bill and answer. But the error was in that Vandevalde, who was concerned most, to speed the cause, accepted a replication to himself alone. So then, he moved. And it was ordered that the plaintiff reply to the other defendants.

Note, now, Vandevalde must examine again as to the other defendants etc.

Another point was moved, which came up by a report made in the cause, *viz.* Borre was a factor for Lewellin, a merchant, and, in the time of Oliver [Cromwell], the Usurper, did steal so much custom and excise [money] as came to alone £600 and, offering an account to the creditors of Lewellin's estate, charged himself with the goods and, then, in discharge, craved allowance of the £600, which the creditors were contented to allow if that he would swear he paid or satisfied it, which he would not.

Fountaine pressed it might be allowed for that it did not belong to Llewellin, nor, consequently, to his creditors, but to the Usurper, according to the law then used. And it is no reason the plaintiff should have that which was not due to them. And between Smith and Oxenden,[1] it was so ruled in this court, for Oxenden, being a factor beyond the sea in the East Indies and Persia for S. Smith on account, would not allow what Oxenden demanded etc., who had not paid the customs in India, and it is true [?] it was so ruled that he should not be charged.

And divers merchants examined by Borre deposed it was the custom of merchants not to charge their factors in such cases.

But, on the other side, there can be no custom maintained grounded on deceit, for it may as well be said that it is a lawful custom to steal the duties and a good custom cannot be grounded on a wrong. Second, if this should be allowed, it would give encouragement to factors and others to defraud the king of England etc. if they should have such a reward. Third, and it would be more strange to make such allowances in a court of conscience and be of very high and ill consequence in example. Fourth, and if the offense had been found out, the merchant would have sustained the loss by the forfeiture of his goods. And so, the factor, if he should not be charged, shall gain. And, if he be espied, the merchant shall lose.

Fountaine: The merchant shall have his action against the factor.

M.: That is no reason why this court shall allow the factor, neither is it equal; the factor may be poor.

Chancellor [Lord Clarendon]: Speak to the King's Counsel to look to the king's interest if the £600 belongs not to the king in this case. The difference is nought between this and the Case of Oxenden. He there hazarded his life. The consequence here is perilous etc. And he would advise on the matter.

1 Chancery Cases 30, 22 E.R. 678

27 October [1663]. Borr v. Vandall.

The factor had stolen the custom of divers goods, of which, the bill was to have an account and to discover whether he paid those customs or no.

The defendant, by an answer, insisted that he was not bound to answer that part of the bill, for that the plaintiff, who was the employer, was not entitled to those customs, nor any advantage, whether they were paid or not.

Exception being taken to this answer, the Master certified the answer sufficient.

Exceptions being taken to the report, the cause came now to be heard upon that. And the cause of Smith and Oxenden, fol. 25, was cited. But, on the plaintiff's side it was insisted that this case was not like that, for that was of customs stolen from a foreign king and this was of customs stolen from our own king and that it would be of evil consequence and an encouragement to evil factors if the court should give an opinion for them in a matter of fraud, as this was.

[1] *Smith v. Oxenden* (Ch. 1663), see above, Case No. 113.

And, whereas it was insisted by the defendant's counsel that it was the course of merchants that factors should have the benefit of customs themselves, and not the principals, because the penalty would fall on the factor if discovered, it was declared that could not be called a custom, being grounded upon fraud. And, therefore, the court ordered that the defendant should answer whether he paid the customs or not.

2 Freeman 174, 22 E.R. 1140

27 October, 15 Car. II [1663]. Lord Chancellor, Master of the Rolls.

The bill was to discover whether the factor had paid customs in England. The factor insisted that, as to that, he need not answer, for the advantage did redound to himself if it were not paid. Exceptions were taken to this. And the Master reports the answer was sufficient.

But, on exceptions to the Master's report, it was resolved that the factor should answer. And the case was not like the foregoing case, for, here, could be no custom of merchants grounded on a fraud to the king. *Vide casum proximum precedentem.*[1]

Nelson 87, 21 E.R. 796

Borre v. Vandall.

A factor had stolen the customs of several goods. And the bill was to have an account and to discover whether he paid those customs or not.

The defendant, by his answer, insisted that he was not bound to answer that part of the bill, because the plaintiff, who was the merchant, was not entitled to those customs nor had any advantage thereby whether the same were paid or not.

And it being referred to the Master whether this was a sufficient answer or not, he certified it was not.

And exceptions being taken to his report, the cause was heard. And it was insisted that it would be of very ill consequence and an encouragement to unjust factors if the court should give any opinion for them in a matter of fraud, as this was.

But it was said for the defendant that, by the law and course of merchants, the factors were to have the benefit of customs stolen, because they were liable to the penalties if discovered, and not the merchants.

But the court declared that could not be a law or custom amongst merchants which was grounded on a fraud, and so ordered the defendant to answer.

[Other reports of this case: 1 Eq. Cas. Abr. 370, 21 E.R. 1109.]

[1] *Smith v. Oxenden* (Ch. 1663), see above, Case No. 113.

120

Rich v. Jaques

(Ch. 1663)

Where a case is removed out of the Mayor of London's Court into the Court of Chancery to have discovery, new matter can be alleged in the Court of Chancery, and that court will retain jurisdiction and grant a remedy.

1 Chancery Cases 31, 22 E.R. 678

29 October [1663].

Rich was the plaintiff upon a *certiorari* bill to remove a cause out of the Mayor's Court, his witnesses being out of that jurisdiction, and the bill here was for an account touching other matters. Witnesses being examined, the defendant moved for a [writ of] *procedendo*, and insisted upon it, for that, if the cause should be heard here, he could not be relieved, not having any bill here, being here but as defendant, though plaintiff in the Mayor's Court.

Whereunto the plaintiff's counsel insisted that no *procedendo* ought to be [had], for that this bill, containing other matters, could not be determined upon the bill in the Mayor's Court and that the bill could not be divided and that the plaintiff, in the Mayor's Court, might file his bill in the Mayor's Court in this court and direct it to the Chancellor and have the same remedy here as he could there.

[It was] ordered that the cause stand to be heard on the bill in this court. And, after the hearing, the cause was dismissed out of this court.

2 Freeman 174, 22 E.R. 1141

29 October, 15 Car. II [1663].

Rich was plaintiff upon a *certiorari* bill to remove a cause out of the Mayor's Court because his witnesses lived out of the jurisdiction of the court. And now, having examined his witnesses here, the defendant here (who is plaintiff in the Mayor's Court) moved for a [writ of] *procedendo*. The plaintiff here insisted that his bill was of a new matter, and desired to be heard here. And so he was, and, after the hearing, the cause was dismissed.

[Other reports of this case: 1 Eq. Cas. Abr. 80, 21 E.R. 893.]
[Reg. Lib. 1663 B, f. 54.]

121

Tew v. Thackwell

(Ch. 1663)

Where a leasehold is diminished in value by a subsequent right of common in third parties in the land, the rent will not be apportioned at common law, and, in such a case, a court of equity will not apportion the rent where the diminished value is still a very generous bargain to the lessee.

1 Chancery Cases 31, 22 E.R. 679

30 October [1663].

The plaintiff was the lessee of divers lands, whereupon an entire rent was reserved. Afterwards, the inhabitants of the town where part of the lands lay claimed a right of common in part of the lands so let. And, upon a trial of their right, they are found to have a right of common there. Now, this, being but a right of common recovered, is no eviction of the land in law, because the soil was not recovered, and so no apportionment could be at law. And, therefore, the bill was to have the rent apportioned in equity.

And Serjeant *Maynard* insisted that such an apportionment had frequently been decreed here.

But, in this case, it appearing that, notwithstanding the right of common, the lands were worth the rent reserved and better, the court would not decree it, but the bill was dismissed.

2 Freeman 174, 22 E.R. 1140

30 October, 15 Car. II [1663].

The plaintiff was the lessee of divers lands whereon one entire rent was reserved. A township recovered a right of common in part of the land. Not being evicted, the lessee could not apportion the rent at law, so he sues here for an apportionment, as there were precedents that he might.

But, it being proved that the land was still worth the rent, the bill was dismissed.

Nelson 69, 21 E.R. 792

Thew v. Thircknell.

The plaintiff was lessee of several lands, out of which an entire rent was reserved. Afterwards, the inhabitants of the parish where part of the lands lay claimed a right of common in that part. And, upon a trial at law, it was found that they had such a right. Now, this being only a right of common which was recovered, it was no eviction in law of the land itself, and so no apportionment of the rent could be made at law. Therefore, a bill was brought to have the apportionment made in equity.

And Serjeant *Maynard* insisted that such an apportionment had been frequently decreed here.

But, in this case, it appearing that, though the right of common was recovered, the lands were still worth the rent reserved and more, the court would decree no apportionment, but ordered the bill to be dismissed.

3 Chancery Reports 11, 21 E.R. 713

31 October, 15 Car. II [1663].

The plaintiff was the lessee of divers lands, whereupon one entire rent was reserved. Afterwards, the inhabitants of the town where part of the lands lay claim a right of common in part of the lands so let. And, upon a trial of their right, they are found to have a right of common there. Now, this being but a right of common recovered, it was not an eviction of the land in law, because the soil was not recovered. And so, no apportionment of this rent could be made at law. And, therefore, this bill was to have the rent apportioned in equity.

And Serjeant *Maynard* insisted that such an apportionment had frequently been here decreed.

But, in this case, it appeared that, notwithstanding the right of common, the lands were worth the rent reserved and better. And, therefore, the court would not decree, but the bill was dismissed.

[Reg. Lib. 1663 B, ff. 38, 160.]

122

Anonymous

(Ch. 1663)

Where the necessary parties to a lawsuit have not been joined, the case will be dismissed.

Lincoln's Inn MS. Hill 125, f. 44v

Michaelmas [term] 15 Car. II, at the Rolls.

An indenture was made 1649 whereby a marriage was to be had between the Lord Grandison, son of the Lady Villiers, and the plaintiff that, by the indenture, the marquess of Dorchester covenanted with the trustees, Sir Edward Hyde, now Lord Chancellor, and others, that the securities for money, amounting to £20,000, should be put in the said trustees' hands, £14,000 *inde*, when received to be laid out in lands to be settled on the Lord Grandison and his wife, now plaintiff, for [. . .], remainder in tail to the Lord Grandison, and other covenants. The Lady Villiers covenanted to renew her lease of lands etc. in Battersea for the dean and chapter of York and put therein the plaintiff's lease and to settle it on the plaintiff for her life. The Lady Villiers having then three [. . .], one whereof was dead, the plaintiff now sued to have this covenant performed.

The securities were never deposited, nor money paid, nor land purchased, and the covenants are mutual. And, though the covenant to renew be expressed in consideration of the marriage, not mentioning to be in consideration of the other articles, yet, in reason, it cannot be presumed that the Lady should intend to do the one but with an eye to the other.

Therefore and because the covenantees were no parties, the bill was dismissed for both reason, but without prejudice to a new bill of etc.

123

Dashwood v. Browne and Dike

(Ch. 1663)

A suit to foreclose a mortgage does not lie against the mortgagor and a second mortgagee.

Lincoln's Inn MS. Hill 125, f. 45, pl. 1

Michaelmas [term] 15 Car. II.

Browne mortgaged to Dashwood for £200 *anno* 1656, and, 1657, he mortgages the same lands to Dike for £300. Now, Dashwood exhibits his bill against Browne and Dike to discharge the equity of redemption which Dike might pretend or that he be paid his money, conveying his interest.

The Chancellor [Lord Clarendon] dismissed the bill.

124

Anonymous

(Ch. 1663)

Where a party dies pendente lite, *his sureties to appear are released.*

Lincoln's Inn MS. Hill 125, f. 45, pl. 2

Michaelmas [term] 15 Car. II.

Webb, being attached by goods in London and condemnation had according to the custom, appeared, and put in bail. And the plaintiff there declared in debt for £300 for [. . .]. And he and his bail complained in Chancery because the party had sufficient [assets] on account in New England, where his business was transacted. And the business [being] judicially examined, the plaintiffs got an injunction. Webb died, whereby the other plaintiffs, his bail, were freed in law by the death of the principal.

They would dismiss the bill, but the court having taken security of them before on granting the injunction (as I take it) to abide the order of the court would not allow it, but ordered them to proceed because of the delay by the injunction.

And now, Michaelmas [term] 15 Car. [1663], the cause being brought to a hearing and the security [?] produced, the bill was dismissed with costs since Webb's death.

125

Serle v. Serle

(Ch. 1663)

For a contract to be enforceable, it must be supported by some consideration.

Lincoln's Inn MS. Hill 125, f. 45v, pl. 1

Michaelmas [term] 15 Car. II.

The plaintiff, being formerly a tenant to the dean of Wells, desired the defendant to agree with the dean in his behalf for a grant of an estate. He did undertake the employment. But, contrary to his trust, he took and dealt for an estate for himself, for which, the plaintiff exhibited the bill.

But [it was] dismissed *quia nudum pactum*, no money [having been] paid by the plaintiff. Yet [it was] objected that here was fraud in the defendant and damage to the plaintiff.

The Chancellor [Lord Clarendon] called for the defendant, who presenting himself in court, it was expected he would have asked him some question or propounded some way of composure, but he only said to him 'when I have an errand to send, you shall not be my messenger'.

126

Wolstoncroft v. Long

(Ch. 1663)

Where a debtor gives lands to be sold for the payment of his debts, the judgment creditors will be paid first and, then, the secured and unsecured creditors will be paid together pro rata.

1 Chancery Cases 32, 22 E.R. 679

6 November [1663].

A debtor upon bonds and simple contract makes a conveyance of lands upon trust to sell for the payment of his debts.

It was declared to be the constant practice, and so ruled and decreed here that all the debts should be paid in proportion and that, if the lands were not sufficient to pay all, all should lose in proportion. And so it is where lands are given to pay debts and legacies; they shall be paid in equal proportion because the land is made liable to the one as well as the other by the debtor himself. But otherwise it is in the case of debts on judgments that, in their own nature, charge the lands.

2 Freeman 175, 22 E.R. 1141

6 November, 15 Car. II [1663].

A debtor in bonds and simple contracts assigns land to sell in trust for the payment of his debts.

It was resolved and declared to be the constant rule that the creditors shall have in proportion, and not the bonds to be first satisfied. So legatees shall have an equal proportion *pro rata*, according to the greatness or smallness, for the land is made debtor, etc. But it is otherwise of judgments, which affect land by their own strength and nature.

3 Chancery Reports 12, 21 E.R. 713

6 November, 15 Car. II [1663].

A debtor upon bonds and simple contract makes a conveyance of lands upon a trust to sell for the payment of his debts.

It was declared to be the constant practice and so ruled and decreed here that all the debts should be paid in proportion and that, if the land were not sufficient to pay, all the creditors should lose in proportion. And so it is where lands are given to pay debts and legacies; they shall be paid in equal proportion, because the land is made liable to one as well as the other by the debtor himself. But otherwise it is in the case of debts on a judgment that in their own nature charge the lands.

[Other reports of this case: 2 Eq. Cas. Abr. 458, 22 E.R. 390.]

127

Baker v. Beaumont

(Ch. 1663)

The Court of Chancery can issue a writ of habeas corpus for the return of its prisoner for a contempt of court.

1 Chancery Cases 32, 22 E.R. 679

6 November [1663].

One of the Fleet [Prison] for the breach of a decree for the not vacating of a judgment, by a judgment in a feigned action in the King's Bench, gets himself turned over thither, and so had liberty to go abroad. And he got the defendant in the judgment taken in execution in Exeter. And, on a [writ of] *habeas corpus*, he was brought hither, and re-committed to the Fleet, and confined to his chamber, and a *habeas corpus* with a long return for the defendant in the judgment was granted.

2 Freeman 175, 22 E.R. 1141

6 November, 15 Car. II [1663].

One was in the Fleet [Prison] for the breach of a decree for not vacating a judgment. And, by a judgment in a feigned action in the King's Bench, he gets himself turned over thither, and so he had liberty to go abroad. And he got the defendant in the judgment taken in execution. And, on [a writ of] *habeas corpus*, he was brought hither and recommitted to the Fleet, and confined to his chamber, and a *habeas corpus* with a long return to the defendant in the judgment was granted.

3 Chancery Reports 13, 21 E.R. 713

Eodem die [6 November 1663].

The defendant being brought into court by [a writ of] *habeas corpus* directed to the Marshal of the Marshalsea [Prison], the plaintiff informed that the defendant was formerly committed to the Fleet [Prison] for a breach of a decree of this court, by which, he was to vacate a judgment which he had against the plaintiff. And he turned himself over to the King's Bench by a [writ of] *habeas corpus* in a signed action set up by himself and, thereby getting liberty to go abroad, he had taken the plaintiff in execution upon the said judgment, and clapped him in execution[1] jail.

And the defendant now refusing to discharge the said execution, it was ordered that the defendant stand committed to the Fleet [Prison] and be confined to his chamber. And a *habeas corpus* was granted to the plaintiff, whereby to remove him, which the court declared should be made of as long a continuance as it could.

128

Ayre v. Ayre

(Ch. 1663)

Where a widow pays the just debts of her deceased husband, she is not liable to his executor for such payments, but will have an allowance for them.

Where there is a rightful executor, there can be no executor de son tort.

1 Chancery Cases 33, 22 E.R. 680

10 November [1663]. The Lord Chancellor, Master of the Rolls.

[1] Exon *MS.* [perhaps Exeter].

The plaintiff, being the widow of her husband, sued the defendant, who was his executor, to have allowance of a satisfaction for several debts of the testator, which she, having possessed herself of his estate, had paid, the executor having gotten all the estate out of her hands. It was much controverted whether she should be helped herein, for the executor of his own wrong shall be allowed all payments made to any but himself, yet she was not executrix of her own wrong, for, where there is a rightful executor, as here, there can be no executor *de son tort*. Yet it resembled that case.

And the court, doubting much what to do in this case, decreed by consent of counsel that she should be allowed for all payments that she had made which were incumbent on the executor to pay, according to the course of law, but that, if she had made any payments out of order and the rule that the law left the executor liable to, that such payments she should not be allowed for if they were to the prejudice of the executors.

129

Sackville v. Dobson

(Ch. 1663)

A gift to a husband and wife with the right of survivorship is a single gift.

1 Chancery Cases 33, 22 E.R. 680

10 November [1663].

A limitation of the trust of a term to a husband and wife and the longest liver of them for life and, after, to the eldest issue of them, none being then born, [is] a good limitation. So the limitation to a husband and wife is but one limitation. And so it was admitted by counsel, it being not controverted, for, though the trust of a term, according to the rule in Goring and Bickerstaff's Case, fol. 4,[1] may be limited to divers persons that are in being, one after another, because the same is transferrable, yet it cannot be good beyond two limitations to a third person not in being. *Ergo*, the limitation to a husband and wife and the longest liver of them was admitted to be but one limitation in this case.

130

More v. Mayhow

(Ch. 1663)

The pleading of a 'valuable consideration' for a contract is sufficient without being specific.

[1] *Goring, ex dem. Alford v. Bickerstaff* (Ch. 1662), see above, Case No. 67.

It was a question in this case whether notice of encumbrances to a purchaser after the purchase but before the execution of if is sufficient to charge the purchaser with notice.

1 Chancery Cases 34, 22 E.R. 680

10 November [1663].

The plaintiff's bill was to be relieved upon a trust. And it charged the defendant with notice of that trust and that he had gotten a conveyance of the lands upon which the trust was had and that, at or before his taking the said conveyance, he had notice of the said trust for the plaintiff.

The defendant, by way of answer, denied that he had any notice of the trust at the time of his purchase or contract. And he pleaded that he was a purchaser for a valuable consideration.

It was insisted the plea was not good, because he did not say what the valuable consideration was, for 5s. was a valuable consideration but yet no equitable consideration.

The court declared that the plea in this case was well enough.

It was further insisted that the plea was founded upon the answer, *viz.* that the defendant had no notice etc. and that the point of notice was not well answered, in that the defendant denied notice at the time of the purchase only and the word 'purchase' might be understood when the contract for the purchase was made and it might be he had no notice then and might have notice after, before, or at the sealing of the conveyance and, if there was any notice before the conveyance to him was executed, that should charge the defendant and that it was so lately decreed in a cause between Sir William Wheeler and [*blank*] and Yarraway and Nicholas, by the Lord Chancellor.

And so the plea was overruled.

2 Freeman 175, 22 E.R. 1141

10 November, 15 Car. II [1663]. Lord Chancellor, Justice Tyrell.

The plaintiff's bill was to be relieved upon a trust, and it charged the defendant with notice and that yet he had gotten a conveyance and yet, on or before the conveyance, he had notice. The defendant, by way of answer, denying that he had notice at the time of purchase, for plea, says he is a purchaser on a valuable consideration.

Objection first: He ought to have expressed the money given for 5s. is a valuable consideration, but not equitable.

Curia: The plea is good as to that.

Second, the plea depends on the answer that he had no notice at the time of the purchase, which is not a sufficient denial of notice, for the purchase is equivocal and may mean the articles on agreement of purchase and so he might have notice at the time of the conveyance executed.

Curia: It has been always ruled that, if the purchaser, after articles, have notice before or at the executing of the conveyance, it shall defeat his title. And, therefore, it was resolved that the plea is not good.

Lord Nottingham, *Prolegomena*, p. 255

If a man enters into articles for the purchase of land and, before he has paid the whole purchase money or any part of it or before any conveyance be sealed, has notice given him of a trust or an equity, which he knew not of before, he may safely proceed without being charged with this trust, because he was innocently and ignorantly engaged before. Sir Thomas Wheeler's Case and several other cases *pro et con*. But the law is thus conceived at this day.

[Other reports of this case: 1 Eq. Cas. Abr. 38, 334, 21 E.R. 857, 1084.]

131

Garfoot v. Garfoot

(Ch. 1663)

A devise of land to be sold by executors is not a mere personal power that cannot be exercised after the deaths of the executors.

1 Chancery Cases 35, 22 E.R. 681

10 November [1663].

Lands were devised to the wife for life, afterwards, to be sold by the executor for younger children's portions. The executor dies. The wife dies. The younger children prefer their bill against the heir.

He demurs because it was but an authority in the executor, which is dead with them.

But the demurrer was overruled.

2 Freeman 176, 22 E.R. 1142

10 November, 15 Car. II [1663].

Lands were devised to the wife for life, afterwards, to be sold by the executors for the young children's portions. The executors die. The wife dies. The younger children prefer their bill against the heir.

He demurs because it is but an authority in the executors, which is now dead with them.

And the demurrer was overruled.

[Other reports of this case: 1 Eq. Cas. Abr. 264, 21 E.R. 1034.]

132

Raynes v. Lewis

(Ch. 1663)

A married woman can sue her husband for her separate maintenance without joining him as a co-plaintiff.

1 Chancery Cases 35, 22 E.R. 681

17 November [1663]. Regnes v. Lewis.

The demurrer was for that a married woman sued without her husband.

But she being to be relieved touching a separate maintenance agreed to by her husband, the court overruled the demurrer, declaring the wife might sue without her husband.

Nelson 88, 21 E.R. 797

The bill was brought by a married woman against her husband to be relieved concerning a separate maintenance agreed to be paid to her by her husband.

The defendant demurred, for that she sued without her husband.

But, for the reason aforesaid, the demurrer was overruled.

133

Williams v. Arthur

(Ch. 1663)

A negligently enrolled decree can be corrected after the death of the parties by means of a bill of revivor, but not by a scire facias.

1 Chancery Cases 37, 22 E.R. 682

24 November [1663]. The Lord Chancellor, Baron Turner.

A decretal order was produced in 1657 for several matters. And, then, after the cause had depended on account three years, a decree was drawn, wherein the first decretal order was recited, but part of the matter thereby decreed was omitted in the decretal part of the decree itself. And, soon after the decree was signed and enrolled, the defendant died. A *scire facias* was sued to revive, and, in the prosecution thereupon, the plaintiff discovered the omission, and so could not have the benefit of that part which was omitted in the decree that way, and, the defendant being dead, could not help that omission by a motion upon the surprise.

The bill now was a bill of revivor to revive so much of the decree as was omitted, as was alleged. Howbeit, in truth, the bill was to the whole decree.

It was pleaded that, the decree being enrolled, a bill of revivor did not lie, but a *scire facias* did.

[It was] ordered that the plea and demurrer be overruled.

2 Freeman 177, 22 E.R. 1143

24 November, 15 Car. II [1663].

A decretal order was pronounced in 1657 after it had depended on account for three years. The decree was drawn up reciting the first order but part of the matter there is omitted in the decretal part of the decree. The decree was signed and enrolled, the defendant died, and a *scire facias* was sued to revive.

But the plaintiff, discovering the omission and that he could not have a remedy that way nor could mend the decree as defective by surprise (the defendant being dead), upon any motion in court, he exhibits his bill of revivor to revive so much as was omitted. And, in truth, the words of the bill extended to revive the whole decree.

It was pleaded that, the decree being enrolled, a bill of revivor did not lie, but a *scire facias* be ordered and that the plea be overruled.

[Other reports of this case: 2 Eq. Cas. Abr. 180, 22 E.R. 154.]

134

Seaborne v. Blackstone

(Ch. 1663)

A creditor can be paid by payments to his wife where she regularly acts as his agent.

1 Chancery Cases 38, 22 E.R. 683

26 November [1663].

The wife received money due on a bond entered into by one to her husband. She usually received and paid the money. He got judgment on the bond.

[It was] ordered that he acknowledge satisfaction thereupon.

2 Freeman 178, 22 E.R. 1143

26 November 1663, 15 Car. II. Master of the Rolls.

The wife received money due upon a bond to her husband. She usually received and paid the money. He got a judgment on the bond.

It was ordered that he acknowledge satisfaction.

[Other reports of this case: 1 Eq. Cas. Abr. 61, 21 E.R. 874.]
[Reg. Lib. 1663 B, f. 121.]

135

Jones v. Done

(Ch. 1663)

An office can be seized in execution by a writ of extent.

1 Chancery Cases 39, 22 E.R. 683

In [this] case, a decree was made, whereby it was decreed that an office was extendible in law or equity.

136

Roberts v. Wynn

(Ch. 1663)

A court of equity can set aside a fraudulent will, though, in this case, no relief was granted.

Lincoln's Inn MS. Hill 125, f. 42v, pl. 1

Michaelmas [term] 15 Car. II, 1663. Wyn v. Roberts.

On a suggestion of divers misdemeanors in Cresset, Wyn obtained an order to examine thereto. Cresset demurred to the interrogatories, being concerning tampering with witness etc.

The court discharged all, because there was no affidavit whereby the charge [was] ascertained and none ought to be examined on oath in such a case unless first charged by an oath.

Mr. Roberts had the like order against Wyn. And his order [was] discharged also.

1 Chancery Reports 236, 21 E.R. 560

The bill is to be relieved against the will of John Bodvile, father of the plaintiff Sarah, pretended to be gotten by fraud and practice of the defendant Wynn, which will tends to disinherit the plaintiff Sarah, the said John Bodvile's only surviving daughter and heir, of a great estate in lands, and to settle the same on the two defendants, Griffith Wynn, son of the defendant, Thomas Wynn, and Thomas Bodvile, infants.

The case is that the said John Bodvile, deceased, upon his intermarriage with Anne, the daughter of Sir William Russel, and in consideration of a £5000 portion, settled the premises on himself and his heirs male on the body of the said Anne, remainder to his right heir. And the said John Bodvile died without issue male, by virtue whereof and of the said settlement, the premises would have descended to the plaintiff Sarah, who married the plaintiff, Mr. Roberts, son of the Lord Roberts, Lord Privy Seal, and who had issue by the said Sarah, two sons and two daughters, in the lifetime of the said John Bodvile, and who was so well satisfied with the said match that he did on the birth of the second son of the said plaintiff become godfather and named him Charles Bodvile Roberts. And he declared he would make him his heir with several other expressions. And he declared that, if the Lord Roberts would settle on his son, the plaintiff, an estate, he would so settle his estate that it should come to his said daughter Sarah and her heirs, whereupon, the Lord Roberts settled £3000 *per annum* upon his son, Mr. Roberts, and his issue on the body of the said Sarah. And, in the year 1660, the said Mr. Bodvile made his will, whereby he gave all his estate to the said Sarah for life, remainder to her son Charles in tail, and made the said plaintiff, Sarah, executrix. And he declared that, though he had since levied fines of all his estate, yet he did not in the least thereby intend to revoke the said will or disinherit his said daughter, nor would he give one foot of land away from his daughter Sarah and his grandson, Charles Bodvile. But, in December 1662, the defendant Wynn, by practice, got the said Bodvile to make another will, who, at that time, was very infirm, and which was twice published, whereby he settled all his estate in trustees for the use of two infants, *viz.*, one named Bodvile, an obscure child, and the other was the said defendant Wynn's son.

The defendant insisted that Bodvile, upon his marriage with the plaintiff Sarah's mother, had a £5000 portion and that Bodvile, upon the settlement made upon the said marriage, did tie nothing upon his daughter but £5000 in money and that upon condition that she married with his consent, and he reserved the power of his lands to himself, lest he should have issue male by a second wife, and, by this will, he gave £5000 to his said daughter, though she did marry without his consent, but with a proviso that they should not question his will or disturb or hinder his executors and that his said daughter Sarah, the plaintiff, married in 1657, but there was no reconciliation until the year 1660. But he had declared he would never settle his estate on his issue female and that the said Bodvile had always a great kindness for the defendant Wynn and his family and that Wynn had no hand in making or contriving the said will. So that the effect of the suit is to have the said will in 1662 set aside and made void.

This court, with the assistance of the judges and on reading several precedents on the plaintiff's part, declared they did not conceive it of any consequence or value that the defendants, for whom the estate is settled in the trustees, were infants and not privy to the fraud, for, if that should be admitted to bar the heir from relief, any third person might, for the advantage of his children or relations, by practice set up a will or deed, and put it out of the power of the court to set aside or make void such a will or deed. And they were also of opinion that the making of this will was not an act of prudence or honesty in Mr. Bodvile, but rather of great injury and injustice, the same tending to disinherit an heir and only child, being innocent and inoffensive, and to introduce strangers without any reason of affinity or merit. And it appeared Mr. Bodvile always intended to leave his estate to his daughter if she married with his consent. And

His Lordship [LORD CLARENDON] farther declared that, although the marriage of the plaintiff Sarah without Mr. Bodvile's, her father's, consent was a high trespass, insomuch that, if his passion had possessed him from that hour and he would have resolved to have punished it with a total disinherison, His Lordship would not have relieved her; nevertheless, it now appeared that he was reconciled before 1660 and well satisfied in the match and that he intended to settle his estate on the plaintiff, as by the will in 1661. And it appeared that the defendant Wynn was the contriver of this will and that Mr. Bodvile's promising to settle his estate on his daughter and her heirs induced the Lord Roberts to make the settlement of £3000 *per annum* on the plaintiff, Mr. Roberts, and his issue by the said plaintiff Sarah, which did carry in it a great circumstance of equity against the pretended will, although there was no such formal agreement executed, which, according to the course of proceedings, could in equity be ground enough of itself for a judicial decree against the said will.

His Lordship [LORD CLARENDON], with the judges, were of opinion that the said will was obtained by great fraud and circumvention of the defendant Wynn, but, by reason the precedents did not fully reach to this case, whereby there might be a decree without creating a precedent, which, if [there were] any one, His Lordship declared he would have decreed the cause. Therefore, His Lordship and the judges find it not fit at present to make a decree finally to determine this cause, yet they declared that there appeared so much fraud in the defendant Wynn in gaining the will and so much equity and justice in the plaintiff's cause that they would not dismiss the plaintiff's bill or relieve the defendants upon their bill. But the matter being fit to be relieved and yet not ripe for a decree, this court gave the plaintiff a year's time to take such further course against the said will as he should be advised and the injunction to continue.

The plaintiff petitioned the House of Lords, who, upon several long debates, referred it back to the Lord Chancellor to decree for either party according to justice and equity, although no precedent should be found for that purpose.

And His Lordship [LORD CLARENDON], with the judges, upon a several days' hearing of the matter, declared they could not relieve either plaintiff in this court, and dismissed the plaintiff's bill without costs, and dissolved the injunction.

[Reg. Lib. 15 Car. II, f. 434.]

137

Simmons v. Cornelius

(Ch. 1663–1664)

A court of equity will not enforce an oral contract where the earnest money paid was insubstantial.

1 Chancery Reports 241, 21 E.R. 561

The bill is to have an agreement in specie to be performed. The defendant demurred, for that there was but 20s. paid as earnest to bind the bargain, which is but an inconsiderable execution of the agreement, and, it being not under hand and seal, the court allowed of the demurrer.

[Reg. Lib. 15 Car. II, f. 73.]

138

Minshal v. Minshal

(Ch. 1663–1664)

A person who holds land without impeachment of waste can cut down and sell the timber thereon.

1 Chancery Reports 242, 21 E.R. 561

The plaintiff got an injunction to stay waste or the felling of timber trees from off the premises.

The defendant moves to dissolve the injunction, insisting that he has sworn in his answer that he has an estate of inheritance in the premises and has for fourteen years cut down timber growing upon the said premises and sold the same without interruption.

And, upon producing the settlement, which was made by the said defendant upon the marriage with his wife, thereby, it appeared that he had an estate in the premises in question without impeachment of waste.

His Lordship [Lord Clarendon] ordered the said injunction to be absolutely dissolved.

139

Field v. Clerk

(Ch. 1663–1664)

Where a debtor makes his creditor his executor, a bond given as a security is discharged, but not the underlying debt.

1 Chancery Reports 242, 21 E.R. 561

The defendant entered into a bond to the testator, and, after[wards], the testator makes the defendant his executor, whereupon the defendant insists the bond is thereby discharged in law.

This court declared that, though the bond was discharged in law, yet, in equity, the defendant ought to account for the arrears of rent thereby secured.

[Reg. Lib. 15 Car. II, f. 790.]

140

Hunby v. Johnson

(Ch. 1663–1664)

After a fair trial and a final judgment in a common law court, a court of equity will not grant any relief against that judgment.

1 Chancery Reports 243, 21 E.R. 562

The defendant won of the plaintiff playing at cards £105, which the plaintiff upon account did own to be due to the defendant, whereupon the defendant brought his action of the case, and declared on *indebitatus assumpsit* for £105 and upon an *insimul computaverunt* for £105, to which the plaintiff pleaded *non assumpsit*. And, upon a trial, a verdict passed for the defendant for £105 damages. And he has since taken out judgment and execution.

And, therefore, in respect there were only damages recovered, whereof the jurors were the proper judges, and for that the bill was exhibited after judgment and execution, as by the records and proceedings duly carried on, according to the rules of the Court of Common Pleas, the defendant demurs, and pleads, and demands judgment, whether he shall farther answer that part of the plaintiff's bill as concerns the verdict and judgment.

This court allowed the plea and demurrer.

[Reg. Lib. 15 Car. II, f. 293.]

141

Curtis v. Smallridge

(Ch. 1664)

A defendant in a common law action will not be relieved in equity against a judgment where he had the opportunity to present all of his evidence and make a complete defense in the common law court.

1 Chancery Cases 43, 22 E.R. 685

26 January [1664]. The Master of the Rolls.

The defendant's wife had pawned her husband's plate to the plaintiff for £110. The defendant in [an action of] trover for this recovered £115 damages against the plaintiff and a judgment for it.

A bill was to be relieved against this judgment, for that the defendant was privy to the pawning and had the £110.

And, the proofs being read, it appeared that the defendant had confessed so much, which, if it had been proved at the trial, it was agreed the defendant could not have recovered in the trover. And there being no proof now that the defendant at law could not by reason of any accident have his witnesses at the trial, the court would not on any neglect of his grant a new trial.

And it was insisted upon as a rule that nothing shall be a ground to direct a new trial to avoid a judgment at law that would not be a ground for a bill of review to reverse a decree, and a confession subsequent to a decree [is] no ground for a bill of review. Nor is the want of any evidence or matter which might have been used in the first cause and of which the party had then knowledge any ground for a bill of review. And here is no proof but that the plaintiff might have had the witnesses that were examined here at the trial.

And so this cause was dismissed.

2 Freeman 178, 22 E.R. 1143

26 January, 15 Car. II [1664].

The defendant's wife had pawned her husband's plate and the husband recovered £1500 in [an action of] trover. The plaintiff exhibited his bill here. And it appeared that the pawning was by the husband's consent and he received the money.

Curia: Because it does not appear that, by any accident, the defendant was hindered of his witnesses at the trial, we will not order a new trial. And it was taken for a rule that the court will not set aside a trial at law for any matter which might be made use of at the trial and, here, nothing appears but the defendant, at the trial, might have produced this evidence and we will not help his negligence. So there can be no bill of review for any matter which might have been made use of in the first cause or for any matter subsequent to the decree as the plaintiff's confession.

[Other reports of this case: 1 Eq. Cas. Abr. 377, 21 E.R. 1114, 2 Eq. Cas. Abr. 173, 22 E.R. 148.]
[Reg. Lib. 1662 A, f. 403.]

142

Byron v. Balston

(Ch. 1664)

A court of equity has the discretion to dispense with the general rule that a bill of review will not be granted before the final decree has been fully performed.

An objection of the lack of a guardian ad litem *for an infant litigant must be raised before the final decree is entered.*

Lord Nottingham, *Prolegomena*, p. 293

28 January, 15 Car. II [1664].

If a decree be made for the payment of money, no bill of review lies until the money be paid and obedience yielded to the decree, which is a just and necessary rule. Yet the court does sometimes dispense with this rule according to circumstances. They did so in the Case of the Lord Biron, who was admitted to his bill of review against Balston without paying £1900 decreed to Balston. But this was by the recommendation of the House of Lords. Yet it has been done often since, in December 1672, by Shaftesbury, Chancellor.

In the Case of Biron and Balston, the error assigned was that the decree was made against Biron, an infant, and Hutchison, his guardian, whereas, in truth, no guardian was assigned in that cause, but Hutchison was the guardian in another cause and only administrator *durante minore aetate* in this. And it was urged to be error in substance to proceed against an infant without a guardian, against whom the infant may have a remedy on faint pleading.

And HALE, Chief Baron, cited a case where depositions against an infant in Chancery were refused to be read in evidence at common law, because the order for assigning a guardian was not produced.

Yet, by BRIDGEMAN [C.J.] and HALE [C.B.], and all the justices, [it was] resolved this was no error: first, because the formality in Chancery should not be too accurate; second, if a guardian be once assigned and the order of assignment be lost, yet the decree is good, for, if a warrant of attorney be lost, the court of common law will cause a new warrant to be filed to salve the error and so the Chancery may cause a new order of assignment to be entered; third, the presumptions of fact that a guardian was once assigned are very vehement, not only by the title of several orders, but by the strenuous defence etc.; fourth, there is an *admittitur* as well as an assignment of a guardian, and an *admittitur* may amount to an assignment; fifth, [there are] no precedents after such a defence of a decree reversed for want of a guardian assigned. Therefore, the decree was affirmed.

[Earlier proceedings in this case: 5 Russell 235, 38 E.R. 1021.]

143

Sands v. Darrell

(Ch. 1664)

Timber cannot be taken from land that is under an order of sequestration for contempt of court.

Lincoln's Inn MS. Misc. 497, p. 162, pl. 1

4 February, Hilary [term] 15 & 16 Car. II.

Lands were decreed to be liable to pay £500 *per annum* for the life of A. etc. And [there was a writ of] sequestration and an injunction for the possession to that purpose. The defendant, against the injunction, enters upon the land and received the profits to the value of £1972, and, thereupon, he was decreed to pay it.

And, after the death of A., it was decreed that the sequestration should continue against the defendant for the payment of that money.

Now, the defendant moved to have liberty to fell timber to raise money for his subsistence, alleging that the sequestrator had only the possession and the perception of the annual profits by the course of the court and, therefore, it would be no prejudice to him to have this granted.

But Sir Harbottle Grimston, Master of the Rolls, refused, for, first, this invades the decree, which is for the quiet possession, which will be disturbed if the defendant enters to cut down timber, second, the defendant not having performed the decree by the payment of the money, he shall not receive any favor of the court while he stands in contempt, third, if he will with the sale of this timber pay the plaintiff his debt and so discharge the sequestration, there might be some reason, but, for him to raise money to other purposes, he shall not be favored, and, unless the plaintiff will consent, he shall not have liberty to fell.

[Other copies of this report: Lincoln's Inn MS. Hill 83, p. 152, pl. 3.]

144

Baker v. Shelbury

(Ch. 1664)

After an apprentice has served his time, he can sue in equity to have his former master sue on his articles within a short period of time or be estopped to do so.

1 Chancery Cases 70, 22 E.R. 700

10 February.

The bill being to be relieved against an apprentice bond and articles and to have them up, upon the hearing, [it was] ordered that the defendant do within a certain time, *viz.* one year, bring his action and go to trial thereupon for his damages or, in default thereof, the bond and articles are to be delivered up. And the reason that was given was that, if it were at the defendant's choice to stay his action as long as he pleased, he would stay until the plaintiff's witnesses were dead. And it was said it was usual in the case after apprentices were out of their time to exhibit a bill to put their master to sue their covenants within a certain time or else to deliver up their indentures.

2 Freeman 184, 22 E.R. 1149

10 February 1664.

It is usual when an apprentice is out of his time to prefer his bill to force his master to sue his covenants within a year or be foreclosed. *Semble in auters cases*, for witnesses may die.

[Other reports of this case: 1 Eq. Cas. Abr. 78, 307, 21 E.R. 891, 1065.]

145

Noble v. Floater

(Ch. 1664)

A court of equity will not give relief against a bond that was given without consideration.

Gray's Inn MS. 35, p. 529, pl. 1

Easter term, 16 Car. II.

At the Rolls, the case was [thus]. The defendant Floater pretended himself vicar of Tillingham in Essex. And being about to leave the living, he desired the plaintiff to collect certain monies due to him from several persons of that parish for tithes to the value of £19 9s., which the plaintiff agreeing to, the defendant gave him a letter of attorney with a particular of the tithes said to be due annexed thereto, [and the plaintiff] gave him a bond of £38 to pay the said sum. And, in truth, he was never the lawful vicar, nor was any of the said tithes then due, but all were paid before. This rested from 1648 to 1662. Then, the defendant sues the bond, and the plaintiff prays relief against it.

But the bill, upon the hearing, was dismissed. And these two things were resolved by the Master of the Rolls [GRIMSTON]. First, if a bond be given without any consideration, this court relieves not against it; second, if a consideration was suggested which was not true and, thereupon, a bond given, as in this case, this court will not relieve against it, for the party might have looked better to it. Roll's Reports 111.[1]

146

Paston v. Crowe

(Ch. 1664)

If both parties have equities on their side, the court of equity will consider all of the points of equity, but, if one party has both equity and common law rights, the court of equity will leave the parties to their action at common law.[2]

[1] *Glanville's Case* (K.B. 1614), 1 Rolle Rep. 111, 81 E.R. 365, also 118 Selden Soc. 440.

[2] This is not what this garbled report says, but it is what the court probably (and should have) said, but the reporter, not being a regular practitioner in the equity courts, misunderstood the holding of the court. This case illustrates the maxim that, where the equities are equal, *aequitas sequitur legem*.

Gray's Inn MS. 35, p. 529, pl. 2

[It was the] opinion of the Master of the Rolls [Grimston], if the plaintiff [Sir Robert Paston] has equity and the defendant has also equity, one shall be relieved without the other. But, if the plaintiff has equity and the defendant has [equity] also and the defendant may have relief at common law, the plaintiff shall have relief and the defendant not.

147

Kingston v. Manwaring

(Ch. 1664)

In this case, the court granted relief for the plaintiff based solely on evidence of a deed without any proof of or production of the deed itself.

1 Chancery Cases 47, 22 E.R. 687

4 May [1664]. The Lord Chancellor, Judge Brown, the Master of the Rolls. Kinaston v. Maynwearing.

The plaintiffs were the children of the defendant's sister. And the defendant's mother, during his minority, as his guardian, managed his estate. And, as to the lands in question, it was pretended those were settled by the defendant's father on the plaintiff's mother, being the defendant's sister and the defendant's mother and guardian, for about two years before the plaintiff's mother's marriage, put her into possession of those lands, and, upon her marriage, articled that those lands should be settled on her and her heirs. And, to those articles, the defendant, then an infant, was a witness.

Upon this matter (though there was no proof of the deed whereby it was pretended the defendant's father settled the lands upon the plaintiff's mother), the court decreed against the defendant upon color of equity for want of the deed.

And yet there was no proof of a deed, which was conceived very hard for the court to raise an equity out of a deed when it was not proved.

Nelson 94, 21 E.R. 798

The plaintiffs were the children of the defendant's sister. And the said defendant being an infant, his mother took care of his estate during his minority and as guardian to him.

And, upon a bill exhibited by the plaintiffs to discover a deed, the question was whether the defendant's father had settled the lands now in demand on the plaintiff's mother.

The proof was that, about two years before her marriage, he had put her in the possession of these lands and had articled upon her said marriage that the same should be settled on her and her heirs, to which articles, the defendant, then an infant, was a witness. But there was not any other proof of such deed of settlement.

Yet the court decreed for the plaintiff.

But it was conceived a hard case for the court to decree an equity upon a deed, which had no other proof.

148

Beautry v. Ibson

(Ch. 1664)

Marriage is a good consideration to support a marriage settlement contract.

In this case, the release in issue was not intended to include a certain lease.

1 Chancery Cases 46, 22 E.R. 687

4 May [1664]. The Lord Chancellor, Baron Turner. Bawtrey v. Ibson.

William Ibson, being possessed of a term for years from the Vicars Choral of York, assigned the same to trustees, and then he buys the inheritance from the trustees for the sale of church land. And, before marriage, he covenants to stand seised to the use of himself and wife for life for a jointure.

In 1659, William Ibson died, having made his will. After his death, his relict entered and held the lands. And then, upon an agreement with his executors for money paid, she released to them the personal estate of the testator and all demands for the same. Soon after, the king being restored, the title of the inheritance under the said purchase became void. The widow married the plaintiff, and they two brought their bill against the executors of William Ibson and the assignees and trustees of the lease. And it was to the end that, though the inheritance was evicted, they might hold for so long of the term as the jointress should live and that the release might not bar her of that because [it was] not intended when the release was given, nor was the lease then looked on as part of the personal estate.

The first question was whether, the inheritance being gone, the lease which was to attend it should go now according to the use in the covenant to stand seised.

[It was] resolved in this case, it being a settlement in marriage and so on a consideration, it should go to the wife for so many years as she lived. But it was said it would have been another case between the heir and executor of the covenantees.

The second question was if the release of the demands to the personal estate should bar the wife of the benefit of the term.

And, it appearing by the proof that the agreement which begot the release was before the title to the inheritance was avoided and concerning that which was then looked upon as a personal estate and not touching the lease and that, notwithstanding the release, the wife continued the possession, it was resolved the release should not bar or prejudice the plaintiff's title in right to the lease. And it was decreed that the plaintiff should hold for so many years as she lived and that, if the lease were renewed, she paying proportionably to her estate for life, that the jointress should hold for so many years as she lived, and then to go to the executors.

2 Freeman 179, 22 E.R. 1145

4 May, 16 Car. II [1664]. Master of the Rolls.

Ibson, possessed of a church lease for years, buys the fee of the trustees for sale, and then covenants to stand seised etc. for his wife for life. His wife releases the personal estate to the executors. The church is restored. And she sues here to have the term against the release as long as she lived.

Curia [Grimston]: The lease was to attend the inheritance, and shall go where the inheritance was to go, *viz.* to the wife etc.

Second, as to the release, it appears by the proof that it was not intended the term should pass, and, therefore, nothing of that shall be included to go to the executor, and the release shall extend no farther than the agreement which begot it.

149

Lord O'Bryan v. Crump

(Ch. 1664)

Where a person bought land with money borrowed from a third person, when the land is later sold, the debt will be repaid from the purchase money.

79 Selden Soc. 884

4 May, 16 Car. II.

It appeared that Crump had been engaged with the Lord Dacres for the most part of the purchase money with which he bought the manors of Downash and Bowles. And, therefore, Lord Dacres took the conveyances in the name of Crump.

It was resolved by the advice of Orlando Bridgeman and Hale that the land ought to indemnify Crump and, when sold, the money to be applied in the first place for that purpose.

150

Freak v. Horseley

(Ch. 1664)

In a suit to foreclose by a mortgagee's heir, the mortgagee's executor is a necessary party.

1 Chancery Cases 51, 22 E.R. 690

12 May [1664]. Freak v. Hearsey.

The heir of the mortgagee exhibited a bill to have the mortgagor pay the money or to be decreed to make further assurance and be foreclosed of the redemption.

The demurrer was because the executor of the mortgagee, who might have a title to the mortgage money, was no party.

And the demurrer was allowed.

2 Freeman 180, 22 E.R. 1145

11 May, 16 Car. II [1664].

The heir of the mortgagee exhibited a bill to have the mortgagor redeem or else be foreclosed.

The defendant demurred, because the executor, who might have title to the money, was not a party.

And the demurrer was allowed.

Nelson 93, 21 E.R. 798

Lord Chancellor and Mr. Justice Brown.

The heir of the mortgagee exhibited a bill to have the mortgagor pay the money or to be decreed to make a farther assurance and also to be foreclosed of the equity of redemption.

The defendant demurred to the bill, because the executor of the mortgagee was not made a party, for, probably, he might have a title to the mortgage money.

And the demurrer was for that reason allowed.

[Other reports of this case: 2 Eq. Cas. Abr. 77, 427, 22 E.R. 67, 364.]
[Reg. Lib. 1663 A, f. 734.]

151

Goodrick v. Brown

(Ch. 1664)

A conveyance ordered by a court of equity to be made to a particular purpose operates only as to that particular purpose in equity, though, in law, it would operate farther.

A conveyance made by a beneficiary of a trust transfers the ownership of the trust.

1 Chancery Cases 49, 22 E.R. 688

11 May [1664]. The Lord Chancellor, the Master of the Rolls, Justice Wyndham,

[It was], first, resolved that, whereas, by a decree of this court, a fine was levied to a particular end and purpose, which would operate farther in point of law than to that end which the decree ordered it, that such fine should not be suffered in equity to work farther than the decree intended;

Second, that the fine or recovery of a *cestui que trust* should bar and transfer the trust, as it should an estate at law if it were upon a consideration, but, otherwise, Justice WYNDHAM doubted of it, for he said he looked upon this court as remedial to those that come in upon a consideration etc.;

Third, that, whereas the person that suffered the recovery was tenant for life in point of law and there had been an agreement precedent to the recovery by the ancestor that was dead for the settling of the premises so as to have made the tenant for life tenant in tail, that the recovery should be good in equity and should work upon the agreement.

Against which, it was objected that the recovery was a willful forfeiture in point of law and was voluntary and [there was] no consideration. And so the truth appeared that the defendant was as near in blood to the first ancestor as the plaintiff. And, if this court would maintain a voluntary recovery of a trust raised upon a conveyance, there was not so much in this case, for here was but an agreement and, though that agreement might upon a bill have been decreed, yet there being never any such bill, the recovery ought not to be supported.

As to this point and the second, the judge would not deliver any opinion. But the court decreed it.

2 Freeman 180, 22 E.R. 1145

11 May, 16 Car. II [1664].

By a decree, a fine levied to a particular purpose shall operate only as to that particular purpose in equity, though, in law, it would operate farther. A fine and recovery of a *cestui que trust* should operate as strongly as an estate at law, and, to the same purpose, if it were on any consideration.

Judge WYNDHAM doubted whether, otherwise, this court would give relief.

Also, one, being tenant for life by a conveyance and, afterwards, the reversioner and ancestor, in consideration of blood etc., articles to settle the estate on him in tail so that, in equity, he had a trust in tail in the estate, the court allowed of his recovery, though but a tenant for life at that time in law.

Yet, it was objected that he ought first to have exhibited his bill and have had his estate decreed to him in tail, according to the articles.

To which, the court answered not, but decreed *ut supra*.

[Other reports of this case: 1 Eq. Cas. Abr. 255, 21 E.R. 1029.]
[Reg. Lib. 1663 A, f. 759.]

152

Thirveton v. Collier

(Ch. 1664)

A contract for an enclosure will be specifically enforced even though all of the persons who might have an interest in the common not be made parties to the suit.

1 Chancery Cases 48, 22 E.R. 688

11 May [1664]. The Lord Chancellor, Master of the Rolls.

The bill was to have a decree for an enclosure upon an agreement. It appeared by the bill that there were to be eighteen allotments and there were but fifteen parties to the suit. And so it was objected by the defendants that all the parties to the agreement were not parties to the suit and also that there were other persons that claimed common on the ground to be enclosed that were not parties either to the agreement or suit and so to decree that agreement would be to do a manifest wrong, and be an occasion of suits and quarrels.

Whereunto, it was answered by the plaintiffs that, though there were eighteen shares, some of the persons were to have two shares so as that made up the eighteen and that there were others [who] had common but by vicinage. But nothing of this appeared to be alleged by the plaintiffs.

It was decreed, nevertheless, that the agreement for the enclosure should be performed. And a commission was awarded to set out each person's title. And the court decreed that, if there were any that had interest and were not parties to the agreement, they could not be bound, and so be at no prejudice, but, however, it should not be in the power of one or two willful persons to oppose a public good.

Nelson 79, 21 E.R. 794

The bill was to have a decree for an enclosure upon an agreement made by the parties for that purpose. But, there being eighteen shares and but fifteen parties to the suit, it was objected that all the parties to the agreement were not made parties to the suit and, also, that other persons claimed a right of common in the soil now to be enclosed, who were neither parties to the suit nor the agreement, and, therefore, to decree that agreement would be to do manifest wrong and occasion many suits and quarrels.

To which it was answered that, though there were eighteen shares and but fifteen parties, yet some of those parties were to have two shares, and that there was one [who] had common but it was by reason of vicinage.

Whereupon, it was decreed that the agreement for the enclosure should be performed. And a commission was awarded to set out the share of each person. And the court declared that, if there were any who were not parties and who had any interest, they could not be bound by this decree and so be at no prejudice, but that it should not be in the power of two or three obstinate persons to oppose and hinder a public good.

3 Chancery Reports 13, 21 E.R. 714

Lord Chancellor, Master of the Rolls.

The bill was to have a decree for an enclosure upon an agreement. It appearing by the bill that there were by the agreement to be eighteen allotments and but fifteen parties to the suit. And so it was objected by the defendants that all the parties to the agreement were not parties to the suit and also that other persons claimed common in the ground to be enclosed that were not parties either to the agreement or suit and so to decree that agreement would be to do a manifest wrong and be the occasion of suits and troubles.

Whereunto, it was answered by the plaintiff that, though there were eighteen sharers, some of the fifteen were to have two shares so as they made up the eighteen and that there were others who had a common but by reason of vicinage. But nothing of this alleged by the plaintiff appeared.

[It was] decreed, nevertheless, that the agreement for the enclosure should be performed. And a commission then was awarded to set out each person's lot. And the court said that, if there were any that had an interest and were not parties to the agreement, they could not be bound by the decree and so at no prejudice and, however, that it should not be in the power of one or two willful persons to oppose a public good.

[Other reports of this case: 1 Eq. Cas. Abr. 103, 21 E.R. 913.]

153

Scott v. Rayner

(Ch. 1664)

A court of equity will enjoin execution of a common law final judgment that was obtained by a fraud on the court.

1 Chancery Cases 50, 22 E.R. 689

11 May [1664]. At the Rolls, the Master of the Rolls.

The defendant had sued the plaintiff at law on a single bond entered into by the plaintiff to the defendant's husband, the defendant suing there as administratrix to her late husband. The bill here was that, in truth, the defendant's husband was not dead.

And there appearing some probable evidence that he was not dead, but concealed himself, and the defendant, pending this suit, having got a judgment against the plaintiff, the court awarded an injunction to stay execution, and directed a trial at law to be whether the defendant's husband was dead or not.

Nelson 93, 21 E.R. 798

An action was brought at law by an administratrix to her late husband upon a single bill for the payment of money due to him.

The defendant in that action exhibits his bill, suggesting that, in truth, the husband was not dead, but concealed himself, and, pending this suit, the administratrix got judgment at law.

But the court granted an injunction, and directed an issue at law to try whether the husband was dead or not.

154

Ward v. Lake

(Ch. 1664)

A demurrer does not lie to a subpoena scire facias.

1 Chancery Cases 50, 22 E.R. 689

12 May [1664].

The demurrer was to a subpoena in the nature of a *scire facias*. And it was because he that brought the subpoena did not thereby allege himself to be heir or executor to him that had the decree.

[It was] resolved that there never was any demurrer of this nature before and the subpoena was no record, nor anywhere filed, and so not to be demurred to. But the cause was to be showed upon the return of the writ on the order. And the order did mention him that brought the writ to be both heir and executor. So this demurrer was conceived very ridiculous, and overruled.

2 Freeman 180, 22 E.R. 1146

12 May, 16 Car. II [1664]. Lord Chancellor, Justice Brown.

A demurrer was filed to a subpoena in the nature of a *scire facias* because the plaintiff therein did not allege himself heir or executor to him that had the decree.

[It was] resolved the demurrer is naught and never were any such before, for the subpoena is no record, nor anywhere filed. But, if there be any defect in the order for the subpoena, cause must be shown at the return of the writ. But the order mentioned the plaintiff to be both heir and executor.

3 Chancery Reports 15, 21 E.R. 714

12 May, 16 Car. II [1664].

The demurrer was to a subpoena in the nature of a *scire facias*. And it was because he that brought the subpoena did not thereby allege himself to be the heir or executor to him in the decree.

It was resolved that there never was a demurrer of this nature before and the subpoena was no record, nor anywhere filed, and so it is not to be demurred to, but the cause to be shown at the return of the writ upon the order. And the order mentioned him that brought the writ to be both heir and executor. And, therefore, this demurrer was conceived very ridiculous and overruled accordingly.

155

Glover v. Portington

(Ch. 1664–1665)

A bill of review cannot be brought by a successful plaintiff on the ground that the judgment was insufficient.

1 Chancery Cases 51, 22 E.R. 690

14 May [1664].

Joss Glover, the plaintiff's father, for securing £50 *per annum* to Anne, his mother-in-law, for life in lieu of £50 *per annum* which she had chargeable on other lands of his which he was about to sell, 11 May, 13 Car. I [1637], surrenders certain copyhold lands (of gavelkind) to Thomas Roll, brother of Anne, and his heirs in trust for Anne upon condition that, if Joss Glover, his heirs, or assigns paid Anne £50 *per annum* during life, the surrender to be void. Thomas Roll was admitted. Joss Glover failing to pay the £50 *per annum* 4 July, 20 Car. I [1644], Thomas Roll surrendered the premises to the use of Anne for life, the reversion to himself and his heirs (but in trust for her and her heirs). She was admitted. Thomas Roll died. The premises descended to his children and grandchildren, some whereof yet infants and one a lunatic. 22 January 1651, Anne, by will, directed that the arrears of the £50 *per annum* should be paid to her executor, which the defendant Portington is, to such purpose as therein is expressed, and declared that her nephews, the sons, and grandchildren of Thomas Roll should permit her executors to receive the rents and profits towards the payment of legacies, and she appoints her said nephew and grandchildren that, if the plaintiff, being heir of Joss Glover, should within three years after her death pay her executor all the arrears of the £50 *per annum*, that they should surrender to the plaintiff and his heirs, and remit the plaintiff £100 thereof, and the interest of the whole, so as he paid the arrears in three parts. And she declared that, if the plaintiff failed to pay the arrears in three years, the premises should be surrendered to her executors. And, the arrears being paid, she wills her executors to pay the overplus to the plaintiff and to surrender to him. And, in July 1654, Anne died.

And, in February next following, the bill was exhibited to have a discovery of what was paid and that, paying all arrears but the £100 and interest, he might have a surrender from the Rolls, who claimed the estate to their own use. This cause was through the infancy of the defendant so delayed that their answers could not be gotten and through the absence of the plaintiff out of England, which was nigh ten years.

And, now, it was decreed that, if the plaintiff would redeem, he should pay all the arrears and interest.

Serjeant *Fountaine* drew a petition to the Master of the Rolls to rehear it on the point of interest, and, afterwards, moved it in court.

And the Lord Keeper [LORD CLARENDON] (the Master of the Rolls [Grimston] being present) recommended it to him to rehear it. And, as to the point of the £100 of the principal, which was to be abated by the will, the bill came within six months after the death of Anne, and it was not safe to go to a hearing without the trustees, whereby to have a surrender, and they were in infancy and a lunatic, which was the principal reason the cause depended so long.

Serjeant *Fountaine* did upon a discourse between him and A.B. agree it was against the plaintiff as to the £100 (though *Churchill* was clear of another opinion), for Serjeant *Fountaine* said that it being a voluntary conditional gift, the plaintiff ought, if he would have the benefit of it, to have performed it by payment within three years, and sought a re-conveyance after. But, as to the matter of the interest that was stronger, for that the will appointed that, the arrears being paid, the land should be surrendered to the plaintiff. And it was said the testator intended a benefit to the plaintiff by the appointment, and, if he should pay the arrears and interest, it was no benefit, for, then, the premises without such appointment ought to be surrendered to the plaintiff, for the same were not forfeited above ten years when the bill was exhibited.

The Master of the Rolls [GRIMSTON], upon the re-hearing 25 June, Car. II, confirmed the first decree. Serjeant *Fountaine*, Master *Churchill*, and Master *Keck* [were] for the plaintiff; Master Solicitor [General] *Finch*, and divers others [were] for the defendants.

And, afterwards, there was a bill of review to reverse this decree, to which Portington demurred and insisted there was no error in the decree.

And this demurrer was argued in Trinity Term, 1665, before the Lord Chancellor [LORD CLARENDON] and Baron RAINSFORD. And, in the debate, it was insisted by the defendant's counsel that this was a bill of review of a strange nature, for that the plaintiff, who had the decree, did by his bill of review complain that he had not enough decreed, whereas, if a review lies, it lies only for him against whom the decree or dismission is. After long debate, the demurrer was overruled.[1]

2 Freeman 182, 22 E.R. 1147

14 May, 16 Car. II [1664]. Master of the Rolls.

[1] Sic in text.

A mortgagee, by a will, remits part of the mortgage money and all interest, provided the rest be paid within three years or, if the rest be paid in three years, the mortgagor, not paying in three years, loses the benefit of that bequest, for the gift was voluntary.

And, in this case, upon a demurrer, it was resolved that, if a man has less decreed for him than he would have, he shall not bring a bill of review. But a bill of review lies only for him against whom the decree or dismission is. And, after long debate, the demurrer was, therefore, allowed.

And note, in the case *supra*, the mortgagor suing to redeem was decreed to pay the whole money *causa qua supra*, and the decree was confirmed on a rehearing. And *Fountaine*, of counsel with the plaintiff mortgagor, agreed it to be so.

Nelson 96, 21 E.R. 799

John Glover, the plaintiff's father, for securing £50 *per annum* to Anne, his mother-in-law, during her life in lieu of so much which was charged on other lands for her life and which he was now about to sell, did surrender certain copyhold lands of the tenure of gavelkind to Thomas Rolt, brother of the said Anne, and his heirs in trust for the said Anne and upon condition that, if the said Glover, his heirs, or assigns paid Anne £50 *per annum* during her life, then the surrender to be void. Thomas Rolt was admitted. And, afterwards, the said Glover failing to pay the £50 *per annum*, Rolt surrendered the premises to the use of Anne for life, remainder to himself and his heirs, but in trust for her and her heirs. Rolt, the trustee, died. The lands descended to his heirs, *viz.* children and grandchildren, some of them infants and one of them a lunatic.

Afterwards, Anne devised that the arrears of the £50 *per annum* should be paid to her executors. And, having made the defendant Partington her executrix and declared that the children and grandchildren of Rolt should permit her said executrix to receive the rents and profits of the lands towards the payment of certain legacies she had bequeathed and that, if the plaintiff, who was the heir of the said Glover, should within three years after her decease pay unto her said executrix all the arrears of the said £50 *per annum*, then they should surrender to him and his heirs. And she remitted £100 of the principal debt and the interest of the whole in case he paid the rest within that time. But, if he failed, then the premises should be surrendered to her said executrix, and, the arrears being paid, then she was to pay the surplus to the plaintiff, and to surrender to him. And soon afterwards, she died.

After whose death, the plaintiff exhibited a bill against the executrix and against the children and grandchildren of Rolt to have a discovery of what was paid and that, upon payment of the arrears, excepting £100 and the interest, the lands might be surrendered to him.

But it was decreed that, if he would redeem, he should pay all the arrears and interest and that, upon payment thereof, the lands should be surrendered.

This cause was afterwards reheard upon the point of interest, for, as to the payment of the £100, it is true the bill came in six months after the death of Anne and a long time within the three years in which it was appointed to be paid. But, by reason of the infancy and lunacy of the defendants and other accidents, the cause depended for many years. And it was not safe to go to a hearing to obtain a surrender without their being made parties. And, for this reason, he suffered the three years long since to lapse.

But all this was not held a sufficient reason to retard the payment of the £100, because, the remittance of it being a voluntary and conditional gift to the plaintiff, he ought to have performed the condition by the payment of the rest of the money if he would have any benefit of the gift. And, if the lands could not be surrendered to him at the time he paid the money in performance of the condition, he should have sought for a surrender afterwards, when it might have been lawfully made.

Then, as to the matter of interest, the counsel insisted that was strongest for the plaintiff, for the will appointed that, the arrears being paid, the lands should be surrendered to him. Now certainly, some benefit was intended for him by this appointment. But it would be none if he should pay all the arrears and interest, for, in such case, the lands must be surrendered whether the will had made any such appointment or not.

But, notwithstanding this reason, the decree was confirmed.

Serjeant *Fountaine*, Mr. *Churchill*, Mr. *Keck*, and Mr. Solicitor [General] *Finch* [were] for the defendants.

Afterwards, there was a bill of review brought by the plaintiff to reverse this decree, to which Partington, the executrix, demurred, and insisted there was no error in it.

And the demurrer being argued before the Lord Chancellor [LORD CLARENDON], assisted by Baron RAINSFORD, it was insisted that this was a bill of review of a very strange nature, because the plaintiff, who had a decree in his favor, *viz.* that the lands should be surrendered to him, complained that he had not enough decreed, when, in truth, a bill of review lay properly for him against whom the decree or dismission was pronounced. And, after long debate, the demurrer was allowed.

Lincoln's Inn MS. Hill 125, f. 48v

Anne Glover had due to her [for] some years an annuity of £50 *per annum* secured to her by a mortgage to her friends by Roger. The inheritance of the land, charged with this annuity and mortgage, was come to the plaintiff. Anne forgives the defendant £100 of the arrears and all the interest if he paid £300 within three years. And she willed her trustees to convey to the plaintiff on the payment of the £300.

The plaintiff exhibited his bill against the defendant, executor of Anne, to pay the money and against the trustees to have a re-assurance. The trustees were in by descent. And one of them [was] an idiot. The other answered not, but stood long in contempt for want of an answer. The bill was exhibited within the three years, but some years passed before the defendants, the trustees, answered. But the defendants, the executors did answer in time.

At the hearing, the Master of the Rolls [GRIMSTON] decreed a redemption but paying the whole arrears and damages, although it was objected that the plaintiff sued within the three years and it was no reason he should pay and not have a re-assurance, the will directing a re-assurance.

A bill of review [was] brought and dismissed. But the reason given by the Lord Chancellor [LORD CLARENDON] was not expressed on the merits, but because the plaintiff did not appeal. Yet, in truth, the plaintiff did appeal, and the Lord Chancellor referred it back to the Master, who confirmed his former order.

[Other reports of this case: 2 Eq. Cas. Abr. 174, 22 E.R. 149.]
[Reg. Lib. 1663 A, f. 751.]

156

Blackston v. Master of Hemsworth Hospital

(Ch. 1664)

Where rents from lands are given to a charitable use, the charity is entitled to receive the full value even though the trustees made leases for less than the full rental value.

Herne & Duke 96

Robert Holgate, late archbishop of York,[1] by his will, dated 27 April 1555, did devise to Sir William Peters, etc., whom he made executor of his will, and their heirs divers houses and lands in Yorkshire to the intent to erect an hospital in Hemsworth [Yorkshire] for one master and twenty brethren and sisters to continue forever and directed an allowance to each of them, being about the then value of the lands and authorized his executors to sell his goods and divers of his lands and that the executors should keep no goods or profits besides their charges in their hands but bestow the same to the glory of God and the health of his soul.[2] The surviving executors proved the will and became seised, and, 17 March 3 & 4 P. & M. [1557], renting a license to erect the said hospital, ordered a common seal, etc., settled 100 marks *per annum* upon the master and brethren, the lands being worth £500 *per annum*. The executor sold the lands, reserving only 100 marks *per annum* to the hospital.

[In] 11 Jac. [1613 × 1614], the vicar and churchwardens of Hemsworth exhibited a bill in Chancery against such as had the lands. And upon the hearing,

[1] H. L. Parish, 'Holgate, Robert (1481/2–1555)', *Oxford Dictionary of National Biography*, vol. 27, pp. 641–643.

[2] W. K. Jordan, *The Charities of Rural England* (1978), pp. 258–259.

Sir Edward Philips, Master of the Rolls, increased the 100 marks *per annum* to £100, declaring that he did not conceive that the defendants' fines with proclamations barred the charity. Afterwards, the master, brethren, and sisters of the hospital, conceiving the former bill to be exhibited by practice, exhibited their bill against the possessors of the land and did set forth that the lands were given to the hospital and that, in breach of trust, the lands had been conveyed away in fee farm, reserving upon all but 100 marks *per annum* to the hospital.

The defendants answered and set forth their titles and claimed the lands, some by descents and others by conveyances and fines for valuable considerations.

The Lord Ellesmere and the judges declared that there had been an apparent breach of trust and that the hospital had been abused by being kept from what, by the donor, was meant unto them, *viz.* the land itself and not only a dry rent, being appointed by the donor for the good and benefit of the hospital. Neither did His Lordship conceive that the fines with proclamations ought to be a bar to the said charitable use and that all the purchasers claiming under the trust, which was broken, and there being a violent presumption that they had notice of the trusts, as well [as] that they that sold the said lands, could not make any title but by the will of the said archbishop, as also for that they did all pay rents to the said hospital.

And in 12 Car. I [1637], this matter came again in question[1] before the Lord Keeper Coventry, who directed a commission to be awarded upon the Statute of Charitable Uses.[2] The commissioners made a decree for the whole lands, to which exceptions were put in by one Brigg, who claimed under a purchase made by one Mr. Wymarke, who, pretending the crown was entitled to the lands, had obtained a patent thereof from Queen Elizabeth as concealed lands. The Lord Keeper, assisted by Judge Hutton, Judge Jones, and Judge Berkeley (no color of proof being offered that the same were concealed lands, as His Lordship [said], but only the patent itself), His Lordship did see no cause to give allowance to the patent to overthrow a charitable use. And His Lordship, having perused the evidences, confirmed the decree as to all but some chantry lands in the patent, which were not the archbishop's, and that the hospital should hold the lands forever. But, because the exceptant had laid out much money in building upon the hospital lands, he should have a lease for one-and-twenty years, at £120 *per annum* being above [the old rent of] £50 *per annum*, increase of what had been formerly paid to the hospital, the lands being above £150 *per annum* above the old rent of £70 *per annum* reserved to the hospital, and so would be worth £130 to the lessees above the rent which they should pay for it, and a lease was made accordingly.

Afterwards, one Blackston put in new exceptions to the said decree, to which the hospital pleaded the former proceedings. And in October, 15 Car. II [1663],

---

[1] Orders of 4 February and 22 May 1637: Public Record Office C.33/171, ff. 152, 161v, 352v.

[2] Stat. 43 Eliz. I, c. 4 (*SR*, IV, 968–970).

the matter was heard before the Lord Chancellor CLARENDON and Mr. Justice TYRELL, and the plea [was] allowed.

And 18 June, 15 Car. II [1663], it was ordered that the exceptant, who had much of the lands, should account for his proportion of the rent of £120 *per annum* reserved upon the lease directed by the Lord Coventry during the term and, since it expired, until Whitsuntide before. It was proposed that the exceptant Blackston, being a great sufferer for His Majesty in the late wars, might renew his lease upon reasonable terms, which was referred to the archbishop of York.[1]

The Lord Chancellor, having advised with the then Lord Chief Justice and Lord Chief Baron upon the merits of the cause and a master's report touching the arrears, declared that he did not see any cause to recede from the former decree of the commissioners nor the Lord Coventry's confirmation in 12 Car. I [1637] and that he could not absolve the exceptant from the £220 certified by the master but decreed the payment thereof and ratified the Lord Keeper Coventry's confirmation and that the hospital should enjoy the lands but a lease should be made to the exceptant for the fine and rent formerly proposed by the archbishop with the consent of the hospital etc.

Public Record Office C.33/221, f. 1010

10 June 1664.

Williamum Blakiston, armigerum, exceptantem; Magistrum, fratres, et sorores hospitii Roberti Holgate quondam archiepiscopi Eboraci in Hemsworth in Comitatu Eboraci, respondentes.

Whereas upon a petition presented to the Right Honorable the Lord High Chancellor of England in the name of the poor brethren and sisters of the said hospital and His Lordship's subscription thereto of the 20th of May last wherein it is amongst other things set forth that this cause commence to be heard the 14th of July last, His Lordship was pleased to refer the matter to the then lord archbishop of York to mediate between the parties for a lease to be renewed to the said exceptant Blakiston upon reasonable terms and that the master of the said hospital without any knowledge or consent of the said petitioners did agree before the said lord archbishop to renew the said exceptant's lease at the old rent without making any provision for the payment of the arrearages and that, on the 24th of October last, this court did recommend the matter to his said Grace to mediate and end as well touching the arrears as all other demands in an amicable way if he could and that he being accordingly attended did propound £111 10s. to be paid to the hospital in two year's time in full of all arrears and to quit all costs but, the hospital having expended above £300 and upon his refusal, they were forced to make a lease to a stranger for security thereof and other monies for which they still stand indebted, did not nor could consent to those propositions

[1] Order of 14 July 1663: Public Record Office C.33/219, f. 857v.

and for that the said agreement made by the said master was very prejudicial to the hospital and they were not privy or consenting to the same, it was prayed that the said hospital might not be bound thereby and that the said hospital may receive the fruit and benefit of a decree made for them by the late Lord Keeper Coventry and that they may either be at liberty to dispose of the premises to their best advantage or may have their full costs and arrears of rent with some improvement of rent for the time to come, the rent reserved being not above a third part of the true value of the lands, whereby they may be enabled to satisfy their just debt so contracted as aforesaid before they shall be compelled to make any new lease of the premises. And to that purpose, it was prayed that some short day may be appointed for the hearing and final determination of the cause.

Whereupon, it was then ordered that the said exceptant should have notice thereof and show cause this day at his peril why the same should not be granted as was desired.

Now, upon opening of the matter this present day unto the court by Mr. Attorney General [*Palmer*], Mr. Solicitor General [*Finch*], and Mr. *Churchill*, being of the exceptant's counsel, who came this day to show cause according to the direction upon the said petition and for cause alleged that the said petitioners preferred in the name of the brethren and sisters without the privity of the master of the said hospital and upon false suggestion, the said exceptant having been in no fault and never refused but was always ready to perform both the award of the said lord archbishop and has, in pursuance of the said last award, tendered £50 for the fine to the said master which he certified saying he was content with the sum His Grace had ordered but insisted his neighbors [?] would be displeased, as by affidavit appears, and that the reason why there has been no proceedings in the courts upon the said award ever since Michaelmas Term last was for that the respondents got the original report from the archbishop under his hand and the exceptant had only a copy, which he could not produce in court, and forasmuch as the solicitor in this cause for the said respondents, who has got the said second award or report of the said archbishop, does refuse to produce the same but does promote the business on purpose to overthrow all that this court or His Grace the lord archbishop have done for the settling the same on purpose to his own designs about his being reported to have taken a lease of the said premises to himself.

And therefore, it was prayed that the said petition so preferred by the said brethren and sisters of the said hospital without the master and all proceedings thereon may be discharged, which this court, allowing the cause now showed, does order the same accordingly, and the said respondents' solicitor is within ten days next to bring in and file the said award and certificate of the said lord archbishop, but, if the said respondents' solicitor be in town, he is to bring in and to file the same within six days upon notice hereof given to the respondents' clerk in court.

Public Record Office C.33/221, f. 949

21 June 1664.

Williamum Blakeston, armigerum, exceptantem; Magistrum, fratres, et sorores hospitii Roberti Holgate quondam archiepiscopum Eboraci in Hemsworth in Comitatu Eboraci, respondentes.

Whereas by an order of the 10th of June instant which recites a former order of the 20th of May last grounded on a petition to the Right Honorable the Lord High Chancellor of England, it was ordered that the said former order should be discharged and that the said respondents' solicitor should within a week next bring into this court and file the second award or certificate of the said late lord archbishop of York Frewen upon notice thereof given to the said respondents' clerk in court, upon opening of the matter this present day unto this court by Mr. Attorney General [*Palmer*] and others, being the exceptant's counsel, it was alleged that, in pursuance of the said order, the said respondents' solicitor has brought in and filed the said award and upon producing the same in court bearing date the 20th of November 1663, it is ordered that the said award and all the matters and things therein contained shall stand ratified and confirmed by the order, authority, and decree of this court to be observed and performed by all parties to all intents and purposes according to the tenor and true meaning thereof unless the said respondents, their counsel, and solicitors, now present in court and offering to take notice thereof now, shall on Thursday next show good cause to the contrary.

Public Record Office C.33/221, f. 955v

25 June 1664.

Williamum Blakeston, armigerum, exceptantem; Magistrum, fratres, et sorores hospitii Roberti Holgate aliquando archiepiscopi Eboraci in Hemsworth in Comitatu Eboraci, respondentes. Et inter praedictum magistrum, fratres, et sorores hospitii praedicti, prosecutores, et dictum Williamum Blakeston, defendentem.

Whereas by an order of the 21st instant, the award or certificate therein mentioned dated the 20th of November last was to stand confirmed unless cause was showed to the contrary, now upon opening of the matter this present day unto this court by Mr. Serjeant *Glynne* and Mr. Serjeant *Fountaine*, being of counsel for the said hospital, in the presence of Mr. Attorney General [*Palmer*], Mr. Solicitor General [*Finch*], and Mr. *Churchill*, being of the exceptant's counsel, and for as much as it was now alleged by the counsel for the hospital that, by an order of reference of the 24th of October last, the matter was referred to His Grace, the late archbishop of York, to mediate an end of the differences, if he could, and thereupon make his certificate to this court and the cause was to be continued and stand in the paper until the last day of causes save one that term for His Lordship's final determination of all matters in controversy and that the exceptant ought to have procured the cause to be set down in the paper accordingly and for as much also as the matter will take up a long debate and cannot conveniently be determined upon a motion, it is ordered that the cause be set down in the paper the first day for causes and exceptions after the term for counsel on both sides to be heard therein, whereupon His Lordship will make such further order therein as shall be meet.

Public Record Office C.33/221, f. 910

4 July 1664.

Williamum Blackeston, exceptantem; Magistrum, fratres, et sorores hospitii Roberti Holgate aliquando archiepiscopi Eboraci in Himsworth in Comitatu Eboraci, respondentes.

This cause standing in the paper this present day for counsel on both sides to be heard therein according to an order of the 25th of June last, it appeared unto this court that the matter upon the exceptions put in by the said exceptant to a decree made 9 April 10 Car. I [1634] by commissioners upon the Statute of 43 Eliz. for Charitable Uses and the plea of the said respondents put in thereunto coming to be heard the 15th of October 1662 before the Right Honorable the Lord High Chancellor of England assisted with Mr. Justice Tyrell, the respondents having, *inter alia*, pleaded a former decree of confirmation made by the late Lord Keeper Coventry 12 Car. I [1637] upon exceptions put in on the behalf of the now exceptant and the exceptant's acceptance of a lease of a lease and enjoyment of the premises in pursuance thereof in bar to the now exceptions, the plea after long debate by counsel on both sides was allowed and the said exceptant having replied to the said plea and witnesses having been examined on both sides, the cause came again afterwards to be heard before His Lordship the Lord Chancellor assisted with the now Lord Chief Justice Hyde and the Lord Chief Baron Hale and the matter upon the exceptions and plea, the will of Archbishop Holgate, the letters patent of 3 & 4 Philip & Mary for incorporating the hospital, the Lord Ellesmere's decree of the 11th *Jacobi*, the decree of the Lord Coventry of 12 Car. I, and an order of the 20th of February 9 Car. I [1634] made by the Lord Coventry with the assistance of Mr. Justice Jones, Mr. Justice Hutton, and Mr. Justice Berkeley in the exceptions and plea mentioned, having by special order and direction of this court been at several times at large and deliberately heard and debated by their lordships in the presence of counsel learned on both sides as well on the 4th of June as on the 10th of June 1663, their lordships did nevertheless suspend their final judgments in the cause and by order of the 10th of June ordered that the exceptant should account before Sir Thomas Estcourt, knight, etc., for his proportion of the 120 *per annum* rent reserved on the lease during the term and since the exceptions thereof after the same rate until Whitsuntide then last and the exceptant was recommended to the master of the hospital to admit him tenant and to renew his lease on reasonable terms in pursuance whereof Sir Thomas Estcourt, by his report of 6 July 1663 certified that there was £582 10s. unpaid of the rent referred. If the said exceptant should be charged with any rent due before Master Hewly's report therein mentioned, the master having reported the matter special as to that point and that for £222 10s., part of the said £582 10s., the same was agreed by the exceptant himself to be due and afterwards, by order of the 14th of July 1663, His Lordship declared his judgment to be that the exceptant ought to have a lease made by the said master according to the ancient constitution of the said hospital and the matter was then recommended to His Grace the archbishop of York to interpose between the parties so as the exceptant might be admitted tenant to the hospital and at liberty to renew his lease on reasonable terms and His Lordship did suspend his final judgment in the cause in the mean time.

In pursuance whereof, His Grace, the said archbishop, by his report of the 14th of October 1663 certified that the exceptant and the master of the hospital had subscribed an agreement that the master should before Martlemas[1] then next seal a lease to the exceptant of certain lands in question for twenty-one years under £60 *per annum* rent and that the exceptant should pay £100 fine £50 at [the] sealing and £50 at six month's end and that the payment of the arrears of rent should be no obstruction to the lease, and, by a subsequent order of the 24th of October 1663, the matter was recommended back to His Grace, the archbishop, to mediate and end as well touching the arrears as all other demands and matters in controversy in an amicable way if he could.

In pursuance whereof, His Grace made an award or certificate therein dated 20th November last, but the hospital not consenting thereto, the poor brethren and sisters, finding themselves aggrieved by the agreement of the master for a new lease without making provision for payment of the arrears, did petition His Lordship and disclaim the said agreement under their common seal as being without their authority and consent and prayed that the cause might be determined on the merits thereof.

And by order of the 10th of June last, His Lordship did discharge the said petition and allowed the cause showed by the exceptant. And the cause now standing in the paper this present day for His Lordship's final determination of the whole matter, in the presence of counsel learned on both sides, the counsel for the respondents insisted that, the former lease being made to Tobias and the exceptant jointly, they after the expiration thereof let a lease for a moiety of the premises to one Henry Blakiston who was assignee to Tobias, one of the lessees, and that they did not oppose the renewing of the lease to the exceptant as to the residue of the leased premises so as the said fine and arrears might be first paid or well secured to them. And His Lordship having advised with the Lord Chief Justice and Lord Chief Baron upon the merits of the cause and having heard the report of the said Sir Thomas Estcourt and both the certificates of His Grace, the said late archbishop, and the said several orders read and having taken de-

[1] Martinmas, 11 November.

liberate consideration of the whole matter after long debate thereof and hearing what could be alleged on both sides declared that he saw no cause to alter the said original decree made by the commissioners nor recede from the decree of confirmation of 12 Car. I made by the Lord Coventry, the same being made upon just grounds, and that he could not absolve the exceptant from the £222 10s., arrears of rent agreed and certified by the said master to be due to the hospital.

And therefore, it is ordered and decreed that the said exceptant shall pay unto the said respondents the said £222 10s. so certified and agreed to be due to the respondents for the said arrears of rent as aforesaid in manner following, that is to say, £55 12s. 6d. part thereof at Martlemas next coming and £55 12s. 6d. more thereof at Whitsuntide next coming and £55 12s. 6d. other part thereof at Martlemas 1664 and £55 12s. 6d. residue thereof at Whitsuntide 1665, and shall also forthwith pay unto the said respondents the sum of £30 for the last half year's rent due for the premises at Whitsuntide last.

And it is further ordered and decreed that as well the original decree made by the said commissioners as the said decree of confirmation of 12 Car. I made by His Lordship the said Lord Keeper Coventry as to any the lands late of the said Archbishop Holgate in Old Malton, Wickham, and Cowhouse in the County of York do stand ratified and confirmed by the decree of this court and that the said master, brethren, and sisters of the said hospital and their successors shall forever hereafter hold and enjoy the same premises against the said exceptant William Blakeston and all claiming by, from, or under him according to the said decrees with this nevertheless that, upon payment of the £100 agreed between the exceptant and the master of the hospital to be paid as a fine for the premises as aforesaid which is to be paid to the respondents at or before Michaelmas next and upon payment of the said £30 for the rent for Whitsuntide last as aforesaid the said respondents shall renew the lease made to the said Tobias and the exceptant in pursuance of the Lord Coventry's decree as to all the residue of the lands, tenements, and premises demised in the former lease not already leased to the said Henry Blakeston for the term of twenty-one years commencing from Lady Day [25 March] 1663 at the yearly rent of £60 with such covenants and provisoes as in the former lease are contained. And for the better security of the payment of the said £222 10s. to the said hospital in manner as aforesaid, it is ordered and decreed that the same shall be procured by proviso and covenants to be inserted in the said now lease so to be made as aforesaid and with [a] clause of re-entry and forfeiture for non payment thereof in such manner as the counsel learned for the said respondents shall devise and think fit.

And it is further decreed that the said exceptions put in by the said exceptant to the original decree of the commissioners be overruled and that the matter of the said exceptions do from hence forth stand clearly and absolutely dismissed out of this court.

157

Proud v. Combes

(Ch. 1664)

A bill of review lies only for errors on the face of the record and not for alleged errors of fact.

1 Chancery Cases 54, 22 E.R. 691

16 June [1664].

The bill was a bill of review. And in drawing up the decretal order, the matter upon which the decree was made was declared to be proved, and the case was stated far different from the fact. The errors assigned by the bill were that the decree was grounded on matters not proved and instanced in particulars and that the matters mentioned in the decree to be proved were not proved etc.

The demurrer was general that the decree contained no error in law and that the matters alleged for error were but a misjudgment.

And, upon debate, it was declared that, upon a bill of review, the causes for review must arise and appear upon the case as it is stated in the fact and that the fact must be admitted as it is there stated and that, touching where the fact is mistaken, upon which the court grounded their judgment, it is proper in such case for that reason to have the cause re-heard before the decree be enrolled; yet, after the decree is enrolled, that is no ground for a bill of review, for the decree enrolled is a matter of record, and can be tried by the record itself after it is enrolled, and must be taken to be true.

And so the demurrer was allowed.

The original case of Comb and Proud was as follows. It was heard at the Rolls in November last. The original bill was to be relieved against an account stated between the mortgagor and the heir of the mortgagee under hand and seal, upon a suggestion that it was agreed upon the sealing that, if there were any mistake in the account, the same should be reviewed and rectified. The defendant denied the agreement, and pleaded the account stated, and three meetings in order to [have] it, and the same was perused first by the plaintiff, and affirmed on his behalf, and then fully consented to and sealed. An issue was taken on the plea, and the plea was proved. Yet it appearing to the court by the quantum of the same that the account was made up of interest upon interest and the court taking the agreement to be proved (howbeit it was not), [the court] decreed the account stated to be set aside and the parties to go to an account *ab origine*.

Observe the reason why the review did not lie was because, as the decree was drawn up, there was no error appeared in it.

2 Freeman 182, 22 E.R. 1147

16 June, 16 Car. II [1664]. Lord Chancellor, Baron Rainsford. Combes v. Proud.

The bill was a bill of review, and, in drawing up the decretal order, the matter on which the decree was [made was] declared to be proved, and the case was stated far different from the fact. Therefore, the errors assigned were that the decree was grounded on matters not proved, and he instanced in particular that the matters mentioned in the decree to be proved were not proved.

This demurrer was general, that the errors assigned were not errors in law and were but misjudgments etc.

And, on debate, it was declared that, on a bill of review, the cause of review must arise and appear upon the case as stated in the decree and that the fact must be admitted as then stated and that, though the fact whereon the court gave judgment were mistaken, yet there is no ground of a bill of review. But the fact in this case must be admitted true and the decree is a matter of record and can be tried only by the record. But, in mistaking the fact, the proper course had been to have gotten the cause reheard before the decree had been signed and enrolled.

2 Freeman 183, 22 E.R. 1148

An account stated is a good plea. But, if there be any agreement to rectify mistakes, it shall not conclude, though under hand and seal.

Nelson 100, 21 E.R. 800

There was an account stated between the mortgagor and the heir of the mortgagee, and it was under hand and seal. And a bill was now brought to be relieved, suggesting that, upon the sealing to the said account, it was agreed between the said parties that, if there was any mistake, it should be rectified.

The defendant denied the agreement, and pleaded the account stated, and set forth the several meetings in order to it and that it was perused by the plaintiff and a friend before it was sealed, and, by him, approved, and he consented to it.

But it appearing to the court upon the hearing that the account was made up of interest upon interest, they set it aside, and ordered the parties to go to a new account *ab origine*.

3 Chancery Reports 18, 21 E.R. 715

15 November.

The principal case was now heard at the Rolls. The original bill was to be relieved against an account stated between the mortgagor and the heir of the mortgagee, under hand and seal, upon a suggestion that it was agreed upon sealing that, if there were any mistake in the account, the same should be reviewed and rectified.

The defendant denied the agreement, and pleaded the account stated, and three meetings in order to [have] it. And the same was perused, first, by the plaintiff and a friend on his behalf and, then, fully consented to and sealed. Issue was taken on this plea, and the plea was proved. Yet it appeared to the court by the quantum of the sum that the account was made up of interest upon interest. And the court, taking the agreement to be proved (howbeit it was not), decreed the account stated to be set aside and the parties to go to an account *ab origine*.

Observe the reason why the review did not lie was because, as the decree was drawn up, there was no error in it.

[Other reports of this case: 1 Eq. Cas. Abr. 164, 21 E.R. 961, 2 Eq. Cas. Abr. 174, 22 E.R. 149.]
[Reg. Lib. 1663 A, f. 974.]

158

Bolton v. Arme

(Ch. 1664–1665)

Rents payable to lessees of the crown by sublessees were discharged by the Act of Oblivion of 1660.

1 Chancery Cases 55, 22 E.R. 692

17 June [1664].

A lessee of the crown made an underlease of a rent. During the Usurpation [1649–1660], the state voided the first lessee's estate, and exposed the crown interest to sale. The underlessee applies to his lessor for protection. He bids him shift for himself. Thereupon, the underlessee pays his rent to the purchaser from the state for some time, and, after[wards], the underlessee purchases his tenement from him that purchased of the state. Upon the king's restoration, the first lessee brings [an action of] debt against his underlessee for the arrears of rent from the time he discontinued payment to him, and he had a judgment by default. The underlessee prayed to be relieved against this judgment, which was by the bill alleged to be by surprise, though no surprise appeared in obtaining the judgment.

[It was] decreed that the judgment be vacated, for that the rent was discharged by the Act of Oblivion,[1] of which, the Lord Chancellor [LORD CLARENDON] said, a court of equity was as proper a judge or interpreter as the judge at law.

2 Freeman 182, 22 E.R. 1147

16 Car. II [1664–65]. Lord Chancellor, Master of the Rolls. Belton v. Anne.

A debt was extinct by the Act of Oblivion. The debtee gets a judgment. The defendant sues here.

[1] Stat. 12 Car. II, c. 11 (*SR*, V, 226–234).

And the judgment was decreed to be vacated. And the Chancellor [Lord Clarendon] said this court might relieve on that Act, as well as any other court.

Nelson 95, 21 E.R. 798

Betton v. Ann.

A lease was granted by the crown to one who made an underlease to another in the time of the Usurpation, rendering rent, etc. Afterwards, the interest which the crown had in the lands was exposed to sale, and the title by which the first lessee held it was defeated. And, by consequence, the underlease was in danger. Therefore, he, who had that interest, applies himself to his lessor to be protected, which he refused. The estate was afterwards sold by the usurpers. And the underlessee paid the rent to the purchaser, and, afterwards, purchased the lands himself of that very purchaser. When the king was restored [in 1660], the first lessee who held under the crown brought an action of debt against this underlessee for all the arrears of rent ever since he had discontinued the payment thereof to him. And he had judgment by default. And, now, the plaintiff, who was the underlessee, exhibited a bill to be relieved against that judgment, which, as he alleged, was obtained by surprise.

And, though that did not appear, yet the judgment was vacated, because the rent was discharged by the Act of Oblivion. Of which, the Chancellor [Lord Clarendon] said a court of equity was as proper a judge as the courts at law.

3 Chancery Reports 16, 21 E.R. 715

17 July, 16 Car. II [1664]. The Lord Chancellor, the Master of the Rolls. Bolton v. Anne.

A lessee of the crown made an underlease at a rent during the Usurpation. The state avoided the first lessee's estate, and exposed the crown's interest to sale. The underlessee applies to the lessor for protection. He bids him shift for himself. The underlessee pays his rent to the purchaser from the state for some time. And, after[wards], the underlessee purchased his tenement from him that purchased from the state. Upon the king's restoration, the first lessee brings [an action of] debt against his underlessee for the arrears of rent from the time he discontinued payment to him. And he had a judgment by default. And, now, to be relieved against the judgment, which was by the bill alleged to be by surprise, though no surprise appeared, the underlessee brought his bill in equity, though no surprise was apprehended in obtaining the judgment.

And [it was] decreed that the judgment be vacated, for that the rent was discharged by the Act of Oblivion, of which the Lord Chancellor [Lord Clarendon] said a court of equity was as proper an interpreter as the judges at law.

159

Backhouse v. Bellingham

(Ch. 1664)

A remainder of a trust of a term limited after another person's dying without an heir is void.

Pollexfen 33, 86 E.R. 503

20 June, 16 Car. II.

The case was touching the limitation of a term in lands limited to these trusts: that Sir John Backhouse should receive the profits during his life, and, as to part, after his death, his lady for her life and the residue to pay debts and legacies and, after their deaths and the debts and legacies paid, the profits to be employed as Nicholas Backhouse should appoint for his own maintenance, and that, after his death, his first, second, third, fourth, and fifth sons, according to their seniority, and the respective heirs male of their bodies to receive the profits for the residue of the term, and, for default of such issue, that William Backhouse should receive the profits during his life, and, after his death, John Backhouse for his life and, after his death, to his first, second, etc. sons, (as before), the remainder to Rowland Backhouse and others, with the like remainders to their sons as before, the remainder to the defendant Samuel Bellingham, and the heirs male of his body during the residue of the term.

Afterwards, Sir John Backhouse and his lady died, he having made his will and William Backhouse his executor. The trustees paid his debts and legacies. And Nicholas Backhouse died intestate without issue male, and administration of his estate was granted to the same William Backhouse. And John Backhouse, the son of William, died also intestate. And administration of his estate was also granted to William Backhouse, who granted the premises and all his estate therein to Lloyd and Turner in trust for himself and his own executor etc. And, then, he made his will and the plaintiff's wife his executrix, and he died. And, afterwards, all the remainders to Samuel Bellingham were spent.

The question [was] whether, by the trust, the residue of the term did belong to Bellingham and the heirs male of his body as limited or to the plaintiff's wife, executrix of William Backhouse.

The Lord Chancellor [Lord Clarendon], at the hearing, declared the limitation of the remainder to Samuel Bellingham and the heirs male of his body to be a void limitation. And he decreed the estate to be conveyed by the first trustees to Lloyd and Turner for the benefit of the plaintiffs.

Lord Nottingham, *Prolegomena*, p. 229

Trinity [term], 16 Car. II.

Sir William Backhouse and wife exhibit a bill against Codrington, the surviving trustee of a term, and Samuel Bellingham to have an assignment. Wherein it was resolved: first, that the trust having been limited to Nicholas Backhouse for life, with remainders to his first, second, third, etc. sons in tail, and, for default of such issue, the remainder to Samuel Bellingham, this remainder was void, because a term could not be so limited in remainder, and, therefore, the residue of the term or possibility of returning did in law belong to the plaintiff as administrator to Nicholas; second, that, seeing that Samuel Bellingham sat out all process of contempt and went away beyond the sea, a decree might well be against Codrington alone without prejudice to Bellingham.

160

Nicholson v. Sherman

(Ch. 1664–1665)

Anyone who gets any of a testator's estate into his hands is answerable for the legacies.

1 Chancery Cases 57, 22 E.R. 693

24 June [1664].

A. bequeaths a legacy, and makes a husband and wife his executors, and dies. The husband, afterwards, makes his will, and makes the wife and his son executors, and dies. The legatee of A. exhibits his bill against the wife and her son, setting forth the case, *ut supra*, and charges that the estate of A., liable to the payment of the legacy, is come all to the hands of the wife and her son.

The demurrer was by the son, for that the wife who was the surviving executor of A. was only liable to his legacies and the son, being an executor of one of A.'s executors that died first, leaving an executor of A. to survive, was not privy in law, nor accountable for the estate of A., which, though it be so in point of law.

Yet, inasmuch as it was charged that the son had gotten the estate of A., the demurrer was overruled, the court declaring that the estate of A., in whosesoever's hands, ought to be liable to his legacies.

And, in Trinity term 1665, this cause was heard and decreed.

2 Freeman 181, 22 E.R. 1146

24 June, 16 Car. II [1664]. Lord Chancellor, Baron Turner.

One exhibits a bill against an executor and a stranger, setting forth that the testator's estate came to both their hands and that the testator had given him a legacy etc.

The stranger demurs because the executor is only suable.

The court overruled the demurrer, for whosoever gets any of the testator's estate into his hands is answerable for the legacies.

And, in Trinity Term 1665, this cause was heard and decreed.

[Other reports of this case: 1 Eq. Cas. Abr. 237, 21 E.R. 1016.]
[Reg. Lib. 1663 A, f. 1004, 1664 B, f. 770.]
[Related cases: Nicholson v. Sherman (1661), T. Raymond 23, 83 E.R. 13, 1 Siderfin 45, 82 E.R. 960, 1 Keble 116, 83 E.R. 846.]

161

Williams v. Owen

(Ch. 1664)

New matter cannot be enquired into upon a bill of review.

A demurrer lies to an answer that adds new matter to a bill of review.

1 Chancery Cases 56, 22 E.R. 692

24 June. The Lord Chancellor, Baron Turner.

The defendant, having answered the bill of revivor [sic], which sought to revive the order on hearing, as to so much as was not within the decree enrolled, had by his answer set forth matter that tended to draw into question and new examination an agreement which was contained within the decree as it was enrolled and thereby fully settled.

Therefore, to so much of the answer as tended again to draw into examination the matters settled by the decree enrolled or by the order on hearing, the plaintiff did demur, for that it would be of evil consequence and introductive of perjury to permit a reexamination of any of those matters.

Upon the debate of this demurrer, which was drawn by Serjeant *Fountaine*, it was averred by the defendant's counsel that a demurrer to an answer was never known before in a court of equity, though Serjeant *Glynne*, for the plaintiff, affirmed he had known of a demurrer to an answer before.

And, though it did seem unreasonable to the court that a defendant should by answer draw again into examination the matters formerly examined unto and settled, yet the court doubted what to do as to the demurrer. Some at the bar said the court should have been moved in this special case for an order to retain an examination of all matters formerly examined and settled.

And it was now ordered that there should be no matters reexamined that were examined to before. This, I take it, was the rule that was given; *tamen quaere*.

2 Freeman 181, 22 E.R. 1146

24 June, 16 Car. II.

The defendant answered the bill of review but so as that some matter in his answer would bring into examination some part of the decree as it was signed and enrolled.

On which answer, as to that part, Serjeant *Fountaine* drew a demurrer, because this would tend to perjury and infiniteness, to re-examine things examined and decreed.

Of which opinion, the court was. But as well the defendant's counsel as the court said there could be no demurrer upon an answer in equity.

Serjeant *Glynne*, for the plaintiff, said he had known it.

The court made an order that there should be no examination of that which had been examined, and that was the rule.

Dickens 8, 21 E.R. 169

24 June, 16 Car. II.

Upon a bill of review and a supplement to carry a former decree into examination, the defendants answer and thereby wanting to draw into question and have a new examination of the matters in the decree, the plaintiff demurred to the answer on that ground.

On arguing the demurrer, it was ordered by Lord Clarendon, Chancellor, that no matter should be re-examined.

[Other reports of this case: 1 Eq. Cas. Abr. 41, 21 E.R. 859, 2 Eq. Ca. Abr. 174, 22 E.R. 149.]

162

Norton v. Rowley

(Ch. 1664)

An agreement to arbitrate can be revoked at any time before the award is made.
A court of equity will not enforce an unjust arbitral award.

Lord Nottingham, *Prolegomena*, p. 309

8 July, 16 Car. II.

The court, on debate, did permit the party to revoke his consent, for there can be no irrevocable submission either in law or equity. And, if the parties at common law consent to a reference by a rule of court, yet no attachment shall be awarded for a breach of the award or for revoking the submission, as all the judges are now agreed.

Second, admit the submission had not been revoked, yet the award here cannot be decreed by [reason of] the apparent injustice of it and also because there is no necessity for decreeing such awards, for the law gives an action for a breach of the agreement, and the rule at law or order of Chancery is a very clear evidence of the agreement.

163

Wright v. Newport Pond School

(Ch. 1664)

Charity commissioners can make void a lease in reversion, and they can order an increased rent for new leases.

Herne & Duke 105

Joyce Francklands, widow, seised in fee of a portion of tithes in Bansted in Surrey, by her last will, dated the 20th of February 1586[/87], devises the same then in lease, for divers years to come at £7 *per annum* to five persons and their heirs to the intent that they and their heirs and assigns should yearly forever employ and bestow the yearly rents, issues, and profits thereof *inter alia* to the erecting, maintaining, and finding of a free grammar school in Newport in Essex of a competent number of scholars of the children of the inhabitants there; if there were but one master, he should have £20 *per annum*, and, if a master and usher, then the master 20 nobles and the usher 20 nobles, and appoints the master of Gonville and Caius College in Cambridge governor.

Joyce died seised. The devisees received the rents and erected a school house and devised the same portion of tithes to Richard Wright for thirty-six years at £7 *per annum*. The devisees, in consideration for the surrender of that lease and of £40 disbursed by Richard Le Wright in suits at law brought against him for the premises, demised the said tithes to Richard Le Wright from Michaelmas then last for fifty years at £7 *per annum*. Richard Le Wright made Robert Le Wright his executor and died [in] 1634. Robert enjoyed the tithes during the residue of the term of fifty years; and the tithes from Richard's death until 1650, were worth £43 *per annum* above the rent. And afterwards, the surviving trustees demise the tithes to Edward Nightingale, after the determination of the lease of fifty years, for twenty-one years at £10 *per annum*. Edward Nightingale, for £150, sold that lease to Robert Le Wright; and, from Michaelmas 1650 until Michaelmas 1660, at which time the lease of fifty years ended, the tithes were worth £60 *per annum* above the rent.

These things being found by inquisition, [the] commissioners, upon the Statute for Charitable Uses,[1] did decree that the concurrent lease made in 1646 at the rent of £10 *per annum* was made contrary to the intent of the donor and was a misemployment of the same tithes and a defrauding the charitable use within the said Statute and that the same lease and the assignment thereof to Robert Le Wright and all mesne assignments of the same should from thenceforth be utterly void and of none effect and that the feoffees should let the same tithes at

[1] Stat. 43 Eliz. I, c. 4 (*SR*, IV, 968–970).

the true value and that no lease should be afterwards made for above twenty-one years in possession.

Robert Le Wright put in exceptions to the decree:

First, that the commissioners had not power to make void the lease in reversion made to R. Nightingale by the feoffees, who had the fee and inheritance of the tithes;

Second, nor to decree a greater rent to be reserved upon any new lease than was reserved at the making of the will;

Third, nor to decree an increase of the rents against him but rather against the feoffees that broke the trust and that R. Le Wright had assigned to one Andrews for a valuable consideration, *viz.* £150.

But the Lord Chancellor [Lord Clarendon], upon full hearing of the said exceptions, confirmed the decree.

164

Thornton v. White

(Ch. 1664)

Where court costs have been taxed, they cannot be re-litigated in another lawsuit.

Lincoln's Inn MS. Hill 125, f. 45v, pl. 2

20 October 16 Car. II.

Burnell sold the Antelope Inn to White [in] 1651, and he gave [a confessed] judgment in £1000 for security against encumbrances to be discovered within ten years. And, after[wards], he sold other lands to the plaintiff. White, discovering a fraudulent assurance of the lands sold to him made by Burnell to Pepper [in] 1656, had a decree to avoid it and costs, which were taxed to £24 and paid to White, who extended now on Thornton the lands which Thornton purchased, who exhibited his bill against White to be relieved, who justified [?] the extent by reason of that and other encumbrances. And he did insist to have damages for his trouble and costs in that suit above the £24. But that is to draw in examination the judgment of the court in the point of costs, which, being accepted, he shall not now question it. And, therefore, that demand [was] disallowed. As for other matters, [it was] referred to [an] account.

165

Fleming v. Walgrave

(Ch. 1664)

Where a gift is made to a woman upon a condition of marriage with consent, and, if not, a power of a gift over is given, the marriage is without consent, but no gift over is made, the woman or her administrator takes the gift.

1 Chancery Cases 58, 22 E.R. 693

28 October [1664].

The case was thus. £900 was secured by a lease for years for a *feme sole* in case she did not marry contrary to the liking of Sir Edward Walgrave and his Lady, and, if she did, then to such persons as Sir Edward and his Lady or the survivor of them should nominate and, for want of such nomination, then to Sir Edward Walgrave and his Lady and the survivor of them. And, in this case, Sir Edward Walgrave and his Lady were lessees in trust. The *feme sole* married without their consent. Sir Edward dies without any appointment, and so did his Lady who survived him, and she had after the death of Sir Edward made a general deed of gift of all her goods and chattels to one Sandal.

The question was between Sandal and Francis Copledike, who was administrator to the Lady and also to the *feme sole*, who should have the benefit of this lease.

The court was of opinion that it was not in the power of Sir Edward and his Lady to have disposed of this lease otherwise than for the benefit of the *feme sole* if she had lived and that Francis Copledike, as administrator to her and also to the Lady, was well entitled to the benefit of the lease, and so decreed it.

[Other reports of this case: 1 Eq. Cas. Abr. 110, 21 E.R. 918.]

166

Rogers v. Walford

(Ch. 1664)

The arrears of a rent charge are recoverable against the terre tenant.

Lincoln's Inn MS. Hill 125, f. 46v, pl. 1

29 October 1664, by the Chancellor and the Master of the Rolls.

The devisee [has] a rent charge out of land in lease, upon which, part, to the value of the rent, is reserved. The heir, Walford, aliens the land to Burrage, another defendant. And, because there cannot be a distress during the lease, a bill exhibited for the rent and the arrears [was] dismissed *quoad* the continuance [?] of the payment. But the arrears [were] decreed against the terre tenant Burrage, as well before as after the purchase.

167

Hill v. Chapman

(Ch. 1664)

An arbitral award against an infant is void and unenforceable.

Lincoln's Inn MS. Hill 125, f. 46v, pl. 2

Michaelmas [term] 16 Car. II.

The father of Chapman, tenant for life, remainder to Chapman in fee, consents to a reference to Justice Hutton, who made an award, the son being an infant.

A bill now exhibited against the son to have execution of the decree [was] dismissed.

168

Backhouse v. Middleton
Lord Cornbury v. Middleton

(Ch. 1664–1671)

A devisee cannot file a bill of revivor, being only in privity of estate.

Depositions taken upon an improper bill of revivor cannot be used in any other litigation.

Lincoln's Inn MS. Hill 125, f. 46v, pl. 3

Michaelmas [term] 16 Car. II, on demurrer. Middleton v. Backhouse.

A., a purchaser, who articled before his purchase but paid not his money until after notice of former articles made for the [. . .] purchase, [was] ruled to answer B.

2 Freeman 132, 22 E.R. 1108

Hilary [term] 21 & 22 Car. II [1670]. Lord Bridgeman.

Bacchus, being a purchaser, exhibited a bill of revivor against the defendant, and revived the suit by order. And the defendant joined in examining witnesses. But, at the hearing, the plaintiff was dismissed, for that the plaintiff, as purchaser, could not maintain a bill of revivor.

And it was now moved that, in an original bill exhibited by Bacchus, he might use the depositions taken in the cause of revivor.

But the court denied it, because, in truth, there was never any bill depending in it, for the bill of revivor brought by a purchaser was void and the depositions, therefore, were taken on no issue, and there was no bill and answer depending, and, consequently, no indictment could lie against the witnesses if they were perjured.

3 Chancery Reports 39, 21 E.R. 722

Hilary [term] 21 & 22 Car. II [1670].

Backhouse, being a purchaser, exhibited a bill of revivor against the defendant, and revived the suit by an order. And the defendant joined in examining witnesses. And the cause coming to be heard, the bill was dismissed, for that the plaintiff, as a purchaser, cannot maintain a bill of revivor, for that there wanted other parties at the hearing.

And it was now moved on an original bill exhibited by the plaintiff that he might use the depositions taken in the cause on the bill of revivor.

But, upon the hearing of counsel on both sides, the court denied those depositions to be used in the new cause, because, in truth, there was no cause depending, for the bill of review, being brought by a purchaser, was void and so the depositions were taken where there was no bill and answer depending. And, consequently, no indictment of perjury could be brought against the witnesses.

Lord Nottingham, *Prolegomena*, p. 198

Trinity [term] 16 Car. II [sic].

At common law, if a judgment be given for a man or an erroneous judgment be given against him and he dies and, by his will, he devises the thing recovered by him or against him, in this case, the devisee can have no *scire facias* to revive the judgment given for the testator, nor no writ of error to reverse the judgment given against him. And the reason is because he who would revive or reverse a judgment given for or against the testator ought to have privity in blood as heir or representation as executor and a mere privity in estate will not suffice. And so it is also in equity.

Bishop articles with Sir Hugh Middleton for a purchase of fourteen shares of 36 in the New River [Company], pays £250 down, exhibits a bill, and dies, having devised it to his wife. She marries Sir William Backhouse, and he exhibits a bill of revivor.

And, at the hearing, the bill was dismissed, because a devisee cannot revive.

1 Chancery Cases 173, 22 E.R. 748

17 June [1670]. Dame Flora Backhouse against Simon Middleton and others.

Sir William Middleton, seised of the king's moiety in the New River Water [Company] in fee, consisting of thirty-six shares, 1646, conveyed the same to Henry Middleton and others upon trust for himself and his wife, during their respective lives, and, after that, the trustees, out of the rents and profits of the premises, should pay his debts and portions for his daughters at certain days, and, after, to permit Sir Hugh Middleton, heir of Sir William, and his heirs to take and receive the rents and profits of the premises. Sir William and his Lady die. Sir Hugh, in June 1657, contracted with William Bishop, former husband of the plaintiff, for the sale of fourteen shares to him of the king's moiety for £7000, whereof £250 was in hand and the rest to be paid as Sir Hugh and Bishop and the trustees should agree, for the daughters' portions, which are ascertained by Sir William at several great sums. In December 1657, the defendant Simon contracted with the same Sir Hugh by articles under hand and seal for all the king's moiety at £15,100, and, in January after, Sir Hugh and his wife and Henry Middleton, the only active trustee, execute a conveyance to Simon according to the articles.

In Hilary [term] 1657, Bishop exhibits his bill against Sir Hugh to enforce an execution of the agreement, which the defendant answered.

Hilary [term] 1658, Simon Middleton brought his cross-bill against Bishop, Sir Hugh, and the trustees to have a conveyance etc. February 1659, Bishop exhibits interrogatories in his cause. November 1660, one witness was sworn thereon. 4 March 1660, Bishop dies, yet the witness sworn was not examined. Bishop having devised the benefit of his contract to the plaintiff, being his wife, and her heirs, 24 January 1661, she brings a bill of revivor. 24 November 1662, she marries Sir William Backhouse, and so her suit abates. 27 November 1663, Simon Middleton's cause was heard and decreed for him. 1 December 1663, Sir William Backhouse, by a petition, gets Simon Middleton's decree stopped. 2 December 1663, he brings a bill of revivor in his own and his wife's name. 18 May 1664, he exhibits a new schedule of interrogatories, and, on those interrogatories, some witnesses are examined. 11 June 1664, this cause was heard, and the plaintiffs' claiming as devisees to the plaintiff in the first cause and the heir of Bishop, whom only it concerned to contest, the devisee being no party and a devisee not being entitled to a bill of revivor, this bill was dismissed without prejudice to a new bill.

Then, an original bill, setting forth the former proceedings and the former dismission, was exhibited by Sir William Backhouse and the plaintiff, his wife, which also abated by Sir William's death and was revived by the plaintiff and answered by the defendants. And, then, issue being joined, the plaintiff moved to have the use of the depositions taken upon the former bill, which was dismissed, made use of in this cause, those witnesses being dead.

This matter was several times strongly debated by counsel on both sides, where, for the plaintiff, it was insisted that, though a bill be dismissed, yet the depositions taken on such bill are to be made use of here or at law and that the bill was not dismissed on the point of right, but for matter of form. And it is usual and frequent to use depositions taken in one cause if for the same matter that is in controversy in another, especially, if against the same defendant, as here it is. Which was admitted by the defendant's counsel. But, as to the using of depositions in a cause dismissed, this difference was taken, that, though, where a cause is dismissed, the matter of it not being proper for equity to decree, yet the fact in this cause proved may be used as evidence in that fact between the same parties whenever it shall come in question again. But, when a cause is dismissed not upon that ground, but upon irregularity, as for that it comes by a revivor, when it should come by an original bill, so that, in truth, there was never regularly any such cause in the court and, consequently, no proofs, these proofs cannot be used, for proofs cannot be exemplified without a bill and answer, nor can they be read at law without the bill on which they were taken can be read. But this bill of revivor could not be read at law, and, therefore, the proofs taken upon it cannot be used here.

And so, upon long debate and after several formal arguments, it was ruled about Michaelmas term 1669 in this very cause by the Lord Keeper [BRIDGEMAN].

And now, upon the hearing of this cause, the endeavor on the plaintiff's part was to prove a notice in the defendant of Bishop's contract, which was opposed by the defendant. But the notice being proved, it was, for the defendant, insisted that there was no ground to decree the agreement made by Bishop, it being made by a *cestui que trust* of the surplus only and the trustees were no parties, and the second agreement by the defendant Simon Middleton is exempted before any bill was brought by Bishop against the *cestui que trust* and the principal trustee, who, being examined as a witness, swears that he did disapprove of the agreement with Bishop and would never consent to it. And it was farther insisted, for the defendant Simon, that the agreement with Bishop was not pursued, nor could Sir Hugh enforce the payment of the £6750, it being to be paid as the trustees and he should agree, so that that was no complete agreement, and, the trustees disagreeing and having executed the other to Simon, the defendant, the agreement with Bishop ought not now to be decreed, especially for the plaintiff, who claimed the benefit of it by a devise only, which, at the best, was a devise of an equity on an equity.

But, for the plaintiff, it was insisted that the trustees had not, by the trust, power to sell, they being to pay the daughters' portions out of the rents and profits.

To which, it was replied by the court that the trustees were not to pay the portions out of the annual rents and profits, but out of the rents and profits, and those portions were to be paid at prefixed days, which the annual profits would not do. And, therefore, he conceived the trustees might sell for that purpose within the intention of the trust, and so he declared he was of opinion to dismiss the bill. But, withal, he said he would think farther of it.

Vide the end of this cause in Cornbury against Middleton.

1 Chancery Cases 208, 22 E.R. 765

July 1671. The Lord Cornbury and Dame Flora, his wife, formerly the Lady Backhouse, against Simon Middleton and others.

This cause begins fol. 173, and, being abated by the plaintiff's intermarriage since the last hearing, a bill of revivor was brought, and the cause was reheard by the Lord Keeper [BRIDGEMAN], assisted with Justice WILDE and Baron WYNDHAM the 3d of March 1670[/71]. And the case appearing to be as before, it was for the defendants insisted that the contract made by Sir Hugh Middleton with Mr. Bishop did not bind and that, he, being but a *cestui que trust* of a surplus, had no power to sell, for that it was against the very essence of the trust for him to have a power to dispose, and it would be a vain thing for any parent to settle his estate by way of a trust to prevent his son's imprudent disposition of it, which Sir William Middleton did here to settle his estate with a design to keep a hand on his son, if, notwithstanding, his son might have a power to sell it when he pleased.

And it was farther insisted on for the defendant that, if the agreement with Bishop were binding, yet the plaintiffs have no title to have the benefit of that agreement, for that the breach of an agreement, as the case was, was not devisable, and so the plaintiff had no title, things in action, as this case is, being not devisable.

To which it was answered by the plaintiffs' counsel that equity consists purely in action, and is only to be come by by the process of this court. And they cited Cole and Moor's Case, 5 Jac. [1607], Moor's Rep. [806].[1]

WYNDHAM was of opinion that the benefit of this agreement is not devisable, for things that consist in privity must be carried on in privity. And Sir Hugh Middleton could not have enforced the devisee, unless she had pleased to pay the money Bishop was to pay, and the remedy ought to be reciprocal.

WILDE: Sir Hugh had an equity to the residue after the debt and portions paid, and it was a crime to sell a thing twice, and the defendant was *particeps criminis*, and so no decree ought to be for him. But he would have Sir Samuel Jones and the other trustees for Sir William Middleton, in whom three parts of the four were vested in point of law, convey fourteen shares to the Lady Cornbury and her heirs.

Lord Keeper [BRIDGEMAN] agrees with WILDE that the clear equity and conscience was with Bishop's title and that the defendant Simon Middleton did interlope. But he did much doubt upon the devise. Yet, forasmuch as Bishop's heir was a defendant and consents to the devise by answer, he did decree that Sir Samuel Jones and the Six Clerks, to whom he had conveyed by order of this court, should convey by consent of the heir of Bishop fourteen shares to the Lady Cornbury and her heirs.

The Lord Keeper [BRIDGEMAN] upon the hearing by himself alone in June 1670, being of opinion to dismiss the bill and the court being now divided in opinion, the defendant Simon Middleton petitioned for a rehearing, and had a hearing accordingly in July 1671 before the Lord Keeper, Master of the Rolls, Rainsford, Wilde, and Wyndham.

And now upon this rehearing, it was, for the defendant Simon Middleton, insisted that the agreement with Bishop did not bind for the reason *supra* and, farther, that the agreement itself was imperfect because the money was to be paid as the trustees should agree and they did never agree to it. But Henry Middleton, the only acting trustee, did, so soon as he heard of it, utterly disagree to it. And also for that the agreement with Bishop was not pursued, for the agreement

[1] *Cole v. Moore* (Ch. 1607), Moore K.B. 806, 72 E.R. 917.

with Bishop was in June 1657 and, by that, the conveyances were to be executed in August next, but those not so much as prepared nor anything done in time and but £250 paid and the defendant Simon had paid above £15,000 and had a conveyance by a deed and a fine of the whole thirty-six shares, Bishop's contract being but for fourteen shares executed above twelve years since, and had been in the possession of the whole thirty-six shares ever since and that the Company of the New River had bought in another waterworks from Sir Edward Ford, which was united to that of the New River and mixed with it and could not be distinguished and that no distinct account could be taken, and so it was impracticable to decree the performance of the agreement with Bishop. Nor could Sir Hugh have compelled him to perform the same. And, if the City, which was lately burnt [in 1666] had not been rebuilt or any other loss had befallen the waterworks, the said Sir Hugh could never have compelled the Lady Cornbury to pay the money. And the heir's consent, though it may bind himself, shall not put a bargain upon another.

But it was, for the plaintiff, insisted that the money Bishop was to pay was enough to pay all the debts and legacies of Sir William Middleton and, thereby, all the trusts precedent to Sir Hugh might have been satisfied and so Sir Hugh had a clear title to the surplus. And he was looked upon as the owner. And the contract with Bishop was in pursuance of the trust, and he might by a bill have compelled the trustees to sell and the reason why the agreement was not pursued in time was because Sir Hugh Middleton's occasions drew him to the Bath. And he wrote a letter to have it respited until he came back, which was not until after August. And the defendant Simon was a willful purchaser with notice of the agreement, and Sir Hugh would have performed with Bishop if Sir Hugh had not been persuaded by Simon. And Bishop did endeavor to take up money of Sir George Prat for that purpose and these doings of Simon were against conscience and, in conscience, the first agreement ought to be performed. And the court ought to decree with, and not against, conscience.

WYNDHAM adheres to his first opinion, *viz.* that the bill ought to be dismissed, for he was not satisfied that Sir Hugh had any such interest as he could contract for, nor is it well come to the Lady Cornbury, though Sir Hugh might by a bill enforce the trustees to sell, for what a man may do himself is not transferrable in all cases and, what a man cannot transfer, he cannot oblige by articles. If Sir Hugh could not grant, he could not by the articles bind. His interest is but a mere possibility contingent; in its creation, it is so. Sir William has a power to charge, and does so by his will. And Sir Hugh could not dispose in his father's lifetime, and what Sir Hugh should have is uncertain, for the trustees might sell so much as to perform the precedent trust. Nor was it intended by Sir William that Sir Hugh should sell. If Sir Hugh had had the possession with this contingent interest, it might have gone far. But Sir Hugh had no possession. If Sir Hugh had covenanted the trustees should convey, equity ought not to decree him to procure them to convey, but to leave the covenantee to his covenant at law.

And, by the agreement, the payment of the money is entangled, and does not pursue the trust. And Mr. Bishop could not enforce his interest, nor is the devisee bound to pay the money, nor shall she take it up or lay it down as she pleases. Cases that rest in privity are to be carried on in privity, and strangers are not to be engaged in it. The heir comes in as improper as the defendant, and that cannot help it.

WILDE: This is a case in equity and in conscience, and this court is to help that side that has conscience. The case is on a trust, and that is proper here. And an interest in a trust is in equity assignable or devisable. And, if land be conveyed for the payment of debts and legacies and what remains to be to the heir, the heir may dispose. And the fine to Simon Middleton by Henry does nothing, for it is but the fine for one tenant in common which passes but his own share. Possibly a fine and non-claim may bar in equity, but not here, for a bill was presently filed. Notice is all in all in the case. And it is against good conscience for Simon Middleton to enjoy. And the court must judge with conscience, and not against conscience. If this be an interest, it is devisable. And it is but a circuity of action to bring the heir to revive, for, if he will not execute the estate to the devisee, she must bring a new bill against him. And he concluded that there ought to be a decree for the plaintiffs, but no action is to be but of the £7650 to be paid by the defendant and to convey fourteen shares of the thirty-six shares and the mesne profits to go against interest.

RAINSFORD conceived the plaintiff ought to be relieved, for Sir Hugh had an equitable interest that might be transferred in equity, though it was in its creation contingent. And we are not to take our measure as it stood in the creation, but as it stood when the contract was made with Mr. Bishop. And he that may transfer may covenant that his trustee shall do it. And Simon Middleton injuriously comes in with notice, and threatens Sir Hugh into this contract. And he conceived Bishop might devise, and he concluded as Wilde did.

The Master of the Rolls [GRIMSTON] agreed with Rainsford and Wilde, and looked upon the agreement with Bishop to be in pursuance of the trust.

The Lord Keeper [BRIDGEMAN], when he first heard this cause, was of opinion to dismiss the bill. But that was on a mistake, for he did conceive that all the trustees had conveyed to Simon Middleton, whereas, it seems that Henry Middleton, who was but one of the trustees, had conveyed to the said Simon. It is a cause of great consequence, and the trustees were trusted as well for Sir Hugh as the others. And he conceived the plaintiffs ought to be relieved. Bishop has the first agreement, and Simon Middleton the second, and equity ought to decree with the first, and the fine and conveyance carries no more from Henry than his fourth part, and carries Sir Hugh's equity no farther. And so he decreed that, out of the three parts remaining, fourteen shares of the thirty-six parts shall be conveyed by the Six Clerks to the Lady Cornbury and her heirs and no account [taken] of mesne profits, but those to go against interest. And, as to Ford's waterworks, if it can be severed, it cannot be taken into the decree, but, if it cannot, there must be an allowance for it. And so it was decreed accordingly. And whereas the said thirty-six parts were charged with a rent of £500 *per annum* to the crown in fee and £100 *per annum* to Henry Middleton for life and Sir Hugh, in his agreement with Bishop, had covenanted to discharge the fourteen shares he had agreed to sell Bishop from those rents, it was farther decreed that the plaintiff should enjoy the fourteen shares discharged of those rents and that the other twenty-two shares should be subject to the plaintiff's indemnity therein, notwithstanding it was insisted that Sir Hugh's covenant to discharge the fourteen shares of those rents was merely personal and did not, nor could, charge the whole rents upon the twenty-two shares.

169

Dickenson v. Knowell

(Ch. 1664)

The question in this case was whether the bond in issue was discharged by the Act of Oblivion of 1660.

1 Chancery Cases 59, 22 E.R. 694

3 November [1664]. The Lord Chancellor, Lord Chief Justice Bridgeman.

The plaintiffs were bound to one Crofts, to whom the defendant was executor, in £600 for the payment of £300. Crofts was sequestered by the Usurper [Oliver Cromwell], and, for £300, which the states owed the plaintiffs, they had an order from the committee to retain the £300 of Crofts for satisfaction. The bond was upon the king's restoration put in suit. To be relieved against which was the scope of the bill. The question was whether the defendant was barred by the Act of Oblivion.[1]

Bridgeman being present, he declared he conceived that the defendant, inasmuch as Crofts still kept the bond and the money was not actually paid, but retained, was not discharged by the Act of Indemnity. But it was referred to make a case.

170

Rand v. Cartwright

(Ch. 1664)

A voluntary or fraudulent conveyance is voidable by a creditor of the grantor; however, it is valid against the grantor and his heirs.

[1] Stat. 12 Car. II, c. 11 (*SR*, V, 226–234).

1 Chancery Cases 59, 22 E.R. 694

3 November [1664]. At the Rolls.

A man makes a voluntary deed and then a mortgage of the same lands. The first deed, upon a trial at law, is found fraudulent. He to whom the deed is made exhibits a bill to redeem the mortgage.

It was held that, though the first deed was fraudulent, because voluntary *quoad* the mortgage money, *et pro tanto*, yet that it was good as to the equity of redemption, and would pass that, for that a voluntary deed will bind the party that makes it and his heirs. But the matter was compromised.

2 Freeman 183, 22 E.R. 1148

5 November, 16 Car. II [1664]. Master of the Rolls. Ramm v. Cartwright.

A voluntary deed was found to be fraudulent against a mortgagee. Yet, the grantee in the said deed may afterwards sue for a redemption, for it is good against the grantor and his heirs and he shall have the equity of redemption.

Nelson 101, 21 E.R. 800

A man made a voluntary grant of his lands. And, afterwards, he mortgaged the same lands. Upon a trial at law against the mortgagee, the first deed was found fraudulent.

And, afterwards, he, to whom that deed was given, exhibits his bill to redeem upon payment of the money to the mortgagee.

And it was decreed that, though the first deed was fraudulent, because, *quoad* the mortgage money and *pro tanto*, it was voluntary, yet it was good as to the equity of redemption, and would pass it, for a voluntary deed is good against the party who made it and against his heir, though not against a mortgagee.

[Other reports of this case: 2 Eq. Cas. Abr. 282, 22 E.R. 238.]
[Reg. Lib. 1664 B, f. 81.]

171

Kennesby v. Parrett

(Ch. 1664)

Underage legatees who are entitled to receive their vested legacies at a future date can be paid a maintenance in the interim.

1 Chancery Cases 60, 22 E.R. 694

15 December [1664]. Rennesey v. Parrot.

The plaintiffs were legatees, their legacies to be paid at twenty-one years of age. They suggest they had no maintenance, and, by their bill, a guardian prays that the defendant, who is the executor of the will, may allow them maintenance.

The defendant demurred, for that the plaintiffs were under age and their legacies were not to be paid until twenty-one and so they had no cause of suit.

Collins [appeared] for the defendant, and none for the plaintiff. The demurrer was overruled.

Response: No doubt, equity may interpose, and order the payment as they see fit; besides, the legacy is *debitum in praesenti*, though *solvendum in futuro*, and, as it shall go to his executors in the case of his death, *a fortiori*, it shall be paid to him to support his life.

2 Freeman 183, 22 E.R. 1148

15 December, 16 Car. II [1664]. Justice Archer *in curia*.

Legatees of portions at twenty-one years of age had maintenance in the meantime allowed them on a suit here.

Nelson 101, 21 E.R. 800

Kinnersley v. Parrett.

The plaintiffs were legatees. But their legacies were not to be paid until they attain their respective ages of twenty-one years. And, because they had no maintenance in the meantime, they exhibit their bill by their guardian, setting forth this matter and praying that the executor might allow them maintenance.

The said executor demurred, for that the plaintiffs were under age and their legacies not yet due, and so they had no cause of suit

But the demurrer was overruled.

172

Crisp v. Nevil

(Ch. 1664)

After a second insufficient answer, the defendant cannot then object to the Master's report on the first set of exceptions.

1 Chancery Cases 60, 22 E.R. 695

16 December [1664].

The plaintiff excepts to the answer. The exceptions are referred. The Master certifies the answer insufficient in the points excepted to. Then, the defendants fully answer to the charge of the bill. But, in truth, the exceptions were longer than the bill. The Master, upon a reference to the second answer, reports the answer insufficient in the points excepted unto. The defendants except unto the report.

And, upon debate, the defendants' counsel insisted they had answered well to the bill and that they ought not to be put to answer any matter but what is in the bill.

But the plaintiff's counsel insisted that, inasmuch as the defendants did not except against the first report, but had since answered, they had admitted they ought to answer to all the matters of the exception.

And so it was ruled.

[Other reports of this case: 1 Eq. Cas. Abr. 35, 21 E.R. 855.]

173

Lord Digby v. Morgan

(Ch. 1664–1665)

In this case, the court found that the lease in issue was valid and enforceable.

1 Chancery Reports 244, 21 E.R. 562

The Lord Digby's bill being to be relieved for a messuage in Queen Street, which was purchased by the earl of Bristol, and, there being then a lease of ninety-nine years made of the premises by one Newton, the said earl took an assignment thereof in the names of Philip Digby and Arthur Everard, and the conveyance of the fee he took in the name of the defendants Broom and Hodges in trust for the said earl. And the said earl, by deed, 23 February 17 Car. I [1642], settled the premises, and therein he declared that his son John Digby should have the premises to him and the heirs of his body, remainder to the plaintiff, John, lord Digby, and the heirs of his body, remainder to George, Francis, and every other of the sons of the now earl of Bristol in tail, remainder to the daughters of the now earl in fee, and that the estate, which Broom and Hodges had, should be subject to the trust aforesaid, with a power of revocation to the said earl. And, in 1651, the said earl, by a will, confirmed the said deed. And, soon after, he died, after whose death, the said John Digby, his son, took the profits. And the said John Digby being dead without issue of his body, the plaintiff, the Lord Digby, claims the premises according to the trust. But the defendant, Diana Digby, taking advantage of John Digby's being beyond the seas and concealing the trust, procured the said Philip Digby and the said Everard to assign their interest in the premises to Newman and Hussey, who, by the said Diana's importunity, mortgaged the same to one Currance for £560. Afterwards, the defendant Langhorne purchased the said lease and inheritance of the premises of the said Diana for a valuable consideration, paying off the £500 to Currance, who, having the said lease forfeited to him, assigned to Langhorne with the consent of the said Diana, and then, in 1663, procured the said John Digby to suffer a recovery of the premises, and declared the use to the said Langhorne. And the said Langhorne insists he is a purchaser without notice of the plaintiff's title and, if any such entail were as the plaintiff pretends, the same is cut off in equity by the recovery.

But the plaintiff insists that the recovery is void in law; the said John Digby having no estate of the freehold, but a trust, [it] cannot bar the plaintiff's equity.

This court, with assistance of the judges, were of opinion that the lease of ninety-nine years was separate from the inheritance and was well conveyed by Newman and Hussey and that the said lease, for so much as was mortgaged to Currance and by him assigned to Langhorne, might not be impeached. And they decreed Langhorne to enjoy for the remainder of the ninety-nine years, as was mortgaged to Currance, and the bill, as touching the lease, is to be dismissed.

[Reg. Lib. 16 Car. II, f. 799.]

174

Brest v. Offley

(Ch. 1664–1665)

An executor of a will does not have an unfettered discretion as to the payment of the legacies.

1 Chancery Reports 246, 21 E.R. 563

The suit is touching a legacy of £200 given by the will of John Wynn to the plaintiff, of which will he made his wife, the plaintiff's sister, executrix, who, since, has married the defendant Offley, his executrix, but the defendants refuse to pay the said legacy.

The defendant insists that the testator made such a will, and, thereby, desired his executrix, the defendant, to give the plaintiff £200, but he left it wholly to the said defendant's own free will how, when, and in what manner to dispose of it to him. And the defendant insists she ought not to be questioned for the same in this court, it not being the intention of the testator to make the defendant liable to the plaintiff's suit for the same, but she does own assets in case the court adjudge the payment of the said legacy in any other manner than is directed by the will.

This court is satisfied that the said legacy of £200 is due and payable from the defendant to the plaintiff, and decreed the same to be paid accordingly.

[Reg. Lib. 16 Car. II, f. 746.]

175

Proctor v. Reynel

(Ch. 1664–1665)

A sequestration will be discharged after the death of the person whose property was sequestered.

1 Chancery Reports 247, 21 E.R. 563

A sequestration was awarded to sequester the manor of Shampton and all the estate, real and personal, of Sir Thomas Reynel to satisfy a decree, out of which manor, the defendant, the Lady Reynel had an annuity, which, during the life of the said Sir Thomas, her husband, was sequestered. But Sir Thomas being dead, she insists that the sequestration ought to be taken off.

The plaintiff insists that the sequestration is particularly to sequester the said manor and all the estate, real and personal, of the said Sir Thomas Reynel and the said annuity was the estate of Sir Thomas in the right of his wife and cannot be accounted a separate maintenance.

The defendant insists that her father settled the annuity on her for life as a maintenance for her in lieu of a jointure, and he gave her no other portion.

His Lordship [Lord Clarendon] declared that this court cannot continue the said sequestration upon the said estate, the said Sir Thomas being dead, for whose offense the same was sequestered. And he discharged the sequestration of the said manor as concerning the said annuity.

[Reg. Lib. 16 Car. II, f. 781.]

176

Fleming v. Taylor

(Ch. 1664–1665)

In this case, the land in issue was held to be subject to an executor's decedent's debt.

1 Chancery Reports 249, 21 E.R. 563

John Fleming, the plaintiff's father, by a deed in 1643, for the securing of £1000 with interest, demised the lands in question by a lease to Samuel Ferrers to be void on the payment of the said £1000 and interest and, after[wards], in trust for the payment of all his debts if he left not sufficient personal estate to do the same and, after[wards], the profits of the premises to go towards the maintenance of the plaintiff, and, upon the payment of his debts as aforesaid, the mortgage was to be void. And John Fleming dying in 1643, being the sole executor of Giles Fleming, his father, he had assets to pay his said father's debts.

The defendant Taylor claims a debt of £500 owing to Samuel Ferrers by the said Giles Fleming on the foot of an account made up betwixt the said Samuel Ferrers and John Fleming over and besides the said £1000, the said Taylor being entitled to the said £500 by virtue of an assignment of the commissioners of bankrupt of the estate of the said Ferrers. And he is now in possession of the said lands in question.

And the only question being whether the said £500 owing to Ferrers by the said Giles Fleming, who left assets enough to pay his debts, shall be charged on the said lease or the mortgage aforesaid made by the said John Fleming as if it were the said John Fleming's particular debt, this court declared the said lease shall be liable to the debts of John Fleming, as he was executor of Giles Fleming, his father.

[Reg. Lib. 16 Car. II, f. 228.]

177

Kingsmill v. Ogle

(Ch. 1664–1665)

In this case, the devise in issue created a trust for the benefit of the plaintiff.

Chancery Reports 250, 21 E.R. 564

Sir William Kingsmil, by a will in writing, devised as follows, *viz.*:

> First, all my lands and tenements, I give and bequeath unto my only son William Kingsmil [the now plaintiff] and his heirs forever, and my will is that my executrix shall from time to time during his minority receive the rents, issues, and profits thereof to be disposed and employed of by her towards his and his sisters' breedings, and the payment of the portions and legacies devised.

And he gave to his daughter Bridget £3000 and to Anne £1500 to be raised out of the profits of the real and personal estate with all convenient speed and to be put out for their best benefit with interest. And the residue of his goods, chattels, and personal estate he gave to Dame Anne, his wife, whom he made executrix. And, at the making of his said will, he declared he only trusted his executrix with the receipts aforesaid for the purposes aforesaid and she to be accountable to the plaintiff William for the surplus and the same should be employed for his use. The executrix proved the will, and married the defendant, and, the defendant's said wife dying, the defendant denies the trust, though his wife had declared the trust. And, before her marriage, he made a deed to one Mason for the better execution of the said trust, in respect she was not fit to manage such affairs. But the defendant insists that the deed was made with a power of revocation, and so is void and that the defendant is entitled to the said profits until the said William attains his age of twenty-one years.

This court was fully satisfied that it was the intention of the testator, and it is so proved, that, after debts and legacies raised out of the real and personal estate, the overplus of the real estate was in trust for the use of the plaintiff William, the testator's son and heir, and decreed the same accordingly and the defendant to account accordingly.

[Reg. Lib. 16 Car. II, f. 560.]

178

Peachy v. Vintner

(Ch. 1664–1665)

Where a proper co-defendant is not so named in a bill of revivor but appears gratis *and participates in the litigation, he or she will be added as a co-defendant without any abatement of the suit.*

1 Chancery Reports 252, 21 E.R. 564

The plaintiff, in a bill of revivor, had omitted to make the defendant Margaret, the wife of the defendant Robert Vintner, who was a defendant to the original bill, in whose right only the defendant claims, a party to the said bill of revivor, which omission the defendant insists will be error in the body of the decree and would have the cause re-heard.

The plaintiff insists that the defendants are now come too late by the course of the court, for to have a re-hearing as to the merits of the cause by way of appeal against a decretal order in Michaelmas 1662, for that the defendants have bound themselves by the said proceedings and have submitted thereto. And, though the plaintiff omitted in the bill of revivor to pray for process against the defendant Margaret, yet the defendants, by their own act, have made her a party. The defendant made several motions in her name, and executed a commission in her name since the decretal order, and named her defendant in the title of several orders. And, now, after a report made that was confirmed *nisi* and a reference to the Master to re-hear the cause, it would be to make a precedent of very ill and dangerous consequence.

His Lordship [Lord Clarendon] declared the defendants came too late for a re-hearing and the defendants ought not to take advantage of their own default, they, by their own act, having made the defendant Margaret a party defendant to a bill of revivor, her name must now be used as a defendant throughout the cause. And he would not relieve the defendant.

[Reg. Lib. 16 Car. II, f. 777.]

179

Carter v. Cummins

(Ch. c. 1665)

A lessee is liable for the rent even though the leased premises be destroyed by an act of God.

1 Chancery Cases 84, 22 E.R. 706

The plaintiff, being a tenant of a wharf which, by an extraordinary flood, was carried all away, brought his bill to be relieved against the paying of his rent.

But all the relief he had was only against the penalty of the bond, which was broken for non-payment of the rent. And the defendant was ordered only to bring [a action of] debt for his rent.

12 Meeson & Welsby 79, 152 E.R. 1119

Carter, being the tenant of a wharf which was carried away by an extraordinary high tide of the River Thames, filed a bill in equity to be relieved against the lessor's claim for rent.

All the relief he had was against the penalty of his bond, which had been broken by the non-payment of the rent. And the lessor was ordered to bring [an action of] debt only for the rent.

180

Cocker v. Bevis

(Ch. 1665)

The time for the performance of a consent decree can be extended in cases of inevitable necessity.

1 Chancery Cases 61, 22 E.R. 695

23 January [1665]. Cocker, Knight, and the Lady Elizabeth, his wife, daughter and heir of Edmund Ludlow, son and heir of Henry Ludlow, against Bevis. The Master of the Rolls.

Upon the hearing and debating of the matter in question between the said parties this present day in the presence of counsel learned on both sides, the substance of the plaintiff's bill appeared to be that Henry Ludlow, having borrowed the sum of £2000 of Peter Bevis, the defendant's father, did for security of £1000 thereof, by an indenture dated September 25, *anno* 5 Car. I [1629], demise unto the said Peter Bevis the manor of Kingston Deveril with its appurtenances for the term of 99 years and, for security of the other sum, did by indenture the 7th of the same month in the year aforesaid, demise several woods called Sawley, Eulel, and Ely and divers grounds unto the said Peter Bevis for the term of 99 years aforesaid. And the said Peter Bevis, by indenture 29 October 5 Car. I [1629], did re-demise the said manor of Kingston Deveril with the appurtenances unto the said Henry Ludlow for the term of 99 years, rendering a yearly rent unto the said Peter Bevis of £100 at Lady Day and Michaelmas by equal portions during the life of Susan, the wife of the said Peter Bevis, and Richard Cubbel and the longest liver of them. And, by another indenture dated 9 October in the same year, he did re-demise the said woods and grounds unto the said Henry Ludlow for the same term, rendering unto the said Bevis £100 *per annum* during the life of Richard Bevis, William Bevis, and Sabastian Isaac, which said lands, at the time of the aforementioned grants, were worth to be sold £8000. And, for six years and a half, the said Henry Ludlow did duly pay the said rent, amounting to £1300, and, for non-payment thereof, about the year 1640, the said Bevis made his entry, and received the profits thereof. Whereupon, John Ridout, Gent., and Elizabeth, his wife, formerly the wife and executrix of Edmund Ludlow, together with the now plaintiffs, about Easter term 1650, exhibited their bill into this court to have a redemption of the said mortgage, paying what should appear due on the said account.

Upon the hearing of which cause in November following, it was ordered and decreed by the consent and agreement of the parties that the then plaintiffs should pay all the arrearages of the said rents at £160 *per annum* and that, upon the payment thereof, the said Bevis should re-convey the said mortgaged premises unto the then plaintiffs or to whom they should appoint. And, to that end, they did appoint an account to be taken by Mr. Rich, then one of the Masters of this court. And what he should find due was to be paid, £200 thereof at Christmas then following and the residue at the end of six months, and six months then next following, by equal portions. Pursuant to which order, the said Master certified there was due to the said Bevis the sum of £4640, which sum was made up of interest during the late troubles at £8 10s. *per centum*, which said £200 was duly paid at the time prefixed for that purpose. But the plaintiff, being a colonel in the king's army and, about the time allowed for the latter payments, being engaged in His Majesty's service at Worcester [in 1651], was forced to leave the kingdom, and was thereby disabled to make satisfaction according to the decree. Nevertheless, he did write to the said Bevis to sell part of the said lands and pay himself what was due to him, who accordingly sold unto Sir James Thynn and others so much of the said premises as raised the whole money. And yet, he continued the possession and received the whole profits of the residue of the lands, and, about four years since, died, whereby the said premises came unto the defendant, his son, as administrator of the said Peter Bevis, his father, who continues the possession thereof. Therefore, that the said defendant might come to an account with the plaintiff for the mesne profits by him received and that he may re-convey the mortgaged premises to the plaintiff or to whom he shall appoint, he being willing to satisfy the defendant if anything shall be found due to him on account, is the scope of the bill.

Whereunto, the counsel for the defendant insisted that there was such a decree as in the bill set forth and that, for the nonpayment of the money computed due, which consisted only of the arrears of rent, without any interest for the same, the said decree became absolute. Upon which, the said defendant rested satisfied, and the sale made to Sir James Thinn was not pursuant to such letter sent by the plaintiff, but sold on the said Peter Bevis's own account, and wherein the said

Peter Bevis has given a general warranty, wherein he has bound himself and his heirs in perpetuity, which he would not have done for a third person's advantage.

This court, nevertheless, after long debate of the matter and hearing what could be alleged by counsel on either side and reading of the whole proofs taken in this cause and of the decree made in the former cause, which appeared to be made by consent, was fully satisfied that the decree was in the nature of a mortgage and but a security for money, although the same was made absolute, and the said lease to Mr. Bevis was confirmed. And, inasmuch as the consent and agreement of the said parties was in part executed by the payment of the said £200 and the conditions of the times being then such that, as appeared by the defendant's own proofs, that part of the lands could not be sold, by which the plaintiffs could not make satisfaction of the said decree, notwithstanding a continued endeavor appeared in the plaintiffs to that purpose, as his desire of a sale of part of the said premises to Sir James Thinn, and a sale made by the said Mr. Bevis, and much monies received by him by fines and otherwise of some of the tenants of the said manor, and it also appearing that this court has very often in such like cases of inevitable necessity and no willful default appearing in the party enlarged the time as to the performance of the decree, notwithstanding such decrees have been signed and enrolled and this appearing to be new matter subsequent to the said decree, [the court] was also satisfied the plaintiffs are capable of relief in this court, and do therefore think fit, and so order and decree that both parties do proceed to an account and that it be taken by Sir Thomas Bird, Knight, one of the etc. and the plaintiff is at liberty to take out a commission in the country for proof of anything relating to the said account. Upon which account, the Master is to allow unto the defendant the whole money decreed with damages for the same since the time the same should have been paid by the decree, deducting the £200 already paid as aforesaid, and that the said defendant Mr. Bevis do also account before the said Master for what he really made and received of the said manor of Kingston Deveril, by granting estates or otherwise as also the profits made by the woods called Sawley etc. by the defendant and his father before the sale thereof unto Sir James Thynn and also in making and confirming the tenants' estates in the said premises, which said estates together with the aforesaid sale to the said Sir James Thynn the plaintiff is hereby decreed to confirm and to discharge the defendant, his heirs, etc. of all covenants entered into thereupon etc. And the said Master is to appoint a time and place for the payment of what shall appear due; upon payment whereof, it is decreed the defendant shall re-convey the said mortgaged premises, unsold as aforesaid, to the plaintiffs or whom they shall appoint, freed of all encumbrances done by him and his father or any claiming by, from, or under the said Peter Bevis, the defendant's said father.

The 18th of February, 17 Car. II [1665], upon re-hearing the said cause, the said order was confirmed.

2 Freeman 129, 22 E.R. 1105

23 January, 16 Car. II [1665].

The defendant had an annuity of £100 *per annum* granted by the plaintiff's father in this manner. A lease was made by the plaintiff's father to Bevis, the defendant, for ninety-nine years, and Bevis leases back for ninety-eight, rendering £100 *per annum* and, if the rent were behind, Bevis was to enter and satisfy himself. Bevis re-enters to satisfy. And the heir desires an account, and offers [to pay] the arrears. They come to an account, which was stated by a Master in this court. And then, by consent, they come to this decree, that the arrears should be paid by such a day; otherwise, the defendant was to keep the land. The plaintiff paid £200, being part of the arrears, at the day appointed, but being a Colonel in the king's army at Worcester, was not able to pay the rest, but was forced beyond the sea.

And, now, the plaintiff desired an account, and that, on payment, he might redeem.

Objection: That the decree by non-payment of the residue was become absolute.

But it was answered and resolved that, this being by agreement and consent, the decree was but in the nature of a mortgage and the agreement was executed in part by the payment of £200. And, then, the other part being hindered in payment by an inevitable necessity, the plaintiff should be admitted to redeem and the defendant to reconvey to the plaintiff or whom he should appoint free from all encumbrances by the defendant etc.

1 Chancery Reports 253, 21 E.R. 565

Coker v. Beavit.

The plaintiff has a decree for the redemption of a mortgage. And the time for the performance is elapsed, of which the defendant would take advantage, the decree being signed and enrolled.

It appearing that this court having very often, in such like cases of inevitable necessity and no willful default appearing in the party, enlarged the time as to the performance of decrees, notwithstanding such decrees have been signed and enrolled, and this being also new matter subsequent to the decree, this court declared the plaintiff was capable of relief, and decreed [the parties] to go to an account.

[Reg. Lib. 1664 A, f. 378.]

181

Woollet v. Roberts

(Ch. 1665)

A bill of complaint cannot be introduced into evidence unless it be proved to have been filed by the original plaintiff or with his permission.

1 Chancery Cases 64, 22 E.R. 697

27 January [1665].

At the hearing, the now plaintiffs offered a bill exhibited formerly by the defendant against the now plaintiffs in evidence, to which it was agreed the now plaintiffs had answered. The now defendants objected that the bill ought not to be read for evidence against them unless the plaintiffs could prove it was exhibited by the now defendant's direction or privity, for any person may file a bill in another person's name.

And the court were of opinion that it should not be read unless it were proved to have been exhibited with the privity of the party plaintiff in it.

But the defendant's counsel did after[wards] admit it to be read.

Nelson 102, 21 E.R. 800

At the hearing of this cause, the now plaintiff offered to give in evidence a bill formerly exhibited against him by the now defendant. It was objected that the bill ought not to be given in evidence unless the plaintiff could prove that it was exhibited by the order, direction, and privity of the defendant, for any man may file a bill in the name of another.

And the court was of opinion that it should not be read unless it was so proved.

182

Bowyer v. Tufton

(Ch. 1665)

Where a married woman files a bill of complaint and her husband refuses to join as a co-plaintiff, he should be made a co-defendant.

Lord Nottingham, *Prolegomena*, p. 319

Hilary [term] 16 Car. II, Sir Edmund Bowyer and Francis Tufton v. John Tufton, Welsh, etc.

[Where] a married woman had cause of suit to examine witnesses *in rei memoriam* and the husband refused to join for conformity, [it was] resolved: first, the wife and the covenantees to stand seised etc. may sue without the husband;

but then, second, the husband should be made a defendant; else, the witnesses in this cause can never be read against the husband and, besides, the husband might exhibit a new bill, and so, after publication of witnesses in his wife's cause, examine the same persons again; third, note also, that, when the husband is outlawed, as in this cause he was, it will be a good policy always to make him a defendant.

183

Colt v. Colt

(Ch. 1665)

A widow does not have dower rights in a trust.

1 Chancery Reports 254, 21 E.R. 565

The plaintiff claims a third part of the said trust for her dower.

This court, to so much of the plaintiff's bill as relates to the dower of the plaintiff Elizabeth claimed by her out of the said trust, ordered that the said bill be dismissed.

[Reg. Lib. 16 Car. II, f. 749.]

184

Sewell v. Freeston

(Ch. 1665–1666)

A court of equity will not re-consider a case after a fair trial and a final judgment at common law.

1 Chancery Cases 65, 22 E.R. 697

Justice Tyrell.

The bill was after a verdict in an action of the case. The equity was that the defendant had written a letter, which the plaintiff could not prove at the trial, which would have discharged the plaintiff. And so he sets forth the substance of it and that the matter lay only in the defendant's cognizance and ought to be answered and that the plaintiff's witnesses were beyond the seas.

The plea was of the verdict and that the effect of the letter was given in evidence at the trial. And the demurrer was for want of equity.

On the debate, it was insisted that there was not any precedent of a bill in a like case after a verdict; but, before a verdict, it might be proper for a discovery. Payton and Humfrey's Case[1] was cited for the plaintiff.

---

[1] *Humphreys v. Sir Robert Payton* (11 November 1663 and 2 May 1664).

But it was answered that was for matter discovered after the trial, but no such matter is pretended here. And, as to the allegation of the plaintiff's witnesses being beyond the seas, if the plaintiff could not have them at the trial, it was answered that, upon an affidavit of that at law, the court there would have stayed the trial. And the case was referred to precedents.

And, after[wards], the plea and demurrer were allowed.

3 Chancery Reports 17, 21 E.R. 715

Justice Tyrell on a plea and demurrer.

The bill was after a verdict in an action of the case. And the equity was that the defendant had written a letter which the plaintiff would not produce at the trial, which would have discharged the action, and he set forth the substance of it, and that the matter lay only in the defendant's cognizance, and so ought to be answered and that the plaintiff's witnesses were beyond the seas etc.

The plea was of the verdict and that the effect of the letter was given in evidence at the trial. And the demurrer was for want of equity.

On the debate whereof, it was insisted that there was not any precedent of a bill in the like case after a verdict, but, before a verdict, it might be proper for a discovery. Peyton *contra* Humphries was cited for the plaintiff.

But it was answered that that was a matter discovered after the trial, but no such matter was here. And, as to the allegation of the plaintiff's witnesses being beyond the seas so that the plaintiff could not have them at the trial, it was answered that, upon an affidavit of that at law, the court would have stayed the trial.

And this case was referred to precedents.

1 Chancery Reports 248, 21 E.R. 563

The bill is to be relieved against a verdict for £200 upon an *indebitatus assumpsit*, whereupon judgment is obtained and a writ of error brought by the plaintiff.

The defendant pleaded the matter was properly examinable before the judges in the court where the action depends, and not in this court, especially, upon a bill exhibited after a verdict, judgment, and writ of error.

This court, on perusal of precedents, conceived the matter of the bill to be of ill consequence, and allowed the demurrer to the bill.

Lincoln's Inn MS. Hill 125, f. 49

28 April 1666. Sewell v. Freeston and Nicholas.

Roger Clarke had letters of credit made by Sewell and directed to Bruce in Scotland to furnish Roger Clark with any sums not exceeding £600 and this by the 22nd of November and to draw a bill for repayment. £280 was accordingly furnished by Bruce to Clerk and, on a bill of exchange, satisfied and all other debts. Afterwards, in January, Clerk borrows on his own account, and not of the plaintiff's, £200. Bruce takes bills of Clerke for his satisfaction and a bond also from Clerke. Then Clerke fails. Bruce sues Sewell, pretending the money [was] lent on his account on the letter of credit. He goes to trial, and was nonsuited. And he died. The defendants, Freeston and Nicholas, commence a new action against the plaintiff upon an *indebitatus assumpsit*, supposing the £200 was their money. And issue being joined, the plaintiff had his witnesses out of Scotland and attended with from Michaelmas and Hilary terms. But the plaintiffs at law proceeded not. But when the plaintiff's witnesses, one of them was in Scotland, the other in Ireland, the now defendants gave but nine days' notice of a trial at law to be had to the now plaintiff's attorney so that it was impossible that the plaintiff should [have] obtained his witnesses to be present. The defendants had a verdict and judgment.

The now bill was to be relieved and have a new trial, the money lent in Scotland and the witnesses living in Scotland. And the bill charged that all the matters etc. were known to the defendants, and charged the delay of trial when the witnesses of the plaintiff were here was done to the end to surprise the plaintiff when his witnesses should be absent and that the matters were known to the defendant.

One of the defendants answered. The other demurred. The demurrer was overruled by a judge, and now re-heard by the Chancellor [LORD CLARENDON]. And, because the bill came in after the verdict and judgment, yet the demurrer [was] allowed.

Myself and *Glyn*, *pro querente*; attorney of the king etc., *pro defendentibus*.

[Reg. Lib. 16 Car. II, f. 795.]

185

Hayne v. Hayne

(Ch. 1665)

An issue out of Chancery to a jury cannot be ordered before the parties are at issue.
Two related cases can be heard together by the court.

Nelson 105, 21 E.R. 801

Pending the suit and after replication and before issue joined, the defendant got a release from the plaintiff, and, at the hearing, he brought a witness to prove it.

It was insisted for the plaintiff that this release could not be produced in evidence, because the reality of it could not be tried, for it might be fraudulent or obtained by surprise.

The court offering a trial at law upon any such issue, it was objected that an issue ought to be first joined in this court upon a point to be tried here before the court could direct a trial at law.

After consideration upon this point, both at the bar and bench, it was ordered that the principal cause should stay and that a new bill should be exhibited against the release, so that the truth of it might be examined and both causes to be heard together.

3 Chancery Reports 19, 21 E.R. 716

29 April, 17 Car. II [1665].

Pending the suit after replication and issue joined, the defendant got a release. And, at the hearing of it, he brought a witness into court *viva voce* to prove it. It was insisted by the plaintiff that this release could not now be read, because the reality of it could not be tried, for it might be fraudulent or by surprise.

Then, the court offered a trial at law upon any such issue.

In answer to that, it was said that an issue ought to be first joined in this court upon the point to be tried before the court could direct a trial.

After a serious consideration in this point, at the bench and the bar, it was ordered the principal cause should stay and a new bill to be exhibited against the release, whereupon the reality of it might be examined and both causes to be heard together.

186

Anonymous

(Ch. 1665)

After a final decree has been entered, the defendant will not be prosecuted for a prior contempt of court.

Lincoln's Inn MS. Hill 125, f. 46v, pl. 4

April 1665.

A decree being against the defendant to convey lands to the plaintiff, the defendant being served with the decree and, thereupon, a [writ of] attachment, now, without any farther process, an injunction for possession [was] prayed and granted, for it is no end to prosecute the person for contempt, *viz.* to examine him etc.

187

Bonfoy v. Rea

(Ch. 1665)

The defense of arbitration and award will not be enforced where there was fraud committed on the arbitrator.

Lincoln's Inn MS. Hill 125, f. 47

12 April 1665, by the Chancellor.

Sir John Rea, as scrivener to Trodley, did put out his monies, took securities, etc., in other names. And, on a difference, the matters [were] referred to Sir Edward Turner. The estate in debts [was] confessed by Rea to be £32,500. An award [was] made of £20,000 of the debts and the securities to be demanded to Trodly, a schedule of them to be made and another schedule of the goods, Rea to depose before a Master in Chancery to the truth of the schedules, and mutual releases. Trodly died. The plaintiffs, executors, received the schedules and consented to the penning of the affidavit [?] which was made and pleaded to be penned in full satisfaction. And mutual release [were] given of all accounts and demands in law or equity.

And yet, now, the plaintiff [sued] on a supposal of divers particulars concealed, and he mentions some and that the intent of the award was that the defendant should have had but £12,500, and that Sir Edward Turner was induced by the false affirmance of the defendant that there was no other estate than in the schedules.

The matter *supra, viz.* the accord, oath, [and] release, [were] pleaded, but overruled.

188

Gallop v. Cardonnell

(Ch. 1665)

Where two merchants have ongoing commercial dealings and also make a specific contract not related to their business dealings, that specific contract will not be included in an account of their ongoing business dealings.

Lincoln's Inn MS. Hill 125, f. 47v, pl. 1

15 April 1665, at the Rolls.

Nicholas Pescod, merchant, on the marriage of Cardonnell, the defendant, covenanted to pay him, *inter alia*, £500 within one year after the death of Pescod etc. Cardonnell and Pescod dealt as merchants together then and after, until Pescod's death, which happened *anno* 1644.

[In] 1663, Cardonnell puts the covenant in suit against the now plaintiffs, executors of Pescod, who exhibit their bill to have an account of Cardonnell, charging great sums of money due to them for Cardonnell as a merchant and that, the same being allowed, Cardonnell was [. . .] pending the bill and had a verdict for £500. And the cause [was] now heard.

An account [was] decreed, but the £500 being a debt collateral to the trading should not come into the account, but he may proceed to his execution.

Yet it was alleged he was an alien and non-solvent and desired and the plaintiff offered to pay etc. on the account, *sed non allocatur.*

189

Gower v. Lady Baltinglass

(Ch. 1665)

A defendant who is in contempt of court for not sufficiently responding to a bill of discovery can be examined on interrogatories.

1 Chancery Cases 66, 22 E.R. 698

26 May [1665].

The bill was to discover a writing, which it is supposed the defendant, the Lady Baltinglass, had concealed, she having gotten a trunk of writings by a trick from a Master of the court. The defendant had put in four insufficient answers, and delayed the plaintiff eight years. And, upon the fourth insufficient answer, she was ordered to be examined upon interrogatories.

And now, upon a motion, it was ordered that one of her counsel should attend in the next room when she was examined to advise her in any matters of law if she should need it. And afterwards, on another day, it was ordered on debate that her counsel should see the interrogatories, but not have a copy.

190

Love v. Baker

(Ch. 1665)

Service of process on one co-defendant is good service on the other defendants where they were acting together in concert.

The question in this case was whether a court of equity can enjoin persons from litigating lawsuits in a foreign country.

1 Chancery Cases 67, 22 E.R. 698

28 May [1665]. Love and others against Baker, Roll, and Clutterbuck.

The defendants brought a joint action at Leghorn against the plaintiffs, and had there arrested the plaintiffs' goods. The defendant Baker being here and the other defendants at Leghorn, Baker answered here, and, by an order, a subpoena left with him was to be good service for the other defendants. And, thereupon, [there was] an attachment for want of an answer. And, upon this, an injunction was granted to stay the defendants' proceedings at Leghorn. Now, the defendants moved to dissolve the injunction, and insisted it was a new case.

The Lord Chancellor [LORD CLARENDON] conceived it to be a dangerous case to stay their suit there and so deprive them of their remedy.

To which, it was answered all parties might have justice and be fully heard in this court. But the plaintiffs would be without a remedy if the defendants proceeded at Leghorn, and got possession of their goods.

And the court declared they would advise with the judges herein. And, afterwards, the Lord Chancellor [LORD CLARENDON] declared he had advised with the judges and that they were of opinion the injunction ought to be dissolved.

Sed quaere, for all the bar was of another opinion. It was said the injunction did not lie for foreign jurisdictions nor [those] out of the king's dominions. But to that it was answered the injunction was not to the court, but to the party.

2 Freeman 125, 22 E.R. 1101

28 May, 17 Car. 2 [1665]. Lowe v. Baker, Roll, and Clutterbocke.

By the Lord Chancellor [LORD CLARENDON] with advice of the judges, an injunction does not lie to stop a suit at Leghorn or any other foreign parts.

Nelson 103, 21 E.R. 801

Both the defendants brought a joint action at Leghorn against the plaintiff, and had there arrested his goods. And the defendant Baker being now here and the other at Leghorn and a bill being filed against them, Baker put in his answer. And it was ordered that a subpoena being left with him should be good service on the other defendant who was at Leghorn. And, thereupon, an attachment [was ordered] for the want of an answer and so an injunction to stay proceedings at Leghorn.

Now, the defendants moved to dissolve that injunction, and insisted that it was a new case.

And the Lord Chancellor [LORD CLARENDON] being of opinion that it might be a dangerous case to stay proceedings there, it was answered that all parties might have justice and be fully heard in this court but that the plaintiff would be without a remedy if distresses proceed at Leghorn and the defendants should get the possession of all his goods there.

Thereupon, the court declared they would advise with the judges. And, afterwards, they declared that they were of opinion that the injunction ought to be dissolved. But all the barons were of another opinion. And, as to the objection that an injunction did not lie to foreign jurisdictions nor out of the king's dominions, it was answered that the injunction was not to the courts there, but to the party, who was the king's subject.

191
Smith v. Pemberton
(Ch. 1665)

When a mortgagor redeems against an assignee of the mortgagee, the debt due and payable is the amount of the principal and unpaid interest at the time of the assignment, i.e. *the amount the assignee paid in good faith to the assignor.*

1 Chancery Cases 67, 22 E.R. 698

30 May [1665].

The mortgagee had assigned the mortgage. The mortgagor comes to redeem. The question was if what was really due to the mortgagee when he assigned for principal and interest and paid him by the assignee should be taken as principal or so much only as the mortgagee first lent.

[It was] ordered that all monies really paid by the assignee that was due to the mortgagee should be principal to the assignee. But the account between the mortgagee and assignee was not to conclude the mortgagor, but the Master was to see what was really due at the assignment and whether he had really paid the money, for, if the assignment was colorable, it would be otherwise.

2 Freeman 184, 22 E.R. 1149

30 May, 17 Car. II [1665].

The mortgagee had assigned for principal and interest. The mortgagor came to redeem. The question was if what the assignee paid should be all taken for principal.

[It was] resolved that all which he really paid and was due should be principal, but the account between the mortgagee and the assignee should not conclude the mortgagor. And, therefore, it was referred to a Master.

[Other reports of this case: 1 Eq. Cas. Abr. 287, 329, 21 E.R. 1050, 1081.]

192
Lord Digby v. Langworth
(Ch. 1665)

A tenant in tail of a trust can bar a remainder in tail to another person.

1 Chancery Cases 68, 22 E.R. 699

30 May [1665]. The Lord Chancellor, Chief Justice Bridgeman, Baron Turner, the Master of the Rolls.

Whether the tenant in tail of a trust, remainder in tail to another, if the tenant in tail by suffering a recovery, that recovery shall bar the remainder, which is no settled interest vested, BRIDGEMAN was of opinion it should not. But it was referred to a case, and the judges to consider of it.

See the Case of Goodrick and Brown, fol. 49.[1]

Lincoln's Inn MS. Hill 125, f. 47v, pl. 2

Trinity [term] 17 Car. II, in Chancery.

A conveyance was made by John, earl of Bristol, in trust for himself for life, the remainder in tail to John, his second son, the remainder to the plaintiff John. The earl died. John, his son, being *cestui que trust* in tail bargains to J.S. by a deed enrolled, and, then, suffers a common recovery, J.S. being tenant and he the vouchee to the use of him and his heirs. And he devises the land to the defendant, his niece. And he dies without issue.

John, the plaintiff, being *cestui que trust* in remainder, exhibits his bill to have the lands according to the limitation.

And [it is] dismissed. The court held the recovery good to bar the equity of him in the remainder though there was no tenant to the *praecipe*.

And Goodrick's Case was cited in accord.

193

Shirley v. Fagg

(Ch. 1665)

A court of equity will not require a defendant to make a disclosure of deeds that might defeat his own title.

Lord Nottingham, *Prolegomena*, p. 204

Sir Thomas Fagg purchased land of the earl of Thanet in Sussex, which was formerly the land of Shirley. The heir of Shirley exhibits a bill against Sir Thomas Fagg, supposing that the land was entailed and that Sir Thomas Fagg had by money and great rewards procured a servant of the family of Shirley, with whom the evidences were entrusted, to deliver up the deed of entail etc., and he prayed a discovery and relief.

Sir Thomas Fagg pleads that he was a purchaser for a valuable consideration without notice of any entail at the time of his purchase.

[It was] ruled by the advice of the judges that he should not answer nor be compelled in equity to deliver or discover any deed against himself, which way soever he came by it, but let the heir recover it at law by [an action of] detinue if he can, for equity will not disarm a purchaser.

[1] *Goodrick v. Brown* (Ch. 1664), see above, Case No. 151.

1 Chancery Cases 68, 22 E.R. 699

1 June. The Lord Chancellor, Chief Justice Bridgeman, Judge Archer.

The plaintiff, by his bill, made a title to the lands in question by an entail of his great-grandfather, 9 Jac. [1611 × 1612], whereby the premises were limited to the great-grandfather for life, remainder to the plaintiff's grandfather by name for life, remainder to the plaintiff's father by name for life, remainder to the first son, which the plaintiff is, and other sons in tail. And he shows how, by virtue of those limitations, the great-grandfather, grandfather, and father did enjoy during their respective lives, and the plaintiff's father died about ten years since, the plaintiff then an infant of ten years old, and that the plaintiff ought to enjoy by that settlement. And the bill complained that Sir John Fagg and the rest of the defendants had entered into several parts of the premises, and did divide the same among them, having gotten the evidences and the settlement, and did conceal the same, which the said Sir John had gotten into his hands from one Walter for a reward to him or otherwise. And he had altered and confounded the bounds and names of the land. And so to have a discovery of the evidences and the deed of settlement and the delivery up of the same was the scope of the bill.

The defendant Fagg pleaded that, for £6870 really paid to the earl of Thanet, he purchased the premises of him by a good conveyance at law. And he demands judgment whether he shall further discover his title or any deeds or evidence to weaken it.

And upon long debate, after a case stated, the whole court was of opinion that the plea was good.

1 Vernon 52, 23 E.R. 304

He [Sir John Fagg], being a purchaser, came into a man's study, and, there, laid hands on a statute that would have fallen on his estate, and put it up in his pocket. And, in that case, he having thereby obtained an advantage in law, though so unfairly and by so ill a practice, the court would not take that advantage from him.

[Other reports of this case: 1 Eq. Cas. Abr. 354, 21 E.R. 1098.]

194

Ridout v. FitzJames

(Ch. 1665)

The Act of Oblivion and Indemnity discharged unpaid bonds made during the Interregnum.

Lincoln's Inn MS. Hill 125, f. 48, pl. 1

Trinity [term] 17 Car. II, at the Rolls.

FitzJames being on the Parliament side [. . .] Ridout, his tenant, being indebted to him for rent, Sir L. Dover, being on the king's party, forced the rent from Ridout. The Parliament party taking Sherborne Castle where Sir L. Dover commanded, FitzJames sent for Ridout's rent so paid to L. Dover. And Ridout gave him a bond for the rent, but paid it not.

Now FitzJames sued the bond. Ridout prefers his bill and grounded his equity on the Act of Indemnity.[1] And he was relieved.

195

Stanley v. Mandesley

(Ch. 1665–1666)

Money due to a deceased creditor-mortgagee is payable to his executors and not to his heir at law.

1 Chancery Reports 254, 21 E.R. 565

The testator lent £1400 to one Pershal, and took a mortgage of lands to him and his heirs in fee, defeasanced to pay the said mortgage money to him, his executors, or assigns.

This court declared the mortgage money belonged to the executor, and not to the heir.

[Reg. Lib. 17 Car. II, f. 599.]

196

Corbet v. Morris

(Ch. 1665–1666)

In this case, the settlor of the trust in issue intended that the plaintiff's deceased husband and devisor should have a share of his, the settlor's, estate.

1 Chancery Reports 254, 21 E.R. 565

The suit is touching £1000, for which the plaintiff, as executrix to her late husband, seeks to be relieved. Sir John Corbet, father of Vincent Corbet, the plaintiff's late husband, by a deed of settlement made in 1652, appoints £1000 apiece to be paid to every one of his children therein named, of which the said Vincent was the eldest, as should be then unmarried or not provided for at the time of the decease of the said Sir John Corbet at their respective ages of twenty-one years successively, one after another, according to seniority of age, and the eldest to be the first. And the question being whether the plaintiff, who was the wife and

[1] Stat. 12 Car. II, c. 11 (*SR*, V, 226–234).

executrix of her said husband, Vincent Corbet, shall have the said £1000 being devised to her by the will of her said husband, although he was of age and married before the said settlement but never had any provision made for him by the said Sir John Corbet, his father.

The defendant insists the plaintiff had no right to the £1000, for that the trust limited by the deed aforesaid was discharged as to the said Vincent Corbet by his intermarriage long before the death of his said father.

The court ordered a case to be made that Sir John Corbet, in 1652, being seised in fee of the Barony of Stoke and other lands, conveyed the same in trust for ninety-nine years, that, out of the profits and rents thereof, the trustees should pay to every of Sir John's children £1000 apiece as should be then unmarried or not provided for after they shall attain the age of twenty-one years and they to pay them in seniority, as above said, with a power for Sir John to revoke or alter any of the said payments with a power also to limit, appoint, or sell the premises to any other uses or persons, that the said Vincent Corbet, the eldest of the said children, was twenty-one and married to the plaintiff in 1642 and before the said settlement without the consent and privity of his father, at which his father was angry. And the said Vincent had £350 with the plaintiff in marriage, which he spent in maintaining himself and his wife, and he never had any provision made for him other than £30 *per annum* for seven years if the father lived so long, but his said father continued the £30 *per annum* to be paid to the said Vincent during his life and to the plaintiff afterwards during the said Sir John Corbet's own life. And, in 1654, the said Vincent made his will, and, thereby, devised in these words *viz.*:

> All my worldly goods and estate, I thus bestow, *imprimis*, if my father, Sir John Corbet, die and leave me, his son, any real or personal estate, then my said wife shall have all the said estate which is or shall be left me by my said father, whether personal or real, and the rents, issues, and profits of all the said estate I give unto my said wife during her life, and, after her decease, the principal, if it be a personal estate, or the rents and profits of a real estate to my brothers and sisters equally to be divided, and, all the rest of my estate in the world, I give to my said wife.

And he make her sole executrix, and he dies before his father. And Sir John Corbet, being requested to settle a yearly maintenance on her for life, she being the relict of his son, Vincent, declared she was well enough provided for already, and would do no more for her. And, after the said Sir John Corbet died, not having altered or revoked the said settlement nor any of the payments and, in his life, made no other provision for the said Vincent or the plaintiff than as aforesaid and there is received of the rents and profits of the premises sufficient to pay off Sir John Corbet's debts and £1000 and upwards, but not sufficient to pay to each of the said children in the said settlement and who were unmarried and unprovided for at the time of his death £1000 apiece, as is directed by the said settlement.

And the question arising upon the said case being whether the plaintiff, who is the devisee and sole executrix of the said Vincent, who was married and died without issue in his father's lifetime, shall have the £1000 limited to her husband by the said deed of settlement and the interest since the same became payable or what part thereof, forasmuch as he never was any otherwise provided for by his father in his lifetime than as aforesaid and notwithstanding the estate falls short to pay all of the portions without interest, as aforesaid.

This court, having considered the case, declared it was the intention of the said Sir John Corbet that his son Vincent, who is first made in the trust, should have a £1000 portion as well as the other children, and, therefore, she, being the relict and devisee and executrix of the said Vincent Corbet, ought to have the benefit of the said portion and interest so limited to her said husband and to be paid equally in proportion with the other children. And [the court] decreed the same accordingly.

[Reg. Lib. 17 Car. II, f. 569.]

197

Goodfellow v. Marshal

(Ch. 1665–1666)

New matter pleaded in a replication that is a departure from the bill of complaint is not allowed as a matter of pleading.

1 Chancery Reports 259, 21 E.R. 566

The plaintiff putting matter in the replication which was not contained in the bill and which matter the plaintiff knew of at the exhibiting of the bill, the defendant pleaded and demurred to the replication, which this court allowed of.

[Reg. Lib. 17 Car. II, f. 546.]

198

Constable v. Davenport

(Ch. 1665–1666)

A freeholder within a manor cannot be compelled to consent to an enclosure where he will receive no benefit therefrom.

1 Chancery Reports 259, 21 E.R. 567

The bill is to compel the defendant, being the only freeholder within the manor, to consent to an enclosure. The defendant demurs for that there are no articles of agreement to compel an enclosure, nor does it charge that the defendant is like to receive any benefit of the enclosure towards the benefit of the church and that, although he be the only freeholder within the manor in the right of his church, yet the same is no ground in equity to compel him to an enclosure.

This court, as to the compelling of the defendant to agree to an enclosure, allowed the demurrer.

[Reg. Lib. 17 Car. II, f. 435.]

199

Hart v. Hart

(Ch. 1665–1667)

A contingent remainderman cannot have a bill of discovery as to his remote possibility nor have security given for its preservation.

1 Chancery Reports 260, 21 E.R. 567

The bill is touching the real and personal estate of Sir Percival Hart, deceased, the plaintiff pretending title and interest in certain lands, household stuff, and plate of the said Sir Percival in reversion or remainder by virtue of some settlement made by the said Sir Percival in his lifetime and also by his last will, whereby it is ordered and appointed that William Hart, this defendant, should have the use of all his plate and household stuff for his life and that, after his decease, the said plate and household stuff should continue to the eldest son of this defendant and so to the heirs of his body and so to the first, second, and third, and other sons to the tenth son of this defendant and the heirs male of their bodies as an heirloom according to the limitation of the lands in the bill, and, for want of such issue, to the plaintiffs and the heirs male of their bodies. So the bill is to discover the plate and household stuff and that the defendant may put in security to leave the said plate or household stuff or the value hereof at the death of the defendant according to the will.

The defendant demurred, for that the plaintiff having but a possibility of a remainder, which is void in law, has no ground or color of relief for the same, either in law or equity, or to have the defendant give security for such personal estate.

This demurrer being argued before Mr. Justice Brown, he held the same good and sufficient.

This court referred the matter to Mr. Justice Archer, who certified the plea and demurrer to be good.

This court confirmed the judge's certificate, and dismissed the plaintiff's bill with costs.

[Reg. Lib. 17 Car. II, f. 525, 18 Car. II, f. 332.]

200

Heyne v. Middlemore

(Ch. 1665–1666)

The administrator of a co-partner can compel an account from the surviving partners.

1 Chancery Reports 261, 21 E.R. 567

The plaintiff, administrator to one partner, sues the co-partner for an account of the intestate's share, which this court accordingly decreed.

[Reg. Lib. 17 Car. II, f. 410.]

201

Stephens v. Baily

(Ch. 1665–1666)

Where a lessee dies before executing the lease agreement, his heir will be ordered to complete the contract, even though the heir has entered as a special occupant.

Nelson 106, 21 E.R. 802

The lessee for another man's life contracts with the plaintiff for a sum of money to convey an estate to him, but he dies before the conveyance was perfected.

The defendant, being the heir of the lessee *pur auter vie*, enters, and holds the land as special occupant. And a bill being brought against him to perfect the assurance, he demurred to it. And it was insisted for him that he was in possession as an occupant and so was not privy to his father who made the contract.

Maynard, on the other side, argued that an occupant is liable to an action of waste and that was the Dean of Worcester's Case[1] and that an occupant was bound by this agreement in equity, that the plaintiff, who was out of his money, ought to have relief, that, where a man contracts for the purchase of lands and dies before the assurance is executed, the heir of the vendor stands trusted for the purchaser and is compellable in this court to execute the estate to him, and that trusts here are of another nature than uses are at common law, that a covenant does not bind an occupant at law, because the estate which he possesses by the occupancy is not assets in law, but here it is a trust, that, if a copyholder takes money and covenants to convey, his heir is not bound at law, yet this court will compel him. So, in this case, the lands are bound by the agreement in whose hands soever they fall.

[1] Perhaps *Bishop of Worcester v. A Copyholder*, 2 Freeman 137, 22 E.R. 1112, 2 Eq. Cas. Abr. 225, 22 E.R. 191.

Mr. *Finch*, for the defendant, insisted that this was not like the case of a copyholder, for the lord is bound to admit the heir and then he is in by descent, and he may have an [action of] ejectment before admittance. It is more like the case of one seised in fee, who contracts to sell and dies before any assurance and without an heir, so that his lands escheat to the lord; this court will not compel that lord to convey to the vendee.

But *Maynard* said the reason was because, by such conveyance, the lord would lose his ancient services which were due before the lands escheated.

To which it was replied that this did not seem to be a tolerable reason, because the lord might make such a conveyance reserving the ancient services.

But it being referred to Justice TYRELL, he certified that, having advised with the judges, he was of opinion that the defendant ought to answer. And so it was ordered.

[Other reports of this case: 2 Eq. Cas. Abr. 54, 22 E.R. 48.]

202

Meech v. Little

(Ch. c. 1665)

In this case, a suit in equity was allowed after a verdict upon a praecipe *at common law.*

Lincoln's Inn MS. Hill 125, f. 48, pl. 2

The defendant had a verdict against the plaintiff on a *praecipe* of the plaintiff to pay the defendant rent as surety for his brother. The bill was that, in truth, the brother prior [?] etc. had paid the rent. The bill [was] after the verdict. A new trial [was] directed.

203

Crispe v. Spranger and Westwood

(Ch. 1666–1667)

Where one co-executor manages a decedent's estate in good faith and solely for the benefit of the estate, he is not chargeable for assets of the estate that came to the hands of his co-executor.

Lincoln's Inn MS. Hill 125, f. 50v, pl. 3

4 February 18 Car. II.

Two executors, one a stranger, B., the uncle, [were] made executors for children. A., one of the executors, sold cattle of the testator, and he delivered the money to B.; B. wasted the money. Then, A. renounced the executorship.

The defendants' being named executors in trust for the children of the testator, they sue A. and B. for an account. The question was whether A., who paid the money to B. should be accountable in case of the insolvency of B. for the payment to B., who had the same title to the money as A. had was no breach of trust nor a *devastavit* in A. and B. was then solvent and it was not done on any design of fraud.

[It was] decreed by the Master of the Rolls [GRIMSTON] that he should be charged, *quod mihi durum videtur.*

After Easter [term] 19 Car. II [1667], the cause was re-heard by the Chancellor, and Spranger was discharged notwithstanding the former order.

Nelson 109, 21 E.R. 802

The plaintiffs, being infants, exhibited their bill against the defendants, as executors in trust for them. And it was to have an account of the profits of the estate with which they were entrusted. The case was thus.

The defendant Westwood, both at the time of the death of the plaintiffs' testatrix and long before, had employed a farm, part of her estate, for her use and benefit in fattening cattle. After her death, he used the farm as before, and fattened cattle, and sent them to Spranger, the other executor, to sell, which he did, and laid out the money in lean cattle, which he sent back to Westwood, who received them, and fattened them on the said farm, and, afterwards, sold them at several markets. Westwood became insolvent.

And it was now endeavored to charge Spranger with the money which he had actually received for the fat cattle and for which he had given several receipts, upon this rule that every trustee ought to be charged with his own receipts. And, thereupon, it was decreed that each executor should be charged for what he had respectively received. This was by the Master of the Rolls [GRIMSTON].

Serjeant *Maynard*, not satisfied with this decree, said it was no *devastavit* for one executor to pay or deliver over the testator's estate to another executor, because each has a title to the whole. And here was nothing done by Spranger but what was for the benefit of the estate. He ought not to be charged with the money for the fat stock when he had returned it to the estate in lean, but the other executor ought to be answerable for the whole.

Afterwards, this cause was re-heard before the Lord Chancellor [BRIDGEMAN], the Master of the Rolls [GRIMSTON] being present.

And Serjeant *Maynard* insisted that Spranger, being not liable at law, ought not to be so in equity, that, if this decree should stand, no trustee could be safe, that the farm was in Westwood's management when the testatrix died, and, after her death, continued still in him, who was a near relation both to her and the children. It is true Spranger acted as an executor, but he is not to be charged, because there is no breach of trust and an executor is a trustee, as well to dispose as to receive, and that he did not break his trust in selling fat cattle, since he laid out the money upon the lean stock to be fattened on the same land, which were actually delivered to Westwood and taken into his possession.

Serjeant *Fountaine*, on the other side, argued that Spranger did suspect Westwood's sufficiency, and, therefore, ought to have kept the money, and not bought lean cattle for him, that, if two trustees give receipts, they shall be both charged, though they did not actually receive the money. See Townly *versus* Chaloner, Cro. 312, *contra.*[1] As to the fat cattle, the value of them before they were sold and the money afterwards was assets in Spranger's hands to charge him by any creditors to whom he was liable and this by receiving the money for which they were sold. And the executors are not bound to manage the farm as in the lifetime of the testatrix, but, upon the first opportunity, to turn the stock into money.

Lord Chancellor [BRIDGEMAN]: Since the farm was in Westwood's possession when the testatrix died, if the cattle had afterwards died or had not been sold, Spranger had not been chargeable. It must certainly be good husbandry for the executors to sell the fat cattle and to buy lean, and Spranger has committed no fault in what he did. As to the allegation that, where the receipts can be distinguished, each trustee is to be charged with so much as he received, it is very true. But Spranger ought not to be charged with his receipts, because he laid out the money for stock to be fattened on the same farm which was afterwards disposed by Westwood. And he did so order and declare and explain the former decree made in this cause accordingly.

204

Drake v. Mayor of Exeter

(Ch. 1666)

A contractual right to renew a lease does not pass to the assignees of a bankrupt.

1 Chancery Cases 71, 22 E.R. 700

February. The Lord Chancellor, Justice Wyndham, Baron Turner.

[There were] a lessor and lessee for years; the lessor covenants with the lessee and his assigns to renew, then the lessee becomes bankrupt, and commissioners of bankrupt assign this covenant. The assignee brought this bill to have the defendant, the lessor, renew to him.

The case was referred to Justice WYNDHAM and Baron TURNER, and they certified the plaintiff ought not to be relieved. And so he was dismissed.

[1] *Townley v. Chalenor* (1633), Croke Car. 312, 79 E.R. 872, also *sub nom. Townley v. Sherborne*, J. Bridgman 35, 123 E.R. 1181, Chancery Repts. *tempore* Coventry 208.

Serjeant *Newdegate*, who was counsel in this case for the defendant, said it had been ruled in this court that commissioners of bankrupt might assign an equity of redemption of a mortgage.

But *quaere*, for it seems to be against the Statute,[1] which enables them to the benefit of a condition that is performed, and not forfeited.

2 Freeman 183, 22 E.R. 1148

February, 17 Car. II [sic].

[There was a] lease with covenants to renew. The lessee becomes bankrupt. The commissioners assign to the plaintiff, who sues the lessor to renew.

And it was resolved that he should.[2]

Serjeant *Newdegate* affirmed that the commissioners might assign the equity of redemption of a mortgage. *Sed quaere quia de hoc*; the statute speaks only of conditions and not conditions forfeited.

Nelson 102, 21 E.R. 801

The lessor made a lease for years, and covenanted with the lessee and his assigns that he would renew the lease. The lessee became a bankrupt. And, afterwards, the Commissioners of Bankrupts assigned this covenant to the plaintiff, who brought his bill against the lessor to have the benefit thereof and that he might be compelled to renew the lease.

The case was referred to Justice Wyndham and Baron Turner. And they certified that the plaintiff ought not to be relieved. And so he was dismissed.

But Serjeant *Newdegate* told Mr. *Keck*, who was of counsel for the defendant, that it had been ruled in this court that Commissioners of Bankrupts might assign an equity of redemption of a mortgage. But this may be a question, because the statutes of bankruptcy[3] do enable them to assign the benefit of conditions which are to be performed, but not conditions which are forfeited.

[Other reports of this case: 1 Eq. Cas. Abr. 53, 21 E.R. 868.]
[Reg. Lib. 1664 A, f. 380.]

205

Digardine v. Swift

(Ch. 1666)

Where a party has absconded and the litigation continues, the solicitors or counsel are liable to pay court costs.

---

[1] Stat. 1 Jac. I, c. 15 (*SR*, IV, 1031–1034); Stat. 21 Jac. I, c. 19 (*SR*, IV, 1227–1229).

[2] Sic in text.

[3] Stat. 1 Jac. I, c. 15 (*SR*, IV, 1031–1034); Stat. 21 Jac. I, c. 19 (*SR*, IV, 1227–1229).

1 Chancery Cases 71, 22 E.R. 700

22 February [1666].

Upon a motion, it was ordered that, where one of the bail at law for the plaintiff had prosecuted a suit in equity in the plaintiff's name in his absence, the plaintiff not being to be found, and the said person's bail acting throughout the cause in this court as party and solicitor, that the solicitor should pay the defendant here his costs. But this was in respect he was solicitor and prosecutor, and not as bail, for, there being other persons that were bail, the court declared they would not charge them with the costs.

And the Master of the Rolls [Grimston], to whom this matter was formerly moved, as concerning the solicitor's paying the costs, desired to see precedents before he made any order. And he declared in this case that, if there were any one precedent, he would make the second.

And note, in the case of scandal etc. in a bill or answer, it is now a commendable practice to charge the counsel with costs.

206

Lawrence v. Brasier

(Ch. 1666)

An annuity out of an office is not payable for those years when the office was non-existent.

1 Chancery Cases 72, 22 E.R. 701

The Lord Chancellor, Justice Wyndham.

A bond was entered into before the wars, conditioned to pay £40 *per annum*, for twelve years out of the profits of an office, which was taken away by the usurpers. And the obligor being sued on the bond and the office revived, he exhibits his bill to be relieved against the bond. The obligee insisted that the office continued some part of the twelve years, and, being now revived, the obligor ought to pay the £40 *per annum* for twelve years or be dismissed, for the obligee having the law with him ought not to be hurt in equity without satisfaction according to the condition.

It was decreed that the obligor should pay the £40 *per annum* for so many years as the office continued, and, thereupon, the bond was to be delivered up.

[Other reports of this case: 1 Eq. Cas. Abr. 85, 21 E.R. 897.]

207

Terwit v. Gresham

(Ch. 1666)

Depositions that were taken in an earlier case involving the same issues can be used in a later case even though the parties are not the same or in privity in both cases.

1 Chancery Cases 73, 22 E.R. 701

March [1666]. The Lord Chancellor, Baron Turner.

It was ordered upon a long debate that depositions of witnesses taken in a former cause thirty years since where the same matters were under examination and in issue as in this (the point being concerning encumbrances and damnification in both cases) should be made use of in this cause, albeit the plaintiff in this cause and those under whom he claims were not any parties in the former cause, inasmuch as the terre tenants were then parties and the now plaintiff's title did not then appear and the witnesses were dead.

And precedents were cited for this between Trinity Hall and Doctors' Commons, where Dr. North's depositions taken in a former ancient cause, where neither of the now parties were party, were read. And the like between Culton and Vaughan.

2 Freeman 184, 22 E.R. 1149

It was ordered upon a long debate that the depositions of witnesses taken in a cause thirty years since about the same matters, being encumbrances and damnifications, should be made use of in this cause, the witnesses being dead, though that suit were between other parties from whom these claim not.

And the case between Trinity Hall and Doctors' Commons was cited and between Charlton and Vaughan.

[Other reports of this case: 1 Eq. Cas. Abr. 227, 21 E.R. 1008.]
[Reg. Lib. 1664 B, f. 337.]

208

Armitage v. Metcalf

(Ch. 1666–1668)

Courts of equity grant relief against accidents.

1 Chancery Cases 74, 22 E.R. 701

16 May [1666].

The cause being heard about 1664 and one point being that the obligor, having paid a debt of his ancestor upon bond, might be reimbursed his money by the executor of the obligor, who had personal assets, the heir being forced to pay the debt by a suit, it was decreed the executor should reimburse the heir as far as there were personal assets come to the executor's hand.

And upon an exception taken to a report in this cause, which came to be heard before Mr. Baron Atkyns, 29 June 1668, there was this point. Whereas A. alone was bound to the testator, the executor delivered up the bond, and took another to himself for the same debt, whereby, as was alleged by the counsel of the executor, the security was bettered. And whether this in equity should be charged as assets in the executor's hands, he having delivered up the old bond was the question. Against the executor, it was insisted that the taking the new bond had altered the property of the debt, so that, if the executor died intestate, his administrator would have the debt; whereas, if it had rested on the old bond, the administrator *de bonis non* of the first testator should have it subject to the first testator's debts. It was admitted that, at law, this did charge the executor as a conversion and receipt of so much of the estate. But it was insisted that, in equity, he having taken the same person and another bound and offering to assign the bond to the heir, it ought not to charge him, especially when the heir is plaintiff in equity, as here.

And it was ruled that the executor should not be charged with the money by altering the security, but that he should assign the security to the heir, for it is not equity that the executor should suffer for his care in taking a new bond with further security and the debt was lost, not by his default, but through accident only, against which equity relieves.

[Other reports of this case: 1 Eq. Cas. Abr. 269, 21 E.R. 1038.]

209

Smallpiece v. Anguish

(Ch. 1666)

In this case, the purported will was found to be forged, the debtors of the decedent were ordered not to pay anything to the executor, and the executor was punished for the fraud.

1 Chancery Cases 75, 22 E.R. 702

25 May [1666]. The Lord Chancellor, The Master of the Rolls.

The bill suggested that the defendant did endeavor to set up a will, pretended to be made by one that died in the great sickness in London, and that the defendant was executor of it, whereas there was no such real will, but [one] obtained unduly and that was contested in the spiritual court. And yet the defendant, in the interim, being insolvent, endeavored to get in the debts due to the estate.

The defendant demurred, for that the bill contained no equity and the suggestion of insolvency might be made against every executor.

But the demurrer was overruled.

And, upon a motion, it was ordered that the debtors to the deceased's estate should forbear to pay any money until the matter be settled in the spiritual court.

And note that, upon examination, this was found to be a forged will, and the defendant stood in the pillory for it. *Quaere*, if it was done without a trial at law.

[Other reports of this case: 1 Eq. Cas. Abr. 238, 21 E.R. 1016.]

210

Bradborne v. Mico

(Ch. 1666)

A bill to remove a case out of a London court must be made upon security to prove the reason for the removal.

The reasons for removing a case out of a London court are examined in secret.

The defendant in a certiorari *must object to the removal before the higher court has accepted jurisdiction of the case.*

Lincoln's Inn MS. Hill 125, f. 49v

[Upon] a *certiorari* bill to remove a bill in equity out of London, [there must] be sureties to prove the suggestions, and, if not, the bill is to be dismissed and a [writ of] *procedendo* granted. And the examinations in such a case are referred to a Master, who, without making either side acquainted with the examinations, makes his report to the court, for neither side must see the examinations nor are they of any use *in futuro*, for all is examined again after the bill is answered.

And, in this case between Bradborne and Mico, security was not well given, and yet the bill was retained, and no *procedendo* was granted, because the defendant moved not until after the Master had reported the suggestions were proved. And so the want [?] of the security obtained, and so the motion was too late.

211

Holford v. Holford

(Ch. 1666–1672)

Every voluntary conveyance is prima facie fraudulent against a conveyance for a consideration.

Lincoln's Inn MS. Hill 125, f. 50v, pl. 2

Trinity [term] 18 Car. II.

The elder brother makes a voluntary assurance whereby he conveys lands to the use of himself in tail and, after, to his second son in tail. And, afterwards, in consideration of marriage and a great portion, he covenants to settle on his second wife and issue by her. The lands were decreed according to the agreement against the issue in tail.

[On] 4 July 1667, the cause [was] reheard, and [it was] decreed that the defendant admit the plaintiff a purchaser on a valuable consideration and then try the validity of the first settlement, if fraudulent or no, at law. The lands lying in Cheshire, the trial [was] to be in Shropshire.

1 Chancery Cases 216, 22 E.R. 769

9 February [1672]. The Lord Keeper, Justice Twysden.

This cause having been formerly heard and the plaintiff claiming under articles of marriage between her father and mother, whereby, in consideration of a great portion, her father did agree to settle the lands in question on himself and his wife and their issue, whose issue the plaintiff is, but, though he lived some years after, he did not execute any conveyance. And the defendant, being the plaintiff's father's brother, claimed by a deed of entail made by the plaintiff's father ten years before the articles, whereby, for failer of issue male on his own body, the lands were limited to the defendant.

It was directed to a trial on this issue whether the deed, by which the defendant claimed, was fraudulent or not and the defendant to admit the plaintiff a purchaser that the fraud might come in issue. A trial was had, and it was found against the plaintiff.

And, now, for the plaintiff, it was prayed there might be a new trial and that the defendant might at such trial admit the plaintiff had a conveyance, for, as it stood upon articles, the defendant's conveyance could not be taken to be fraudulent against the articles, nothing passing in law thereby and yet it would be fraudulent against a conveyance. And, therefore, it was insisted, the defendant ought to admit the plaintiff had a conveyance, though not such a one as to bar the estate tail, yet a conveyance by way of a lease and release, as if the plaintiff's father was seised in fee, and then the matter of the fraud would properly come in issue, which the court denied, and so dismissed the bill.

And, in the arguing of this cause, it was admitted that every voluntary conveyance is *prima facie* fraudulent against a conveyance for a consideration.

212

Hotly v. Reynolds

(Ch. 1666)

A fraudulent act cannot discharge a contempt.

Lincoln's Inn MS. Hill 125, f. 50, pl. 1

19 July 1666.

A [writ of] sequestration being granted against the defendant for the non-performance of the decree, the defendant's tenant was served with process, and examined on a contempt for disobedience. But the same being for some irregularity discharged, new process was taken against him. But, before service thereof, he paid his rent to the defendant, and, then, he was served.

The payment did not discharge him, for it was held collusive and fraudulently done.

213

West v. Diddlefold and Otway

(Ch. 1666)

A final judgment at common law is res judicata to a later suit in equity.

Lincoln's Inn MS. Hill 125, f. 50, pl. 2

West, possessed of a mill, contracted with Diddlefold to assign his term at an increase [?] of rent and covenants. Other differences happening, then, they made mutual releases, before which, Otway had arrested West, supposing the contract for him. Yet, there was a judgment by a [?] verdict for £5 and costs.

West prefers his bill because of the surprise, being by default for want of a plea.

The cause at issue here [was] fully proved with West. But the bill [was] dismissed because [it was] after the judgment.

214

Anonymous

(Ch. 1666)

Where a seller of land dies before executing a conveyance, the occupant of the land will be ordered to make the conveyance.

Lincoln's Inn MS. Hill 125, f. 50, pl. 3

Michaelmas [term] 18 Car. II.

This term, [it was] decreed on debate. A tenant *pur auter vie* covenanted to assign his estate, and he died before the assurance; the occupant, after his death, was decreed to assure according to the agreement.

215

Knipe v. Jesson

(Ch. 1666)

Where an agent for an exporter does not pay foreign import duties that were due, he does not have to account for them to his principal.

1 Chancery Cases 76, 22 E.R. 702

13 November [1666]. The Master of the Rolls.

The defendant employed the plaintiff as his factor beyond the sea, and brought an action of account against the plaintiff here at law, and had a judgment *quod computet*.

The plaintiff brought his bill here to have an allowance upon the account for what he had saved in not paying the customs for those goods, which could not be allowed before the auditor, as was said.

And an allowance was decreed to the plaintiff for the same against the defendant, the employer. And so it was referred to a Master to take the account.

Vide Smith and Oxenden, f. 25, and Borr against Vandale, f. 30.[1]

216

Hampden v. Brewer

(Ch. 1666)

Where a co-executor's power as executor ceases, all continuing actions and consents, such as consents to arbitration, cease ab initio.

A bill of revivor cannot revive an invalid consent.

1 Chancery Cases 77, 22 E.R. 703

19 November [1666].

Richard Hampden made the plaintiff and his widow executors under this condition, that, if the widow married, her executorship to cease and the plaintiff to be sole executor. The plaintiff and the widow exhibited the bill, to which the defendant answered, and several orders were made, one (*inter alia*) by consent to refer the matters finally to be determined. Then, the widow married. And it became a question in this case whether the plaintiff might proceed upon that bill, wherein there was no mention that the widow's executorship was conditional, but the bill was by both as executors general, or whether he must bring a bill of revivor.

---

[1] *Smith v. Oxenden* (Ch. 1663), see above, Case No. 113; *Borre v. Varde* (Ch. 1663), see above, Case No. 119.

And upon a reference of that point to Chief Justice BRIDGEMAN, he was of opinion he must bring a bill of revivor, though Serjeant *Fountaine*, upon producing the will under seal, whereby it appeared the widow's executorship was conditional, *ut supra*, did insist that there was no need of a revivor. This was the result of the former debates.

A bill of revivor was brought, which was to revive all the former proceedings, and particularly the order by consent.

The defendant did demur to the bill, for that it sought to revive that order, whereas the wife was a party to it and she being married since her executorship, consequently, her consent was determined.

And upon debate, which was the only work of this day, the demurrer was allowed.

Nelson 108, 21 E.R. 802

Richard Hamden made the plaintiff and his widow joint executors of his will, but, upon this condition, that, if his widow married, her executorship should cease and then the plaintiff should be the sole executor.

A bill was exhibited by the executors, and an answer was put it. And several interlocutory orders were made. And, amongst the rest, an order by consent [was made] to refer the whole matter in difference to the arbitration of another person. Then, the widow died,[1] and now the question was whether there could be any farther proceedings on this bill or whether there must be a bill of revivor.

And it being referred to the Chief Justice BRIDGEMAN upon this point, he was of opinion that there must be a bill of revivor.

Serjeant *Fountaine* opposed it. But, notwithstanding, a bill of revivor was brought, and it was to revive all the former proceedings and, particularly, that order made by consent.

To this bill, the defendant demurred, for that it sought to revive the order made by consent, to which the woman was a party, and she being married since her executorship, her consent was determined.

And, upon debate, the demurrer was allowed.

[Other reports of this case: 1 Eq. Cas. Abr. 1, 21 E.R. 828.]

217

Underwood v. Staney

(Ch. 1666)

A loss is as good a consideration for a promise as a benefit or a profit.

[1] Sic for married.

1 Chancery Cases 77, 22 E.R. 703

24 November [1666]. In court, the Master of the Rolls.

The obligee in a bond of twenty years old exhibits his bill against the administrator of the principal and the surety upon the loss of his bond. The administrator says by his answer that he has no assets.

Upon hearing the cause, it was directed to a trial whether the surety had sealed and delivered the bond. And a verdict had passed against the surety, *viz.* that he had sealed and entered into the bond. And the cause coming back to this court and the plaintiff's counsel praying a decree for the plaintiff's debt against the surety, Serjeant *Fountaine*, not of counsel on either side, said it was doubtful whether equity should in this case bind the surety, who was not obliged in law, but in respect of the lien of the bond and, that being lost and the surety having no benefit by (nor consideration for) being bound, he thought equity after so long a time should not charge the surety.

The Master of the Rolls [Grimston] said he would see to moderate and mediate this matter between the parties, in order to which, he was several times attended by the plaintiff. And the defendant making default, he decreed for the plaintiff.

And, afterwards, the cause was upon a case made brought before My Lord Chancellor [Lord Clarendon], who was of opinion with the Master of the Rolls and decreed it for the plaintiff.

It was in the debate of this case said that, if a grantee in a voluntary deed or an obligee in a voluntary bond lose the deed or bond, they should have a remedy against the grantor or obligor in equity. *Tamen quaere.* But, if so, there was no mistake in the principal case, where the bond was for money lent. And, though the surety had no advantage, yet the obligee had parted with his money, and a loss is as good a consideration for a promise as a benefit or a profit.

218

Poole v. Pipe

(Ch. 1666)

In this case, a title to land was confirmed by the court in affirmance of an award and against a lease that was not performed.

3 Chancery Reports 20, 21 E.R. 716

The plaintiff had land descended to him from his brother, who had bought it. But the defendant brought an [action of] ejectment upon a lease for 500 years. And an award [was] made concerning the title under which the plaintiff claimed, and the party that had the lease had not performed, but kept the lease, and it came to the defendant. And the bill is to hold the land.

And it was decreed if it had been enjoyed under the award, 14 Jac. [1616 × 1617], and a perpetual injunction against the lease.

219

Doyly v. Doyly

(Ch. 1666)

The intent of a grantor cannot invalidate his express words.

Lincoln's Inn MS. Misc. 499, p. 205, pl. 2

Note that the Chancery will not relieve against the express words of a deed or make a construction of it contrary to the words, even though the intent be proved to be otherwise, because it will be to incur confusion and there would be no certainty.

And this was the Case of Doyly of Turville Court in Oxfordshire.

220

Rex v. Earl of Dorset

(Ch. 1666–1669)

The questions in this case were whether a certain public charity was properly established and, if not, whether the royal patent creating it could be challenged by means of a scire facias.

T. Raymond 154, 83 E.R. 82

Upon a *scire facias* against Richard, earl of Dorset, and others, members of Sackville College in East Grinstead in Sussex, to show cause why the letters patent which incorporated and constituted the said hospital should not be repealed as they concerned Edward, earl of Dorset, and the heirs males of Robert, earl of Dorset,[1] who was the founder of the said hospital, and cancelled, and the enrollment of them vacated. The *scire facias* recites the will of Robert and that he devised to his executors, by which it was provided that his executors should found and endow the said hospital and make by-laws and that the heirs of Robert should have the patronage and visitation of the hospital and the king, by letters patent, intending to incorporate the said hospital according to the said will and that the charitable cure might be performed according to the intent of the founder, constituted the corporation and granted a licence to purchase the endowment intended. And he farther granted that Edward, earl of Dorset, who was heir male

[1] M. A. R. Graves, 'Sackville, Robert, second Earl of Dorset (1560/61–1609)', *Oxford Dictionary of National Biography*, vol. 48, pp. 541–542.

of the founder, should have the patronage and visitation. The *scire facias* recites that the Lady Thanet and the Lady Compton are heirs of the founder and that Edward, earl of Dorset, had taken upon him the patronage and visitation of the hospital to the disinherison of the said ladies. And, upon this *scire facias*, the earl of Dorset demurs in law.

Finch, Solicitor General, for the earl of Dorset: And he said that this *scire facias* is rather the process in the name of the king than the process of the king himself and such process does not consist with the interest of the crown. And he reduced his argument into five heads: first, this *scire facias* need not to be brought in the name of the king; second, this *scire facias* does not lie at the suit of a subject; third, a *scire facias* does not lie to repeal part of a patent; fourth, this patent is good *in toto*; fifth, admit it is not good *in toto*, yet it is not fit to repeal this patent at this time.

As to the first, because the conclusion of the writ is *ad damnum* of a particular subject, and the king cannot have a *scire facias* but where the thing is *in deceptionem regis* or *ad gravamen populi*. 10 Co., Magdalen College's Case. The king is called *sponsus regni*, and the writ of *ad quod damnum* is *ita quod patria non gravaretur*, but, if the writ be not brought against a public injury, the king cannot make a private quarrel himself. And no *scire facias* lies to repeal a patent but in two cases: first, a *scire facias* to repeal a prior patent is always at the suit of a subject, 2 Edw. III, 7b; Hil. 16 Edw. III, Fitz., *Grant*, 53, the Case of The Burgesses of Wells, 17 Edw. III; Dyer 269a, pl. 18, lands held of the bishop of Winchester were conveyed to the king by covin to make the bishop lose his seigniory, and the king *sede vacante* granted them to the brothers Carmelites, and this grant was repealed by a *scire facias*; Mich. 21 Edw. III, 47a, pl. 68; and in the Prince's Case, 8 Co., the king brought the *scire facias*, but the king there had an interest, and the prince could not have those lands without the king by seizure.[1] Second, here, it does not appear to the court that the ladies ever petitioned to the king to have any such writ of *scire facias*. Pas. 27 Eliz., Sir Henry Nevil, in Chancery, brought a *scire facias* to repeal a patent, and the writ was *unde nobis supplicavit*.

Objection: The king may maintain this *scire facias* because it is in *deceptionem domini regis*.

Response: Admit that it is; yet no deceit will be a sufficient ground for any such writ if it be not to his damage or to the damage of his people. Second, the king here is not deceived, because he recites the will, and yet it goes contrary to it, which is according to his prerogative. And there is a difference where the king

---

[1] *Warren v. Smith* (1615), 11 Coke Rep. 66, 77 E.R. 1235, also 1 Rolle Rep. 151, 81 E.R. 394, 2 Bulstrode 146, 80 E.R. 1021, Croke Jac. 364, 79 E.R. 312; YB Hil. 2 Edw. III, f. 7, pl. 20 (1328); YB Hil. 16 Edw. III, Rolls Ser. 31b, vol. 7, p. 109, pl. 38, Fitzherbert, Abr., *Graunt*, pl. 53 [bis] (1342); *Anonymous* (1567), 3 Dyer 268, 73 E.R. 596; *Earl of Kent's Case* (1347), YB Mich. 21 Edw. III, f. 47, pl. 68; *The Prince's Case* (1606), 8 Coke Rep. 1, 77 E.R. 481.

takes notice of the estate of the testator and where he has not notice, but only by the suggestion of the party.

To the second point, such a *scire facias* does not lie at the suit of a subject for two reasons: first, because, although the king may bring a *scire facias* in Chancery to repeal a patent, yet, when a subject repeals a patent of another, not upon privity but grievance, there, it ought to be repealed in Parliament. Hil. 16 Edw. III, Fitzh., *Brief*, 651; Mich. 21 Edw. III, 46b, pl. 65.[1] It ought to be grounded on matter of record, and not upon a suggestion of a matter of fact only. If the king grants two patents of the same thing, the second patentee cannot have a *scire facias* against the first. Mich. 7 Edw. IV, 22b, by Catesby; Dyer 176, 277a, pl. 54.[2] Where the title of a subject appears upon record, there, he may have a *scire facias*; otherwise not. 11 Hen. IV, 67, Fitzh., *Scire Facias*, 70; 12 Ric. II, Fitzh., *Forfeiture*, 20; 41 Assise, pl. 25, Fitzh., *Scire Facias*, 133; Pas. 49 Edw. III, 11, Fitz., *Traverse*, 19.[3]

To the third point, a *scire facias* does not lie to repeal part of a patent. Letters patent may be void in part and good in part. But they cannot be repealed in part: first, because the record of the patent is entire; second, the form of the entry of the judgment in a *scire facias* to repeal a patent is *quod literae patentes vacentur*, and not part of them. Dyer 197.[4] In the Prince's Case, they are repealed *quoad maneria etc.*, but it does not appear there were other lands. And there is a difference between a *scire facias* and a *quo warranto*, for a *quo warranto* may be good for part and ill for another part, because the record is not to be touched by it. But, upon a *scire facias*, the record is to be cancelled; 5 Ric. II, *Rotuli Parliamenti*, 89, the Case of Laystoffe, reversal of records in part; Cro. Jac. 303, King versus Marlborough and Croker, in [an action of] ejectment against an infant and others reversed against all; Hil. 1653, King's Bench, Symonds versus Bockle.[5]

Objection: English's Case, where a fine is reversed *quoad* an infant and good for the other, and F.N.B. 98b, a fine of lands in ancient demesne and at common law [is] reversed as to the lands in ancient demesne and it stood as to the others.[6]

---

1 YB Hil. 16 Edw. III, Fitzherbert, Abr., *Briefe*, pl. 651 (1342); *Master of Merton College v. Prior of St. Austin's* (1347), YB Mich. 21 Edw. III, f. 46, pl. 65.

2 YB Mich. 7 Edw. IV, f. 22, pl. 25 (1467); *Anonymous* (1560), 2 Dyer 176, 73 E.R. 387; *Basset v. Corporation of Torrington* (1568), 3 Dyer 276, 73 E.R. 617.

3 *Earl of Suffolk v. Queen of England* (1410), YB Pas. 11 Hen. IV, f. 67, pl. 26, Fitzherbert, Abr., *Scire facias*, pl. 70; YB Trin. 12 Ric. II, Ames Found., vol. 6, p. 19, pl. 10, Fitzherbert, Abr., *Forfeiture*, pl. 20, Bellewe 196, 72 E.R. 84 (1389); YB 41 Edw. III, Lib. Ass., f. 256, pl. 25, Fitzherbert, Abr., *Scire facias*, pl. 133 (1367); YB Pas. 49 Edw. III, f. 11, pl. 3, Fitzherbert, Abr., *Travers*, pl. 19 (1375).

4 *Rex v. Toly* (1561), 2 Dyer 197, 73 E.R. 436.

5 *The Prince's Case* (1606), 8 Coke Rep. 1, 77 E.R. 481; *Case of Kerkley Roads*, G. Martin and C. Given-Wilson, edd., *Parliament Rolls* (2005), vol. 6, p. 254; *Rex v. Marlborough* (1611), Croke Jac. 303, 79 E.R. 259.

6 *English's Case*, 1 Coke Rep. 76, 76 E.R. 176; A. Fitzherbert *Natura Brevium*.

Response: Upon the *Book of Entries*, it appears a rational difference, for, if a fine be reversed, generally, the writ issues to the Custos Brevium to cancel the fine. Coke's *Entries* 252, Gage's Case; Rastal's *Entries* 278a. But, when there is a reversal as to part, there is no such writ. Coke's *Entries* 257b, Peirs and Parmiter's Case.[1] So a fine may be reversed in part, but not cancelled in part. And, as to the case of ancient demesne, the fine may be reversed by a writ of deceit, but the judgment is only *quod dominus rehabeat curiam suam*. Rastal's *Entries* 100b; 7 Hen. IV, 44, Countess of Kent's Case.[2] In the case of an obligation for performance of covenants, the obligation may be good for part and not good for the other part, but the obligation cannot be cancelled for part and stand good for another part. And, here, the judgment ought to be *quod literas patentes cancellentur.* There are precedents in point, Pas. 27 Eliz., Privit versus Ward, in a *scire facias* to reverse a patent for a walk in Cranburn Chase. The judgment ought to be given in the King's Bench when the record is brought there to try the issue, but judgment was not given. 28 Eliz., The Countess of Bath brought a *scire facias* to repeal a patent for a market; *vide* such a *scire facias*, Mich. 11 Hen. IV, 5, pl. 13.[3]

Objection: Then, all the patent is to be repealed if any part be defective.

Response: It cannot be repealed upon this writ; second, then, the whole corporation is dissolved, and all the revenue returns to the defendant.

To the fourth point, this patent is good in the whole, because, although the king takes notice of the will of Robert, yet he is not tied to pursue those rules in the erection of the college prescribed in the said will, because a corporation is a creature of the king. 11 Hen. VII, 27b and 28; 21 Edw. IV, 7a, by Choke.[4] Second, *ab inconvenienti*, if any variance will destroy corporations, Sutton's Hospital and the School of Sevenoak in Kent and many others would be destroyed. Third, I will go over the desire of this writ of *scire facias.*

To the fifth point, it is not fit to repeal this patent at this time, because the court will not repeal the patent without calling the guardians and assistants of the hospital, and, here, they are not parties. Keilway 194, Sir John Savage's Case.[5]

Maynard, serjeant, *contra.*

And it was adjourned.

---

[1] *Tawier v. Gage* (1597–1599), E. Coke, *A Booke of Entries* (1614), 'Error', pl. 9, f. [250], also 5 Coke Rep. 45, 77 E.R. 124, Jenkins 258, 145 E.R. 184, Noy 171, 74 E.R. 1130; W. Rastell, *Entries*; *Parmiter v. Pearce* (1610), E. Coke, *A Booke of Entries* (1614), 'Error', pl. 11, f. 255b.

[2] W. Rastell, *Entries*; *Countess of Kent's Case* (1406), YB Pas. 7 Hen. IV, f. 44, p. 10.

[3] YB Mich. 11 Hen. IV, f. 5, pl. 13 (1409).

[4] *Master of Runceval's Case* (1495), YB Trin. 11 Hen. VII, f. 27, pl. 12; *Abbot of St. Benet's v. Mayor of Norwich* (1481), YB Pas. 21 Edw. IV, f. 7, pl. 21.

[5] *Savage's Case* (1517), Keilway 194, 72 E.R. 372, also 2 Dyer 151, 73 E.R. 329, 3 Dyer 259, 73 E.R. 574.

Lincoln's Inn MS. Misc. 499, p. 443

Trinity term 20 Car. II (1668).

Robert, lord Buckhurst, had an intention to found a hospital in Sussex for thirty-one poor and unmarried men and to make a provision for their sustenance. And he conveyed divers lands (to be settled by the grant and license of the king) for the maintenance of the said hospital. And by his will, he declared that, if he did not finish it in his lifetime, that it will be perfected by his executors. And, by the said will, he devised that his heirs will have the nomination of the persons and the supervision of the lands of the said hospital by the grant and license of the king. And the King Charles I, reciting this will, incorporated the said hospital and granted the said nomination and supervision to Edward, earl of Dorset, who was heir male but not heir at common law to the devisor and his heirs and, upon this, two of the daughters of the said lord Buckhurst, being heirs at common law, prayed a *scire facias* out of the Chancery with an intent to repeal this part of the grant to Edward, earl of Dorset, and his heirs which give to them the nomination and supervision, because, by the will, the heirs at common law of the divisor and not his heirs male should have the nomination and supervision of the persons and lands of this hospital.

And upon this, two points were moved: first, whether a patent or grant of the king could be good in part and void in part; second, whether a *scire facias* in this case lies for the repealing of this part of the said patent of incorporation that touches the nomination and supervision only.

Maynard, King's Sergeant, for the *scire facias*: And he held that this patent is void in part, that is to say as to the nomination etc. because the king has not pursued the will in this point and though in all other points, the will is well pursued, yet, as to this part, which is against charity and the intention of the founder, the king is deceived in it. And, on account of this reason, [it is] void. And this variation from the will changes the founder and alters the primary intention of the foundation. And, in this case, it is not a nude charity only that such poor persons should be maintained but it is a qualification of the nomination in the heirs general of the founder. And if the prime intention had been pursued, this hospital in the process of time would become a donative to the heirs of Robert. And for the difference between donative and presentative, see 9 Hen. VI, 32.[1] Also, the formal and essential part of this hospital is the persons and not the house. And, on account of this, the persons who should nominate should be respected. And the profits of the hospital are alienable, but not the foundership. Mitton's Case, 10 rep. 110.[2] And it is harsh that the maintenance will be taken according to the will but the foundership according to the same will not pursued. And the hospi-

[1] *Rex v. Abbot of Fountains* (1430), YB Mich. 9 Hen. VI, f. 32, pl. 3.

[2] *Vowe, ex dem. Vowe v. Smith* (1578), 10 Coke Rep. 110, 77 E.R. 1096, also 2 Anderson 19, 123 E.R. 523, Moore K.B. 298, 417, 72 E.R. 591, 666.

tal, in the eye of the law, had an existence by the will and is capable of a limitation though not perfected before incorporation. Fitzh., *grant de roy*, 56. And, though the king is the founder of the legal hospital, yet the devisor is the founder of the charitable hospital and, by reason of the foundation and dotation, he will be the patron. And, if the king had not mentioned any person to have the nomination, without question, the heirs general of the founder would have it, and it is not material who is the legal or the notional founder, because it is not any gratification except the honor. And the executors are not patrons or founders, but they are only the conveyers of the charity. *Et pietas circuitu non tollitur*, because lands given to A. to hold of a stranger is not good unless to a charitable use, as to found a hospital or maintain a bridge etc. Also he observed that, in this patent, there are two clauses and grants, one of the incorporation, and this is good. The other is *ulterius concessimus* Edward, earl of Dorset, and his heirs the nomination etc. And this *ulterior concessio* is void, and it could be well repealed without prejudice to the other part of the grant because it is substantive of itself and it does not depend on the other. And he said that a patent for substance can be good in many things and void in some, as when the king grant liberties to a corporation, some of monopolies is included, yet it is good for the legal [parts] and void for the unlawful things.

To the second point, he argued that a *scire facias* in this case lies to repeal a void part of a patent. And he said that, when there is any obstacle to the justness of a cause made by the king, that the king is bound in honor to repeal this unjust grant and [there is] no way as proper as by a *scire facias*. And here, in this case, it is a prejudice to the heirs general in actuality and not only in potentiality. And these authorities prove that a *scire facias* lies where grants are void and other remedies allow, because by them, there is a color of tort, as Dier, 197, 199; 17 Edw. III, 59; 12 Ric. II, 40. And that a *scire facias* to repeal a patent in part lies is proved by Prince's Case, 8 rep. [*blank*].[1] But he admitted that it cannot be cancelled in part nor repealed in part if it was entire. But here, the patent contains right and wrong distinctly, and, for the wrong, it can be well taken away, and it stands with the honor and justice of the king to maintain right and to suppress wrong.

Sir Heneage Finch, Solicitor General, against the *scire facias*: And he held: first, that the patent is good in all; second, if it was not good in all, yet the course taken to avoid it is not good.

As to the first, the king is not deceived in law or fact nor by *suppressionem veri* or *suggestionem falsi*, because, in this case, the king made this nomination by virtue of his prerogative, and not in pursuance of the will, though the will is

---

[1] *Rex v. Toly* (1561), 2 Dyer 197, 73 E.R. 436; *Galle v. Galle* (1561), 2 Dyer 199, 73 E.R. 439; YB Mich. 17 Edw. III, f. 59, pl. 59 (1343); YB Trin. 12 Ric. II, Ames Found., vol. 6, p. 19, pl. 10, Fitzherbert, Abr., *Forfeiture*, pl. 20, Bellewe 196, 72 E.R. 84 (1389); *The Prince's Case* (1606), 8 Coke Rep. 1, 77 E.R. 481.

recited. And, on account of this, it is not similar to Mitton's Case, 10 rep. 111. And, though Edward, earl of Dorset, is mentioned in the patent of incorporation to be heir male to Robert, yet this is not anything to ground it, but it is only a description of the person who will have the nomination. And the king is not bound *ex debito justitiae* to pursue the direction of a subject in the foundation of a hospital. And, if the will of the founder was not observed, the executors could refuse to endow it. And, for this, he cited 11 Hen. VII, 27, 28; 21 Edw. IV, 70, because, in the cases of Sutton's Hospital and the Hospital of Sevenoaks in Kent, there is a variation from the founder's direction, yet [they were] good; thus here. Edgar and Sorrell's Case, Cro. El., fo. [*blank*].[1]

And he enforced his argument with a consideration of the Statute of 39 El., ca. 5,[2] that, before it, a subject could not found a hospital without the power of the king, which imports that, before this statute, all hospitals were in the power of the king. And he cited this verse *patronum faciunt dos aedificatio fundus.*

As to the second part, he said that the king cannot sue to repeal any patent but where he is prejudiced in honor or interest. Also, the king could not sue to repeal a patent for a subject except in such a case where the thing before granted is granted to another subject. And, for this, he cited Dier 197, 198. None of which things are in this case in question. Also the two coheirs, who prayed the *scire facias* here, should petition for the *scire facias* and entitle themselves by an inquisition that will find all of the will so that the court could be apprized whether the will is truly recited or not. And, for this, he relied on 29 Ass. 13, cited in the case of the Commonalty of Sadlers, 4 rep. And the patent here cannot be repealed in part, as 4 Instit. 88, where the judgment in a *scire facias* is general that all the letters patent be revoked etc. *Novel Entries* 257.[3] And he took a great difference between a *scire facias* and liberties because a [writ of] *quo warranto* well lies for the forejudging of part of liberties and an *eat sine die* could be for another part. But otherwise it is in a *scire facias*. And he admitted that the tenant of part of the estate as to the whole but not one part of the whole in the tenant could be set aside.

Adjornatur, Chief Baron HALE assisting the Lord Keeper.

[1] YB Trin. 11 Hen. VII, f. 27, pl. 12 (1496); YB Mich. 21 Edw. III, ff. 67, 70, pl. 53 (1481); *Baxter v. Sutton* (1612), 10 Coke Rep. 1, 77 E.R. 937, also Jenkins 270, 145 E.R. 194; *Edgar v. Sorrell* (1629), Croke Car. 169, 79 E.R. 748.

[2] Stat. 39 Eliz. I, c. 5 (*SR*, IV, 902–903).

[3] *Tenants of Wilton's Case* (1355), YB 29 Edw. III, Lib. Ass., f. 159, pl. 13; *The Sadlers' Case* (1588), 4 Coke Rep. 54, 76 E.R. 1012, also 1 Anderson 180, 123 E.R. 418; E. Coke, *Fourth Institute* (1644), p. 88; *Tawier v. Gage* (1597–1599), *ut supra*.

T. Raymond 177, 83 E.R. 93

Twysden, Justice, for the plaintiff: The questions in this case are three: first, if these grants are repealable and are void; second, if this be an apt *scire facias*, being to repeal part of a patent; third, if this writ may conclude to the exheredation of the heirs.

As to the first, these letters patent to Edward, earl of Dorset, and his heirs male are void, and ought to be repealed, and may be repealed though void. Hil. 12 Hen. VII, Kelw. 19a, by Keble. And that these letters patent are void appears, first, because they are contrary to the intention of the king; Hob. 223, Anne Needler's Case; 10 Co. 110b, Vowe's Case;[1] second, the king cannot deprive the patron of those rights which are appendant to him, which is *jus patronagii et jus visitandi*, which are in Earl Robert and his heirs.

As to the second, this grant may be repealed in part, Dyer 276b, pl. 53,[2] because it consists of things of several natures and, as a patent may be good in part and naught in part, so it may be repealed for part and stand for another part.

As to the third, here are apt persons, because the heirs are concerned, because the question is who is the *dotator*, not the executors, but Earl Robert and his heirs, and the executors are only instruments. And the conclusion *ad damnum* of the heirs does not vitiate, because the court knows to whose damage the patent is.

Objection: If this grant shall be repealed, the endowments of the hospital will fail.

Response: It was subject to repeal originally in the creation.

Hale, Chief Baron, *contra*: I premise three things: first, why I cannot give an opinion to repeal these letters patent without grand cause; second, how the case stands here upon the patent and the will; third, the reasons why this writ of *scire facias* will not lie in this case.

As to the first, this is the first case in which clauses which have a general influence through the whole patent may be repealed; second, it is a case of great moment in particular, because, by this repeal, the endowment is void; as the Case of the Abbey of Fountain is;[3] and, here, no master nor other officers may subsist; third, because there is no necessity to repeal them because there are void clauses, and they may be tried at law. And that is the reason that judgment upon an issue tried in a *scire facias* to repeal a patent in the King's Bench is not there given, but the record is to be returned into this court, which is not in another case. And those things are of long continuance, *viz.* from 6 Jac., for then was the will, and the letters patent were 7 Car. I, and it cannot be known what transactions have

[1] *Needler v. Bishop of Winchester* (1615), Hobart 220, 80 E.R. 367, also 1 Brownlow & Goldesborough 162, 123 E.R. 730; *Vowe, ex dem. Vowe v. Smith* (1580), *ut supra*.

[2] *Basset v. Corporation of Torrington* (1568), 3 Dyer 276, 73 E.R. 617.

[3] *Rex v. Abbot of Fountains* (1430), YB Mich. 9 Hen. VI, f. 32, pl. 3.

been passed between the king and the heirs of Richard, earl of Dorset, during the time.

As to the second observation, upon the patent and the will: first, no will of Robert appears by other record than by recital in these letters patent; second, although Richard, son and heir of Robert, was dead at the time of the letters patent, it appears not; third, although, *de facto*, Edward was the father of Richard, it appears not; fourth, it does not appear that the land, upon which the hospital was built, was the endowment of the hospital, and, if no endowment, no hospital. First, it cannot be understood that Edward was heir to Robert, because here is an averment contrary, and he might be heir male in vulgar appellation; second, the clauses are not substantive and independent clauses, but have an influence through the whole letters patent, and so, by the repeal of them, the patent shall be vitiated, *viz.* the naming and appointment of the several officers, making of rules, constitutions, and by-laws, and, in this particular, this patent is not like to the patent in the Prince's Case; third, if here were not derogatory clauses, *viz.* to create a corporation according to the intention of the will, this will create a right to the heir to nominate, but here are derogatory clauses in it *secundum voluntatem*, which shall be according to the king's pleasure, otherwise, the name shall be altered; fourth, the licence to amortize; fifth, those clauses are not simply void, but only voidable, because the king takes notice of the will of Earl Robert; sixth, the grant made to Edward to make by-laws is to him and the heirs male of his body, but, concerning election of members, this is to Edward and the heirs male of the body of Robert.

As to the third, such a *scire facias* lies not in point of form: first, a patent may be repealed in part, but this shall be only in clauses independent; Fitzh., *Petition*, 19;[1] second, there will be an infinite inconvenience if, by this way, part of this patent may be repealed, for, by this way, a good patent may be made naught and *e contra*; third, the king has said how he will have this corporation qualified, and he is dead, and now we will make other patrons after his death; fourth, the king has said how it shall be governed, and not otherwise, and here is no necessity to repeal this, because, if there be void clauses, they may be tried in assize.

And, therefore, the writ is ill: first, it does not lie for the matter; second, because the king takes notice of the clauses in the will which are desired to be repealed, and, therefore, he is not deceived in this grant.

In the creation of the hospital, *sunt tres actores fabulae*: first, Earl Robert; second, the king, whose right is to grant the incorporation; third, the executors, which ought to endow this hospital; second, the executors are not at any prejudice, because they are not compellable to endow this corporation if it be not according to the will of Earl Robert; third, if the executors have endowed the hospital, being so created, it is a breach of trust.

[1] YB Hil. 46 Edw. III, Fitzherbert, Abr., *Peticion*, pl. 19 (1372).

Objection: The king cannot dispose of the right of another, and here the founder was Earl Robert.

Response: There is no patronage until the foundation of the hospital, and the heir of Robert has not to do with it until the foundation, and the executors do not break the trust.

The Lord Keeper [BRIDGEMAN] would advise, and so it was adjourned.

[Argument of counsel: Lincoln's Inn MS. Maynard 24, f. 88.]

221

Ismoord v. Claypool

(Ch. 1666–1667)

Even after the enrollment of a final order of foreclosure, a court of equity can allow the debtor to redeem the mortgage.

1 Chancery Reports 262, 21 E.R. 568

This court, upon a motion made by the defendant, ordered that, notwithstanding the signing and enrolling of the said decree, the defendant shall have six months' longer time to pay the mortgage money, interest, and costs.

9 Simons 316, 59 E.R. 380

Notwithstanding the signing and enrolling of the decree of foreclosure, let the defendant have six months' longer time to redeem.

[Reg. Lib. 18 Car. II, f. 597.]

222

Gore v. Blake

(Ch. 1666–1668)

The question in this case was whether, where a lease of land is devised to pay the testator's debts and the executor pays the debts and legacies in full, the remainder of the lease goes to the executor or to the heir of the testator.

1 Chancery Reports 263, 21 E.R. 568

William Gore, being seised of lands, made his will, and he thereby appointed the yearly profits of all his lands, over and above what was given to his wife, should for the term of fifteen years be disposed, employed, and improved by his wife, whom he made executrix, for the benefit of the persons in the will named for the payment of their legacies. And, after the expiration of the said fifteen years, he gave all his lands to the plaintiff Gore and his heirs male. After the testator's death, Elizabeth, his wife, received the profits two years. And she married the defendant Blake, and they received the profits until 1661, at which time, Elizabeth died. And after[wards], the defendant Blake received the profits. The plaintiffs Singer and Hammond, being heirs at law, claim the interest of the premises during the fifteen years and the overplus of the profits after the debt and legacies paid. The defendant Blake claims the same in the right of Elizabeth by virtue of his marriage. The defendant Kent claims the same as executor to Elizabeth under an agreement made before the marriage with Blake and that she should have a power to make a will and, by agreement, to receive the profits.

Now the question being to whom the lease of fifteen years and the overplus of the rents and profits belong, whether to the plaintiffs Singer and Hammond as heirs at law or to the plaintiff John Gore, to whom the remainder is limited, or to the defendant Blake by survivorship, who married with the executor, or to the defendant Kent, her executor, who has taken administration *de bonis non* of the testator William Gore, this court, with the judges, were clearly of opinion that the surplus of the rents and profits of the premises after debts and legacies paid during the fifteen years belonged to Elizabeth, the testatrix, and it was the intent of the testator, William Gore, her former husband, by his will, that she should enjoy the same and receive the surplusage of the rents and profits during the said fifteen years and, since her death, to the defendants Blake and Kent as under her right. And this court dismissed the plaintiff's bill.

1 Chancery Cases 98, 22 E.R. 712

The case, being stated by an order, came this day to be determined. And, in effect, it was thus. A., by his will, whereof he makes B. his executor, devises (*inter alia*) that B. shall take the rents and profits of his lands of inheritance for fifteen years in trust to pay his debts and upon other trusts. And, after several particular legacies, he bequeaths all the residue of his goods and chattels to B., his executor. It falls out that all the debts are paid and all the trusts are performed and there is an overplus of the fifteen years besides what was sufficient to pay the same.

The question was between the heir and the executor of B. who shall have the remainder of the fifteen years after the debts paid and the trusts performed.

For the heir, it was said there was a difference between this term, being out of the inheritance, and a bare chattel and that the overplus of this term, being out of the inheritance, should attend it. And there was not any intention in the testator to give the executor the profits for fifteen years, otherwise than to make a provision for the payment of his debts and those other trusts and, that, the end being satisfied, the residue of the term did cease and return to the inheritance.

But for the executor, it was insisted that the fifteen years was a term and then the devise of the residue of the goods and chattels did pass.

Curia: The term is in the devisee, and there passed an interest. And, if it had been devised, the executor should take the profits for fifteen years and then the appointing of the debts to be out of the profits and the other trusts does not alter it. So [the court] conceives the residue of the term belongs to the executor, and not to the heir. And it was so decreed.

Tamen quaere. And note this *quaere* is well made, for that, in all doubtful cases, the heir is to be preferred before the executor, for, wherever lands are given or devised to pay the debts etc., the heir, after payment made, shall have the lands. 2 Can. Cases 115.[1]

[Reg. Lib. 18 Car. II, f. 353.]

223

Glide v. Wright

(Ch. 1666–1667)

Interest earned by a trust payable at marriage or eighteen is payable for the beneficiaries' maintenance until the corpus is distributed.

1 Chancery Reports 265, 21 E.R. 568

The testator left £1200 in trustees' hands to be paid to the plaintiffs or to the survivor of them at eighteen years of age or days of marriage, which first happens. The defendants, the trustees, refuse to pay interest in the meantime towards the maintenance of the plaintiffs, because none is expressed nor any notice taken or direction given what shall become of the interest.

This court decreed the defendants do from time to time henceforth pay to the plaintiffs for their maintenance the interest, profits, and increase of the said £1200 until the same becomes due together with all arrears of interest.

[Reg. Lib. 18 Car. II, f. 633.]

224

Hawtre v. Wallop

(Ch. 1666–1668)

A court of equity can interpret and enforce a will.

Where a plea is overruled and the defendant is ordered to answer upon interrogatories, the defendant must be given a copy of the interrogatories and can answer with the advice of counsel.

[1] *Culpeper v. Austin* (Ch. 1673–1676), Lord Nottingham, *Prolegomena*, p. 259, 2 Chancery Cases 115, 221, 22 E.R. 873, 919, 1 Eq. Cas. Abr. 272, 21 E.R. 1040, 73 Selden Soc. 443.

1 Chancery Reports 265, 21 E.R. 569

The suit is to have an account of the profits of the lands and testamentary estate of Sir Thomas Wallop, father of the plaintiff Jane Hawtre, and that she may have an equal share thereof with the younger children of the said Sir Thomas, who, having issue by Dame Hester, his first wife, Sir William Wallop, Anne Wallop, and the plaintiff Jane, and, by Dame Mary, his second wife, Thomas Wallop, Mary, the wife of the defendant Hide, and the other defendants, did, by his will in 1649, give £1000 to the plaintiff Jane to be paid her at her marriage. And he devised the rents of divers lands and his personal estate to raise portions for his younger children and every of them to have equal portions with a proviso that what any of his children have formerly received of him or the feoffees to be part. In the year 1651, Jane was married, and had a £1000 portion, and, about March following, the said Sir Thomas made a second will, and he devised lands, together with his personal estate, to his executors, for the use of his children, not disposed of nor provided for, to raise portions for them. And, when the said Thomas attained the age of twenty-two years and James twenty-one years, then a dividend was to be made, and every child, William and Thomas excepted, were to have an equal part, deducting what they had formerly received. And he made one Hall and Clithero executors, and the defendant Dame Mary was to have an equal power with them, during her widowhood. And the said Sir Thomas Wallop, before and after the time of the making of the said second will, that the plaintiff Jane and Anne, the late wife of the said Hall, one other of the daughters by his first wife, should have an equal share with his younger brother, allowing for part what they have received of him upon their marriage and, by a paper writing of his own hand, written after the making of his second will and found with his will after his death, he so declared. So the plaintiff's bill is to have an equal share with the younger children, deducting the £1000 received, as aforesaid.

The defendants insisted that Sir Thomas, by his second will, all of his own handwriting, devised the rents and profits and testamentary estate for the benefit of his children not disposed of nor provided for to raise them portions and to bring them up, and he explained his mind as to the words 'not disposed of nor provided for' should not exclude his son James from his part of the estate, from whence the defendant's counsel enforced that the plaintiff Jane, whose name is not at all mentioned in the second will, is absolutely excluded from having any part of the testamentary estate by force of the second will, she being before the making thereof disposed of in marriage and received £1000 from her father, and so could not be intended to be undisposed of or unprovided for, nor yet one of the children that was to be brought up, and that the paper writing aforesaid ought not to be deemed as a declaration for the disposing of any part of the estate to the plaintiff Jane, contrary to the express words of the will, the said paper writing being only a draught of a letter not sealed. And it was endeavored by the plaintiff to have been proved as a codicil in the spiritual court, where a sentence was pronounced that it was no codicil. And the defendants insist that the said paper writing by all circumstances was made before the second will, and so it ought not to be countenanced or alter the same, nor to be a ground for a decree that the plaintiff should come in for an equal share of the testamentary estate, directly contrary to the express words of the second will.

The plaintiff insisted that the paper writing was written after the making of the second will and was found in the box after the said Sir Thomas Wallop's death laid between both the said wills, and, although the said paper does not amount to a codicil, yet it is a good declaration of the said Sir Thomas to his executors that his intention was that the plaintiff Jane should have an equal share of the rents and profits and testamentary estate of the younger children.

The said paper writing was referred to law, whether it was written and made before or after the second will. A verdict passed for the plaintiff that the paper writing was written after the making of the second will of the said Sir Thomas Wallop.

This court, with the assistance of the judges, upon the reading of the second will of the said Sir Thomas Wallop, whereby he declared that, for an explanation of his mind as to the gift to his children, was that an equal dividend should be made against them, and every child, William and Thomas excepted, should have an equal part, deducting what they had formerly received or had been paid to or for them. And also reading the said note, they confirmed the Master of the Rolls' decree, which was that the said Lady Wallop should account for the rents and profits of the lands and the testamentary estate of the said Sir Thomas Wallop devised by him, as aforesaid, according to the will (except the adventure in the East India Company) and the Master to make a dividend of the rest of the estate. And, the plaintiff Jane bringing the £1000 portion, which her father gave her, into hotchpot with the rest of the estate so to be accounted for, she, the said Jane, should have her equal share and proportion of the said estate with the rest of the younger children.

Nelson 119, 21 E.R. 805

Hawtry v. Trollop.

The defendant pleaded to the bill, which plea, upon hearing the cause, was overruled, and the defendant was ordered to perfect her answer upon interrogatories. And, afterwards, upon a motion, it was ordered that she should have a copy of the interrogatories and answer by the advice of counsel.

And on the other side, it was insisted that this was against the course of the court for any person who was to be examined on interrogatories to answer by advice of counsel. Yet, upon debate, the matter was settled that she should have a copy of the interrogatories and answer by advice of counsel. And so it has been practiced in like cases since.

[Reg. Lib. 18 Car. II, f. 357, 19 Car. II, f. 131.]

225

Greenwood v. Hare

(Ch. 1666–1667)

A contract to surrender copyhold lands is specifically enforceable in favor of the deceased purchaser's personal representative and against the deceased seller's personal representative.

1 Chancery Reports 272, 21 E.R. 571

John Hare, the defendant's father, did purchase part of the manor of East Carry for the lives of himself and his two sons, Richard and William Hare. And he alone paid the fine for the same to the lord of the said manor. And, by virtue thereof, the said John Hare became entitled to the said premises, and, according to the custom of the said manor, he had a good power to surrender the same, as well for the lives of the said William and Richard as for his own life. 15 Car. I [1639–40], the said John Hare covenanted and agreed by deed with the plaintiff's father to surrender and assign all their title and interest in the said copyhold premises to the said plaintiff's father, his heirs, etc. And the said John, soon after and before the making of any surrender, died, having made his will and Agnes, his wife, executrix. And, soon after, the said plaintiff's father died, having made his will and his wife and the plaintiff executors. And, since, the said wife, the plaintiff's mother, died. And the plaintiff being the survivor ought to have the benefit of the said deed and agreement made with the said defendant's father. And to have the said copyhold premises surrendered to the plaintiff's use, according to the covenant aforesaid, and to compel the defendant to surrender is the scope of the bill.

The defendant insists that he ought not to be concluded by the said agreement or contract, the surrender not being made in the defendant's father's lifetime. And he insisted they were neither parties nor privy to the said contract or agreement, so as the same ought not in any sort impeach the said defendant's estate for life in the said premises, and the defendant has entered and brought his action for a recovery of the premises as by custom is warranted in case the said defendant's father had surrendered in his lifetime.

This court, forasmuch as the defendant insisted that the surrender being not made in his father's lifetime, and so ought not to oblige the defendant to surrender the said premises, being a copyhold for lives, and not a copyhold in fee, being satisfied of the said agreement, purchase, and payment of the purchase money by the said plaintiff's father, and that, by the custom, the defendant's father could have surrendered all the three lives, does leave the defendant to precedents touching the said point and the distinction between the copyhold estates held in fee or for lives, where relief has been given in such case of copyhold for life, it being offered by the defendant's counsel that it ought to be made against a copyholder in fee. And, if the said defendant shall not find precedents, then it is decreed that the said agreement be performed and that the defendant do surrender the premises to the plaintiff's use according to the custom and an injunction for quiet enjoyment [to be issued].

No precedents could be found.

[Reg. Lib. 18 Car. II, f. 528.]

226

Walker v. Sydenham

(Ch. 1666–1668)

The question in this case was the existence of an alleged trust made under difficult circumstances.

1 Chancery Reports 270, 21 E.R. 570

The bill is to compel the execution of a trust created by Alexander Portrey by a deed in 1642 whereby the premises were to be sold to pay the debts of the said Alexander and the remainder of the money to be divided into three parts, whereof Katherine, the wife of the said Alexander, to have one-third, and Jane and Mary, her daughters, the other two parts and to have several sums paid to the plaintiff, which were disbursed by the said Katherine about the premises and payments of debts and otherwise, the plaintiffs claiming the same as executors of the said Katherine, who was executrix of Hurlstone, her late husband. The said defendants Jane and Mary aforesaid, being co-heirs of the said Katherine, deny they know of any such trust, and insist that the said Katherine, in her answer to a former bill exhibited against her by Owen Feltham and his wife, had sworn the deed aforesaid was not upon any such trust, but was made without any consideration and merely to preserve the estate from hazard.

This court dismissed the bill against the executors and legatees in regard the said Katherine had sworn in a former answer, as aforesaid.

But the cause being re-heard with the assistance of judges, the plaintiffs, the executors and legatees, insisted that what the said Katherine had sworn was to a bill exhibited against her by the said Feltham to have a third part of the premises and with whom she was very much displeased, and she used her utmost endeavor to hinder and keep him from the estate. And she only swore that the said deed of trust was (as she believed) made to preserve the estate from sequestration and that she might make use thereof or not as she saw cause. And, for other reasons now expressed, the plaintiffs insist the bill ought not to be dismissed, especially after two trials at law and both found for the plaintiffs that it was a good deed of trust.

The defendants insisted that, at the said trials, no trust was proved nor to be tried by the issue, but only the sealing and delivery of the deed of trust. And they insist also that there ought not to be any execution of the said trust after twenty-two years, the said Katherine always opposing the same and refusing to consent thereto. And again they insisted upon Katherine's former answer as aforesaid, and, if the said Katherine had been living, she could not have been relieved upon the said trust against her own oath. And they cited a precedent in this case between Edwards and Whitehorne[1] to the same purpose. And the plaintiffs, claiming by her will only, are in the same condition with her, and cannot set on foot or be relieved upon the said trust.

This court declared they were not satisfied with the dismission of the plaintiffs' bill after two verdicts, and conceived the plaintiffs ought not to be determined by the said Katherine's answer, her business being then but to disturb and obstruct Mr. Feltham.

This cause was re-heard by the Lord Keeper Bridgeman, and he confirmed the dismission of the first hearing, and set aside the Lord Clarendon's order, and was quite of another opinion to the whole matter therein.

[Reg. Lib. 18 Car. II, f. 431, 19 Car. II, f. 126.]

227

Feltham v. Harlston's Executors

(Ch. 1667)

If a testator devises lands for the payment of his debts and makes an executor and leaves a personal estate, his personal estate does not go towards the payment of his debts, but, if there is no executor, his administrator should pay his debts out of his personal estate.

1 Levinz 203, 83 E.R. 369

In this case, it was said by Serjeant *Fountaine* to have been resolved in this court, and now admitted by the Master of the Rolls [Grimston], he being only in court, to be reasonable, that, if a man devises lands for the payment of his debts and makes an executor and leaves a personal estate, that no part of the personal estate shall go to the payment of the debts, because, by the making of an executor, the testator's intent appears that the executor should have the goods, for that the testator had made another provision for the payment of his debts. But, if a man disposes of lands for the payment of his debts and, after[wards] dies intestate, the personal estate shall be chargeable in the administrator's hand to the payment of the debts, for, thereby, either the most part of the land remains unsold for the benefit of the heir or the most part of the money for which the land

[1] *Whitehorn v. Edwards* (1656), 1 Chancery Reports 173, 21 E.R. 541.

was sold shall remain to the heir and no intent appears that the administrator shall have anything.

[Other reports of this case: 1 Eq. Cas. Abr. 271, 21 E.R. 1039.]

228

Smith v. Smoult

(Ch. 1667–1668)

Upon a redemption of a mortgage, the mortgage money is payable to the mortgagee's executor, not to his heir.

1 Chancery Cases 88, 22 E.R. 708

21 January [1667]. The Master of the Rolls.

The question was whether the mortgage money should be paid to the heir or the executor of the mortgagee. And it was for the heir insisted that it was ruled in a case between Tilley and Egerton, in Michaelmas 1660,[1] heard by the Lord Chancellor, assisted by the Lord Bridgeman, there being no defect of assets in the executor's hands, that the heir should have the money, who is to convey the estate. And this was said to be the first precedent of this kind. The court will see precedents.

And afterwards, about Michaelmas or Hilary term 1667[/68], the principal case was heard before the Lord Keeper BRIDGEMAN, where the order in the Case of Egerton was produced. But, in the principal case, there appeared to be a bond for the payment of the mortgage money, which goes to the executor, and the condition of the redemption was upon the payment of the money to the executors etc. (without naming the heir). So it was ruled in the principal case that the money should be paid to the executor. But the Lord Keeper [BRIDGEMAN], said that, if the condition of the redemption had been to pay the money to the heir or executor and no bond were in the case nor no want of assets of the personal estate, it might have been otherwise. And, in the Case of Egerton, in reading the order, it did not appear how the condition was penned. But the court now took it that the money was payable to the heir by the condition. St. John against Grabham, 11 Car. I,[2] adjudged by the Lord Keeper that the heir, and not the executor, should have the money, being payable by the condition to the heirs or assigns of the mortgagee.

---

[1] *Tilly v. Egerton* (Ch. 1660), see above, Case No. 4.

[2] *St. John v. Wareham* (Ch. 1635), 73 Selden Soc. 202, 3 Swanston, 631, 36 E.R. 1001, 15 Viner Abr. 455, n.

229

Thorndike v. Allington

(Ch. 1667)

A court of equity will give a remedy where the common law remedy is inadequate.

1 Chancery Cases 79, 22 E.R. 704

26 January [1667]. The Master of the Rolls.

A devise was made to the plaintiff by the defendant's father, whose son and heir the defendant was, of £20 *per annum* out of a rectory with a clause of distress for nonpayment.

The glebe belonging to the rectory was but of 40s. *per annum* and the tithe not being subject at law to a distress and so there was no sufficient remedy at law for the rent, thereupon, the plaintiff brought his bill to have the whole rectory liable to the rent and the defendant decreed to pay it.

On the defendant's part, it was insisted that this court ought not to extend a remedy beyond what the devisor appointed and the plaintiff must take such remedy as by law he might.

To which, the plaintiff's counsel replied that the devisor gave the annuity out of the whole rectory and intended the tithe as well as the glebe should be liable to it and that, in the case of a rent seck, where the grantee had no seisin, this court had frequently given relief by decree here.

But the defendant's counsel insisted that that was not like this case because, in that case, there was no remedy at law at all.

The court decreed that the whole rectory be liable to pay the annuity and that the defendant do pay the arrears and costs.

Yet note this seems to be otherwise held since, *viz.* though equity will grant a remedy where there is none at law, yet it will not where there is one at law, though it be not effectual.

230

Beversham v. Springhold

(Ch. 1667)

Where a jury has ruled against a purported will, a court of equity will enjoin the parties from proffering it for probate in an ecclesiastical court.

1 Chancery Cases 80, 22 E.R. 704

11 February [1667]. The Master of the Rolls.

A perpetual injunction was awarded against the defendant not to prove a will touching a personal estate only in the Prerogative Court.

But note that, in this case, it was directed by this court to be tried at law whether a will or no. And it was found against the will, and then this injunction was awarded.

231
Gilpen v. Smith
(Ch. 1667)

Where a testator makes a testamentary trust for the payment of his debts, his debts are payable by his trustees and executors and their spouses who received the settlor's assets and, if his heir be forced to pay the debts, the heir should be reimbursed out of the testator's personal estate and by they who received it.

1 Chancery Cases 80, 22 E.R. 704

Gilpen against Smith, Knight, and Dame Dorothy, his wife, and Zouch. Upon a re-hearing before the Lord Chancellor.

Sir Edward Zouch, seised in fee of lands, settled them on trustees after his death for the payment of his debts. And he dies, leaving the defendant Zouch, his son and heir, an infant, and the defendant Dame Dorothy, his widow. She enters upon the lands, and takes the profits, the trustees not at all acting. Then, she marries Lloyd. After the marriage, he continues to take the profits during his life, as she had before. He dies. Then, the defendant, Sir [*blank*] Smith intermarries with Dame Dorothy, and, she being in receipt of the profits until that time, the defendant Smith continued to receive the rents until the defendant Zouch came of age. The plaintiff was a creditor of Sir Edward Zouch, and his bill was against the heir of Smith and his wife and the trustees to have his debt paid.

This cause being first heard at the Rolls, it was there decreed that the plaintiff's debt should be paid and that both the lands and Smith, in respect of the profits taken by Dame Dorothy and Lloyd and himself, should be liable to the payment thereof with this, that, if it fell on the heir to pay the debt, he should have the benefit of the decree to reimburse him against Smith so far as the profits taken by Dame Dorothy, Lloyd, and Smith did extend.

From this decree, Smith and his wife appealed.

And for Smith it was insisted that he ought not to be charged with the profits taken by the lady or Lloyd, her former husband, and farther, that she had assets of Lloyd's estate, to whom she was executrix. The argument on Smith's part was thus. Either the profits taken by the Lady and Lloyd were taken by right, for there was a pretense she entered on the lands as part of her jointure, or by wrong; if by wrong, then Lloyd the wrongdoer being dead, the tort was dead with him and so there was no remedy to be answered for that wrong. And he compared this case to a trespasser and the trespasser dead. If by right, then he is not answerable over for them.

Serjeant *Maynard*, for the heir, insisted that both by law and equity Smith and the Lady were answerable for the profits taken by the Lady and, after, by Lloyd, as if a wife, tenant *pur vie*, marry and the husband does waste and dies, waste lies against the wife. And he compared it to the case where a wife executrix takes a husband that wastes the testator's estate; a *devastavit* lies against the wife after the husband's death for the waste of the husband. And the wife, by her entering and meddling, had made herself liable to answer what she had taken as a debt. And Lloyd, her husband, upon his marriage, continuing to take the profits as she did, it is a continuance of the wrong she did, and, by color of her having entered before and taking the profits, made her liable for her own receipts, as a debt owing by her. And her marriage with Lloyd, which is her own act, cannot discharge herself. And the husband must be looked upon as acting in this case by reason of the wife's so acting before.

And so, upon the whole matter, the court conceived the decree just and that Smith must take his wife chargeable with this debt. But, upon the proof that the mother and the son were related to the earl of Anglesey, it was referred to him to moderate the matter, if he could; if not, then they directed a case to be made.

[Other reports of this case: 1 Eq. Cas. Abr. 60, 21 E.R. 873.]

232

Harrison v. Lord North

(Ch. 1667)

The question in this case was whether a rent is payable during the time that a third party kept the lessee out of possession and no remedy lies over against that third person.

1 Chancery Cases 83, 22 E.R. 706

25 April [1667]. Sir John Harrison against the Lord North, executor of the Lady Montagu. The Lord Chancellor, the Master of the Rolls.

The plaintiff was tenant to the Lady Montagu of a house in London at a certain rent. He left the house, and went to Oxford to the late king, and then sent his servant with the key of the house to the Lady, and desired her to reenter and accept the surrender. She said she would advise with the defendant, her son-in-law, who then sat in the House of Commons and acted with them. Afterwards, she refused to accept of a surrender. The house was made a hospital by the Parliament for maimed soldiers. The defendant, as executor to the Lady, brought [an action of] debt at law against the plaintiff for the rent incurred while the house was so used and, all the time, to be relieved against which action was the scope of the bill.

Finch, for the plaintiff: It is but reasonable that, if a tenant be put out by such against whom he can have his remedy over, that he, notwithstanding, be liable to pay his rent to the lessor. But, here, the plaintiff has no remedy over. And it was an act of force in the Parliament, which is pardoned by the Act of Oblivion,[1] and so there is no remedy over, and the king has pardoned all his arrears of rent. The law of England is *ex vi termini* stricter in the matter of rents than other nations, for *redditus et reddere* is accepted as *restituere*, and render implies *apprendre*.

Maynard, for the defendant: The plaintiff has a pitiful case, but not such as this court can relieve, for the law and equity is all one in this case. And, if the matter be no good bar at law, it is not good in equity. And he insisted that, if rebels, the king's own subjects, do an act of force and hold a tenant out, that is no equity to excuse him from the payment of his rent. And he cited the case of Carter and Cummins,[2] about two years since, in this court, where the plaintiff, being a tenant of a wharf, which, by an extraordinary flood, was carried all away, brought his bill to be relieved against the paying of his rent, but all the relief he had was only against the penalty of the bond, which was broken for non-payment of the rent. And the defendant was ordered only to bring debt for his rent. And he insisted that a surrender of lands is no cause for apportionment of rent, which is stronger than the principal case.

The Lord Chancellor [LORD CLARENDON] took time to advise, but he declared, if he could, he would relieve the plaintiff.

12 Meeson & Welsby 79, 152 E.R. 1119

The Parliament, during the civil wars, turned a house into a hospital for sick and maimed soldiers, and so prevented the lessee from having any beneficial occupation thereof for several years, notwithstanding which the lessor brought an action of debt for the rent. No question appears to have been made but that the lessee was bound by law to make good the rent.

The lessee, consequently, brought his bill in equity for relief on the ground that he had no remedy over against the wrongdoers, because it was an act of force in the Parliament, which had been pardoned by the Act of Oblivion. But it does not appear that he got relief even in equity.

[Other reports of this case: 1 Eq. Cas. Abr. 365, 21 E.R. 1106.]

233

Frank v. Frank

(Ch. 1667)

A contract to convey land is valid and enforceable where it is under the grantor's hand though not sealed.

---

[1] Stat. 12 Car. II, c. 11 (*SR*, V, 226–234).

[2] *Carter v. Cummins* (Ch. c. 1665), see above, Case No. 179.

1 Chancery Cases 84, 22 E.R. 706

17 May [1667].

A man, seised in tail of freehold lands, with a remainder to his elder brother, and of copyhold lands in fee, devises his lands to his younger brother, and the copyhold lands to his elder brother, and dies. The devisees agree by writing under their hands that the lands should be enjoyed by them respectively accordingly. And, to draw on this agreement, the younger brother pretends the devisor did suffer a recovery of the freehold lands, and he produced an exemplification of a recovery. Upon a search, it was found there was a writ of entry brought and a warrant of attorney to appear was entered so that, had the party that suffered the recovery been living, he might have perfected the recovery. But there is no recovery of record. The elder brother, being informed there was no recovery upon record and so the devisor could not devise the freehold lands from him and he being, in truth, entitled to the copyhold as heir at law, and not by the will, no surrender being made to the use of it, brought his action at law to recover the freehold lands.

The younger brother exhibits his bill upon the agreement, and pretends there was a recovery, howbeit the record was embezzled. And he prays he may hold according to the agreement between him and his brother.

And, upon a hearing at the Rolls, it was decreed that he should enjoy the freehold land. And an injunction was awarded to stay the elder brother's suit.

From this decree, the elder brother appealed by a bill of review. And, upon a hearing of the bill of review, it was insisted for the plaintiff therein that the agreement between the two brothers was parol only and that the pretense of a recovery was a fraud, there being none, and that, if there was an intention and it was never executed, that intention can never found a decree against the Statute *de Donis*,[1] and that the agreement does not alter the case, it being introduced by fraud, there being in truth no recovery nor no surrender of the copyhold to the use of the will so that the plaintiff in a bill of review ought to have both the freehold and the copyhold.

Maynard, for the decree: The question is not whether the recovery shall bar or not, but whether here is not enough to fortify and execute the agreement. He insisted farther that the plaintiff had departed from his title to the freehold lands. And, though the agreement was not sealed, yet it was under hand so that the certainty of it was not to be disputed. And so he relied upon the agreement and that, in that respect, the decree was well grounded.

And, thereupon, the bill of review was dismissed with costs, for *modus et conventio vincunt legem* so that, in this case, the agreement of the party upon a conceit he had not (when in truth he had) a title to permit another to enjoy lands shall forever bind him.

[1] Stat. 13 Edw. I, Westminster II, c. 1 (*SR*, I, 71–72).

And yet this agreement does appear to be upon no valuable consideration.

[Other reports of this case: 1 Eq. Cas. Abr. 24, 21 E.R. 845.]

234

Rooks v. Deacon

(Ch. 1667–1668)

In this case, the Court of Chancery found that the trustees of a charitable trust had not misemployed the trust income and the charity commissioners' findings to the contrary were reversed.

Public Record Office C.33/228, f. 555v

14 May 1667.

William Rooks and Edward Potter *ex parte* that part of the Parish of St. Giles extra Cripplegate within the liberty of London, exceptants; Richard Deacon *ex parte* that part of the same Parish of St. Giles extra Cripplegate of London lying and being in the County of Middlesex, respondents.

The matter upon the exceptions taken by the said exceptants to a decree made the 13th of October 1663 by certain commissioners for the County of Middlesex by virtue of a commission grounded upon the Statute of Charitable Uses made 43 Eliz.[1] coming this present day to be heard before the Right Honorable the Lord High Chancellor of England in the presence of counsel learned on both sides for and touching a charitable bequest of £100 given by the last will and testament of Mrs. Mary Chambers then living in the Parish of St. Giles without Cripplegate, London, in these words following: 'Item, I give and bequest unto the church wardens and overseers for the poor of the Parish of St. Giles without Cripplegate aforesaid the sum of £100 of lawful money of England to be paid unto them for the increase of their parish stock and better maintenance of the poor there.' And it being found by inquisition that there are and time out of mind have been distinct church wardens and overseers for the poor of the said parish living in London and for the poor of the said parish living in Middlesex and that the executor of the said Mary Chambers' will paid the said £100 to two of the church wardens of the said parish, who put out the same at interest for the use of the poor of the same parish and that in July 1663 the exceptants, Rooks and Potter, being church wardens for that part of the parish that lies within London, received for the interest thereof £3 and disposed thereof to and amongst one hundred poor persons living in that part of the parish in London and no part thereof to that part of the parish within the County of Middlesex. It was thereupon adjudged and decreed by the said commissioners for the charitable uses that the

[1] Stat. 43 Eliz. I, c. 4 (*SR*, IV, 968–970).

said exceptants misemployed 30s. of the said £3 and therefore should pay unto Henry West and Hugh Shipley, the church wardens of that part of the parish which lies in the County of Middlesex, for the use of the poor there the sum of 30s. and 1s. for damages and £10 for costs to the respondent Deacon, the prosecutor, whereunto the exceptants for exception set forth that the said parish has two distinct stocks and almshouses for the poor in London and for the poor in Middlesex and distinct officers and distinct rates and it has been the constant usage and practice where a charitable gift has been made to the said parish or other parishes which lie part in London and part in Middlesex if it be in the donor's will expressed that the parish is in London to apply it to the poor there only and if expressed that the parish is in Middlesex to apply it to the poor there only and that the will of Mrs. Chambers only mentions the Parish of St. Giles Cripplegate, London, and that a complaint being heretofore brought by the respondent Deacon against the exceptant Rooks and one Dormer for misemploying the said gift, they have since distributed the product of it to the relief of the poor in that part of the parish within London only suffered himself to be nonsuited therein and afterwards upon another plaint brought by the said Deacon before the said commissioners against Isaack Bennett and one John Paddwick, executors of Edward Dobson, which Bennett and Dobson had been church wardens of that part of the said parish in London, the same was tried and, after two hours debate, the jury found for the said Bennett and Paddwick and the exceptants have since paid the £3 in question to one hundred poor people of the said parish living in London in pursuance of the said verdict, they conceive it is no misemploying thereof and therefore ought not to pay 31s. abovesaid nor the £10 decreed to the prosecutor for costs, the commissioners not being empowered by the Statute to tax any costs.

But the respondents' counsel insisted that the difference before the commissioners being only in point of law, it was agreed that the matter of fact being agreed on both sides should be found specially, which was accordingly done, and upon hearing counsel on both sides, it was adjudged that the law was for the respondents, and it was further insisted that it does not appear by the will of Mrs. Chambers that her meaning was only to have the money in question to go to that part of the parish called The Freedom and no other intent can be proved than what is expressed in the will.

Whereupon and upon debate of the matter and reading some proofs in the cause and hearing what was alleged on both sides, His Lordship does think fit and so order that a case be made and agreed upon by the counsel on both sides upon the will of the said Mrs. Chambers and the proofs taken in this cause and that it be also made part of the case whether that the executors of Mrs. Chambers having paid the money in question to the church wardens of the said parish and they having paid the same to the poor of that part of the said parish within London only, the same shall be taken to be a misemployment of the charity. And

His Lordship being attended with the said case after it is stated and agreed upon will be pleased to advise thereupon and afterwards deliver his opinion.

Herne & Duke 109

The matter, upon the exceptions put in by the exceptants to a decree made in this cause by the commissioners upon the Statute of Charitable Uses coming this present day to be heard and debated before the Right Honorable [Sir Orlando Bridgeman] the Lord Keeper of the Great Seal of England in the presence of the learned counsel on both sides, the substance of the matter upon which the said decree is grounded being that one Mary Chambers, by her last will in writing, 7 June 1654, did devise unto the churchwardens and overseers of the poor of the parish of St. Giles without Cripplegate, London, the sum of £100 to be paid to them for the increase of their parish store, which said £100 was accordingly paid unto the then churchwardens of that part of the said parish lying within London for the use of the poor aforesaid and the said money was by them placed out at interest for the use aforesaid and that the said exceptants, being churchwardens of that part of the said parish which lies within London, did, on or about the first of July 15 Car. *nunc regis* [1663], receive £3 for interest of the said £100 and disposed thereof to the poor of that part of the said parish which is in London, no part thereof being paid to the poor of the other part of the said parish lying in Middlesex, upon which complaint being made, the commissioners empowered for that purpose did thereupon decree that the said exceptants should pay unto Henry West and Hugh Shipley, the churchwardens of that part of the said parish which is in Middlesex, for the use of the poor there 30s. and 1s. for damages and £10 to the respondent or prosecutor for costs.

The exceptants have excepted thereunto:

[First], for that they, being churchwardens for the poor of that part of the said parish which is in London, they received the same and employed the same for and towards the relief of the said parish lying in London;

Second, and the exceptants are in no fault, they not misemploying the same but paying it to the poor as aforesaid. And the exceptants' counsel insisted;

Third, that their predecessors, churchwardens of that part of the said parish which is in London, have done the same in cases of like nature and have by the commissioners been indemnified therein;

Fourth, and that the prosecutor, upon a trial before the commissioners touching the matter in question, has been nonsuited;

Fifth, and, upon another trial at law, verdict passed against him;

Sixth, that the money was not misemployed; and

Seventh, that by the words of the will and by the custom of the parish, the poor in London only ought to have the said monies.

Whereupon and upon long debate of the matter and hearing what was insisted upon by the counsel on either side, His Lordship allowed the exceptants' exceptions put in to the said decree, they having paid the money to the poor of that part of the said parish in London as aforesaid and in pursuance of the verdict and nonsuit aforesaid and not converted the same, or any part thereof, to their own uses or misemployed the same. And His Lordship conceived the said decree, made by the said commissioners aforesaid, to be erroneous and therefore does order and decree the same to be reversed and set aside.

235

Wallis v. Crimes

(Ch. 1667–1668)

In this case, the trust in issue was a condition precedent in the nature of a penalty that never occurred, and, thus, it did not defeat the mortgage in issue.

Lincoln's Inn MS. Hill 125, f. 51v, pl. 3

4 May 19 Car. II and opinion and judgment 4 July 19 Car. II.

Sir Thomas Crymes, the grandfather, conveyed the lands in question to the use of himself and his wife, Margaret, for three lives, remainder to Scott and Moore and their heirs in trust that, if Sir George, his son, secure £500 to the use of the daughters within six months after the death of Sir Thomas and Margaret, then, after such security first given, the trustees should convey the premises to Sir George or to such others as he should appoint, and, until the time limited for giving security, the trustees to stand seised in trust for the defendant, Thomas, the grandchild, and, in default of such security, the trustees to convey to the grandchild and his heirs. Sir Thomas and Margaret die. No security was given. The trustees claim to the use of the grandchild. Sir George, the father, mortgaged the premises for £2000 for 1000 years.

The mortgagees are plaintiffs to have their mortgage made good against the trustees and the grandchild.

And [it was] decreed, excepting as to the £500 by the Chancellor on a case made. The objection was because Sir George, the mortgagor, had no title but a possibility on payment of the £500 and, until then, the trust [was] expressly limited to the grandchild etc. Yet [he] decreed etc.

[On] 28 October 1668, this decree [was] confirmed by Sir Orlando Bridgeman, Lord Keeper, because, else, if the son have the lands [there is] no remedy by the daughters for the £500 and then the intent to the father securing the £500. The bill of review [was] dismissed.

1 Chancery Cases 89, 22 E.R. 708

4 June [1667]. Elston Wallis and others, executors of Anne Smith, against Sir Thomas Crimes, Baronet, John Scot, Esq., and others.

In 1656, Sir George Crimes, father of the defendant Sir Thomas and whose eldest son the defendant Sir Thomas was, demised the lands in question to Anne

Smith for £2000 for 2000 years by way of a mortgage, Sir George then being in possession and taken to be the absolute owner. 19 January 1643[/44], Sir Thomas Crimes, father of Sir George, had conveyed the premises to the defendant Scot and others and their heirs upon trust that, if Sir George, within six months after his father's death, secured to the trustees £500 for the benefit of Sir George's younger children, then (after such security first given to the trustees) to convey the premises to Sir George and his heirs as he should appoint, and, until the time limited for giving the security, the trustees to stand seised to the use of Sir George's eldest son, which Sir Thomas is, for his maintenance, and, in default of such security, the trustees, at the request of Sir George's eldest son, to convey to him.

This appearing to be the case in proof upon a bill exhibited by the plaintiffs to enforce a redemption or to hold discharged of equity, the court decreed that the plaintiffs do hold and enjoy the premises for security of the £2000 with interest against the defendants and all claiming under them, charged with the £500 to Sir George Crime's younger children from the time the plaintiff came into possession and that the defendants do accordingly execute conveyances, unless the defendant Sir Thomas Crimes do pay the mortgage money and interest by a day.

The defendant brought a bill of review to reverse this decree. And, for error, he showed that, in default of giving security six months after Sir Thomas's death, the trustees were to convey to the defendant and his heirs and the security was first to be given before Sir George was to have anything in the lands and that, Sir George being dead, that was impossible, he having not given any security.

But, upon the debate of the matter upon an answer put in to the bill of review and the hearing of the cause before the Lord Keeper Bridgeman, 28 October 1668, he declared he saw no cause to reverse the decree, but looked upon the condition precedent to be in the nature of a penalty, and would regard the intent of the trust, which was to secure £500 to the younger children, which, with the way the plaintiffs went in this bill of review, could not be. And so he dismissed the bill of review.

[Other reports of this case: 1 Eq. Cas. Abr. 107, 21 E.R. 916.]

236

Barker v. Kellet

(Ch. 1667–1673)

Where a mortgage is redeemed against an assignee of the mortgagee, the original mortgagee must be made a co-defendant, and the money due and payable is the original debt, not the amount paid by the assignee to the mortgagee.

2 Freeman 127, 22 E.R. 1103

Trinity [term] 1667. Lord Bridgeman.

The bill was preferred by the plaintiff as heir to the mortgagor to have a redemption against Mr. Kellet, who was the assignee of the mortgagee, and to know what he paid for the assignment and, on payment of the money Mr. Kellet paid for the assignment, to have a reconveyance.

Kellet demurred to that part which required him to set forth what he paid for the assignment and because the bill had not made the first mortgagees parties.

And it was ruled a good demurrer, for that he should not discover what he paid on the assignment and, if the plaintiff will redeem, he shall pay what was due upon the original mortgage.

Nelson 117, 21 E.R. 804

Baker v. Hellett.

The heir of the mortgagor exhibited his bill against the assignee of the mortgage, setting forth that he had bought in several encumbrances for a very small consideration and would now subject the lands for the payment of more than he had really advanced, therefore, he prayed that the defendant, who was an attorney, might set forth what he had justly paid to buy in those encumbrances and that the plaintiff might be relieved etc.

The defendant, for answer, sets forth that he did not desire more than what was really due. But, as to that part of the bill which sought a discovery of what he had really paid, he demurred, and insisted that he ought not to answer, for, if he bought in the encumbrances for less than was due, there was no reason the plaintiff should have any benefit of the bargain.

And, upon debate, the demurrer was allowed.

3 Chancery Reports 23, 21 E.R. 717

15 January, 19 Car. II [1668].

The plaintiff's bill is to discover the defendant's title to the lands of her father and what they paid to buy in several encumbrances chargeable thereon and to have a reconveyance on the payment of so much as they paid for the same.

The defendant demurred, for that he ought not to take less than was due on the encumbrances. And, therefore, he demands judgment whether he shall answer what he paid.

And it was allowed because the first mortgagees were no parties.

Lord Nottingham, *Prolegomena*, p. 212

27 January 1672[/73], Shaftesbury, Chancellor, and Wilde, Justice.

If a purchaser without notice buy in a precedent statute or mortgage, which is satisfied, he shall make no other use of his purchased encumbrance than thereby to defend himself. But he shall not be suffered to offend another.

Lord Nottingham, *Prolegomena*, p. 338

27 January 1672[/73], by Shaftesbury, Chancellor. Kellet v. Barker.

A redemption was decreed and encumbrances were allowed to the mortgagee only *pro tanto* what he has really paid to purchase them in, and, if he has made a good bargain, the mortgagor shall have the benefit of it, *quod mirum*.

237

Harrison v. Middleton

(Ch. 1667)

In this case of money due to the crown before the Interregnum, the court decreed that no interest was payable after 1644 and what money had been paid but not expressly designated as interest was paid to reduce the principal debt.

Lincoln's Inn MS. Hill 125, f. 51, pl. 1

Trinity [term] 19 Car. II. Harrison and farmers etc. v. Middleton.

The farmers borrow £10,000 of Smithsby [in] 1641. They secured it by a bond of £15,000 and the interest by five other bonds. The money was borrowed to lend to the king. Smithsby, as it was taken to be the case, had oppressed the farmers in the time of the Troubles.

The interest on the bonds [was] paid, and divers other sums, by agreement after, [were] paid. But *non constat* if paid on account of principal or interest only, no interest [was] paid *eo nomine*.

The question was whether the money should go on account of the interest to sink that first, as the ordinary rule of the court is, or to sink the principal.

[It was] decreed the defendants to have no interest after 1644, when the last interest secured by the bond was due, and the moneys paid since 1650 to sink the principal. But what was paid for interest [was] to stand as paid for interest.

[There was a] like decree against Mr. Delmahay for James Maxwell's debt, before.[1]

238

Reeve v. Reeve

(Ch. 1667)

In this case, the devise to the plaintiff did not vest, and the action to enforce it was dismissed.

[1] Note *Cranborne and Demahoy v. Crisp* (Ch. 1671), see below, Case No. 428.

Lincoln's Inn MS. Hill 125, f. 51, pl. 2

A termor devised to Mary, his wife, [and] if she died within the term, to Richard, his son, and his executors and assigns during all the term if he or any issue of his body so long live, otherwise to John, the plaintiff. And he died. Mary died. Richard assents, being executor, and makes his will, *viz*. 'I hear my brother John enquires after my death, but I leave him nothing but what my father has left him. I give all my estate to my wife.' Richard dies. John sues the wife of Richard.

[The suit is] dismissed.

239

Tovey v. Strangeway and King

(Ch. 1667)

In this case, the intent of the testator was that the devise in issue did not vest before the life tenant died, and the land passed to the remainderman.

Lincoln's Inn MS. Hill 125, f. 51v, pl. 1

Richard King, having ten acres, devised the lands to be so conveyed as that R., his son, might at his age of twenty-three have them to him and the heirs male of his body, the remainder to the plaintiff. And he died. His son, before twenty-three, suffered a recovery. He died without issue. The plaintiff entered by the trust.

And the court adjudged for Tovy because it seems the father's intent was that he should not have the land as present owner [?] until twenty-three. The recovery was to enable him to make a jointure. The decree was *circa* 15 Car. II [1663].

240

Callow v. Fenwick

(Ch. 1667)

The grantee of a conveyance after a final judgment at common law takes subject to that judgment.

Lincoln's Inn MS. Hill 125, f. 52, pl. 1

4 July 19 Car II.

Fenwick after a judgment in an action on the case against him for [. . .] conveyed lands and leases in trust. [It was] decreed to be subject to the execution.

241

Anonymous

(Ch. 1667)

The question in this case was whether the filing of an answer cures a contempt for not timely answering such that court costs are not to be awarded.

Lincoln's Inn MS. Hill 125, f. 52, pl. 2

4 July 19 Car. II.

The defendant appeared, and departed without answering. Process continued against him until sequestration.

The Master of the Rolls [GRIMSTON] discharged the process on answer. But the plaintiff [was given] no costs because the attachment was not entered with the Register where the defendant was to enter his appearance on the contempt.

But, on debate, it was referred to the Six Clerks if the process was regular.

242

Herne v. Mayor of Newcastle

(Ch. 1667)

In this case, a Master's report was confirmed nisi causa.

Lincoln's Inn MS. Hill 125, f. 52, pl. 3

5 July 1667.

A report for Herne against the Mayor and Commonalty of Newcastle upon Tyne [was] confirmed *nisi* upon giving eight days' notice because he could not be present at the Corporation and render [. . .] a report but that which was confessed by the answer of the defendants.

243

Bond v. Henley

(Ch. c. 1667)

There must be a hearing to confirm or not a report of a Master in Chancery.

Lincoln's Inn MS. Hill 125, f. 52, pl. 4

Bond v. Henly, executor of Wolrich.

The bill is to be relieved against a mortgage of lands made to Wolrich and against a [confessed] judgment to perform the covenants of the mortgage, on which money was levied and the plaintiff imprisoned. The defendant had had possession for twelve years and had an injunction, bringing into the court £600 and entering a recognizance to abide the order of the court at the hearing. And, on an offer of the plaintiff that it being a matter of account only and the debt certain and the time how long the defendants had been in possession by twelve years certain and confessed by the answer, as also the yearly value during all that time, *viz.* £72 *per annum*, that, therefore, it might be referred to a Master to take the account, which, by assent, was also ordered. The Master took the account, and made a report of a great sum due on the mortgage.

The defendant moved for a confirmation.

And [it was] ordered *nisi causa* on notice. But the order was that the money reported be decreed. Notice [was] given; the defendant drew up a decree. And it was referred to the Six Clerks if the decree, being enrolled, were regularly done, who certified it was.

But the Lord Keeper [Bridgeman] adjudged the proceeding irregular. The defendant ought not to have had a decree, but he might have moved to dismiss the injunction. And, though, where a decree is to account, that may be enrolled and another decree [had] after for payment, but here, the cause was never brought to a hearing. (It was Christmas 1667.) And [it is] to [go] back and begin where the error first happened, as in a case of repleader, and so the party may put in exceptions to the report etc.

244

Wyndham v. Wyndham

(Ch. 1667–1670)

Where a father buys land as a joint tenant with his son and pays all of the purchase price and receives all of the profits of the land and then dies, the son will succeed to the land by the right of survivorship, and not be considered as a mere trustee for his father. The purchase will be considered as an advancement and not as a trust.

A consent decree that touches and concerns land binds later purchasers of the land without notice of the decree.

2 Freeman 127, 22 E.R. 1103

Lord Keeper, Justice Twysden.

A decree by consent for a lease or other personal estate shall bind the purchasers. Otherwise, said the Lord Keeper [Bridgeman], you will blow up the Court of Chancery.

3 Chancery Reports 22, 21 E.R. 717

Lord Keeper Bridgeman and Justice Twysden.

[It was] ordered that a decree for a lease and other personal estate by consent shall bind purchasers for a valuable consideration; otherwise (said the Lord

Keeper) you will, like gunpowder, blow up the whole Court of Chancery. A trustee has been examined as a witness. Anthony Keck.

Lincoln's Inn MS. Hill 125, f. 53v

15 February 1667[/68].

Thomas Windham purchased divers little parcels of lands lying several among other his estate and manors of several persons in fee in the name of his son, John, and himself. The purchase money was paid by himself. He took the profits, made leases himself, reserving the rents. And from the purchase until his death, he and his lessees had the possession. And, being so seised and being also seised of other lands of his own purchase, by his will, *inter alia*, he devised all his copyhold lands and freehold lands of his own proper purchase in A., B., and C. etc. to certain persons in trust provided, if his son, John, disturbed his trustees etc., then the uses and trusts of them limited to John etc. should cease, and he devised then to his son Thomas.

First, the Lord Keeper [BRIDGEMAN], assisted with Justice WYNDHAM, declared and decreed, when the father purchased jointly with his son, no trust should be taken to be in the son for the father, though he paid the money, had possession, and leased etc., although it might be that he purchased these parcels for the convenience of sortication[1] among his other lands and though some proof was offered that the son (some years after the purchase), that is son John, should not have them. And the Lord Keeper [BRIDGEMAN] said that no declaration of the father after the purchase [was] made could alter the case. The Lord Keeper [BRIDGEMAN] noticed the Case of the earl of Lincoln, who purchased in the name of him and his daughter and told them that [. . .].

Secondly, the devise could not, either in the will or the proviso thereof, extend to these lands because that there were other lands purchased to satisfy the words of the will. But, if they had been devised by particular names or descriptions, then the will, in devising part, would not pass them, yet the proviso would have reached them.

Lord Keeper [BRIDGEMAN]: There is a mental and a legal intention; they are within the mental or son's intention. I believe [them] to have been devised, but not within a legal intent. The difference, said he, I learned from the Lord Hobart.

It was objected that the legal intent was to be made out because, in some of the vills named, there were some of the joint purchased lands and none of his sole purchase.

Lord Keeper [BRIDGEMAN]: That is but in general [. . .].

Third, Thomas, the father, devised to John divers lands under the condition, if he disturbed his executors, the estate in the purchased lands devised to him to cease. The executors refused to prove the will, by which certain goods in specie

[1] Sic in MS.

were appointed to John for his use and a stock on the grounds in like manner, concerning which he was to give a bond of £2000 to the executors to leave them at his death. He exhibited a bill against the executors to discover the lands particularly devised etc. that he, knowing them, might not disturb etc. and, thereby incur a forfeiture on that occasion, as articles of agreement were entered into, by which the wife of Thomas relinquished her dower and the administration of Thomas's goods which belonged to her on the refusal of the executors. And John was to perform the will. Whereupon, the articles were by consent decreed. John takes administration, but performs not according to the decree and articles. He aliens some of the lands on consideration of marriage and a portion, which, by the will of Thomas and the articles and decree, should have come to Thomas, the plaintiff.

[It was] decreed that, though the decree was a decree by consent, it should bind the defendant, who came in by purchase, though she had no notice of the decree.

But whereas John, testator to his wife, the defendant, whose executrix she was, had broken the decree and, therefore, she was to make satisfaction so far as she had assets of the estate of John, it was decreed that a trial should be [had] on that point, assets or no assets.

The counsel of the plaintiff prayed that there might be an issue joined in an action supposing a judgment at law against the defendant John for that, in this case, a decree should be taken to be as strong as a judgment at law.

Lord Keeper [BRIDGEMAN]: If the decree had been for a certain sum of money, assets should be, as in the case of a judgment at law. But, here, it is a decree to perform articles that sound in damages, and not a certainty. And, therefore, with the advice and consent of Justice TWISDEN, he did deny to have it tried, as in the case of a judgment at law, but as a covenant. And a special issue [was] to be framed accordingly.

Lord Nottingham, *Prolegomena*, p. 241

Hilary [term] 21 Car. II.

The father made his son a joint tenant purchaser with him of certain copyhold lands, and not only paid all the money, but took all the profits whilst he lived.

Yet it was resolved that no trust for the father was implied in this case, for the father might lawfully take the whole profits as joint tenant, and yet this might stand well with an intent to advance his son, which shall be supposed rather than a trust implied.

[Other reports of this case: 2 Eq. Cas. Abr. 280, 22 E.R. 237, 73 Selden Soc. 226, Repts. *tempore* Finch 267, 23 E.R. 147.]

245

Harding v. Nelthrope

(Ch. 1667–1668)

Fraud is a ground to set aside a lease.

Nelson 118, 21 E.R. 804

The defendant purchased several lands charged with a rent of £40 *per annum*, and sold part thereof for a valuable consideration to the plaintiff, and covenanted that the same were free from all encumbrances done or committed by him.

Afterwards, the grantee of the rent distrained on these lands for the arrearages of the rent. Now, though this was not an encumbrance within his covenant, yet the plaintiff exhibited his bill to be relieved, for that the vendor knowing of the encumbrance and concealing it, he, by fraud, brought the plaintiff to purchase, and, therefore, he ought to indemnify him against this encumbrance.

The Lord Keeper [BRIDGEMAN] inclined to relieve him, because the vendor did know the lands were charged with the rent and it was a fraud to sell them without discovering that encumbrance, like the case in Croke, where a counterfeit stone was sold for a jewel, knowing it to be counterfeit, it was held that an action of debt would lie.[1] And now, in the principal case, a trial at law was directed to try whether the vendor did know that the lands were charged with the rent when he sold them, so that, if it was found that he did know it, the court seemed to incline that he ought to be relieved, because he was drawn in by a fraud to make the purchase.

246

Phillips v. Henning

(Ch. 1667 × 1672)

A bill of review does not lie to enforce a decree.

Lord Nottingham, *Prolegomena*, p. 295

By Lord Bridgeman, Keeper.

By the course of the court, if a defendant make default, no decree is to be made against him without a day to show cause given. Yet, when the omission of this form was assigned for error on a bill of review between Phillips and Henning, the court would not reverse the decree by reason of the antiquity of it, in

[1] *Glanville's Case* (1614–1615), Croke Jac. 343, 79 E.R. 294, also 118 Selden Soc. 440.

which case, they would rather presume that it was done, though the entry of it does not appear.

247

Henn v. Coningsby

(Ch. 1667–1668)

In this case, the bankrupt third party was not the agent of the creditor to receive the repayment of the debt in issue, and the payment to the third party did not discharge the debt.

1 Chancery Cases 93, 22 E.R. 710

25 October [1667]. Sir Henry Henn against Sir Henry Conisby.

Money of the defendant was lent out by one Yarway to the plaintiff upon the security of a mortgage and a recognizance, and the security was taken in one Cambel's name in trust for the defendant. The money was lent 1659, and paid in to Yarway in 1663 and all interest for the same. And Yarway, during that time and a year after, paid the interest to the defendant, but the defendant himself kept the security. Yarway failed. And the question was whether the payment of the money to Yarway, who had not paid it over to the defendant, should be taken as a good payment to conclude the defendant.

For the plaintiff, it was laid down by his counsel as a rule that, where one places money in a scrivener's hands with this general trust for him to put it out where he pleases, there, by that general trust or authority, the payment back to the scrivener is a good payment.

And it was proved by witnesses that the defendant had said he had trusted Yarway with the greatest part of his estate and he feared he should be cozened, which the plaintiff's counsel insisted on as evidence to prove that the defendant trusted Yarway with his money.

But, as to that, it was answered by the defendant's counsel that Conisby lent Yarway other monies on his own security, which he lost. So he might say he was like to be cozened by the said Yarway. But it was farther insisted by the defendant's counsel that the defendant kept the security himself, which clearly showed that Yarway did not act under such general authority, as was alleged by the plaintiff's counsel. And it was insisted that that one circumstance would rule the case. And no man will pay the money due upon a mortgage and recognizance (no not on a bond) without having the security up. And the payment of the money by the plaintiff to the scrivener without having up his security was an evidence that he did trust the scrivener more than the defendant did (who always kept the security himself), and he that trusted most is to be cozened.

A case between Sir Gilbert Gerrard and Baker[1] was cited by the defendant's counsel, where money was paid to one that did usually receive for the obligee, yet, the obligee not trusting the receiver with the bond, it was held no good payment.

The court conceives the case is against the plaintiff in regard the defendant kept the security, but will see precedents. English against Lee was a precedent cited by the plaintiff, in 1655.

And, after the court had perused the precedents on both sides, in Easter [term] 1668, judgment was given for the defendant that the payment to the scrivener should not conclude him. But he was ordered to take the principal without costs.

[Other reports of this case: 1 Eq. Cas. Abr. 145, 21 E.R. 946.]

248

Deta v. Dickinson

(Ch. 1667–1668)

Where an enrollment of a decree is lost, the court can order a new enrollment.

3 Chancery Reports 20, 21 E.R. 716

A docket and enrollment of a decree was lost, and it was ordered to be new enrolled.

249

Owen v. White

(Ch. 1667)

Where a creditor-mortgagee devises the mortgage to his executor, upon a redemption of the mortgage, the devisee-executor is to receive all of the money, and the mortgagee's heir must join in the reconveyance.

2 Freeman 126, 22 E.R. 1102

6 November 1667. Lord Keeper Bridgeman, Justice Morton.

The bill was preferred by the mortgagor against the heir of the mortgagee in fee and his executors, praying that they might interplead who should have the money. The mortgagee had devised all his mortgages to the executor.

Therefore, the court decreed the whole money to the executors.

[1] *Gerrard v. Baker*, 1 Eq. Cas. Abr. 145, 21 E.R. 946.

The counsel insisted that the heir ought to have part, for that the mortgagee had not given all his fee away, for the words 'for ever' were wanting, nor any words of the heir or heirs of the executor.

But it was decreed *ut supra*.

3 Chancery Reports 20, 21 E.R. 716

6 November 1667. Justice Morton in court.

The bill was preferred by the mortgagor against the heir of the mortgagee and his executors, to whom the mortgagee had devised all his mortgages, that he might pay his money and have a reconveyance.

And the defendants interpleaded to whom he should pay his money.

And it was decreed that the executor's devisees should have the whole money. And the heir was decreed to join in this reconveyance, notwithstanding his counsel insisted that they might have a proportion of the money, it not being devised to the executors and their heirs forever. But yet he was decreed to re-convey.

[Reg. Lib. 1667 B, f. 221.]

250

Otway's Case

(Ch. 1667)

An injunction can be issued against a member of Parliament, but not a writ of arrest.
A consent decree made by an infant can be set aside by the infant at any time.

2 Freeman 126, 22 E.R. 1103

10 November 1667.

The Lord Keeper [Bridgeman] granted an injunction for want of an answer against a Parliament man, but he ordered no [writ of] attachment should be taken out.

3 Chancery Report 21, 21 E.R. 716

10 November 1666 [sic]. Lord Keeper Bridgeman.

Upon a motion for an injunction for want of an answer, upon an affidavit of a subpoena served upon Mr. Otway, a Parliament man, after deliberate consideration upon the said case, [the court] did grant an injunction, but did order them not to enter an attachment against them.

But [the court] denied to grant an injunction for quieting possession of an office, though an affidavit was made of three years quiet possession before the bill was exhibited.

If an infant suffer a decree against him by consent, he may at any time reverse it for that error of his being an infant. [It is] otherwise if he be a defendant by an adversary bill and a decree [be] pronounced.

251

Harrison v. Haynes

(Ch. 1667–1668)

A final decree not enrolled cannot be stayed on the ground of a matter of fact omitted, but the party must proceed by a bill of review or an appeal.

A court of equity has the sound discretion, in appropriate circumstances, to moderate or discharge court costs and interest.

2 Keble 279, 84 E.R. 173

Tuesday, 12 November [1667]. Harrison etc., customers against Hayns etc., executors of Smythsby.

Note by Bridgeman, Lord Keeper, that a decretal order not enrolled cannot on an allegation of matter of fact omitted be stayed, but the party must have a bill of review. But, if the matter of fact be omitted, this is cause to appeal into the House of Lords.

Second, it was said by the opinion of the judges that interest may be abated if unreasonable, and, by the same cause, may be taken away by the court; and this upon an order to set down the cause this day on the question, whether, for the former reasons, it should be reheard or not. And it was ruled that it should not be reheard, but the party defendant was put to his bill of review.

1 Chancery Cases 105, 22 E.R. 716

19 May [1668]. Haynes and others, executors of Smithby, against Harrison and others, farmers of the Customs. The Lord Keeper, Justice Tyrell, Justice Rainsford.

The bill was a bill of review to reverse a decree made by the Lord Chancellor Hyde, for that, by that decree, all interest due on several securities by bond and judgments and costs at law suffered before the first bill in suing those securities were taken away upon a pretense that the money lent the defendants by the plaintiffs' testator was paid by them to the king in consideration of the farm of the Customs, which they did not enjoy, whereas their testator was not concerned in the bargain. And, if the disposing of money by the borrower and any accident befalling it afterwards should create an equity against the creditor, it would destroy all commerce. And, by the course of the court, which is the law of the court, where interest is due on a bond and the debtor pay any sum less than the interest, the payment is to be accounted interest only, yet the decree allows such payments, although they were much less than the interest then due, for principal. And the court has also taken away the plaintiffs' costs at law, though, by the decree, £800 is still due to the plaintiffs on legal securities and the proceedings and costs at law were before any considerable part of the principal was paid, taking the interest for the principal, as the decree does, so that the proceedings were legal. And, without those, the plaintiffs' testator could not recover his debt, and so ought to be allowed those costs.

The defendants demurred, and insisted that there is no error in the body of the decree, nor new matter to reverse it. And they insist that this court ever had a power, upon circumstances, to relieve against penalties, judgments, and executions and to abate and moderate and sometimes discharge damages and costs. And it was insisted it had exercised such power in the Lord Keeper Coventry's time.

And the court did declare this court had a power, upon circumstances, to abate and moderate costs and interest and sometimes to discharge them. And they must take the decree as they found it, whereby it appears Smithby's debt was ill made up and that the farmers became bound in consideration of the farm, which they did not enjoy, and costs are in the discretion of the court and costs were discharged there, because there was no oppression. And so the whole court declared they could not go out of the decree, and saw no cause to reverse it, and so dismissed the bill.

252

Gerrard v. Stanley

(Ch. 1667–1668)

Disputes over land in the County Palatine of Lancaster should be litigated in the Court of Duchy Chamber, and not in the Court of Chancery.

1 Chancery Reports 278, 21 E.R. 572

The bill is that the defendants may discover their title to certain lands in the County of Lancaster, which the plaintiff claims as heir male of Miles Gerrard. The defendants, having possession, claim by a conveyance to one John Davis of London and also a title to the defendant Margaret, as heir at law to the said Miles Gerrard.

The defendants plead the jurisdiction and privilege of the counties Palatine of Chester and Lancaster and that the lands lie in the County Palatine of Lancaster and that the defendant, by several acts of Parliament, ought not anywhere else to be impleaded.

This court, upon the reading of a precedent produced by the plaintiff against the jurisdiction of the County Palatine of Chester, wherein was also cited several other precedents to the purpose, His Lordship, notwithstanding the said precedent, declared the said plea to be good as to the title and possession of the said lands or for any accounts of the profits.

[Reg. Lib. 19 Car. II, f. 509.]

253

Pitt v. Pelham

(Ch. 1667–1672)

Where a will appoints land to be sold, if no person is appointed to sell, it is intended that he shall sell who has the estate.

1 Chancery Reports 283, 21 E.R. 574

The case is that William Shirley, in 1650, being seised in fee simple of lands, upon his marriage with Jane Hecked for her jointure, settled the said premises to the use of himself and Jane and the heirs of their two bodies and, for want of such issue, to the right heirs of the said William forever. In 1657, the said William, having no issue, made his will, and, as to so much thereof as concerns the matter in question, devises in these words, *viz.*:

> I appoint my dear wife my sole executrix. My land at Blandford, which is my wife's jointure, I do confirm unto her, and, after her decease, I do appoint it to be sold, and the money that is made thereof to be divided by equal portions amongst these four, namely, one part to be disposed of by my wife, the other three parts are my nephews', William Major, Ezra Shirley, and Jonadab Savage. I give to my cousin Roger Higham £20, and, in case any of my three above named nephews shall die before the decease of my wife, that, then, my cousin Roger Higham shall have that portion of the money, which upon the selling of the land at Blandford, should have fallen to that nephew.

And the said William Shirley, five days after the said will was made, died without issue, and Jane, his wife, proved the said will and possessed the said premises. And, afterwards, she demised the same to the plaintiff Pit. And the said Ezra Shirley died in the lifetime of the said Jane. And the said William Major, in 1664, for £125, sold the said premises and his right and interest therein and all his part and share of money, which he, his executors, etc. might claim or have out of the said money to be raised by such sale by virtue of the said will or otherwise, and he covenanted for further assurance. And the said Jonadab in like manner sold his interest to the said Pit. And the said Roger Higham, being entitled to a fourth part of the premises by the death of the said Ezra Shirley, sold in like manner all his interest to the said plaintiff and with like covenants as the said other plaintiffs had done. And the said Jane, for £300 secured to her by the said plaintiff Pit payable after her death, sold all her interest in the said fourth part of the inheritance of the said lands expectant after her death and her share of what money should be raised by the sale thereof and she covenanted for further assurance. And, in 1666, the said Jane died, having made her will and the said Roger Higham and one Harris executors, who proved the said will, and received the said £300, so that, according to the said William Shirley's will, the said lands ought to be sold, there being a trust raised thereupon for the benefit of the said Major, Savage, and Higham, and the assignee of the said Jane. And, thereupon, the plaintiff Pit, who is a purchaser of all the other plaintiffs' interest as aforesaid and is also assignee of the said Jane, seeks to have the defendant Pelham and Mary, his wife, and Mabel Shirley, which said Mary and Mabel are sisters and co-heirs of the said Ezra Shirley, who was the son and heir of Ezra Shirley, brother and heir of the said William Shirley, convey the said premises to the plaintiff Pit and his heirs, the other plaintiffs offering to join with them therein.

But the defendants insist that, if such a will was made, yet the said defendants, co-heirs, not being therein appointed to sell or convey the said premises nor any person, by the said will appointed particularly to sell the same, and the lands not devised by the will, but appointed to be sold, therefore, the said lands are well descended to the said co-heirs, and they are neither in law or equity obliged to sell or convey the same. And they submitted to the judgment of this court to do as this court shall direct in case the will be a good will. And they also insisted that there was as good equity in this case for the heir as for the devisees and these lands being descended on the defendants as heirs, they hope this court will not compel them to disinherit themselves and that the plaintiff's purchase was after a suit commenced depending in this court for the same thing.

The plaintiffs insisted that the will was a good will at the death of the said William Shirley and that the lands were charged with a trust to be sold and that no act since can invalidate the same and that the said former bill was only to preserve testimony for proving the said will and the plaintiff Pit, being a real purchaser in the lifetime of the said Jane, he has a proper and equitable suit in this court to have the said will performed and the trust executed.

This court ordered a case to be made upon the said will, taking this to be a case of great consequence and weight in the precedence of it and admitting the said William Shirley was seised in fee and made such a will and that the said Ezra Shirley, brother of the defendants Mary and Mabel, died in the lifetime of the said Jane and that the plaintiff Pit made such purchases as aforesaid.

This court, having perused precedents in this case and advised with the judges thereupon, declared his opinion to be for the better clearing of the cause for his determination, and ordered that a trial should be had at law in a feigned action by a wager whether Jane, the relict and executrix of the said William Shirley, had a power and could by the will have made a sale of the lands in question and also, in the next place, whether a sale by her executors, admitting such sale to be actually made, be a good sale. And, in pursuance thereof, a trial has been had upon the point aforesaid and a special verdict thereon found and several solemn arguments and debates thereof have been before the judges of the Common Pleas, who have given a judgment therein for the defendants. And the cause

[came] again to be heard on the equity reserved before the Lord Keeper assisted with the judges, and they, having considered of the precedents offered by the plaintiff and compared the same with the case in question, find a great difference between them and this case, upon the circumstances thereof.

This court, upon the whole matter, the will in question being adjudged void in law in the very constitution thereof, saw no cause or color to make good the same in equity, and dismissed the plaintiff's bill. But [the court] declared this should not be a precedent.

The plaintiff appealed to the Lords in Parliament, who adjudged and resolved that the plaintiff ought to be relieved, and they ordered the Lord Keeper to set aside the said dismission, and adjudged the defendants, the heirs at law, to convey the said premises to the plaintiff Pit and his heirs, which this court, in obedience to the said order, ordered accordingly.

Lincoln's Inn MS. Misc. 500, f. 24

Easter term 21 Car. II.

The case was thus, A., seised in fee of lands, took a wife, and made a jointure to him for her life of them. And, afterwards, A., by his will, reciting the said jointure, confirmed it for the life of his wife, and devised that the said lands will be sold after the death of his wife and the money arising from the sale to be paid and disposed to such persons who were in the nature of legatees. And, afterwards, he died having made his said wife executrix. And, afterwards, the wife died, not having sold the lands. And the said legatees preferred their bill in equity to be relieved and to compel the heir of A. to sell the lands and to dispose the money according to the will.

And, upon this, the Lord Keeper [Bridgeman] took to his assistance Twysden and Wilde, J. And these points were moved, first, if the said lands could have ever been sold by force of this will, inasmuch as they were to be sold after the death of the wife, and not before, and none could sell them except the executrix inasmuch as no vendor was named. And the executrix could not sell because they were not to be sold but after the death of the wife. And thus it seems to be the opinion of the two justices. But the Lord Keeper [Bridgeman] inclined that this will, as to the sale was not void in the creation because it could be that the intent of the testator was that such estate that was in the land after the death of the wife could be sold by the wife during her life, and it is only in the nature of a reversion.

Second, it was moved if the executors of the executrix in this case or the executor of an executor in any other such case where lands are devised to be sold could sell.

Wilde, thought that they could; Justice Twysden, not.

Third, as the wife in this case had not sold, but was dead, if there was any equity for the legatees to compel the heir at law to sell or if there is not any difference when lands are devised to be sold for the payment of debts or raising portions for younger children (these being things at the making of which the law of nature and conscience binds) and when lands are devised to be sold for raising voluntary sums in the nature of legacies, at the making of which, there is not any obligation upon the devisor, as there is in the other cases.

Adjornatur.

1 Chancery Cases 176, 22 E.R. 750

4 July [1670]. Pitt and others against Pelham and his wife and Mabel Shirly.

William Shirly, seised of the lands in question, settled them on Jane, his wife, for a jointure, remainder to the heirs of their two bodies, remainder to his own right heirs. Afterwards, in 1657, he made his will in writing in these words:

> I make my dear wife my sole executrix; my land at Blandford, which is my wife's jointure [which is the land in question] I confirm unto her; and, after her death, I appoint it to be sold, and the money that is made of it to be divided in equal portions amongst these four, namely, one part of it to be disposed of by my wife, and one to William Major, one to Ezra Shirley [who was heir at law], and one to Jonadab Savidge, and, in case any of my three above named nephews shall die before the death of my wife, my cousin Roger Higham shall have the portion of money, which, upon selling my land at Blandford, should have fallen to that nephew.

And he dies, leaving Ezra his heir. Ezra Shirly dies before Jane, leaving the defendants, the women, his sisters and co-heirs. Jane, the executrix, Major, Savage, and Higham, in 1663, exhibit their bill against Mary and Mabel, the defendants, to prove the will, and compel them to sell. They answer. And, in 1664, witnesses are examined. Pending this suit, the now plaintiff, being only tenant of part of the lands from year to year, purchases of Major, Savage, Higham, and Jane their interest given them by the will. Jane dies in 1666, and makes Higham and Harris her executors. The now plaintiffs Pitt, Major, Savage, Higham, and Harris exhibit their bill to compel the co-heirs to convey the land to Pitt and his heirs.

The cause was first heard before the Master of the Rolls. And it was then ordered that a case should be drawn up and heard before the Lord Keeper.

And, on the hearing before the Lord Keeper, 7 November 1668, because the cause appeared to be of weight and consequence, His Lordship [Bridgeman] ordered copies of the case to be delivered to Justice Twysden and Justice Wilde, and he will advise with them and appoint a day to deliver his opinion.

29 April 1669, the cause was heard by His Lordship [Bridgeman], assisted with those judges, at which time, it was by Serjeant *Maynard* insisted, for the plaintiff, that the will was good in law if the same was executed. But [they] could not compel an execution at law, and, therefore, equity ought. And, as to the pretense that there was no person named to sell, he said that, when the intention is clear, all means, without which that cannot be attained, must be supplied by a

court of justice. Dyer 371b; 2 Leon. Rep. 220, a case in point.[1] And the devisor has a power to dispose as he pleases. And, though the devise be not of an estate, but of an authority to sell, it is good within the Statute.[2] And, if a devise be to an heir upon a condition that he sell, this condition is void, but yet it is good by way of a trust in equity, for it lies within the power of an ancestor to charge his lands with a trust and the heir must sell. And the precedents of the court do run that the heir is to sell. And he cited Batersby and Prince, in the Lord Coventry's time, and Tenant against Brown, 18 February 1659.[3]

Serjeant *Fountaine*, for the plaintiffs: Originally, this is a good will, and the land might have been sold. And, if, by any accident, it be prevented, as by the death of the executor, this court ought to help it. And it is not denied that, if the will had been to sell to pay debts, it had been good and the heir should have sold. And there is no difference between a debt and legacies. And, here, the money is given for legacies, but shall be raised by the sale. And he relied on it that the executor might have sold.

Mr. Solicitor [General] *Finch*, for the defendants: There are two questions: first, what the law is; second, what the equity is. The law is against the plaintiffs. If land be appointed to be sold for the payment of debts and no person is appointed to sell, the executor shall sell, because the soul is concerned, which the executor is to take care of. But it is otherwise in a voluntary disposition, as here. And it is not like the case of Howel and Barns, 1 Cro. 382, for, there, the executors were appointed to sell.[4]

Serjeant *Ellis*, for the defendants: The devise is a void devise in the creation, because no person is appointed to sell or, if good in the creation, is void *ex post facto*, for no bond of the ancestor binds the heir, unless he be expressly named.

The Lord Keeper [BRIDGEMAN] doubted whether the will be void in the creation, for it is against a rule in law to make it void if, by any construction, it can be made good.

TWYSDEN doubted that the executor of the executor cannot be compelled to sell in this case, the sale not being to be made until after the death of the executor.

WILDE conceived the devise good in the creation, the intent appearing, and the case in Leonard is the very case. And he was of opinion that the executor of the executor shall sell. But he doubted whether the heir be compelled to sell.

Precedents on both sides were given in to the Lord Keeper and the judges. And 18 May 1669, the Lord Keeper [BRIDGEMAN], after advice with the judges,

---

[1] *Anonymous* (1580), 3 Dyer 371, 73 E.R. 832, 110 Selden Soc. 382; *Anonymous* (1574), 2 Leonard 220, 74 E.R. 493.

[2] Stat. 32 Hen. VIII, c. 1 (*SR*, III, 744–746).

[3] *Tenant v. Brown* (Ch. 1659), 1 Chancery Cases 180, 22 E.R. 752.

[4] *Houell v. Barnes* (1634), Croke Car. 382, 79 E.R. 933, also W. Jones 352, 82 E.R. 185.

in order to [aid] the determination of the cause, ordered a trial of these points in a feigned action: first, whether Jane, the executrix, had a power, and could by the will have sold the lands; second, whether a sale by her executors, admitting such sale to be actually made, be a good sale. And, after the trial, either party is to resort to the court for a final determination.

Upon the trial, by consent of counsel, a special verdict was found, and, upon several solemn arguments thereon by counsel on both sides at the Common Pleas, the court gave judgment unanimously on both points for the defendants. Thereupon, the defendants move to dismiss the bill. And it is ordered that the cause be set down for a hearing before the Lord Keeper upon the equity reserved.

And, now, upon the hearing thereof before His Lordship [BRIDGEMAN], it was, for the plaintiff, insisted that it was plain by the will that the lands should be sold and no person, by law, can sell but the heir, and, therefore, the heir must sell and that matter was not tried, but the matter tried was improper, for it was not to the purpose. And the precedents of the court run that the heir should sell, and, therefore, though the other issues tried are against the plaintiff, that is not, but remains in justice for the plaintiff.

And [there were] cited divers precedents, *viz.* Hughes and other plaintiffs against Collis, defendant, 1 February 16 Car. I [1641]. The case was thus. The plaintiffs were creditors of the testator. The defendants were his executors, and the daughters [were] legatees. The bill was to enforce the sale of the testator's lands for the payment of his debts by the executors, who, by answer, submit to sell if the court thought fit, having in truth sold part before. And the words of the will were thus:

> as for my lands, tenements, goods, and chattels, I give and bequeath as follows: after my debts be paid, to my five daughters £100 apiece and to be paid at their ages of twenty years; also I give to my wife, whom I make my executrix, all the rest of my lands and tenements, goods, and chattels.

The personal estate was not sufficient to pay the debts, nor could the executrix, out of the profits of the premises, being but £63 *per annum*, raise money to pay the debts and the daughters' portions, being £500. Therefore, the court conceived it was intended by the will that the executrix should raise money to pay the debts and legacies, and decreed the executrix to sell accordingly and, by the sale, to satisfy the plaintiffs. But, before the executrix was to receive any part of the purchase money, she was to give security to pay the daughters their portions at their ages of twenty years, they being then in their infancy, and that the daughters should, when they came of age, release the lands to the purchaser.

Another precedent was Lockton against Lockton. 13 November 13 Car. I [1637].[1] Where lands were devised to be sold and the monies to be distributed to

[1] *Locton v. Locton* (1637), 2 Freeman 136, 22 E.R. 1111.

several persons and no person was named to sell, there, by consent of counsel, it was decreed that the executor should sell.

Another precedent [was] Asby and others, creditors of Walker, against Doyl and others, heirs of Walker. The words of the will were these:

> my will and mind is and I do hereby authorize that my executors hereafter named shall sell my lands and woods thereupon growing to any person or persons and their heirs for the best value, and, with the monies thereby raised, to pay all my just debts.

16 February 1655. The Lords Commissioners, assisted with Judges, the executors being dead, upon a view of precedents, decreed the heirs to sell.

Tenant and others against Brown and others, 18 February 1659. The sale being to be made expectant upon a contingent estate, which did not happen in the executor's time, that was decreed to make the sale, but, happening after his death, his executor and those that claimed the land after his death, were decreed to sell.

And, for the plaintiff, in the original case, it was strongly insisted that it was all one where lands were devised for the payment of legacies or younger children's portions and for the payment of debts and that was as much a trust of lands in the principal case that it should be sold and the money paid as it is where monies are appointed to be paid out of the profits of the lands.

The Lord Keeper [Bridgeman]: This is not like the case where a father makes provision for younger children, for a parent is bound to provide for them, nor is it like to the case of a sale to pay legacies at large. But, here, they are sums in gross. And he conceived a difference may be taken between the principal case and monies appointed to be raised out of the profits of lands; that does not amount to a total disherison, but only a charge upon the land in the heir's hand, and so that savors more of a trust than in the principal case. And so he decreed the bill to stand dismissed, but with directions that this should be no precedent.

2 Freeman 134, 22 E.R. 1110

Ro. Pitt v. Ro. Pelham *et uxor*, and Mabel Sherley.

William Sherley, clerk, in the year 1650, having jointured his wife in lands, by his will, confirmed her estate, and devised that the lands should be sold and the money disposed by his wife and to three of his nephews by name and, if one of them died in the life of the wife, then his part of the money to his cousin Higham. The same nephew died in his wife's life. The two other nephews, the wife, and Higham sold to Pitt the reversion on a full consideration, by the advice of great counsel, that they might sell, and the sale be established in a court of equity.

The plaintiff, therefore, exhibited his bill against the defendants, being the coheirs of the devisor, that they might be decreed to convey to the plaintiff.

And, at the hearing, a trial at law was directed, whether the wife, being, in truth, executrix, might sell in her lifetime or whether the executors of that executrix. On which point, judgment was against the plaintiff in the Common Pleas. And now, on the equity reserved, they came to a hearing.

And the court dismissed the plaintiff's bill, but ordered that this be not drawn into a precedent for the future.

Notwithstanding which, it is conceived that the decree is erroneous, according to several precedents in this court, and that the defendants ought to convey to the plaintiff Pitt, the intent for which they should be sold being certain and the lands certainly denominated and that it should be judged in equity a trust in the heir to sell or that, the same being sold by the legatees, the heir should not impeach the same, but confirm them. And they cited precedents, orders 11 June 1639, 26 November, 3 Jac., 9 July, 4 Jac. [1606–07], decreed by the Lord Chancellor assisted by the judges, and a case between Hyer and Wordale.[1] Thomson devised lands to be sold after the death of his wife, but he says not by whom, and the money is to be raised by the sale to be divided amongst his children; he makes his wife executrix. The elder brother and the executrix leased for 1000 years, part to Nicholas, a brother, and part to another brother, who sold to the defendant Wordale, which sale was adjudged fraudulent to overthrow the will. And there was a decree that the land should be sold and the money divided amongst the children.

The ground of the Statute of Wills, 32 Hen. VIII,[2] is the good of children and posterity, and, though, in the principal case, here are not children, yet the legatees are the nearest of posterity.

The plaintiff Pitt's Case, upon a petition to the House of Lords, was then heard upon an appeal from the aforesaid decree, and it was declared the lands ought to be sold according to the will. 17 December 1670.

Lord Nottingham, *Prolegomena*, p. 240

19 December 1670.

A man makes his wife sole executrix, and confirms her jointure, and appoints the land to be sold after her death and the money to be distributed amongst his kindred.

[It was] resolved: first, *per Curiam* Common Bench, a void devise, because nobody was appointed to sell, and the law does not imply the executor here, because the purposes are not testamentary for debts or legacies, but voluntary distributions, and so it differs from all the books, 15 Hen. VII, 12; Perkins, *Profitable Book*, 105.[3]

---

[1] *Hyer v. Wardell* (Ch. 1597), 117 Selden Soc. 217, Tothill 121, 21 E.R. 142.

[2] Stat. 32 Hen. VIII, c. 1 (*SR*, III, 744–746).

[3] YB Trin. 15 Hen. VII, ff. 11, 12, pl. 22 (1500); J. Perkins, *Profitable Book*, 105.

Second, it was urged in Chancery that, however, the heir ought to be compelled to join in the sale, for, though the will be defective, yet it amounts to a declaration of a trust, which shall charge [the land], and which the heir shall be compelled to execute. And many precedents were cited where the heir has been decreed to join in a sale when the will appointed [land] to be sold without saying by whom, *viz.* the cases of Hyer and Wardor, which depended from 39 Eliz. to 4 Jac., and 13 Car. I, Locton and Lowth; and 24 Car. I, Smith and Allesby,[1] for it was conceived in these cases the law did imply a trust in the heir to sell rather than the will should be defective. And so was the opinion of great lawyers in this case before Mr. Pitt became a purchaser.

Yet the Lord Keeper [BRIDGEMAN] would not compel the heir to join in a sale, because, in the precedents cited, the ends of the sale decreed were either for natural or moral considerations. Here are neither. Wherefore, by the advice of two judges, he dismissed the bill.

But, afterwards, on appeal to the Lords, the dismission was reversed, and it was adjudged that Pitt ought to be relieved, and, with this direction, it was sent back, and was accordingly decreed.

T. Jones 25, 84 E.R. 1130

On a special verdict, the case was such. J.S., seised in fee, devised that his lands should be sold after the decease of his wife and that she should dispose the money to divers of his kindred, and he made his wife executrix, and died. The wife proved the will, and made her will and died. The wife's executors sell to J.N. And his lessee brings an [action of] ejectment against the heir of the devisor.

Baldwin, Serjeant, for the plaintiff: The sale in this case is good, for the wife being made executrix and no other person appointed to sell and the will appointing that the wife should distribute the money to be raised by the sale, the law will adjudge that the sale shall be made by her. And this power not being executed by her, her executors shall perform it. And, although it be said that the sale be after her death, the intent of that was to give an estate to the wife for her life, not to hinder the sale of the reversion by her. He said also that the law favors the intent of devisors, and will not suffer his will to be void if it may be made good by any reasonable construction. Giles Bridges made his cousin his sole heir and executory, yet, in the King's Bench, 13 Car. II, it was adjudged that this was a good devise of his land. 20 Hen. VII, 12b, Dyer 371; Perkins, sect. 547.

Ellis, Serjeant, for the defendant: The devise is void. He agreed that, if land be devised for the payment of debts, the executor shall sell if no other be appointed to do it, 15 Hen. VII, 12; Dyer 371, for it is the office of an executor to pay debts, and the money raised by the sale shall be assets. And also the executor

[1] *Hyer v. Wardell* (Ch. 1597), *ut supra*; *Locton v. Locton* (1637), *ut supra*; *Smith v. Alterly* (1648–1649), 2 Freeman 136, 22 E.R. 1111, 3 Chancery Reports 93, 21 E.R. 739.

shall sell where the devise is for a charitable use. But, in the case at bar, the money shall be distributed in voluntary benevolences to the kindred, and this belongs not to the spiritual court, and distribution may be made by any person. He said also that, admitting an executor not named may sell, yet, in this case, the wife cannot, for the devise is that the land shall be sold after her death, and, therefore, the sale here is contrary to the express words of the will that she should sell. 15 Hen. VII, 12; 1 Co., Albany's Case, 111, for this clause excludes the wife, 1 Inst. 112; Dyer 219; Leon., part 2, 220. A devise that feoffees, after their decease, shall sell is void. 19 Hen. VIII, f. 12; 17 Hen. VII, 45; Keilway 8.[1] And, here, no part of the money is given to the wife, but it only appoints that she shall dispose the money, which she might do by a will or otherwise in her lifetime, though the sale be after her death. Admitting that the wife could sell, her executors cannot, for this is no testamentary interest, but a bare authority. Cro. Car. 182.[2] And this power is not given to the executor *quatenus* executor, for an executor may refuse to prove, and, notwithstanding, a sale by him is good. He agreed that, if a devise be that the heir shall sell, the heir of the heir may sell. 9 Hen. VII, 10. It is otherwise of executors, for executors of executors, in his opinion, were not chargeable at common law, nor before 25 Edw. III;[3] 27 Hen. VII, 45. But the case here is of a thing of freehold, and not within the Statute 19 Hen. VIII, 9.[4] And so he prayed judgment for the defendant.

I did not hear the arguments of the judges, but was informed by Ellis, who was a judge at the time that he told it me, the unanimous opinion of the court was that the devise was void for not naming a vendor, and judgment was entered for the defendant. He said also that this case was sent into the Common Pleas from the Chancery and that, there, after the judgment, it was so decreed with the assistance of the other judges. But, afterwards, on an appeal to the Lords in Parliament, the decree was reversed, and a decree was made that the vendees should have the land.

1 Levinz 304, 83 E.R. 419

A man devises lands to his wife for her life and that, after her death, the reversion shall be sold, and the money arising thereby distributed between his heir and three nephews. The heir refuses to sell or to join with the wife in the sale.

---

[1] YB Trin. 15 Hen. VII, ff. 11, 12, pl. 22 (1500); *Grendon v. Albany* (1585–1586), 1 Coke Rep. 107, 76 E.R. 246, also 4 Leonard 133, 219, 74 E.R. 778, 833; E. Coke, *First Institute* (1628), f. 112; *Anonymous* (1580), *ut supra*; *Anonymous* (1574), *ut supra*; YB Trin. 19 Hen. VIII, f. 12, pl. 10 (1527); *Lord Willoughby de Broke v. Lord Latimer* (1497), Keilwey 8, 72 E.R. 161, YB Mich. 12 Hen. VII, f. 8, pl. 5, 115 Selden Soc. 312.

[2] *Houell v. Barnes* (1634), *ut supra.*

[3] Stat. 25 Edw. III, stat. 5, c. 5 (*SR*, I, 321).

[4] Perhaps YB Trin. 19 Hen. VIII, f. 9, p. 4 (1527).

And, on a bill exhibited in Chancery against him to compel him to join in the sale, the bill was dismissed by the Lord Keeper BRIDGEMAN, who held the will to be void as to the sale of the reversion, it not being said who shall sell.

But, in the House of Peers, they, on advice with the judges, reversed the dismission, and decreed that the heir should sell, for, when no person is appointed to sell, it ought to be intended that he shall sell who has the estate, which is the heir.

See 5 Hen. VII, 12b, by Hide, Fenwick, and Fineux;[1] a devise that lands should be sold and not said by whom, they shall be sold by the executors; and to the same intent when they are to be sold for the payment of debts.

[Other reports of this case: 1 Eq. Cas. Abr. 265, 21 E.R. 1034.]
[Reg. Lib. 1667 B, f. 875, 1668 B, ff. 52, 572, 659, 1669 B, f. 979.]
[Judgment was given for the plaintiff in the House of Lords, Michaelmas term 22 Car. II, Lincoln's Inn MS. Misc. 500, f. 121.]

254

Bois v. Roswell and Dickins

(Ch. 1668)

Where a settlor declares how the profits of the trust are to be distributed, the corpus of the trust will be distributed in the same manner as the profits were.

1 Levinz 232, 83 E.R. 383

Dickins, seised in fee, enfeoffed Roswell in trust for himself for life, and, afterwards, to pay the profits to John, Robert, and Nicholas Dickins in ratable and equal manner, and also, when they should come to the age of twenty-one years, in like sort, to convey the premises to them and their heirs. John dies, leaving Susan, his sister and heir, in the life of the feoffor. Susan marries Bois, and has issue, the plaintiff Bois, and dies. Nicholas dies without issue, leaving Robert, his brother and heir.

Bois exhibits his bill to have an account of the third part of the profits and also to have the third part of the inheritance conveyed to him.

Robert Dickins, the defendant, claims the whole.

And the only question was if this trust was a joint tenancy and so should survive wholly to Robert or a tenancy in common, so that the third part should go to the heirs of John.

And it was decreed by BRIDGEMAN, Lord Keeper, assisted by the judges RAINSFORD and MORTON, that it was a tenancy in common and that as well for the inheritance as for the profits and as well in the case of a deed of trust as in a will, in both which the intent is to be considered. And the inheritance here was

[1] YB Trin. 15 Hen. VII, ff. 11, 12, pl. 22 (1500).

to be conveyed in like sort as the profits, and that was in a ratable and equal manner, which, in a will, would make a tenancy in common.

255

Moyser v. Peacock

(Ch. 1668)

Where a suit in equity is dismissed for lack of jurisdiction, any depositions taken can be used de bene esse in a subsequent action at common law.

3 Chancery Reports 22, 21 E.R. 717

Hilary [term] 1667[/68].

A bill was to have ten groats a year and the arrearages to be paid for a pretended rent issuing out of the defendant's houses. But it was dismissed at the hearing for want of equity.

Yet the Master of the Rolls [GRIMSTON] said and allowed the plaintiff to use the depositions in this cause at a trial at law, in the case of the death of the witnesses, though the bill did not pray to perpetuate the testimony.

256

Anonymous

(Ch. 1668)

A default judgment cannot be had in a court of equity against a defendant who has not appeared.

A defendant cannot be held in contempt in a court of equity unless he has been served with process.

3 Chancery Reports 22, 21 E.R. 717

[In] an original bill or bill of revivor, if the defendant has not appeared, but stands out all process of contempt to a serjeant at arms returned, no decree can he had against him or the bill taken *pro confesso* unless he had appeared and stood in contempt for want of an answer.

No process of contempt is to be taken out against a defendant for the disobedience of an order unless he be served with a writ of execution of that order under the seal of the court.

257

Dagnall v. Thomas

(Ch. 1668)

The question in this case was whether an executor can enforce a decree after the benefit of the decree has been given away to a legatee.

Lincoln's Inn MS. Hill 125, f. 53, pl. 1

13 January 1667[/68].

Dagnall, conusee of a statute acknowledged by Samuel Thomas, brother of the defendant, and extended, obtained here a decree to hold the extent until [. . .]. And, by his will, he devised the extent and estate to his daughter, and made his wife executrix. And she consented to the legacy.

The executrix sued now a subpoena *scire facias* to execute the decree, and prosecuted for the contempt. [. . .] report after witnesses [were] examined to the contempt.

The defendant insisted that the estate being now transferred, the executrix could not prosecute and, if that the defendant should be now acquitted on his title [. . .] his defense was a matter of title, then the devisee, not being a party, is not concluded by the depositions here.

The Lord Keeper [Bridgeman] overruled this point.

But on the point of title, a trial was directed, and the contempt [was] suspended in the meanwhile.

258

Priaulx v. Aldworth

(Ch. 1668)

The question in this case was whether a defendant can appear and plead after a writ of attachment has been issued against him but before the sheriff makes his return.

Lincoln's Inn MS. Hill 125, f. 53, pl. 2

An attachment with proclamation issued against the defendant returnable the first return of Michaelmas term. The sheriff made no return of the writ actually made until 6th December. And then the sheriff endorsed the writ *cepi corpus et paratum habeo etc.* After the writ [was] delivered to the sheriff and the time of the return and before the endorsement thereof, the defendant put in a demurrer. The question [was] if it be timely come in after the day when the writ was returnable and executed but not returned.

259

Thomas v. Porter

(Ch. 1668)

A court of equity will enforce a forfeiture for a willful waste by a copyholder.

In this case, the court found as a fact that no waste had been committed, and granted relief against the forfeiture in issue.

1 Chancery Cases 95, 22 E.R. 711

8 February [1668]. Mary Thomas, widow, against Edward Porter, Phineas Porter, and Robert, bishop of Worcester.

The plaintiff was a tenant *durante viduitate* of the lands in question, being copyholds of a manor, whereof the defendant, the bishop, was the lord, remainder to Edward Porter. The defendant had felled trees, which, at a court baron was presented and found a waste and, consequently, a forfeiture by the homage. And the defendant Edward was afterwards at another court, after an entry made by the bishop for the forfeiture, admitted. And he brought [an action of] ejectment, and, before a judge of assize, he had a verdict.

To be relieved against which was the bill, which did suggest that the timber that was cut was worth but 40s. and the estate £60 *per annum* and that there was £300 worth of timber standing and that, if, upon examination, it should appear to be waste, the plaintiff would make satisfaction.

The defendant Porter, by an answer, insisted that the waste was voluntary, and declared to be so by the judge of Assize before whom the judgment was and that the timber felled was worth £60. Upon the proofs, there was a great difference touching the value of the timber felled. And there was some proof of a load or two of boards that were carried off the premises by the plaintiff, which, for her, was insisted were carried to another copyhold within the same manor. But there was not any proof that the plaintiff had sold any of the timber she felled. And it was proved the copyhold in question was much out of repair.

And, for the plaintiff, it was insisted that, with that timber, she intended to repair the same.

The Lord Keeper [BRIDGEMAN]: It was not clear there was any willful forfeiture, for that the defendants, before the plaintiff had applied the timber, took advantage of the forfeiture, and the defendants were ever forward therein. And yet withal, he declared that, in the case of a willful forfeiture, he would not relieve. And then he referred the cause to the bishop, the defendant, to be chancellor in this cause.

Upon this, the bishop certified the waste to be willful and no ground to relieve the plaintiff.

Upon this certificate, the cause coming to be heard before Justice TYRREL (in the absence of the Keeper), he pronounced an order to dismiss the bill, which, being stayed by a petition to the Lord Keeper, 11 November 1668, he re-heard the cause, at which time, it was insisted for the plaintiff that the Lord Keeper could not delegate his jurisdiction to the bishop, as the order on the first hearing did mention. Which was admitted. And it was made out by affidavits that the bishop's son had taken a bond from the defendant Porter for £50 if the cause went for the defendant Porter.

Upon this hearing, it was referred to a trial at law upon this issue, whether the primary intention in felling the timber was to do waste. But, as the order was drawn up, the issue to be tried was whether the supposed waste was willful or not.

And, upon two several trials, it was found for the plaintiff. And so, after these two trials, it was decreed the plaintiff should be relieved and the defendant was to deliver possession and account for the mesne profits.

[Other reports of this case: 1 Eq. Cas. Abr. 121, 21 E.R. 927.]

260

St. John v. Holford

(Ch. 1668)

A debtor who mortgages land to secure a debt and, afterwards, borrows more money from the same creditor must pay off both debts in order to redeem the mortgage.

He who seeks equity must do equity.

1 Chancery Cases 97, 22 E.R. 712

9 February [1668]. The Master of the Rolls.

The defendant's grandfather, whose heir and executor the defendant is, became bound with the plaintiff's father, whose heir the plaintiff is, in several bonds as his surety for £4000. The plaintiff's father conveyed the manor of Colwerton by way of a mortgage to the defendant's grandfather to counter-secure him against the said bonds for £4000. The plaintiff's father prevailed with the defendant's father to become bound with him afterwards for £2000 more. Then, the plaintiff's father paid off £1500 of the £4000 debts by bond.

The bill was to be admitted to redeem upon payment of what the defendant's grandfather or himself had paid off or been damnified by the bonds for the £4000 and what remained unpaid of the £4000.

And the question was whether the plaintiff (inasmuch as there was no agreement proved that the mortgage was to be a security to the defendant's grandfather against the bonds for the £2000 as well as those for £4000) should be admitted to redeem upon payment of the £4000 without the £2000.

And it was ruled and so decreed that, if the plaintiff would redeem, he should reimburse and save harmless the defendant, as well touching the £2000 as the £4000, upon this rule, he that will have equity to help where the law cannot shall do equity to the same party against whom he seeks to be relieved in equity.

Serjeant *Maynard* and *Fountaine* were of counsel this case with the plaintiff, and did without any debate rest in this order. Serjeant *Fountaine* said it was a just decree.

Hilary [term] 1667[/68], upon an appeal to the Lord Keeper BRIDGEMAN, the decree was confirmed.

Lord Nottingham, *Prolegomena*, p. 305

Hilary [term] 1667/68. Bridgeman, Keeper.

Holford is bound for St. John in £4000, and he has a counter-security. Afterwards, Holford is bound for St. John in £2000 more, and has no other counter-security nor any agreement that the first counter-security should continue for the whole. Holford pays £6000 for St. John.

Then, St. John exhibits a bill to have up his counter-security on repayment of the £4000 for which it was made.

But it was dismissed unless he should pay the other £2000.

79 Selden Soc. 885

A conveyance was made to Holford in trust for the payment of debts in a schedule and particularly to indemnify him for £4000 wherein he stood bound for St. John. Afterwards, Holford became bound for St. John in £2000 more, yet his indemnity remained for that too, when once possessed of a security.

Lord Nottingham, *Prolegomena*, p. 322

St. John mortgages several lands in Leicestershire to Sir R. Holford in 1639 to secure £4000. After this, in 1641, St. John sells part of the mortgaged lands to Dr. Hamy. And Sir R. Holford, who knew of Dr. Hamy's proceedings all along and was made acquainted with them, suffers Dr. Hamy to proceed and never tells him of his own precedent mortgage.

It was decreed in 1653 that Dr. Hamy should enjoy his purchase against Sir R. Holford and all claiming under him, for *qui tacet consentire videtur*;[1] else, Holford should cozen Hamy, and enable St. John, with Hamy's money, to pay part of Holford's debt, yet keep the land too.

1 Vernon 448, 23 E.R. 577

It appeared that the lands mortgaged to Mr. Holford were subject to a mortgage prior to his and that the mortgagor had made a deed of trust of those lands, amongst others, for the payment of his debts.

[1] *Liber Extra*, 5, 12, 43.

And, upon hearing of that cause, it was decreed that the now plaintiff should be only paid in proportion with the other creditors. And, not liking that decree, he brought this cause to a hearing on the bill and answer.

And, in regard the lands by the deed of trust were subjected to the payment of more debts than the same were worth to be sold, the defendant would now go back from the offer in his answer and be contented to be foreclosed.

[Other reports of this case: 1 Eq. Cas. Abr. 324, 21 E.R. 1077, 79 Selden Soc. 465.]
[Reg. Lib. 1676/77 B, f. 203.]

261

Dodsworth v. Place

(Ch. 1668)

A new trial can be granted where there was conflicting evidence between a party and a witness.

Lincoln's Inn MS. Hill 125, f. 55, pl. 1

The plaintiff, upon a promise to pay money, was dismissed. And, in a cross-bill, he swore the promise made in Honey Lane, London. The plaintiff, after[wards] sued at law, and had a verdict by the testimony of R.P. And the defendant brought his cause to a hearing because [of] the suit here by the plaintiff and [there was but] a single witness and a variance of the testimony, for the answer, for the witness swore the promise at another place.

A new trial was ordered by the Lord Keeper [BRIDGEMAN].

262

Long v. Clopton

(Ch. 1668–1687)

Where a mortgagor or his successor in interest settles an encumbrance for less than the debt due on it, he is entitled to reduce his debt to the creditor-mortgagee only in the amount he paid for the settlement, but, where the creditor settles, he is entitled to the entire bargain he made.

Lincoln's Inn MS. Hill 125, f. 55, pl. 2

E. Clopton, father of the defendant, mortgaged land whereof he was seised in fee for £1000 for 500 years. And he mortgaged other lands in fee. And then the plaintiff's husband had a judgment against him for £600. His heir bought in both the mortgages in the other defendants' names. The plaintiff, as executrix of her husband, sues the plaintiff to set aside the [. . .] or mortgage for 500 years, paying what [was] due to the defendant. The heir questions. The heirs purchased in a mortgage for years in other names for less than [was] due to the mortgagees. The question was whether, if the court shall let in the judgment, what shall be allowed the heir, *viz.* the debt or only so much as he compounded for, as in the case of executors.

Lincoln's Inn MS. Hill 125, f. 55 [bis], pl. 2

12 May 1669.

The heir purchased in by way of composition some mortgages precedent to the plaintiff's statute for lesser sums than what was due to the mortgagee.

Curia dubitante, and will advise if the heir shall be allowed more than what he paid with damages, as in a case of an executor.

But costs expended in suits by the heir to defend the title against a superior title and that, if it had prevailed, would have destroyed the plaintiff's title as well as the heir's were allowed in proportion, rating the benefit the heir and the mortgagees reaped by the defense.

The plaintiff's suit was as adverse to a conusee of a statute to set aside or satisfy precedent mortgages and so to extend.

1 Vernon 464, 23 E.R. 590

Eodem die [8 June 1687].

On a Master's special report, to whom the account in question was referred to be taken, it was determined by the court that an heir or any other shall not, as against a real purchaser, be allowed more on any encumbrance bought in than what he actually paid for the same without regard to what was really due on such encumbrance and that, where a prior encumbrancer buys in a subsequent encumbrance with notice of an intervening security, he shall not be allowed the same. And the Case of Borough and Frances[1] was cited.

[Raithby's note: The case by the Register's Book appears to have been that a bill was exhibited against the defendant, as heir of his father, against whom a judgment had been obtained to discover the real and personal estate of his said father liable thereto and for an account of profits of the said estate and that, at the hearing, an account was directed of what had been received and paid for preceding encumbrances for principal and interest and for charges in defense of the title. And the defendant having compounded several encumbrances, the court reserved the matter whether the defendant should have the benefit. And it was agreed that the encumbrances being particular and charged on several parts of the estate, some of which estates were of far greater value than the money lent thereon, over and besides all general securities that effected the same, the plaintiff ought to be admitted to a redemption to such particular estates as he should think fit and not be bound to redeem the whole. And the decree was that the defendant, though he be an heir,

[1] *Burgh v. Francis* (1673), Reports *tempore* Finch 28, 23 E.R. 16, 73 Selden Soc. 14, 3 Swanston 551, 36 E.R. 971, 1 Eq. Cas. Abr. 320, 21 E.R. 1074.

yet ought not to be allowed the benefit of the composition to the prejudice of plaintiff's debt, but ought to be allowed what he had really paid for principal, interest, and charges, as well on account of encumbrances precedent to the plaintiff's judgment as subsequent, until he had notice of the said plaintiff's judgment and that the plaintiff ought not to be admitted to a redemption of any part of the estate without redeeming the whole and paying what should appear to be due to the defendant upon the account. And, as to the account, Lord Chancellor [JEFFREYS] declared that the defendant, being charged with the rent of the lands for the time he held it, ought to be allowed taxes, repairs, and all incidental charges annually and the costs and charges he had been put unto in relation to the title of the premises and that defendant ought not to be charged with any rents or profits while any of the encumbrancers were in possession of the premises or with any more than he raised or received out of said estate. Reg. Lib. 1686 B, f. 652.]

263

Labyne v. Alley

(Ch. 1668)

A final decree can be enrolled after the death of the defendant.

3 Chancery Reports 27, 21 E.R. 718

22 February 20 Car. II [1668].

A decree was made and ordered that, if the defendant died before Easter, yet that the plaintiff may afterwards enroll it.

264

Douglasse v. Waad

(Ch. c. 1668)

The marriage is a good consideration to a marriage contract so as to make the parties thereto purchasers.

Voluntary conveyances are prima facie *considered to be fraudulent against creditors, unless the contrary be made to appear.*

1 Chancery Cases 99, 22 E.R. 713

Sir Joseph Douglasse and his wife against William Waad.

James Waad, the defendant's father, having married a first wife, did in her lifetime many years before her death by several fines and deeds settle the several manors of Buttles and Payton Hall to the use of himself for life, remainder to his first and all his other sons in tail. Afterwards, the first wife dies without issue. Then, James Waad marries with the daughter of Eltonhead. But, before the marriage, he agrees with Eltonhead that, in consideration of a £1000 portion, which Eltonhead was to pay her, to settle her a jointure of £300 *per annum*, of which it appeared in the case Buttles Manor was to be part. But what the other lands were that were to make up the £300 *per annum* did not appear. James Waad had issue by his second wife, the defendant, and he died, leaving the second wife, who married Douglasse, the plaintiff.

Their bill is against the defendant to have him decreed to settle the jointure on the defendant's mother and to set aside the settlement made by James Waad against the jointress as fraudulent.

When this case was first brought to hearing, there was no proof of payment of the £1000 portion by Eltonhead. It was proved that Eltonhead maintained James Waad and furnished him with money for other uses.

And it was insisted on the plaintiff's part that the marriage was a good consideration to make the jointress a purchaser and it was her father that was to pay the £1000 and not she. And so she was clearly a purchaser. If a man secures his purchase money, it is a payment.

And to this opinion that she was a purchaser, the Lord Chancellor [BRIDGEMAN] inclined.

And the plaintiff's counsel, Serjeant *Maynard* and *Fountaine*, insisted that the jointress being a purchaser, the settlement, being after the marriage of the first wife, was fraudulent as to the jointure, which the second wife claims by the marriage agreement.

On the defendant's part, it was insisted the first conveyance was good and cannot be set aside by the marriage agreement, for it was not in the power of the father, after the first settlement, to avoid it. And every voluntary conveyance is not fraudulent. The Chancellor of Oxford's Case; Merry and Littleton's Case, 10 Jac.;[1] fraud is not to be presumed. And this conveyance was by a fine, and, so, notorious and upon record. And there could not be any intention of fraud as against the second wife. And it is rare that this court takes upon them to judge a deed fraudulent.

To which it was replied fraud is only cognizable here and was only proper here before the Statutes.[2] And every voluntary conveyance is presumed to be fraudulent, unless he that claims by it can prove the contrary.

The Lord Chancellor [BRIDGEMAN] inclines that the jointress is a purchaser and, whether the deed be fraudulent, he proposes to have it tried. But, after[wards], he referred it to a case. And a case being stated to the effect *ut supra* with this more, that there was a release given by James Waad for the portion, 25 February, 19 Car. II [1667], the cause came to be heard before the Lord Chancellor [BRIDGEMAN] and Baron TURNER. At which time, the court declared the marriage was a good consideration to make the wife a purchaser and, besides, upon the release for the portion, it was clear she was a good purchaser and that

---

1 *Chancellor of Oxford's Case* (1613), 10 Coke Rep. 53, 77 E.R. 1006; *Tirer v. Littleton* (1612 × 1613), 10 Coke Rep. 55, 77 E.R. 1010.

2 Stat. 13 Eliz. I, c. 5 (*SR*, IV, 537–538); Stat. 29 Eliz. I, c. 5, s. 1 (*SR*, IV, 769).

all voluntary conveyances are *prima facie* to be looked upon as fraudulent against purchasers, unless the contrary be made to appear. And so they decreed the settlement by James Waad to be set aside as fraudulent.

The defendant brought a bill of review, and assigned for error that it was not cognizable here whether a deed were fraudulent, but that was only triable at law. And, besides, there was no color of fraud against the jointress, for the deed, as appears by the decree, was made in the life of the first wife, who lived ten years after, and the second wife was not then thought on. And the settlement, being by a deed and a fine, ought not to be presumed fraudulent without proof. And it was farther assigned for error that, by the decree, the settlement as to Payton Hall was to be part of the jointure and she was not, as appeared, any purchaser as to that. And so there was no reason to set aside the settlement as to Payton Hall under the notion of the jointress's being a purchaser, for that it did not appear that that was within her pretended purchase.

To this bill of review, the defendants demurred, and insisted that the decree was well grounded.

And, upon debate thereof before the Lord Chancellor and Baron Turner in Trinity vacation, 19 Car. II [1667], the demurrer, as to the points above, was allowed.

But as to another particular, touching the mesne profits (which point I [*Keck*] have not stated), the plaintiff in the bill of review was upon the arguing of the demurrer relieved, and the decree so far explained (that is to say) whereas, by the decree, the defendant was to answer and pay all the arrears of the £300 *per annum* to the jointress since his father's death, whereas it appears by the decree that, by a former decree of the court, the mesne profits had been applied first to the payment of Eltonhead's debts and, afterwards, been taken by the Lady Waad and the defendant was neither charged as heir or executor to his father nor had any assets to answer the arrears, it was ordered that the defendant should be chargeable only with so much arrears as he had received out of the lands.

265

Devering v. Cooper

(Ch. 1668)

Where the enrollment of a decree was lost many years before, the case can be reheard.

3 Chancery Reports 27, 21 E.R. 718

13 April, 20 Car. II [1668].

An enrollment of a decree in 10 Car. I [1638] being lost, the counsel, after so long a time, [was] ordered to be re-heard.

266

Pearson v. Pulley

(Ch. 1668)

An assignee of a mortgagee in possession, upon a suit to redeem, is required to account only for the profits received by himself, and not by his assignor.

1 Chancery Cases 102, 22 E.R. 714

25 April [1668]. The Lord Keeper, the Master of the Rolls.

The bill being to redeem a mortgage made in 1632 and it being insisted on by the defendant that he came in as an assignee at the third hand and so it would be hard to put him to an account now, the Lord Keeper [BRIDGEMAN] said that, in regard there had been no stint put to the time a mortgage is to be redeemed, the defendant shall come to an account. But, in regard he comes in at an old hand, he shall not account but so far only as goes in discount of his money, but not for the surplusage. And he said he would have a rule to limit to what time a mortgage shall be redeemable. And he conceived twenty years to be a fit time, in imitation of the Statute of Limitation of real actions.[1] But he gave no rule in that, but only he directed that, when a bill came to redeem an old mortgage, the defendant should plead or demur to it, that so the judgment of the court might he had upon it.

267

Jenkins v. Kemis

(Ch. 1668)

The marriage is a consideration for a marriage contract, and it supports the entire marriage settlement.

1 Chancery Cases 103, 22 E.R. 715

28 April [1668]. David Jenkins, Esq., against Sir Charles Kemis, Baronet, and others.

Edward Kemis, Esq., devised the lands in question after other estates tail (which are all spent) to Sir Nicholas Kemis for life, remainder to his first son and the heirs male of his body, with other remainders over. Sir Nicholas has issue Charles, father of the defendant Charles. In 1637, the defendant's father married Blanch, the daughter of Mansel, with whom he had £2500, which Sir Nicholas had. And, thereupon, Sir Nicholas and Charles, his son, levied a fine, and suffered a recovery. And, five years after, *viz.* 1 April, 18 Car. I [1642], by an in-

[1] Stat. 21 Jac. I, c. 16, s. 1 (*SR*, IV, 1222).

denture tripartite, whereto Sir Nicholas and Charles, his son, are both parties named, and, though Charles never sealed, yet he consented to the use thereof, reciting that Nicholas was tenant for life, the remainder to his son Charles *prout* and the marriage of Charles *prout* and that his wife's portion was £2500 and that Sir Nicholas had it and the fine and recovery was had thereupon and, in consideration thereof, the uses of the fine and recovery are declared to be to Sir Nicholas for life, the remainder to his son, Charles, and the heirs male of his body begotten on the body of Blanch, the remainder to the heirs male of Sir Nicholas, the remainder to the heirs male of the body of Sir Charles, the defendant's father, the remainder to the right heirs of Sir Nicholas, with a power to Sir Nicholas by deed or will to charge the land with £2000, as he should think fit.

After[wards], in January, 18 Car. II [1667], the marquis of Worcester borrows of the plaintiff's father £2000, which was applied to the king's service. And he prevails with Sir Nicholas Kemis and Charles, his son, then both under his command, by lease and release to convey the premises to the plaintiff's father in fee by way of a mortgage, wherein they covenant to make farther assurance. The mortgagors continue possession and die.

The defendant is the eldest son and heir of the said Charles Kemis by a second wife, Blanch being dead without issue, but he claims the premises as issue in tail by the settlement as son and heir of his father. The mortgagee brought [an action of] ejectment against the defendant. And, thereupon, there is a special verdict *ut supra*. And, upon the argument, it was ruled against the plaintiff, whereupon the plaintiff, being as well executor as heir to his father, brings his bill in equity, suggesting the tripartite deed was antedated and however to be merely voluntary and fraudulent as to the defendant, he not being the issue of Blanch, and so it is not within the consideration of the tripartite deed and settlement and the plaintiff being a purchaser and the defendant's father or grandfather being taken by the plaintiff's father to be seised in fee when they made the mortgage. And it was farther insisted on by the bill that Sir Nicholas having a power to charge the premises with the payment of £2000 and the mortgage being for £2000, though it were by way of conveyance of the lands and not by a charge of the lands and so, according to strictness of law, was not good, yet, in equity, it ought to be taken as in execution of the power and that nice legal defect ought, therefore, to be supplied in equity to the plaintiff, who is in under a purchaser.

For the plaintiff, it was farther insisted that Sir Nicholas's power ought to be knit to his interest, and so come in supply of his interest to make the mortgage good. And, if a person that has a power to charge lands for a sum of money do for the like sum convey lands to another and covenant to make further assurance (as here), equity will compel him to execute his power to the benefit of the person from whom he has received the money. And the defendant was heir to Sir Nicholas and his farther, and bound by their covenant to make farther assurance.

Whereunto, it was answered by the defendant's counsel that the defendant does not claim as heir to his father or grandfather, but by the settlement, and that he was heir male of the body of his father, and was within the consideration of the £2500 portion which the grandfather had and which belonged to the father. And, however, if that settlement had not been made, the defendant was issue in tail by the settlement made by Edward Kemis' will. And it was farther insisted that the settlement, by which Sir Nicholas had power to charge the lands, was discharged by the mortgage, he having conveyed all his interest out of him thereby and that so he was disabled to execute his power after. And it was also insisted for the defendant that equity in this case ought to follow the law, the defendant claiming by precedent title to the plaintiff in such manner that there was no equity to bind it farther than by law it is bound. And, in truth, it did appear, howbeit it was not found in the special verdict, that Sir Nicholas did after the mortgage to the plaintiff's father in pursuance of his power charge the premises with the £2000 debt which he owed, which debts the defendant's father paid accordingly.

The Lord Keeper [Bridgeman] conceived the power was not destroyed by the mortgage, because it was by a lease and release, and not by a fine or a feoffment. Yet both he and the Master of the Rolls [Grimston] were of opinion that the plaintiff could not be relieved in equity. Nevertheless, at the plaintiff's importunity, he directed a case to be made, and, after Michaelmas term 1668, he dismissed the bill.

1 Levinz 237, 83 E.R. 386

Sir Nicholas Keymes, being tenant for life, the remainder to his son Sir Charles in tail, they, about the year 1641, in consideration of a marriage to be had between Sir Charles and Blanch Mansel and a £2500 portion paid, levied a fine to the use of Sir Nicholas for life, the remainder to Sir Charles and Blanch for their lives, the remainder to the heirs of the body of Sir Nicholas, Sir Charles, of the said Blanch begotten, the remainder to the heirs of the body of Sir Charles, with a power for Sir Nicholas to charge the premises with £2000. Sir Nicholas and Sir Charles, about the year 1642, joined in a lease and release to David Jenkins, the Welsh judge,[1] and his heirs for £2000 on condition of payment of £2000 with interest some years after to be void, and covenants, on default of payment, to make further assurance. And, about the year 1643, by indenture between Sir Nicholas of one part and Sir John Awbry of the other part, Sir Nicholas reciting the power, it is said in the indenture that he charged the premises with £2000 for the payment of his debts. But it is not said that he granted anything to Sir John Awbry nor that he charged the lands to Sir John Awbry or to any other person, but (only) that he charged them. Blanch, afterwards, dies without issue. Sir Charles marries another wife, by whom he had issue, Sir Charles, the defendant, and dies. David Jenkins dies, and leaves David Jenkins, the plaintiff, his heir and execu-

[1] C. W. Brooks, 'Jenkins, David (1582–1663)', *Oxford Dictionary of National Biography*, vol. 29, pp. 948–950.

tor, who brought an [action of] ejectment in the Exchequer Chamber.[1] And, on a special verdict, it was adjudged, as before appears, that the lease and release was no good execution of the power at common law.

And, now, he brought his bill in equity on these grounds: *viz.* first, that the consideration of the marriage of Blanch and the £2500 paid with her did not extend to the defendant, being an issue by the second wife, and so the estate in remainder, whereby he claimed, was voluntary; secondly, that the father, tenant in tail, joining in the conveyance (who might by fine have barred the defendant) if his issue could not be obliged by his covenant for further assurance, to make that assurance good, which his father had made; thirdly, if not, then, though the power be not well executed as to the intent, yet whether it shall not be made good in equity as to the £2000.

And, upon the bill and answer with this further, that Sir John Awbry having £500 due to him and suing here for relief, his bill was dismissed, Sir Nicholas only having sealed the deed and no proof that Sir Charles assented thereto, which was now made to appear. (Query.) And it also appeared that the defendant had paid other debts of Sir Nicholas due by bond to the value of £2000.

And, now, on the said points, it was declared by the Lord Keeper BRIDGEMAN, as to the first, the consideration of £2500 paid on the first marriage should extend to the issue by the second wife, and, as to the second, that the issue in tail was not bound by the covenant of his father to make that assurance good, which his father might have made good by a fine, although it was said that it had been so done formerly, and that the Lord Chancellor Hyde was of that opinion. And, as to the third, the Lord Keeper [BRIDGEMAN] held that Sir Nicholas and Sir Charles joining in the conveyance to Jenkins and covenanting, on default of payment, to make further assurance cannot be taken to be an execution of the power at all, but as a common mortgage, and, although that the deed to Awbry was not a legal execution of the power, for default of a person to whom it should be charged, yet it being intended for an execution of the power, it shall be aided in equity before that to Jenkins, and that the defendants, having (though not the executors) paid to the value of £2000 in debts, may apply it in execution of the power to the discharge of the lands, being terre tenants.

[Other copies of this report: British Library MS. Hargrave 65, f. 92.]

1 Chancery Reports 275, 21 E.R. 571

The bill is to have the benefit of a mortgage of lands, whereof Sir Nicholas Keymeys and Charles Keymeys, his son, the defendant, Sir Charles's father and grandfather, were seised in fee, who, 1 January 18 Car. I [1643], mortgaged the premises to the plaintiff's father for £2000, [and] notwithstanding added a deed

[1] *Jenkins v. Keymish* (Ex. 1664–1666), Exch. Repts. *tempore* Car. II, 26, Hardres 395, 145 E.R. 515, 1 Levinz 150, 83 E.R. 343.

tripartite 1 April, 18 Car. I [1643], made by the said Sir Nicholas and Charles Keymeys, whereby the defendant claims the premises as the heir in tail of the body of the said Charles, for that it is a mere voluntary conveyance to the said Charles without consideration and for that there was a proviso therein that Sir Nicholas should have a power to charge the premises with £2000 at any time by a will or deed, and the conveyance made to the plaintiff's father ought to be and is a good execution of the power according to the said proviso. And, in the deed of mortgage to the plaintiff's father, there was a covenant for the payment of £2000 by Sir Nicholas and Sir Charles Keymeys to the plaintiff's father. And the subsequent deed [of] 22 October 20 Car. I [1644], mentioning the deed, proviso, and power, does not appoint any person to levy the £2000 and to pay debts, and Sir Charles, the defendant's father, has not paid near £2000 of the said Sir Nicholas's debts such as this court will allow of and prefer before the plaintiff's debts.

The defendant says Sir Nicholas and Sir Charles were not seised in fee of the premises, for that Edward Keymeys, uncle of Sir Nicholas, being seised thereof by a will, 8 January 5 Jac. [1611], devised to David Keymeys, son and heir to Rees Keymeys, the premises during life and, after[wards], to his first son and heir male of his body, with a remainder to the said Nicholas for life, and, after[wards], to his first son and the heirs male of his body. And Sir Nicholas, the said David dying without issue, entered, and was seised for life, remainder to his first son and the heirs male of his body with a remainder over. And on the marriage of Charles, his son, the plaintiff's father, with Blanch, the daughter of Lewis Mansel, and in consideration of a £2500 portion, a fine and recovery was had of the premises and the said deed tripartite was to the use of the said Sir Nicholas Keymeys for life, remainder to the use of the said Charles, afterwards, Sir Charles, the defendant, Sir Charles, his father, and the heirs male on the body of Blanch, remainder to the body of Sir Charles, which the defendant is. And so he does not claim by a voluntary conveyance, the portion and marriage of Sir Charles being a consideration extending to all his issue. And, in the tripartite deed, there was a proviso for the said Nicholas to charge the land with £2000, as aforesaid, who charged the same accordingly. And, not long after, the said Sir Nicholas died indebted £2000 at least, which Sir Charles, the defendant's father, paid, so as the lands ought not to be subject in law or equity to the plaintiff's demand, the rather for that the plaintiff endeavored to recover possession in the Exchequer, but a verdict was found for the defendant's title as heir male of his father. And he enjoys both by the will of Edward Keymeys and the settlement by the tripartite deed. And the defendant insists that the £2000 was not borrowed by the said Nicholas and the said Charles, but by the marquess of Worcester, and they only secured it, as aforesaid.

The plaintiff's counsel agreeing this case to be against the plaintiff, the court dismissed the bill.

[Reg. Lib. 19 Car. II, f. 406.]

268

Morley v. Elways

(Ch. 1668)

In this case, the debtor was allowed to redeem a mortgage, and the creditor was required to account for any profits received from the mortgaged land.

Upon the redemption of a mortgage, all the money paid as a surety shall be reckoned as principal money from the time of the payment, and interest is to be allowed accordingly.

1 Chancery Cases 107, 22 E.R. 717

1 June [1668]. Cuthbert Morley, Esq., against Jerome and Henry Elways.

The end of the plaintiff's suit is to have the redemption of a mortgage made by the plaintiff and his father, James Morley, Esq., in December 1641 to Jerome Elways, father of the defendants Jerome and Henry.

Against the plaintiff's relief, the defendant set up a release made by the plaintiff in 1646 of all his equity of redemption and a decree made by the Lord Chancellor Hyde in this cause in 1663, which decree is penned as if made by consent. This decree being signed and enrolled and the plaintiff, not able to perform the same, could not have a bill of review, nor could he be relieved by such a bill if it had been brought, the release barring all his pretenses and, that being upon a secret trust, he could not prove the trust positively, the witnesses being dead, and so he was not relievable, neither in law nor equity.

Whereupon, the plaintiff and Baron Greenvil, Esq., [sic] petitioned the Lords' House the last sessions of Parliament for relief against the said decree and release.

The cause held many debates at the bar of the Lords' House before Christmas 1667, the great question being whether the release was made in trust or *bona fide* for a valuable consideration. The proofs offered to evidence the trust were circumstantial and not direct, positive proofs. One thing offered by the plaintiffs to evince the truth of their assertion to Their Lordships in affirming the same to be only a trust was that Their Lordships would please to consider what debts were due from the plaintiff or his father to the defendant when the release was made and, with that, to take notice of the value of the estate released at the time of the making thereof. As to the reading the proofs to both these, the Parliament being to adjourn in two days and there not being time, Their Lordships adjourned the consideration of these two things. And, reading the proofs to the value of the estate, they desisted until their next meeting after Christmas.

The Lord Keeper [Bridgeman] was present thus far.

But the next meeting after Christmas, the Lord Keeper being absent, the Lord Privy Seal sat on the wool pack. And the cause had two days' hearing when all the plaintiffs' and defendants' proofs were read to the values. And the House [of Lords], after several days' debate of the matter, being satisfied that, by the proofs, it clearly appeared that the value of the lands was much greater than to make a satisfaction for the debt for which it was released, did adjudge the said release to be a farther trust to pay £80 *per annum* to the comptroller for life, and set aside the decree aforesaid, and referred the cause back to the court to proceed as in the case of an equitable mortgage, which Their Lordships adjudged this to be.

Monday, 1 June 1668, this cause was heard in court, when a decree was made for the defendants to come to an account and the plaintiff to be admitted to the redemption of his estate. The ordering part is as follows, first, that Jerome Elways come to account for all the profits of the lands in question, which he or his father or any other to his or their use or by their direction or appointment, have or might without their own willful default have received; [second], that Sir William Glascock should take the account, but with this direction, that, in case the lands mortgaged in fee were not a sufficient security for the money due to the defendant's father and for which he now stands engaged for them and the pre-engagement that was thereupon at the time of the defendant's father's taking the sequestration over and besides the other lands mortgaged, in which, at the time of the defendant's entry and the release made, the plaintiff had only one estate for life that then the defendant shall be charged in the account no more for the lands held for the plaintiff's life, than the Master shall really judge them to be worth without respect to the benefit that has happened by the continuance of the plaintiff's life.

The plaintiff, aggrieved with this direction, procured a rehearing by the Lord Keeper [Bridgeman], assisted with the Lord Chief Justice Vaughan, and Chief Baron Hale, and they confirmed this order, and that in respect of the contingency of the estate, and not for what was made, the mortgage being above twenty years old.

For the plaintiff, it was insisted that this was a new direction without a precedent and that it was safer to judge what was than what might have been and that, at this rate, the Western estates would not be mortgageable.

The plaintiff, by petition, complained of this direction to the Lords in Parliament, and, upon a solemn hearing at the bar of the House, he was relieved, and the Lord Keeper was ordered to direct the mortgagee to account for the whole profits of the estate for life, as in the case of other mortgagees.

2 Keble 376, 84 E.R. 235

1 June.

Note Bridgeman, Lord Keeper, and Grimston, Master of the Rolls, declared it as a rule and course of the court, on a reference to a Master to state an account upon a mortgage, that all money paid as a surety shall be reckoned as principal money from the time of the payment and interest is to be allowed accordingly.

And, second, if lands in fee and for life be joined in a mortgage, if the fee be not sufficient at the time, the life [estate] shall be valued only as it was at the time, six or seven years' purchase, and not according to the enjoyment since, be it twenty years or more.

269

Pitt v. Scarlet

(Ch. 1668–1670)

A creditor can bring a bill in equity for discovery and relief against the executors of his deceased debtor.

3 Chancery Reports 26, 21 E.R. 718

Trinity [term] 20 Car. II [1668].

The plaintiff brought a bill to be relieved as obligee in a bond against the defendant as executor of the obligors and to discover assets for the payment.

The defendant demurs, for that the plaintiff had brought no action at law against him, whereto the defendant had pleaded *plene administravit.*

Nelson 127, 21 E.R. 807

The plaintiff brought a bill against the defendant, as executor of the obligor, to discover assets and to compel the payment of the debt.

The defendant demurred, for that the plaintiff had brought an action against him at law, to which the defendant had pleaded *plene administravit.*

But the demurrer was overruled, and the defendant was ordered to answer without payment of costs.

270

Rex v. Squibb

(Ch. 1668)

A final judgment cannot be amended in another term from that in which is was entered.

A writ of error does not lie from the Court of Chancery to the Court of King's Bench, but only to the House of Lords.

Lincoln's Inn MS. Misc. 499, p. 445

Trinity term 20 Car. II [1668].

Judgment was given in Chancery upon a *monstrans de droit* for an office of Teller in the Exchequer in this manner: *Ideo consideratum est quod praedictus Edmundus Squibb forisfaciatur dicto domino regi officium illud et quod dictum officium resesiretur in manus domini regis tanquam forisfaciatur,* where in truth it should not be *Edmundus* but *Arthurus*,[1] and it should not be *forisfaciatur* but *resesiretur* (because those words do not purport a present forfeiture by the judgment, but a future), but it should be *ideo consideratum est quod officium praedictum sit seisitum in manus domini regis tanquam forisfactum*. And whether such as amendment could be made was the question.

And it was argued that it could be amended.

And, as to the mistake of the name, *Winnington* cited the case of Cro. El. 865,[2] where a name, after a judgment and writ of error, was amended.

And, for the other part of the judgment, *Sir Heneage Finch*, Solicitor General, cited the Case of Gibbon and Kent, King's Bench, Trinity [term] 1650, 1 Rolls 205, and the case of 1 Rolls 206, 8,[3] and 209 and 210, where amendments in as material points, as here is desired, were made. And this case is more strong, being the case of the king, because, at common law, there were amendments for the king, though none for the subject.

But [it was said] by the Lord Keeper [BRIDGEMAN], Chief Baron HALE assisting to him, it is not any ground to make the judgment '*seisitum*', because this is a new judgment and the court cannot amend their judgment in another term. And so the amendment was denied by the court.

Lincoln's Inn MS. Misc. 499, p. 466

Michaelmas [term] 20 Car. II. Chief Baron Hale, assistant to the Lord Keeper.

A judgment in a *monstrans de droit* for an office of Teller in the Exchequer was given in Chancery against the defendant. And, upon this judgment, the defendant brought a writ of error in the [Court of] King's Bench. And whether this writ lies in the King's Bench or only in the Parliament was the question.

And the Lord Keeper [BRIDGEMAN] called Chief Baron HALE to his assistance.

Sir Heneage Finch, Solicitor General, argued for the king that this writ lies only in Parliament because, if it be brought in the King's Bench if this Court of King's Bench be once possessed of the record, it never will be remitted into this court, as Bro., *Jurisdiction*, 48, and it will be inconvenient. And he said that, notwithstanding the opinion of Lord Coke, 4 Inst. 80, that says the Court of Chancery is inferior to the King's Bench, *quia addicio probat minoretatem*, yet he said that Chancery is *officina justitiae*. And it is expressly adjudged by the cases of 18 Edw. III, 25, and 17 Assizes 24, which are one and the same case, that such a writ lies in Parliament. And thus also are 37 Hen. VI, 13, 14; Fitzh., *Error*, 71; 11 Edw. IV, 9; Statham, Abr., *Error*, fo. 37; Compton, *Jur.*, 12b; 21 Edw.

[1] A. Woolrych, 'Squibb, Arthur (d. 1679/80)', *Oxford Dictionary of National Biography*, vol. 52, p. 14.

[2] *Wolf v. Stepney* (1601), Croke Eliz. 864, 78 E.R 1091.

[3] *Gibbon v. Kent* (1649–1650), 1 Rolle, Abr., *Amendment*, pl. F, 3, p. 205, also Style 212, 82 E.R. 654; *Belch v. Pate* (1640), 1 Rolle, Abr., *Amendment*, pl. F, 8, p. 206.

III, 46;[1] Wilson and Wilson's Case, in this court, 1659; Lenthall and Day, in this court, 24 Car. I. And he urged that, from the time of 18 Edw. III until 15 Eliz., Dier 315,[2] there is not any mention of a writ of error brought in the King's Bench. And, in the Petty Bag [Office], there is not any precedent of any judgment reversed in the King's Bench, but all precedents [are] of judgments reversed in Parliament.

And, as to the objection that Parliament could be prorogued and thus the subject delayed and other inconveniences ensue, he said that the same objection takes place at this day of judgments given in the King's Bench by original and other judgments before the Statute of 27 El., ca. 8.[3]

Baldwin, for the defendant: And he argued that a writ of error in this case lies in the King's Bench. And, for this, he cited Dier 315; 1 Rolls 745; Plowd. 393; 4 Inst. 80. And he said that the books of 37 Hen. VI, 13 and 14, and 10 Edw. IV, 9, are only opinions *pone obiter.*[4] And he argued that the King's Bench is superior to the Chancery as to the Latin side, which makes it to be a court of record and that no issue could be tried in the Chancery, but in the King's Bench only, as 1 Rolls 534, 50; Kelway 34; Stanf., *Prerog.*, 77; Latch 3.[5]

Also, in Chancery, there is only one judge, but, in the King's Bench, four or five. And, if the King's Bench is admitted to reverse the errors in the Common Bench, where there are four or five judges, *a fortiori*, they could be admitted to reverse judgments in Chancery, where there is only one judge. And he observed the inconvenience of a prorogation of Parliament.

Chief Baron HALE [held] that the Court of King's Bench sometimes reverses judgments given by the court itself for error. And, for this, he cited the case of one Payton, *circa* twenty years past, where he, being under age, entered into a

---

1 24 Edw. III, f. 45, Brooke, Abr., *Iurisdiction*, pl. 48 (1350); E. Coke, *Fourth Institute* (1644), p. 80; YB Trin. 18 Edw. III, f. 25, pl. 17, YB 17 Edw. III, Lib. Ass., f. 52, pl. 24 (1344); *Reynolde v. Knott* (1459), YB Hil. 37 Hen. VI, f. 13, pl. 3, 51 Selden Soc. 147; Fitzherbert, Abr., *Errour*, pl. 71; *Barrowwick v. Hawes* (1471), Chancery Repts. Middle Ages 173; 1 N. Statham, Abr., *Errour*, pl. 37; R. Crompton, *Authority et Jurisdiction des Courts*; *Master of Merton College v. Prior of St. Austin's* (1347), YB Hil. 21 Edw. III, f. 46, pl. 65.

2 *Anonymous* (1572), 3 Dyer 315, 73 E.R. 714.

3 Stat. 27 Eliz. I, c. 8 (*SR*, IV, 714).

4 *Anonymous* (1572), *ut supra*; 1 Rolle, Abr., *Error*, H. 'En quel Court', p. 745; *Dawkes v. Peyton* (1650), 1 Rolle, Abr., *Error*, pl. I, 13, p. 747, also Style 216, 218, 82 E.R. 657, 659; *Earl of Leicester v. Heydon* (1570), 1 Plowden 384, 393, 75 E.R. 582, 594; E. Coke, *Fourth Institute* (1644), p. 80; *Reynolde v. Knott* (1459), *ut supra*.

5 *Rex v. Holland* (1648), 1 Rolle, Abr., *Courts, Bank le Roy*, pl. G, 3, p. 534, also Style 90, 94, 82 E.R. 554, 557, Aleyn 14, 82 E.R. 889; W. Staunford, *Exposition of the King's Prerogative*; *Blackston v. Martin* (1625), Latch 3, 112, 274, 82 E.R. 245, 300, 383, also Benloe 161, 73 E.R. 1026, 3 Bulstrode 305, 81 E.R. 253, W. Jones 82, 90, 82 E.R. 44, 47, Palmer 410, 81 E.R. 1147, Paynell K.B. 20, 49.

recognizance, and, upon a *scire facias*, he appeared by an attorney in proper person where he should have appeared by a guardian, and, upon a trial, judgment was given for the plaintiff in the King's Bench, and the same court reversed this judgment for this error.

And, as to the case of 18 Edw. III, 25, he questioned whether this case was not upon a partition where there were two joint tenants of land *in capite*. And the Lord Chancellor made several liveries that amounted to a partition, yet there was not any judgment, and, if there was not any judgment in this case, it is not any authority for this case in question. But he said that there are some authorities that a writ of error lies in the King's Bench and he wished [?] to see any that lay in Parliament.

Adjornatur.

And, afterwards, it was ordered by the Lord Keeper [Bridgeman] that inasmuch as that the Parliament meets before the next term, that the writ of error will be brought in Parliament for expedition.

But Hale was not there, nor did he deliver his opinion, which was by all thought to be that it lay in the King's Bench.

M. Hale, *Jurisdiction of the Lords' House* (1796), p. 49

In a case of a judgment given in the Chancery upon a *rege inconsulto* upon an aid prayer, in the case of Squibb for a Teller's office in the Exchequer, the then Lord Keeper would not grant a writ of error in the King's Bench, but only in the Parliament. And the only reason that can maintain this decision and give a difference between this and a judgment in a *scire facias* or suit by privilege must be this, because this is one of the cases which is before the Keeper or Chancellor and the *consilium regis*, whereunto the judges are or should be called and give at least their advice. And so it is one of those cases above mentioned, which are of a higher nature than ordinary cases. And it is no reason the judges, who are presumed at least to give advice in these cases, should be the judges of the errors of that judgment, wherein, by the constitution of the courts themselves, they are to be public assistants and advisers.

271

Delamere v. Smith

(Ch. 1668)

The question in this case was whether the contract in issue should be strictly enforced or whether a small delay in the payment was substantial performance.

1 Chancery Cases 110, 22 E.R. 718

The plaintiff having had great dealings with Smith, the testator, for malt and other things bought by the plaintiff, by that means, he became indebted to the defendant's testator in several great sums, for which he gave him security by mortgage, bond, and otherwise.

Afterwards, the plaintiff became a great loser by the badness of the malt he bought of the defendant's testator and other accidents. And, thereupon, Smith and he came to a new agreement that, in consideration of £80 lately before paid and of £70 paid on the plaintiff's behalf by one Tubbing, the plaintiff's father-in-law, and of £40 more promised by Tubbing at a short day that, if the £40 were paid accordingly, that then, if the plaintiff should pay Smith £800 in four years by £200 *per annum*, that the said Smith would deliver up to the plaintiff all his securities etc.

The money was all paid to Smith, the testator, but £104, though not at a precise day. So to have those securities up, paying what was unpaid upon the last agreement with damages from the time it should have been paid, is the scope of the bill.

In this case, it was insisted for the defendant that, where a greater sum is due by specialty and a less [sum is] agreed to be taken for it to be paid in certain sums at certain days, if the agreement be not strictly pursued and the monies paid precisely at those days, but part of the money be paid at other days, a court of equity ought not to oblige him that made that agreement (in favor of the person failing to perform it) to stand to it upon payment of so much as will make up the money paid since the last agreement with damages for the same from the respective times the same should have been paid by that agreement to the times the same were paid and damages for what remains unpaid until the same be paid. But, if the plaintiff would have any benefit by the agreement, he ought, literally, to have performed it, which was in his favor, and without any penalty. And, therefore, he insisted that the plaintiff was not to have any benefit by that agreement.

The Baron [Turner] ordered this matter to be made into a case.

But, as yet, nothing has been done therein. And it is to be observed in this case that part of the consideration of the agreement was that Tubbing, who was not obliged by any former security, had paid Smith £70 and undertook to pay him £40 more; so Smith bettered his security etc.

[Later proceedings in this case: 73 Selden Soc. 148.]

272

Degg v. Osbaston

(Ch. 1668)

In this case of a bankrupt third-party trustee, the creditor was ordered to receive his principal debt but not any interest due on it, and the debtor was given additional time to pay.

1 Chancery Cases 111, 22 E.R. 719

[This was] the like case with that of Hen and Coninsby, *ante* f. 93.[1] And, upon solemn debate, it was ruled as that was. And, in both these cases, the mortgagee was ordered to take his principal without his interest, and time was given for the payment of the principal, *viz.* a year's time.

273

Booth v. Sanky

(Ch. 1668–1669)

A contract to surrender a bond can be specifically enforced.

3 Chancery Reports 26, 21 E.R. 718

Michaelmas [term] 20 Car. II [1668], Trinity [term] 21 Car. II [1669].

The plaintiff was indebted unto the defendant, and one Browne was indebted to the plaintiff. Browne gave a [confessed] judgment to the defendant for the debt, and the plaintiff gave a bond to pay it if Browne did not. And to have up the bond upon a promise of the defendant that, if the plaintiff would at his charge extend Browne's land, he would deliver up the bond, was the bill.

The defendant denied the promise.

But upon a verdict that he did make such promise and proof of the extent, the bond was decreed to be delivered up, although Browne failed in his verdict.

Nelson 128, 21 E.R. 807

The plaintiff was indebted to the defendant by bond. And one Brown was indebted to the plaintiff. Brown gave a [confessed] judgment to the defendant for the debt which was owing to him by the plaintiff, and the former bond was delivered up, and a new bond given by the plaintiff, that he would pay the money if Brown did not. Afterwards, the defendant promised the plaintiff that, if, at his own charge, he would extend Brown's lands, he would deliver up the new bond.

[1] *Henn v. Coningsby* (Ch. 1667–1668), see above, Case No. 247.

And, it being proved that he did make such a promise and that he did at his own charge extend the lands, the bond was ordered to be delivered up, though the extent would not satisfy the debt. And Brown became insolvent.

274

Lord Gorge v. Dillington

(Ch. 1668)

Where a mortgagor in possession forfeits, the mortgaged land goes to the administrator of the mortgagee, and not to the heir.

1 Chancery Reports 279, 21 E.R. 572

Sir William Lisle mortgaged the inheritance of the manor of Appleford to Sir Robert Dillington, the defendant's grandfather, by way of a lease and release, for £1000, in which there was a proviso that, if the said Sir William Lisle, his heirs, or assigns did not pay to the said Sir Robert, his executors, administrators, or assigns the sum of £1300 at days therein limited, then the said Sir Robert and his heirs to enjoy the mortgaged premises, with a covenant for farther assurance to the said Sir Robert and his heirs upon the non-payment of the said money, which said mortgage was forfeited in the said Sir Robert's, the grandfather's, lifetime, whereby he had an absolute estate of inheritance therein to him and his heirs. And, thereupon, the defendant, since the said Robert's, the grandfather's, death, being his heir, has entered on the mortgaged premises, and hopes to enjoy the same, there being a large personal estate and no debts.

But the plaintiff, the executor, insisted that, though the said mortgage was made to the said Sir Robert, the grandfather, and his heirs, yet it ought to be accounted part of his personal estate, being made payable to him, his executors, or administrators and a covenant on the mortgagor's part to pay it to his executors or administrators, not mentioning his heirs, not forfeited in Sir Robert's lifetime, and the interest was duly paid to the said Sir Robert, the grandfather, in his lifetime, and the heirs of the mortgagor are still in possession.

The defendant insists it is proved the mortgage was forfeited in Sir Robert's, the grandfather's, lifetime. And, therefore, where there is a contest of this nature between an heir and an executor or administrator and there are no debts in the case and, if there were, yet where there is no defect of assets, as there is not any in this case, this court does never take it from the heir. And [he produced] a precedent of this court with the like nature of this case.

This court conceived a clear difference between the cases, the money being only made payable to the executor or administrator, and not to the heir, and a covenant to pay the same to the said Sir Robert, the grandfather, his executor, or administrator, and the interest money paid during the grandfather's life, and no entry made by the grandfather, the principal money not payable until November 1668, but the heir of the mortgagor was still in possession, and the interest money was paid since the grandfather's death, and being fully satisfied, that what has been already received by the defendant on the said mortgage ought to be accounted as part of the personal estate, and so ought to go to the administrator of the grandfather, and not to the heir. And [the court] does decree the same accordingly, and the defendant is to convey the said mortgaged premises unto the plaintiff and his heirs.

And touching the £250 secured by a lease for years in the name of one Tucket in trust for Sir Robert, the grandfather, the defendant insisted that a lease was made by the said Sir Robert, the grandfather, of part of his lands of inheritance to one Coleman for years for a fine of £250, for the securing whereof, the said Coleman did assign all his term to the said Tucket, in which assignment, there was a proviso for the payment of the money to the said Sir Robert or to his heirs, executors, or administrators, and the said Tucket, accordingly, declared the trust for the said Sir Robert, his heirs, executors, and administrators, and has since the death of the said Sir Robert, the grandfather, surrendered the said lease to the defendant, as heir, according to the said trust, the said Coleman not having paid his said fine and the assignment being absolute in law, and so the defendant ought to enjoy the said lands without any account for the said fine.

But the plaintiff insisted, and so it appeared to the court, that Coleman, being indebted £250 for a fine, as aforesaid, secured the payment thereof by an assignment of the said lease to Tucket under a proviso to pay £250 and in trust for the said Sir Robert, the grandfather, his heirs, executors, or administrators. So the plaintiff insisted that, if Tucket had surrendered to the defendant, it is a breach of trust. In regard of its being a chattel, it belongs to the administrator, and not to the heir, and the money secured belongs to the plaintiff, and, if any surrender was made, it was after the death of the said Sir Robert, the grandfather, or the defendant's administration granted to him *pendente lite*.

But the defendant's counsel insisted that the surrender was made before the granting of the administration *pendente lite*, and produced a surrender made by Tucket in September 1665.

This court declared that, in case the administration to the defendant was before the surrender, that, then, the lease to Coleman cannot be thought to wait on the inheritance, but ought to go to the administrator, for the defendant had it as administrator, and so took the surrender as a trust. And, therefore, in such a case, he ought to pay the £250 with damages from the time of the surrender or else make a new lease to the plaintiff of the premises surrendered by Tucket, as effectual in law as that which was made to Coleman, for the same term, same covenants, and rents, as in the former lease, and the defendant to account for the profits by him received.

73 Selden Soc. 204

21 October, 20 Car. II, between the Lord Gorges and Sir Robert Dillington.

Sir William Lisle mortgaged in fee to Sir Robert [Dillington], proviso to be void on the payment of the principal and interest to Sir Robert, his executors, and administrators, and he covenants to pay the money accordingly. Sir Robert dies before the principal is due but after the forfeiture for non-payment of interest, leaving Sir Robert, the defendant, his son and heir.

It was decreed by LORD BRIDGEMAN, Lord Keeper, that the plaintiff, as administrator, should have the money and the defendant, the heir, should convey the security to the administrator. And this was right and just.

[Other copies of this report: 3 Swanston 633, 36 E.R. 1002.]
[Reg. Lib. 19 Car. II, f. 730.]

275

Attorney General, ex rel. Smith v. Parkhurst

(Ch. 1668)

The question in this case was whether a lunatic who has lucid moments can make a valid contract or be a party to an action.

1 Chancery Cases 112, 22 E.R. 719

26 October [1668]. Sir Geoffry Palmer, the King's Attorney General, on the behalf of Jerome Smith, a lunatic, against Sir Robert Parkhurst and others.

The bill did suggest that, by an inquisition taken before the Mayor of London by virtue of a writ to him directed, the said Jerome Smith was the 23d of June 1664 found a lunatic, and he had lucid intervals, and he had not sufficient government of himself, his lands, and goods, and that he was lunatic the last of June 1647, and, during his lunacy, he had several sums of money due to him, which he had wasted, and had alienated divers goods. But, to whom, the jurors were ignorant. And they did charge that one Archibald owed the lunatic, during his lunacy, £1300 by good security and that, in 1656, the defendant caused the lunatic to assign Archibald's debt to him, and had received the same upon color of a satisfaction given to the lunatic for the same, whereas that pretended satisfaction was not valuable, and was done in prejudice of the lunatic. And to have an account of the £1300 and to be relieved was the scope of the bill.

The defendant sets forth by answer that he sold the said Jerome Smith in 1656 a manor, which he much desired to buy at £1200, it being the place of his birth. Jerome Smith assigned Archibald's debt for to satisfy himself the purchase money and pay the overplus to Smith, which he did, and he did convey the said manor to Smith. And he insisted that Smith was not a lunatic at that time, but did usually buy and sell etc.

This being the nature of the case, it came first to be heard before Justice TYRELL, who, although it did appear that the defendant had conveyed the said manor to Smith for the said £1200 and that Smith did at that time usually barter and was not found a lunatic until eight years after, with a retrospect of seventeen years, did order the defendant to account for the £1300, being Archibald's debt, and to satisfy the same with damages without any provision for the defendant's having the manor again or account for the mesne profits. And, though it was stood upon at the hearing that, in the case of a lunatic, where the king has no interest in his estate, but, as *pater patriae*, commits him to another to manage it for him, the lunatic, in case he recover his senses and wits, shall have his estate again, and, if not, it will go to his administrators, the lunatic himself (as in the case of an infant) ought to have been party.

Yet that opinion was overrated by the judges and by the Lord Keeper [BRIDGEMAN] on a rehearing. But the Lord Keeper did stay the passing of the decree, and gave liberty to the defendant to traverse the inquisition.

[Other reports of this case: 1 Eq. Cas. Abr. 278, 21 E.R. 1044.]

276

Carter v. Church

(Ch. 1668)

A devise to executors until a child attain a certain age is vested, and continues in the devisee-executors until the child would have come to that age, even though the child die beforehand.

1 Chancery Cases 113, 22 E.R. 719

28 October [1668]. Carter and others, creditors of Church, against Church, *alias* Westin, and others.

Church devises some part of his lands and tenements to his executors to sell for the payment of his debts. And the rest of his lands, he devised, to marry his daughter, in fee, being then a year old. And he declares that his executors shall receive the profits of those lands until his daughter come to the age of twenty-one years towards the payment of his debts and legacies. The daughter died at five years old.

The Lord Keeper [BRIDGEMAN] was of opinion that the charging the profits until the daughter attained twenty-one (though she died before) amounted to a term until she would have attained that age if she had lived. And he cited Boraston's Case, 3 Cro.,[1] and a case in Dyer, where lands were given to a mother for the education and maintenance of the daughter until eighteen years old; the daughter died before eighteen, yet it was adjudged a good term to the mother un-

[1] *Hynde v. Ambrye* (1587), 3 Coke Rep. 16, 76 E.R. 664, also 1 Eq. Cas. Abr. 190, 194, 21 E.R. 980, 984.

til she would have attained eighteen had she lived. And he said that the principal case was much a stronger case.

Lincoln's Inn MS. Hill 125, f. 55, pl. 3

[There was] a devise of lands to J.S. until his daughter came to the age of twenty-one for the payment of his debts and, after that his daughter should come to [the age of] twenty-one, to her and her heirs, provided always that, if his daughter died before twenty-one, then he gave his lands to [. . .] and his heirs. The daughter, after the death of the devisor, died before twenty-one. The interest of the trustee did not determine.

[This was] decreed by the Lord Keeper [Bridgeman].

277

Tattle v. Bradshaw

(Ch. 1668)

All persons who are accused of diverting assets of a charity have a right to be heard before the jury upon an inquisition by commissioners of charitable uses.

2 Eq. Cas. Abr. 202, 22 E.R. 172

Michaelmas term 1668.

Upon an order of reference out of Chancery to Lord Chief Justice Keeling and all other judges of exceptions there taken to a decree made by the commissioners of charitable uses in Michaelmas 1668, the judges certified that they found that, by an inquisition taken before some of the commissioners for charitable uses in the absence of the exceptants, it was found that several houses and lands therein mentioned were given by several persons, some in the time of Edward III, some in the time of Queen Elizabeth and since, to several uses within the said parish, *viz.* some to the poor, some to the repairs of the church, and some for preaching sermons, and that, since the year 1646, the rents and profits had been received by thirteen several persons, and not employed to the aforesaid uses and that the commissioners thereupon caused a charge to be drawn up of those rents and profits, amounting to £3847 10s. and, because the exceptants did not discharge themselves of that sum, they have decreed the exceptants and every of them, being five of the said thirteen persons, to pay the said £3847 10s. and to alter the feoffees, which decree they, *i.e.* the judges, conceived to be altogether erroneous, and ought to be reversed:

First, because the exceptants were by order of some of the commissioners debarred from being heard before the jury until after the inquisition was found;

Secondly, for that it did not appear to them, *i.e.* the judges, but that as much or more has been yearly paid to and for several charitable uses directed by the donors, as is required by their respective wills and gifts, though the same has not been mentioned to be paid out of the rents of the respective houses and lands by them given;

Thirdly, because they, *i.e.* the judges, found that all the parish rents and monies within the time mentioned in the said decree have been by the exceptants and the preceding and succeeding churchwardens paid and accounted for and those accounts audited and allowed according to the ancient usage of that parish.

And they, *i.e.* the judges, conceived that the way used by the exceptants and other churchwardens of that parish touching the leasing out of the premises, receiving the rents, and accounting for the same is fit to be continued. And, for an expedient to prevent the frustrations of commissions upon the Statute for Charitable Uses[1] by the wilfulness of any person, they, the judges, conceived it is requisite that the persons who are complained of for diverting the charity be heard before the jury and have liberty to answer for themselves before the inquisition be found and, thereby, they will have less, if any cause at all, to put in exceptions to decrees made against them.

4 Viner Abr. 499

The report of myself [Kelyng] and all other the judges made to My Lord Keeper [Bridgeman] upon a reference to us of exceptions taken in the Chancery to a decree made by the commissioners of charitable uses in Michaelmas term 1668 [is] as follows. According to an order made in the High Court of Chancery on Tuesday the 11th of June last past in a cause here depending between Ralph Tattle, John Lee, Grace Harding, Thomas Rock, and Nathaniel Humphreys, exceptants, and John Bradshaw, rector of the parish church of St. Michael, Crooked Lane, London, and others, respondents, we have called all parties, *viz.* their counsel, before us, and, upon consideration of the decree mentioned in the said order and hearing what was alleged on the other side, we find that, by an inquisition taken before some of the commissioners for charitable uses in the absence of the exceptants, it was found that several houses and lands therein mentioned were given by several persons, some in the time of Edward III, some in the time of Queen Elizabeth and since to several uses within the said parish, *viz.* some to the poor, some to the repair of the church, and some for preaching sermons, and that, since the year 1646, the rents and profits had been received by thirteen several persons and not employed to the aforesaid uses and the commissioners, thereupon, caused a charge to be drawn up of those rents and profits, amounting to £3847 10s., and, because the exceptants did not discharge themselves of that sum, they have decreed the exceptants and every of them, being five of the aforesaid thirteen persons, to pay the said £3847 10s. and to alter the feoffees, which decree we do conceive to be altogether erroneous and ought to be reversed:

[1] Stat. 43 Eliz. I, c. 4 (*SR*, IV, 968–970).

First, because the exceptants were by the order of some of the commissioners debarred from being heard before the jury until after the inquisition was found;

Secondly, for that it does not appear to us but that as much or more has been yearly paid to and for several charitable uses directed by the donors, as is required by their respective wills and gifts, though the same has not been mentioned to be paid out of the rents of the respective houses and lands by them given;

Thirdly, because we find that all the parish rents and moneys, within the time mentioned in the said decree, have been by the exceptants and the preceding and succeeding churchwardens paid and accounted for and those accounts audited and allowed according to the ancient usage of that parish.

And we conceive that the way used by the exceptants and other churchwardens of that parish, touching leasing out the premises, receiving the rents, and accounting for the same, is fit to be continued. And, for an expedient to prevent the frustrations of commission upon the Statute for Charitable Uses by the willfulness of any person, we conceive that it is requisite that the persons who are complained of for diverting the charity be heard before the jury and have liberty to answer for themselves before the inquisition be found and thereby they will have less, if any cause at all, to put in exceptions to decrees made against them, all which we humbly certify and refer to Your Lordship.

278

Seabourn v. Chilston

(Ch. 1668–1669)

A bill to perpetuate testimony lies to prove or disprove an alleged forged deed in order to preserve the evidence of a common law title.

Nelson 125, 21 E.R. 806

The plaintiff's father and mother, in their own right, were seised in fee of the lands in question, in which one Price had an estate for life. And, in the year 1643, they covenanted to levy a fine thereof to the use of the father and mother for life and to the longest liver of them, remainder to their first son, *viz.* the plaintiff, in tail male, with several remainders over. The father survived, and then, as the bill suggests, forged another deed, declaring the uses of the fine to be to the father and mother and to the survivor of them and to his or her heirs, under which deed the defendant purchased the lands of the father, who is since dead. And Price, the tenant for life, being still living, the plaintiff exhibited his bill to perpetuate the testimony of his witnesses to prove the true, and to disprove the forged, deed.

The defendant demurred to the bill, for that he was a real purchaser under the pretended deed, believing it was a true and real deed. And, therefore, inasmuch as it was to draw under examination a matter of forgery against a dead person who could not answer for himself and to get aid to impeach a real purchaser, the defendant did insist upon it that he ought not to answer nor the plaintiff be permitted to proceed any farther.

And, upon debate, it appearing that the tenant for life was still living, so that the plaintiff could not try his title at law, and that this court is obliged in justice to preserve a title at law, which, by such impediment, could not at present be tried, the demurrer was overruled.

279

Langton v. Ashley

(Ch. 1668–1669)

The questions in this case were whether a conveyance to a trustee to pay the settlor's debts is revocable by the settlor and whether a purchaser of the settled land with knowledge of the trust confirms the trust.

Nelson 126, 21 E.R. 807

Ashley became a purchaser from a person who had conveyed the purchased lands to one Tracy in trust for the payment of all his debts, and he had a conveyance both from the person himself and from the trustee Tracy.

The plaintiff, being one of the creditors, exhibits his bill against Ashley, as being a purchaser under that trust to pay debts etc.

It was insisted for Ashley that the conveyance to Tracy being general, *viz.* for the payment of all his debts, who made the conveyance, and none of his creditors being parties to it, that it was revocable at his pleasure and merely voluntary and that it had been so adjudged by the Lord Keeper Coventry that such conveyances are ambulatory and that, if a man make a conveyance to another in trust to pay all his debts mentioned in a schedule and all other his debts, that, as to all the debts, besides those mentioned in the schedule, such conveyance is fraudulent against a purchaser.

But, for the plaintiff, it was insisted that, if the deed to Tracy was revocable by the party that made it, yet Ashley, purchasing under that conveyance, had now confirmed it.

280

Ash v. Gallen

(Ch. 1668)

The question in this case was whether a trust can arise from a use upon a use.

1 Chancery Cases 114, 22 E.R. 720

18 November [1668]. The Lord Keeper, Justice Wyndham.

It was declared that a use upon a use will not rise by a bargain and sale. Dyer 155, and Chudley's Case, Co. Rep.[1]

But, for the plaintiff, it was insisted that, though a use could not rise as a use upon a use, yet, as a trust, it would in equity.

And a case was ordered to be made which was this. Isaac Ash, with his own money, bought lands of £100 *per annum*, and took the conveyance by indenture in these words, 'grant, bargain, sell, alien, enfeoff, and confirm to Isaac Ash, his executors, and assigns to the use of Isaac for life, remainder as to one-third to his wife for life, remainder to Jacob Ash and to his heirs', whose heir the plaintiff is, with a letter of attorney to make livery. The deed is acknowledged, and duly enrolled in Chancery. Two months after enrollment, livery is made, and endorsed on the deed. The plaintiff and the defendant's wife were both grandchildren to Isaac Ash, who, by a lease and release, did convey the lands in question, the one moiety to the plaintiff and the other moiety to the defendants and their heirs. And the plaintiff did not except to this disposition in Isaac's life, which, if he had, Isaac would (as was insisted for the defendants) have otherwise provided for them, he having given every grandchild to the value of £50 *per annum* but the defendants, to whom he gave nothing but the moiety of the premises.

For the plaintiff, it was insisted that Isaac intended to take the estate by feoffment and that the enrolling of it first was only for safe custody of the deed and that, however the uses upon a use would not rise in law, yet, in equity, they were good by way of a trust.

For the defendant, it was argued thus upon private discourse of counsel, that Isaac having by the deed an election to take it either by a feoffment, which, if he did, it would not be in his power otherwise to dispose it, or by a bargain and sale, whereby he might have a power to dispose the estate as he pleased and he having elected to take it by enrollment and disposed the same by an act executed in his life, it was apparent he intended to take it so as to dispose it. And, therefore, there was no reason in equity to make any other operation of this conveyance than the law made.

There was some diversity of opinion amongst counsel touching this case. But the parties agreed among themselves, and it was not argued at all.

281

Read v. Read

(Ch. 1668–1669)

A writ of ne exeat lies to enforce a final decree for alimony in an ecclesiastical court.

---

[1] *Tyrrel's Case* (1557), 2 Dyer 155, 73 E.R. 336, also Benloe 28, 73 E.R. 951, 1 Anderson 37, 123 E.R. 341; *Dillon v. Freine* (1589–1595), 1 Coke Rep. 113, 76 E.R. 261, Popham 70, 79 E.R. 1184, also 1 Anderson 309, 123 E.R. 489.

1 Chancery Cases 115, 22 E.R. 720

25 November [1668]. The Lord Keeper, Justice Twysden.

The Lady Read, wife of Sir John Read, had by petition got a [writ of] *ne exeat regno* against her husband, upon a suggestion that, she having gotten a sentence for alimony against him in the spiritual court, he refused to obey it, and, in avoidance of it, threatened to go beyond the sea.

The husband moved for a [writ of] *supersedeas* of this writ. And whether it lies in this case was the question.

For the husband, it was said that every man may travel where he will, unless he be prohibited by the king's writ. Dyer 296. This writ is a prerogative writ, which the king may use, as he has the care of his people. 2 Inst. 54.[1] A writ *de securitate invenienda* not to go beyond the seas lies not against a layman, but a clergyman only, *qui habet curam animarum*, and they are to maintain the laws of the Church, which, if they went beyond the seas, they might adhere to the pope, and they have no temporal estate to oblige them to stay here. And this writ ought to be endorsed *patronus sequitur hoc breve*, but, in this case, there is no patron [and] no clergyman. 19 Jac. [1621–22] in the Case of Welby and Stevens, at the suit of his creditors, which were many, there this writ was granted, but a bill was filed, and none is here. Crisp against Bishop, 16 Car. II [1663–64]. The writ was granted upon a suggestion he was indebted, but, on the putting in of security, it was superseded.

On the other side, for the maintaining of the writ and on the behalf of the Lady, it was said the king may restrain a subject from going out of the realm. Knowls against Luce, Moor 109; Selden's *Janus Angliae*, 92, says it extends *tam laicis quam clericis*.[2] There is no other writ but this. And, if this go not to a layman, then there is no writ to a layman. It is true all writs in the Register are '*clericis*', but that is but an addition. The ground of the writ is that a person is going beyond the sea to the prejudice of the king, and the writ is to give security not to go until the king license him. Leigh against Bever, 9 Jac. [1611–12]. A precedent is 9 Car. I [1633–34], Mead's Case, a *ne exeat regno* was awarded for a private matter. Hilary [term] 1652, Boyl against Slugborough, it was a question whether this writ was grantable at the suit of a private person.[3]

But the court resolved this writ well lies in the principal case, and will not supersede it.

Lincoln's Inn MS. Misc. 500, f. 31v, pl. 2

Easter term 21 Car. II (1669). Sir John Read's Case.

---

[1] *Anonymous* (1570), 3 Dyer 296, 73 E.R. 664; E. Coke, *Second Institute* (1642), p. 54.

[2] *Knowles v. Luce* (Ex. 1580), Moore K.B. 109, 72 E.R. 473; J. Selden, *Jani Anglorum Facies Altera*.

[3] *Boyle v. Scarborough* (1653), Style 395, 82 E.R. 807.

The wife of Sir John Read of Bishop's Hatfield in the County of Hertford sued her husband for alimony in the ecclesiastical court, and she had a sentence. And, afterwards, she doubted that her husband will depart out of the realm. And she, by her counsel in Chancery, moved for a writ of *ne exeat regno* to be directed to the sheriff of Oxford, where Sir John at this time was, to take security of the said Sir John, that he *ne exeat regno* without the license of the king or otherwise to take him and commit him to jail until he do it according to the writ, F.N.B., fo. 85, D, which was granted upon argument notwithstanding that it was prayed at the instance of the subject and notwithstanding that Sir John was a layman, and not a clerk, as this writ is, because the Lord Keeper [Bridgeman] was satisfied in both of these cases.

And the sheriff returned that he *accessit* to the house of the said Sir John and that the doors were closed, by which he could not take him.

And, upon this return, it was argued whether the sheriff upon this writ of *ne exeat regno* could break the doors as he could upon process where the king is a party, according to Semayne's Case, 5 rep. 91b.

Query if this is such a process and if any contempt. *Vide* 3 Inst. 178, 179, 180, and the authorities cited in the margin.

Ex relatione Holt of Gray's Inn, who argued this case in Chancery upon the return of the sheriff for the Lady Read.

2 Chancery Reports 19, 21 E.R. 604

This case is touching the granting of a [writ of] *ne exeat regno* against the defendant. The defendant insisted that the said writ ought not to be issued out, for that the affidavit of the Lady Read did not contain a ground sufficient to warrant it, for that the writ is a writ of prerogative on behalf of the Crown and the reason of granting it is that the party against whom it is prayed intends to convey away some considerable treasure out of the kingdom or do some other matter prejudicial to the king or his government, which the affidavit does not specify, and, if that were, yet no writ does regularly lie in this case against a layman to find security, as this writ is, but only against a clergyman, neither is the writ endorsed, as formerly it ought to be. And, therefore, it ought to be superseded. And several cases were offered and precedents were produced on the behalf of the defendants.

But the plaintiff insisted that, by the affidavit, Sir John Read, the defendant, conveying and making over his estate to others, standing out an excommunication, and absconding his person, and giving out that he intends to go beyond the seas, the said writ is well warranted. And, for justification thereof, several cases and precedents were urged. And, it appearing that the only matter which carries any countenance or pretense of irregular issuing the writ, that it ought to be for a clergyman to find security, and not for a layman, is an opinion taken up in a posthumous work of the Lord Coke, being called his *Third Institute*, contrary to the general authorities, precedents, and practice of granting writs of *ne exeat regno* in former and later times, which are as usual against a layman to find security, as well as a clergyman, or else there can be no writ at all to be found in the Register against a layman to find security in any case or any *ne exeat regno* against a layman, neither is there in the Register any such form endorsing the writ as is suggested, but what is inserted in the Register is but a note of some observer.

So His Lordship [Bridgeman], with the judges, are of the whole matter that there is no ground to grant a *supersedeas* of the said writ of *ne exeat regno*, but that the same was well granted and ought to stand, and ordered it accordingly.

[Reg. Lib. 20 Car. II B, f. 146.]
[Related cases: Read v. Read (1671), 2 Keble 853, 84 E.R. 540; Rex v. Reade (1671), 2 Keble 736, 84 E.R. 465; Attorney General v. Read (Ex. 1671), Exch. Repts. *tempore* Car. II, 229; Attorney General v. Read (Ex. 1676), 1 Freeman 327, 89 E.R. 242, 2 Modern 299, 86 E.R. 1083, Dodd 256; Lord Paget v. Read (Ch. 1683), 1 Vernon 143, 23 E.R. 375, 1 Eq. Cas. Abr. 61, 21 E.R. 874, Chancery Repts. *tempore* North 82.]

282

Every v. Gold

(Ch. 1668–1669)

In this case, the legatees' portions did not vest in their lifetime, and their administrators were not entitled to have them.

2 Chancery Reports 1, 21 E.R. 599

The bill is to be relieved for two legacies of £1500 apiece, which the plaintiff claims as administratrix to her daughters, Susanna and Martha Every, given and secured to them by several conveyances and by the last will of William Every, their grandfather.

The case is, *viz.*, that the said William Every, the grandfather, in consideration of a marriage between William Every, his son, and the plaintiff Martha, a daughter of Sir John Pool, by deed 22 April, 7 Car. I [1631], did provide that, if William, his son, should die without issue male by him on the body of the said plaintiff Martha begotten and should have two daughters by the plaintiff Margaret then living or if the said William should fail to have issue male which should be living until the same daughters should respectively attain eighteen years of age or be married, that then the recoveree therein named should stand seised of the premises to the use of the recoverors and their heirs for the raising £1500 apiece for the portions of the said daughters and £20 apiece *per annum* for each of their maintenance in the meantime, to be paid at their respective ages of eighteen years or days of marriage, which should first happen, and, if either of the said daughters should die before that age or marriage, the portion of her so dying to be distributed to the survivor, and, if all the said daughters should die, their portions not paid or payable, then the same should be paid to the next heir of William Every, the grandfather.

William Every, the son, had issue by the plaintiff, one son, named William, and two daughters, the said Susan and Martha. And, by a deed of bargain and sale and a release thereupon, both dated in December 1651, in which release, so much of the tripartite indenture as relates to the daughters' portions is recited, William Every, the grandfather, conveys to Gold, Doble, and Holloway and their heirs lands in Somersetshire to the use of William, the grandfather, for life and, after[wards], to Gold, Doble, and Holloway for 200 years, with other remainders over, upon trust, out of the profits or by granting leases or estates, to pay his debts first and, then, for raising to and for the said Susan and Martha so much money as should supply and advance their respective portions to them severally thereafter to be given by William, the grandfather, either ready money or otherwise, to be limited by any act thereafter to be executed in his lifetime or by his last will to the sum of £1500 apiece together with £20 *per annum* until the said £1500 apiece should be paid unto them, the same to be in satisfaction of all monies that they might claim by force of the said indenture tripartite, with a proviso that, if the said William, the grandfather, should by a will or otherwise appoint them £1500 apiece or £1500 to the survivor of them for their portions with such yearly maintenance, as aforesaid, so as the same should be well and truly paid unto them accordingly or, if, before such portions should be paid, the said William Every, their brother, should die without issue male, whereby the said premises should be charged for the raising of portions and maintenance aforesaid, that, then, the trustees should not levy the portions by that indenture limited, other than what should be paid in the lifetime of William Every, their brother. And it is thereby declared that, in case the said Susanna or Martha or either of them should die before their portions (in and by the said last indenture to them limited) should become due and payable to them, that, then, the said portion and portions of them or either of them so dying should not go or be to the survivor of them or to any the executors, administrators, or assigns of them or either of them, but should go to whom the said William, the grandfather, by a writing or will should appoint and, for want thereof, to his executors or administrators. And it is further declared that the said Susan and Martha shall not have any benefit in case that they or any other of them should take any advantage or benefit by means of the said indenture tripartite or any proviso therein contained.

And then, the 9th of March 1651, William, the grandfather, makes his will, therein reciting that he had by several deeds, all dated February 21 Car. I [1646], granted to Knight, Cade, Webber, and Ford certain lands in the County of Dorset for terms of years determinable upon the death of certain persons therein mentioned upon trust and for the use and benefit of such person or persons to whom he should by his last will give, limit, or appoint the same. And, by his will, he gave, limited, and appointed all the said estates and terms so by him granted to the said Knight, Cade, Webber, and Ford to the defendants Gold and Doble, in trust, that the said Gold and Doble or the survivor of them or the executors or administrators of the survivor of them should dispose of all the rents and profits of the said lands or should otherwise sell, assign, and convey the said estates and terms as to them should seem most convenient towards the raising of £1500 apiece to the said Susan and Martha. And he did thereby give and appoint to each of the said Susan and Martha £900 to be paid unto them severally out of his personal estate, whereof he should die possessed, accounting therein all such monies which he had or should lend upon the specialties taken in the names of Gold and Doble towards the farther raisings of their said portions to £1500 apiece, having (as by his will is expressed, by his deed dated the last day of December then last past) made provision for advancing their said portions to the value out of his lands in the County of Somerset, which said portions, his last will and meaning was, should be paid unto them, the said Susan and Martha severally, at their respective ages of twenty-one years or sooner if they should be respectively married with the consent of the said Gold and Doble or the survivor of them with a proviso that, if William Every, his grandson, should happen to die without issue male of his body lawfully begotten before the said respective portions should become payable to the said Susan and Martha, according to the time before limited, whereby the said Susan and Martha should be entitled to £1500 apiece by virtue of the said indenture tripartite made upon his deceased son's marriage, then, the said legacies or appointments or portions unto Susan and Martha thereby made should be void. And, of his will, he made Gold and Doble executors.

And the plaintiff, as administratrix of her said two daughters, Susan and Martha, exhibited her bill against Gold and Doble, executors of William, the grandfather, and Webber, the surviving trustee in the deed of the lands in Somerset, and against John Every, the heir in tail of William, the grandfather, and seeks to be relieved upon the deeds and will before mentioned for the £1500 apiece given to Susan and Martha, her daughters.

The defendants say that William, the grandfather, died in the lifetime of William, the grandson, and that the personal estate of William, the grandfather, came to £4000 and that William Every, the grandson, was buried 23 November 1660, and was about twenty years old when he was buried, and Susan, the plaintiff's daughter, was buried 25 July 1655, and was about eighteen years old when she was buried, and Martha, the plaintiff's daughter, was buried 4 July 1660, and was about twenty years old when she was buried. And it appears there was sufficient personal estate to satisfy the several portions demanded.

Which case the Master of the Rolls [GRIMSTON] having considered and upon the hearing before him declared that he was satisfied with £1500 apiece by the deed and will aforesaid for portions to Susan and Martha, daughters of the plaintiff, was a debt or duty well fixed in them by the said deeds and will and by their deaths did accrue and belong to the plaintiff, their mother, as administratrix to them. And, therefore, he did decree the same should be paid accordingly.

From which opinion and decree the defendants appealed to the Lord Keeper [BRIDGEMAN], who being assisted by the judges and upon reading the deeds and will aforesaid, were all clear of opinion that the indenture tripartite of 27 June, 7 Car. I [1631], is not, as the case now stands, material or conducing to the state of the case or to the limitation of the time for the payment of the portions, for that the same is by a deed of bargain and sale and release thereupon, in 1651, barred, and a new provision is made for raising the said portions in such manner as he should limit by any act in his lifetime or by his last will. By which deed, the survivorship between the two daughters is barred, and a provision is made that, if either of them die in the lifetime of William, the grandson, the portion of her so dying shall not go to her executors, but to the grandson. And William, the grandfather, having by his will of the ninth of March 1651, wherein he recites the deed of December 1651, limited and appointed £900 apiece to be paid to his daughters severally out of his personal estate towards the raising of their portions to £1500 apiece, having (as is recited) made a provision by his deed dated the last of December 1651 for advancing their portions to that value. And he does by his will declare and appoint that such portions should be paid unto them, the said Susan and Martha, severally at the respective ages of twenty-one years or sooner if they should be married and both of them dying unmarried before they or either of them attained the age of twenty-one in the lifetime of William, the grandson, and the said deed of December 1651, relating to the will and both of them making one entire provision and limitation of the said portions how the same shall be raised and what time paid.

His Lordship [Bridgeman] and the judges were all clear of opinion there was no ground for the former decree made by the Master of the Rolls or a pretense of claim to either of the said portions of £1500 by the plaintiff, as administratrix to Susan and Martha. And they discharged the decree, and dismissed the bill.

This dismission was confirmed by the Lords.[1]

[Reg. Lib. 20 Car. II, f. 921.]

283

Beauchamp v. Silverlock

(Ch. 1668–1669)

Where the administrators of a decedent's estate pay the assets of the estate to a receiver upon security, who later becomes insolvent, the administrators are liable to the estate only for any unsecured funds.

[1] *Gold v. Emery*, 2 Chancery Reports 290, 21 E.R. 681.

2 Chancery Reports 9, 21 E.R. 601

William Beauchamp, the plaintiff's father, being a freeman and citizen of London, by his last will, gives a third part of his lands and tenements, whatsoever and wheresoever, to the plaintiff. And he appointed Dorothy, his wife, guardian to his children, and made her sole executrix and Richard Camden, Robert Cheslyn, John Pace, and Hogan Hovell overseers. And the said Dorothy makes her will afterwards, and gave the greatest part of her estate to the plaintiff. And she willed her brother, Hogan Hovell, and her sister, Margaret Cheslyn, and the survivor of them to be guardian to her children. And she made the said Hogan Hovell and Margaret Lovell her executors, and she died. By articles of agreement between Hogan Hovell, Robert Cheslyn, and Margaret, his wife, reciting the will of Dorothy Beauchamp, whereby they agreed to administer the estate to the best benefit of the children and exhibit a true inventory into the Prerogative Court and that they should with the consent, and not without the consent and knowledge of each other, use their best endeavors to get in the estate, and not to release any part of it without each other's consent, and that, if Hogan Hovell should die and Margaret survive, then, the executors or administrators of Hogan Hovell to make a true account to Margaret of all the estate which he should receive of the said testator and pay the same to Margaret or to such person who shall by the consent of the said William Beauchamp, the plaintiff, be chosen as guardian to receive the same or to such person to whom, by right or law, the same ought to be paid. And the same agreement and covenant is if the said Margaret should die and Hovell survive.

Robert Cheslyn died, and the said Margaret married the defendant, James Silverlock.

And Hogan Hovell possessed himself of the greatest part of the personal estate of the plaintiff's said father and mother, and received the profits of the lands of the said Margaret, receiving only title as executor.

Hogan Hovell made his will, and Mary, his wife, executrix. And, afterwards, the guardianship of the plaintiff, the orphan, is at his friend's decree committed to Sir William Bateman. The said Mary Hovell, the executrix of Hogan, exhibited an account into the Orphans Court of the money received by her husband, belonging to the plaintiff, out of which, allowances being made, there rested due to the plaintiff £933. And, afterwards, the defendant Silverlock and Margaret, his wife, the surviving executrix of Dorothy, did by their deed empower Sir William Bateman, then reputed a man of great estate, to receive of Mary Hovell, executrix of Hogan Hovell, who was the other executor of the said Dorothy, the said £933 to the use of the plaintiff, and to give a discharge for the same. Sir William Bateman received it accordingly, and gave a discharge for it in the name of Silverlock and his wife, and he gave security after that to the Court of Aldermen to pay the plaintiff £800.

Mary Hovell died, and made executors.

The plaintiff did several times after he came of age own Sir William Bateman to be his debtor for the £933, that the plaintiff received of Sir William Bateman £440, and gave acquittances for it, the first was on the fourth of January 1663, the last on the twenty-fifth of July 1666. The plaintiff came of age in December 1663, and the said Sir William. Bateman became insolvent at Christmas 1666.

The question was touching the said £933 claimed by the plaintiff and whether the same should be charged on the defendant Silverlock and the surviving executor of Dorothy Beauchamp or on the defendant Sir William Bateman, who had given security to the Chamber of London, as aforesaid, for the plaintiff's use.

This court, as to the executors of Mary Hovell, declared there was no reason to charge them therewith, but that they ought to be discharged and dismissed from being accountable for the same. And, as to the defendant Silverlock, the case being as aforesaid, [the court] declared that there was a clear intention of all parties to perform the articles aforesaid and that the said defendant Margaret never received any estate during Hogan Hovell's life and that, Sir William Bateman being chosen by the consent of the friends of the plaintiff and by the order of the Court of Orphans appointed guardian to the plaintiff, she, the said Margaret, gave in an account to the court and empowered Sir William Bateman to receive the money, who before had given security to answer the same or the greatest part thereof, and, when the plaintiff came of age, he admitted and owned Sir William Bateman to be his guardian, and received several sums of money from him, and Sir William was proved not insolvent until three years after, and so, there being no default in the said defendant Margaret, there was no reason to charge her, the said Margaret, with the same, but that she ought to be dismissed and discharged from the same. But Sir William having given security to the Court of Orphans for £843, part of the said £933 by him received by order of the defendant Margaret, and that for the residue, being £90 10s., there was no security given by the said Sir William, this court declared that the defendant Margaret ought to be charged with the same, and decreed accordingly, but not with interest for it.

[Reg. Lib. 20 Car. II, f. 765.]

284

Wyndham v. Love

(Ch. 1668–1670)

After a term is devised to one and the heirs of his body, no further limitation can be of it nor any appointment by way of an executory devise, because the law will not presume any term to have a continuance so long as there can be issue of the body and a limitation of it after a death without issue is too remote a possibility.

2 Chancery Reports 14, 21 E.R. 602

The bill is that the Dean and Chapter of Winchester, June 17 Jac. [1619], granted the premises to Gilbert Searle, his heirs, or assigns during the lives of the two defendants, Barnaby, Robert, and Nicholas Love,[1] sons of Dr. Nicholas Love [d. 1630], and to the survivor of them in trust for the said Dr. Love. And the said Gilbert Searle, in July 17 Jac. [1619], demised the said premises to the said Dr. Nicholas Love for 99 years if the said Nicholas and the defendants, Barnaby and Robert Love, the sons, or any of them should so long live. And the said Dr. Love had the original lease made by the Dean and Chapter delivered to him by the said Searle. And, afterwards, the premises, by mesne conveyances, came to Nicholas Love, the son, who claimed the same absolutely to himself during the said term, and was the reputed owner thereof. And, in the late usurping times [1649–1660], the said Nicholas, the son, had the premises confirmed to him, and the said defendants never pretended any right, possibility, or executory estate in the said premises after the death of the said Nicholas, the son. And the said Nicholas, the son, by an act of Parliament[2] declared, forfeited his estate to His Majesty upon account of treason, and His Majesty granted the premises to the duke of York and his heirs. And he, 18 Car. II [1666–67], granted the premises and all the writings to the plaintiffs, their executors, administrators, and assigns during the residue of the term.

The defendants insist that the said Dr. Love, the plaintiff's father, by his will, 15 Car. I [1639–40], did devise the premises to Dulcibella, his wife, for life, for so many years of the said ninety-nine years as should be spent in her life and, after her death, then to the said Nicholas Love, the son, for so many years of the said term as he should live and, after the death of him and the said Dulcibella, unto the defendant Barnabas, his executors, administrators, and assigns for all the residue of the said term. And he made the said Dulcibella his executrix, who assented to the said will and executory devise. And she enjoyed the premises during her life. And, after her death, which was about 1656, the said Nicholas Love, the son, entered, and, by virtue of the will, possessed the premises for the residue of the said term as was not spent, and not by virtue of any assignment, nor otherwise than the said executory devise, and, if the said Nicholas did purchase the premises of the usurpers, the same ought not to prejudice the defendant Barnaby's right and interest in the premis].es by the said executory devise, which he claims after the death of Nicholas, the son, by virtue of the said will of his father, as aforesaid. And they say that Nicholas, the son, had no other estate therein but in expectancy of the death of Dulcibella.

---

[1] S. Kelsey, 'Love, Nicholas (bap. 1608, d. 1682)', *Oxford Dictionary of National Biography*, vol. 34, pp. 503–504.

[2] Stat. 12 Car. II, c. 30 (*SR*, V, 288–290).

This court referred it to be tried at law upon this issue, *viz.* whether the defendant Barnaby, by the will of the said Dr. Love, has or shall have any estate or interest or possibility in the premises after the death of the said Nicholas Love, the son, if the term so long continue.'

The said issue was tried, where a special verdict was found that Gilbert Searle, being possessed of the premises for the lives of Nicholas, Robert, and the defendant Barnaby, demised the premises to Dr. Nicholas Love for ninety-nine years if either of the three live so long and that the said Doctor, afterwards, made his will, and devised the premises to Dulcibella, his wife, for her life and, after, to Nicholas, his son, for his life and, if he died without issue, then, to the defendant Barnaby, and made the said Dulcibella executrix, who assented to the said devise. In Easter term last, the special verdict was argued in the King's Bench, and, upon great debates, judgment was given for the plaintiff.

This court declared that the defendant has no right or title to the premises, and decreed the plaintiffs, their heirs, and assigns to enjoy against the defendant.

[Reg. Lib. 20 Car. II, f. 100, 21 Car. II, f. 741.]

1 Ventris 79, 86 E.R. 55

1670. Love v. Wyndham.

An action upon the case upon an issue was directed out of Chancery. Upon a special verdict, the case was George Searl, being seised of the manor of N., demised the same to Nicholas Love for 99 years if three lives should so long live. Nicholas Love devised it to Dulcibell, his wife, the remainder to Nicholas, his son, for life, and, if he the said Nicholas, the son, should die without issue, then to Barnaby Love, the plaintiff. The executor assented. And whether the devise to Barnaby were good was the question.

Jones, for the plaintiff: This is a good possibility. I shall make two points:

First, if a termor devise first to one and then to another, whether he may devise it over;

Secondly, whether the limitation here after the death without issue be a good limitation over.

First, he may make a third limitation, which is a possibility upon a possibility. At least, he may make two or three such limitations over. I cannot certainly say where it will end. It cannot be denied but that a termor may devise first to one for life and after to another. 8 Co. 95.[1] But I say he may go further and that will appear by reason and authority.

First, by reason, the reason given why the executory devise in the first case is good is because it is, in construction of law, as much as if he had devised it to the last first, if the first man should die within the term, and then had devised that the first should hold during life. And, without such a transposition, it cannot

[1] *Clark v. Manning* (1609), 8 Coke Rep. 94, 77 E.R. 618.

be good. Now, this being the way of operation, there is no reason why he may not devise it to one after the death of two, as well as after the death of one. This would be so in grants were it not that a certainty is required in them, 1 Cro. 155,[1] which is not required in devises.

1 Modern 50, 86 E.R. 724

Upon an issue out of Chancery, the jury find a special verdict, *viz.* that one Gilbert Thirle was seised of the lands in question for three lives, and demised the same to Nicholas Love, the father, for a term of years if the *cestui que vie*s or any of them should so long live. He, being so possessed, made his will, and devised them in this manner, *viz.* to his wife for her life and, after her decease, to Nicholas, his son, for his life and, if Nicholas, his son, should die without issue of his body begotten, then he devises them to Barnaby, the plaintiff. Then, they find that the wife was executrix and that she did agree to this devise.

And whether this be a good limitation to Barnaby or not is the question.

Jones: I conceive it is a good limitation to Barnaby. I shall enquire, first, whether a termor having devised to one for life and, after his death, to another for life may go any further and, secondly, admitting that he may go further, whether the limitation in our case, which is to begin after the death of the second without issue of his body be good or no.

For the first point, he said the reason given in Plowden and in Coke[2] why an executory devise of a term is good in law is because the law takes it as devised to the last man first and, then afterwards, to the first man, without which transposition, it is not good, for, if it should be a devise to the first man first, there would be nothing left for the last but a possibility, which is not grantable over. Now then, if a man may devise a term after the death of another, then he may devise it after the death of two others. It is true, this cannot be in grants, for they are founded upon contracts and there must be a certainty in them, according to The Rector of Chedington's Case.[3] Now, if a devise may be good after the death of one or two, it is all one if it be limited after the death of five or six. Now that a contingency may be devised upon a contingency, I take it that the authorities are clear. In the Case of Colton v. Herle, it was so resolved by three justices and

[1] *Goshawke v. Chiggell* (1629), Croke Car. 154, 79 E.R. 734, also W. Jones 205, 82 E.R. 109.

[2] *Welcden v. Elkington* (1578), 2 Plowden 516, 75 E.R. 763; *Clark v. Manning* (1609), 8 Coke Rep. 94, 77 E.R. 618.

[3] *Lloyd, ex dem. Roberts v. Wilkinson* (1598), 1 Coke Rep. 153, 76 E.R. 343, Moore K.B. 478, 72 E.R. 707.

also in the Case of Rethorick v. Chappel.[1] As for the Case of Child v. Bayly,[2] I conceive it is not against our case, for they held the devise to be void, not because it was a contingency upon a contingency, but in respect of the remoteness of the possibility and because the term was wholly devised to a man and his assigns; so that, by the express authority of the two first cases and by the implication of this case, I do think that a devise to a man after such a manner is good, provided that it do not introduce a perpetuity; so that, where there is not the inconvenience of a perpetuity, though there are many contingencies, they are no impediment to the devise. Therefore, where a devise is upon a contingency that may happen upon the expiration of one or more men's lives and where it is upon a contingency that may endure forever, there is a great difference. The reason of The Rector of Chedington's Case was because of the uncertainty, for, in the case of a grant of a term, there is a great uncertainty, but ours is in the case of a devise, which is not taken in the law by way of a remainder; so that I conceive a contingency may be limited upon a contingency, provided that it be not remote.

The second point is whether this devise thus limited be a good devise. Now, I conceive the limitation is as good as if it had been to his wife for her life and, after her death, to Nicholas for life and, after his death, to Barnaby. I agree, that, if these words 'if Nicholas die without heirs of his body' shall not be applied to the time of his death, it will be a void devise. But the meaning is that, if at the time of his death, he shall have no issue, then etc. Now that they must have such a construction, I prove from the words of the will. The limitation of the remainder must be taken so as to quadrate with the particular estate, as if there be a conveyance to one for life and, if he die without issue, to another; this is a good remainder upon a condition, and the remainder shall rest upon the determination of the particular estate if the tenant for life have no issue when he dies. But, if a man convey to one and the heirs of his body and, if he die without issue, to another, there, it must be understood of a failure of issue at any time, because the precedent limitation goes further than his life. But, admitting there were no precedent words to guide the intention and that common parlance were against me, yet, if there be but a possibility of a good construction, it shall be so construed. And they may very well be understood of his dying without issue of his body at the time of his death. In the case of Goodyer v. Clerk, in this court,[3] I confess it was adjudged that it would be understood of a failure of issue at anytime. But, in our

---

[1] *Cotton v. Heath* (1638), Pollexfen 26, 86 E.R. 500, 1 Eq. Cas. Abr. 191, 21 E.R. 982, Chancery Repts. *tempore* Coventry 287; *Retherick v. Chappel* (1612), 2 Bulstrode 28, 80 E.R. 932.

[2] *Child v. Bayley* (1623), Palmer 48, 333, 81 E.R. 972, 1109, W. Jones 15, 82 E.R. 9, Croke Jac. 459, 79 E.R. 393, 1 Eq. Ca. Abr. 192, 21 E.R. 982, 2 Rolle Rep. 129, 81 E.R. 704, 1 Rolle, Abr., *Devise*, pl. L, 5, p. 612.

[3] *Goodiar v. Clarke* (1661–1663), 1 Siderfin 102, 82 E.R. 996, 1 Keble 73, 78, 169, 246, 462, 83 E.R. 819, 822, 880, 926, 1054.

case, if you shall not understand it of a failure of issue at the time of his death, it cannot have any construction at all to take effect. I think there are no express authorities against me. Those that may seem to be so, I will put, and endeavor to give an answer to them. As for the Case of Child v. Bayly, reports differ upon the reason of that judgment, for Croke says it was held to be a void devise, because it was taken if he die without issue at any time during the term. But Serjeant Rolle goes upon another reason, for he says it is void because given absolutely to the son and his assigns before. In the Case of Leventhorp v. Ashly,[1] the remainder there is said to be void, because, when he had devised the term to A. and the heirs male of his body, it shall go to the executors of A., and the remainder there was to begin upon his dying without issue at anytime. The Case of Saunders v. Cornish[2] will not come to ours, for there were many limitations for life successively to persons not in being etc. In the case cited in the First Report,[3] of an estate for life limited to one and to every heir successively an estate for life, the limitation was naught, because it would make a perpetual freehold. And nobody would know where the absolute estate should vest. So he prayed judgment for the plaintiff.

Coleman for the defendant: I conceive this to be a void limitation. Mr. Jones would make this a middle case. I shall discharge him of the first point, though he has taken pains to argue it. And I shall rest upon this, that the limitation of a term after the death of a man without issue of his body is void. The case is put as a middle case to these two, *viz.* if a man, possessed of a lease for years, devise it to J.S. for life, the remainder to J.N. for life, the remainder to J.G. for life, these remainders are good. But, if he devise to J.S. and the heirs of his body, the remainder over, this remainder he admits to be void, because it depends upon so remote a possibility as may never happen. Now I conceive it is the same thing to limit it to one for life and, if he die without issue, then to another for life, as to limit it to one and the heirs of his body, with a remainder over. He would tie it up from the ordinary and legal construction, *viz.* to the issue at the time of his death. If it be to be understood of dying without issue at anytime, then Child v. Bayly and Cornish's Case are full authorities in the point. There, a lessee for years devises to one for life and, after[wards], to Williams and his assigns, and, if he die without issue then living, the remainder to J.G., this, they say, is good in the case of a fee simple. But they will not allow it in the case of a term for years. Now Mr. Jones would by construction bring the words 'then living' into our case. The legal construction of the words 'dying without issue' is if there be a failure of is-

[1] *Leventhorpe v. Ashbie* (1635), 1 Rolle, Abr., *Devise*, pl. L, 1, p. 611.

[2] *Saunders v. Cornish* (1631), 1 Rolle, Abr., *Devise*, pl. L, 2, p. 611, Croke Car. 230, 79 E.R. 801.

[3] *Dillon v. Freine* (1589–1595), 1 Coke Rep. 113, 135, 76 E.R. 261, 305, Popham 70, 79 E.R. 1184, also 1 Anderson 309, 123 E.R. 489.

sue at anytime to come. In the Case of Pell v. Brown,[1] if the words 'then living' had not been in the will, the case had not been so adjudged.

KELYNG, Chief Justice: You go up hill a little. Can Barnaby take so long as there is any issue in being of Nicholas?

Jones: He cannot.

KELYNG, Chief Justice: Then Barnaby's interest depends upon a contingency that may never happen.

Jones: I grant, if Nicholas has issue at the time of his death, that Barnaby shall never take, but, if he has none, he shall.

KELYNG, Chief Justice: If I devise lands to A. for life and, if he die without issue of his body, to B., A. shall have an estate tail. So, in this case, the words and limitation are the same, though, the devisor having but a lease for years, there cannot be an estate tail of it. Yet he intended not that Barnaby should have an estate as long as there were any issue in being of Nicholas's body.

TWYSDEN, Justice: It appears to me upon the reason of the cases that have been cited that the remainder to Barnaby must be void, because of the remote possibility.

If a tenant of a term devise it to B. for life, the remainder to C. for life, the remainder to D. for life, I have heard it questioned whether these remainders are good or not. But it has been held that, if all the remaindermen are living at the time of the devise, it is good. If all the candles be alight at once, it is good. But, if you limit a remainder to a person not in being, as to the first-begotten son etc. and the like, there would be no end if such limitations were admitted. And, therefore, they are void. And some judges are of the same opinion to this hour.

But, then, there will be a question to whom the remainder of the term will go if Nicholas die without issue, whether to the executors of Nicholas or to the executors of Dr. Love.

If I devise a term to A. for life, after the death of A., his executors shall not have it, but it shall go to the executors of the devisor. But, if it be devised to A. generally without saying 'for life', it shall go to his executors after his death. But a devise for life vests in him only during his life, and you may make a limitation over.

KELYNG, Chief Justice: I take it that A. carries the whole term when devised to him for life, because an estate for life is larger than the longest term.

TWYSDEN, Justice: As a term for years does admit of remainders, so it does of reversions if you will have it so. And, when he devises to A. during his life, A. shall have it for his life, but the reversion shall be to the devisor's executors. But, if he devise it to A. for life and if he die without issue of his body, the remainder to B., what shall become of the reversion then?

---

[1] *Pell v. Brown* (1620), Croke Jac. 590, 79 E.R. 504, Palmer 131, 81 E.R. 1012, 2 Rolle Rep. 196, 216, 81 E.R. 746, 760, Godbolt 282, 78 E.R. 165, J. Bridgman 1, 123 E.R. 1157.

Kelyng, Chief Justice: You start a new point.

The Court: You shall have our judgments this term.

1 Levinz 290, 83 E.R. 412

A man possessed of a term for years devises it to his wife for life, remainder to his first son for life, and, if he died without issue, to his second son. The first son died without issue. And if the remainder to the second son was good was the question on a special verdict, for it was objected that, here, it is not to him and his issue, in which case, it was agreed it should go to him and his executors and the remainder over be void. But, here, it is devised to him for his life and, if he die without issue, the remainder to the second brother; so that, hereby, he had only an estate for life with an executory devise to the second son on the contingency that he had no issue when he died. And he cited 2 Roll. Abr. 406, No. 8, 9. A devise of a term to one so long as he has issue, remainder over, is good.

But, after divers arguments, it was adjudged that the remainder to the second son was void and that a devise to one and his issue with a remainder over is all one with a devise to one for life and, if he dies without issue, to another, for a remainder of a term shall not depend on a possibility so remote as the dying without issue.

2 Keble 637, 84 E.R. 401

In an action upon the case on an issue out of Chancery, if the plaintiff had any estate, interest, or possibility in a lease for 99 years, determinable on three lives, whereof the plaintiff's is one, by a devise of his father, to whom one Searle, seised to him and his heirs as tenant for the three lives, demised it to the father for 99 years, who devised to Dulcibell, his executor, for life, and, after[wards], to Nicholas for life and, if Nicholas die without issue of his body, then to Barnaby, the plaintiff

And by *Jones* this is a good possibility. And, first, a termor, as Manning's Case, 8 Co. 94, may after a devise to two for lives limit it to a third, though it be a possibility on a possibility, as well as to one for life, and, after[wards] to another, which is clear he may. And the reason of both is the same on Com. 519, Welden and Elkington, the construction in both being taken by way of transposition of the latter devise in remainder first in favor of devises. And, unless grants required more particular certainty, it would be so in grants, as for so many years as are to come after the death of J.S. is void by a grant, but good by a devise, as if a lease be made for 99 years to begin from the making to begin after another is good, as The Rector of Chedington's Case, 1 Co. 153, and that a contingent on a contingent is devisable, 14 Car. I, Cotton and Heath, 1 Roll. 612, is express, Hilary [term], 9 Jac., 2 Cr. 461, Rhetorique and Chapell, there, is two degrees farther than in the case at bar. Yet it is not denied in the Case of Child and Baily, 2 Cr. 459, and 1 Roll 613, which opposes not this point, being only adjudged on the remoteness of the contingency, not on that a contingency cannot be on a contingency, which may be. So the inconvenience of a perpetuity does not attend it, but that the contingency may ordinarily happen on the lives of one or two men, and cannot by possibility endure forever. This appears by the reason of Pell and Brown's Case, 2 Cr. 591, in *Devise*, Br. 1, where a fee simple on a remote contingency is void, as on the death without issue male etc. whether the remoteness depend on the act of God or of the party, 3 Cr. 359; Com., Fulmerston and Steward, and whether the contingent be incident or collateral, as 1 Cr. 577, the Mayor of London and Alport, a failure of payment of rent by J.S. or his heirs is too remote.[1] So in The Rector of Chedington's Case, which was by a lease, not by a devise, and it was held void for the uncertainty rather than the contingency. And 12 Ass. 5, cited to prove it, warrants not that a possibility cannot be upon a possibility, but the lessor could not recover, because, by a livery, an estate for life passed, until which be ended, the lessor could not recover by an assize, which, *Condition*, Br. 102, is observed.[2]

Second, this particular devise is good at bar. And the dying of Nicholas without issue is void, were it intended on a failure of issue, but, being devised to Nicholas but for life, it must be intended that, if he have no issue at the time of his death, then to Barnaby, the plaintiff, which must the rather be so, because the estate of Nicholas determines by his death, and it must go to the plaintiff or to the executors of the devisor. But, where the first limitation is to the heirs of the body, there, the dying without issue is so intended. But it is otherwise here, as vulgar and common parlance demonstrates, albeit in formedon and pleading it is otherwise. But were there no precedent words to guide nor common intendment, yet, to support the devise, it shall be thus taken when it can be made good by no other construction. And, on this reason, the case of Trinity [term] 12 Car. II, rot. 1043, Goodier and Clerke, was taken in the contrary sense to support a conveyance, and there was a contingency that might take effect at the time of the death and also another. But, in this case, it cannot be taken otherwise. The Case of Child and Baily was a devise of the whole term to the son and his assigns, and, on his death without issue, then to another; this is void. 1 Roll. 611, Leventhorp and Ashby, is on the same reason. And Nicholas, the devisee, was never any perfect owner, but limitedly. And the Case of Saunders and Cornish, 1 Cr. 230, pl. 268, comes not to the case in question, being remote possibilities to persons not *in esse*; so 1 Co. 138, an estate to everyone that should be his heir for life is void, making a perpetual freehold.

Coleman, for the defendant: The limitation to Barnaby is void. And the conclusion of the verdict is whether Barnaby takes anything or not. So whether the term shall go after is not material. Also he agrees that a limitation may be to

---

[1] *Fulmerston v. Steward* (1554), 1 Plowden 102, 75 E.R. 160, also 1 Dyer 102, 73 E.R. 225; *Mayor of London v. Alford* (1640), Croke Car. 576, 79 E.R. 1095.

[2] YB 12 Edw. III, Lib. Ass., f. 34, pl. 5, Brooke, Abr., *Conditions*, pl. 102 (1338).

one, two, or three lives, but a limitation cannot be made of a term after the death of J.S. without issue, which is the same as if it were before devised to J.S. and his heirs of his body. And, therefore, the case of Pell and Brown was adjudged good, because the limitation was on dying without issue living at the time of the decease of the devisee. And it would otherwise be void as well in cases of a fee simple as of leases. It is much stronger, being uncertain when the first devisee dies without issue. And whatever Nicholas takes, yet the plaintiff shall not take it until the issue fail, though it go to the executors or others in the meantime. And the cases of Child and Baily and 1 Cr. 230; 1 Roll. 611, Cornish and Saunders, are express authorities in this point. And albeit, in that case, it were limited on dying without issue then living, yet it was held void in the case of a term. And, in the Case of Saunders and Cornish, it was to each for life only, but such a limitation after, as here, which was held void. And there is no difference when it is limited to the issue of the body, for they cannot take the term, as Leonard Lovy's Case.[1] And the case in the Common Bench of Goodier and Clerke was adjudged on the same reason. But, in the King's Bench, before, it was ruled on the particular intendment of the provision for a daughter to be in the lifetime of the party.

KELYNG, Chief Justice: The plaintiff goes up the hill, for Barnaby cannot take while Nicholas has issue, and, if not, then the contingency is too remote. Also, the words are 'if Nicholas die without issue of his body', not if he die without any issue then living.

TWYSDEN said this is as fully within the reason of Child and Baily's Case as possibly can be. Also Nicholas cannot here have but for his life. Therefore, it is more disputable who shall have it after. And he said the executors of the devisor should have it. But he conceived that, if all be living when all the candles are lighted together, the devise of term may be to twenty, one after another, but not else.

And so it was ruled, RAINSFORD and MORTON according.

But RAINSFORD, KELYNG, Chief Justice, and MORTON agreed that, on the devise of a term to A. for life, the whole term is in the devisee, and, on his death within the term, nothing reverts to the devisor's executors.

Adjornatur.

1 Siderfin 450, 82 E.R. 1211

The case was Dr. Love took a lease of a farm in Hampshire of the dean and chapter of Winchester. And it was to Searle and his heirs for the lives of Nicholas Love, Barnaby Love, and Robert Love, which was in trust for Dr. Love. Searle leased it for 99 years to Dr. Love if the said three lives live so long. Dr. Love, being thus possessed, made his will. And he devised the premises in such a manner,

[1] *Prowt v. Worthen* (1613), 10 Coke Rep. 78, 77 E.R. 1043, also 2 Brownlow & Goldesborough 103, 123 E.R. 839.

'to Dulcibella, my wife, for her life and, after her decease, to Nicholas, my son, and, if Nicholas die without issue, then, I devise the same to Barnaby, my son'. The testator died; Dulcibella, the wife died; Nicholas, the son, dies without issue. Windham, the defendant, claiming under Nicholas, *scil.* by a patent of the king, who was entitled by the attainder of treason by Parliament of the said Nicholas Love, obtained the possession of the farm. The plaintiff, pretending title by Barnaby Love, suggested in Chancery that the defendant was not entitled. And, by an order of the court, an issue was directed to be tried here what the defendant had by any will made by Dr. Love or otherwise, a title to the premises. And upon this, such an issue was joined here in a feigned action upon the case, which was tried in Hampshire.

And, by a special verdict there, the aforesaid will etc. was found. And upon it, the sole question argued here was whether this devise of this term be good to Barnaby after the death without issue of Nicholas. And it was agreed after argument at the bar by all of the justices that the devise to Barnaby Love was a void devise because as the term was devised to Nicholas 'and, if he die without issue, then to Barnaby', Barnaby cannot be entitled until the death without issue of Nicholas. And so it is to the same effect as it had been to Nicholas and to the heirs of his body, remainder to Barnaby, which devise to Barnaby had been clearly bad, because, after a term is devised to one and the heirs of his body, no further limitation can be of it nor any appointment by way of an executory devise because the law will not presume any term to have a continuance so long as there can be issue of the body. And a limitation of it after a death without issue is too remote a possibility.

And so it was adjudged in Child and Bayly's Case, Cro., 2, 461; Ro., tit. *Devise*, 613; Cro., 1, 230, Sanders and Cornish's Case. And by Rolle, above, it appears that it will be void to Barnaby though it to Nicholas had been more respective, *scil.* if it had been to Nicholas and, if he died without issue living at the time of his death, the remainder to Barnaby, it had been void to Barnaby.

And the Court of Chancery was accordingly informed by this court that Barnaby did not have any title.

But Twysden, Justice, was of the opinion that [neither] the executor nor the assignee of Nicholas Love will have this term, but the executor of the first devisor would.

But the Chief Justice [Kelyng] was *fortiter contra, scil.* that the executor or the assignee of Nicholas, the devisee, will have it.

Note [it was said] by Twysden, Justice, that the law is now settled. And, if a term be devised to one for life, remainder to another for life, remainder to a third for life etc., and so to twenty, one after the other, that this is a good devise to them all, notwithstanding the objections of possibilities upon possibilities if all of the persons were *in esse* at the time of the devise because all of the candles are lit at once. But, if the devise be to one for life who is not then *in esse*, as to the first son, there, no limitation of a term can be beyond it. And, of this opinion, all of the court seemed to be, *quod nota.*

[Other reports of this case: 1 Eq. Cas. Abr. 191, 21 E.R. 982, 73 Selden Soc. 206.]
[Entered: Trinity, 21 Car. II, rot. 1605.]

285

Mosely v. Maynard

(Ch. 1668–1669)

A court of equity can enforce the provisions of a will.

2 Chancery Reports 17, 21 E.R. 603

This suit is to have the will of Sir Edward Mosely decreed, which, upon a trial, has been found a good will.

This court, with the assistance of judges, declared they saw no cause to decree the said will. This cause also is touching alteration of possession, the point touching the decreeing of the said will heard and argued again.

The plaintiff insisted that it is the proper justice of this court to settle estates in peace and quietness, and pressed to have the will decreed, especially, for that no purchaser would meddle under the title of the will and that the plaintiff was by the will to raise £10,000 to be paid according to the directions of the said will by a time therein prefixed or else he forfeited his estate therein.

But the defendants insisted it is altogether improper to decree a will in this court, especially, to the disinheriting of a married woman and her son, an infant, and that this court had refused to decree the same in a former order with judges.

This court ordered a new bill to be brought.

The point touching the condition in a will, settled on a bill of review, the proofs in the original cause were not allowed to be read.

[Reg. Lib. 20 Car. II, f. 999, 22 Car. II, f. 274.]
[Related cases: 73 Selden Soc. 38, 142, 344, 399, 79 Selden Soc. 761.]

286

Macklow v. Wilmot

(Ch. 1668–1669)

After the enrollment of a final decree, the court will not order a defendant to make a discovery of deeds.

2 Chancery Reports 18, 21 E.R. 604

The plaintiff would have the defendant examined on interrogatories to discover deeds and writings and to be examined to other matters.

The defendant insists that what the plaintiff now moves for may be of dangerous consequence, being to discover the estates of purchasers to whom the said defendant has sold most of the land in question. And it is now long since the cause was heard and many attendances on the Master and examinations before him, and the decree is enrolled by the plaintiff, wherefore, the defendant ought not to be examined on interrogatories, being to put up the order on a hearing in a point that the plaintiff at the hearing did not think fit to move for.

This court, in regard the examining of the defendant on interrogatories is omitted out of the decree, would not now order it.

[Reg. Lib. 20 Car. II, f. 548.]

287

Dixon v. Read

(Ch. 1668–1673)

If a defendant pays money ordered by a decree to be paid, he can have a bill of review, but, if a plaintiff seeks relief against a bond and it is denied and he pays the money, no bill of review lies.

2 Chancery Reports 21, 21 E.R. 604

The bill is that, the plaintiff being sued by the defendant Read in the Sheriffs' Court in London upon a bond of £200 for the payment of £100 to the said defendant by the plaintiff, when the said defendant, being a solicitor, should recover a verdict on the behalf of one Thrale, upon which bond, though the defendant was so far from being instrumental in getting any such verdict, that he acted for Thrale's adversary, yet the defendant has gotten a verdict on the said bond, whereupon the plaintiff removed the cause into the Mayor's Court and, from thence, into this court by [a writ of] *certiorari*, and the plaintiff, according to the proceedings in such cases, proved his suggestions. Yet the defendant, without a [writ of] *procedendo*, has removed the proceedings back out of the Mayor's Court into the Sheriffs' Court, and has there taken out execution, and taken the plaintiff's bail thereupon and levied £102.

This cause was heard by the Master of the Rolls [GRIMSTON], who saw no cause in equity to relieve the plaintiff against the penalty and interest of the said bond.

This cause came to a re-hearing before the Lord Chancellor [BRIDGEMAN], being assisted with the Lord Chief Justice HALE, who were of opinion with the Master of the Rolls, and they confirmed his decree.

Lord Nottingham, *Prolegomena*, p. 302

29 July 1673.

If a defendant has submitted to the decree by the payment of money, that performance is a means to entitle him to a bill of review. But if a plaintiff submits to a dismission by the paying of the money, against which he sought relief, and taking in his bond on which he was sued at law, he shall not have a review or a rehearing of such dismission.

79 Selden Soc. 534

29 July 1673.

A plaintiff prayed relief against a bond and was dismissed. And, then, he paid the money, and took up his bond, after which submission to the dismission by the payment of the money, he brought a bill of review.

It was adjudged by SHAFTESBURY, C., it would not lie.

[Reg. Lib. 20 Car. II, ff. 46, 561.]

288

Smith v. Holman

(Ch. 1668–1669)

A party who prevents another party for examining witnesses can be held in contempt of court.

2 Chancery Reports 22, 21 E.R. 605

The defendant caused the plaintiff's bill at law to be arrested soon after the plaintiff and defendant had joined in a commission for the examining of witnesses, which was for the same matter here in question. And also, about two days before the execution of the commission, the said defendant caused the plaintiff to be arrested when he was preparing for the said commission, so that the plaintiff could not execute the same.

The plaintiff prays that the defendant, for such his abuse, being against the ancient privilege of this court to suitors that are in the management of their causes in this court, may stand committed, and pay the cost of the last commission and damages sustained by the said arrest.

The defendant insisted he was ignorant of such privilege and that the plaintiff was now in execution.

This court, in favor of the defendant, spared the commitment, but ordered him to pay the plaintiff's costs of the last commission, as also his costs and damages sustained by reason of the arrest, imprisonment, and prosecution thereon, and referred it to a Master of this court to tax. And, the plaintiff giving a new [confessed] judgment for the debt in question, the defendant shall at his, the defendant's, charges presently release and discharge the said plaintiff out of execution. And the defendant is to be at the charges of a new commission, and the plaintiff to take an injunction until the hearing of this cause.

[Reg. Lib. 20 Car. II, f. 192.]

289

Wiseman v. Foster

(Ch. 1668–1669)

In this case, the plaintiff did marry with consent, and the court ordered her legacy to be paid to her.

2 Chancery Reports 23, 21 E.R. 605

The plaintiff's father, George Brigges, by a will, devised to the plaintiff Anne £500 for her portion, which was appointed to be paid her at the age of twenty-one years or day of marriage, and he made the defendant, Dame Anne Foster, his then wife, and his son, George, his executors. And, by a subsequent clause in his will, he declared that it should be in the power of his executors to order and dispose of the plaintiff's portion, according to their discretion, to the use of the rest of the children, unless the plaintiff should marry by the advice and consent of the defendant, Dame Anne, and others, who were overseers of his will, or the greater part of them. And the defendants insist that the plaintiff has married without such consent [and], therefore, ought to have but £250.

Whereas the plaintiff insists that the said clause was intended only *in terrorem* and awe to the plaintiff Anne to induce her to take heed how she married, and not that she should lose any part of her portion, so as she married one who deserved the same, which she has done with the consent of the major part of the overseers.

The defendants insist that the plaintiff marrying, as aforesaid, ought to have but £250, as by the memorandum in the will, and the rest to be distributed amongst the other children of the testator.

But the plaintiff insists that, in this case, there was not by the will any devise over to the said other children.

This court, upon reading the proofs touching the approbation of the major part of the overseers and their consent to the plaintiff's marriage, decreed the defendants to pay the £500 and damages.

[Reg. Lib. 20 Car. II, f. 731.]

290

Rowley v. Lancaster

(Ch. 1669–1670)

In this case, the legacy in issue vested in the decedent, and it was ordered to be paid to his administrator.

2 Chancery Reports 25, 21 E.R. 606

Matthew Lancaster bequeathed to John Creeke £100, thus, *viz.* £50 in one month after the expiration of his apprenticeship and the other £50 within one whole year after the expiration of the said apprenticeship. And he made the defendant executor. The apprenticeship expired 29 September 1664, but John Creeke dying before the legacy was paid, the defendant refuses to pay it to the plaintiff, the administrator of the said John Creeke.

The defendant insists that he paid the £50 due within a month after the expiration of the said apprenticeship and that the said John Creeke died before the whole year after the expiration of his apprenticeship was expired, and, therefore, the other £50 was not due to the plaintiff.

This court, being assisted with judges, were clear of opinion that the said legacy was a *debitum in praesenti solvendum in futuro*, and decreed the said £50 to be paid to the plaintiff with damages.

[Reg. Lib. 21 Car. II, f. 993.]

291

Darrell v. Whitchcott

(Ch. 1668–1672)

Where a royal patent grants a new trust, the terms of a former trust of the same res do not carry over to the new trust.

2 Chancery Reports 59, 21 E.R. 615

The plaintiff had a trust in a lease of a coal farm by a patent from the late king, which lease was afterwards renewed by the king, and other trustees were named therein, and the defendant, being one of the trustees, insists he was a joint patentee for the valuable consideration of £500. But the plaintiff insists the defendant comes in as the plaintiff's trustee, and is not to be subject to the same trust in the new lease, as he was under the old lease.

But the defendant insists the new patent was to the new trustees for service done by them to this king and this defendant's £500 and this defendant was not a trustee for the plaintiff, but was in for his own use, which patent, this defendant had pleaded, and it was allowed.

Yet the plaintiff insisted there was a continued trust and the defendant and the king declared he had a respect for the old tenants and the defendant, coming in under the tenants' interests, ought to be in trust for the plaintiffs and that, though there be no tenant right against the king, yet the king did consider the tenants and that this case is but the same with that where a mortgagee or trustee renews a church lease, in which, in this case, the court had given relief.

This court with the judges declared their opinion that there was no ground at all to relieve the plaintiff, and so dismissed his bill.

Lord Nottingham, *Prolegomena*, p. 242

4 May 1672.

The case, by way of admittance, was allowed to be this. Perrot was possessed of the fifth part of a coal farm in trust for Mr. Darrel by virtue of a lease from the Crown which would expire in 1661. Sir Jeremy Whitchcott gets an assignment from Perrot after full notice of the trust for Darrel, and, in the year 1659, takes a new lease from His Majesty, then in Holland, to himself and the Lord Mordant and Sir Thomas Peynton for thirty-one years.

Darrel exhibits a bill supposing that the new lease by implication of law shall be likewise in trust for him as to a fifth, because it was grafted upon the old lease, to which the customary favor, though not right, of renewing is incident. And it was compared to the mortgage of a church lease, which, if the mortgagee renew, the former equity of redemption will infect the renewed lease. So, here, the former trust will go along with the new lease which was built upon it.

But Bridgeman, Keeper, Hale, Chief Justice, and Vaughan [Chief Justice] denied that any trust did rise by implication, and [said] such constructions were not to be favored, because it tended to make a great uncertainty in men's titles, and, since no lessor is bound to renew, it follows that he who gains a new estate, for a valuable consideration, especially, ought to keep it. And Turner, Chief Baron, though absent, was of the same mind. And they denied the case of the church lease.

Lord Nottingham, *Prolegomena*, p. 287

In the case of Darrel and Whitchcott, Hale, Chief Justice, cited a case before himself *in Scaccario, viz.* Cage mortgaged a lease to Holgate, who renewed the lease from the Dean and Chapter of St. Paul's for twenty-one years before the former expired. Cage exhibited [his] bill in the Exchequer to redeem the new lease, and prayed an account of the profits as well since the old lease expired as before. [It was] resolved no account of the profits since the new lease [should be allowed] nor any redemption of it.

But the precedents in Chancery are otherwise in Greenvill and Elme's Case. And there is reason against it, for, then, any mortgage of a lease for years forfeited may by speedy renewing bar all redemption.

[Reg. Lib. 20 Car. II, f. 516.]
[Later proceedings in this case: 73 Selden Soc. 27, 79 Selden Soc. 687.]

292

Savage v. Whitebread

(Ch. 1668–1669)

A minor pleading error made by an infant's counsel can be corrected by the court.

3 Chancery Reports 24, 21 E.R. 717

Sir Thomas Savage, the plaintiff's father, sold land to the defendant's ancestors, and covenanted that they were free of encumbrances, and gave a collateral security by other lands also. And the purchaser having entered on the security for damnifications, the bill was to have the collateral security reconveyed. Whereto, the defendants having set forth divers encumbrances on the purchased lands and (*inter alia*) a lease of twenty-one years of parcel thereof, the plaintiff replied generally.

And, at the hearing, a reconveyance was decreed on satisfaction of the damnifications. And, upon the report, the plaintiffs excepted against the lease, that it was no encumbrance, because they had proved the purchaser had notice of it at the time of the purchase. Whereto, the defendants insisted that the notice was not in issue in the case.

Yet Lord Keeper Bridgeman would not conclude the infant by a slip of her counsel in not putting it in issue upon the replication, but he ordered a trial whether the purchaser agreed to take the lands charged with that lease.

293

Pridgeon v. Pridgeon

(Ch. 1668)

The question in this case was whether a widow can make a binding contract with a future husband to retain her ownership in rents and profits of land.

A court will not grant a remedy where the case is not ripe for adjudication.

Lincoln's Inn MS. Hill 125, f. 56

15 December 1668. Prujean v. Lord Gorges.

Dame Margaret Prujean, relict of Sir Francis Prujean, kt., plaintiff; Richard, lord Gorges, Dr. Stanley, Mr. Pearse, executors of Sir Francis, in trust for Robert Prujean, his grandson, and the said Robert, defendants.

This cause came to be heard before the Lord Keeper [Bridgeman] assisted with the Lord Chief Baron [Hale] and Mr. Justice Archer, the case then appearing to be that the plaintiff being the relict and executrix of Thomas Fleming, Esq., being seised for life of lands worth £500 *per annum* and possessed of household stuff as executrix to Fleming, about 1663, there was a treaty for a marriage to be had between her and Sir Francis, upon which it was agreed between them and others on her behalf that marriage should be solemnized and that the rents and profits of her jointure lands and all her goods and chattels should be at her disposal after the marriage took effect.

In pursuance of the agreement, Sir Francis permitted the plaintiff, by herself and servants, to receive the rents of the lands and to dispose thereof and of her personal estate to her own use without account. And he gave her other gifts to be at her disposal. In April 1665, he made his will and devised to her £2500 besides what he had formerly given her, his coach and horses, plate, household stuffs, goods, and chattels in his house in the Old Bailey, and he made the defendants executors in trust for Robert.

The plaintiff became entitled to the legacies bequeathed. And, by the agreement, she claims the rents of her jointure lands and the goods that were Mr. Fleming's with which Sir Francis, by the agreement, was not to intermeddle. The defendants, the executors, refuse to submit upon the pretense that they are but trustees for Robert.

And the plaintiff, being in danger to be sued for the rents and goods, has exhibited her bill to have the agreement confirmed by a decree and an injunction to stay suits at law touching the rents or goods.

The agreement being fully proved and the execution thereof during Sir Francis's life by permitting her to receive the profits of the jointure lands and to dispose the same at her will as freely as she did before her intermarriage, the question upon the case as it now stands being whether the court shall decree the agreement or how far before any suit commenced against the plaintiff touching the rents or goods the court shall make a provisional relief for the plaintiff upon the said agreement, some precedents [were] insisted on by both sides.

His Lordship [Bridgeman], before he delivered his judgment, does order that the Lord Chief Baron [Hale] and Mr. Justice Archer be attended with this order and precedents and His Lordship will advise with the Lords, the Judges, thereupon. The Judges, having been attended with the case and the plaintiff's precedents, have appointed Friday, the 29th of October to deliver his judgment and the Lords, the Judges, are desired to be then present.

Precedents read at the hearing on the plaintiff's part:

Carew Georges, plaintiff; Toby Cancy *et al.*, defendants; Order of 12 November 15 Car. I [1639].[1] Sir William Chancy and his lady being separated, he agreed with her friends to allow her £170 *per annum* for alimony out of which

[1] *Gorges v. Chancey* (Ch. 1639), British Library MS. Harley 1576, f. 233v, pl. 3, 1 Chancery Reports 125, 21 E.R. 527, Tothill 97, 21 E.R. 134, Public Record Office, C.33/177, f. 226v.

she saved £200 and delivered it to the defendant Gibbs in trust to be put out at interest for the plaintiff, her grandchild. Bonds were taken in the defendant's, Chancy's, name. A month before her death, she gave the bonds and money to the plaintiff. Chancey released the bonds, alleging that Sir William's father gave a power to the lady, his wife, to dispose her estate to the defendant. The court declared that, for things in action or upon trust, a married woman might dispose by will of the same without any assent of her husband, the defendant assented to pay the money, and it was so decreed.

Atkins v. Stepkin, order of 13 April 19 Car. [1643]. [There was] an agreement before marriage between the defendant and his wife that she should make over an estate to the plaintiff for her separate maintenance, and he did so. She saved several sums of money, and put them out in the plaintiff's name at interest. The defendant procured the money to be paid unto him by the debtors. He was decreed to pay the money to the plaintiff according to the trust.

Precedents read on the defendant's part:

Earl of Suffolk v. Greenvill, 6 June 7 Car. I [1631].[1] The plaintiff's bill was to be discharged of £600 *per annum* decreed against him at the Lady Greenvill's suit before her marriage with Sir Richard in respect of an assignment made by the lady before her marriage to one Cuttiford upon a verbal agreement made between the defendant before her marriage that she should have the power and sole disposal thereof and which she and Cuttiford had released to the plaintiff. But the deed of assignment could not be produced, being alleged to be in Sir Richard's hands. The court ordered the defendant and Cuttiford to be examined upon interrogatories for the discovery of the deed, who, having been examined, the court was not satisfied what the true contents of the same was nor how the same could be of any validity. The Lord Keeper [Lord Coventry] and judges assistant [Hutton and Whitelock] declared they had considered of the points in question and were of opinion, first, that there was not sufficient matter nor proof produced to bar the defendant, Sir Richard, of the execution of the decree or to relieve the plaintiff, for that the arrears of the £600 *per annum* decreed to the lady being a thing in action to be had merely by the process of this court cannot be assigned so as the assignment to Cuttiford, if it had been proved, had been void in law and ought not to be maintained against the rule of law in a court of equity, no consideration appearing to support the same to make it better in equity than at law, Sir Richard's verbal agreement in consideration of marriage being in subversion of the grounds of the law and right of marriage. The court was clear of opinion that, unless the agreement had been so settled by a legal assurance as it might be good in law, it was not fit for a court of equity to give any such power to a mar-

[1] *Earl of Suffolk v. Grenville* (Ch. 1631), Lincoln's Inn MS. Maynard 75, f. 46v, pl. 2, British Library MS. Hargrave 174, f. 18, pl. 2, British Library MS. Hargrave 99, f. 56, pl. 1, 2 Freeman 146, 22 E.R. 1119, 3 Chancery Reports 89, 21 E.R. 738, Nelson 15, 21 E.R. 778, Public Record Office, C.33/159, ff. 400v, 520, 653v.

ried woman, as the defendant, the lady, pretends. Things in action, though not assignable in law, yet may be turned over by a letter of attorney. The court declared, if that had been done, yet, by the marriage, the letter of attorney [were] determined and also Sir Richard's promises and agreements made unto her before marriage and the disposal of her estate [were] extinguished. If it had been an effectual letter of attorney made to Cuttiford and had a continuance, yet he could not by force thereof make a release in his own name, as in this case, being void in law.

He remains a party interested, and ought not by his own oath, being a single witness, no other besides him swearing to the contents of the deed, be admitted a fit witness, there being other exceptions against him and so he swears for himself etc.

[They] dismissed the bill.

1 Chancery Cases 117, 22 E.R. 721

Dame Margaret Pridgeon, relict of Sir Francis Pridgeon, against the executors of Sir Francis Pridgeon in trust for Robert Pridgeon etc.

After several debates on both sides before the Lord Keeper [Bridgeman], this cause came to be further heard by him in November 1668, assisted with the Lord Chief Baron Hale and Judge Archer. And the case was thus.

The plaintiff, being a widow, at her marriage with Sir Francis Pridgeon, suggests an agreement precedent to the marriage between him and her and others on her behalf that, notwithstanding her marriage, the rents and profits of all her own estate and what personal estate and goods she had should be at her own disposal and that she was possessed of certain goods etc. before her marriage with him, which the defendants, the executors of Sir Francis, claimed, as being his executors in trust for the said defendant Robert, his nephew and heir, which, by the said agreement, she claimed.

For the defendants, it was insisted that, if any such agreement were with Sir Francis before the marriage, it was extinguished by the marriage. And they so cited Smith and Stafford's Case, Hob. 216, and the Earl of Suffolk and Greenvill's Case.[1] And [it was] insisted such like agreement ought not to be countenanced in equity, being derogatory to the rights and privileges of marriage.

And on the debating the matter of this cause, a case between Scot and Brograve, about 1639, in this court, was cited, which was thus. The wife of an improvident husband had, unknown to him, by her frugality raised some monies for the good of their children, which she had disposed for that purpose, being otherwise unprovided for. And this disposition of the wife, the Lord Coventry had established by a decree. But afterwards, upon a review and assistance of the

[1] *Smith v. Stafford* (1618), Hobart 216, 80 E.R. 363, also Hetley 12, 124 E.R. 302, Noy 26, 74 E.R. 996, Hutton 17, 123 E.R. 1069, 1 Brownlow & Goldesborough 181, 23 E.R. 638; *Earl of Suffolk v. Grenville* (Ch. 1631), *ut supra*.

judges, this decree was reversed, as being dangerous to give a wife power to dispose of her husband's estate.

And another case between Gorges and Chancy, which was about Michaelmas term 1639, was cited, which was to this effect. A husband and wife, by agreement, separated and lived apart, and they agreed that the wife should have £150 *per annum* separate maintenance, out of which she had saved some money and put it out to interest and took bonds in a friend's name and disposed of the money by a will. And this, upon debate, was established a good disposition. And this was now declared to be a just order.

But note that, in this case, it was an agreement after marriage with friends in the behalf of the wife for a separate maintenance. But, in the principal case, the Chief Baron [Hale] declared that, though, where an agreement is between the husband and the wife before marriage that the wife may by will dispose of part of her estate or for a thing which is future to the marriage, such an agreement is not dissolved by the marriage; yet, where an agreement is to have execution during the coverture, as in the principal case, there, the marriage extinguishes such an agreement.

And the whole court concluded the plaintiff had no ground for relief, and declared she had no cause of suit but by way of anticipation, for the executors did not claim the goods, but she feared the other defendant, the infant, for whom they were executors in trust, would claim the goods etc. Yet the court declared that they would farther consider the matter, and the cause has not yet received any farther hearing.

294

Anonymous

(Ch. 1669)

In this case, a suit in equity was allowed for a debt dispute despite a final judgment at common law on the merits for the same debt.

3 Chancery Reports 25, 21 E.R. 718

Hilary [term] 20 & 21 Car. II [1669].

The bill is to be relieved against an action brought by the defendant against the plaintiff as executor for money due to the defendant upon a trade between the testator and him. And it charges that the defendant was in the testator's debt, and prays a discovery of the truth.

The defendant pleaded that, the differences being referred to arbitrators by the testator and him, he gave the testator an account, whereon rested due £164 17s. 2d. And, no end being made, he had sued the plaintiff, the executor, and obtained a verdict for £100 damages besides costs. And he says he is advised such a bill is to be admitted before a trial, and not after a verdict, and only damages recovered, and that judgment is since entered.

But the plaintiff, on a petition, got an order that the bill shall be taken as filed before the trial, and the plea be set aside, but that the defendant may plead, answer, or demur *de novo*.

The defendant pleaded the said matter again and that he had no notice of the bill nor was served with a process until after the verdict nor that the bill was filed before the verdict. Yet he must answer.

295

Whitewick v. Sherer

(Ch. 1669)

A bill of review does not lie in an action that has abated.

Lincoln's Inn MS. Hill 125, f. 59v, pl. 1

Whitewick, executrix of Mary Studly, executrix of John Studly against Susan Sherer.

The bill was to have an account of a joint stock in trade, whereupon, in a former cause, all the partners being parties and the cause referred to account, the Master referee stated the account, and divided to each party what was due, *inter alia* a thirteenth part to the plaintiff's testator.

The bill abated by the death of Richard Sherer, the defendant.

The plaintiff exhibits a bill of review *quoad* her share, she being executrix to one of the partners.

And [it was] dismissed.

296

Hall v. Salter

(Ch. 1669)

A surety is not liable until the secured debt or claim has been liquidated.

A surety can defend in a court action the secured claim.

Lincoln's Inn MS. Hill 125, f. 55v, pl. 1

27 January 1668[/69]. Hall and Salter and Sir John Lenthall.

Wollaston, indebted to divers persons and in the custody of Sir John Lenthall, gave a bond to Sir John Lenthall £2000 for his true imprisonment. And the plaintiff was one of his sureties in that bond. And, after[wards], he became indebted to the defendant Salter, who arrested him, and had a judgment against him, and he was in the custody of Sir John Lenthall. And, in execution, he did escape. Sir John Lenthall, being sued for the escape, assigned his bond to the defendant, who put the bond in suit. And he had a judgment by *nihil dicit*. The plaintiff in execution on this judgment sued for relief because that Sir John Lenthall was not damnified and [there was] no judgment on the escape against him nor had he paid any money.

[It was] decreed that [they] go to a new trial on the escape and the plaintiff to make a defense in Sir John Lenthall's name.

297

Marquess of Winchester v. Child

(Ch. 1669)

An account can be ordered for the misuse of funds belonging to a charity.

Lincoln's Inn MS. Hill 125, f. 55v, pl. 2

27 January 1668[/69].

Divers monies being in the corporation's hands for particular charitable uses to lend to the poor with every [. . .] his successor [?] at his coming in with the securities etc. laid out £30 on occasions of the corporation.

[He was] decreed to account to the plaintiff on the charitable use, for, as to the charity, it was a misemployment. But the plaintiff [was] to reimburse the defendant out of the proper stock of the corporation.

298

Goddard v. Complin

(Ch. 1669)

A creditor secured by a mortgage has priority over a jointress where the creditor had no notice of the jointure.

If a tenant in tail confess a judgment and suffer a recovery to any collateral purpose, that recovery validates all his precedent acts and encumbrances.

1 Chancery Cases 119, 22 E.R. 722

27 January [1669].

A tenant in tail demises his lands for ninety-nine years by way of mortgage, and, after[wards], he marries and, in consideration thereof and of a £500 portion, he suffers a recovery to enable him to settle a jointure. And, afterwards, he takes up more money of the mortgage upon the former security. The jointress was plaintiff. And the question was whether the defendant should be allowed money lent after the recovery and marriage.

And the court declared that, if the defendant had no notice of the jointure when he lent the new money, he must be allowed it.

Another question was whether the defendant had proved payment of the money supposed to be lent. And, as to that, there was the receipt in the deed of the mortgage, the condition of redemption on repayment of the money, and the defendant's oath that he had paid it, which was insisted on was evidence enough of payment after ten years against any person.

And so the court inclined.

But the plaintiff standing upon it that it was not sufficient evidence as against the plaintiff, who claimed as a jointress, there was farther evidence.

There was also this question put, a tenant in tail mortgages for years, and, afterwards, upon marriage, in consideration thereof, he suffers a recovery to settle a jointure etc., whether this recovery should enure to make good the mortgage, it being designed for the marriage settlement only.

Which was answered, if no recovery had been, there could have been no jointure, and the jointress could not have avoided the mortgage, and she is in by the act of her husband, and no subsequent act of the husband could avoid his own act precedent. And it was also declared that, if a tenant in tail confess a judgment etc. and suffer a recovery to any collateral purpose, that recovery shall enure to make good all his precedent acts and encumbrances.

299

Duncumban v. Stint

(Ch. 1669)

An executor of a will can be required to give security for the payment of a legacy when it should become due.

1 Chancery Cases 121, 22 E.R. 723

1 February [1669]. Duncumban, an infant, against Stint, executor of Stint.

The defendant's testator gave the plaintiff £1000 to be paid at the age of twenty-one years. The bill suggested the defendant wasted the estate, and prayed he might give security to pay this legacy when due.

And the Master of the Rolls [Grimston] did accordingly decree the defendant to give security.

[Other reports of this case: 1 Eq. Cas. Abr. 78, 21 E.R. 891.]

300

Eton College v. Beauchamp

(Ch. 1669)

A rent issuing out of land is payable by the occupant even where the land is intermixed with other land so that distress cannot be had.

Lincoln's Inn MS. Hill 125, f. 55v, pl. 3

5 February 1668[/69].

The bill was to have the arrears of a pension of money paid and future payments continued and a discovery of the lands liable.

The bill pretended a confusion of bounds, by reason whereof they knew not where to distrain. The arrears were demanded. Part grew due in the life of the testator of one of the defendants and who was husband of the other and, being seised in fee, had made her a jointure.

The arrears in the husband's life were not charged on the jointress in equity, but the executor (though of a tenant in fee) was charged therewith as far as he had assets.

Nota in esse nova lex condita.

1 Chancery Cases 121, 22 E.R. 723

5 February [1669].

There was a rent or pension of £1 14s. *per annum* granted by King Henry VI to that College, issuing out of lands. Riggs was the executor of the terre tenant. And to be relieved for the arrears of rent incurred in his testatrix's lifetime was this bill brought, which did suggest that the College did not know the lands out of which the rent went and so would not distrain. Beauchamp was the present terre tenant. And, though the person of the terre tenant was not chargeable with the rent at law, but only the land by way of distress, yet, forasmuch as the testatrix held the land and did not pay the rent, it was said that, thereby, the personal estate of the testatrix was augmented.

And so the Master of the Rolls [Grimston] decreed the executor to pay the arrears as far as he had assets of the testator's estate.

Dickens 216, 21 E.R. 251

The Provost and Fellows of Eton were possessed of a rent or pension of £1 14s. *per annum* granted by King Henry VI to that College, issuing out of the lands. The defendant Biggs was executor of the tenant. And the bill was brought for a satisfaction of the arrears of rent incurred in his testator's lifetime. And it suggested that the College did not know the lands out of which the rents were issuable, and so could not distrain. And, though the person of the terre tenant was not chargeable with the rent at law, but only the land by way of distress, yet, forasmuch as the testatrix held the land and did not pay the rent, it was said that, thereby, the testatrix's personal estate was augmented.

And, therefore, the Master of the Rolls, SIR HARBOTTLE GRIMSTON, decreed the executor to pay the arrears as far as he had assets of the testatrix.

[Other reports of this case: 1 Eq. Cas. Abr. 32, 21 E.R. 852.]

301

Collet v. Jaques

(Ch. 1669)

Even though the nature of a rent be uncertain, a tenant who has constantly paid the rent in the past will be ordered to pay the arrears and to pay it in the future.

1 Chancery Cases 120, 22 E.R. 723

8 February [1669]. The Master of the Rolls.

The bill was for £3 for a rent of 5s. *per annum* arrear for twelve years.

The plaintiff suggested that the deeds by which the rent was created were lost and also the rent for the future. And there was proof of a constant payment of it until the last twelve years.

And the Master of the Rolls [GRIMSTON] decreed the defendant to pay the arrears and growing rent, because he said it was uncertain what kind of rent it was, and so there is no remedy at law. And, here, the person is made liable for the rent, which, for aught appeared, he was not at law.

[Other reports of this case: 1 Eq. Cas. Abr. 32, 364, 21 E.R. 852, 1105.]

302

Slingsby v. Hale

(Ch. 1669–1671)

A devisee cannot file a bill of review.

1 Chancery Cases 122, 22 E.R. 723

14 February [1669]. The Lord Keeper, Justice Tyrell, Justice Morton.

The bill was a bill of review to reverse a decree made about twenty years since, wherein the mortgagor being plaintiff against the mortgagee to have a redemption, it was decreed accordingly, paying the money to be found due on account. And, for that purpose, it was referred to a Master to take the account. And it was also decreed that, if the plaintiff failed to take the money at a day to be set by the Master, the defendant should hold discharged of all equity of redemption.

Pending the reference, the suit abated by the death of one of the parties defendant, yet the account went on without any notice taken to the court of the abatement. The executor, being a defendant to the original bill, the Master was attended on the behalf of both sides, and made up his report, and that was confirmed and decreed. And that decree was enrolled near twenty years since. And, now, the plaintiff, being a devisee of the mortgagor, by a bill of review, assigns these errors, and now excepts against the decree: first, for that, in respect of the abatement, there was no cause in the court when the account was stated, and the decree drawn up and enrolled; secondly, that it was error for the court to make a decree for the defendant to hold free of the equity of redemption on the plaintiff's bill.

The demurrer was *in nullo erratum*, and the plaintiff not entitled to a bill of review.

To the first, it was answered it was only an exception in point of form, and not in point of right, and that the account, being stated and settled, ought not after such a length of time to be let loose or ravelled into. And, as to this point, they cited the Case of the Lady Cranbourn and Mr. Dalmahoy.[1]

And as to the second, it was said that circuity of action is to be avoided and that there were many precedents of decrees in this manner for the defendant and that what was decreed for the defendant was most just and could not be denied upon the account of justice.

And the court declared they saw no cause to alter the decree, and so allowed the demurrer, and dismissed the bill.

After a complaint of this in the Lords' House, the matter of the demurrer was reheard March 9, 1670, by the Lord Keeper [BRIDGEMAN], Chief Justice HALE, and VAUGHAN. And on long debate, they seemed to incline against the plaintiff, but took time to consider. And after, 21 July 1671, they all three delivered one uniform opinion clearly that the plaintiff, being a devisee, is not entitled to a bill of review, being not in privity to the testator, against whom the decree was, as, if a judgment be against land and the owner aliens the land, the alienee cannot bring a writ of error, nor the vendor. And so they dismissed the bill for this reason principally. Yet the Keeper and Chief Justice HALE were of opinion that the error assigned was no sufficient error to avoid the former decree, but, notwithstanding the abatement, the account ought to conclude and stand as an account stated.

Lord Nottingham, *Prolegomena*, p. 198

21 July 1671, 23 Car. II.

And again in the Case of Slingsby and Hale, it appeared Sir Anthony Caye exhibited a bill against Rose Hale and Rowland to redeem. Pending the suit and

[1] *Viscountess Cranborne v. Delahay* (Ch. 1663), see above, Case No. 104.

after an order to account, Rose dies. Yet the cause carried on after her death, the account was stated, and the plaintiff was decreed to redeem or be foreclosed. Sir Anthony Caye having devised the land to his daughter, Mrs. Slingsby, who was not his heir, she and her husband bring a bill of review.

It was resolved by BRIDGEMAN, Keeper, and HALE and VAUGHAN, Chief Justices, the devisee shall not have a bill of review.

Lord Nottingham, *Prolegomena*, p. 292

23 Car. II.

If a bill be exhibited against two for an account and one dies and the bill abates and then the account is carried on against the survivor and [it is] decreed, this is error ordinarily, but, after some length of time, the court will presume an order by consent, which salves all.

[Other reports of this case: 1 Eq. Cas. Abr. 164, 21 E.R. 961.]

303

Weymberg v. Touch

(Ch. 1669)

The Court of Chancery has jurisdiction over international disputes where witnesses are to be examined out of the jurisdiction.

1 Chancery Cases 123, 22 E.R. 724

24 February [1669].

The bill was to be relieved against an action of debt for money due to the defendant as a merchant from the plaintiff for wares sold in Denmark. The equity was that, in the time of hostility between that crown and this, the defendant being a subject to this crown, the plaintiff was forced to pay the money he owed the defendant to commissioners authorized in that behalf to the king of Denmark and that, in the articles of peace between the two crowns, it was agreed that all monies so exacted from each others' subjects should be compensated by setting one against the other and that the parties that paid the money to either of the kings' orders should be discharged against the creditor.

To this bill, the defendant demurred, and insisted there was no equity and that, if the articles did bind private persons, they were as good at law as here, but, at law, they did not bind, for the defendant had a verdict.

For the plaintiff, it was insisted that the Chancery was a court of state and that the articles of peace were enrolled there and that the bill was to have witnesses examined beyond the sea.

The judge [WILDE] ordered the defendant to answer.

304

More v. Grice

(Ch. 1669)

A court of equity can enforce the terms of a marriage settlement.

1 Chancery Cases 124, 22 E.R. 725

The plaintiff Marah [More's] mother was sister of the defendant [Nicholas] Grice. And, by articles of agreement made between Thomas More, the plaintiff's father, and Nicholas Grice, the defendant in behalf of his sister, the plaintiff's mother, it was agreed that, in consideration of £800 agreed to be given with the plaintiff's mother in a portion to the plaintiff's father, whereof £600 was Nicholas's own free gift, that the said Nicholas should stand seised in trust of the lands in question as a jointure for the proper use of the plaintiff's mother for and during her natural life, the remainder to the issue of her body, which the plaintiff only is, the remainder to the right heirs of Thomas More. These lands were in truth mortgaged by More before, and the defendant did pay him £500 of the portion, and was wrought upon by him to deliver up the articles and, for £5, to release to More the lands. And More and his wife had by a deed and a fine sold the lands away. And so to be relieved against the breach of trust was the intent of the bill.

And, for the plaintiff, it was insisted that the defendant ought to make good to the plaintiff the value of the lands ever since her mother's death, who died about twenty years since, and the full value of the lands, if to be sold (by the agreement, the lands being to come to her immediately after her mother's death).

But, for the defendant, it was insisted that, if there were a breach of trust, it was no ill intent in him, nor anything to his benefit, but to comply with the necessity of the plaintiff's father, who is still living, and, if a settlement had been made according to the articles, it might have been so awarded that he and his wife might have prevented the estate from coming to the plaintiff. And they did after[wards] sell the lands by a fine. And, however, the plaintiff's father, according to the true meaning of the articles, was to have had at least an estate for life in the lands, for it was absurd to think that the husband in marriage should settle his lands on his wife and her issue and exclude himself for life and, being mentioned in the articles, that the wife should have them for a jointure, and after[wards] to her issue, the very word 'jointure' did imply that the husband should have an estate for his life as well as the wife, and that was the usual way of settling jointures for life on the husband and then in remainder to the wife for life. And it was said that, if a bill had been brought against More to compel him to make a settlement according to the articles, the court would never have excluded him of an estate for his own life.

And, of this opinion, the Lord Keeper [Bridgeman] declared he was, as to the husband's estate for life, and that he ought to have the premises, by the intention of the agreement, for life. And, therefore, and inasmuch as £600 of this portion was agreed to be given by the defendant as a free gift of his own and it was uncertain what the value of the lands might be after the plaintiff's father's death and there was £300 of the £800 unpaid, the Lord Keeper [BRIDGEMAN] proposed that the plaintiff should have the said £300 with damages and the defendant to pay it to her accordingly. And so it was decreed.

[Later proceedings in this case: 79 Selden Soc. 533.]

305

Bluck v. Gore

(Ch. 1669)

Where a plaintiff alleges title to land by a conveyance, he need not allege the details of the conveyance.

3 Chancery Reports 28, 21 E.R. 719

Easter [term] 21 Car. II [1669].

The plaintiff alleges by the bill that M.W. and K.W., by a good and sufficient conveyance and assurance in the law, had granted to him and his heirs their third parts of the premises in question. And he prays relief against the defendant, who was in possession by a mortgage from an ancestor.

The defendant demurred, for that the plaintiff set not forth what kind of conveyance or assurances were made to him or when executed, so as the court might judge whether the plaintiff had any title. And, therefore, he demanded judgment and whether he should be called to any account for any profits, it appearing the plaintiff was never in possession.

And it was overruled.

306

Pary v. Juxon

(Ch. 1669–1670)

A trust can arise by parol.

An executor can become a trustee by the will of the testator.

A member of Convocation has the same privileges of suit as a member of Parliament.

Where a husband and his wife, in the right of the wife, exhibit a bill in equity and the husband dies, the wife may proceed in the litigation without a bill of revivor.

3 Chancery Reports 38, 21 E.R. 722

Easter [term] 21 Car. II [1669].

The bill was against the defendant, the executor of the late Archbishop Juxon.[1] And it charged that the bishop, having the next presentation to the mastership of St. Cross, did in his lifetime direct Sir William Juxon, his executor, to give it to Doctor Pary.

And, upon the hearing, the Lord Keeper [Bridgeman] directed a trial at the King's Bench bar whether it were in trust in Sir William Juxon or not.

And, at the trial in the King's Bench, the judges declared a trust might arise by parol and that the executor might become a trustee by the will of the testator, though nothing be mentioned in the written will or what is proved in the spiritual court. And the verdict there was found for Doctor Pary.

Note Doctor Pary, being a member of the Convocation, had his privilege allowed him in this suit, as a privilege in Parliament.

Nelson 135, 21 E.R. 809

The bill was against the defendant, Sir William Juxon, as executor of the late archbishop of that name. And it sets forth that he had the next presentation to the Mastership of St. Cross and that, in his lifetime, he did direct Sir William to give it to Dr. Porey.

Upon the hearing, the Lord Keeper [Bridgeman] directed a trial at law whether this was a trust in Sir William Juxon, the executor, or not.

And, at the trial, the court declared that a trust might arise by parol or that the executor might be a trustee by the will of the testator, though it was not mentioned in the written will. And a verdict was found for Dr. Porey.

2 Freeman 132, 22 E.R. 1108

He [Dr. Pery] had his privilege allowed in a suit depending in Chancery as a member of the Convocation, the same with the privilege of Parliament.

3 Chancery Reports 40, 21 E.R. 722

It has been judged, where a plaintiff and his wife in the right of the wife, exhibited a bill and the husband died, the wife, if she please, may proceed without a bill of revivor.

[It was] so adjudged in the Commissioners' time, *ex relatione Magistri Amhurst.*

And, therefore, Dr. Pary's wife went on, notwithstanding the death of her husband.

[Other reports of this case: 1 Eq. Cas. Abr. 1, 21 E.R. 828.]

[1] B. Quintrell, 'Juxon, William (bap. 1582, d. 1663), archbishop of Canterbury', *Oxford Dictionary of National Biography*, vol. 30, pp. 848–852.

307

Witham v. Witham

(Ch. 1669)

A public rudeness to an officer of the Court of Chancery is punishable as a contempt of court.

3 Chancery Reports 41, 21 E.R. 723

4 May 1669.

The plaintiff moved to commit the defendant, for that, when the plaintiff told him he came to serve him with an order from the Master of the Rolls, the defendant said 'the Master of the Rolls [can] kiss my arse'.

But the Master of the Rolls [GRIMSTON] only ordered a [writ of] attachment for the familiarity, but said he believed the Lord Keeper would have committed him.

308

Hele v. Stowell

(Ch. 1669)

Where a widow acts in good faith under a will that was afterwards proved to have been revoked, any legacies paid by her will be allowed, but she must account for all profits received by her and any second husband.

Lincoln's Inn MS. Hill 125, f. 55v [bis]

8 May 21 Car. II.

Hugh Stowel, father of the plaintiff, devised his lands to his wife for her life with a power to make leases for one, two, or three lives. And, after[ward], he revoked the will. And he died, leaving his wife, the defendant, *enceinte* with the plaintiff. The wife, having no notice of the revocation etc., enters of the lands, pays debts [and] legacies, and makes leases and takes fines of the lessees to a full value. And then she marries, and her husband takes the profits, before the age of fourteen of the plaintiff, and continues to take them until his age of nineteen. The husband dies. The plaintiff, as heir, sues for an account. And he is decreed to have an account.

First, [it was] decreed that the legacies paid by the wife, if she had no notice of the revocation of the will, ought to be allowed in her account. And [it was] so decreed because [there was] no proof of notice. It was only proved that she had notice before payment that her husband had made a later will, but not what it was. But, if she had had notice of the revocation, the Lord Keeper [BRIDGEMAN] said he would have given other directions touching the account.

Second, she was to give an account as guardian in socage of what her husband received after the marriage though her husband was dead.

But whether she should account for the profits received by her husband after fourteen, when her title as guardian ended and the husband chargeable as bailiff [?], the Lord Keeper [BRIDGEMAN] would advise because that was a new title. But he seemed to incline she should because [it] but continued her possession.

Third, [there was] no allowance of the leases though p[. . .] by the revoked will etc. and though she had covenanted for enjoyment and [was] liable thereby to the lessees.

1 Chancery Cases 126, 22 E.R. 725

8 May [1669].

The husband devised his lands to his wife during the minority of his son, and dies, and has only a posthumous son, and, by his will, gives his wife a power to make leases to raise money to pay debts etc. The wife enters, and takes the profits, and then marries a second husband, and he lives some years, and takes the profits, and dies. And the wife continues to take the profits of such part of the land as she had not let, for she did let some part according to the will. This son attains his age, and proves a revocation of the will, and prays his mother may account.

It was ordered that she shall account for all the profits that herself or her husband took. And the reason was that she should be said to take them until the infant was fourteen years of age as guardian and after[wards] as bailiff. And she was to answer as to what her husband took, as in a *devastavit*.

The wife, having no notice of the revocation, had paid legacies charged on the lands by will. It was ordered that she be allowed those. But, as for the leases she had made, though they were for fines and full rents, though she offered to account for the fines and rents, the court would not make them good, because the mother could not set or let lands.

309

Holcomb v. Rivers

(Ch. 1669)

There is no jus accrescendi *among merchants.*

An action of account lies against an administrator or executor of a deceased factor.

An action of account can be barred by laches.

Where account books have been lost, an account can be proved by the oath of the accountant.

1 Chancery Cases 127, 22 E.R. 726

10 May [1669]. Holstcomb v. Rivers.

The defendant and one Collins were factors for the plaintiff in Spain before 1654. In that year, they sent him to London on account and charged themselves with divers goods of the plaintiff in specie. In 1656, there happened an embargo on English ships and goods in Spain and a seizure of all the goods in the defendant's and Collins' hands and on their books, and the defendant was cast in prison on that account.

And the bill was now to call the defendant to an account, Collins being dead, without making his executrix a party.

For the defendant, it was insisted that, by reason of the seizure and imprisonment, he could not account, having lost his books and never seen them since, and that the plaintiff had been twice over with Collin's executrix and she was no party and that, after this length of time, it would be hard to draw the defendant to an original account.

By the court, it was resolved for law that, though *inter mercatores jus accrescendi* has no place, yet the surviving factor was to account for what was made by himself or a co-factor. And yet it was agreed that, in this case, an account lies against the executrix of the dead factor. And so it was ordered that, in respect of the length of time since the account was sent and there was no clear proof of any exception to it until after the seizure and that, when the account was sent over, the plaintiff was written to to send his exceptions speedily, if any he had, that the account should not be ravelled into. But they ordered the defendant to account for and satisfy what had been made by sale of the goods remaining in specie in the former account before the seizure. But, in regard of the length of time and the loss of the books, which the defendant had sworn by his answer, it was ordered that the defendant should not be charged in this account for more than, according to his own oath, what was made or he did remember or believe was made by the sale of those goods.

And, with these directions, it was referred to merchants to take the account, who made a direction tending to draw a harder direction from the court upon the defendant in the way of his accounting.

Whereupon His Lordship [BRIDGEMAN] appointed to rehear the cause, and the same was, accordingly, re-heard by him, assisted by Mr. Justice RAINSFORD, and Mr. Justice WILDE. And, upon long debate, the former order was confirmed.

Nelson 139, 21 E.R. 810

The defendant and one Collins were factors for the plaintiff in Spain before the year 1654. And, in that year, they sent him an account to London, in which they charged themselves with several of the plaintiff's goods remaining there in specie. Afterwards, *viz.* in the year 1656, there happened to be an embargo on English ships and goods which were in Spain. And all those goods were seized, and the defendants were imprisoned.

And now, Collins being dead, a bill was exhibited against the defendant, being the other surviving factor, to have an account of those goods, to which bill, the executrix of the dead man was not made a party.

It was insisted for the defendant that, by reason of the said seizure and imprisonment, he could not account, having lost his books in the seizure and never seen them since and that he had been twice in England with the executrix of Collins since the embargo and that she was made no party and that, in this length of time, it would be hard to draw him into an original account.

The court declared and resolved for law that, though, amongst merchants, *jus accrescendi* has no place, yet the surviving factor is to account for what was made or received by himself or a co-factor. And yet it was agreed in this case that an account lies against the executrix of the dead factor.

And it was ordered that, since there was no exception to the account which was sent thither nor any until after the seizure, that, therefore, the defendant should only account for and satisfy what had been made by the sale of the goods in the former account before the seizure and that he should not be charged for more than what upon his own oath he should declare to have made.

Lord Nottingham, *Prolegomena*, p. 269

Holcomb v. Rives.

Ryves and Collins were joint factors for Holcomb in Spain. Ryves sends an account, which remained two years with Holcomb without exception. Afterwards, in 1653, the account books were seized by the embargo in Spain and lost. Ryves returns. Holcomb continues in trade with Collins, the other factor, until his death. And then, in 1660, he exhibits a bill against Ryves for an account.

[It was] ruled: first, no account [was due] for anything since the embargo; second, in the account for matters before the embargo, the defendant's own oath is to discharge him without proof.

[Other reports of this case: 1 Eq. Cas. Abr. 5, 21 E.R. 831.]

310

Pratt v. Colt

(Ch. 1669)

The question in this case was whether an heir who inherited land is liable for his ancestor's debts.

1 Chancery Cases 128, 22 E.R. 726

11 May [1669].

The plaintiff had a judgment against George Holt, and he brought his bill against his heir to subject certain lands, which he had a decree of this court for upon a trust for his father and his heirs, to satisfy his debt.

And the defendant demurred.

And this demurrer was allowed. And the Lord Keeper [Bridgeman] conceived it all one with Bennet and Box's Case.[1]

But *quaere*, since the Statute of Frauds and Perjuries.[2]

2 Freeman 139, 22 E.R. 1114

Colt's father had given a [confessed] judgment to the plaintiff, Sir George Pratt, for £1000, and Colt's father had the trust of the fee of £300 *per annum*, which descended to the defendant, his son and heir, who sued the trustee in this court, and had the estate in law conveyed to him. And now Sir George Pratt would by the aid of this court extend those lands by this judgment.

And it was argued that, if this had been a term for years and the trust had come to the executor, it had been assets in equity, and so, in this case, where the defendant claims as heir.

The defendant demurred to this bill.

And the Lord Keeper [Bridgeman] ruled the demurrer good. And, for reason, he said the executor claimed *in autre droit*, but the heir to his own use.

But note that this has not been taken to be a good demurrer by the old and best practicers, as little according with good reason, for the heir at law is as much chargeable with the ancestor's judgment as the executor with the testator's debts. And so equity ought to follow the law, and the above-said difference is immaterial.

311

Neville v. Bambridge

(Ch. 1669)

A settlement of a claim cannot be unilaterally revoked.

Lincoln's Inn MS. Hill 125, f. 55 [bis], pl. 1

11 May 1669.

[There was a] suit to relieve an ancient mortgage. The order and decree was entered as made by the consent of the defendant to take £3 10s. *per annum* for damages or interest until a certain time. The defendant made oath.

And Sergeant *Fountaine*, Mr. *Peck*, and others of the defendant's counsel averred to the court that they consented not, and moved for damages as in other cases.

It was strongly pressed several days.

---

[1] *Bennet v. Box* (Ch. 1662–1664), see above, Case No. 68.

[2] Stat. 29 Car. II, c. 3, s. 5 (*SR*, V, 840).

Lord Keeper [Bridgeman]: I have advised with judges. They and myself hold it inconvenient to change or recede and that [would be an] evil precedent if it should be permitted. And the judge of the court where the cause was heard affirms the consent. And, therefore, he would not alter the order.

312

Meek v. Hyde

(Ch. 1669)

A devise to charitable uses can be enforced even though the will was never found or admitted to probate.

Herne & Duke 110

John Meek, clerk, seised in fee of divers messuages and lands in East Smithfield, in St. Katherine's, and Aldgate in Middlesex, by his last will in writing, dated in November 1665, did give £100 *per annum* forever to ten poor scholars to be chosen out of the Free School of Worcester and placed and educated in Magdalen Hall in Oxford, to wit, to each of them £10 and what his lands should fall short of £100 *per annum* should be supplied out of his personal estate by his executors and, if the rents should increase, then more scholars should be elected, etc. and have £10 *per annum* apiece. And 14 February 1665[/66], he died seised of lands of the value of £84 *per annum*. This will was suppressed, and a nuncupative will set on foot by one Magwick, and *pendente lite*, letters of administration were granted to Dr. Hyde, principal of Magdalen Hall and syndic of the University of Oxford, and the nuncupative will was afterwards set aside. And one John Meek was heir at law and refused to convey the lands according to the written will, and no rent was paid but lay in the tenants' hands and Dr. Hyde, as administrator, had received £100. Which matters were proved by witnesses and found by inquisition and further that the lands and tenements ought to be settled on the chancellor, masters, and scholars of Magdalen Hall in the University of Oxford.

Whereupon, commissioners, by virtue of the Statute for Charitable Uses,[1] being of opinion that the written will was not revoked or made void, though concealed, did decree that the chancellor, masters, and scholars of the University of Oxford and their successors should forever then after stand seised of the said lands and tenements and should receive the rents and pay them over to Magdalen Hall to the uses in the will and that the heir should be forever excluded and debarred, that Dr. Hyde should, out of the money in his hands, lay out £320 in the purchase of so much land as would make the lands whereof Mr. Meek died seised £100 *per annum* and £41 to make up the arrears of the £100 *per annum* for three years, and that the lands to be purchased should be settled as the other

[1] Stat. 43 Eliz. I, c. 4 (*SR*, IV, 968–970).

lands were, and that the tenants should pay the remaining rents in their hands to the University for the purposes aforesaid and should deliver the possession of the lands to the University, and that leases should be made for twenty-one years in possession, and that the will should be performed.

To which decree, Christopher Meek put in exceptions:

First, that the decree was *felo de se*, for that the inquisition found that he was heir to John Meek and that he made a will but did not find that ever any such will was produced or was ever seen after the death of John Meek, and so the decree was grounded upon the imaginations of jurors and fancies of commissioners without ground for *omne testamentum morte consummatum est*, so [it is] no will until after his death and, if any, annihilatory and revocable, *in articulo mortis* and of no effect and was not his will in propriety of speech or legal understanding until his death;

Second, that John Meek made no such will but died intestate, and the lands descended to the exceptant;

Third, that no evidence was given to the jurors but depositions taken in the prerogative court, which was no evidence at law or equity;

Fourth, that the jurors did not find that John Meek died seised in fee, and so nothing could pass by the pretended will;

Fifth, that the decree was grounded upon a void and insignificant inquisition;

Sixth, that the commissioners have determined a right and set up an estate in a corporation no way at all concerned, mentioned, or intended by John Meek in the pretended will, *viz.* the chancellor etc., and they to stand seised to the use of a hall, being no corporation or body politic capable in law or equity to receive the lands without any respect of any right or foundership or visitation, which at least ought to have been reserved and saved to the exceptant as heir at law and others of his blood ought to have been preferred in the elections; and the commissioners had forever barred his heirs of all demand in case of breach of trust in the University;

Seventh, they ought not to have decreed the £320 to purchase lands etc.

To which the respondents answer:

First, that the inquisition and decree were well warranted by the Statute;

Second, that in the inquisition, sufficient matter did appear of truth, fact, and right, whereby the commissioners might bar the exceptant, although the will was not produced nor proved to be seen after his death;

Third, that it was proved to the jurors that John Meek made such a will in writing, as in the inquisition is mentioned, and that John Meek, a little before his death, declared that he had not altered nor would alter that will;

Fourth, and that Jonathan Magwick did embezzle the will; and the exceptant did say that his uncle did tell him that he had made his will and had given his land to Magdalen Hall for the maintenance of poor scholars and had promised to settle the lands accordingly.

And divers other answers were given to the exceptions.

And, on the 26th of June, 21 Car. II [1669], the matter was heard before the late Lord Keeper BRIDGEMAN, and His Lordship having heard the exceptions and answers and what was alleged on either side, His Lordship, being fully satisfied that there was such a will made by the testator and the decree made thereon, saw no cause to reverse the decree and therefore confirmed the same.

Public Record Office C.33/232, f. 976

29 June 1669.

Christopher Meeke, exceptant; James Hyde, M.D., *ex parte* Master and Scholars of Oxford University for Magdalen Hall in the same university, respondents.

The matter upon the exceptions taken by the exceptant to a decree made by commissioners upon the Statute of Charitable Uses coming this present day to be heard and debated in the presence of the counsel learned on both sides, the substance of the inquisition taken by virtue of the said commission appeared to be that John Meeke, clerk, late of Popler in the County of Middlesex, deceased, being seised in his demesne as of fee of and in several messuages, lands, and tenements in East Smithfield in the county aforesaid in November 1665 did make his will in writing in two sheets of paper and published the same in the presence of divers credible witnesses whereby he did devise £100 *per annum* forever to ten poor scholars to be taken out of Worcester School and placed in Magdalen Hall in Oxford at £10 apiece and they to enjoy the same for seven years and then others to be chosen and what his said lands should fall short of that sum the same to be made up out of his personal estate and that in February 1665[/66] the said John Meeke died seised as aforesaid of lands to the yearly value of £84 in the possession of Richard Sturges and John Curtis and also possessed of a considerable personal estate, all debts and disbursements being discharged, that afterwards the administration of the same was granted to the respondent Dr. Hyde on the behalf of the charity *pendente lite* a nuncupative will having been set on foot by one Magwick and opposed by the respondent, and it further appeared by the said inquisition that the said exceptant is heir at law to the said donor and that the said tenants were in arrear three years at Christmas last, *viz.* Sturgis £138 and Curtis £114 and that so much ought to be taken out of the personal estate as will purchase £16 *per annum* to supply the said lands and make up £100 *per annum* forever to be settled on the said chancellor, masters, and scholars for the use of the said poor scholars and Hall forever.

And upon opening the said decree made by the said commissioners and grounded on the said inquisition whereby the said chancellor, masters, and scholars are decreed to stand seised of the premises as aforesaid and that the said respondent Hyde shall lay out £320 of the personal estate in his hands to purchase lands to make up the said sum £100 *per annum* forever and that he do dispose of £48 to make up the arrears £100 *per annum* for three years and that he shall be discharged in so doing and that the said exceptant shall be forever debarred of all claims and demands of and to the same. The exceptant's counsel insisting that there did nothing appear to the jurors to find that the testator made such a will for that the same was never seen or read by any person after the said Meek's death neither in truth was there ever any such will but the said John Meeke died intestate and the same premises ought to descend to the said exceptant as his heir.

Upon long debate of the matter and hearing of the proofs in the cause read and what was alleged on either side, His Lordship [BRIDGEMAN] being fully satisfied there was such a will made by the said testator and there being a decree made thereon, he saw no cause to reverse the same in any part and does therefore think fit and so order and decree that the said decree and all the matters and things therein contained shall stand confirmed by the decree of this court. And in order to the execution thereof, His Lordship does further order and decree that the said respondents shall forthwith lay out the said sum of £320 out of the donor's personal estate to purchase lands or rents to make up the premises devised £100 *per annum* and that, when there shall be lands and rents so purchased, that then the said exceptant shall make a conveyance of the fee of the premises devised by the said will to the said chancellor, masters, and scholars and their successors for the use of Magdalen Hall forever and that the said chancellor, masters, and scholars shall at the same time make back a lease of the same premises devised as also of the lands and rents to be purchased to the said exceptant for forty-one years at £100 *per annum* clear yearly rent without any deductions whatsoever to the end what overvalue after the expiration of the lease or leases in being will arise out of the said premises the same in gratification may redound to the said exceptant who is the heir at law to the said donor.

And it is further ordered and decreed that the arrears due not only before but since the said commissioners' decree now remaining in the hands of the said Richard Sturgis and John Curtis as also all rents that shall accrue before the making of such new lease shall be paid to the chancellor, master, and scholars for the use of Magdalen Hall aforesaid according to the said commissioner's decree and to the uses therein directed and that the said Sturgis and Curtis do pay the said arrears and growing rents accordingly and that the said respondent shall continue in his hands £8 out of Meeke's personal estate to make up the arrears for [the] half year ending at Midsummer now last past £100 *per annum*, and it is hereby referred to Sir Justinian Lewin, knight, etc., to settle the said conveyance and lease and to take care that the said rent of £100 *per annum* be clearly reserved as aforesaid and that the said lease do contain such covenants, provisos, and reservations as other leases of this nature usually have and contain.

313

Wood v. Saunders

(Ch. 1669)

A remainder of a trust of a term limited after another person's dying without an heir is void.

Pollexfen 35, 86 E.R. 503

1 July, 21 Car. II.

Edward Saunders, having issue, John, Edward, and the defendant Nicholas, and being possessed of several bullaries of salt water for several terms of years, by two deeds, assigned the same to Thomas Watts and others in trust for himself for sixty years if he so long lived and, after his death, in trust for Elizabeth, his wife, for sixty years if she so long lived and, afterwards, as to part thereof in trust for John, his son, in case he survived Edward, the father, and Elizabeth for the residue of the terms, and he directs the trustees to assign to John accordingly, and, if John die in the lifetime of the father and before assignment, having a son, then, to assign the whole term to his eldest son, and, if no son to his daughter, if any, and, if John die without issue before assignment or having issue, if his issue die before assignment, then, in trust for Edward, the son, and the heirs of his body, and, for default of such issue, in trust for the defendant Nicholas for the residue of the term, and, as to the residue after the deaths of Edward, the father, and Elizabeth in trust for Edward, the son, in case he survive Edward, the father, and Elizabeth for all the residue of the terms. And he directs the trustees, upon request, to assign the same accordingly and, if Edward, the son, before assignment die, having issue, then, to assign to his eldest son, if any, and, if none, to his daughters, and, if Edward, the son, die without issue and before assignment or, having issue and his issue die before assignment, then, the trustees to permit John and the heirs of his body and, for want thereof, to Nicholas and the heirs of his body and, for want thereof, to the executors etc. of Edward, the son, to hold the same during the residue of the terms.

John died without issue in the lifetime of Edward, his father, and Elizabeth. And, then, Edward, the father, and Elizabeth died, and Edward, the son, survived them and entered and enjoyed the whole. And he died before any assignment was made to him, without issue, intestate. And administration of his estate was granted to the plaintiff, Elizabeth, his relict, who married the other plaintiff, Simon Wood.

the question [was] whether the trusts of the terms did belong to Simon Wood and Elizabeth, his wife, as administratrix of Edward Saunders, the son, or to Nicholas Saunders, either as administrator of Edward Saunders, the father, and John Saunders or by the remainders limited to him in the trusts *prout*.

The Lord Keeper [Bridgeman], assisted by Mr. Justice Twysden, Mr. Justice Rainsford, and Mr. Justice Wilde, agreed in opinion, and declared that, the estate limited to John being but in the nature of a contingency, no estate ever vested in him and that Wood and his wife, as administratrix of Edward, the son, were well entitled to the trusts of all the term. And he decreed the same accordingly.

1 Vernon 304, 23 E.R. 485

Where the trust of a term was limited to the husband for life, remainder to the wife for life, with a remainder to their eldest son, and, if he died leaving issue, then, to that issue, but, in case he should happen to die in the lifetime of the husband or wife without issue, then the remainder over was limited to another son of the husband and wife.

And this remainder, by the advice of the judges, was held to be good, the remainder to the eldest son being but a contingency.

Lord Nottingham, *Prolegomena*, p. 228

July 1669, 21 Car. II.

There was the famous case where a long lease was assigned in trust for the father if he live so long, then to the mother if she so long live, then to John the [eldest] son and his executors if he survive the father and mother, but, if [he] die in their lives having issue and the issue be living at the death of the father and mother, then to such issue, but, if he die without issue, living the father and mother, or, having issue, he and his issue die living the father and mother, then to Edward, a second son, in tail, and, for default of such issue, then to Nicholas, a third son, in tail etc. John dies intestate and without issue. Then the father and mother die. Edward enters and receives the profits, and, dying intestate without issue, his wife, Elizabeth, takes out administration to him. Nicholas, the third brother, takes out administration to John, and also procures the trustees to assign to him.

But it was decreed for the administratrix of Edward. First, the remainder to Nicholas was absolutely void; so he could claim nothing in his own right. Second, neither could he claim anything as administrator to John, for the limitation to John was merely on a contingency which never happened, so nothing vested in John, nor, by consequence, his administrator. Third, the remainder to Edward was good, because, though the whole term might have vested in John or his issue if the contingency had happened, yet that never happening and the contingency being to wear out in so short a time as two lives, *viz.* of the father and mother, the remainder was good, by the unanimous [opinion] of Lord BRIDGEMAN, Keeper, TWYSDEN, and RAINSFORD.

Dodd 43

Decreed by Bridgeman.

A trust of a term limited to A. for ninety-nine years, if he lived so long, remainder to B. for ninety-nine years if he lived so long, remainder to C. for life and, if C. died without issue in the lifetime of A. and B., the remainder over was adjudged to be a good remainder.

1 Chancery Cases 131, 22 E.R. 728

1 July [1669]. The Lord Keeper, Justices Twysden, Rainsford, Wilde.

A long term of years was assigned upon a trust to permit the father to receive the profits for sixty years if he live so long and, after his death, to permit the mother, his wife, to receive the profits for sixty years if she so long live and, after the death of the father and mother, to permit John, the son, his executor, etc. in case he survive his father and mother, to receive the rents etc., and the trustees, at the request of John, after the death of his father and mother, should assign to him, his executors, etc., but, if John die in the lifetime of his father and mother and leave issue, which shall be living at the death of his father and mother, then, the trustees to assign the premises to such son of John which shall be his eldest son at that time etc., but, if John die without issue before any such assignment, then the trustees shall permit Edward, another son of the said father and mother, and the heirs of his body and, in default of such issue, Nicholas, a third son of the same father and mother, and the heirs of his body and, for default of such issue, the executors etc. of Nicholas to receive the profits of the premises during the term to their own uses. John dies intestate in the life of his father and mother and without issue, and, before any assignment, the father and mother die. Edward, the son, enters and receives the profits, and dies intestate without issue. Elizabeth, his wife, takes administration, enters, and receives the profits. Nicholas, the third son, takes administration to John, his brother, and procures the trustees to assign to him.

The question was who has a right to this lease, whether Nicholas, the administrator of John (who died in his father's life), or the administrator of Edward, who enjoyed during life, or Nicholas, the third son, in his own right.

It was unanimously resolved that, where the trust of a term is to one for life, the remainder for life, the remainder to a third person for the whole term if he outlive the tenants for life, the remainder to another as heir to Edward, the son, and the heirs of his body, that the remainder to the third person, *viz.* John, being merely contingent, was not so vested in him as that his executors could have it, he dying before his father and mother. And the contingency not happening, he dying in the life of the tenant for life, the remainder over to Edward was well limited after such a contingent remainder.

Vide, as to this point, the Case of the Duke of Norfolk.[1]

[1] *Howard v. Duke of Norfolk* (1681), 1 Vernon 163, 23 E.R. 388, 3 Chancery Cases 1, 22 E.R. 931, 2 Swanston 454, 36 E.R. 690, Pollexfen 223, 86 E.R. 568, 2 Chancery Reports 229, 21 E.R. 665, 2 Freeman 72, 80, 22 E.R. 1066, 1070, 79 Selden Soc. 904, 922, 999, Dodd 42, Oxford Bodleian Library MS. Rawlinson C.347.

314

Vachel v. Vachel

(Ch. 1669)

In this case, the legacy in issue passed specific items to the ultimate legatee with a right to the decedent's widow to use them during her life.

1 Chancery Cases 129, 22 E.R. 727

1 July [1669]. The Lord Keeper, Justice Twysden, Justice Wilde, Justice Rainsford.

Tanfield Vachel, by his last will in writing, devised to the effect following, *viz.*:

> I give the use of all my several paintings and books of print, my colored collection of medals in gold, silver, and brass; all my rare turnings of ivory and guaiacum, with my press of books, and chest of drawers with the perspective in it, to my dearly beloved wife [the defendant, Rebeccah Vachel] during the term of her natural life. And my will is that, if she be with child of a son, that then after her decease, the same paintings, books of print, etc. shall be left, remain, and come to the same son. But, if my wife be not with child of a son or if the same son shall die without issue male of his body, then my will is that all the said paintings, books of print, etc., after the decease of my said wife and the death of such son as my wife is now with child of, shall come and remain to the use of Thomas Vachel [the father of the plaintiff], of which my will is that the said Thomas Vachel shall have the use only during his life and that he leave them to my kinsman Thomas Vachel, his son [the plaintiff], and that he shall, as far as in him lies, so dispose thereof to him that shall by God's blessing next succeed himself in my manors and lands in the County of Berkshire, that they remain as an heirloom and go and remain to such person and persons as shall inherit my said manors and lands, who I desire may prove lovers of learning, ingenuity, and arts.

Which clause, the defendants insisting to be revoked by a codicil and the matter, as to that point, having been fully heard, His Lordship [Bridgeman], having had the opinion of the civilians therein, did on the first of May last declare his judgment to be that the use of the aforesaid rarities was well settled by the will of the said testator upon the plaintiff Thomas Vachel after the death of the said defendant Rebeccah Vachel and not revoked.

But the defendants' counsel then insisting that, though they were admitted to be agreeable to the civil law, yet, the very limitation in the clause of the will of the rarities to the plaintiff was void by the common law, His Lordship [Bridgeman], for the defendants' farther satisfaction, declared he would have the opinion of the Lords, the judges therein, upon that single point of the limitation of the rarities, whether the same were a good or void limitation.

And the cause now standing in the paper for a determination in that point, His Lordship [BRIDGEMAN] declared he had advised with the Lords, the judges, and now assisted with Mr. Justice RAINSFORD and Mr. Justice WILDE, upon deliberate consideration had of the clause aforesaid in the will whereby the use of the rarities are devised to the plaintiff after the death of the said Rebeccah Vachel and, forasmuch as the said Thomas Vachel, the plaintiff's father, died in the lifetime of the said Tanfield, and the defendant Rebeccah being not with child of a son, so as the contingencies upon which the limitation was made never happening, His Lordship with the Lords, the judges, were all clear of opinion that the devise to the said Thomas Vachel, the son, was an absolute devise, and good in law, and that the defendant Rebeccah Vachel ought only to have the use of the said rarities during her life only, and the plaintiff is to have the same after her death, according to the said will. And he does order and decree the same accordingly and that the defendant be examined upon interrogatories for the discovery of the particulars of the rarities and matters so devised and that an inventory of the said rarities be made according to the said order of the first of May.

And, as touching security now prayed by the plaintiff's counsel and other matters for the final completing of this decree, the court declared that the same was not the proper business of this day and they would not now determine the matter, but leave the plaintiff to move this court therein, and, then, such farther order shall be made as shall be just.

Lincoln's Inn MS. Misc. 12, p. 52, pl. 2

A man gives his son 1s. by his will, and declares he should have no other advantage out of his estate but what he had given him by the will. And he having made no disposition of the surplus of his personal estate, the son brought his bill for his distributive share thereof.

And it was decreed to him by the late Master of the Rolls.

But, upon an appeal to the House of Lords, that decree was reversed.

315

Hilliard v. Leicester

(Ch. 1669)

The question in this case was whether a demurrer lies to a bill of discovery on the ground that the defendant has no legal interest in the dispute.

3 Chancery Reports 27, 21 E.R. 718

Trinity [term] 21 Car. II [1669]. Baron Turner.

The plaintiff's wife being the daughter of one Constable and his heir, she married the defendant's father, who is dead. And the land being descended to her, she and the plaintiff brought a bill, and alleged that the defendant Leicester claimed some estate in reversion after her death and had levied a fine to the other persons, who had brought a *quid juris clamat* against her. And, therefore, they prayed a discovery of what settlements were made, that he might know whether to plead an estate in fee or for life to the *quid juris clamat* and to what uses and to what considerations the fine was levied.

The defendant demurred, for that the defendant had not a sufficient title whereby the court could make a decree as touching the fine.

316

Parry v. Parry

(Ch. 1669)

A defendant can deny that the plaintiff is entitled to equitable relief by either a plea or a demurrer.

Gray's Inn MS. 35, p. 622, pl. 1

Trinity vacation 1669.

An answer was put in, which denied all the suggestions of the bill on which relief in equity was to be founded, and then a demurrer as to relief.

It was moved strongly by *Hecke*, junior, that it ought to have been pleaded by a demurrer, and not an answer and demurrer, for a demurrer is properly to what is contained in the bill or to what is brought in by a plea, which was agreed to be the formal way.

But for that Serjeant *Fountaine* and Mr. *Churchill* did agree that it had been allowed both ways, it was allowed by Lord Keeper BRIDGEMAN at Essex House on the demurrer.

317

Nurse v. Guillem

(Ch. 1669)

A plaintiff can give evidence under oath of a defendant's contempt of court.

2 Freeman 132, 22 E.R. 1108

Michaelmas [term] 1669. Lord Bridgeman.

Nurse was examined as a witness, though plaintiff, to prove the service of a decree.

And, on debate, the deposition was allowed. And it was ruled that the plaintiff's oath was sufficient to convict the defendant of a contempt unless the defendant swear quite contrary. And, on an exception to a Master's report, the defendant was found in contempt.

3 Chancery Reports 39, 21 E.R. 722

Michaelmas [term] 1669.

Nurse was examined as a witness, though he was the plaintiff in the case, to prove the service of the decree.

And, upon debate, his deposition was allowed toward the proving the defendant in contempt. And it was then ruled that the plaintiff's oath is sufficient to convict the defendant, unless the defendant in his examination swear clear contrary, and, then, the defendant's oath being against the plaintiff's, it shall not convict the defendant. And the defendant in this cause, upon exceptions to the Master's report, was found in contempt.

[Other reports of this case: 2 Eq. Cas. Abr. 413, 22 E.R. 351.]
[Reg. Lib. 1669 B, ff. 74, 115, 136, 488.]

318

Voll v. Smith

(Ch. 1669)

A court of equity will order specific performance of a contract for the sale of land.

3 Chancery Reports 28, 21 E.R. 719

Michaelmas [term] 21 Car. II [1669], at the Rolls.

The bill is that the plaintiff agreed with the defendant for the purchase of a house for £290 to be paid, and he paid 20s. in hand, and tendered the rest at the day.

And he was relieved.

319

Glanvill v. Jennings

(Ch. 1669)

A court of equity can order a bond to be cancelled on the ground of a fraudulent inducement.

Nelson 129, 21 E.R. 807

The bill was to be relieved against two bonds, one given by the plaintiff and another by his wife. The defendant telling the plaintiff that his wife, who was his kinswoman, was a good fortune and that he would help her to the plaintiff for a wife, for which he must give him something for his pains, whereupon the plaintiff gave him a bond of £400 with a condition to pay £200 on a certain day. And, afterwards, the defendant went to the woman, and got another bond from her of the same penalty and upon the same terms. And the equity was that this was a cheat, for neither the husband nor the wife had any fortune.

But the defendant proved that the plaintiff had £1200 with his wife, and, therefore, he insisted that the bond given by him was good. But the woman being cheated, for that her husband had no estate, but was a broken merchant, her bond was ordered to be delivered up and cancelled.

3 Chancery Reports 31, 21 E.R. 720

Michaelmas [term] 21 Car. [1669]. Justice Rainsford.

The bill was to be relieved against two bonds, one given by the plaintiff and the other by his wife, to the defendant, for that the defendant told the plaintiff that the plaintiff's wife, who was the defendant's kinswoman, was a good fortune and that he would help her to the plaintiff for wife, but that, if he did, he must give the defendant something for his pains, whereupon, he sealed a bond to the defendant of £400 penalty to pay £200 absolutely. And then the defendant went to the woman, and, upon the same ground, got another bond from her for the like sum, and that the equity was that it was a chouse or fraud and that the woman had nothing, nor the man had nothing either.

But the defendant proved that the plaintiff confessed that he had £1200 with his wife and, therefore, that the bond given by him was good. But the woman being cheated, for that her husband had nothing, but was a broken merchant, her bond was decreed to be delivered up.

320

Nelthrop v. Hill

(Ch. 1669)

The question in this case was whether a legatee must make a refund where other legacies under the same will cannot be fully paid when they become payable later.

1 Chancery Cases 135, 22 E.R. 730

6 October [1669]. Nelthrop and Margaret, his wife, against Hill, Biscoe, and Anne, his wife. The Lord Keeper, Justice Wyndham, Baron Turner.

This cause was heard first before the Lord Keeper. The case [was] the plaintiff Margaret and the defendant Anne were the two daughters of Smith, who having made his will eighteen years since and Hill executor and curator of the children, both then in infancy, by his will, gave several legacies, and then he gave the residue of his personal estate to be equally divided between his two daughters, Anne and Margaret. And, if both die before marriage or full age, then, he devises it over to another. Biscoe marries Anne, the eldest sister, and, then, one moiety of the estate, which was good and in the hands of the executor, is paid to Biscoe and his wife, and Biscoe settles a jointure for this on his wife, and gives the executor a discharge. Afterwards, the executor puts out the other moiety, Margaret being still in minority, on security, and part of it is lost. Then, Margaret marries Nelthrop.

And they bring this bill against the executor and Biscoe and his wife to have a contribution towards the loss borne by them and to have Biscoe refund.

Upon the first hearing, it was so decreed, unless Biscoe showed precedents to the contrary.

Now, upon a farther hearing this day, *viz.* 10 January 1669, before the Lord Keeper [BRIDGEMAN], Mr. Justice WILDE, and Mr. Baron TURNER, it was for Biscoe insisted that, by the marriage of Anne, her moiety became due and the devise over is defeated, so that, if Biscoe and his wife had brought their bill for it, the executor could not have denied payment of it, and so Biscoe has done no default, who has not his money until it be due, and he is not concerned to look any farther. And, in lieu of the portion, a jointure is made, and a release for the legacy is given. And, probably, if the executor would not have paid, Anne might have lost her preferment. And the executor was by the will the curator of the children. And it was said that, by Anne's marriage first, she became first entitled. And it was insisted that, where legacies are payable at several times and the legacy that is first due is paid when due and there is money in the executor's hands to pay the other legacies, that, if a loss fall on that afterwards, there is equity in that case to put the first paid legatee to refund.

For the plaintiff, it was insisted that there was in this case no time limited for the payment of either and that, by the marriage of Anne, the devise over being defeated, both became due and payable, the devise being indefinite, without any express time of payment. And the plaintiff Margaret's infancy ought not to turn to her prejudice. And it was the testator's intention that they should have it equally, one as much as the other. And, if Biscoe had sued, the executor might have required security to refund.

And it was said and admitted by the court that, if executors pay out the assets in legacies and, afterwards, debts appear and they be forced to pay them of which they had no notice before the legacies were paid, that the executors, by a bill here, might force the legatees to refund.

But, as to that, it was answered that case was not like to this, for there was not enough to pay all when the legacies were paid, but here was enough when the legacies were paid to pay all, and the loss was since.

And, for the plaintiff, it was farther insisted that a division could not be made without the plaintiff Margaret called to it. And the case of Grove and Banson[1] was insisted on, where Banson had a conveyance and a statute for his wife's legacy, and yet he was put to refund.

[1] *Grove v. Banson* (Ch. 1669), see below, Case No. 331.

But, as to that case, it was answered there was not any payment, but a security, and, by that, he would have had a redemption, so this payment was not paid, but executory. And the plaintiff cited the case of Picks and Vincner[1] upon Sir Henry Martin's certificate, which was 29 October 1639 and was in substance thus, that an executor may not pay one if he has not enough to pay all and an executor is not bound to pay a legacy without security to refund if there be want of assets to pay either debts or legacies. Which there was not, as is said, to this purpose, there being at the time when this legacy was paid enough to pay all.

It was ordered the cause be set down to be re-heard originally, as well against the executor as the legatee Biscoe and his wife.

Quaere, if there be not a difference between debts and legacies thus, debts may appear to the executors, but legacies appear in the will. And *quaere* if, therefore, executors be not bound more strictly to take security against legacies that do appear than debts that do not.

321

Fry v. Porter

(Ch. 1669–1672)

A condition of a gift that the donee not marry without permission is valid and enforceable where there is a gift over, because the gift over makes it a limitation and not a condition.

Notice of a condition to a donee or the lack thereof does not affect its validity.

1 Chancery Cases 138, 22 E.R. 731

13 October [1669]. Charles Fry, Gent., and the Lady Anne, his wife, and Mountjoy Fry, an infant, by their guardian, against George Porter, an infant, by George Porter, his uncle and guardian. The Master of the Rolls. First hearing.

Mountjoy, earl of Newport, had two daughters, Isabella, who, by his consent, married Nicholas, earl of Banbury, whose daughter the plaintiff the Lady Anne is, and Anne, who, without her father's consent, married Thomas Porter, Esq., by whom she had George, the defendant, the infant.

The earl of Newport, being seised of Newport House in fee, by his will in writing, devises in these words:

> Item, I give and bequeath unto the Lady Anne, countess of Newport, my dear wife, all that my house called Newport House and all other my tenements in the County of Middlesex for her life and, from and after the death of my said wife, I do give my said house and all other my tenements in Middlesex unto my grandchild the Lady Anne Knowles, the daughter of

[1] *Vintner v. Pix* (Ch. 1637–1640), Chancery Repts. *tempore* Coventry 284.

> Nicholas, earl of Banbury, by the Lady Isabella, my late daughter, and the heirs of her body to be begotten, provided always and upon condition, that my said grandchild, the Lady Anne Knowles, do marry with the consent of my said wife and of Charles, earl of Warwick, and of Edward, earl of Manchester, or the major part of them. And, in case the Lady Anne Knowles do and shall marry without the consent of my said wife or the major part of my trustees aforesaid or shall happen to depart this life without any issue of her body, then, I will and bequeath all my said premises unto my grandchild George Porter, son of my deceased daughter, the Lady Anne, late wife of Thomas Porter, Esq., and to his heirs forever.

The plaintiff Fry, after the death of the Lord Newport, stole away the plaintiff, the Lady Anne, in the night from Newport House, where she lived with her grandmother, over the garden wall. And, so soon as she was missed by her grandmother and she was informed of this fact, she sent to the earls of Warwick and Manchester to inform them of it, who both protested against the marriage as unfitting for the young lady, who was at that time about fourteen years of age, and declared their utter dislike of it. Afterwards, these two earls, being examined for the plaintiffs as witnesses in the cause, say that they do assent to the marriage and that they do not know but that, if their consents had been asked for before the marriage, such reason might have been given as they might have consented to it. And they and other witnesses speak as to the earl of Newport's intent and frequent declarations that the plaintiff the Lady Anne should have Newport House, which the plaintiff's counsel would lay weight upon to interpret the meaning of the will to be *in terrorem* only, and not to defeat the devise to the Lady Anne.

The bill was to be relieved against the condition and the breach of it.

And, for the plaintiffs on the first hearing, which was before the Master of the Rolls only (in the Lord Keeper's absence), it was insisted on by Serjeant *Fountaine* that there were three things in equity upon which the plaintiff ought to be relieved against this penalty:

First, that there was no other reason for this condition and penalty but to prevent the Lady's marriage without consent, and, therefore, it was to be expounded *in terrorem* only;

Secondly, that this young lady was but fourteen years old, and knew nothing before her marriage of the condition;

Thirdly, as she was in her infancy and knew nothing before her marriage of the condition, so soon after as she did know it, she did go to the two earls, her grandmother being dead, and they did approve of the marriage.

For the defendant, it was insisted that the infancy or want of notice to her of the condition was of no weight, for that there was not by the will any provision made or any directions given to give her notice, but, as she takes by the will as a purchaser, so she must take it subject to such condition as the will has subjected it to, and is to take notice at her peril. And an infant may break a condition. And this act of hers in marrying was but what the earl had reason to expect she would do before she came to the age of twenty-one years, it not being usual for ladies of her quality so stay until twenty-one before they marry. And, as to the pretense that this condition was *in terrorem*, it was said that it was a limitation and that it was by the will limited over to the defendant in case of the Lady Anne's marriage without consent *pari passu* to her dying without issue. And, though the civil law may construe the limitation in a personalty over in such cases as this to be void and to be but *in terrorem*, yet, in this court, in the case of inheritances, as this is, nay even in the case of personalty, where it was limited over, as here, this court has not any time avoided such limitation over, the constant difference taken in this court being betwixt a condition to make the devise void without limiting over to another and the limiting over to another. In the first of which cases, the court has usually construed the condition to be *in terrorem* only, because there is no other person appointed to take, as in the case of Sir Henry Bellasis, now cited (which you may see before, fol. 22).[1] But, where it has been limited over, it has been always taken otherwise, as in the case of Davis against Halton, November 1664, the matter here being £1000, part of what was given to the party who broke the condition. And so, though it were for a personalty, the limitation over is good.

The Master of the Rolls [Grimston]: There is no difference in this case whether it be a condition or a limitation, for the penalty is the same in both. And this must be understood to be *in terrorem*. And the infant had no notice of the condition. And so he decreed against the defendant and that the plaintiff, the Lady, and the heirs of her body should hold and enjoy against them.

The defendant appealed from this order by a petition, and prayed the entry of it might be stayed. And it was so, and ordered to be reheard by the Lord Keeper [Bridgeman], assisted with the Lord Chief Justice Kelyng, Chief Justice Vaughan, and, Chief Baron Hale, 22 April 1670.

At which hearing, it was insisted by Serjeant *Fountaine*, for the plaintiff, that this was a penalty *in terrorem* that the daughter might not rashly marry, but she was then an infant without notice of it, and the earls do approve the marriage.

Serjeant *Maynard*, for the defendant: It is a limitation, not a condition. A will would not pass lands by the common law; it is by the Statute.[2] And that says the will shall stand. And, for notice, the law requires no notice to be given, nor did the earl, the devisor, require any. And who should give notice? The defendant is an infant, and could we give notice? *Mente testatum ratum est.*

Mr. Solicitor [General] *Finch*, for the defendant: There can be no decree, for the subsequent approbation works nothing, and was extorted by compulsion, for, when the earls were first acquainted with the marriage, they disallowed it, and the estate was divested out of the Lady by the marriage without consent. And the subsequent assent cannot revest it. The primary intention was *in terrorem*, to

---

[1] *Bellasis v. Erwin* (Ch. 1663), see above, Case No. 107.

[2] Stat. 32 Hen. VIII, c. 1 (*SR*, III, 744–746).

restrain the Lady from an imprudent disposal of herself. But the secondary intention was that, if she did marry without consent, she should lose the lands. The grandfather could not have settled it stronger than he has. And that the grandfather may impose such a condition on his children is not to be denied. And, if this court should relieve against it, it is to encourage disobedience in children to parents. And this is a case purely at law, and the matter of notice and other circumstances are all to be considered at law as well as here. And, if not relievable there, it is the same here. And, if notice is necessary, as I conceive it is not, that is purely at law. And, possibly, it may be found at one trial that there was not notice and, at another, it may be found there was notice. And it being a matter of inheritance and freehold, the defendant ought to be at liberty to try it *toties quoties*.

Serjeant *Fountaine*: A limitation may be at law, and yet be relievable here, as, if the condition lie to have the consent in writing and the consent is had without a writing, this court will help in that case. And he doubted whether a father can so provide or limit an estate as that a court of equity shall have no power over it, for it cannot be so provided by agreement of the parties in the case of a mortgage that this court shall not give relief. And equity is part of the law of England. And there are emergencies and cases which a man cannot provide for, as, suppose the plaintiffs had sent to the parties for their consent and the messenger never went but said he did and had their consent and, upon this, she had married, she should certainly be helped in equity. And the end of the will is performed. She was to marry such person as the earls should like of, and they have approved, and so the substance is performed. And whether it be a limitation or a condition is equally penal. And a limitation over of personal legacies is void by the civil law, I grant. But, in some cases of a limitation over, there may be equity; it clearly follows in this, upon the circumstances of infancy, and not notice, and assent subsequent.

The court would see precedents. And, then, 30 May 1670, upon perusal of all the precedents, the whole court agreed in one uniform opinion to dismiss the bill, and, accordingly, it was dismissed.

Chief Baron HALE argued thus: first, it is to be considered whether this be a good condition or limitation; secondly, whether any relief be to be given against it; thirdly, whether, upon the circumstances, it is relievable here.

First, he conceived it a limitation and condition both in law and equity, because it is collateral to the land. She may marry if she will. But, if it be without consent, there is a penalty.

Secondly, it is a condition, because it is to contain the party in that due obedience which law and nature oblige her. And she should have applied to her grandmother for her consent, though there had been no such condition. And, although in the civil law, in the case of a mere personalty, the limitation over is to be void, yet this is a devise of the lands not governed by that law. Estates governable by the law of this kingdom without relation to another form ought not to be influenced by another law. And this being a good condition, it cannot be in law defeated. And there being a full breach of the condition, as law will not, equity cannot help. And, as to the objection, if there may not be relief against a breach of conditions in equity, there will be a great shatter in decrees already made, this case is not like the case of a mortgage, where the condition is for the payment of money, because, there, if the money be not paid at the day, there may be a compensation made by a payment at another day with damages.

Thirdly, again, this breach is not relievable in equity, because it is a voluntary disposition throughout, both *in aequali gradu*, as to the settlement and as to the blood of him that made the settlement. And it appears by the will of the earl of Newport that made the settlement, that he did as really intend it should go over for marrying without consent as the Lady's dying without issue. And he rests much on it that there is no precedent of any relief given in this case, for, upon a view of all the precedents, he does not think any of them come to this case, and it is not fit to go further than the court has gone already, for, if they should, there would be no end, and it is fit to set bounds. And, as to what was offered from the proof, that it was the earl's intention that the Lady should have Newport House and that, therefore, it was *in terrorem*, he said that no collateral averment to expound the will ought to be admitted, for, if there should, there would be no certainty in any case. And, as to the earl's approving the marriage since, he said they were charitable therein and, though equity will favor infants, yet an infant may be bound by law to a performance of a condition. And, inasmuch as this condition is annexed to an act, marriage, which she, as an infant, might do, the infancy will not help. And, as to the point of notice, I will not determine here whether notice be requisite and necessary, for that is at law, and the want of it, if necessary, will avail there. I will not say what equity may do in a case of a want of notice, but that fact is not settled whether notice or not. It would be hard, because there is not full notice proved, to conclude here is no notice. And so he would have the bill dismissed.

Kelyng agreed, and said it is fit to keep those bonds which parents impose to hold their children at obedience strait and it is not fit for a court of equity to relax them.

Vaughan: As to the consent subsequent, that signifies nothing, for a man cannot be said to consent to a thing which is not capable of consent, as to say a man consents that his heir is of such a color is nonsense, for that is not an object of his consent. And, after the marriage, their consents signify no more in that case.

The Lord Keeper [Bridgeman] declared he was clear of opinion that equity ought not to interpose in this case, and was glad to see that a parent could settle his estate that it might be out of the power of a court of equity. And so the bill was dismissed.

Note that, upon a trial and an argument after this hearing in the King's Bench, it was adjudged that notice was not necessary to be given.

2 Chancery Reports 26, 21 E.R. 606

The earl of Newport, deceased, by his will, devised to the plaintiff, the Lady Anne, the messuage called Newport House with the appurtenances thus, *viz.*

> I do give and bequeath unto the Lady Anne, countess of Newport, my dear wife, all that my house called Newport House and all other my tenements and hereditaments whatsoever in Middlesex for her life and, after her decease, I do give and bequeath the said house and all other my tenements and hereditaments, as aforesaid, to my grandchild, the Lady Anne Knowles, the daughter of Nicholas, earl of Banbury, by the Lady Isabella, my late daughter, and to the heirs of her body lawfully to be begotten, provided always and upon condition that my said grandchild, the Lady Anne Knowles, do marry with the consent of my said wife and of Charles, earl of Warwick, and Edward, earl of Manchester, or the major part of them. And in case the said Lady Anne Knowles do and shall marry without the consent of my said wife and the major part of my trustees aforesaid or shall happen to depart this life without any issue of her body, then I will and bequeath all the said premises unto my grandson, George Porter, son of my deceased daughter, the Lady Anne, late wife of Thomas Porter, Esq., and to his heirs forever.

The bill is to be relieved against the forfeiture of the said estate for not performing the said condition in the will and marrying against the consent of the trustees and the mother. Yet the said mother was told that the plaintiff was about to marry, and said nothing to the contrary; whereupon, the plaintiff married and has issue. The plaintiff insisting that, if any error was committed in marrying, it was through ignorance and not obstinacy, she, the plaintiff, being very young, and knew not of the proviso or condition in the said will. And it would be very unreasonable to make the happiness of the plaintiff to depend upon the consent of strangers in the point of marriage, to put it into their power to keep her during her life, either from marrying or from her estate, and thereby make them masters of her affection or fortune, and to disinherit her and her children.

But the defendant insists that the reason of inserting the said proviso into the said will was that the plaintiff, the Lady Anne, might be disposed of in marriage without disparagement, and, therefore, that she should marry with the consent of the said countess and the two earls or the major part of them and of that other clause, *viz.* that, if she married without such consent, then he gave the said house and premises to the said defendant, George Porter, the infant, and his heirs forever, and that the said Lady Anne having married a person very unequal to her fortune and without such consent, as aforesaid, having little or no estate, had made a willful breach of the said proviso or condition in the said grandfather's will. And the said George Porter claims the said house to him and his heirs by virtue of the said condition and limitation over to him by the said will, the construction whereof is to be made out of the will itself, and not otherwise. And the said Lady Anne had notice of the said will before the marriage, there being discourse of it by the trustees to her. And so the Lady Anne ought not to be relieved against the said forfeiture or limitation aforesaid.

This court, with the judges, and on a perusal of precedents, are clear of opinion and fully satisfied that the plaintiff ought not to be relieved against the said forfeiture and that the same was such as ought not to be relieved in equity. And they dismissed the plaintiff's bill.

Gray's Inn MS. 35, p. 655, pl. 2

Easter term 1670.

The case was the earl of Newport, by his will in writing, devises the reversion of Newport House to W., a married infant, his grandchild, and her heirs on condition she married with her grandmother's consent, and, if she did not, then to two other married infants, his grandchildren, and their heirs. The first devisee married to Fry, the plaintiff, she being under age and without the consent of her grandmother. After the marriage, the grandmother did consent. The other two grandchildren married the other two defendants, Porter [and Porter], who by [an action of] ejectment recovered the house.

Fry and his wife exhibited their bill in Chancery to be relieved against the judgment at law.

And, upon a hearing of the cause before the Master of the Rolls, *viz.* Sir Harbottle Grimston, it was agreed for the plaintiffs, and a perpetual injunction was granted.

On appeal to the Lord Keeper Bridgeman, the case was several times argued before him and before Kelyng, Chief Justice of the King's Bench, Vaughan, Chief Justice of the Common Bench, and Hale, Chief Baron of the Exchequer, whom he called to his assistance. And, upon a solemn argument by all four *seriatim*, the bill was dismissed, and the injunction was dissolved. Their reason were [as follows].

First, the conditions to be performed by the first devisee were no more than by the law of nature ought to be performed, she being a natural parent as grandmother that was to consent and see her grandchild disposed of in marriage. And that differenced this case from other conditions of payments of moneys etc., which are relievable in this court, for, there, the moneys to be paid is the only scope of the condition, and, on the performance thereof with interest, though not at the precise time, in satisfaction [is] sufficient to the parties. Yet, in cases of moneys to be paid where there is a limitation over, as the case may be, there may be no relief. But, in this case, the consent and apt disposing in marriage can never be supplied and the purpose of the devisor can never be served after the breach.

This case is also differing from many cases of legacies paying on conditions which have been construed *in terrorem* only and from cases where the consent of strangers is enjoined and they totally refuse to consent though the match propounded be ever so advantageous. Yet, in that case, they may be compelled by this court to consent if all advantageous circumstances apt to serve of the purpose of the disseisor be concurring. And, in such like cases at common law, strict rules have been laid aside, as infants' suffering recoveries. *Vide* above 451; Hobart 196.[1]

Also in this case, all the grandchildren were *in aequali gradu* to the devisor, and, by common law, equally entitled to the estate, so that is it a mutual designment of the house to the other two, on the disobedience of one contrary to nature's laws.

As to the consent after marriage, it was held insignificant, for, after marriage, when the same could not be helped, the consent was only out of pity to the party disobedient and cannot be intended such a consent as was to serve the design of the devisor. Besides, by the limitation over on the condition broken, the estate was vested in the other two and cannot be re-vested by any subsequent consent at law. And Chancery shall not help, alter, or abridge the law operating consentaniously to the law of nature.

And, though it did not appear on the case that the first devisee had notice of the will, yet notice may be intended, and the will was proved and so on record. And, by Chief Baron [Hale], any ordinary notice is sufficient, as common talk etc.

This report I [Charles Cremer] had by information, from which it was appealed into the House of Lords, and heard Michaelmas term 1670. And the decree was confirmed.

Lincoln's Inn MS. Misc. 500, f. 89v

Easter term 22 Car. II (1670).

The plaintiff and the Lady Anne Knowles, his wife, who was the daughter of Nicholas, earl of Banbury, and Isabel, his wife, who was the daughter to the earl of Newport, deceased, and Montjoy Frye, their son, exhibited their bill in Chancery against the defendant, who was the son and only child of the other daughter of the earl Newport. And the case was [thus].

The earl of Newport, seised in fee of a house called Newport House and other tenements in Middlesex, made his will in writing. And, by it, he devised them in the manner following:

> I give to the Lady Anne, my wife, Newport House and other my lands and tenements in Middlesex with their appurtenances for the term of her life and, after her decease, I give the same to my grandchild, the Lady Anne Knowles, and the heirs of her body lawfully begotten, provided always and upon condition that my said grandchild do marry with the consent of my said with the consent of my said wife and of Charles, earl of Warwick, or Edward, earl of Manchester, or the major part of them. And, in case she

[1] *Lord Camden's Case* (1661), Gray's Inn MS. 34, p. 451, pl. 1; *Blount's Case*, Hobart 196, 80 E.R. 343.

> marry without the consent of my said wife and the major part of my said trustees shall happen to depart this life without issue of her body, then I give and bequeath the premises to my grandchild, George Porter, and his heirs.

The Lady Anne Knowles, being only fifteen years of age and not having notice of this proviso and condition, married the said Fry without any consent of her grandmother, the countess of Newport, or of the said earls of Warwick and Manchester precedent to the said marriage. But, upon the proof, it appeared that, after the marriage, the said countess sent for the said Lady Anne and entertained her. And, before the said marriage, the said countess proposed the Lord Morpeth in marriage to the said Lady Anne, whom she refused, and, for this the said countess said that she no more will propose any matches for her nor would concern herself in her marriage (but it did not appear whether it was said in anger or otherwise.) And afterwards, the said countess died, and the earls of Warwick and Manchester, after the marriage, gave their assent to it and said that perhaps they might have consented to the marriage if they had been asked beforehand, or words to such effect.

After which marriage, the defendant entered into the premises devised for the condition broken by the Lady Anne's marrying without consent, as before, upon which the plaintiffs preferred their bill to be relieved against the condition broken, and had a decree and perpetual injunction against the defendant made by the Master of the Rolls [Grimston]. From which decree, the defendant appealed to the Lord Keeper, who called Kelyng, Chief Justice of the King's Bench, Vaughan, Chief Justice of the Common Bench, and Ward, Chief Baron, to his assistance. And, after hearing the plaintiff's counsel, that is to say, Fountaine, Ellis, and Baldwin, serjeants, and Churchill, and Winnington, for the plaintiffs, and Maynard, King's Serjeant, and Finch, then the King's Solicitor [General], and Peck, for the defendants, and great consideration of the matter and view of precedents, the said chief justices and the Chief Baron delivered their opinion *seriatim* that the plaintiffs could not nor should not be relieved in this. And the Lord Keeper [Bridgeman] concurred with them in opinion. And the decree made by the Master of the Rolls was set aside, and the plaintiff's bill was dismissed, notwithstanding that the Lady Anne Knowles had not any other legacy given by the said earl of Newport, though the defendant had a legacy of £5000 given him by this will. And their principal reasons and arguments were as follows.

Chief Baron Hale observed the general question to be whether the decree as drawn up should pass and be confirmed. But, in this case, he considered those particulars, first, whether the condition or limitation in the will is good, second, whether relief in equity will be against it, third, if there will not be relief against the conditions or limitations of such nature generally, yet whether this particular case in question has such circumstances that will induce or merit a relief.

As to the first, he held that it is a good conditional limitation in law and equity and it absolutely ended the estate of the plaintiffs and vested the premises in the defendant, first, because it is a collateral limitation of the land and no restraint of marriage, second, because that the Lady is not bound to anything but only her duty to be advised by her grandmother, who is *in loco parentis*, third, that it was in the power of the earl of Newport to dispose his estate upon what condition it pleased him. And though such a limitation of a legacy in ecclesiastical law is not good, as Swinburne, *of Wills*, 4th part, ca. 12, fo. 270, 271, etc., yet the devise in question is different inasmuch as it respects land and inheritance and not personal things as legacies. And, on account of that, here, the estate vested by the limitation over will not be defeated.

As to the second particular, he held that in general cases, there will not be relief against such conditions or limitations, but not upon the reason that the estate is settled by the will, and, on account of that, it has the sanction of the art of Parliament of 32 Hen. VIII, ca. 1, which enables a devise of lands, because he held that there could be relief against breaches in wills, otherwise many estates in England will be unsettled. And, for this, he cited Fish and Seamon's Case in Chancery, [*blank*] Car. I, and Salmon and Bartman's Case, 6 May 12 Car. I,[1] nor upon the reason that it is a limitation and not a condition, because there could be relief against a limitation.

As to the third particular, he held that there will not be relief in this particular case considered with all the circumstances of it, first, because it is not similar to the condition or limitation of an estate for the payment of money at the certain day, because, upon a non-payment of it at the precise day, there could be a compensation by a payment at another day. But, in this case, there could not be any compensation for marrying without consent, second, because it is a condition to contain the Lady to due obedience to the law of nature and reason, third, because the settlement by the earl of Newport was voluntary to the plaintiff and defendant and both being *in aequali gradu* as to the devisor, it is not equity to take away an estate vested by law in the defendant and to give it to the plaintiff in a case of such parity, fourth, because it appears by the body of the will that the devisor's intent was that the estate given to the plaintiff will go to the defendant as well if the plaintiff marry without consent as if she died without issue, he having made the same limitation for one as for the other, and, on account of this, the same reason to relieve in equity for one as for the other, fifth, because this case is without precedent, none of the precedents produced being similar to this. And, on account of this, he agreed here with the reason of the judges in Mathew Manning's Case, 8 rep. 94, and Lampet's Case, 10 rep. 47,[2] to bound themselves

---

1 *Fish v. Seaman* (Ch. 1628), Chancery Repts. *tempore* Coventry 78; perhaps *Salmon v. Vaux* (Ch. 1635–1636), Tothill 105, 21 E.R. 137.

2 *Clark v. Manning* (1609), 8 Coke Rep. 94, 77 E.R. 618; *Lampet v. Starkey* (1612), 10 Coke Rep. 46b, 77 E.R. 994, also 2 Brownlow & Goldesborough 172, 123 E.R. 880.

as far as they will go in construction and admission of such estates and to give themselves bounds and limits that they not exceed. And, though precedents are not [. . .] variation in equity where there is parity of cases, yet precedents many times enlighten and furnish with reason.

And he said, by the ordinary distributive justice of the land, this case is not relievable in equity, because a court of equity should not relieve in all cases, but to be confined and limited within certain bounds, because Parliament only is of an unlimited jurisdiction.

And as to the allegation [of] offer for the plaintiff, first, that that proviso is *in terrorem* only, he said that he was not satisfied with it being a collateral averment against the express words of the will, and, if such averments will be admitted, great uncertainty and confusion will be introduced, second, allegation that the effect of the testator is obtained by the assent subsequent as whether the lady had married with their consent precedent, as to this, he held that no response because the dissent of the trustees *ex post facto* will be vain at this day and they would not know of what opinions they would have been if they had a contemplation of this marriage before it has been solemnized. And if the variation from the will had been in a circumstance, there could be a pretense of equity. But, here, it is in substance. The allegation [was] that the lady at the time of her marriage was an infant and thus to be favored in law and equity. He said that this is not any reason in this case inasmuch as the condition here depends upon the act that is in the sole power of the infant. And infants are bound to perform conditions in fact, which it is here.

[As to the] fourth allegation, that the lady being an infant had no notice of the conditions, he said that notice or no notice is not triable here, but in a court of law. And on account of this, if the plaintiff has title, he can try it at law upon this point of notice, because public intimation in the house can amount to notice in equity. But, if notice [is] necessary in this case, this can be legal notice, which is only determinable upon a trial at law. And, thus, upon all the matter, he concluded against the plaintiffs, relinquishing the notice to the law.

Chief Justice VAUGHAN held that this case is not proper for nor relievable in a court of equity, inasmuch as there is not any fraud or trust in it. And he agreed that there could be relief against a conditional devise upon non-payment at the day upon the reason of a recompense to the other day and that such a condition in a personal legacy is not good. But this is ruled by another law. But his great argument, upon which he much relied, was the sanction and sacredness of the act of Parliament 32 Hen. VIII, ca. 1, which provides that every man will have free liberty by his will in writing to devise his lands etc. for any estate at his free will and pleasure and the will in question was made in observance of this Statute, which cannot be altered by a decree in this court, because last wills, where they do not cross the rules of law, are to be preserved unalterable. And he held that this general statute is as strong in this case and will settle and will vest the estate devised by the will in question in the same manner as those estates here devised have been settled by a special act of Parliament. And, if the case in question will be relieved, all other matters in Westminster Hall, by the same reason, could be relieved in equity.

And, as to notice or no notice, consent or no consent, if it come into question, they are to be determined by a trial at law and not in a course in equity.

And, as to the words of the grandmother and trustees, they signify nothingm because though the grandmother said that she will not propose again any match, yet this does not discharge the Lady Anne from procuring her assent to the marriage. And the words of the trustees that, perhaps, if they had been asked, they might have consented are dubious and will serve for little or nothing, because consent and dissent must have an object upon which the could operate and be in the power of the person that could give his consent or dissent, either to consent or to dissent, at the time of giving it. But, here, it is impossible because the trustees cannot consent to the marriage of which they would not know, and it was vain to dissent after it was done. And, on account of this, their freedom and election of assent and dissent was taken away, inasmuch as nothing was said to consent to a thing that is not in his power to alter as the color of his hair etc.[1] Also, he did not say that he would have consented because he could know nothing of what opinion he will be in the circumstance of an act of which he never had made a trial.

And, thus, he concluded against the plaintiffs in equity but would leave them to the [common] law upon [the issues of] notice and consent.

Chief Justice Kelyng said that it us an unreasonable thing to give relief here, inasmuch as it will destroy the prudence of parents and will introduce disobedience in children and corruption of persons entrusted with heiresses etc. but, to the contrary, it is more equitable to hold those bonds and obligations upon children firm. And he said that the precedents produced do not reach this case. And he agreed with Hale that, in a case of a limitation over for non-payment of money at the day certain, there could be relief, inasmuch as there could be a recompense, but here none. And the condition here is not to be intended *in terrorem*, because there is a limitation over; [it is] otherwise is [there were] no such limitation.

And he held that all cases upon wills are not irremediable in equity, but the difference depends upon matters of substance (as here marriage without consent generally is) and matters of circumstance as (in Yelverton's Case, 36 El., in Chancery) marriage without consent in writing, where, if consent there was, though not in writing, it is good, because equity does not relieve against substantial matters in wills or conveyances, but against emergencies upon them only. And, here, a parol averment against a will is not to be admitted.

And he held that, if the trustees are obstinant and refused or neglected to give their consent without good cause, they would be compelled in equity.

[1] Matthew, chapter 5, verse 36.

And infancy in this case is not relievable, because it will destroy the care of parents. And, at the common law, an infant in wardship marrying himself without consent will lose the value of his marriage.

And the fault of notice does not help inasmuch as it is the act of the party herself. Also, Fry will be intended to have notice, inasmuch as it is presumed that no one will steal shorn sheep, as he termed it.

And, thus, he concluded that it is a just and prudent condition and not to be violated in law or equity.

The Lord Keeper [BRIDGEMAN] concurred in all with the chief justices and the Chief Baron. And he declared himself to be satisfied that there is a delivery to this error, that parents could not put a restraint upon their children to marry without consent. And he said that as he agreed as before, yet he held these things considerable to move the Master of the Rolls to make the decree as *supra*, first, that the defendant had a £5000 legacy by the will and the plaintiff nothing; second, the subsequent assent of the grandmother and trustees such as it was; third, that no time is limited in which the trustees will give their consent to the marriage, and it could be forty years to come.

But his reason against these things was that parents, by the law, could restrain their children to marriage without the consent of friends and that it is the duty of children to be ruled by them in such a case, especially as in this case where the countess was *in loco matris* to the Lady Anne. And he held that notice is not necessary, but everyone is bound to take and none to give notice, especially in this case, where the plaintiff is not the heir.

And he held that acts of Parliament could be defeated by the course of law, as if an act of Parliament entail lands to A., remainder to B., A. could dock the remainder by suffering a common recovery, *quod nota*.

The bill was dismissed, and this [was] the 13th of May 1670.

Note, in the last case, the court took the difference between such devise of lands and goods, because, in the case of goods, they seemed to agree that the condition had not been good according to Swinburne, *Wills*, 4th part, ca. 12, fo. 270, 271, etc., and Moore 857.[1]

1 Modern 300, 86 E.R. 898

1670, Charles Fry and Anne, his wife, against George Porter.

The case was [thus]. Montjoy, earl of Newport, was seised of a house called Newport House, etc. in the County of Middlesex. And he had three sons, who were then living and two daughters, *viz*. Isabel, married to the earl of Banbury, with her father's consent, who had issue Anne, the plaintiff, and Anne, married

[1] H. Swinburne, *Brief Treatise of Testaments and Last Wills*; *Gresley v. Luther* (1614), Moore K.B. 857, 72 E.R. 953, also 1 Brownlow & Goldesborough 18, 123 E.R. 638.

to Mr. Porter, without her father's consent, who had issue D. Both these daughters died.

The earl of Newport made his will in this manner:

> I give and bequeath to my dear wife, the Lady Anne, countess of Newport, all that my house called Newport House and all other my lands [etc.] in the County of Middlesex, for her life. And, after her death, I give and bequeath the premises to my grandchild Anne Knollis [*viz.* the plaintiff] and to the heirs of her body, provided always and upon condition that she marry with the consent of my said wife and the earl of Warwick and the earl of Manchester or of the major part of them. And, in case she marry without such consent or happen to die without issue, then I give and bequeath it to George Porter [*viz.* the defendant].

The earl died. Anne, the plaintiff, married Charles, the plaintiff, she being then about fourteen or fifteen years old, without the consent of either of the trustees.

And, thereupon, now, a bill was preferred to be relieved against this condition and forfeiture, because she had no notice of this condition and limitation made to her etc. To this the defendant had demurred, but that was overruled. Afterwards, there were several depositions etc. made and testified on each side, the effect of which, was this.

On the plaintiffs' part, it was proved by several that it was always the earl's intention that the plaintiff should have this estate and that they never heard of this purpose to put any condition upon her. And he believed that he did not intend to give away the inheritance from her but that this clause in the will was only *in terrorem* and cautionary to make her the more obsequious to her grandmother. The two earls swore that they had no notice of this clause in the will, but, if they had, they think it possible such reason might have been offered as might have induced them to give their consents to the marriage and that now they do consent to and approve of the same. Some proof was made that the countess of Newport had some design that the plaintiff should not have this estate, but that the defendant should have it. But, at last, even she, *viz.* the countess, was reconciled, and did declare that she forgave the plaintiffs' marriage, and that she showed great affection to a child which the plaintiff had and directed that, when she was dead, the plaintiff and her child should be let into the possession of the premises and should enjoy them etc. It was proved also that, when there had been a treaty concerning the marriage between My Lord Morpeth and the plaintiff and the plaintiff would not marry him, her grandmother said 'she should marry whom she would, she would take no further care about her'. (The countess was dead at the time of this suit.) It was proved that Mr. Fry was of a good family and that the defendant had £5000 appointed and provided for him by his grandfather by the same will.

On the defendant's part, it was sworn by the said late countess of Newport, *viz.* in an answer made formerly to a bill brought against her by the now defendant for preserving of testimony, which was ordered to be read, that the marriage was private and without her consent and approbation and that she did not conceive it to be a fit and proportionable marriage, he being a younger brother and having no estate. The like was sworn by the earl of Portland, the said countess's then husband, and that it appeared she leaped over a wall by means of a wheelbarrow set up against it to go to be married and that, as soon as the trustees did know of the marriage, that they disavow and dislike it, and so declared themselves several times, and said that had they had any hint of it, they would have prevented it. Others swore that the earl of Portland declared upon the day of her going away 'that he never consented thereto' and that the countess desired then that he would not do anything like it and that the earl of Warwick said he would have lost one of his arms rather than have consented to the said marriage.

On the hearing of this cause before the Master of the Rolls, *viz.* Sir Harbottle Grimston, bart., the plaintiff obtained a decretal order, *viz.* that Anne, the plaintiff, and her heirs should hold the premises quietly against the defendant and his heirs and that there should be an injunction perpetual against the defendant and all claiming under him.

And now, there was an appeal thereupon, and a rehearing before Sir Orlando Bridgeman, kt., then Lord Keeper, assisted by the two Lord Chief Justices and the Chief Baron, before whom it was argued thus.

Maynard, Serjeant: The plaintiff ought not to have relief in this case. The plaintiff's mother had a sufficient provision by the earl of Newport's care and, therefore, there is less reason that this estate should be added to the daughter. The noble lords the trustees, when the thing was fresh, did disapprove the marriage, however they may consent thereunto now. The devise was to the plaintiff but in tail and, afterwards, to the defendant. We disparage not Mr. Fry in blood nor family. But people do not marry for that only, but for recompense and like fortune. There was a public fame or report (it is to be presumed) of this will in the house. And, were there not, yet it was against her duty and against nature that she should decline asking her grandmother's consent. And Mr. Fry, in honor and conscience, ought to have asked it. And, therefore, this practice ought not to receive the least encouragement in equity. It is true, when there was a demurrer, it was overruled, because the bill prayed to be relieved against a forfeiture, for which there might be good cause in equity. But now, it does not appear there is any in the case. The estate is now in the defendant, and that not by any act of his own, but by the devisor and the plaintiff. This is a limitation, not a condition, for My Lord Newport had sons. It is somewhat of the same effect a condition, though it is not so. We have a title by the will of the dead and the act of the other party without fraud or other act of us. And, therefore, it ought not to be defeated. I take a difference between a devise of land and money, for land is not originally devisable, though money is. By the civil law and amongst civil lawyers, it has been made a question, whether there shall be relief against such a limitation in a devise. But be that how it will, chattels are small things, but a freehold settled ought not to be divested thus. No man can make a limitation in his will better and stronger to disappoint his devise, conditionally, than this is made. If My Lord Newport had been alive, would he have liked such a practice upon his granddaughter as want of notice? In Organ's Case and Sir Julius Caesar's Case,[1] there was a grant to an infant on condition to pay 10s. and no notice given thereof before it was payable; yet, because nobody was bound to give notice, it was adjudged against the infant.

Sir Heneage Finch, Solicitor General: The witnesses who swear that the earl said he would give the estate to her, prove nothing to the purpose, for he did so but upon a condition that they did not hear. The after-consent of the earl or the countess ought not to make it good, which consent at last perhaps was extorted by importunity or compassion, for, at first, they disapproved of the marriage. Marrying without consent and dying without issue are coupled in the same line, and the estate shall as effectually pass over to the defendant upon the one limitation as the other, for such consent is matter *ex post facto* and suspiciously to be scanned, for we ought in this case by law to proceed strictly, and not derogate from My Lord Newport's intent, which plainly appears by the letter of his will, that his grandchild should ask consent of such he had thereby appointed to consent before her marriage were solemnized, the actual solemnization of which was an act so permanent that it would admit of no alteration or dissolution, an act of such force and efficacy, tending clearly and immediately to the ruin of their right and title to the estate in question and rendering it wholly incapable of reviver by any other means than what the common and civil laws of this realm do permit. The *post* consent, therefore, will not avail the plaintiffs in this court. Otherwise, the defendant claiming by this limitation should have indeed advantage, but such as is inconsiderable, being liable to alteration by the pleasure of this court. And, for a strict observation of the testator's words, the same ought to be in equity as well as at law. What great respect the old heathens paid to the wills of deceased persons may appear in these following verses: *Sed legum [est] servanda fides, suprema voluntas, quod mandat, fierique jubet, parere necesse est.*[2]

The countess saying, likely in passion, that 'she might marry whom she would', etc. did not amount to a dormant warrant to her to marry without consent. I am upon conjecture still that the plaintiffs will insist upon these particulars, for it looks as if they would, because they read them. Doubtless the primary intention of the clause was *in terrorem*, but the secondary was that, if she offended, she should undergo the penalty. His intention is to be gathered out of the words only, and whatever they say the earl intended does not press the question.

[1] *Organ v. Gardiner* (1674), 1 Chancery Cases 231, 22 E.R. 776, 1 Eq. Cas. Abr. 82, 21 E.R. 895; *Springe v. Caesar* (1636), 1 Rolle, Abr., *Condition*, pl. F, 1, p. 420, pl. D, 1, p. 469, W. Jones 389, 82 E.R. 204, *sub nom. Cooper v. Edgar* (1624), Winch 103, 116, 124 E.R. 87, 97.

[2] W. Sheppard, *Touchstone* (1841), p. 240.

Our freehold is settled in us by virtue of an Act of Parliament. I lay it down for a foundation that a father may settle his estate so as that the issue shall be deprived of it for disobedience, and not be relievable in equity. And now it is not possible that any counsel could advise a man to do it stronger than it is done in this case. And shall a child break these bonds and look disobedience in the face here? If it had been only provided that she should marry with the consent etc. and no further, it might have been somewhat, but, since he goes on, and makes a limitation over etc., he becomes his own chancellor. And, upon this difference, are all the precedents and even those of devising portions, *viz.* devising them over or not, as I have understood. Infancy can be no excuse in case of the breach of a condition of an estate in which the infant is a purchaser so that nothing rests now in this case but the point of notice. And why should not the infant be bound to take notice in this case, as he is to take notice in case of a remainder wherein he is a purchaser? But, if notice be necessary, it is not to be tried here now. If we had brought an [action of] ejectment and (supposing notice had been necessary) we had failed in the proof thereof, should we have been barred forever, as, by this perpetual injunction, we should be? And shall it be done now without proof? If we are not bound to prove notice at law, much less are we bound to prove it here. This case is epidemical, and concerns all the parents of England that have or shall have children, that the obligations which they lay upon their children may not be cancelled wholly and this court, under color of equity, protect them in it, and be a city of refuge for relief of such, the foulness of whose actions deny them a sanctuary.

Pecke: If infancy would excuse, such a clause would signify nothing, for most persons, especially of that sex, marry before full age. The lords give no reason why they changed their opinions.

Fountaine, Serjeant: The case of Yelverton v. Yelverton is a precedent in the point for us, and Shipdam's Case[1] is much like it. This being of a devise of land, and that of money, which, if it were paid, the land was to go over. The grand objection is that here is an estate vested by a settlement, which is not to be avoided or defeated. But I doubt whether a man can lay such a restraint that there shall not be relief in any case of emergency and contingency. It is a part of the fundamental justice of the nation that men should not make limitations wholly unalterable, as, by the common law, men cannot make a fee unalienable. You give relief every day where there are express clauses that there shall be no relief in law or equity; where a thing is appointed to be etc. without relief in law or equity, you relieve against them, and look upon them to be void. In our case, suppose she had married a great lord or suppose a person had brought notice of the trustees' consent, would you not have given relief? But, secondly, I deny the assumption. This case is not so. I agree it had been well done if they had asked My Lady Newport's

[1] *Shipston v. Booler* (1661), 1 Siderfin 25, 82 E.R. 948.

consent. But is there a word in the will that, if the plaintiff did not, he should have no relief in equity? The estate was devised to My Lady Newport during her life (so that the plaintiff could not be in possession), and she might have lived until the plaintiff was twenty-one years old. Could not My Lady Newport have said 'have a care how you marry, for you forfeit the estate if you marry without the consent of two of us three'? All ingredients and circumstances must be taken in a matter of equity. It is an argument to say he has no estate, therefore, take away his wife's estate, then there will be nothing to maintain her. It is agreed that, if the approbation had been precedent, it had been well. Now, she had no notice before the marriage that it was necessary, and, when she had that notice, she got the approbation. And that, though subsequent, is good enough, because it was asked and gotten as soon as she had notice that she ought to have it. The will is hereby sufficiently observed, for the intent of the will was that she should have such a husband as those persons should approve, and this marriage is so approved. I rely upon this matter, but especially upon the word of notice.

Ellis, Serjeant: There was a case of a proviso not to marry but with the consent of certain persons first had in writing. Consent was had, but not in writing, and yet you ruled it good. Had this been a condition in law (as it is in fact), the law would have helped her. If the estate had been in her, there might have been some reason that she should have taken notice how it came to her and of the limitation etc. Had the earl been alive and consented to the marriage after it was solemnized, he would have continued his affection, and the plaintiffs have had the estate still. Why now, the consent of the Lords and countess is as much as his consent. He had transferred his consent to them. This is a *ratihabitio*, you cannot have a case of more circumstances of equity; first, an infant; secondly, no notice; thirdly, consent after; fourthly, their declaration that they thought My Lord meant it *in terrorem etc.* What if two of the trustees had died, should she never have married? Surely you would have relieved her.

Baldwin, Serjeant: Here is as full a consent to the marriage, as could well be in this case, for, since the plaintiff had no notice of the necessity of the earl's consent before the marriage, it had been the strangest and unexpectedest thing in the world that she could have gone about to have asked it. The heir could not have taken notice of such a forfeiture. And why should a man that is named by way of remainder? In the case of a personal legacy, this were a void proviso by the civil law, for I have informed myself of it. It is a maxim with them, *viz.* '*matrimonium [debet] esse liberum*'.[1] This amounts to as much as the condition that the person should not marry at all, for, when it is in the trustees' power, they may propose the unagreeablest person in the world. It is a most unreasonable power, and not to be favored. Sir Thomas Grimes settled his land so, that his son should pay portions, and, if he did not, he demised the lands over, and it was adjudged

[1] Matrimony should be free.

relievable.[1] If I limit that my daughter shall marry with the consent of two etc. if each of them have a design for a different friend, if you will not relieve, she can never marry. Is it not more probable that, if the earl had lived, he would rather have given her a maintenance than have concluded her under perpetual misfortune and disherison?

Kelyng, Chief Justice: I do not see how an averment or proof can be received to make out a man's intention against the words of the will. In Vernon's Case, though it were a case of as much equity as could be, it was denied to be received, and so in My Lord Cheney's Case.[2] Here was a case of Sir Thomas Hatton,[3] somewhat like this case, wherein no relief could be had.

Vaughan, Chief Justice: I wonder to hear of citing of precedents in matter of equity, for, if there be equity in a case, that equity is a universal truth, and there can be no precedent in it. So that, in any precedent that can be produced, if it be the same with this case, the reason and equity is the same in itself. And, if the precedent be not the same case with this, it is not to be cited, being not to that purpose.

Bridgeman, Lord Keeper: Certainly precedents are very necessary and useful to us, for, in them, we may find the reasons of the equity to guide us. And, besides, the authority of those who made them is much to be regarded. We shall suppose they did it upon great consideration and weighing of the matter. And it would be very strange and very ill if we should disturb and set aside what has been the course for a long series of time and ages.

Thereupon, it was ordered, that they should be attended with precedents, and then, they said they would give their opinions.

Three weeks after, they came into Chancery again, and delivered their opinions *seriatim*, in this manner, *viz*.

Hale, Chief Baron: The general question is whether this decree shall pass. I shall divide what I have to say into these three questions or particulars.

First, I shall consider whether this be a good condition or limitation or conditional limitation, for so I had rather call it, it being a condition to determine the estate of the plaintiff and a limitation to let in the defendant. I think it is good both in law and equity. And my reasons are, first, because it is a collateral condition to the land, and not against the nature of the estate, and she is not thereby bound from marriage.

---

1 *Wallis v. Crimes* (Ch. 1667–1668), see above, Case No. 235.

2 *Vernon v. Vernon* (1572), 4 Coke Rep. 1, 76 E.R. 845, Benloe 210, 123 E.R. 147, 3 Leonard 28, 74 E.R. 519, 3 Dyer 317, 73 E.R. 718; *Lord Cheyney's Case* (Wards 1591), 5 Coke Rep. 68, 77 E.R. 158, Moore K.B. 727, 72 E.R. 867.

3 Perhaps *Hatton v. Long* (1673), Repts. *tempore* Finch, 23 E.R. 7, 73 Selden Soc. 9, or *Hatton v. Gray* (1684), 2 Chancery Cases 164, 22 E.R. 895, 1 Eq. Cas. Abr. 21, 21 E.R. 843.

Secondly, it obliged her to no more than her duty. She had no mother, and, in case of marriage, she ought to make an application to her grandmother, who was *in loco parentis*. And, since the estate moved from the grandfather, she was mistress of the disposition and manner of it. It is true, by the civil ecclesiastical law, regularly such a condition were void, and, therefore, if the question were of a legacy, there might be a great deal of reason to question the validity of it, because, in those courts wherein legacies are properly handled, it would have been void. But this is a case of land, a devise. Indeed, it is agreed that this is a good condition, and not to be avoided in itself.

Thirdly, this being a good condition and limitation over, the question is whether there be relief against it in equity, admitting it were a willful breach. I think there ought not to be any. I differ from the reasons pressed at the bar, as, first, that it was a devise by a will by virtue of the Statute etc. But that does not stick with me, for, if there may not be a relief against a breach of a condition in a will, there would be a great shatter and confusion in men's estates, and some of those settled by great advice, and there have been precedents of relief in such cases: Fitz v. Seymour and Salmon v. Bernard. Secondly, it has been urged there could be no relief, because there is a limitation over. But that I shall not go upon neither. There have been many reliefs in such cases. I will decline the latitude of the objection, for that would go a great deal further than we are aware. But yet I think there ought to be no relief in this case. It is not like the case of payment of money, because, there, the party may be answered his debt with damages at another day and so may be fully satisfied of all that is intended him. But here, my first reason is that it is a condition to contain the party in that due obedience which law and nature require. Secondly, it is a voluntary settlement to the granddaughter in tail, and the remainder over is so too, and both these parties are *in aequali gradu* to the devisor. And, therefore, they being both in a parity, it would be hard to take the estate from him to whom and in whose scale the law has thrown the advantage. Thirdly, it appears by the body of the will that the earl did as really intend it should go over if she married without consent as if she died without issue, for they are both in the same clause. There may be as much reason to turn it into a fee simple, in case she had died without issue, as in this case, for so I doubt the penning of this decretal order does. And fourthly, I rest upon this, it is a case without a precedent. I remember after that Lanyett's Case had been adjudged, that in the sixth [year] of Charles I, there was a case, I suppose Saunders v. Cornish,[1] of a limitation in tail and a devise over, and it was adjudged void, and the judges said 'so far it is gone, and we will go no further, because we do not know where it will rest'. I know there is no intrinsic difference in cases by precedents, but there is a great difference in a case wherein a man is to make and where a man sees (and is to follow) a precedent; in the one case, a

[1] *Lampet v. Starkey* (1612), *ut supra*; *Sanders v. Cornish* (1631), Croke Car. 230, 79 E.R. 801.

man is more strictly bound up, but, in the other, he may take a greater liberty and latitude. For, if a man be in doubt, *in aequilibrio*, concerning a case, whether it be equitable or no, in prudence, he will determine according as the precedents have been, especially if they had been made by men of good authority for learning etc. and have been continued and pursued. Here must be some boundary, or we shall go we know not whither. It were hard a court of equity should do that which is not fit to be done in any court below a Parliament. The precedents do not come home to the case. Most of them are in cases of money legacies, and, in some of those cases, we may give allowance in respect of the law of another forum to which they belong. But this is in a case of land only. Indeed, he is no authority, but there is a very good exemplification of this matter.

I shall consider the allays and circumstances which are observed, and offer to qualify this case and induce relief.

First, it is said that this clause was only *in terrorem*, and some witnesses have been examined to prove it. But I am not satisfied how collateral averments can be admitted in this case, for, then, how can there be any certainty? A will will be anything, everything, nothing. The Statute appointed the will should be in writing to make a certainty. And shall we admit collateral averments and proofs and make it utterly uncertain?

Secondly, it is said in this case, the effect of the proviso has been obtained, for the trustees have now declared their consent. I must say it is not full, for they do not say they would have consented, but that, possibly, such reasons might have been offered as they should have done it. And possibly, I say, not. They, like good men, have only declined the showing an ineffectual contradicting of a thing which is done, and cannot now be recalled, undone, or altered. Besides, if there had been but a circumstantial variation, the consent afterwards might have been somewhat. But, here, it is in the very substance. In this case before cited at the bar by Mr. Serjeant Ellis, where the consent was to he had in writing and it was had only by parol, there was great equity that it should be relieved, because it was only a provident circumstance and wisdom of the devisor, *viz.* for the more firm obliging the party to ask consent, which the devisor considered might be pretended to be had by slight words in ordinary and not solemn communication or else in passion and heat (as in this case, when the plaintiff would not consent to the approved marriage with the Lord Morpeth, the countess said 'she might marry where she would', which words imported a neglect of care for the future over the plaintiff because she would not be ruled by the countess in accepting the tender of so commendable a marriage), as also for the benefit of the devisee (in the case aforesaid) that, in case the devisee did marry with the consent of the trustee, he might not after (through prejudice etc.) avoid it by denial of such consent, and so defeat or perplex the devisee for want of proof of such his consent.

Thirdly, it is said the party is an infant. Why, an infant is bound by a condition in fact, by law. It is true we are now in equity, but, in equity, since this refers to an act which she though an infant is capable of doing, *viz.* to marry, it were unreasonable that she should be able to do the act and not be obliged by equity to observe the conditions and terms which concern and relate to that act; so that it is all one as if she had been of full age. The Statute of Merton, cap. 5, provides, that usury shall not run against infants, and yet the same Statute, cap. 6, appoints that, if an infant marry without the licence of his lord etc., he shall forfeit double the value of his marriage.[1] And it is reasonable, because marriage is an act which he may do by law while he is under age.

As to the point of notice, first, whether notice be requisite or no, in point of law, I will not determine. But I must needs say that it must be referred to law. But, secondly, if it be not requisite in law, how far a court of equity might relieve for want of it, I will not now take upon me to determine. I will not trench upon matters *gratis*, of which I know not what will be the consequence. But I conceive in this case, the fact is not yet settled whether there were notice or not. And it were a hard matter that, because no notice is here proved, it should be taken for granted there was none, for, here, are several circumstances that seem to show there might be notice, and a public voice in the house, or an accidental intimation, etc. may possibly be sufficient notice. I shall therefore leave it as a fit thing to be tried. And, until that, the case in my understanding is not ripe. And, therefore, I will add no more. I think this decree ought to be altered, if not set aside. But, as this case is, there ought to be no relief.

VAUGHAN, Chief Justice: I shall conclude as My Lord Chief Baron did, that, as this case is, there ought to be no relief. I will single out this case from several things not material to it, as My Lord Chief Baron did etc. I think, if land be devised on condition to pay legacies and that the devisee has paid almost all and fails in one or so, there may be good cause of relief, because he has paid much and is somewhat in the nature of a purchaser. This is not like a legacy. This is upon the Statute, where it is said, 'a man may devise at his will and pleasure', *i.e.* absolutely, upon condition, upon limitation, or any way that the law warrants. Suppose there had been a special act of Parliament disposing as the earl has done, in this case; could there be any color in equity to alter or vary this law? And here it is equally as concluding as that, since the Statute gives a man power to dispose as expressly and, otherwise, equity would alter and dispose of all property and all things that came in question. But let notice or consent etc. be requisite or not, it is triable at law. But I stand upon this, that there ought to be no relief in equity. It was insisted that her grandmother gave a kind of consent. But I take that for nothing, for, though the grandmother would not have offered or proposed a marriage, yet she ought not to marry without her consent. Nor is the lord's *post* consent anything, for consent cannot be had for things which cannot be otherwise, as a man cannot be said to consent to his stature or the color of his hair etc. A man may know of what opinion he is or was. But it is impossible for a man to know of what opin-

[1] Stat. 20 Hen. III, cc. 5, 6 (*SR*, I, 3).

ion he would have been in the circumstances of an action which he never tried. I conclude the plaintiffs ought not to have relief in equity. But, if any matter in law will help them, they are not excluded from it.

Kelyng, Chief Justice: I think there ought to be no relief in this case. I have considered it as well as I can, and I think nothing is more fit to be observed than chief customary rules for children; they are very good restraints for children, and ought to be made good here to encourage obedience and discourage those who would make a prey of them. And, if there were not hope for men to hasten their fortunes by this means, there would be few adventures of this nature. I have looked upon the precedents etc., and I find they come not to this case, except only one, and that is but seven years old, and the others are for money, for which there is reason, because the party may be substantially relieved and satisfied otherways. If there had been no limitation over, there may be some reason why it may be intended that it is only *in terrorem*. I do not think all cases upon wills are irremediable here (because of the Statute). If the breach of the condition be in a circumstance only, as in the case where the consent was given, but not in writing, as it ought, it may be relieved, for that was a caution to the consentor that he should not give consent before strangers and trust to the swearing of a parol consent. I never yet saw any devise obliging to have any such consent after the party's age of twenty-one years; so that there is no great hardship in it. And, if there should be any ill design in those who have the trust and power to consent in withholding their consent, it might be relieved here. I think none would make a decree that, if she died without issue, the defendant should have it. And this is the same. But equity can never go against the substantial part of a conveyance or will, but that must be governed by the party's agreement or appointment. Equity ought to arise upon some collateral or accidental emergent. It is not *in terrorem* indeed without a penalty. There can be no collateral averment, being an infant is nothing, for this is only a provision while she is an infant. Besides, the case of the forfeiture of the double value is a very good instance for the notice. If she had notice of this will, yet they that came to steal her knew it not, for they did not come to take a shorn sheep. And, therefore, no relief is deserved by the plaintiff. In honesty and conscience, those bonds ought to be kept strict. I confess I would not have the plaintiff tempted to a further suit. But, indeed, in saying that, I go further than I need.

Bridgeman, Lord Keeper: If I were of another opinion, yet I would be bound by My Lords, for I did not send for them not to be bound by them. But I was of their opinion from the beginning. And I am glad now that we are delivered from a common error and that men may make such provisions as may bind their children. But to justify the decree a little: first, here are £5000 appointed to George Porter; so that ample provision was made him, and it may the rather be intended that this estate was wholly designed for the plaintiff; secondly, here was a *post* consent, and those persons were *in loco parentum*. Now, if the earl had, as posibly he might have, thus pardoned and been reconciled to the marriage, he would probably have given the plaintiff the estate, and that is a reason to induce us to the same, for I think it clear that an estate by an act of Parliament is liable to the same relief, regulation, etc. as any other estate. An estate tail, though that be by Statute, yet is liable to be cut off etc. If there had been a time limited, then there had been more reason to bind her up to have consent. But there ought to be a restraint put in these cases. That of the double forfeiture was truly and well observed. Where nobody is bound to give notice, it is to be taken by the party, but, besides, she is not an heir, for that might have made a great difference. This I thought not to say. Upon the whole, I am of opinion with My Lords, and I am glad I have their assistance. Let the bill be dismissed.

1 Modern 86, 86 E.R. 752

Michaelmas term, 22 Car. II, 1670, Roll 392. Williams, on the demise of Porter against Fry.

[In a feigned action of] ejectment on a special verdict, the case was [thus]. A man devises to A. for life, the remainder to one and the heirs of his body upon condition that, if he marry without consent of such and such or die without heirs of the body of his mother, that then the estate shall go to another and his heirs. The devisee marries without their consent, and he in the remainder enters.

Finch, Attorney General: The first question will be whether this proviso be a condition or a limitation. Secondly, whether notice be requisite in this case or not.

For the first, I take it to be a limitation and that it must so be expounded and not as a condition, as in the cases of Wilford v. Wilford; in Scholastica's Case; in Plowden's Queries; in Englefield's Case; in Jennour v. Hardy; in Gibbons v. Wallyard; in Wiseman v. Baldwin and the same case in Owen's Reports, that, in a case of a devise, a condition must be construed as a limitation.[1] There seems, indeed, to be an authority against me in Mary Portington's Case,[2] in a reason there given, but it is an accumulative reason, and does not come to the point adjudged. I shall insist upon Wellock v. Hamond, as reported in Leonard, and as it is reported likewise in Boraston's Case, and Lord Coke says that it does resolve

[1] *Wilford v. Wilford* (1556), 2 Dyer 128, 73 E.R. 279; *Newis v. Lark* (1571), 2 Plowden 403, 412, 75 E.R. 609, 621; Plowden, Quaeries, no. 108, p. 17, 75 E.R. 880; *Attorney General v. Englefield* (K.B. 1590), Moore K.B. 303, 72 E.R. 595, 7 Coke Rep. 11, 77 E.R. 428, Popham 18, 79 E.R. 1139, 1 Anderson 294, 123 E.R. 480, 4 Leonard 135, 169, 74 E.R. 779, 800; *Jennor v. Hardie* (1587), 1 Leonard 283, 74 E.R. 258; *Gibbons v. Maltyard* (1611), Popham 6, 79 E.R. 1129, 8 Coke Rep. 130, 77 E.R. 671, Moore K.B. 594, 72 E.R. 780; *Wiseman v. Baldwin* (1595), Owen 112, 74 E.R. 938, also Croke Eliz. 377, 78 E.R. 624, 1 Rolle, Abr., *Condition*, pl. K, 5, p. 411, Gouldesborough 152, 75 E.R. 1060.

[2] *Portington v. Rogers* (1613), 10 Coke Rep. 35, 77 E.R. 976, 2 Brownlow & Goldesborough 65, 138, 123 E.R. 817, 860.

a query in Dyer 317; so that express words of condition may by construction in a will amount to no more than a limitation.[1]

The second point is whether he shall be excused for a breach of this condition for want of notice. And I shall consider it in respect of the person and in respect of the grounds of notice in any case.

First, in respect of the person, now, he may be considered in two capacities, as an infant and as a devisee. Now, his infancy cannot excuse him, for the condition was annexed to the devise expressly, because he was an infant.

Secondly, he is a purchaser. Now, if an infant purchase an advowson and the incumbent die, a lapse shall incur, though he had notice of the death of the incumbent. And there is the same reason in this case, where he is a devisee.

Thirdly, an infant is bound by all conditions in a deed, though not by conditions in law, as appears in the Case of Winbolt v. Tailbury; indeed, 31 Assize 17 is against it; but, in Brooke's Abridgment, [*Condition*, pl. 114], that case is said to be no law, and Brooke agrees with Plowden in the Case of Stowel v. Zouch.[2]

Secondly, consider him as a devisee, and, then, there will be less ground to excuse the want of notice. I take it to be a good difference betwixt lands devised to an heir upon condition and lands devised to a stranger upon condition. To the heir, notice must be given, but not to a stranger, for the heir is in by descent, and a title by law is cast upon him, and he may very well be supposed to take no notice of a devise, because the law takes no notice of a devise to him. Now, a stranger, as he must needs take notice of the estate given, so he may very well be obliged to take notice of the terms upon which it is given. 4 Co. 82.[3] As for the grounds and reasons of the law, when notice in any case is requisite and when not. First, I take it for a rule that every man is bound to take notice when none is bound to give him notice. 1 Hen. VII, pl. 5; 13 Hen. VII, pl. 9; Sir Henry Constable's Case; Burleigh's Case, in the Exchequer; and 1 Cro. 390; Roll. 856; Litt., sect. 350. Secondly, that, where persons are equally privy and concerned, there needs no notice, as in Leviston's Case; Mallorie's Case; and 14 Hen. VII, pl. 21.[4] The

[1] *Wellock v. Hammond* (1590), 2 Leonard 114, 74 E.R. 403, 3 Coke Rep. 20, 76 E.R. 672, also Croke Eliz. 204, 78 E.R. 460; *Vernon v. Vernon* (1572), 3 Dyer 317, 73 E.R. 718, *ut supra*.

[2] *Wimbish v. Tailbois* (1550), 1 Plowden 63, 55, 75 E.R. 63, 89; YB 31 Edw. III, Lib. Ass., f. 188, pl. 17, Brooke, Abr., *Conditions*, pl. 114 (1357); *Stowel v. Lord Zouch* (1569), 1 Plowden 353, 75 E.R. 536.

[3] *Corbet's Case* (Wards 1599), 4 Coke Rep. 81, 76 E.R. 1058, also 2 Anderson 134, 123 E.R. 585, 1 Eq. Cas. Abr. 196, 21 E.R. 985.

[4] YB Mich. 1 Hen. VII, f. 5, pl. 8 (1485); YB Pas. 13 Hen. VII, f. 22, pl. 9 (1498); *Constable's Case* (1601), 5 Coke Rep. 106, 77 E.R. 218, also 1 Anderson 86, 123 E.R. 367, British Library MS. Lansdowne 1088, f. 69, S. A. Moore, *A History of the Foreshore* (1888), pp. 224–241 (Sir John Constable's Case and Sir Henry Constable's Case); *Gurney v. Saer* (1584), 3 Leonard 95, 74 E.R. 563; *Pearce v. Bacon* (1595), Croke Eliz. 390, 78 E.R. 636; *Gimlet v. Saundrey* (1635), 1 Rolle, Abr., *Estate*, pl. N, 1, p. 856, also *sub nom.*

third consideration arises from the circumstances and strict formality of all notice. You must not give notice of a will by word of mouth, but you must leave a copy of it. He compared Fraunces' Case.[1] Now, the infant in remainder is incapable of observing these circumstances, and they, being both strangers, are both to take notice at their peril.

Now, to answer objections. One is that the condition is penal, and inflicts a forfeiture of an estate, and that, therefore, notice ought to be given.

I say this is rather a declamation than an argument in law. I will put a case, where he that is subject to a penalty must give notice to preserve himself, Poph. 10,[2] so that penalty or no penalty is not the business, but privity or no privity guides the case. And Fraunces' Case was ruled upon the privity, not upon the penalty. The Case of Curtis v. Woolverston and a case adjudged in this court, Lee v. Chamberlyne, seem against me, but they differ from ours, and the Case of Alford v. The Commonalty of London is an authority for me.[3]

Mr. Solicitor [General] *North*, for the defendant: I will not speak much to that point, whether it be a condition or a limitation. I shall rely for that upon Mary Portington's Case that express words of condition cannot be construed to be a limitation. Dyer 127.[4] Now, if this be a condition, then, the heir regularly ought to enter, which he cannot do in this case, because a remainder is here limited over. The law does interpret conditions according to the nature and circumstances of the thing, and not strictly always according to the letter. I do not observe that in any case the law suffers a man to incur a forfeiture where he has not notice or is not in law supposed to have notice. And he cited the Case of Molyneux v. Molyneux and Fraunces' Case. He said it was not the intention of the party that the devisee should be stripped of his estate and be never the wiser. The Case of Saunders v. Gerard is for me, of which I have a private report. He urged also the Case of Curtis v. Woolverston and Pennant's Case.[5]

It is objected that they that are to have the benefit of the estate ought to take notice.

Gymlett v. Sands, Croke Car. 391, 79 E.R. 942; T. Littleton, *Tenures*, sect. 350; *Albany v. Bishop of St. Asaph* (1585), 1 Leonard 31, 74 E.R. 29, also Croke Eliz. 119, 78 E.R. 376; *Mallory v. Payn* (1601), 5 Coke Rep. 111, 77 E.R. 228, Croke Eliz. 805, 832, 78 E.R. 1033, 1058; YB Hil. 14 Hen. VII, f. 18, pl. 7 (1499).

1 *Milner v. Fraunces* (1609), 8 Coke Rep. 89, 77 E.R. 609, also 2 Brownlow & Goldesborough 277, 123 E.R. 940.

2 *Ward v. Downing* (1593), Popham 10, 79 E.R. 1132.

3 *Curteis v. Wolverston* (1605), Croke Jac. 56, 79 E.R. 48; *Mayor of London v. Alford* (1640), Croke Car. 576, 79 E.R. 1095.

4 *Warren v. Lee* (1556), 2 Dyer 126, 73 E.R. 276.

5 *Molineux v. Molineux* (1607), Croke Jac. 144, 79 E.R. 126; *Milner v. Fraunces* (1609), *ut supra*; *Curteis v. Wolverston* (1605), *ut supra*; *Harvey v. Oswald* (1596–1597), 3 Coke Rep. 64, 76 E.R. 775, Moore K.B. 456, 72 E.R. 692, Croke Eliz. 553, 572, 78 E.R. 798, 816, 2 Anderson 90, 123 E.R. 561.

I answer the same objection might be made in Fraunces' Case.

Another reason given to excuse the not giving of notice is that the condition imports no more than nature teaches.

But I answer, in case the executor consent, it is no matter whether the grandmother consent or not. And, for their authorities, I shall rely upon the Case of Gimblet v. Sands and upon Fraunces' Case for answering them.[1]

So he prayed judgment for the defendant.

HALE, Chief Justice: All the difference betwixt this case and Fraunces' Case is that, in that case, there is an heir at law, and not in this. Now the Chancery is so just as to observe the civil and canon law as to personal legacies, but not as to land.

T. Raymond 236, 83 E.R. 123

Michaelmas 22 Car. II, 1670, Rot. 392, King's Bench. Williams *versus* Fry.

[A feigned action of] ejectment [was brought] for Newport House of the demise of George Porter. Upon *non culpabilis* [pleaded, there was] a special verdict. The earl of Newport was seised in fee, and had issue three sons yet living, and two daughters, Anne and Isabel. Isabel married the earl of Banbury, by whom she had issue Anne, now defendant. The other sister, Anne, was married to Thomas Porter, by whom she had issue George Porter, the lessor of the plaintiff. On 8 February, 18 Car. II [1666], the earl of Newport made his will in writing, and devised the house to his wife for her life, remainder to the defendant Anne and the heirs of her body, under this condition (on which the case depends) *viz.*

> Provided always and upon condition that, if my said grandchild do marry without the consent of my said wife, Charles, earl of Warwick, and Edward, earl of Manchester, and the major part of them, and, in case the said Lady Anne Knowles do or shall marry without the consent of the major part of my said trustees or shall happen to depart this life without issue of her body, then I will and bequeath the said premises unto my grandchild George Porter, son of my said deceased daughter Lady Anne, late wife of Thomas Porter, and his heirs forever.

18 August 1667, Anne marries Christopher Fry without the consent of the countess of Newport, earl of Warwick, and earl of Manchester, and the said Anne had not then notice of the will of the said earl of Newport, and, then, she was but of the age of fourteen years.

[It was] resolved, first, it is a limitation and not a condition, though the words are the express words of a condition, yet they must always be conformable to the intention of the parties. Dyer 317, pl. 5; 3 Co. 21; 3 Cr. 833, 2, 591, 3, 376;

[1] *Gymlett v. Sands* (1635), *ut supra*; *Milner v. Fraunces* (1609), *ut supra*.

2 Leon. 31; Owen 8;[1] Roll. Abr. 411. By which cases, it appears that words of condition in a will shall enure as a limitation, and, though in Mary Portington's Case, 10 Co., it is said otherwise, yet that is but an accumulative reason, which was not necessary.

[It was] resolved, second, notice of the condition was not necessary. First, none is appointed by the devisor to give notice; second, nobody is concerned to give notice, the heirs and executors have nothing to do therewith; third, all parties had equal means of coming to notice, and, if notice be requisite, it might be a means to avoid the will of the devisor. 2 Cr. 119, 1, 575; 4 Co. 82, 5, 110; 1 Co. 391;[2] fourth, it is a thing which concerns his own interest, which is the true reason of Sir Andrew Corbet's Case; fifth, it was not impossible for the defendant to have inquired and informed herself, and, if she remains ignorant and not informed, it is her own folly. 1 Roll. Abr. 463; Hob. 68.[3]

As to Francis's Case, 8 Co. 92,[4] there, the party had other means to claim besides the will, and should not need to take notice of the will. But, in our case, the will is the only way to claim the estate, and, therefore, the defendant ought to take notice thereof. As to the Case of 2 Cr. 144, Molineux,[5] it lies there properly in the conusance of the younger son that the legacies be paid or not etc., and differs from this principal case.

And so judgment was given by the whole court (*absente* Morton) for the plaintiff.

Finch, Attorney General, *Jones*, King's Counsel, for the plaintiff; *North*, Solicitor [General], and *Winnington*, for the defendant.

2 Levinz 21, 83 E.R. 434

Michaelmas term, 23 Car. II, 1671. Williams against Fry.

[In an action of] ejectment and upon *non culpabilis* and a special verdict, the case was this. The earl of Newport, being seised and having three sons now living and two daughters, one of which daughters had issue the wife of the defendant, devised the messuage in question, called Newport House, in the parish of St. Martin's, Westminster, to the wife of the defendant in tail, provided that, if she married without the consent of the earl of Manchester and others or died without issue, then to the lessor of the plaintiff, being then and still an infant. She, not

---

[1] *Spittle v. Davis* (1587), Owen 8, 55, 74 E.R. 860, 895, also Moore K.B. 271, 72 E.R. 574, 2 Leonard 38, 74 E.R. 339.

[2] *Corbet's Case* (Wards 1599), *ut supra*; *Gymlett v. Sands* (1635), Croke Car. 391, 79 E.R. 942, also 1 Rolle, Abr., *Estate*, pl. N, 1, p. 856.

[3] *Shepheard v. Frie* (1651), 1 Rolle, Abr., *Condition*, pl. A, 14, p. 463; *Richards v. Carvamel*, Hobart 68, 80 E.R. 217.

[4] *Milner v. Fraunces* (1609), 8 Coke Rep. 89, 77 E.R. 609, also 2 Brownlow & Goldesborough 277, 123 E.R. 940.

[5] *Molineux v. Molineux* (1607), Croke Jac. 144, 79 E.R. 126.

having notice of the condition and being of the age of fourteen, married without the consent of the earl of Manchester etc. to the defendant Fry. He entered, and the lessor brought an [action of] ejectment.

And the case was argued this and Hilary term following by *Jones* and *Finch*, Attorney General, for the plaintiff, and by *Winnington* and *North*, Solicitor General, for the defendant. And three points were argued by the counsel:

First, if this was a condition or a conditional limitation, the plaintiff is not heir, and so has no right to enter; otherwise, if it be a conditional limitation;

Second, be it the one or the other, if notice thereof ought to have been given to the devisee before the estate shall be determined;

Third, if notice were necessary, whether the infant of both parties (for the lessor as well as the devisee, wife of the defendant, were both infants) will alter the case.

And, afterwards, in Easter term following, all the judges concurred in opinion and gave judgment for the defendant:

First, that, in this case, the proviso does not make a condition, but a conditional limitation, although a proviso and the words *et si* be express words of condition, contrary to what is held in 10 Co. Rep. 40b,[1] and that, in respect of the remainder, which is here limited over not to the heir, but to a stranger, for it cannot be a reasonable construction of the intent of the devisor that, if there be a breach by the wife of the defendant, it shall forfeit the estate of the lessor in remainder, but only that it shall work a determination of her own estate. And, for this, were cited 1 Rol. 411; 3 Co., Wellock and Hamond's Case, cited in Boraston's Case, *ibid.* 20b; 2 Cro. 56; Hilary term 1649, King's Bench, rot. 758, Saunders's Case; 3 Cro. 753; Dyer 317.[2]

Secondly, that the infancy in this case is not material, for the infant takes by purchase and is not to have age, and this is a conditional limitation express and infants are not privileged against conditions in a deed. Co. Litt. 233;[3] Plowd. 57, 375; Bro., *Condition*, 114.

Thirdly, no notice of the condition was necessary, and, therefore, want of notice will not excuse in this case, as it did in Corbet's Case, 4 Co. 2, because the devise here is to a stranger, and not to the heir, and the devisee might as well take notice of the condition as of the estate devised to him. [It is] otherwise where the devise is to the heir upon such a conditional limitation, for the heir might enter upon his general title as heir without notice of the will or condition. Here the defendant had no title but by the will, and yet entered. And this difference was taken and agreed, where a devise is to one upon condition and another is concerned

[1] *Portington v. Rogers* (1613), *ut supra.*

[2] 1 Rolle, Abr., *Condition*, p. 411, or *Wassell v. Yelton* (1616), 1 Rolle Rep. 411, 81 E.R. 573; *Wellock v. Hammond* (1590), *ut supra*; *Curteis v. Wolverston* (1605), *ut supra*; *Saunders v. Ritch* (1651), Style 278, 82 E.R. 709; *Vernon v. Vernon* (1572), *ut supra.*

[3] E. Coke, *First Institute* (1628), f. 233.

and more privy, he that is most privy shall give notice to the other, but, where both are equally privy and equally concerned, as the lessor and the defendant in this case, neither of them is obliged to give notice. 2 Cro., Molineux's Case; 3 Leon. 95; Dyer 354; Poph. 10; 3 Co. 72, Westby's Case; 1 Cro., Jean against Thornhill; 22 Edw. IV, 27, 28; 1 Rol. 409, Spring and Caser's Case.[1]

And judgment was given for the plaintiff by the whole court.

2 Keble 756, 84 E.R. 478

Wednesday, 17 May 1671. Williams against Fry.

In [a feigned action of] ejectment of Newport House on a demise by Porter, the title of both parties was under the devise by the earl of Newport, who devised to his daughter, who married the defendant, on condition that she marry by consent of his wife and trustees or the major part, the reversion to another daughter, whose issue is the lessor of the plaintiff. And the defendant, being an infant but fourteen years old, conceived notice ought to be by the party that is to take avail by a forfeiture.

But *curia contra*, as in The Orphans of London's Case and in Hungate's Case,[2] which *Maynard* said he argued and it was adjudged notice was needless.

But the parties agreed to a special verdict, and would not insist on a subsequent assent, which they had.

2 Keble 787, 84 E.R. 498

Friday, 30 June 1671. Williams against Fry.

The earl of Newport, seised in fee, devised to A. for life, the remainder to Ann, the daughter, and her heirs, provided she marry by the consent of the trustees or a major part, and, in default thereof to the lessor of the plaintiff. And it is found she married without consent to the defendant, but that she had no notice and that the trustees did after[wards] consent, and the heir, that should give it, was within age. This was a special verdict in ejectment tried at the bar the last term. The court inclined strongly it is a breach. *Adjornatur.*

2 Keble 814, 84 E.R. 515

Tuesday, 31 October 1671. Williams against Fry. Michaelmas term, 22 Car. II, Rot. 322.

[1] *Molineux v. Molineux* (1607), *ut supra*; *Gurney v. Saer* (1584), 3 Leonard 95, 74 E.R. 563; *Barrough's Case* (1576), 3 Dyer 354, 73 E.R. 793; *Ward v. Downing* (1593), *ut supra*; *Westby v. Skinner* (1595–1597), 3 Coke Rep. 67, 76 E.R. 783, also Croke Eliz. 365, 78 E.R. 613, Popham 85, 79 E.R. 1197, Moore K.B. 688, 72 E.R. 841; *Juxon v. Thornhill* (1628), Croke Car. 132, 79 E.R. 716; YB Mich. 22 Edw. IV, f. 27, pl. 77 (1482); *Springe v. Caesar* (1636), *ut supra*.

[2] *Mayor of London v. Alford* (1640), Croke Car. 576, 79 E.R. 1095; *Springe v. Caesar* (1636), *ut supra*.

A special verdict in [a feigned action of] ejectment of Newport House finds Mountjoy had issue, three sons and two daughters, Isabell and Ann, married to the defendant. And, by a will, he devised to his wife for life, remainder to the defendant and the heirs of her body, provided that she marry with the consent of the trustees by name or the major part, and, if she married without, the remainder to Isabell, married to Porter, the lessor of the plaintiff. The defendant was fourteen years old when married after the testator's death, and had no notice of this condition. The lessor of the plaintiff was eight years old then, and, after[wards], Ann married without consent; then the wife died.

Jones, for the plaintiff: The defendant without notice shall forfeit her estate.

First, where there is a devise to one on condition, the reversion to another without other circumstances, there needs be no notice, because the testator has appointed no notice, and, as the devise and estate was in the devisor's power, so was the manor as to notice. And, when the testator is silent and puts this on neither, it is hard for the court to put more burden and hardship on one than on the other, and the party may be remote. Therefore, if notice, which is here intended personal, should be necessary, 2 Cr. 145,[1] the condition might be prevented before notice could be given or the person found, and the devisee ought to take the estate as the devisor has given it.

Second, this condition is annexed to the estate, and contained in the same will; so the devisee has as much reason to know, one as the other. And, if the devisee for life should do waste before notice, it would be no excuse to say he had none. And it is as hard to know whether the devisee have an estate for life, as to know that it is conditional. And it is no objection to say this is *ignorantia juris*, which does not excuse, but this is ignorance of the fact. And, in some cases, men shall be bound to take notice of other's acts, as Gaulet and Sands, 1 Cr. 391, 1 Roll. 856,[2] on a forfeiture by a collateral warranty. And, by the same reason, the devisee shall take notice of all circumstances incident to the estate.

Third, this notice is as much in the party that is to lose, as in her that is to gain an advantage for not doing, in which case, as upon a resignation to an ordinary, which incurs no lapse without notice to the patron, 5 Co. 113, Mallory's Case, on a bargain and sale of a reversion, the bargainee must give notice; so 3 Cr. 353, pl. 10, Tavernor's Case; 3 Cr. 505, a copyholder shall not forfeit by absence three court days without notice, but, where the party has the easiest means of notice, he must give it, but, as 18 Edw. IV, 18, the defendant cannot plead no notice of arrears found by auditors; also Hub. 14, the high sheriff need not give notice to the under sheriff of an escape;[3] so Doctor and Student 149, the party must give notice of an appointment on condition to repair, but, of an appoint-

---

[1] *Molineux v. Molineux* (1607), *ut supra*.

[2] *Gymlett v. Sands* (1635), *ut supra*.

[3] *Taverner v. Lord Cromwell* (1584), Croke Eliz. 353, 78 E.R. 601, also 4 Coke Rep. 27, 76 E.R. 940, 3 Leonard 107, 74 E.R. 571; *Crisp v. Fryer* (1596), Croke Eliz. 505, 78

ment by a stranger, there needs no notice, because both are alike privy, and there is no reason of 8 Co. 93, Francis's Case, the difference between a condition of a bond and of estates, for, in both 6 Hen. VII, 4; Perkins 151, where the parties have equal means of notice they are all one, it being the subject matter that makes notice necessary.[1] Second, the particular circumstances here that the defendant was an infant when the condition was broken, this will make no alteration, being in the case of a purchase, in which case the parol shall not demur, and infants shall lose their estates on breach. 1 Inst. 233, and 8 Co., Whitingham's Case, as well on a condition of law, as of fact. Also the plaintiff's lessor was but eight years old and so not of discretion, as the other. Second, it is found the devisor has an heir, a son, yet living, and so the defendant seems not so privy to the condition, but she is still in by purchase if she had been heir, so she ought to take notice. Also notice is more requisite to an heir who takes himself generally to be in by descent, than to a stranger who is in by purchase. The authorities of 8 Co. 118, Francis's Case, who was an heir at law, is a resolution *ex abundanti*, and a breach resolved before that and it is not founded on a want of notice of the condition, but of things concurring to the breach, as who were executors and what the will was. Also, here, the executors that were to have advantage of the condition were the chief parties privy to the condition. Also, in this case, the acts were continuing from time to time, but the condition at bar relates to one single act of marriage. Second, the Case of Curteis, of copyhold, 2 Cr. 56, does not come to the matter in question, being not notice of the condition, but of the age of the daughters. Also, this was not equally in both. And, for 2 Cr. 144, Molineux's Case, it receives the same answer. Beside that, the ground here is different, the case in question where the party that is to have advantage has no knowledge of the matter of breach. And 8 Edw. IV, 1,[2] is no law on which that case is founded. And 4 C. 81, Andrew Corbet's Case, is strong in the point in question, being resolved that, had a stranger entered, the devisee should take notice of his estate by the will. But, because the heir concealed the will and kept possession, he should have no advantage thereof; Hilary term 9 Car. I, Common Bench, Spring and Ceasar, Roll 469, was adjudged by both courts that notice of payment was not necessary to be given to the heir, the assurance appointing none, Michaelmas [term] 1656, Southell's Case, devise to A., remainder to B., paying £500, on a trial at the bar, it was resolved the £500 was to be paid presently and the reversion was forfeited by non-payment without notice; and 1 Cr. 575, The Mayor of London and Alport, differs not from our case in reason.

E.R. 755, also Moore K.B. 350, 72 E.R. 621, Noy 58, 74 E.R. 1026; YB Mich. 18 Edw. IV, f. 18, pl. 23 (1478); *Norton v. Simmes* (1614), Hobart 12, 14, 80 E.R. 163, 165.

[1] *St. German's Doctor and Student* (edd. T. F. T. Plucknet and J. L. Barton, 1974), 91 Selden Soc. 267; *Milner v. Fraunces* (1609), *ut supra*; YB Trin. 6 Hen. VII, f. 4, pl. 3 (1491); J. Perkins, *A Profitable Book*.

[2] YB Pas. 8 Edw. IV, f. 1, pl. 1 (1468).

Winnington, for the defendant: Here is no forfeiture without notice, being penal. But, where there is no penalty, as in 22 Edw. IV, 27b, the party may be bound to take notice at his peril, so Keily and Bulkly, on error, notice was held not necessary; so 2 Cr. 391, Sir Baptist Hicks and Goats,[1] the same difference; and 5 Co. 113, Mallory's Case.

Second, the devisor being silent, he has left it to the construction of law who shall give notice, and the law prefers the saving of an estate before the destruction of an estate, as 18 & 19 Eliz., Dyer 354, Barrow's Case; Poph. 1, pl. 7, a voluntary conveyance, provided that, if a conusee paid etc., the conusee tenders at the place, and, by Wray, Dyer, and Manwood, no time certain being appointed for him in remainder to come to receive the money, he that is to pay it must give notice, though he knew the conveyance itself, as is implied; and 8 Co. 92b, in Francis's Case, it is held the estate did not cease without notice; so Lit. Co. 211, and the person that is to take advantage of the condition is the person that, by law, ought to give notice, which is evident on a supposition that notice is requisite; and Francis's Case is stronger than ours, being in a case of a settlement, and a will is more guided by intent, which cannot be presumed, so [it is] penal without notice; and Easter term, 19 Jac., King's Bench, Saunders and Kerwell,[2] one, seised in fee, by will, devises to a married woman on condition to pay money, and the wife's husband was by when the will was made; after the testator's death, the wife of the testator concealed the will, and, on a bill in Chancery to discover the estate after a trial at bar, it was held the wife ought to have notice. And Francis's Case was affirmed for law; also, the husband's being by was not sufficient, nor would notice to him, but only to her personally, by the Chief Justice Fleming, and Chamberlain, Dodderidge, the other [justice] being absent, and, there, it was said the devisor could never intend a forfeiture without personal notice, and [it was] agreed that he that is privy or is to take advantage must give notice. And, where both parties are infants, the law favors preservation of the estate against the forfeiture; and 4 Co. 81, Corbet's Case, a devise for years to raise portions has no appointment of notice by law, for here is no penalty, for the trustees have a remedy against a stranger on an entry; and Winch 104 and 117, Cooper and Edgar's Case, the same as 1 Roll 469, of Spring, it is held the heir ought not to have notice, because his ancestor had notice, and the heir cannot be in a better case than his ancestor; and 1 Cr. 416, of Alport, went off on the fine and non-claim, and the point of notice is left as a doubt.

Hale, Chief Justice, said this case was in Chancery, and there [it was] agreed a good condition by the two Chief Justices, and himself, then Chief Baron.

Second, they resolved there was no equity in case the law made it a forfeiture without notice. It is considerable whether there be not a difference between a devise to an heir, who without difficulty on 8 Co. 92, Francis's Case, ought to have

[1] *Hicks v. Goates* (1616), Croke Jac. 390, 79 E.R. 334.

[2] *Saunders v. Carwel* (1621), Palmer 164, 81 E.R. 1028.

notice, having the estate generally cast on him without the settlement. And, in Spring and Caesar's Case, the wife, tenant for life, the remainder to Hungate, an infant, in tail, and both joined in a fine to the use of the wife or her trustees in fee, proviso, if the heir did not pay 10s. at Michaelmas, and it was doubted if the money might be paid by the heir or were determined by the party's death. Second, as to notice, it was agreed it was not requisite, because Hungate, party to the deed and the fine, had notice; so this does not come home to this case.

Third, it was agreed, if a condition be precedent, whether notice be requisite or not, no use rises without performance of the condition, as, where money is not paid to J.S. and his heirs, the estate being until then suspended. But, in this case, it was agreed to be a condition subsequent, and no notice [is] requisite, because nobody is appointed to give it. And the Case of Kerwell, of Sir Jeoffry Palmer's reporting, he remembered as cited. Also, the court, against Lovy's Case, agreed, as has been resolved, to be a limitation, though the words be upon a condition if she marry or die without issue, the remainder to the lessor of the plaintiff, and so more than once or twice since 10 Co., Mary Portington's Case, it has been resolved, which Justice Twysden much doubted that, against express words of condition, it cannot be said a limitation.

HALE, Chief Justice, said there may be reason to relieve against such provisoes in legacies, because the ecclesiastical law, whom they follow, did relieve, as Swinborn, but, in a case of land, it is unreasonable the Chancery should relieve against such a power, which is the only hold parents have on their children.

Adjornatur.

2 Keble 867, 84 E.R. 548

Thursday, 1 February 1672. Williams against Fry.

In [a feigned action of] ejectment on the demise of Porter of Newport House, a special verdict finds Monjoy, seised in fee, had three sons yet living and three daughters, one married to the earl of Banbury, the other to Porter, lessor of the plaintiff, and he devised to the Lady Ann Knowles in tail, and, if she die without issue, then, to George Porter in case Ann married without the consent of his wife and trustees, she being fourteen years old without notice.

Mr. Attorney [General] *Finch*, for the plaintiff: All the agitations in Chancery were to pray a perpetual injunction after dismission, of which an appeal was in Parliament by the defendant for delay, which was overruled.

And, now, the first point is that this proviso is no condition, for that makes an end of the case, belonging to the heir and not to the plaintiff, but it is a limitation, of which the plaintiff may take the benefit, especially in a case of wills which are guided by intent, which would be frustrated as to the remainder should the heir enter, because he is in of his ancient estate. But, here, the intent is consonant to law, and as Dyer 317, pl. [*blank*], the fee simple to the wife and, after[wards], to his son works as a conveyance. So, here, it shall work to the Lady Ann until she marry without licence. If a man devise a particular estate and limit an interest over, it shall work as a limitation. But, where the condition gives but an authority as to executors to sell, Pl. Quaeres 108, it is no limitation. Also, if the remainder be limited over to the heir of the devisor, it remains as a condition. Michaelmas [term], 27 Eliz., in the Common Bench, Ruddal and Millers, Moor 212, and better in a manuscript of the Lord Cook.[1] But, where the remainder is to a stranger, it must be a limitation and not a condition, whatever the words be, as 29 Eliz., 1 Leond., pl. 383; and 29 Eliz., 2 Leond. 51; and Poph. 6 and 7; Fulmerston's Case, and Easter term, 37 Eliz., Rot. 341, King's Bench; 1 Roll. 411; Wiseman and Baldwin, Owen 112; and Aynsworth and Pretty, 3 Cr. 833;[2] and the only book that calls this in question is 10 Co., Mary Portington's Case, the second resolve, notwithstanding which, Wellock and Hammond's Case, 3 Co., in Boraston's Case, is not well answered, that paying is indifferent to a condition or a limitation; for Dyer 127, pl. [*blank*], is not else well resolved. And all the cases of executory devises must fall to the ground, unless this be a limitation, which has been in peace ever since The Serjeant's Case. And second, the Lady Ann Fry shall not be excused by non-age, because the condition was therefore imposed because she was an infant and the infant is a purchaser. And so 28 Edw. III, 99, in Coney's Case, 9 Co. 85, he shall not have age, and Co., Bosvill's Case, an infant purchaser loses an inheritance by usurpation; the same where an advowson is devised to an infant. Also, an infant is bound by all conditions in a deed, though Lit. Co. 233, not by conditions in law; Com. 57, Wimbish and Talboys, if an infant enfeoffs J.S. *contra* to a condition, it is a breach; so the heir of the feoffor, though an infant, (31 Ass. 17[3] is not law); Cond. Br. 114, and Com. 375, and Lit., sect. 234, must tender the money or lose the land.

Second, as she is a devisee, there is less reason to excuse her for want of notice, for, if lands be devised to an heir on condition, he that will take advantage of the condition must give the heir notice, for he is in naturally by descent, and the devise he need not take notice of, but he that will determine his estate must give notice. Also, a devise to an heir as such is void, unless specially to make him a purchaser, as, on a conditional estate, he shall have notice, but a stranger is bound to take notice of the estate devised, 4 Co. 82, Corbet's Case, and, consequently, of the conditions thereof. And the rather here, because the jury have not found any suppression of the will, but George Porter and the devisee are equally strangers to the will. Second, in respect of the legality of the condition, nothing excuses, for, notwithstanding Swinborn, 4 part, § 12, p. 272, the books in 43 Edw.

---

[1] *Rudhall v. Milward* (1585–1586), Moore K.B. 212, 72 E.R. 537, also 1 Leonard 298, 74 E.R. 271.

[2] *Fulmerston v. Steward* (1554), 1 Plowden 102, 75 E.R. 160, also 1 Dyer 102, 73 E.R. 225; *Haynsworth v. Pretty* (1601), Croke Eliz. 833, 919, 78 E.R. 1059, 1140, also Moore K.B. 644, 72 E.R. 813.

[3] YB 31 Edw. III, Lib. Ass., f. 188, pl. 17 (1357).

III, 6, *per* Kirton,[1] and Dyer 343b, and 1 Leond. 283, pl. 383, are that conditions not to marry are allowable, especially not to marry without consent, but, if there be no remainder over, it is but *in terrorem*. And as this is a lawful condition. So it is to be favored not to marry without consent, being no more than duty obliges.

Third, where notice stands simply on a condition, it is not necessary, for the mere breach of the condition defeats not the estate until entry, but, by a limitation, the estate is *nolens volens* put upon him in remainder. Also a condition descends in privity; so an heir may give notice, but he in remainder is a stranger. Also, upon the rules of law that are the measures of notice, no notice is here requisite. Where nobody is bound to give notice, the party must take it at his peril. 1 Hen. VII, 5, of Awards; 13 Hen. VII, 9b, on Eschete; and 5 Co., the like of a wreck and estray, and on [a plea of] *riens per descent*, the heir is bound by a false plea by a deed whereof he knew nothing. 25 Eliz., in the Exchequer, Gurney's Case, 3 Leond. A lease by the king reserving rent with a condition of reentry after another like lease is made, the first lessee surrenders, the rent incurs, the second lease is forfeit without notice, and 1 Cr. 390; and 1 Roll. 856, Gimlet and Sands; and Lit., § 352, the wife must take notice by feoffment of her husband. Second, where both parties are equally privy or strangers, notice needs not. But, where one is more privy than another, notice must be as, in common cases of *assumpsit*s, where no notice is averred. Easter term, 21 Car. I, Villars and Trussell's Case; and Bayfield and Collard's Case; and Leviston's Case. And this is the reason of the common law why a bishop shall take the benefit of lapse, 27 Eliz., Albany against Bishop, 1 Leond. 31, of St. Asaph, and Dyer 327, and, upon this ground, 5 Co. 117, Mallory's Case; and 14 Hen. VII, 21. A bargainee must give notice; so, of a feoffee, who have best notice shall give it.

Also third, wherever notice is requisite, notice of a will in the testator's life is not sufficient, but, after his death. And 8 Co., Francis' Case, and Sanders and Charwell's Case, not only by word, but by delivery of a copy of the will, with strict precise formality, which an infant cannot well understand, also the nature of the thing requires she would take notice, for she might marry the next day, or have a general notice. The sum of all objections is in this argument, that it is a penal condition that forfeits the estate, which is rather a declamation than an argument. And no case turns upon this single reason, for, in Poph. 10, Ward and Downing,[2] the party must give notice of the condition, though to subject himself to a penalty of payment, because the matter lay best in his knowledge. And the authorities objected are without regard to the penalty, as 8 Co., Francis' Case, the reasons whereof are plain, the conveyance being to secure the executors, whom the son could not disturb without knowing who they were, and the executors were more privy to the will and the feoffment than the son; Richard, one of the executors being the *cestui que use*, by one proviso; 2 Cr. 56, Curteis and Woolver-

[1] YB Hil. 43 Edw. III, f. 5, pl. 13 (1369).

[2] *Ward v. Downing* (1593), *ut supra*.

ston's Case; and Easter term, 19 Jac., King's Bench, Sanders and Carwell,[1] lands were devised to a married woman on condition to pay money, notice to the husband was not sufficient, but must be to the wife herself, which was not on a plea or a special verdict, but an opinion of Lee, Chief Justice, and Chamberlain, on the evidence, whereby it also appeared there was a concealment of the will, and, for aught appears, the wife was heir of the devisor. But, here, the Lady Ann Fry is not the heir. And 1 Roll., Spring and Caesar, though a precedent condition or subsequent, and 11 Car. I, 1 Cr., the Mayor of London and Alport, are authorities unanswerable, and Jones and Berkeley were of opinion that no notice was requisite.[2]

North, Solicitor [General], for the defendant: The entry of the plaintiff is not lawful. On 10 Co., Mary Portington's Case, words of express condition cannot be a limitation, but words indifferent may; and Dyer 127, pl. [*blank*], the whole argument takes it for a condition; and 2 Cr., Wood and Ingersole, might have been a strain by an executory devise, yet it was not supported; so, in Snow and Cutler, the intent of the party shall rather fall to the ground than the rules of law be changed.

But, second, the point which he mainly relied on was the want of notice of the will and condition, without which there is no default in the defendant, whether it be a condition or a limitation; both have a reasonable construction by the intent of the party's condition or estates. And bonds and time to dispense with them differ; they are altered by circumstances. And this, being a condition subsequent, shall not defeat the defendant's estate. No man shall in any case incur a penalty where he has not or cannot be presumed to have notice. 5 Co. 117, Mallory's Case; a feoffment in the absence of the lessee is not sufficient to enter for non-payment of rent, though it be to distrain; 2 Cr. 193, Wats and Ogwell; 22 Edw. IV, 27b, the like. And, in all cases of covenant and *assumpsit*, there is no penalty but only damages on an actual undertaking; 18 Edw. IV, 18. But here is no undertaking by the party, but a subsequent condition, which, without default, shall not be forfeit, especially this being a mere penalty without profit or loss to the defendant. 2 Cr. 144, Molineux's Case; and he relied on 8 Co., Francis' Case, for, if this would not defeat the estate in the case of a condition, much less in the case of a limitation. Also Francis' Case was but of a chattel; this is of an inheritance. In Sanders and Charwell's Case, all the court agreed there must be notice; and 2 Cr., Curteis and Woolverston, the reason of which was not that the legacy was demandable, as in personal legacies of rent, for a sum in gross is to be paid at his peril; therefore, the only excuse is want of notice. Dyer 354a, the like. And the objections that he that has the estate must take notice of the condition might

[1] *Curteis v. Wolverston* (1605), *ut supra*; *Saunders v. Carwel* (1621), Palmer 164, 81 E.R. 1028.

[2] *Springe v. Caesar* (1636), *ut supra*; *Mayor of London v. Alford* (1640), Croke Car. 576, 79 E.R. 1095.

have been made in Francis' Case. But, if the defendant had had no estate vested, but, by the condition, it may be presumed notice was, as where the devisee is in immediate possession, and, though no particular person is bound to give notice, yet, if the defendant, Dyer 354, have it any way, it is sufficient. And, where all the world may give notice, it must be given by the parties that will have the advantage of it. Also, nothing leads to the performance of the will but the notice of it. Also, Co., Corbet's Case, does only save the heir from prejudice, but here is no more prejudice to him in remainder than there would be by performance. And 1 Cr., notice excused only non-entry after five years on a fine, and 1 Cr. 391, Gimlet and Sands, differs a condition from that case.

HALE, Chief Justice, said, in Caesar's Case, it was adjudged a precedent condition as to the estate for life and the remainder, but a condition subsequent as to the fee simple. And, if, in the case at bar, this be not a breach at the time of the marriage, it can never be. But in a case of payment, the money, by possibility, may be carried over. Also, there is no difference between this and Francis' Case, but that, there, the heir had a just pretension to the estate without any settlement, and, here, the defendant has none but by the settlement, which concerns her to search after. And notice or not is no question in Chancery but at common law.

And the court inclined that the defendant must take notice, etc. *Adjornatur.*

3 Keble 19, 84 E.R. 570

Easter term, 24 Car. II, 1672, in the King's Bench. Williams and Fry.

On a lease of George Porter, a special verdict was found. the earl of Newport, seised in fee, had issue, three sons and two daughters. Isabel was married to the earl of Banbury; Anne was married to Charles Porter *alias* Fry, the defendant. The earl of Newport devised to the Lady Anne Knowles provided and on condition she marry by consent of the trustees and, if she marry without, remainder to the lessor of the plaintiff. She married without consent to Fry, without notice of the will. Porter was then under age.

RAINSFORD held this proviso to marry by consent is a limitation, though there be express words of condition, on 1 Roll. 411, p. 5; and Owen 112, Wisman and Baldwin's Case; and 3 Cr., Wellcock's Case; and 2 Cr. 56, here being a remainder limited over to the lessor of the plaintiff. And here is a future devise.

Second, the infancy of the devisee, 8 Co. 42, and Lit. Co. 234, does not avail her, the condition being in fact and imposed because she was an infant.

Third, no notice is necessary of the will or condition, but she must take notice of both at her peril. But, where a devise or conveyance is made to the heir at law, he must have notice of both, else, 8 Co., Francis' Case, he shall lose nothing. But, where the devise or conveyance is to a stranger, if one of the parties be not more knowing nor privy than the other, but equally and indifferently strangers, the devisee must take notice of the condition, which appears by 2 Cr. 145, Molineux' Case, where the younger children must give notice to the executors, and 5 Co., Mallorye's Case, a bargainee must give notice before avowry for rent; so

3 Leond. 95, Gurney's Case, before entry for a condition; thus, 4 Co., Holland's Case, notice of a resignation must be by ordinary computation; and Dyer 354; Lit. Co. 211, the like on a revocation of uses, where time or place is uncertain; so Popham 10. But, as in an action upon the case, 22 Edw. IV, 27 and 28, a lessee for years must remove in convenient time after the death of the tenant for life at his peril, thus a lapse by death incurs without notice. And this is the reason of 1 Roll. 856, Gimlet and Sands; 1 Cr. 391; and 1 Roll. 469, Spring and Caesar's Case, where there was none to give notice. So 1 Cr. 575, The Mayor of London and Alport, though the case were adjudged on a non-claim, and the third resolution in 4 Co., in Sir Andrew Corbet's Case, is full in this point or stronger, for the heir must have given notice to the executors to discharge his land. And, in the verdict at the bar, it is not found that Porter had notice of the will before the condition broken, but the contrary presumption, and no will was concealed. Nor it is not found the trustees had notice of the will, and the executors are not found but, however, it would not be proper to give notice as to the inheritance. Also the inheritance is here given from the heir. And, as to the main objection of Easter term, 18 Jac., King's Bench, Saunders and Carvel, it is so uncertainly reported by Palmer, that it is hard to make anything of it, and it appears the will was concealed a year. And *non constat* whether the condition were to be performed in that time. And the question was rather what was notice, than whether notice were necessary.

TWYSDEN, Justice, for the plaintiff, [held] also that this proviso and upon condition, contrary to 10 Co., Mary Portington's Case, shall work as a limitation, where there is an estate limited over, and, being in the case of a will, where a construction shall be meant to support the will, as 1 Roll., Saunders and Rich, Hilary term 1649, rot. 758, where S. was seised of lands and a portion of tithes, and he devised all his free lands to J.S. on condition to permit his wife to enjoy his fee simple lands in H., in which he had only that portion of tithes, and [it was] adjudged that they passed, as 1 Roll. 611, Burbridge and Knaseborough's Case, and 1 Co. 8, Corbet's Case, *et loquendum ut vulgus*, this is said on condition, and is in common use. Therefore, [it] shall not destroy the subsequent limitations, as Poph., Martidale and Martin, a devise in fee on condition to perform the will are expounded as a limitation.[1] And Owen 112, Wiseman and Baldwin's Case, was upon condition to pay; yet [it was] adjudged a limitation, and, on that point, reversed. And an executory devise is as a remainder or as a new devise in a will is, which are but *pugna verborum*, and 3 Cr. 383, and 1 Roll. 411, a devise to the eldest son on condition to pay the youngest £10 [was] adjudged a good limitation and an executory devise to the youngest; 1 Leon. 283, pl. 383, Imot and Saun-

[1] *Martidale v. Martin* (1592), Croke Eliz. 288, 78 E.R. 542.

ders. All which are of greater authority than Dr. Butt's Case, and 2 Cr. 590 was stronger than the case in question.[1]

Second, notice needs not, being not provided for by the devisor, nor by the law. Nor is it said if she, having notice of the will, marry contrary etc., for then notice must be proved by somebody. So 1 Cr. 132, Juxton and Thornhill's Case,[2] in [an action of] *assumpsit* to pay what B. appoints, notice is needless. And so upon arbitraments which the party is not bound further to perform, then notice is requisite; as an obligation to pay the rent, it must be demanded. And I rely upon Spring and Caesar's Case, which was discharged in the House of Lords on a petition lately, and the land was enjoyed by non-payment without notice. And Gurney's Case was cited to be, the lease to be void by non-payment and the second lease to begin on the forfeiture, adjudged the second lessee is bound to take notice of the time of non-payment by the first, but, of a private surrender, by Wray, there, he must have notice. And 1 Cro. 575, the reason of division was by the words, if, through oblivion, they aliened etc., which was conceived impled notice was requisite, but, else, it was clearly agreed that notice was not necessary.

HALE, Chief Justice, for the plaintiff also:

First, it is no question, but this is a limitation, because the words of condition when joined with another clause are interpreted by it what the testator meant, and this has received as many resolutions as any one point of the law where the remainder is limited over. 2 Cro. 590, and Owen 112, Baldwin, and Wiseman and Pain's Case, and 3 Cro., Ainsworth and Pretiman. It is all one as a provisoes if she marry without licence, her estate [will] cease; and there is nothing but the by-opinion in 10 Co., Mary Portington's Case, that can stumble only young students.

Second, the estate devised to Anne has one limitation by law, until she died without issue, and another limitation of fact, that she do not marry without licence, on the determination of either of which, the estate is presently actually in the lessor of the plaintiff without entry or claim, and all one as a devise for life. And, if she marry, then it remain to Porter. This is all one with the estate *quamdiu sola vixerit*. And, if the want of notice be not a breach, it can never be broken, she being married without licence. So, if notice were necessary, it would be now fruitless. But, where the condition may be performed after notice, there it has been doubted, as Altham's Case, whether notice be necessary. But here, the condition is discharged by the marriage, and nobody can know the will but upon enquiry. And the same means that one has to know all have. Therefore, he that is to have an advantage must make the best enquiry he can, for he that made the will is dead, and cannot give notice. Therefore, lying merely in enquiry and

[1] *Butt's Case* (1557), 10 Coke Rep. 41, 77 E.R. 986; *Pell v. Brown* (1620), Croke Jac. 590, 79 E.R. 504, also Palmer 131, 81 E.R. 1012, 2 Rolle Rep. 196, 216, 81 E.R. 746, 760, Godbolt 282, 78 E.R. 165, J. Bridgman 1, 123 E.R. 1157.

[2] *Juxon v. Thornhill* (1628), Croke Car. 132, 79 E.R. 716.

the plaintiff and the defendant equally concerned to take notice, she that has the estate to know upon what terms and he to know the state of this reversion and neither is preferred. Therefore, rather than this condition or limitation shall be perpetually discharged, there needs no notice. He that has given the estate having appointed no notice, the court have no reason to supply it unless the law strongly presumed it, which it does not here, because no person is bound to give notice, not the heir because disherited, not the executors because not concerned with the inheritance, not the trustees because they have but their labor for their pains. Also it is equally in all to use the same means to enquire. Therefore, the defendant must take the hazard of her own want of notice at her peril, for it is her interest to take advantage of the estate. And, therefore, she must take notice of the incidents to that estate, as 4 Co., Sir Andrew Corbet's Case, and as, when an executor proves a will, it is doubtful, where the rent is more than the land, whether he shall be charged in the *detinet*, but, if under, no doubt but he is bound to take notice of all conditions. So, on a devise to the wife *durante viduitate*, by the same reason, by marriage before notice, she would have an absolute estate for life. No man is presumed to be ignorant of his own interest. Therefore, he must take it with all its faults. Also it is not impossible for the defendant to make an enquiry. Therefore, she shall not take advantage of her own laches; as Frie's Case, a condition to pay £40 when he married the obligor's kinswoman, and, in [an action of] debt, the defendant pleaded performance, and an issue [was] tendered that the obligor had notice, and [there was a] demurrer thereto, and [it was] ruled notice was not material, because, though this was in the privity of the obligee, yet it was also in the privity of the obligor's kinswoman of whom he might have enquired, which is Hilary term 1655, rot. 2851, Shepheard and Fry,[1] and judgment [was] for the plaintiff.

Third, the defendant's infancy is no protection without question, the plaintiff who is to give notice being an infant likewise. But, however, this being not a condition in law, but in fact, an infant has no more avail than others. Also she is as much concerned in this restriction of marriage, being above twelve as any. Thus, the Statute [of Merton], that *usurae non corrunt contra infantem*, does provide that such marrying against consent shall forfeit the double value, this condition is laid on her with respect to her condition, that she cannot so well provide for herself, and the testator might intend she should have no succession if she married without licence, and Harwood's Case,[2] the marriage of an orphan in Kent without notice was finable, because it was his business to enquire whither she was or was not, for the authorities, Saunders' Case may be good law if the condition of the will were known whether, if she refused to pay or to pay and no

---

[1] *Shepheard v. Frie* (1651), 1 Rolle, Abr., *Condition*, pl. A, 14, p. 463.

[2] *Rex v. Harwood* (1672), 1 Eq. Cas. Abr. 153, 21 E.R. 953, 2 Levinz 32, 83 E.R. 439, 1 Ventris 178, 86 E.R. 121, 1 Modern 77, 79, 86 E.R. 745, 747, 2 Keble 847, 855, 84 E.R. 536, 541.

time [was] limited and then, being a legacy, there must be a demand precedent also, the words might import notice [to be] necessary. But this not appearing, nothing can be made of it. And, as for Hungate's Case, the son and heir of the Lady Caesar, who died before the day of payment, it was ruled by all that the heir was bound without notice because none could give notice and the ancestor had notice as the party to the deed by which the money was to be paid; so that comes not wholly to this case. And Molineux's Case quite differs from this, being a devise to those to whom the money was to be paid, and notice to the executor was there ruled necessary, because the money lay in demand and was a rent or, at best, but a legacy. Also, the younger children were to have the rent and the estate by non-payment; therefore, he ought to give notice. But Porter here was not concerned in the marriage. Also, there could be no default in the executor until demand. And had Francis's Case been to the younger son, his disturbance had been a breach without notice. But the heir without a conveyance was entitled; therefore, he must have notice of any clog by a conveyancer. 1 Cro. 575, was a devise to the executor on condition to pay yearly and, if by oblivion or other means, they failed, then to London; there was a question whether oblivion imported notice precedent. But it is not disputed but that, if it had been, if they do not pay, there needed no notice, but a fine and a non-claim could not bar without a breach, which rather implies no notice was necessary.

And, *per curiam* (Morton, [was] for the plaintiff also, but [was] sick and absent), judgment was for the plaintiff.

1 Freeman 31, 89 E.R. 26

Easter term, 1672. Porter v. Frye. In the King's Bench.

The defendant was a grandchild to the earl of Newport. And he, by his will, devises the lands in question to the countess for life and, afterwards, to the defendant, provided that she marry with the consent of trustees by him nominated, and, if she did marry without their consent, then to the plaintiff. She married without the consent of the trustees. The great question was whether notice ought to be given to her of the condition or whether she ought to take it at her peril.

[It was] argued by *Jones* that she ought to take notice at her peril for these reasons:

First, the testator has appointed no notice to be given, and it was in his power to give the estate upon what conditions he pleased;

Second, this condition is annexed to the estate, and is contained in the same deed, and the devisee has the same means to come to the knowledge of the condition as of the estate;

Third, this condition is as much within the notice of the party that is to lose the estate, as of him that is to gain the estate. Where the party that is to take advantage of the condition has not an easier way to come to the knowledge of it than the party that is to lose by it, there shall be no need of notice. 5 Co., Mallorie's Case; Cro. Eliz. 353; Hob. 14; 18 Edw. IV, 18; 8 Co. 92; 6 Hen. VII, 4; Perk. 151.

Objection: The defendant was an infant at the time of the breach of the condition, *viz.* fourteen years of age.

Answer: First, though she be an infant, yet she is a purchaser; second, an infant shall in many cases lose his estate by the breach of a condition; third, the plaintiff is an infant too, *viz.* eight years old, and, if that be any plea, it is the stronger for the plaintiff.

Cases objected were 8 Co. 89, Frances' Case; 2 Cro. 56; 2 Cro. 144; 8 Edw. IV, 1; cases *pro querente*, 4 Co. 81; 1 Roll. 463; Cro. Eliz. 577.

Winnington, pro defendente: Where a penalty is incurred, there, notice ought to be given. 22 Edw. IV, 27, 28; 2 Cro. 391; Winch 104, 107; Cro. Car. 416.

Afterwards, as I have heard, judgment was given that it is not necessary to give notice. And the justices relied on Sir Andrew Corbet's Case, in 4 Rep. 82.

1 Ventris 199, 86 E.R. 135

Easter term, 24 Car. II, 1672, in the King's Bench. The Lady Anne Fry's Case.

In an [action of] ejectment by Williams, lessee of George Porter, Esquire, against the Lady Anne Fry. The case appeared to be this upon a special verdict.

Mountjoy, earl of Newport, was seised of a house called Newport House, in the County of Middlesex. And he had three sons, who are yet living, and he had two daughters, Isabel, married to the earl of Banbury, by whom she had issue Anne, the defendant, and Anne, married to Porter, by whom she had issue George Porter, lessor of the plaintiff. And he made his will in this manner:

> I give and bequeath to my dear wife, the Lady Anne, countess of Newport, all that my house called Newport House and all other my lands etc. in the County of Middlesex for her life, and, after her death, I give and bequeath the premises to my grandchild, Anne Knolles [*viz.* the defendant] and the heirs of her body, provided always and upon condition that she marries with the consent of my said wife, and the earl of Warwick, and the earl of Manchester, or the major part of them, and, in case she marries without such consent or happen to die without issue, then I give and bequeath it to George Porter [*viz.* the lessor of the plaintiff].

The earl of Newport dies. And the Lady Anne Knolles, being of the age of fourteen years, marries with Fry without the consent of her grandmother or either of the earls. And it was found that she had no notice of the will until after the marriage and that George Porter, at that time, was of the age of eight years and that, after the death of the countess, she entered, and George Porter entered upon her, and made the lease to the plaintiff.

This case having been twice argued at the bar, *viz.* in Michaelmas term by Sir William Jones, for the plaintiff, and Winnington, for the defendant, and, in

Hilary term last, by Finch, Attorney General, for the plaintiff, and Sir Francis North, Solicitor General, for the defendant, it was this term resolved by the court, *viz.* Hale, Twysden, and Rainsford (Morton being absent) for the plaintiff upon these reasons.

Rainsford: Here have been three questions made.

First, whether the words in the will whereby the marriage of the defendant is restrained make a condition or a limitation. If it be a condition, then none but the heir can enter for the breach. But it is clear that they must be taken as a limitation to support the intent of the devisor and to let in the remainder which he limits over. 1 Roll. 411.

Secondly, whether the infancy of the defendant shall excuse her in this breach. And clearly it cannot, for a condition in fact obliges infants as much as others (*vide* 8 Co., Whittingham's Case,[1] the difference between conditions in fact and conditions in law), especially in this case, the nature of the condition showing it to be therefore imposed upon her, because she was an infant.

Thirdly, (and the main point of the case) whether the want of notice shall save the forfeiture of the estate. As to that, let the rules of law concerning notice be considered.

First, I take a difference where the devisee, who is to perform the condition, is heir at law and where a stranger. The heir must have notice, because he having a title by descent, need not take notice of any will unless it be signified to him. And so is Fraunces' Case, 8 Co., where the heir was a devisee for sixty years upon condition not to disturb the executor in removing the goods, and [it was] resolved that he should not lose his estate upon a disturbance before he had notice of the will. But, where the devisee is not heir, as in this case, he must inform himself of the estate devised to him and upon what terms.

Another rule is, when one of the parties is more privy than the other, notice must be given. But, where the privity is equal, notice must be taken by the party concerned. A bargainee shall not enter for a condition broken before notice, for the bargain and sale lies in his cognizance and not the lessee's; so, if a lease be made to commence after the end of the former, if the first be surrendered, the lessor shall not enter for a condition broken for non-payment of rent until notice given of the surrender. 3 Leon. 95. And, therefore, there shall be no lapse to the ordinary upon a resignation without notice. If a man makes a feoffment upon condition to enter upon payment of such a sum at a place certain, he must give notice to the feoffee when he will tender the money. Co. Lit. 211a; Dyer 354. And, upon this reason, is Molineux's Case, 2 Cro. 144, where a devise was that his heir should pay such rents and, if he made default, then his executors should have the lands, paying the said rents, and, if they failed of payment, then he devised the land to his younger children, to whom the rents were to be paid. It was

1 *Whittingham's Case* (1603), 8 Coke Rep. 42, 77 E.R. 537.

resolved non-payment by the executors should be no breach until they had notice that the heir had failed, which was a thing that the younger children must be privy to. But, in 22 Edw. IV, 27, 28, a tenant for life lets for years, and dies; the lessee must remove in convenient time, to be reckoned from the death of the tenant, whether he had notice of it or not, for he in reversion is presumed to be no more privy to it than himself. So Gymlet and Sand's Case, 3 Cro. 391, and 1 Roll. [Abr.] 856, where a husband and wife were tenants for life, remainder to the son in tail, remainder to the right heirs of the husband, the husband makes a feoffment with warranty and dies, then the wife and son join in a feoffment; this is a forfeiture of the estate of the wife, though she had no notice of the feoffment or warranty, whereby the right of the son was bound. So Spring and Caesar's Case, 1 Roll. 469, A. and B. join in a fine to the use of A. in fee if B. do not pay £10 to A. before Michaelmas, and, if he does, then to the use of A. for life, remainder to B.; B. dies before Michaelmas; the heir of B. is bound to pay the £10 without any notice given by A. The reason given, which comes home to our case, is for that none is bound to give notice, and then it must be taken, though indeed a second be added, for that B., from whom his heir derives, had notice. The Mayor and Commonalty of London against Alford, 3 Cro., where a devise was to six persons to pay certain sums for the maintenance of an almshouse etc. and, if, through obliviousness or other cause, the trusts were not performed, then to J.S. upon the same condition and, if he failed by two months, then to the Mayor and Commonalty of London upon the same trusts. The six did not perform the trusts, J.S. enters, J.N. enters upon him, and a fine with proclamations was levied, and five years passed, and the better opinion was that the Mayor and Commonalty of London were bound to pay the money appointed by the will, although they had no notice that the six persons or J.S. had failed, though, indeed, the case is adjudged against them, as being barred by the fine and non-claim. Sir Andrew Corbet's Case, 4 Co., is very strong to this purpose; where a devise is to J.S. until he shall or may raise such a sum out of the profits of the land; if a stranger enters after the death of the devisor, though the devisee had no notice of the will, yet the time shall run on, as much as if he had the land in his own possession.

These rules being applied to the present case, it will appear no notice is to be given.

First, the defendant is as privy to the will as anyone else, *viz.* as George Porter, who is found also to be an infant. It is not found whether there were any executors; if it had, they were not concerned to give notice, nor did it import the heir, for he could have neither benefit nor loss by the condition. The two cases which have been chiefly relied upon for the defendant were, first, Frances' Case, which differs, because it was in the case of an heir.

Secondly, the Case of Saunders and Carwell, 8 Jac., in a private report of Sir Geoffry Palmer, the Attorney General, in which there is no clear account of the case and we cannot find the roll, it was a devise to his wife for life, remainder to the daughter in tail upon a condition to pay money, and it was held that the non-payment would be no breach unless she had notice. First, it was an opinion only upon evidence, and Lee and Chamberlain only in court; secondly, for aught appears, the daughter might be the heir, and, then, it is good law; thirdly, it appears there was a foul concealment of the will for four years' time, within which time (for aught appears) the condition was to have been performed.

TWYSDEN was of the same opinion. But I omit his argument, because I could not hear him perfectly.

HALE was of the same opinion. As to the first point, I shall discharge the case of it, as not fit to be called in question, for, without peradventure, though the word 'condition' be used, yet limiting a remainder over makes it a limitation, for so it is plain the testator meant, and it is as much as if he had said, 'and if she marries' etc., then to remain, without the word 'condition'. And this has received as many resolutions as ever any point did, *viz.* Wiseman and Baldwin's Case, 18 Eliz., 1 Roll. 412; Hainsworth and Pretty's, 3 Cro. 833, and 2 Cro., Pell and Brown's Case, with a great many more;[1] and nothing but the opinion in Mary Portington's Case, 10 Co. 41, is against it.

When Finch, Attorney General, argued this case, he observed that Coke himself was of another opinion in the 3rd Report, in Wellock and Hammond's Case, cited in Boraston's Case, for, though, there, it is the word 'paying' only, which is adjudged a limitation, yet Coke says the query in Dyer 317 is, upon that, well resolved, and the case in Dyer is upon the word 'condition' expressly.

Then, to proceed to the other matters. Here is an estate tail devised to the defendant, subject to limitations, the one of law, *viz.* dying without issue, the other express and in fact, *viz.* marrying without the consent etc. And both are coupled together; so that, whenever she marries without consent etc., her estate determines and is transferred to him in the remainder, without either entry or claim. It is all one as if the estate had been devised to her for life, and, if she marries, then, to remain, which had been but an estate *quamdiu sola vixerit.* And it is to be observed that, if her marriage here be no breach of the conditional limitation (for so it is properly called) because she had no notice, then it can never be broken; so that the question must be whether such a marriage shall discharge the estate of it and make it become absolute.

It is true, where the condition requires such an act to be done, as may be done after notice, it has been questioned, whether the law shall not protract the time limited for performance, until notice be had, 3 Cro., Alford's Case, which was a condition for payment of money. But this is a thing of that nature that, being done, no subsequent notice can ever retrieve.

---

[1] *Wiseman v. Baldwin* (1595), *ut supra*; *Haynsworth v. Pretty* (1601), *ut supra*; *Pell v. Brown* (1620), Croke Jac. 590, 79 E.R. 504, also Palmer 131, 81 E.R. 1012, 2 Rolle Rep. 196, 216, 81 E.R. 746, 760, Godbolt 282, 78 E.R. 165, J. Bridgman 1, 123 E.R. 1157.

Then, it is to enquire how far the want of notice will excuse. It must be considered that it is a will made by a person now dead, who can give no notice, neither can any come to the knowledge of it without enquiry, and one has the same means to obtain it with another. And the person who would take advantage of it must make the best enquiry he can. If a devise were made to the defendant, it was her concern to enquire upon what terms. Until then, how can it be ascertained whether she will take it? And so it was Porter's business to enquire. [There is] no difference between them in this respect so that, upon these five accounts, it will appear that no notice is requisite to be given in this case.

First, because the testator has not appointed any notice to be given, for he which was the disposer might give upon what terms he pleased, and this matter of notice shall not be added unless it were in a case wherein the law would very strongly require it.

Secondly, because there is no person who can reasonably be engaged to give notice, *viz.* not the heir, for he is disinherited; not the executors, for they are not concerned in the freehold; nor the trustees, for they have but their labor for their pains; nor Porter, for he is no more bound to give than she to take notice.

Thirdly, because each party have the same means of informing themselves of the will, *i.e.* by enquiry.

Fourthly, it more imported the defendant to know it, as relating to her own interest. The will which gives the estate gives it upon this conditional limitation. Corbet's Case, 4 Co., comes very close; where, if the devisee stays while the time wherein the money might be raised is elapsed, he shall never raise it after. Suppose a man dies possessed of a term upon which a great rent is reserved; shall the executor, after that he has proved the will, throw up the term, as pretending not to have known of it? An estate is devised to one *durante viduitate*; shall she marry and, because she had no notice of the will, hold the estate absolutely for her life? There is the same reason in this case, for this proviso is a part of the limitation of the estate itself. No man is presumed to be ignorant of his own interest. And, as he must take notice to acquire, so also of the manner of the estate he gains. But he that gave it thus was not obliged to do so much.

Fifthly, it was not impossible for the defendant to have made enquiry, and she must not take advantage of her laches. A bond with a condition to pay £50 when the obligee shall marry the obligor's kinswoman, in [an action of] debt upon this, it was resolved that the obligee was not bound to give notice of the marriage, though it lay in his own privity, because the obligor might have known it by other means. Hilary term, 1650, between Try and [*blank*], Rot. 1081, King's Bench. It was proper for the defendant to have enquired whether her grandfather gave her anything. And so it was for him that should marry her. Harwood's Case, adjudged here (Hilary *ultimo*),[1] was upon this reason; he married a City orphan in

[1] *Rex v. Harwood* (1672), *ut supra.*

Kent, and was fined by the Court of Orphans, because he had not first applied himself to them for their licence etc., according to the custom of the City, and the fine was resolved here to be well imposed, though he had no notice that she whom he married was an orphan, because it was his business to enquire of the condition of her whom he will make his wife.

The next thing to be considered is the infancy of the defendant. And that is nothing in this case. Porter, who was the probablest person to give notice, is found to be an infant too. Conditions in fact bind infants. Again, the condition here relates to an act, which she is capable of doing. The Statute of Merton enacts *non currant usurae etc.*, whereby infants are exempted from penalties, yet, in another chapter, it gives the forfeiture of the said double value to the lord where his ward marries without his consent. It is a restraint laid upon her in a matter proper for her condition and with respect to her condition that, being an infant, she might advise with her friends about her marriage. The cases which have been objected do not come to this case, as the opinion in Saunders and Carwell's Case, which might be good in law, if it could be known what that case was, for the words might either explicitly or implicitly require notice, as if it were, if he refused to pay, etc. or it may be no time might be set for payment, for, in Molineux's Case, there, rents were granted, and, after[wards], a devise for the payment of them which naturally lie in demand.

Secondly, there, it concerned the younger children to give notice, for the rents were not only to be paid to them, but, upon failure of payment, the land was devised to them; so that was a concurrence of concern in them, as to the performance of the condition and the estate they should acquire by the breach. Whereas the plaintiff in this case is not concerned in the performance of the condition.

Thirdly, the penning of the condition there quite differs, for it is upon default of payment, which implies notice must be first had. In Frances' Case, there would have been no need of notice if the devise had not been to the heir, which is the only thing wherein it differs materially from this case. In Alford's Case, the debate was occasioned by the special penning, for it was thus, that, if, through obliviousness, the trusts should not happen to be performed. Now there could be no oblivion of that [which] they never knew. Therefore, there is some opinion there that the Mayor and Citizens of London ought to have had a precedent notice. Yet the judgment is contrary, for they could not have been barred by the fine and non-claim if notice had been necessary to the commencement of their title, and it is not found whether those to whom the estate was devised before had notice; so that this cause proves rather that there needs no notice in this case than otherwise. Wherefore, the plaintiff must have his judgment.

When My Lord Chief Justice [Hale] had concluded, Rainsford said, he had spoken with Justice Morton, who declared to him that he was of the same opinion.

[Other reports of this case: 1 Eq. Cas. Abr. 111, 282, 333, 21 E.R. 918, 1047, 1083.]
[Reg. Lib. 21 Car. II, f. 568.]

322

Norcliff v. Worsely

(Ch. 1669)

Entailed lands in a third person's hands cannot be sequestered to enforce a debt due from a decedent's estate.

3 Chancery Reports 29, 21 E.R. 719

23 October 1669, Michaelmas [term] 21 Car. II, at the Rolls.

Thomas Worsly, the great-grandfather, 21 Jac. [1623 × 1624], by articles, covenanted upon the marriage of Thomas, his son, the grandfather, to settle lands upon Thomas, the grandfather, in tail. And Thomas, the grandfather, dying before the great-grandfather, leaving issue, Thomas, the father, before any settlement was made, Thomas, the father, and his mother, who was to have part of the lands for her jointure, exhibited a bill against Thomas, the great-grandfather to have such settlement. And it was decreed 20 October, 15 Car. I [1639].

Thomas, the great-grandfather, having conveyed away the land, another bill was brought against him and John, his second son, by Thomas, the father, and a decree was made the 18 February 1651 that the conveyance should be made according to the covenant and that they should account for the profits to him, which were after settled at £2304 14s. 4d.

Thomas, the father, having issue, Thomas, the son, afterwards, married Penelope, the plaintiff's wife, and Thomas, the father, having possession without a conveyance and dying, left the said Penelope, his then wife, executrix. And she being married to the plaintiff, he claimed the £2304 14s. 4d. And, 13 July, 12 Car. I [1636], he obtained a sequestration against the defendant to sequester his lands for the same. And he had sequestered the said entailed lands, which belonged to Thomas, the son, an infant, as issue in tail, as the estate of John, and disturbed the tenants, whereas the plaintiff ought to have recourse to John's peculiar estate. Thomas, the son, moved and prayed the order for sequestration might be discharged.

Whereupon, the court declared the mesne profits was a personal duty upon the great-grandfather and John ought to be satisfied by them, and not out of the lands. [The court] decreed [and] ordered, unless cause [be shown]. And upon showing cause, [the court] ordered that the sequestration extend not to any of the land. [And it was] decreed by Lord Keeper Bridgeman.

[Later reports of this case: 1 Chancery Cases 234, 22 E.R. 777, Repts. *tempore* Finch 128, 23 E.R. 70, 73 Selden Soc. 85.]

323

Smith v. Palmer

(Ch. 1669)

A party is not bound by his own pleadings in a former action between different parties.

1 Chancery Cases 133, 22 E.R. 729

25 October [1669].

Upon a difference between the plaintiff and one John Browning, an award was made that Browning should pay the plaintiff £5 in hand and £23 at several days and, for that purpose, Browning was to enter into a bond of £50 penalty. This bond was taken in the name of Brown.

Browning exhibits his bill against Smith and Brown, suggesting a fraud in obtaining the said bond and that the same was in trust for Smith.

Smith and Brown join in an answer to that bill, and, there, Smith swears that he was indebted to Brown more than £23 and that, Browning being awarded to pay him that £23, Brown did accept of that bond for so much of what Smith owed Brown. And so he said it was not upon any trust for Smith, but taken to Brown's own use, Brown being dead and the defendant his executor.

The plaintiff Smith, by his now bill, seeks to have the bond out of Brown's executor's hands, and charges his name to have been used in trust for the plaintiff.

The defendant pleads the former answer in the other cause and that, thereby, the now plaintiff had denied any trusts in Brown for him, and swore the bond was taken in Brown's name for his own use, *prout*.

The plaintiff replied that Brown was his solicitor in the other cause and that he answered by his advice and that he advised it was fit to answer to them and, for that purpose, advised the now plaintiff, before he put in that answer, to enter into a bond to Brown for more money that so he might swear as he did in that answer, which bond he promised Smith to deliver back when he had put in his answer. And he did so. And he averred he was at the whole charge in defending the suit and that Brown, after that answer, owned the trust in that bond of £23 for the plaintiff. And there was proof of that.

And, upon the hearing of this cause, it was taken to be a fraud in Brown to draw the plaintiff in to put in such an answer upon oath in the other cause, that the bond was in trust for him. And the defendant was decreed to deliver up the bond to the plaintiff with a letter of attorney to put it in suit.

324

West v. Knight

(Ch. 1669)

The Court of Chancery can enforce a bequest to a parish for charitable purposes that are indefinite.

1 Chancery Cases 134, 22 E.R. 729

27 October [1669]. Richard West, clerk, and divers others the churchwardens and overseers of the poor of Great Creaton, against Knight and his wife, executrix of John Palmer. At the Rolls. The Master of the Rolls.

John Palmer had by will given £50 to the parish of Great Creaton, where he was born, without saying to what use. The minister, churchwardens, and overseers for the poor exhibited this bill for the £50, suggesting that he intended it for the benefit of the poor.

The defendant, the executrix, confesses the devise, and offered, if she were bound to pay it, to assign some security for money owing to the testator to satisfy it.

10 May 1669, this cause was first heard by the Master of the Rolls [Grimston]. And it being then insisted by the defendant's counsel that the devise was void and that the parish, being no corporation, could not sue for it by an original bill and that it was a void devise, for that there was no use limited touching the £50, whether it were for the poor or for the repair of the church or the highways etc. And it was stood upon that, if the plaintiffs had any ground of relief, it must be by a commission of charitable uses, and not by a bill.

The Master of the Rolls [Grimston] ordered precedents to be produced before he would deliver his opinion.

And now at this day [27 October 1669], upon farther hearing the cause, a decree of this court, of 30 June 1657, was produced, St. John's College against Platt,[1] where, upon the advice of four judges, it was resolved that, upon an original bill, the Chancery might relieve within the Statute of Charitable Uses.[2] And, therefore, inasmuch as the £50 was the personal legacy, and no devise of lands, he decreed that the £50 be paid as far as the defendants have assets of their testator, and he directed it to an account to see what assets, and the Master to whom it was referred, to see the money disposed for the benefit of the poor of the parish.

---

[1] *Platt v. Master of St. John's College* (Ch. 1641 × 1642), Herne & Duke 92.

[2] Stat. 43 Eliz. I, c. 4, s. 3 (*SR*, IV, 969).

325

Borrington v. Borrington

(Ch. 1669)

A purchaser of land will not be required to make a discovery of his title deeds so as to impeach his own title.

3 Chancery Reports 32, 21 E.R. 720

14 November, 21 Car. II [1669], at the Rolls.

A recovery was suffered by a tenant in tail, but it was defective as to much of the land for want of a good tenant to the *praecipe*, it being out on estates for lives and he that suffered the recovery devised the lands to the defendant and his heirs in trust to pay debts and portions.

The bill is by the heirs at law to have the counterparts of the lease for lives in being at the time of the recovery from the defendant to go to law for the title.

The defendant answered, and confessed several counterparts. But he said, he being a purchaser, hoped he should not produce them to impeach his own title to enable the plaintiff to go to law. And he had brought the counterparts into court.

Whereupon, it was ordered that they be delivered back to him and the plaintiffs to take what remedy they can at law. And, if, upon a trial, a verdict pass for the defendant, then to bring back such as concern the land recovered.

326

Pyne v. Matthew

(Ch. 1669)

Joint tenants are each entitled to their proportional shares of the profits of their land.

3 Chancery Reports 29, 21 E.R. 719

24 November 1669, Michaelmas [term] 21 Car. II, at the Rolls.

The plaintiff was seised of three-fourth parts of the farm of Southbark in the County of Devon, and the countess of Bath was seised of the other fourth. And she lets her part to the defendant for lives or years determinable on lives. And he took the profits of all.

A division is decreed to be made by commissioners during the defendant's term and title.

327

Pew v. Cadmore

(Ch. 1669)

A successor administrator of a decedent's estate can suspend an order that was made but not entered.

3 Chancery Reports 33, 21 E.R. 720

2 December 21 Car. II [1669].

The plaintiff was an administrator. And, after a decree was pronounced, he died before the entry of the order, and the entry is suspended by the administrator *de bonis non etc.*

328

Trevor v. Perryor

(Ch. 1669)

The question in this case was whether an equity of redemption that descended to the heir of the debtor is assets of his personal estate.

1 Chancery Cases 148, 22 E.R. 736

4 December [1669].

The plaintiff was an executor to an obligee. And the bill was to have an equity of redemption, which descended to the heir of the obligor by his death, made assets in equity. To this bill, it was demurred, [as] in Bennet and Box's Case.[1]

And on debate, the Lord Keeper [BRIDGEMAN] inclined to think it was all one with that case.

But, for the plaintiff, it was insisted that that case was a hard case to be established in a court of equity and that this is a stronger case, for, here, the lands were once in the obligor and never absolutely put out of him, but conditionally by way of a pledge for money. And the equity of redemption he had was as considerable as the redemption, which was assets at law.

So the Lord Keeper [BRIDGEMAN] ordered [the defendant] to answer, but he saved the benefit of the demurrer to the hearing of the cause.

---

[1] *Bennet v. Box* (Ch. 1662–1664), see above, Case No. 68.

329

Davy v. Davy

(Ch. 1669)

The sole remedy for the non-payment of a rent charge is distress unless the right of distress is defeated by some fraud.

1 Chancery Cases 144, 22 E.R. 734

11 December [1669].

The plaintiff was the eldest son by a second marriage, and the defendant was the eldest son and heir by the first marriage. And the bill was to be relieved for a rent charge of £200 *per annum*, of which there was half a year due.

The bill did suggest that the defendant kept not any stock upon the ground, but converted it all to tillage, so that the plaintiff had not a sufficient distress, and so was without a remedy save in equity. And he prayed a decree against the defendant for the arrears and the growing payments.

The defendant demurred, for that, the lands only being charged with the rent at law, there was no equity to charge the defendant's person.

But this demurrer was overruled, it being laid in the bill that there was a legal defect in the assurance, which ought to be made good in equity, the grant being on a good consideration.

The defendant answered, and denied the converting the premises always to tillage or that the same were not overt to a distress. But he said there had been divers times a stock worth £250 upon them.

After the proofs were published in the cause, it was heard before the Lord Keeper [Bridgeman], 20 November 1667. And the only equity, there, insisted on for the complainant was that the defendant employed all the lands to tillage, so that the plaintiff could not distrain, there being no cattle kept on the premises.

But the defendant did insist that he did keep a stock of cattle thereon sometimes worth £250 at a time and that the plaintiff endeavored to charge the defendant's person with the rent, which was not liable at the law. But the plaintiff's counsel replied that, though possibly he might have a remedy at law, yet it was usual to settle matters of this nature in Chancery.

Whereupon and upon reading the proofs in the cause, the court declared they would be attended with precedents where cases of this nature had been relieved, and then would give their opinion. 8 November 1668, the court ordered the cause to be set down again on the precedents, which the plaintiff was to deliver to the defendant.

One precedent was this, Seymor Boreman and Francis Yeat, plaintiffs, against John Yeat, Esq., defendant.[1] The bill was grounded upon an agreement

[1] *Boreman v. Yate* (Ch. 1660–1667), see above, Case No. 8.

made upon the marriage of John Yeat, the father of the plaintiff Francis, with Frances, his mother, and a tripartite deed 15 Car. I [1639–40], in pursuance thereof, whereby John, the father, became seised in tail, and, after the death of Thomas's father, covenants to levy a fine to the intent Elizabeth, mother of Frances, his second wife, after the death of Thomas and himself, and her assigns should have during her life out of the premises £150 *per annum* if John should have heirs male of his body that should so long live, and to the heirs male of the body of John by the said Elizabeth, another £150 *per annum* during the life of the said Elizabeth and that the heirs male of the body of John and Elizabeth have £300 *per annum* out of the premises with a clause of distress and a covenant to make further assurance. A fine was levied accordingly, August 1663. John, the father, died in the life of Thomas, his father. Elizabeth sold her right to the £150 limited to herself after the death of Thomas to the plaintiff Boreman. And, in October, before the bill, Thomas died, whereby the plaintiffs became entitled to the several rents, the lands descending to the defendant as heir to his grandfather, being the eldest son of John by a former marriage. And he had all the deeds, and refused to pay the rents, pretending the lands were not sufficient, and the limitation in law was defective. And the lands lying intermixed with others and the boundaries confused, the plaintiffs could not distrain, and so they prayed relief here. And they charged also that the defendant's father agreed that, if the lands were too small in value or defective in title, he would make both good. To have that done and to discover the buttals and boundaries and to have the rents arrear and growing rents paid was the scope of the bill. The defendant, by answer, insisted that the plaintiff's proper remedy was at law and that Boreman had not a good title, because he had not any attornment, for aught appeared, or any good conveyance from Elizabeth, and justified the detainer of the deeds.

On the first hearing, 25 January 12 Car. II [1661], [the court] ordered a commission to go to set out the lands, and Boreman's title to be determined on the return of the commission. The commissioners certified that they had set out the lands, the present rents whereof were but £70 *per annum* and that the lands charged were £300 *per annum*. And then the cause came again to be heard before the Lord Chancellor and the two Chief Justices, 12 January 1660[/61]. And, as to Boreman's title as assignee to Elizabeth, by which he claimed the arrears from Thomas Yeat's death, during Elizabeth's life, the matter stood upon was that he did not prove he had paid any purchase money. The court conceived that was not material, he claiming under Elizabeth, who was entitled by the marriage agreement, and so capable of relief.

And the next point was as to the other plaintiffs to £100 *per annum* during Elizabeth's life, and £300 after to him and the heirs male of his body. Whereupon, the court declared that, though the limitation of these rents were defective in law, so as the plaintiff could have no remedy at law, yet, by the true meaning of the marriage agreement, the plaintiff Francis is well described to take the rent, and both the plaintiffs were well entitled and ought to have relief so far forth as the lands and rents reserved on the leases, and the lands, as they shall come out of the lease, shall be of a value to make good the same and that Boreman ought to be first paid. And they decreed the same accordingly and the defendant to account for the mesne profits etc. and for the future the rents reserved. And the lands out of which the rents and profits are issuing at the highest yearly value, not exceeding £200 *per annum*, after the leases expire, should be liable to the payment of those rents to the plaintiff Boreman during Elizabeth's life and, after, £300 *per annum* to the plaintiff Francis, according to the true meaning of the deed.

The difference between the two cases was, first, in the principal case, the rent was well limited to the plaintiff in point of law by the name of the first son of the second marriage, and he may distrain, and, having seisin, may bring an assize. But in Boreman's Case, neither himself had any remedy at law for want of attornment and by reason of intermixture with other lands, nor had the other plaintiff by reason he was not heir male to his father, but that defendant was by a former marriage; so the limitation was not good in law. And observe, in Boreman's Case, the lands only are made liable, not the person.

Another precedent delivered by the plaintiff to the defendant was 22 June 1644, Elizabeth Ferris against Newby, where an annuity being devised by will and by the same will the same lands devised to a half-brother of the devisee of the annuity, this being a rent seck without seisin and no power of distress and the devisee of the lands having promised to pay it, the court did decree the devisee of the lands to give seisin of the rent to the devisee of the annuity, which case, as was conceived, was against the plaintiff in the principal case, it being in his power to have seisin when he would. And the court, in this case, did not decree the lands to be liable.

And now, upon a further hearing of the principal case, the plaintiff's counsel did not think fit to insist upon or so much as to mention their precedents, but stood only upon the defect of a distress and that the arrears of the £200 *per annum* were now £100 and the land but £200 *per annum*.

The Lord Keeper [BRIDGEMAN] declared on the debate of the principal case that, unless there did appear a fraud to hinder the plaintiff of his distress, he could not have relief here and that all he could do was to refer it to a trial at law, whether there was any fraud to hinder the plaintiff of his distress. And, accordingly, at the plaintiff's desire, he did refer it to a trial.

Nelson 120, 21 E.R. 805

Darcy v. Darcy.

The plaintiff was eldest son by a second marriage, and had a rent charge of £200 well settled on him. And the defendant was the eldest son by the first marriage. The bill was to be relieved for this rent charge of £200 *per annum*, for which there was half a year then in arrear, suggesting that the defendant did not keep any stock upon the ground, but converted the same into tillage, so that there was not sufficient [goods] for the plaintiff to distrain and that he was without a remedy but in equity. And, therefore, he prayed a decree against the defendant for the arrears and growing payments.

To which, the defendant demurred, for that the lands being only charged with the rent at law, there was no equity to charge the person of the defendant.

But, because it was further alleged in the bill that there was a legal defect in the assurance which ought to be made good in equity, it being made upon a good consideration, therefore, the demurrer was overruled.

Then the defendant answered, and denied that he always converted the lands to tillage or that the same were not open to a distress. But he said that there had been often a stock worth £250 upon the same.

Upon hearing the cause, the only equity insisted on was that the defendant employed all the lands to tillage and kept no cattle on the same. The court would be attended with precedents.

One precedent [was], 20 January 1666[/67], between Seymour Boreman and Yate, *viz.* Thomas Yate, the father, John Yate, the son, and Francis, the grandson. The bill was grounded on an agreement upon the marriage of John Yate, with Frances, his first wife, by a tripartite indenture, 15 Car. I [1639–40], by which Thomas was made tenant for life, remainder in tail to John, who had issue by that marriage, the defendant, his eldest son. The said John did afterwards upon the marriage with Elizabeth, his second wife, and mother of Francis, the plaintiff, covenant to levy a fine to the intent that Elizabeth might after the death of Thomas and the said John have and receive £150 *per annum* out of the lands for her life, and, if he should have heirs male, then those heirs male should have another £150 out of the lands during the life of Elizabeth, and, after her decease, the heirs male of his body and of Elizabeth should have £300 *per annum* with a clause of distress and a covenant to make further assurance. John died in the lifetime of Thomas, his father; then Elizabeth sold her right to the £150 to the plaintiff Boreman; then Thomas died, and the lands descended to the defendant as heir to the grandfather, being the eldest son of John by the first marriage, and he had all the deeds, and refused to pay the rents, pretending the lands were not sufficient and that the limitation was defective in law and that the lands lay intermixed with others and the boundaries [were] confused, so that the plaintiff could not distrain. Therefore, he prayed relief and to discover and set forth the boundaries and the rents arrear and that the same might be decreed etc. The defendant, in his answer, set forth that the proper remedy was at law and that Boreman had not a good title, because the grantee for life did not attorn and so the conveyance of the rent to him from Elizabeth was not good.

On the first hearing, a commission was directed to settle the boundaries, and the commissioners certified that it was done and that the present rent was but £70 *per annum*. On the second hearing, the point was that, though the limitation of £150 *per annum* was defective in law, for Francis being not named in the limitation, that being to the heirs male, and he was not the heir male, for John, his father, had a son by another marriage, the now defendant, yet the court was of opinion that, by the true meaning of the marriage agreement, the plaintiff Francis is a person well described to take the rent, and yet to be relieved, and the rent to be paid to the plaintiff during the life of Elizabeth.

The difference between these cases was *viz.*, in the principal case, the rent was well limited to the plaintiff Darcy in point of law, by the name of the son of the second marriage, and he might distrain, but, in Boreman's Case, he had not any remedy at law for want of an attornment, and, by reason the lands lay intermixed, nor had Francis, the other plaintiff, any remedy at law, because he was not heir male to his father, but the defendant by another marriage was his heir male, yet they were relieved.

Another precedent [was], 22 June 1644, Terrers *versus* Noby. An annuity was devised, and, by the same will, the lands were devised to another, this being a rent seck and without seisin and no power of distress, and, the devisee of the lands having promised to pay the annuity, the court did decree him to give seisin of the rent.

And now, in the principal case, it was insisted for the plaintiff that here was a defect of distress and that the arrears of £200 *per annum* were now £1000 and the land but £200 *per annum*.

But the court declared that, unless there was a fraud to hinder the plaintiff from distraining, they could not give relief here, and that it should be referred to a trial at law whether there was any fraud or not. And a trial was thereupon directed.

[Other reports of this case: 1 Eq. Cas. Abr. 32, 21 E.R. 852.]

330

Sherman v. Withers

(Ch. 1669)

The Statute of Limitations applies to bar inland merchants' accounts, but not those of merchants trading abroad.

1 Chancery Cases 152, 22 E.R. 738

11 December [1669].

The plaintiff was an inland merchant, and the defendant was his factor. And the bill was for an account of fourteen years' standing.

To all but what was within six years before the bill, the defendant pleaded the Statute for Limitation of personal actions, 21 Jac., c. 16.[1]

[1] Stat. 21 Jac. I, c. 16 (*SR*, IV, 1222–1223).

And, upon the debate of the plea, the Lord Keeper [BRIDGEMAN] conceived the exception in the Statute, as to the merchant's accounts, did not extend to this case, but only to merchants trading beyond the sea.

331

Grove v. Banson

(Ch. 1669)

Where a decedent's estate is insufficient to pay all of the legacies, the legacies abate proportionably.

Where a marriage settlement is given in the form of a legacy, it is a legacy and not a debt, and it abates proportionably if the decedent's estate is insufficient to pay all of the legacies.

The largest legatee of a mortgagor is the one who has the right to redeem the mortgage.

1 Chancery Cases 148, 22 E.R. 736

14 December [1669]. Huttoft Grove against Banson and his wife and Thomas Grove. The Lord Keeper, Justice Wilde.

Huttoft, the plaintiff's grandfather, possessed of a great personal estate, gave the plaintiff £5000 and £500 to his sister, Banson's wife, and made the defendant Thomas Grove his executor, who had purchased the manor of Beeren Hall with part of the testator's money and mortgaged it to Perryor, and forfeited it. Upon the marriage of his daughter to Banson, he agrees her portion to be for a legacy, interest, and what more he would give her, £1000. And he enters into a statute to Banson for the same, and then he grants the equity of redemption and the reversion, for the mortgage was but for a long term of years, to Banson as a farther security.

The bill was to be admitted to redeem the mortgage and to have the legatees lose in proportion. And, though Banson had a statute and a mortgage *prout*, whereby it was said his £1000 continued no longer a legacy, but was as much a debt to him as if he had lent the money and he took it as so much portion or else he would not have married, yet the Lord Keeper [BRIDGEMAN] declared that, inasmuch as the legacy was not paid, but only secured, he conceived it equitable for each legatee to lose in proportion, there not being enough of Thomas Grove's estate to pay all. And he would not admit Banson to redeem, but the plaintiff, for that his was the greater debt. And so he ordered that he should redeem and Banson should lose of his wife's portion in proportion with the plaintiff.

And, in this case, the case of Pink and Vincner, 1639,[1] by the advice of the civilians, was cited where it was resolved that an executor was not bound to pay a legacy but on security to refund in case there should be a defect of assets to pay

[1] *Vintner v. Pix* (Ch. 1637–1640), Chancery Repts. *tempore* Coventry 284.

debts and legacies. But that, as was said, was not applicable to the principal case, for the testator had left ample assets, but Thomas Grove had wasted them, and was insolvent.

1 Vernon 454, 23 E.R. 580

14 December 1669. Huttoft Grove *versus* Banson and his wife and Thomas Grove.

One Huttoft, by his will, devised £5000 to the plaintiff and £500 to the plaintiff's sister, who, afterwards, married Banson. And he made the defendant, Thomas Grove, his executor. And, upon the treaty of that marriage, the executor agrees that there was £500 and interest due for the legacy and that he would make that up £1000. And he enters into a statute for payment, and also assigns the equity of redemption of a mortgage for further security, and dies, having much wasted the testator's estate and without assets sufficient to make compensation.

And the plaintiff's bill was that Banson might have his £500 legacy only in proportion with him.

And it was so decreed accordingly, and the plaintiff was preferred as to the redemption of the mortgage, he having a £5000 legacy, and the defendant but £500.

332

Higgon v. Syddal

(Ch. 1669)

A purchaser cannot be required to make a discovery of notice of prior encumbrances that might defeat his own rights.

1 Chancery Cases 149, 22 E.R. 737

15 December [1669]. Higgon and others against Syddal, Calamy, and others.

The case was this. Syddal arrented a rent charge of £300 *per annum* for £2000 to the plaintiff, and after[wards] mortgaged the premises for £1200 to Calamy. Then, those that have Calamy's interest, he being dead, buy in a judgment precedent to the grant of the rent charge.

The plaintiff exhibits his bill to discover what estate the defendant claims, and charges that Calamy had notice of the plaintiff's rent before his mortgage.

The defendants plead the mortgage to Calamy and that, afterwards, hearing of precedent encumbrances, they bought in a legal title precedent to the plaintiff's, and offer that, if the plaintiff will pay all due on the mortgage and on their new acquired title, to assign all to him. But, if he will not, they stand upon it they ought not to discover what that estate is they have bought in nor ought their title to be drawn under examination in equity. And, by way of answer, they denied that, to their knowledge or belief, Mr. Calamy had any notice of the rent charge when he lent the £1200.

And, on the debate, the plea was allowed as good.

333

Style v. Martin

(Ch. 1669)

War and infancy are excuses for laches.

1 Chancery Cases 150, 22 E.R. 737

16 December [1669]. William Style, by an original bill, against William Martin and Elizabeth, his wife, relict and administratrix of Richard Bosvile, Esq., and Robert Bosvile, son and heir of the said Richard, by a guardian. The Lord Keeper, Justice Wilde.

The bill was an original bill to set aside a decree in 1664 obtained by the defendant on a bill of revivor, to which the now plaintiff is no party, against John Style, heir of Sir Humphrey Style, and others, as obtained by fraud. The case was thus.

Sir Humphrey Style's Lady, mother of the said Richard Bosvile, had by his request mortgaged a manor of hers for £3000 borrowed by Sir Humphrey 8 November, 8 Car. I [1632]. And Sir Humphrey had agreed with his Lady that, if he did not pay off that £3000, that then his lands in Kent should stand obliged to pay £1500 of the £3000 for the ease and benefit of the said Lady and her heirs. And, 15 November 8 Car. I [1632], he conveyed his Kentish lands to trustees, which the defendants say was for that purpose, but there was no such express trust. Trinity [term] 1641, the Lady Bosvile being dead, Richard Bosvile, her son and heir, exhibited his bill against Sir Humphrey and the trustees of the Kentish lands to have the benefit of this agreement. And, in Trinity [term] 1642, two witnesses were examined to the proof of the agreement against Sir Humphrey Style. And the conveyance of the Kentish lands was on that trust. The wars coming on, there was a rest and no farther proceedings until 1663. In 1665, Richard Bosvile, who was a recusant, died, his heir then and yet an infant. Michaelmas 1663, Marton *et uxor* and the other defendant, the infant, brought a bill of revivor against John Style, the heir of Sir Humphrey, and the heir of the surviving trustee. And, in 1664, after the answer of John Style, who, by an answer, said he was willing the plaintiffs in the bill of revivor may have their money if he may have the rest of the lands, and replication, and farther proof taken and published, it was decreed that the plaintiffs in the bill of revivor should hold the lands against John Style and his heirs and all claiming under Sir Humphrey Style since the first bill until the £1500 with costs and interest were paid off. Of which bill of revivor, the now plaintiff had due notice given him, and he might, if he had pleased, come in by a cross-bill etc. before the decree. The now plaintiff made title by an entail of Sir Humphrey Style on him in 1638, precedent to the original bill, so that title was not bound by the decree. But that settlement being, in truth, revoked in 1643, he made another title by the will of Sir Humphrey Style in 1658.

And, for the now plaintiff, it was insisted that there was a collusion in getting the decree, the defendant John Style admitting it by answer to it on the matter, and the now plaintiff, who was terre tenant, no party to it. And the report of the Master who had computed the £1500 and interest to amount to £3600 was confirmed without any defense by John Style. And the rule for binding titles *pendente lite* (which is the rule of the practice at this day), was the Lord Bacon's Rule, and that rule is that *lis pendens* binds if it be in full prosecution. But here was above twenty years cessation and the plaintiff had in that time bought in encumbrances and improved the lands, and the notice given the plaintiff of the bill of revivor was too late, issue being joined, so that he could not come in. And it is said, where judgment is obtained against the land and the terre tenant is no party, a writ of deceit lies for the terre tenant. And so, in a parity of reason, this bill was maintainable for the now complainant. Spencer's Case, 5th Report,[1] was cited. And it was further said for the plaintiff that there was no such agreement between Sir Humphrey Style and his Lady, as the decree was grounded upon.

For the defendant, it was said that the plaintiff was estopped to say there was such an agreement by decree.

Lord Keeper [Bridgeman]: A stranger may falsify at the common law. And, if the decree be by fraud, the plaintiff may then be admitted to falsify the agreement. But it is not by the form, but the substance of a decree, that all be bound that come in *pendente lite*.

But the defendant's counsel insisted that there was no fraud, for the main witnesses, which were to the agreement, were examined in Sir Humphrey Style's lifetime. Those which were examined after were to prove the payment of the £3000, the mortgage money, which was paid afterwards. And notice was given to the now plaintiff before any examination of the bill of revivor, and could go no otherwise, unless they would have betrayed the infant, for, if he had gone by original bill, they must have lost the witnesses examined on the first bill.

Lord Keeper [Bridgeman]: The war and infancy excuses the laches, and the witnesses to the main were examined in Sir Humphrey's life. And so the pretense of the plaintiff's improvement and taking off encumbrances are nothing of that in the bill, but in the replication. And so he dismissed the bill.

[1] *Spencer v. Clark* (1583), 5 Coke Rep. 16, 77 E.R. 72.

334

Attorney General, ex rel. Woolrich v. Woolrich

(Ch. 1669)

In an action brought for the benefit of a lunatic, the lunatic must be made a party.

1 Chancery Cases 153, 22 E.R. 739

Michaelmas [term] 1669. Sir Jeffery Palmer, the King's Attorney General, on the behalf of Woolrich, a lunatic, against Woolrich.

A bill was brought by the Attorney General in the nature of an information for the benefit of a lunatic, as in the Case of Jerome Smith, fol. 112.[1]

The defendant demurred, for that the lunatic was no party, which was ruled a good demurrer, the Lord Keeper [Bridgeman] declaring it was as needful to make the lunatic a party as an infant, where a suit was on his behalf. But, in the case of an idiot, it must be otherwise. But a lunatic may recover his understanding, and then he is to have his estate in his own disposing.

But observe the difference between this case and that of Smith's. Smith's Case was to be relieved against an act done by the lunatic in assigning a debt, because he was a lunatic at that time, so that, if he had been a party, it had been to stultify himself, which the law does not admit. *Vide* Beverly's Case, 4 Rep.[2] And *quaere* how it can be done by an information on his behalf. But, in Beverly's Case, the king has the custody of his person, of his lands, and his goods, so as to provide for the idiot to prevent an alienation. And, therefore, by a *scire facias*, he may avoid a feoffment and other disposition made by the idiot. But the book says that that is not a breach of the rule that a man cannot be admitted to stultify himself, because the idiot is not a party to the record in a *scire facias*. And, in that case, it is the same thing, and the writ is the same as to the alienation of a *non compos mentis* or a lunatic or of an idiot, and the king shall protect those that cannot protect themselves. And the alienation of a *non compos mentis*, as well as of an idiot, being found by an office, shall be avoided.

Tamen quaere. And, upon that ground, I [Keck] suppose it was that those bills were grounded, for it was declared by the court that those bills were proper to be brought by the Attorney [General]. And, in Woolrich's Case, the bill was to be relieved upon a marriage agreement for the benefit of the lunatic before he was a lunatic so that he, being a party to that bill, did not tend to stultify himself, and it may be the reason why he should be a party to it. And the other bill, tending to stultify himself, may be a reason why he should not be a party to it.

---

[1] *Attorney General, ex rel. Smith v. Parkhurst* (Ch. 1668), see above, Case No. 275.

[2] *Snow v. Beverley* (1603), 4 Coke Rep. 123, 76 E.R. 1118.

335

Jones v. Lenthall

(Ch. 1669)

A party is not bound by his own pleadings in a former action between different parties.

1 Chancery Cases 154, 22 E.R. 739

Michaelmas [term] 1669. Cadwallader Jones, Esq., against John Lenthall and his lady. The Master of the Rolls in the absence of the Lord Keeper.

The bill was to be relieved for a debt owing by a bond from Sir James Stonehouse, to whom the defendant, the Lady, was his executrix, which debt and bond the plaintiff, in his answer to a former bill, had sworn was fully satisfied to him, but that was to avoid a sequestration of the debt, as was alleged.

And the Master of the Rolls [Grimston], though that answer was set forth in the defendant's answer in this cause, would not suffer the answer to be read against the plaintiff. And so he decreed the defendants to satisfy the debt.

[Other reports of this case: 1 Eq. Cas. Abr. 36, 21 E.R. 856.]

336

Wray v. Brandsing

(Ch. 1669)

A creditor can sue for his debt to be paid out of a trust that was created for the purpose of paying the deceased settlor's debts, and this without making the debtor's executors parties.

Lincoln's Inn MS. Hill 125, f. 59v, pl. 2

8 December 1669. Demurrer.

A conveyance is made to trustees to pay debts, not mentioning the particulars. A creditor, *post mortem* of the grantor, sued the trustees for his debt out of the trust. And [it was] well, though the executors [were] not parties, by the opinion of Lord Keeper [Bridgeman].

337

Alford v. Pitt

(Ch. 1669–1670)

A court of equity can enforce an arbitral award.

2 Chancery Reports 30, 21 E.R. 607

The plaintiff's suit is to have the benefit of an award. To which, the defendant demurred, and says that the plaintiff ought to take his remedy at law.

This court overruled the demurrer.

[Reg. Lib. 21 Car. II, f. 181.]

338

Langton v. Tracy

(Ch. 1669–1670)

In this case, one of the conveyances in issue created a valid trust for the payment of debts, but the other deed was fraudulent as to creditors and thus voidable.

2 Chancery Reports 30, 21 E.R. 607

The bill is to have the several debts due to the plaintiffs, being the creditors of the defendant Roberts, paid. The case is *viz.* that Thomas Roberts conveyed the manor and lands in question to the defendant Tracy for the payment thereof and of his other debts. But, before that conveyance to Tracy, the defendant Nicholas standing engaged as surety for the said Roberts for several of the debts, the said Roberts made the said Nicholas a lease of the premises for sixty years at a peppercorn rent.

And such lease being made and no care taken for satisfying the debts, the plaintiffs sue the said Roberts for their debts. So to avoid such prosecution, they made the aforesaid conveyance to Tracy in fee upon special trust to pay all his debts. But Tracy combining with the defendant Astrey, who had procured the said Nicholas to assign the said lease to him, after notice of the trust, contrived a conveyance of the premises from Tracy to him the said Astrey, by way of a bargain and sale enrolled, so that Astrey pretends himself a purchaser of the premises from the said Thomas Roberts, and not under the said deed of trust or lease and assignment, and he pretends the trust is destroyed, the said conveyance being not enrolled, whereas the said deed was well executed, and the trust accepted, by which the said deed cannot in equity be made void until payment of the said debts.

The defendant Astrey insists that the deed to Tracy for the payment of debts was a void deed as against a purchaser, there being no creditor party or privy thereto nor any schedule of debts thereunto annexed and that the said conveyance was voluntary and made only between Roberts and his wife and Tracy, and the creditors are not parties thereto. And, by the said conveyance, Roberts was to have all such money out of the premises from time to time as he thought fit for the livelihood and subsistence of himself, his wife, and family. And the said conveyance to Tracy being voluntary and in its nature but in trust for Roberts and revocable by him after the conveyance to Astrey and Roberts having exhibited a bill against Tracy to set aside the said conveyance, Tracy surrendered the same to Roberts, who revoked it, and both cancelled it. And, afterwards, Roberts and his wife conveyed the premises to Astrey, and levied a fine thereon.

But the plaintiff insists that, after the conveyance to Tracy was made, he declared he would pay the plaintiff's debts, which is proved by the plaintiff, Sir John Knight.

The Defendant insists that Sir John Knight is interested and entitled to some of the debts in question, and continued a plaintiff throughout the cause, and is not struck out of the bill, and is but a single witness, and his evidence was denied by the defendant's answer, and, therefore, his deposition ought not to be read.

This court declared they would see precedents where a conveyance made voluntarily for the payment of debts and no creditors were named or appearing in any fixed certainty of the persons and with a proviso for the grantor to have maintenance out of the premises conveyed for himself and family without limitation of how much, whether such a conveyance be revocable by the grantor and grantee.

This court, with the assistance of the judges, were clear of opinion that the deed from Thomas Roberts to Tracy and the trust thereby created were made and created with an honest intention to pay the debts of the said Thomas Roberts and that the same was not fraudulent, though no certainty of the debts appear therein, but the same being made on a trust, which was a good foundation and a just and honest consideration, and none of the creditors complaining of any fraud, the same ought to be taken as a good deed, and the defendant Astrey coming in under this deed and having notice of this trust and paying the debts under it, ought to receive no countenance in this court, but the estate ought to be charged with the same, in whose hands soever the same shall come. And [the court] decreed the deed of purchase from the said Roberts to Astrey to be set aside and Astrey to account for the profits etc. and the plaintiffs and all the creditors to be paid their debts out of the said estate.

[Reg. Lib. 21 Car. II, f. 376.]

339

Eyre v. Good

(Ch. 1669–1670)

In this case of a voluntary contract to arbitrate, the court refused either to vacate or to confirm the award.

2 Chancery Reports 34, 21 E.R. 608

The bill is to be relieved against a bond of £1000 penalty for the performance of an award, whereby possession and profits of lands are awarded to the defendant.

The defendant insists that there was no surprise in the said award, but the said award was by the direction of the plaintiff's friends, and he says it ought not to be set aside, which, if it was, it would involve many suits. And he insisted that the said award is in the nature of an agreement, and ought to be performed.

This court taking notice that the award in question was not made by the order of this court, but that it proceeded from the voluntary submission of the parties, two judges, being chosen by themselves, who declared their opinion that they saw no cause to decree the award to be set aside nor, on the other side, to confirm it or to relieve the plaintiff, but [the court] ordered both bills to be dismissed. The plaintiff electing to go to law, this was heard by Justice Tyrell.

This cause was to be re-heard before the Lord Keeper [Bridgeman], being assisted with Judge Wilde, who confirmed the order above.

[Reg. Lib. 21 Car. II, f. 211.]

340

Hale v. Acton

(Ch. 1669–1670)

In this case, the testator intended that the legacy in issue was to be in satisfaction of a portion, but not in addition to it.

2 Chancery Reports 35, 21 E.R. 609

Edward Eltonhead, by his will, gave the defendant, Mrs. Gilbourne, £1000 to be first paid after his debts, besides a share out of the dividend of the estate when, as, after the making of the said will, the said Edward Eltonhead and Henry Gilbourne, father-in-law to the defendant, Mary Gilbourne, before her marriage, came to an agreement for what the said Mary should have out of the said estate, and that there should be but £1100, and the same was to be in full of what was intended her thereout, and that the said Edward Eltonhead often so declared, and, in his lifetime, he paid £500, and, after his death, his executor paid £100 more in pursuance of the said agreement, so as the chief point then controverted being whether the said defendant, Mrs. Gilbourne, ought to have the £1100 portion and the £1000 legacy mentioned in her father's will or that he intended to give her any more out of his estate than the said £1100.

The Master of the Rolls [Grimston] declared that the £1100 ought to be in full [satisfaction] of what the defendant Gilbourne was and ought to have out of the said estate. And he decreed accordingly.

This cause came to be re-heard before the Lord Keeper BRIDGEMAN, who declared he saw no cause to alter the said former decree, and so confirmed it.

[Reg. Lib. 21 Car. II, f. 409.]

341

Brabant v. Perne

(Ch. 1669–1670)

Copies of lost depositions in a different action will not be established by a court of equity.

2 Chancery Reports 36, 21 E.R. 609

Depositions of witnesses under the hand of a Six Clerk, then in a cause between Butt and Perne, about thirty years since, the plaintiff in this cause prayed the same might be recorded, the record of the original depositions in that cause being lost.

But the defendant Perne's counsel insisted it would be of dangerous consequence and precedent to suffer copies of depositions to be recorded and used as evidence in a case of title of land, there being no cause in court or parties to the said former suit, there being since the dismission of the said former suit two trials brought by the said Butt concerning the said things in question, upon both which two nonsuits passed against the said Butt's title, the witnesses which were examined in this court being all then living and two verdicts upon full evidence on both sides and one other verdict since 1664 has been found for the defendant's title against the now plaintiff's title. And some of the witnesses at the said trial have sworn otherwise than is expressed in those copies of the depositions, which the plaintiff would have now recorded and exemplified.

This court would not allow the said copies of the depositions to be recorded or exemplified, but, they being before ordered so to be by the Master of the Rolls, it is ordered they shall be vacated and made void and cancelled and taken off the file.

[Reg. Lib. 21 Car. II, ff. 146, 344.]

342

Alexander v. Alexander

(Ch. 1669–1670)

An administrator of a decedent's estate can be ordered to account to a creditor of the decedent.

2 Chancery Reports 37, 21 E.R. 609

The suit is to discover the estate of Richard Alexander, deceased, which is come to the defendant's hands to satisfy a debt of £300 due to the plaintiff from the said Richard Alexander.

The defendant insisted that the plaintiff ought not to have relief in this court, in regard the assets in the defendant's hands were legal assets and nothing appeared but that the plaintiff had her proper remedy at law, having not proved anything more to be in the defendant's hands than was confessed in the defendant's answer.

But the plaintiff insisted that this court has directed accounts in cases of this nature to avoid circuity of action and further charge and trouble of suits and that, this court being possessed of the cause and the parties at issue on proofs, the same was as proper for this court as at common law.

This court ordered precedents to be searched, where this court has directed accounts and given relief in this case.

And the cause coming to be heard on the precedents and merits thereof and the plaintiffs insisted that there is sufficient assets of the said Richard Alexander come to the defendant's hands to satisfy the plaintiff's debt with an overplus, this court decreed the defendant to come to an account for the estate of one Blackhall, unadministered.

[Reg. Lib. 21 Car. II, f. 324.]

343

Yate v. Hooke

(Ch. 1669–1670)

In this case, the mortgage money owing to the decedent was payable to his executor and not to his heir at law.

2 Chancery Reports 39, 21 E.R. 610

John Hele, on the 23d December 1654, for £2000 mortgaged Long's Court and other lands to Jasper Edwards, his executors, administrators, and assigns for ninety-nine years. And the said Edwards, on the 25th of December 1654, re-demised the same to the said John Hele for 98 years at a peppercorn rent on condition that, if the said John Hele, his heirs, executors, administrators, and assigns did not pay to the said Jasper Edwards, his executors, administrators, and assigns £2150 at a certain day therein mentioned, that then the said re-demise to be void. And he covenanted for him, his heirs, executors, and administrators to pay the same accordingly. And, in Hilary term 1654, the said John Hele acknowledged a judgment of £4000 to the said Jasper Edwards for the performance of the covenants in the said demise and re-demise. And after[wards], in 1656, the said John

Hele, for £500, mortgaged the said premises to Joseph Jackson, his executors, administrators, and assigns, reciting the said mortgage to Jasper Edwards, to have and to hold the said premises to the said Joseph Jackson, his executors, administrators, and assigns for the residue of the said term demised to the said Jasper Edwards and to hold the reversion to the said Joseph Jackson, his heirs, and assigns for the use of the said Joseph Jackson, his heirs, and assigns forever on condition that, if the said John Hele, his executors, etc. paid to the said Jackson, his executors, etc. £515 in June next following, then the said deed of mortgage to be void, and the said John Hele to re-enter as in his former estate. And the said John Hele covenanted with the said Jackson, his heirs, etc. to pay the said £515, and, for further confirmation, granted to the said Jackson all his equity of redemption. And, afterwards, the said Edwards and Hele, for £2000 paid by Jackson to the said Edwards, the said Edwards and Hele assigned the said premises to Jackson, with a condition or proviso that, if the said Hele, his heirs, or executors should pay to the said Jackson, his executors, etc. £2060, then the said demise from Hele to Edwards to be void. And, afterwards, in 1657, Edwards assigned the said judgment of £4000 to the said Jackson, his executors, etc. And the said Hele, in 1660, died, leaving the said defendant, Sir Thomas Hooke, his nephew and heir.

And the said Jackson having made his will and devised to his daughter, Sarah, wife of the defendant Alford, £2000 and to the said Joseph Jackson, his son, £2000 with his lands, tenements, etc. and to the heirs of his body and, for want of issue, then the one-half of his lands so given to his daughter, Anne Yate, and the other half to his daughter, Earle, and the issue of their bodies equally, and that, in case his personal estate fell short, then every legatee to abate in proportion to make it up the one-half, and, the other half, his son, Joseph, should make good out of what he had bequeathed to him. And he made the defendants, Yate, Earle, and Aldworth executors. And, if his estate should amount to more than he had bestowed, then the said Joseph and Sarah should have the one-half of it, and his son, Yate, and his wife and his son, Earle, and his wife and what child he should have living at his decease the other half. Afterwards, the said Joseph Jackson, having in his account accounted the said mortgage money as part of his personal estate in 1661, died, leaving the said Joseph Jackson his heir. No entry had been made, either by the testator in his lifetime or by the said Joseph, his son and heir, upon the said mortgaged premises. But the said John Hele and Sir Thomas Hooke had received all the rents and profits.

So the question was whether the said mortgage monies are due and payable to the heir or executor of the said testator, Joseph Jackson.

This court, upon reading the said deeds and will, conceived that there was no question in the case, but that the said several sums of £2000 and £500, being the mortgage money, ought not to go to the heir, but to the executors and to be accounted part of the testator's personal estate, he having by his will given his real estate by name to his heir, besides his portion of £2000 and one-fourth part of the overplus of his personal estate, the rather, for that it was not in the power of the heir to discharge the judgment or the mortgage and the monies, by the several provisos being made payable to the executor, and not the heir, and the original mortgage being but for years, though altered by act in law, and the testator having by will charged the lands devised to his heir to supply the deficiency if the personal estate should not be sufficient, whereas, if he had not taken the mortgages to be part of his personal estate, he would have supplied the same out of the mortgages. And [the court] decreed Sir Thomas Hooke to redeem and he to pay the plaintiffs, the executors, the mortgage money with interest.

[Reg. Lib. 21 Car. II, f. 939.]

344

Tolson v. Lamplugh

(Ch. 1669–1670)

Depositions in a former action can be used in a later action where the parties are in privity of estate with the former parties.

2 Chancery Reports 43, 21 E.R. 611

The plaintiff prays liberty to make use of depositions taken in a former cause, wherein Henry Tolson, the plaintiff's late father, deceased, was plaintiff, against Abraham Molline and his wife, and Mr. Winstanley, defendants.

The defendant Lamplugh insisted that there is no color or ground for the using the said depositions taken in the cause, wherein the said Henry Tolson was plaintiff at the trial, directed those depositions, being taken in a cause whereto neither of the defendants, the Lamplughs, are parties. And there is more difference of the title between the defendants, the Lamplughs, and Mr. Molline and Winstanley, than between the said Lamplugh and the plaintiff Tolson.

The plaintiff Tolson insisted that the defendants, the Lamplughs, claimed and derived their title under Mr. Molline and his wife and Winstanley, and so the said depositions ought to be used at the trial, which the defendant denied.

This court declared that the depositions in the said former cause ought not to be used against the now defendants, the Lamplughs, unless they claim under the said former defendants. But, if they do, then, the said former depositions ought to be admitted as evidence against them.

[Reg. Lib. 21 Car. II, f. 786.]

345

Floyer v. Hedgingham

(Ch. 1669–1670)

A copyholder cannot be admitted to any copyhold estate by a letter of attorney.
No one can swear an oath by an attorney.

2 Chancery Reports 56, 21 E.R. 614

No copyholder ought to be admitted to any copyhold estate by a letter of attorney, for that he ought to do fealty at the time of his admittance, which cannot be done by an attorney, but it ought to be done in person, by reason that no man can swear by an attorney.

[Reg. Lib. 21 Car. II, f. 809.]

346

Dennis v. Badd

(Ch. 1670)

When a mortgage is redeemed by a decedent's estate, the land goes to the heir, and the debt is paid out of the decedent's personal estate.

1 Chancery Cases 156, 22 E.R. 740

31 January [1670]. Bridget Dennis, by Sir Alexander Frazer, her committee, against Sir Thomas Badd, Frances Dennis, his daughter, and others.

The case of Sir Thomas Badd was that he was guardian to Edward Dennis, whose sister and heir the plaintiff is, and, at fifteen years of age, married him to the defendant Frances, his daughter. Sir Robert Dillington had a mortgage of £200 of part of the infant's estate, which mortgage Sir Thomas Badd paid off and took the same assigned to other persons. The infant, after[wards], at seventeen years of age, made his will, and the defendant Frances, his wife, executrix.

The bill was that, though Sir Thomas Badd had paid off the mortgage with the infant's own money, yet he now pretends it was not for the benefit of the infant, but that he paid it with his own money. And, for what money he had of the infant's, he was accountable to his own daughter, the executrix, and so he would leave the whole mortgage money still on the mortgage lands, which belong to the plaintiff as sister and heir to the infant.

The defendant, Sir Thomas Badd, by answer, said that the money he had paid Sir Robert Dillington was his own money and that he had not near enough of the infant's to pay the same and that, if he had had enough of the infant's money, yet he could not justify the disposing of it.

It was proved that, when Sir Thomas Badd paid off the mortgage, he called in about £100 of the infant's money and that that was applied that way.

And, in this case, the Master of the Rolls [GRIMSTON] declared that Sir Thomas Badd ought to employ what he had of the estate of the infant as far as it would go to pay his debts. And he did decree a redemption of the mortgage and that Sir Thomas Badd should account and that, what he had of the infant's in his hands when the mortgage was paid off, should be applied in discount of the mortgage money and, upon the payment of what was more due to the plaintiff, to redeem.

1 Vernon 436, 23 E.R. 569

The committee of an idiot had bought in a mortgage that was upon the idiot's estate. And the estate descended to another idiot. And, though the mortgage was kept on foot by an assignment in trust, yet, in that case, it was decreed on a bill brought by the committee that the lands should go to the heir and that the mortgage should not be taken as a personal estate and an heir shall by the course and justice of this court have the personal estate applied in ease of the real and to discharge mortgages, though there be no covenant for the payment of the mortgage money. And, in case the trustees had come to this court and shown how it would be for the benefit of the infant to have had this money thus laid out, he did not doubt but that the court would have decreed it accordingly.

[Other reports of this case: 1 Eq. Cas. Abr. 261, 21 E.R. 1033.]

347

Read v. Howet

(Ch. 1670)

Where an heir of a beneficiary of a trust of a leasehold dies without issue, the right to the leasehold passes to the administrator of his estate and not to his heir at law.

3 Chancery Reports 61, 21 E.R. 729

Hilary [term] 1670. *Per* Lord Keeper Bridgeman and Justice Wilde.

The case was Joseph Warren made a lease to trustees to the use of Edmund, the son, which Edmund had issue, Edmund, Joseph, and Jane. The lease came to young Edmund, who had married Read's wife, her former husband being dead. And he [Edmund, Jr.] died without issue, and she is the administratrix. The bill was to have the trustees assign to her, and is against the heirs of Edmund.

And, young Edmund having left no issue, it was decreed accordingly.

348

Anonymous

(Ch. 1670)

A case in the Court of Exchequer that is dismissed without prejudice can be later sued in the Court of Chancery.

1 Chancery Cases 155, 22 E.R. 740

Hilary term 21 & 22 Car. II.

The cause had been formerly heard in the Exchequer, where two several trials had been directed, will or no will. And, in both, there was a verdict for the plaintiff. Yet the Chief Baron had dismissed the bill there, but without prejudice in law or equity.

And now, by an original bill, the plaintiff has sought relief here for those matters he sought relief in the Exchequer and to examine witnesses in order thereunto *in perpetuam rei memoriam*.

The defendants pleaded the examination and dismission in the Exchequer and that there ought not to be a new examination, the matter having been there full in issue.

On the first hearing of this demurrer, the court gave time to search for precedents, where, after a cause heard upon the merits and dismissed in the Exchequer, a new bill had been admitted here. And, none being to be found, now, upon a farther hearing of the demurrer, it was for the plaintiff insisted that this was a special dismission, it being without prejudice either in law or equity, which words must be considered to signify something, but they did not signify anything unless it were meant the dismission should not hinder the plaintiff from seeking his relief in any other court of law or equity.

And so the court did conceive, and ordered that the plaintiff might examine any witnesses that were not examined in the Exchequer and that, as to the matters examined unto there, the plaintiff might examine the same witnesses *de bene esse*. And how far those *de bene esse* [depositions] should be used, the court would farther consider.

349

Seymour v. Nosworthy

(Ch. 1670–1674)

The question in this case was whether a plea of a purchase of land for a valuable consideration without notice but not alleging that the title came from an ancestor of the other party is a good plea or not.

2 Freeman 128, 22 E.R. 1105

Hilary [term] 1670. Lord Bridgeman.

The defendant pleaded himself a purchaser for a valuable consideration.

But it was ruled no good plea in regard he did not plead himself a purchaser from some of the plaintiff's ancestors, for a purchase from a stranger without a title was held no good plea. And, therefore, the defendant was ordered to answer.

Hilary Vacation, 1674, being the second seal before Easter Term, on a motion by Mr. Nosworthy, the plea was held good by the Lord Keeper FINCH, and all the subsequent proceedings were set aside.

Nelson 135, 21 E.R. 809

The defendant pleaded that he was a purchaser for a valuable consideration.

But this was ruled to be no good plea, because he did not plead the purchase was made from one of the plaintiff's ancestors, for a purchase from a stranger who might have no title was held no good plea. And the defendant was ordered to answer.

3 Chancery Reports 40, 21 E.R. 723

Michaelmas [term], Hilary [term] 1669–70.

The defendant pleaded himself a purchaser for a valuable consideration.

But it was ruled not a good plea, in regard he did not plead himself a purchaser from some of the plaintiff's ancestors, for a purchaser from a stranger without a title was held no good plea. And the defendant was, therefore, ordered to answer.

[Other reports of this case: 2 Eq. Cas. Abr. 69, 22 E.R. 61, *sub nom.* Bassett v. Nosworthy, Repts. *tempore* Finch 102, 23 E.R. 55, 73 Selden Soc. 37, 62.]
[Reg. Lib. 1669 B, f. 484.]

350

Dolbin v. Prettiman

(Ch. 1670)

Tradesmen and shopkeepers cannot charge their customers interest when they are not paid at the time of the sale.

2 Freeman 133, 22 E.R. 1109

Lands were devised for the payment of debts. The Master of the Rolls [GRIMSTON] would not allow any interest for shop debts of twelve years' standing, because, he said, tradesmen selling on tick sold at a rate accordingly.

Nelson 136, 21 E.R. 809

Lands being devised by Mr. Houghton for the payment of his debts, the creditors exhibit their bill against the heir and executor to have the lands sold. And they had a decree for that purpose. And now the creditors by book and by simple contract move to have interest for their debts, which had been proved before the Master, and to be standing out above twelve years, alleging that there was sufficient [money] to pay all.

But it was denied by the court, for that shopkeepers sold their goods at a price accordingly when they were not paid in ready money.

3 Chancery Reports 64, 21 E.R. 730

Master of the Rolls. Dolman v. Pritman.

Lands being devised by Mr. Houghton to pay his debts, the plaintiffs were the creditors who brought their bill against the heir and executor to have the lands sold. And they had a decree for the same. And, now, the creditors, by book and simple contract, moved to have interest for their debts allowed by the Master, which had been standing out twelve years, there being estate enough to pay all. But the court denied it, saying shopkeepers sold at a price accordingly when they were not paid in ready money. But the order was not entered.

An executor is not bound to pay legacies without security to refund in case there be not sufficient [assets] to pay debts and all legacies.

Per Anthony Keck: If a witness will not appear and be examined upon the return of a subpoena, the party may take a [writ of] attachment against such witness, and, if examined on the other side, suppress his deposition.

[Reg. Lib. 1667 A, f. 519, 1669 A, f. 68.]

351

Butler v. Wallis

(Ch. 1670)

In a suit in equity for a legacy, the plaintiff's legacy will not have any priority over the other legacies, but all of the legacies will be paid proportionably.

2 Freeman 134, 22 E.R. 1110

The suit was for a legacy. The defendants demanded an allowance for their own legacies first.

But it was denied, and ordered that an account be taken for the whole estate and the defendants and plaintiffs to abate equally and proportionably for what the estate falls short. And so it is not like the case where executors pay their own debts first at common law or him that first sues his debt in equal degree before the other.

[Other copies of this report: 2 Eq. Cas. Abr. 552, 22 E.R. 464.]

352

Acourt v. Chambers

(Ch. 1670)

In actions based on accounts, where the plaintiff cannot prove his accounts otherwise than by parol evidence, the defendant is allowed also to prove his discharge by parol evidence.

Lord Nottingham, *Prolegomena*, p. 270

8 February 1669, by Lord Bridgeman, Keeper. Acourt, executor of Acourt v. Chambers.

Acourt dies in the Indies, and makes Chambers, now Sir Thomas Chambers, overseer. He burns the books, and pretends to do it by the direction of the testator and for his benefit that the East India Company might not know of Acourt's unlawful trade and breach of covenant with them. Then, Chambers draws up an account, and sends it into England to Acourt's friends, wherein he was himself a debtor to Acourt's estate [for] £4000 and a creditor for the like sum, and so the balance was even.

[It was] ruled: first, that, generally, where the plaintiff cannot charge but by his own proper oath, there, the defendant's oath shall likewise be a discharge; second, but not so here, because the burning of the books by the defendant has disabled the plaintiff, wherefore the defendant's own charge [as a debtor] shall be taken [as proved], but his discharge [as a creditor] must be proved.

Lord Nottingham, *Prolegomena*, p. 272

But, in the same case of Acourt v. Gifford, because Gifford was not privy to the burning of the books and could not otherwise be charged than by his own account, his own oath was accepted in discharge.

353

Attorney General, ex rel. v. Newman

(Ch. 1670)

The Attorney General can sue in the Court of Chancery to enforce a devise to a charitable purpose.

1 Chancery Cases 157, 22 E.R. 741

10 February [1670]. Sir Jeffery Palmer, the King's Attorney General, on the behalf of the king and Trinity College in Cambridge, against George Newman, Esq.

The information suggests that Stephen Newman was seised in fee of the lands in question and was possessed of books and goods, and, out of a pious intent to provide for the maintenance of poor scholars in that College, by his will in writing, he devised to the Master and Fellows of that College the lands in the information mentioned and all his monies, goods, etc. And he appointed the premises to be employed for the buying of lands for the maintenance of scholars in the said College etc. with this clause, that, 'if any, by cavilation concerning the law of maintenance, should go about to hinder this bequest or, if any of his bequest might not be suffered to go to the College', then the defendant should enjoy all his lands, goods, etc. that, by the will, the premises are to be established with the College. But the defendant combines with others unknown, either lords of whom the lands are held or heirs at law, and pretends that, by the Statute of Mortmain,[1] the devise is ineffectual, and so raises cavils to defeat the charity, and so has got the possession of the lands and goods and refuses to let the Master and Fellows have them, that, if by the Statute of Mortmain the said charity be avoidable, yet, by other laws for the establishing of charitable uses and according to equity, the charitable use ought to be made good. Wherefore and inasmuch as the preservation of charitable uses is of public interest and concern unto His Majesty and the College and in respect of the Statute of Mortmain and the cavilation aforesaid, they have no remedy by reason of the latter clause of the will to be relieved in the premises, they exhibited this bill.

The defendant answered, and confessed the will etc.

And, upon the hearing, it was declared by the court that the king as *pater patriae* may inform for any public benefit for charitable uses before the Statute of 30 Eliz., for charitable uses.[2] But it was doubted the court could not by bill take notice of that Statute so as to grant a relief according to that Statute upon a bill, but that the course prescribed by that Statute by a commission of charitable uses must be observed in cases relievable by that Statute.

But no positive opinion was delivered, for the defendant consented to a decree. And so what was done was by his agreement, and not the judgment of the court.

1 Levinz 284, 83 E.R. 409

The information [was] that Stephen Newman, seised of lands, devised them to Trinity College in Cambridge for the maintenance of a scholar there. And, in the will, was this clause, that 'if any by cavil shall hinder this devise or that the same cannot go to the College by reason of the Statute of Mortmain, then, I devise them to Robert Newman and his heirs'. And, under this pretense, that, by the

[1] Stat. 7 Edw. I (*SR*, I, 51).

[2] Stat. 43 Eliz. I, c. 4 (*SR*, IV, 968–970).

Statute of Mortmain, the College cannot have them, Robert Newman entered, and kept the possession of the lands.

For which, the Attorney General brought this information to have the land established to the College.

And this whole matter appearing on the bill and answer and it being a charity, it was held by the Lord Keeper BRIDGEMAN that it ought to be established to the College by virtue of the Stat. 43 Eliz., notwithstanding the Statute of Mortmain and notwithstanding the clause in the will. And so it was decreed. And the Lord Keeper said that it did not differ from Lloyd's Case, in Hob. 136.[1]

354

Wilmer v. Kendrick

(Ch. 1670)

A power of attorney must be strictly executed or it will fail at common law.

1 Chancery Cases 159, 22 E.R. 741

17 May [1670]. Wilmer and his wife against William Kendrick and Jo. Vylet.

William Kendrick, seised in fee of the lands in question worth £90 *per annum* and of other lands in all worth £100 *per annum*, by indenture 23 April, 17 Car. I [1641], conveys the lands in question to the use of Thomas, his eldest son, for life, the remainder to trustees for 99 years for the benefit of Martha, the wife of Thomas, for a jointure, the remainder of those and all other the lands, of which, by that settlement, Thomas was tenant for life, after William's death, to the first son of Thomas in tail.

Thomas has issue Martha, the plaintiff's wife, and another daughter and the defendant Kendrick, his only son. And, by the settlement, there was a power given to Thomas, at any time during his life by any writing, to convey or appoint all or any of the lands in question, being but £90 *per annum*, to any future wife that Thomas should marry for a jointure or to any child or younger children of Thomas, so as that conveyance or appointment be made to commence after the death of Martha, Thomas's wife, for life or lives only of such child or children and for their preferment. Thomas, having no other way to provide for his daughters' younger children, 5 May 1657, for love etc. to them and for a provision of portions for them, grants, bargains, and sells the lands in question to the defendant Vylet, *habendum* to him and his assigns for the lives of the plaintiff Martha and her sister and for their only use and benefit to remain from the death of Thomas Kendrick and Martha, his wife.

[1] *Flood's Case* (1616), Hobart 136, 80 E.R. 285, *sub nom. Case of Jesus College*, Herne & Duke 32.

The plaintiffs, by their bill, suggest that the plaintiff Martha had no provision but this and that her father did look upon it that he had well pursued his power in the grant to Vylet or else that he would have taken the wood of the other lands of greater value, which he knew were by the settlement *supra* to come to the defendant. And they complained that the defendant, taking advantage that the power was not literally pursued, did stand upon it; whereas, it was in substance pursued and the estate granted to Vylet was less than by the power Thomas had power to grant, for, by the power, he was to grant to commence on the death of Martha, his wife, only, and he made it to commence on the death of himself and Martha, which was less than he had a power to do. And the mistake did happen by reason that, in the settlement, the lands were limited to Thomas for life, the remainder in trust for a jointure for Martha.

And it was charged by the bill that, in equity, the mistake and defect ought to be helped, the younger children being otherwise utterly unprovided for. And, so, to be relieved was the intent of the bill.

To which the defendant Kendrick demurred, for that the deed of settlement and the deed to Vylet were void in law. And, being defective in the execution of the power, it ought not to be supplied in equity. In the arguing of which demurrer, it was insisted that, both the conveyances being voluntary, the case was the same here as at law, and there was no reason to help here against law at all. And it was said that, if such defects should be supplied in equity, it would be in vain to employ men of skill in drawing conveyances and settlements, but every unskillful man might do it as well. But, if it had been a consideration of money, it was admitted it might be otherwise. And it was farther insisted that it did not seem to be a mistake in the case, but was done designedly, for, if the estate had been to commence upon the death of Martha, Thomas's wife, then Thomas himself had lost his own estate for life after Martha.

The court was all of opinion that, the law being against the plaintiff (as it was admitted it was), equity could not help the plaintiff. Yet they did mediate with the defendant to pay the plaintiff Martha £20 for her life.

And the cause having been formerly argued on the demurrer and a day given to the plaintiff to produce precedents where, in a like case, the court had relieved, the plaintiff produced a precedent, 6 July 40 Eliz. [1598], Prince and his wife, plaintiff, against Green, defendant,[1] where in effect the case was thus. The father, seised in fee of a great estate, by a covenant to stand seised, settles the same to himself for life, the remainder to his eldest son with a power to himself to lease a small part for forty years, who accordingly made a lease for the benefit of a younger child, which came by assignment to the plaintiff, which the defendant, the eldest son, would avoid at law, the power not being well raised by the covenant to stand seised.

[1] *Prince v. Greene* (Ch. 1598), 117 Selden Soc. 267, Tothill 128, 21 E.R. 144.

But it appearing to the court the eldest son was greatly advanced by the father and that the conveyance, which was by a covenant, was intended to be by livery, which he was advised would be as well by a covenant, the court did decree the plaintiff should hold until the defendant evicted him by law, and did decree the defendant to admit the power to make the lease good in law if he did not prove an entail paramount to the settlement, as he pretended.

Nelson 113, 21 E.R. 803

Miller v. Kendrick and Vylett.

William Kendrick, seised of lands in fee worth £90 *per annum*, settled the same to the use of Thomas, his eldest son, for life, remainder to trustees for 96 years if Thomas should so long live to preserve contingent remainders, remainder to Martha, the wife of Thomas, for life for her jointure, remainder of these and all other his lands, of which Thomas was tenant for life, to the first son of Thomas in tail male, with divers remainders over, in which settlement, there was a power for Thomas, at any time during his life by any writing etc., to limit and appoint the said lands of £90 *per annum* to any other wife that Thomas should have for life or to any of his younger child or children or to any other person for their use, so as such appointment be made to commence after the death of Martha and for the life or lives only of such child or children and for their maintenance.

Thomas had issue, Martha, now the wife of the plaintiff Miller, and another daughter and one son, the defendant Kendrick. And, having no other way to make provision for his daughters, he, in May 1657, for the natural love and affection which he bore to them and for their education and maintenance, grants, bargains, and sells these lands to Vylett to have and to hold to him and his assigns for the lives of his said daughter, Martha, and her sister, etc. to commence after the death of Thomas and Martha, his wife, whereas the power given to him was that he might limit it to them to commence after the life of Martha, his wife, only.

And now, the plaintiff suggests that she had no other provision but what she had under this deed and that her father apprehended he had well pursued the power which he had to make provision for her but that the defendant taking advantage that it was not literally pursued, whereas it was in substance pursued, and the estate granted to Vylett was not more, but less, than Thomas had power to grant, for he had power to grant it to commence after the death of Martha, his wife, and he had granted it to commence after his own life and the life of Martha, and this mistake did happen, by reason that, in the settlement, the lands were limited to Thomas for life, remainder to trustees for a jointure for Martha.

And it was charged in the bill that, in equity, that mistake ought to be rectified; otherwise, there would be no provision for the younger children.

The defendant Kendrick demurred, for that the deed of settlement and deed to Vylett were both voluntary and, it appearing by the bill that the deed to Vylett was void in law, being defective in the execution of the power, it ought not to be supplied in equity, for, if such defects should be helped here, it would be in vain to employ men of skill to draw conveyances and settlements, for any man might do it. It is true, if the deed had not been voluntary, but in consideration of money really paid, it might have been otherwise. Besides, this did not seem to be a mistake, but designedly done, for, if the estate had been made to commence upon the death of Martha, then Thomas himself would have lost his estate for life.

The court was of opinion that, the law being against the plaintiff, equity would not help, but ordered to search precedents. And, thereupon, a precedent was produced for the plaintiff, 6 July, 40 Eliz. [1598], Price and his wife against Green, *viz*. the father, being seised in fee, settled the lands by a covenant to stand seised to the use of himself, remainder to his eldest son in tail, reserving a power to himself to make leases of part of it for forty years, who, accordingly, made a lease for the benefit of a younger child, which came by assignment to the plaintiff, and which the eldest son would have avoided, because the power was not well raised by a covenant to stand seised.

But it appearing to the court that the eldest son was greatly advanced by the father and that the conveyance, which was by a covenant to stand seised, was intended to be by livery and, being advised that it would be as well by a covenant to stand seised, the court did decree that the plaintiff should hold until the defendant evicted him by law, and did decree, likewise, that the defendant should admit the power to make the lease good in law if he did not prove an entail paramount to that settlement.

355

Yeavely v. Yeavely

(Ch. 1670–1672)

A final decree made between living parties will not be reversed because it was enrolled after the death of one of the parties without having been properly revived.

3 Chancery Reports 44, 21 E.R. 724

Monday 19 May, *anno regni* Car. II, *vicesimo secundo* [1670]. *Inter Jacobum Yeavely, querentem, et Ricardum Yeavely et alios, defendentes.*

This cause being this day heard and debated upon a bill of review brought by the said plaintiff to review and reverse a decree heretofore made in two causes, one wherein Katherine Yeavely, the relict of Thomas Yeavely, then deceased, an attorney, was plaintiff, against Anthony Yeavely, the plaintiff's father and heir at law to the said Thomas Yeavely, deceased, defendant, and, in the other, whereof the said Anthony Yeavely, the now plaintiff's father, was plaintiff against the said Thomas Yeavely, the attorney. And the scope of this bill being that the said Thomas Yeavely, the plaintiff's uncle, deceased, being seised in fee of several lands and tenements in the bill mentioned of the value of £200 *per annum*, 1

Car. I [1625–26], dying so seised, leaving the said Anthony Yeavely, his cousin, and Katherine, the relict of the said Thomas, the plaintiff's great-uncle, together with the assistance of one Thomas Yeavely, the attorney, did set on foot a will supposed to be made by the said Thomas, the great-uncle, seventeen years before his death, whereby the premises in question were settled on the said Katherine for life, the remainder on the said Thomas, the attorney, and the heirs male of his body, remainder over to other persons, and that the said Katherine and Thomas, the attorney, brought their bill in this court against the said Anthony, the heir of the said testator, to have the deeds from him touching the premises. And the said Anthony exhibited his cross-bill against them, suggesting his title as heir at law and praying an examination of evidences, in which cause several proceedings being had and, at last, a submission of the parties, by the then Lord Keeper Coventry, being proposed thereupon, in Michaelmas term 1638, one moiety of the premises was decreed to Thomas, the attorney, and his heirs, and the other moiety to Anthony and his heirs, unless a tenure *in capite* by knight's service appeared by the end of the term, in which case two-third parts was to go to Anthony and his heirs, and the other part to Thomas and his heirs. And 14th December 1638, though the tenure was insisted upon, yet a decree passed for the moieties. And yet the plaintiff's father petitioning against the signing and enrolling of the decree, the same was stayed during the life of the Lord Coventry. And the said Katherine and Anthony died before the said decree was signed and enrolled. But the same was, afterwards, by the order of the Lord Keeper Finch, signed and enrolled.

And the premises decreed to Thomas, the attorney, are since, by his death or otherwise, descended or come to the defendants, the Yeavelys and German Buckstone, the said Buckstone pretending a title by a fine levied in Michaelmas term 1653. And the plaintiff did shortly after the attainment of his age of twenty-one years make his entry and claim into and upon the premises.

And he has now brought his bill of review. And, for error contained in the decree, he set forth, amongst other things, that the bill, on which the decree was founded, is only for evidences touching the premises in question, and not for the lands, and it charged the lands to be entailed. And yet the decree does decree the lands themselves and an estate in fee simple. And, for further error, he does charge that the plaintiff Katherine died before the hearing of the cause, and Anthony, the defendant, under whom the plaintiff claims, died before the decree was signed and enrolled, and no bill of revivor was exhibited. And, therefore, to have the said decree reviewed and reversed is the scope of the bill.

And the counsel for the defendant in this bill of review, admitting the plaintiff's entry and claim and that, albeit the plaintiff's father were dead before the decree was signed and enrolled, which, nevertheless, was not admitted, yet that the plaintiffs ought not to have any relief nor the decree reversed, the same being made by a submission of the parties to the Lord Coventry, who, after hearing both sides, the 31st of October 1638, decreed that, if Anthony, the plaintiff's father, should make appear a tenure *in capite* before the end of that term, then the lands in question were to be divided into three parts, the plaintiff's father was to have two parts and Thomas Yeavely, the attorney, one-third part, but, if such tenure should not be made to appear, then, the land to be divided by moieties and the plaintiff's father was to be discharged of the costs. And, though the plaintiff's father, the said 14th of December 1638, still insisted upon the tenure, yet the decree passed for moieties. And a division was afterwards made by Sir Robert Rich, then one of the Masters of this court, as appears by his report of the 19th of March 1638. And the decree not being yet completed and Anthony, the plaintiff's father, endeavoring to waive his submission, upon a pretense that he had sold a great part of the premises to Ashenhurst and Bretland, another reference was made to Sir Robert Rich, to examine whether the purchaser came in *pendente lite*, who certified the said purchases to be *pendente lite* and that they ought to be bound by the decree. Which certificate, the Lord Coventry declared to be just, and, 13th December 1639, he ordered the decree to pass, both against the plaintiff's father and against Ashenhurst and Bretland, without further motion, unless cause were showed to the contrary the first day of the next term, before which time, the Lord Coventry died. And, 8th February 1639, no cause being shown, though notice was given, the decree passed in the time of the Lord Finch, and was then signed and enrolled. And both parties have sold away all or the most part of the lands divided to them.

But the plaintiff's counsel insisting that his father died in January before the signing and enrolling of the decree and that the decree was therein, as well as for other matters, erroneous, upon debate thereof and hearing what was alleged on either side, His Lordship declared that he would not reverse the said decree, other than as to the signing and enrolling thereof. And, if the same shall be so far reversed, the defendants must be left to a new bill or bills of revivor, as they shall be advised, to enforce a performance of the decree.

And, upon reading the proofs touching the time of the death of the plaintiff's father, the same appeared very doubtful. It was, therefore, ordered that the said parties do proceed to a trial on this point at law, whether the said Anthony, the 8th of February 1639, the time of signing and enrolling the decree, was dead or not, which trial is to he had at the next Assizes to be held for the County of Derby, for which purpose, the said defendants are to appear *gratis*, naming an attorney, and accept a declaration, and plead to issue. And the sheriff of the county was to attend the Prothonotary with the books of freeholders, who is to return forty-eight persons, out of which, each is to strike out twelve, and the remaining twenty-four to be impaneled as an indifferent jury to try the said issue, and, after the trial had, the parties are to resort back to this court for such further orders as shall be just. And, at the trial, either party is at liberty to make use of the depositions taken in this court of such witnesses as are either dead or, being sick or beyond the seas, cannot be brought to the trial. And, in case the parties do differ upon the issue, then Sir Mo. Brampton, Kt., etc. is to direct the same.

A verdict was afterwards found that the plaintiff's father was dead before the decree was enrolled. And a new trial was directed, Michaelmas [term] 1670.

3 Chancery Reports 73, 21 E.R. 732

30 February 1671. Lord Keeper Bridgeman, Lord Chief Justice Hale, Justice Wilde, and Baron Wyndham.

The case appeared upon the order in folio [*blank*], and a verdict is for the plaintiff that his father was dead before the signing and enrolling of the decree. And it coming to a hearing 11 November 1671, before the Lord Keeper [Bridgeman], and Chief Justices Vaughan and Hale, before any determination of the cause, they would be satisfied with precedents where a decree, signed and enrolled after the death of the party has been, for that cause only of the death of the party before the signing and enrolling, was reversed.

And this day, they produced for precedents, *viz.*:

Frere, plaintiff, against Ewre, defendant, which was heard 20 January, 9 Car. I [1634], where the defendant Ewre would have had the administration of Frere to sign and enroll a decree pronounced in Frere's lifetime, and, upon a reference to the Six Clerks, they certified they could not by the course of the court;

13 April, 20 Car. II [1668]; an enrollment of a decree in 10 Car. I being lost, the cause, after so long a time, was ordered to be re-heard;

22 February, 20 Car. II [1668]; a decree was made and ordered that, if the defendant died before Easter, yet that the plaintiff may afterwards enroll it;

2 December, 21 Car. II [1669]; the plaintiff was an administrator, and, after a decree pronounced, he died before the entry of the order, and the entry is suspended by the administrator *de bonis non etc.*;

19 May, 22 Car. II [1670]; money, after a decree was enrolled, was certified due to the executor of the plaintiff, and, upon exceptions to the report, they being no parties in court, it was disallowed.

But these precedents did not satisfy, and, thereupon, the bill is dismissed unless cause.

Lord Nottingham, *Prolegomena*, p. 294

17 February *post* Hilary [term] 23 & 24 Car. II.

A decree was made 13 Car. I [1637], by Lord Coventry between Yeavly and Yeavly, and the docket thereby was signed by Finch, Keeper, and afterwards enrolled. Thirty years afterwards, a bill of review is brought, and error is assigned that the defendant was dead before the decree was signed and enrolled. That fact was referred to a trial at law, and found so to be, and the Six Clerks also certified that, by the course of the court, no decree can be signed and enrolled after the death of the party without a bill of revivor first brought. And the counsel at bar compared it to a judgment at law against a dead person, which is erroneous.

Nevertheless, Lord BRIDGEMAN, with the assistance of HALE, Chief Justice, affirmed the decree, and resolved: first, death of the party before the decree be pronounced is error; second, death after the decree be pronounced and before the signing and enrolling is not so, for the pronouncing of the decree is the material thing and the enrollment is only the testimonial of it. And, therefore, if regularly it cannot be enrolled after the death of the party, yet, if *de facto*, it be done, *factum valet*. So, if a bargain and sale be enrolled in the Common Bench *de facto* after the six months ended, but entered as of a term precedent within the six months, this is well enough, for these are not properly matters decreed, but matters of fact recorded. And, for that reason, decrees are not to be compared to judgments at law. Besides, at common law, if judgments are pronounced in term, which the Prothonotary has not time to enter until the vacation and the party dies in the meantime, yet the judgment is usually entered as of the term precedent. And, in this case, after a search directed, no precedent could be found where any decree has been reversed for this cause.

356

Cullum v. Dove

(Ch. 1670)

A final decree made between living parties will not be reversed because it was enrolled after the death of one of the parties without having been properly revived.

3 Chancery Reports 63, 21 E.R. 729

19 May, 22 Car. II [1670].

Money, after a decree enrolled, was certified due to the executor of the plaintiff. And, upon exceptions to the report, they being no party in court, [they were] disallowed. But these precedents did not satisfy. And, thereupon, the bill is dismissed unless cause.

357

Prat v. Allen

(Ch. 1670)

The question in this case was whether the equity of redemption in issue was barred by the mortgagor's laches.

3 Chancery Reports 55, 21 E.R. 727

The bill was that the plaintiff's great-great-grandfather devised a lease to the plaintiff's great-grandfather and his heirs with a proviso to be void unless he paid Alice, Katherine, and Elizabeth, three daughters, £40 apiece at their marriage and, in default of payment, he devised the house to the daughters and their heirs.

The plaintiff's great-grandfather being seised of a close worth £20 *per annum*, in 1602, died. And Margaret, his relict, and Nicholas, his son, the plaintiff's grandfather, sold the house to Gouning in fee. And, for a security against the legacies, 6 November 1602, he devised the close for 500 years upon a proviso that, if Margaret and Nicholas or his heirs paid the legacies, to be void. The plaintiff's grandfather paid one £40 to Alice, and, before the other is due, Katherine and Elizabeth died, leaving a son two years old and Katherine, a daughter, the plaintiff's mother, four years old. And Margaret leaving only an estate for life and had no personal estate, the close was forfeited for the non-payment of the other two £40. And Gouning entered in 1615, and, ever since, enjoyed. And, in 1626, the close came to the defendant's uncle, who had notice of the mortgage, who, about 1653, settled it on the defendants.

The plaintiff's uncle died within age without issue, and Katherine, the plaintiff's mother, his sister and heir, continued married until 1662. And the bill is to redeem and to have an account of the profits since the plaintiff's uncle's death.

The defendant pleaded, answered, and demurred. And, by the plea, he set forth a purchase in 1656 for £240 by the defendant's uncle of the close from Gouning for the remainder of the 500 years. And, by the answer, he denied notice of the mortgage. And he demurred, for that the close had been enjoyed sixty years under the lease and, upon the antiquity, he ought not to account.

The arguments were two why old mortgages ought not to be redeemed: first, because the parties will be involved in long accounts, but the bill prays an account out of the defendant's receipts; second, a power of claim, which, in this case, was not, for there was infancy and coverture until 1662.

And, therefore, the plaintiff is to reply to the plea and answer, and the benefit of the demurrer is saved until the hearing.

358

Gascoigne v. Stut

(Ch. 1670–1672)

If property be sold at an under-value at a sheriff's sale to a bona fide purchaser for value, neither the judgment creditor nor the judgment debtor have a remedy. However, if either of the parties be the purchaser, a court of equity can order an accounting and a reconveyance.

3 Chancery Reports 57, 21 E.R. 727

20 May, 22 Car. II, 1670.

The bill was to have a judgment vacated, whereupon, a lease was extended and sold by the sheriff to one Parker in trust for the defendant, the conusee of the judgment, and to have the bill of sale set aside and an account for the profits since the sale and writ of restitution of the possession, the lease being alleged to be of far greater value than extended at.

The defendant demurred, for that it is inconsistent with the rules of equity, after a judgment executed by a seizure of a chattel lease duly appraised and sold by the sheriff, to dispossess a real purchaser of what he has purchased for valuable considerations upon a bare pretense that it is of greater value than it was appraised and sold by the sheriff, who is no party, nor [was there] any offer by the bill to reimburse the purchaser what he is really out. Also the defendant, by an answer, denies tampering with the sheriff to have the lease sold at an undervalue.

Whereupon, it was ordered that the plaintiff reply to the answer, notwithstanding the demurrer, and proceed to the examination of witnesses and the hearing of the cause. But no costs were allowed. And, upon the hearing before the Lord Keeper BRIDGEMAN, 5 February 1671, a decree, was made to account and re-convey.

Nelson 143, 21 E.R. 811

Gascoigne v. Sturt.

The bill was to have a judgment vacated, by virtue whereof a lease was extended and sold by the sheriff to one Parker in trust for the defendant, who had obtained the judgment, and that the same, together with the bill of sale made by the sheriff, might be set aside and an account of the profits since the sale, and, likewise, that the possession may be restored, it being alleged, that the lease was of a far greater value than what was really due on the judgment.

The defendant demurred to the bill, for that it is not consistent with the rules of equity, after judgment executed by seizure of a chattel lease duly appraised and sold by the sheriff, to dispossess a purchaser for a valuable consideration, but upon a bare pretense that the lease is of greater value than what was due upon the judgment and than what it was appraised and sold for by the sheriff, who is an indifferent party, neither did the plaintiff offer by his bill to reimburse the defendant what he really paid for the purchase. And the defendant denied by his answer that he used any indirect means with the sheriff to have the lease sold at an under value.

But it was ordered that the plaintiff should reply to the answer, notwithstanding the demurrer, and proceed to examine witnesses and hear the cause. So the demurrer was overruled, but without costs. And, upon the hearing, the defendant was decreed to account and to reconvey.

Lord Nottingham, *Prolegomena*, p. 324

Hilary [term] 24 Car. II [1672]. Gascoigne v. Strutt.

[It was] resolved: first, if a sheriff on [a writ of] *fieri facias* sells a term to the party himself, he shall be compelled in equity to answer the overvalue; second, the same law is if [it be] sold to a stranger in trust for the plaintiff or if there be any combination between the plaintiff and a stranger to become a purchaser; third, if a sheriff sell to a stranger *bona fide*, though at a great undervalue, [there is] no remedy in equity.

359

Grimston v. Rand

(Ch. 1670)

Where a defendant does not object to an insufficient bill of complaint and the plaintiff replies fully to the defendant's plea, the plaintiff's insufficiency is waived.

Lincoln's Inn MS. Misc. 500, f. 84, pl. 3

Easter term 22 Car. II (1670).

The plaintiff brought a *scire facias* upon a recognizance against the defendant, being executor, in which the defendant entered. And it was conditional to pay such a sum such a day for a legacy devised by the testator. And it was to be paid out of the assets that the defendant had in his hands at the time of the recognizance.

The defendant pleaded *quod non habuit* (but he did not say what) assets at the time of the recognizance.

The plaintiff replied that the defendant *habuit* assets at the time of the recognizance, *viz*. 40s.

The defendant demurred. And *North* and *Webb* showed for cause that the replication was short and insufficient because it must have replied also that the defendant had not paid the legacy. And, for this, was cited Raymond and Gerard's Case, in the King's Bench, 19 Car. II; and the opinion of Gaudy in Bayly and Taylor's Case, Yelv., 24, 25.[1]

But the plaintiff had judgment by the Lord Keeper [Bridgeman] and by the advice of Justice Twysden and Justice Wilde, who were assistants to the Lord Keeper, upon the reason of the three judges in Bayly and Taylor's Case, before cited, because, by the denial of the assets, the defendant has confessed that he has not paid the legacy that was to be paid out of the assets and, on account of this,

[1] *Hayman v. Gerard* (K.B. 1667), Lincoln's Inn MS. Misc. 499, p. 330, pl. 4, also 1 Williams Saunders 99, 102, 85 E.R. 108, 109, 2 Keble 275, 84 E.R. 171; *Baily v. Taylor* (1602), Yelverton 25, 80 E.R. 18.

it is not necessary that the plaintiff will plead the non-payment in his replication specially, as this case is that the defendant's plea in bar is insufficient in not saying that it was that he had not assets, and also that the plaintiff in his replication had pursued the defendant's plea in bar *verbatim*, which latter matter was the great reason of the judgment.

360

Gladwyn v. Savile

(Ch. 1670–1671)

A purchaser cannot be compelled to make a discovery that might defeat his own title.

3 Chancery Reports 41, 21 E.R. 723

20 May 1670, 22 Car. II. Lord Keeper Bridgeman and Justice Wilde.

The plaintiffs and defendants are all creditors of one Steer, a bankrupt, who was a lead merchant. And he was found a bankrupt the 19 January, 18 Car. II [1667] by the commissioners, and the commissioners assigned the estate to the plaintiffs and others in October, 19 Car. II [1667].

But the defendants being in possession, the plaintiffs brought an action of ejectment, wherein the deeds [debts] were dated in February and March after Steer was found a bankrupt. The plaintiffs in the action became nonsuit, for the defendants had verdicts and judgments so that, in effect, Steer was no bankrupt in those conveyances, which made the plaintiffs bring a new bill to discover whether the defendant did not know at the time of the deeds that Steer was a bankrupt and the fraud of obtaining them and to have new trials and a commission to perpetuate their witness's testimony.

The defendants plead their deeds and verdicts and that Steer was really indebted to them at the times thereof, and demanded judgment whether they shall discover anything to weaken their estates or whether the plaintiffs shall examine against them as purchasers.

And, upon long debate [it was] allowed [and] that the plaintiffs may at any time bring any new action.

Nelson 141, 21 E.R. 810

The plaintiffs and the defendant were all creditors of one Steer, who was a lead merchant and who, on 19 January 18 Car. II [1668], was declared a bankrupt. And the Commissioners assigned his estate to the plaintiff and others in the month of October *anno* 19 Car. II [1667].

The defendant was then in possession of this estate, and, refusing to deliver it to the assignees, they brought their [action of] ejectment. Now, though the deed under which the defendant held the lands was dated in February, after Steer was declared a bankrupt, yet the plaintiffs were nonsuited. Then, they brought a bill, to discover whether the defendant did not know at the time of executing his deed that Steer had committed an act of bankruptcy and so to set forth the fraud of obtaining the deed and to have a new trial.

The defendant pleaded his deed and that Steer was really indebted to him at the time it was executed, and demanded judgment whether he should discover anything to weaken his title.

And, upon long debate, the plea was allowed.

Lord Nottingham, *Prolegomena*, p. 204

Gladwyn v. Bullock.

As the heir, so likewise the creditor shall have no relief against a purchaser. Steer was declared a bankrupt 1 January. The commissioners assign to Gladwyn. Bullock purchases of Steer 1 March following.

And, in [an action of] *ejectione firmae* brought against Gladwyn for the land, the jury finding that Steer was no bankrupt until 3 March, Gladwyn exhibits a bill against Bullock, surmising that Bullock knew Steer to be a bankrupt 1 January, before his purchase, and prays discovery and relief.

Bullock pleads his purchase, and demurs.

It was ruled by Lord Bridgeman, Keeper, and Wilde, Justice, he shall not answer, first, because retrospection and the Statute of Bankrupts[1] to overreach a purchaser ought not to be favored, second, *utcunque* purchaser shall not be bound to discover matter against himself though creditors be concerned and though the commissioners might have examined Bullock as a witness before they made their declaration.

361

Barker v. East

(Ch. 1670)

A bill in equity in the Court of Chancery does not lie to have a new trial in an action in the Petty Bag Office.

3 Chancery Reports 42, 21 E.R. 723

20 May 1670, 22 Car. II. Lord Keeper Bridgeman and Justice Wilde.

The defendant brought an action of trover in Easter term 1668, and, the record being brought down, the wife withdrew it, and, to prevent a challenge, the next term, suggested upon the roll that one Gladwyn, who was the *cestui que trust* to the defendant and a creditor to Steer, the bankrupt, to whom the defendant was an assignee, was a sheriff, whereupon, a *venire* was awarded to the coroners,

[1] Stat. 21 Jac. I, c. 19 (*SR*, IV, 1227–1229).

who all used to return the writs. But Wilkinson, one of the coroners, being newly come to the office, did not join in the return of the jury.

The defendant got a verdict *ex parte*, supposing both coroners had returned both the *venire* and the *distringas*, whereas Wilkinson alone returned the jury of indifferent persons, though he promised not to return the writs alone, but to take Fletcher's advice, who had appointed a meeting, yet Wilkinson, before the time appointed, returned the jury. And Fletcher, perceiving it, refused to sign the writs. And the plaintiff, perceiving the defendants could not have gone on, made no defense, the rather for that Wilkinson persuaded him to keep his witnesses at home, and, afterwards, he returned the writs in both coroners' names, and so the defendant obtained a verdict, which, being a personal action, the plaintiffs cannot try again.

And, therefore, they bring a bill, and seek to discover nothing criminal, but to have a new trial, their witnesses being beyond the seas or in places remote.

The defendants demur, for that Wilkinson's pretended misdemeanor is examinable in the court where the action was brought, and not elsewhere, and that no equity was shown to induce a new trial.

And [the demurrer was] allowed.

362

Bagg v. Forster

(Ch. 1670)

In this case, the court found that the marriage settlement in issue had been performed as agreed.

3 Chancery Reports 50, 21 E.R. 725

22 May.

The bill [was] that James Bushel was seised of the premises in the bill. A treaty was had in August 1648 for a marriage between him and Dorcas, the plaintiff's mother. And, before the marriage, August 31, 1648, he became bound to Francis Goodwin and Francis Holloway, trustees nominated by Dorcas, in £1000, that, if he conveyed and assured the said lands and premises to them and their heirs within two months after or else if he and his heirs purchased so much other lands as amounted to £100 *per annum ultra* reprises within three months and make the like conveyances thereof, then, the bond to be void. And, afterwards, the marriage took effect. But James did not, as the plaintiff can anywise discover, at any time, convey the premises or purchase other lands, but yet, after the time mentioned in the condition of the bond, by indenture dated 20th November 1648, in consideration of the love he bore to the said Dorcas and other considerations therein expressed, covenanted with the said Goodwyn that he and his heirs and all others, being then seised of the said premises, should from thence stand seised to the use of himself for life, without impeachment of waste, and, afterwards, to Dorcas for life, and, after[wards], to the first and tenth sons and their heirs male, and, after[wards], of his own right heirs. And, after the bond of conveyance, James had issue by the said Dorcas, a son, which died without issue. And, afterwards, James died without other issue, and Dorcas, afterwards, married the plaintiff Bagg's father. And they had issue, the plaintiff, their only son and heir. And, about two years since, Dorcas died. And the plaintiff ought, according to the agreement made upon the said marriage, to enjoy the premises to him and his heirs in regard James died in Dorcas's lifetime without issue and he is the heir of Dorcas. And, therefore, he ought to have an execution of the said marriage agreement, according to the condition of the said bond and the defendants, in whom the estate in point of law is, may convey to him accordingly, is the scope of the bill.

Whereto, the defendant Forster, as to two-third parts of the said premises, has pleaded that he is a purchaser for a good and valuable consideration without notice of the said bond and he and his wife, who are entitled, as she is heir at law. And, to the other part of the premises, they have demurred, for that it appears of the plaintiff's own showing that the bond being entered into in 1648, twenty-two years since, to Goodwyn and Holloway, trustees for the plaintiff's mother, that James, in November following, by an indenture between him and the said Goodwyn, made a settlement of the same premises to himself for life and, after[wards], to the plaintiff's mother for life, and, after[wards], to their first and other sons in tail, with remainder to his own right heirs and that there is no issue of James and the plaintiff's mother living, but the plaintiff is a mere stranger to James and a child of Dorcas by another husband, which conveyance, being so accepted as advised, ought reasonably to be intended a performance of the said pretended agreement and condition of the pretended bond and agreement, at least that the plaintiff shall have no relief in equity and for that Goodwyn, the pretended obligee in the bond, nor the executors nor administrators of James Bushel, for aught appears by the bill, are made parties, either as plaintiffs or as defendants thereto, and for that no title in equity appears in the bill for the plaintiff, therefore, they demur thereto.

Upon debate whereof and hearing what could be alleged on either side, it is ordered that the said plea be allowed, but the plaintiff may reply thereunto as he shall be advised. And, as touching the said demurrer, the court, being assisted with Mr. Justice Wilde, adjudged the same to be good and sufficient and the plaintiff is to pay to the defendant the ordinary cost of allowing a demurrer, but with this proviso nevertheless, that the plaintiff may be at liberty to amend his bill or to bring in any new bill upon the said marriage agreement, as he should be advised.

1 Chancery Cases 188, 22 E.R. 755

The Lord Keeper, Justice Wilde.

William Bushel, on his marriage with Dorcas, his wife, enters into a bond of £1000 to trustees to her use in August 1648 conditioned to be void if he did not within two months settle the land in question on those trustees to the use of himself and Dorcas and their heirs in November next. After[wards], William Bushel covenanted with one of the trustees to stand seised of those lands to the use of himself for life, remainder to Dorcas for life, remainder to his first and tenth son in tail, remainder to his own right heirs. William Bushel dies without issue. Dorcas survives many years, and marries with one Bagg, by whom she has issue, the plaintiff, her son and heir, an infant. And, now, in his behalf, the bill is brought against the defendant, who claims under the heir of William Bushel to enforce a conveyance according to the condition of the bond.

For the defendant, it was demurred unto, for that the bond was in 1648 and William Bushel, in November after, made a settlement, *ut supra*, to which one of the trustees was a party and for that there is no issue of the plaintiff's mother and William Bushel and the plaintiff, a mere stranger to William Bushel, being the child of Dorcas by another husband and that the conveyance, *ut supra*, ought reasonably to be intended for a performance of the marriage agreement and, at least, that the plaintiff ought not to have any relief in equity, it not appearing that any possession has gone according to the bond or that any relief was until now sought, though it be twenty-one years since.

On the argument of the demurrer, it was, for the defendant, insisted that there being no agreement but what was in the condition of the bond and [there being] no articles or agreement besides and the bond was twenty-two years old and such settlement, *ut supra*, made unto one of the obligees of the same land mentioned in the condition, though not to the same uses, and Dorcas never questioning it in her life and the agreement being secured by a penalty, which was relied upon, that this case did differ much from an agreement by articles to settle lands, for, here, the party rested on a penalty and there was no reason to turn such an agreement as this was into a collateral execution by decreeing the land, which the court did conceive reasonable, and so allowed the demurrer.

363

March v. Lee

(Ch. 1670)

A junior creditor purchaser having notice of a precedent purchaser cannot protect himself by the buying in of a senior encumbrance.

A subsequent purchase of a prior encumbrance pendente lite *is not material.*

When a third mortgagee purchases in the first mortgage, the second mortgagee has no equity against the third mortgagee.

When a junior purchaser has bought in a precedent encumbrance, he shall not be required to account in equity whether it be satisfied or not.

Lincoln's Inn MS. Misc. 500, f. 84, pl. 4

Easter term 22 Car. II (1670). Lee v. Marsh.

English, seised in fee of two manors, mortgaged part of one for £1000 to A. And, afterwards, he entered into a statute to B. And, afterwards, he mortgaged both of the manors to D. for £7000, and, afterwards, he mortgaged both of these manors to R. for £1000, all of the mortgages being in force at the same time and the statute also. The last mortgagee not having notice of the prior mortgages or statute at the time of his mortgage, afterwards, purchased in the first mortgage and statute. D., the intermediate mortgagee, sued the last mortgagee in Chancery to be relieved, and he offered to pay the first mortgage and statute.

But, by the Lord Keeper [Bridgeman] and Chief Baron Hale and Rainsford, Justice of the King's Bench, the later mortgagee will not be compelled to grant his first mortgage and statute that he had purchased in to D., but he will retain it, because the last mortgagee, as well as D., in respect of his own mortgage has not more than equity to purchase in the first encumbrances. But as the last mortgagee has purchased in those, he has gained a legal estate also in the premises that will not be divested by any equity that D. could pretend, especially as the last mortgagee did not have notice.

And Hale said that the last mortgagee had done prudently. And he cited the saying *redime te captum quam queas minimo.*[1] And this purchase was only a *tabula post naufragium*. And, in this case, D. will not be let in until as well the last as the first mortgage and statute are paid.

1 Chancery Cases 162, 22 E.R. 743

30 May [1670]. Elizabeth March, Richard Chaworth, and Henry Mallory, executors of Jane Duppa, against John Lee, senior, and John Lee, junior. The Lord Keeper, Chief Baron Hale, Justice Rainsford.

The cause coming to be heard and argued on a plea before the Lord Keeper [Bridgeman], he directed a case to be stated, and then would farther consider of it. And now the case being stated, it was thus.

Trinity [term] 1669, the plaintiffs, by their bill, set forth that the nineteenth of January 1662, Henry English, by indenture and fine, wherein the wife joined, conveyed to the plaintiffs, Sir Richard Chaworth and Henry Malory, and their heirs the manor of Monfield in the County of Sussex to the use of Mistress Duppa for 500 years as a mortgage for the security of £4000 payable the fourth of March 1664 with interest in the meantime. On the fourth of March 1664, Mr. English mortgaged to Mistress Duppa the manor of Wigsel in the County of Sussex for 500 years for the security of £3000 more, payable the fifth of June after, with interest, and covenanted in both deeds that the premises were free from encumbrances. 6 August 1664, Mr. English acknowledged to Mistress Duppa a

[1] Terence, *Eunuchus*, 74–75.

recognizance in this court of £2000 for the payment of £1000 and interest. The 7th of December after the 21st of October 1665, the mortgages and recognizances being forfeited, Mistress Duppa died before payment, having made her will and the plaintiffs her executors, who proved the same.

Trinity term 1667, the plaintiffs, having brought several [actions of] ejectment, exhibited their bill here against Mr. English and his wife that Mr. English might discover encumbrances and redeem by a day or that his equity of redemption might be barred. Whereto Mr. English and his lady, after they had stood in a contempt to a commission of rebellion, put in their answer, but did not discover any encumbrances. Michaelmas Term 1667, Mr. English suffered judgment in ejectment at the plaintiff's suit with a *cesset executio* until May after. 18 May 1668, the *cesset executio* being expired, Mr. English, notwithstanding any arguments the plaintiffs' counsel could make, obtained an order of this court for a stay of the plaintiffs' proceedings at law upon the judgment in ejectment until a hearing and another order. 5 June 1668, the cause coming to be heard, the court decreed that Mr. English should pay what was due to the plaintiffs in a twelvemonth or, in default, the plaintiffs should enjoy the premises discharged of all equity of redemption against him and all claiming under him. 26 November 1668, the Master, to whom it was referred to take the account, reported £8530 14s. payable to the plaintiffs the 6th of June 1669. 5 February 1668, the report was decreed, and the decree thereupon signed and enrolled.

The bill farther charges that the defendants, designing to elude the said decree and defeat the plaintiffs of the benefit thereof and of their judgment in ejectment, pretended that Mr. English had mortgaged to them in June 1665, in fee, the manor of Wigsel for the security of £2000 payable the twenty-seventh day of June 1666, which, for non-payment, was become forfeited.

The defendants, having had notice and being acquainted with the contents of the plaintiffs' bill and the proceedings thereupon against Mr. English and their securities and titles to the premises, about a week before the same came to hearing, exhibited their bill here against Mr. English and the plaintiffs to discover the reality of their securities and what was due thereupon and prayed relief therein upon the title of their mortgage. 20 October, the plaintiff moved the court again, which was between the times of the decretal order and pending the reference to the Master, upon an affidavit that Mr. Burrel and several others had encumbrances on the premises precedent to the plaintiffs, to discharge the order of the eighteenth of May last, whereby their proceedings at law for the recovery of the possession of the premises had been stayed and that they might be at liberty to proceed upon their judgment in ejectment to recover the possession, which the court, however, thought not fit to grant, but continued the former order. The Lees, by means thereof, ceased the prosecution of their suit in this court against the plaintiffs. And, while the plaintiffs were tied up by the order of this court from getting possession, they bought in a mortgage made in 1649 by Mr. English to Mr. Burrel of part of Wigsel for £1000 and a statute in 1656 acknowledged by

Mr. English to Mr. Burrel of £800 for the payment of £400, and have extended the statute on both the manors at not above the third part of the value, and, by virtue thereof, intend to evict the possession and to pay themselves as well the £2000 and interest as the £800 and £1000 and interest before the plaintiffs shall have any fruit of their decree. And the defendants ought and the plaintiffs have offered them, upon their payment to them of the £8530 14s. and interest, to assign their securities or else the defendants would accept what is due upon the statute and mortgage to Burrel and, thereupon, assign them to the plaintiffs. And yet they refuse to do it.

And, so, to be relieved in the premises is the prayer of the bill.

Michaelmas [term] 1669. The plea and answer of John Lee, senior, with the answer of John Lee, junior, [was] the defendant, John Lee, the elder, to so much of the bill as seeks relief concerning the manor of Wigsel by setting aside or prejudicing any title he or the other defendant has or for discovery thereof until he be satisfied the money in his plea mentioned, for plea, says that, about the twenty-first of June 1665, the said English affirmed that he was seised in fee of the manor of Wigsel free of encumbrances and the defendant, finding him in possession and believing that he was so seised and knowing nothing to the contrary, in consideration of £2000 paid by him, took a conveyance of the inheritance of fee simple thereof from Mr. English in his and the other defendants' names for the security of £2000 payable the twenty-ninth of June 1666, whereof no part is paid, but the estate is absolute. The defendant, at the time of the conveyance or before, had no notice of the plaintiffs' securities or any of them, but, long after, hearing that Mr. English had encumbered the premises with the plaintiffs' securities and, by a prior mortgage to Mr. Burrel for £500 for securing £1000, which was forfeited in November 1649, had encumbered part of Wigsel, and, in November 1655, had acknowledged a statute to Mr. Burrel of £800 for the payment of £400, which was also forfeited, did by advice of his counsel for the securing of the premises convey to him and the other defendant for £1090 by him paid purchase in Mr. Burrel's mortgage, and agree with him to extend the premises, and, for £430, to assign the same as the defendant should direct. The statute was extended, and the defendant paid Burrel £430, who assigned the extended premises as the defendant did direct. The defendant made the purchase of Burrel principally to secure his title and to protect from encumbrances the premises conveyed to him and the other defendant and to reimburse the several sums of money by him paid with damages or, at least, so much as shall be really due on the said Burrel's mortgage and statute. And he demands judgment. And, by answer, he says that, after this purchase, and not before, he heard of the plaintiffs' encumbrances and heard also of Burrel's mortgage and statute and, before he bought Burrel's mortgage and statute, he had notice of some proceedings by the plaintiffs had in this court against Mr. English touching the premises, but were no parties thereto. But what the same were, he referred to records there and proceedings at law. And, thereupon, by advice of counsel, he did purchase the said mortgage, lease, and extent

November 27, 1668. The agreement for the mortgage and statute with Burrel was entire, though perfected with several instruments, and the consideration was mentioned to be several, and Burrel refused to extend the statute and assign the extent unless the defendant paid him what was due on his mortgage and statute. The defendant submits, if the plaintiffs will let him enjoy his purchase lands free from encumbrances, to pay him the purchase money and damages, and will pay him what he paid Burrel with damages and costs if he will accept it. The rest of his answer is to the effect of his plea.

John Lee, junior, by his answer, says that he claims nothing in the premises to his own use, his name being only used in trust for the other defendant, and he had no notice of the plaintiff's title a long time after the defendant's purchase, and he refers in all things to the plea and answer of the other defendant.

In this case, these queries were made on the plaintiffs' part:

First, whether, upon the paying to the defendants what is due to them upon the mortgage and statute to Burrel, the plaintiffs ought not to have the same assigned to them and, if not, whether the statute, being but an encumbrance, and no estate, ought to be made use of as to the manor of Monfield by the defendants, wherein the defendants have no estate and the title the defendants would protect is but a mortgage or encumbrance, and not to protect the title of an absolute estate.

Second, whether the plaintiffs having a judgment in ejectment for the possession long before the defendants bought in Burrel's mortgage and statute and after the defendants had notice of the plaintiffs' title and proceedings in this court and notwithstanding their endeavors to the contrary, being stayed by the order of this court from recovering the actual possession, they might be looked on as actually in possession. And, in that case, whether shall the defendants make any use of Burrel's mortgage and statute bought in pending the injunction and after the decree against English, other than to reimburse themselves the money thereon due.

Third, and, if not, whether, by the defendants' getting in the statute in the manner as is before expressed, he shall be at liberty to make use of it only against Monfield in the plaintiffs' hands and so force them to pay off the penalty of the statute or clear the same, which Burrel himself could not have done, but all the lands must have been charged with the satisfaction of Burrel's statute, as well those in the defendants' hands as the plaintiffs'.

And these queries were made on the defendant's part.

First, whether the defendant Lee, being a real purchaser, *bona fide*, of Wigsel for £2000 from English then in possession without any notice of any of the plaintiffs' encumbrances preceding to his purchase, might not purchase in the mortgage lease of Wigsel made by English to Burrel and the extent of Burrel's statute preceding to the plaintiffs' encumbrances, both forfeited in point of law, and protect his purchase of Wigsel until the £2000 and interest be paid. And whether there is any equity against him for the plaintiff any way to weaken his legal securities for the enjoying of his purchase until the £2000 and interest be paid, admitting that nothing had been due on Burrel's mortgage or statute in equity and the defendant had paid nothing for purchasing in that mortgage and extent.

Second, whether the defendant, having paid to Burrel £1520 for the mortgage, lease, and extent of the statute, shall be restrained from taking the benefit of the law by the said mortgage, lease, and extent, so far upon any the lands of English in the hands of the plaintiff or any others to recover what [was] really paid to purchase in the same, so as they, after such satisfaction, make no other use of the said Burrel's mortgage or extent than only to protect his own purchase lands until the £2000 and damages be satisfied.

Third, whether the defendant having paid his aforesaid purchase for a valuable consideration without notice of the plaintiff's encumbrances and, by answer, offers to take the mortgage money and damages and the money paid for Burrel's mortgage and extent and damages and costs and quit the whole or else to enjoy the mortgage free from encumbrances and be paid what he paid Burrel with damages and costs and make no further use of Burrel's extent than only to protect his purchased lands from encumbrances, that a court of equity shall give any further relief against him to his prejudice, being a purchaser without notice, and, if any, what relief.

Fourth, whether the defendants, who are no parties to nor at all concerned in the former suits between the plaintiffs and English or concerned in any of the orders or proceedings therein, shall be in any sort affected with or prejudiced by any of those orders.

The court unanimously agreed that the defendant ought not in any sort be impeached in equity as to Wigsel, but he might keep his statute and security on foot to protect his mortgage and that the proceedings in Chancery against English by the plaintiffs did not at all influence this case. But, as to the manor of Monfield, in which the defendants had no estate before they bought in the statute, the court inclined that so much of Wigsel as was not in Burrel's mortgage (for he could not extend on himself) Monfield should be accounted for at the real value in order to discharge Monfield of the extent, but not so as to prejudice the extent in the course of law as to Wigsel, but that the statute ought to protect Wigsel as far as by any course of law it might.

On the argument of this case, was produced Higgon against Udal, and Meddleton against Shelleh, 19 June, Car. I, for precedents.[1] On the hearing of that case, which was a parallel case, the court would be satisfied there by precedents before they would give any relief against purchasers in of encumbrances to protect a real title. And the cause went no further here. But the plaintiff, as

[1] *Higgon v. Syddal* (Ch. 1669), see above, Case No. 332; *Middleton v. Shelly* (Ex. 1666), 1 Levinz 197, 83 E.R. 366, British Library MS. Hargrave 65, f. 65v, pl. 3, Exch. Repts. *tempore* Car. II, 96.

the Chief Baron [HALE] now said, brought his bill in the Exchequer afterwards, and was there dismissed.

And in the principal case, the plea was allowed.

Lord Nottingham, *Prolegomena*, p. 205

A famous case happened between Marsh and others, the executors of Mrs. Ann Duppa, [plaintiffs] and John Lee and his son, defendants.

Mrs. Duppa had three several securities from Mr. Henry English for £8000: first, a mortgage for 500 years of the manor of Monfield in Sussex for £4000; this was dated the 19 January 1662[/63] and the money was payable 4 March 1664[/65]; second, another lease for 500 years of the manor of Wigsell in Sussex for £3000, dated the 4 March 1664[/65] and redeemable 5 January 1665[/66]; third, a recognizance of £2000 for the payment of £1000 dated 6 August 1664 payable 7 December 1664.

After all these securities and without notice of them, Mr. Lee, finding Mr. English in possession, lends him £2000 and, for his security, takes a mortgage of Wigsell dated 27 June 1665 redeemable 29 June 1666.

In October 1665, the plaintiffs, as executors to Mrs. Duppa, exhibit a bill against Mr. English to redeem or be foreclosed.

Mr. Lee, though no party to this suit, had notice of it, and, coming thereby to understand his danger, discovers some encumbrances precedent to Mrs Duppa's, *viz.* a mortgage of part of Wigsell for £1000, dated in November 1649, and also a statute of £800 for the payment of £400 and acknowledged to Mr. Burrell November 1655 and forfeited. Pending the suit against Mr English, he buys in these encumbrances to protect himself, and paid £1090 and £436 for them.

Then, the executors, in Trinity [term] 1669, exhibit a bill against Mr. Lee and his son, praying to redeem Burrell's mortgage and statute or otherwise offering to assign their securities to Lee paying them their £8000.

To which Lee pleads the matter *ut supra*, and offers by answer to let them redeem Burrell's mortgage and statute, so he may enjoy his mortgage from English or otherwise to surrender that too and let them take all if they will pay all.

This plea and answer and the case stated upon it came to be heard, Easter [term] 22 Car. II [1670], by Lord BRIDGEMAN, HALE, Chief Baron, and RAINSFORD, Justice. And the plea was allowed. And these points were resolved:

First, if a man becomes a puisne purchaser having notice of a precedent purchaser, he shall not protect himself by the buying in of an ancient encumbrance; [it is] otherwise if without notice;

Second, if a puisne purchase by Lee had been *pendente lite* against English, there, perhaps, he would have been bound as English. But the original purchase by Lee being precedent to the bill against English, the subsequent purchase of the prior encumbrance *pendente lite* against English is not material, because Lee was engaged before and concerned to help himself;

Third, [it is] not material that Lee was out of possession when he purchased the prior encumbrance, for still he had the same right to protect himself;

Fourth, when the third mortgagee does purchase in the first mortgage, *viz.* Lee buys in Burrell, Duppa, the second mortgagee, shall never impeach him in equity, for, if Lee can save himself by law, Chancery shall never disarm Lee, who has both law and equity on his side, in favor of Duppa, who has only equity. That were only *tollere tabulam post naufragium*;

Fifth, the offer of Duppa's executors to pay off the mortgage is not material, for they must redeem all or none;

Sixth, when a puisne purchaser has bought in a precedent statute, he shall not be called to account in equity whether the statute be satisfied or not. Now, by law, in a *scire facias ad computandum*, the conusee must only account according to the extended value, unless there be a casual profit by mines etc., and must hold it until he be satisfied the whole penalty, costs, and damages, and the reason is because the debtor may aid himself if the extent be too low; the creditor aids himself against the extender if it be too high. And, therefore, if Duppa can avoid this statute by an account according to the extended value, it is well. Otherwise, equity shall not force a purchaser to account contrary to the rule of law, for so long as the extent can live by the law, so long it ought to continue;

Seventh, because the statute attaches on the residue of Wigsell not mortgaged and also on the reversion of that which was mortgaged in 1649 and also on Monfield, it may be reasonable that Lee shall account to let in Duppa's mortgage on Monfield, but not to abridge the fullness of the extent.

And, afterwards, the parties, seeing the opinion of the court, compounded *in facie curiae* to redeem Burrell's mortgage and statute and to permit Lee to enjoy his first mortgage of Wigsell.

3 Chancery Reports 62, 21 E.R. 729

Michaelmas [term] 1670. Lord Keeper, and Judges, Chief Baron Hale, *et al.*

The bill was to be let into Drake's estate after prior encumbrances to the defendant be satisfied.

But the defendant pleaded that there were prior encumbrances of all the plaintiffs claimed to the defendant and that the defendant had a puisne encumbrance to the plaintiff of part of a statute for collateral security.

And the question was whether the defendant should hold all, both to satisfy the prior encumbrance and what was his own security or only to satisfy his own money.

And, he having a statute extended, it was by all adjudged for the defendant, on a demurrer.

2 Ventris 337, 86 E.R. 473

The case was thus. One English being seised of the manor of Wicksall and of the manor of Monfield, in 1649, mortgages part of the manor of Wicksall to Burrell for £1000. Afterwards, in 1655, he acknowledges a statute to Burrell of £800 for the payment of £400. Afterwards, in 1662, English mortgages both these manors to Mrs. Duppa for £7000. Afterwards, in 1665, English mortgages the manor of Wicksall to Lee for £2000, Lee having no notice of the former mortgages. But, afterwards, Lee, coming to have notice of the mortgage to Duppa, purchases in the two encumbrances to Burrell, *viz.* the mortgage of part of the manor of Wicksall and the statute. And now Marsh, executor of Duppa, sues Lee, who pleads this whole matter.

My Lord Keeper [BRIDGEMAN], assisted with HALE, Chief Baron, and Justice RAINSFORD, held, that Lee might make use of these encumbrances to protect his own mortgage, for they said that he had both law and equity for him.

First, he had law, for that he had a precedent mortgage in 1649 (which indeed was but upon part) and also the statute in 1655, so that, while these remained in force, Marsh could not come in.

Next, he had equity, for he having a subsequent mortgage yet, it being without notice, he ought to be relieved in this court.

And, therefore, my Lord Chief Baron [HALE] put the case as, if the first mortgage had been of the manor of Wicksall to Burrell and, afterwards, it had been mortgaged to Duppa and, afterwards, to Lee, not having notice, if, afterwards, Lee bought in Burrell's mortgage, he shall hold the estate against Duppa until he be satisfied for both the money which he paid Burrell and also his own money lent upon the last mortgage. And, for that, he said, that it had been so adjudged in the Exchequer Chamber, in the court of equity, since the king came in, in one Shelley's Case.[1] Next, he put the case of the statute which English entered into to Burrell in 1655, and was, afterwards, bought by Lee from Burrell. He held that Duppa shall not bring Lee to any account upon this statute here in equity any otherwise than he may do at common law.

Note it was agreed that the lands were extended upon the statute at the third part of the true value. Now, at common law, the conusor or he that claims under him must bring a *scire facias ad computandum*, as in the case at 4 Co. 69b.[2] But, then, the conusee shall not account according to the true value, but according to the extended value, and also for the whole statute. And, if the conusee is satisfied by the extended value, the conusor shall recover or, if the conusor will pay down the rest of the money which is behind with damages, he shall also recover. But, if

[1] *Middleton v. Shelly* (Ex. 1666), *ut supra*.

[2] *Libb v. Hynde* (1591), 4 Coke Rep. 68, 76 E.R. 1037, also 1 Anderson 285, 123 E.R. 475.

the conusor will sue the conusee in a court of equity, then, he shall bring him to account for what he has received of the profits above the extended value.

Now then, our case here is somewhat more, for Lee has also equity on his side, and, therefore, Duppa shall not bring him to account for what he has received above the extended value unless he has also received enough to satisfy his own mortgage of £2000 as well as the statute. And, therefore, if Marsh will take off this statute by a suit in this court, he must be content that Lee does account upon the extended value for the whole £800 and damages.

Secondly, they held that, whereas part of the manor of Wicksall was mortgaged to Burrel but that now the whole manor was mortgaged to Lee, that yet the first mortgage should not extend to protect more than that part of the manor which was first mortgaged to Burrel.

And My Lord Chief Baron HALE put the case thus. If a man is seised of sixty acres, and mortgages twenty to A. and then mortgages the whole to B. and then mortgages the whole to C. and, afterwards, C. purchases in the first mortgage, that shall not protect more than the twenty acres, but it shall protect those twenty acres so as B. shall never recover that until he pay C. all the money upon the first and last mortgage.

But HALE said that he thought that, in this case, inasmuch as the mortgage to Lee was only of part of Wicksall that, therefore, Marsh might bring Lee to an account upon the extended value, whereupon these two manors were extended upon the statute, and, if Lee had received the money due upon the statute by the receiving of the profits according to the extended value or if she will pay down the residue of the money due upon the statute or if she will pay down so much as the proportion will come to for Monfield, that then she may discharge the manor of Monfield.

But then My Lord Keeper [BRIDGEMAN] asked him how he would have it appointed and how much should be laid upon Monfield and how much upon Wicksal, for that part of Wicksall is under that extent.

To which HALE answered that, if Marsh did sue Lee for the discharge of this statute from Monfield, that Monfield should be discharged by her paying down as much as the proportion comes to or when Lee shall have received such according to the extended value and that he thought there might be a proportion found out by the court.

Note *Sir H. Finch*, counsel for Lee, cited Primate and Jackson's Case; Grove and Grove's Case; and Mrs. Calamy's Case,[1] all which were resolved in this court that a purchaser or a mortgagee coming in upon a valuable consideration without notice and purchasing in a precedent encumbrance, it shall protect his estate against any person that has a mortgage subsequent to the first, though before the

---

[1] *Grove v. Banson* (Ch. 1669), see above, Case No. 331; *Higgon v. Syddal* (Ch. 1669), see above, Case No. 332.

last mortgage, though he purchased in the encumbrance after he had notice of the second mortgage.

[Other reports of this case: 1 Eq. Cas. Abr. 322, 21 E.R. 1076.]

364

Hurst v. Goddard

(Ch. 1670)

A widower can assign his deceased wife's unpaid portion to a third party, because the assignment is made of his own right and not as an administrator to his wife.

1 Chancery Cases 169, 22 E.R. 746

7 June [1670].

The case was thus. There was a sum of money provided by a settlement of lands to be raised for daughters' portions. One of the daughters marries, and dies before her portion is paid. Her husband takes administration to her, and assigns all his interest in that portion to his son by a former wife. The son, by this title, the father being dead, sued in equity for this money.

It was insisted for the defendants that, though things in action might be assigned here on a consideration by the party that had the interest and were recoverable here by the assignee and that a release afterwards by the assignor, unless it were without notice and on consideration to him, to whom the release was, would not hurt the assignee, yet, here, the assignment being by an administrator, and not the person that had it in his own right, this had never been good, for there might be a creditor to satisfy the intestate etc.

The Lord Keeper [Bridgeman] did think there was a considerable difference between the assignment of the party and of the administrator, where the administrator was a stranger or had not right before and no color of right, but merely by the administration. But, here, in this case, the administration was *pro forma* only, for, here, he had a right to the money as a portion or provision for his wife and every man has not ready money to give daughters, but their portions are to be provided for by this means. And, therefore, it is reasonable to advance or promote the establishing of them, so that they might be disposable by the husband, who settles a jointure, as money itself may be. And so, he decreed for the plaintiff.

365

Martin v. Seamore

(Ch. 1670)

As to an estate mortgaged to secure a debt, the creditor's rights are subordinate to a prior marriage settlement in favor of his wife, but superior to a later gift to his child.

1 Chancery Cases 170, 22 E.R. 746

13 June [1670]. The Lord Keeper, the Master of the Rolls.

Robert Seamore, being seised of the lands, being copyhold in fee, surrenders them to the plaintiff by way of a mortgage for money lent. And, in a few days after, he surrenders them to the use of his will. And, then, by a will, he devises them to his wife for life, remainder to his daughter in fee, and dies. There was a failer to present the plaintiff's surrender at the next court. But the wife got herself admitted.

The plaintiff's bill was to be relieved for this mortgage money and to set aside this surrender and will, being voluntary, unless the wife and daughter would pay him.

For the wife, it appeared there was an agreement of the husband, in consideration of the marriage, to settle the premises on her for life. And she insisted that the will and surrender to her was pursuant to that consideration and agreement.

For the plaintiff, it was insisted that, if a copyholder, for money [borrowed], had agreed to sell or mortgage his copyhold, that, by such agreement, he stands trusted for the vendee and that no voluntary disposition afterwards could prejudice the vendee nor no disposition for money with notice of that agreement and that the plaintiff, having a surrender, ought not to be in a worse case than if he had only an agreement.

The court, as to the wife, she, being in pursuant to a precedent agreement to the plaintiff's title, would not impeach her estate. But, as to the daughter, hers being purely a voluntary estate, it was ordered that, unless she would pay the plaintiff his money, he should hold and enjoy the premises against her.

366

Stowell v. Long

(Ch. 1670)

The Act of Oblivion pardoned the accounting for profits received from land that was confiscated by the government during the Interregnum.

1 Chancery Cases 172, 22 E.R. 747

14 June [1670]. George Stowel, Esq., against George Long, executor of George Long.

Sir John Stowel, whose heir the plaintiff is, was indebted to the defendant's testator by a judgment and counterbond, the defendant's testator having paid the debts he was bound in as surety for him. Sir John was sequestered, and his estate was exposed to sale by the Parliament for his loyalty to the late king. The defendant's testator bought a farm of the trustees for sale, part of Sir John's estate, and, in the purchase, had an allowance of his debt by the judgment and on the counterbond, and he paid the rest of the purchase money, as was usual, by bills etc. The defendant's testator's purchase was in 1652, and he entered and held until 1660, the king's restoration. He being dead, the plaintiff, who claimed under Sir John Stowel, exhibited a bill to call the defendant to an account, and suggested that the land was conveyed by the trustees in satisfaction of the judgment and that, by the profits taken, the judgment was satisfied, and, therefore, the plaintiff ought to hold the lands against the judgment which was extended for the defendant.

It was insisted that, for all the profits the defendant's testator took under the sale, it was pardoned by the Act of Indemnity[1] and that the defendant's testator, besides this judgment and this bond, paid a great sum of money for the purchase. And yet it was offered to come to an account if the plaintiff, on account, would pay the defendants the debt due by the judgment and on the counterbond and the money paid for the purchase.

And, upon that offer, the court decreed it to an account, though it was for the plaintiff strongly opposed that the debt Sir John owed him by the counterbond (it not being within the judgment) should not be brought into the account or allowed the defendant. But, inasmuch as that debt was allowed the defendant as part of the consideration in the purchase of the estate, the Lord Keeper [BRIDGEMAN] did order that to be brought into the account and allowed the defendant. And he declared that, if the defendant's counsel had not offered to account, he would not have ordered an account, for that all monies received by the profits are pardoned by the Act of Oblivion.

367

Troner v. Hassold

(Ch. 1670)

A ruling on a demurrer can be stayed until after the defendant has answered.

[1] Stat. 12 Car. II, c. 11 (*SR*, V, 226–234).

1 Chancery Cases 173, 22 E.R. 748

16 June [1670].

[This was] the very same case with that of Wembergh and Tough, before, fol. 123,[1] save that the debt was by bond and entered into here.

And upon a demurrer, the Lord Keeper [BRIDGEMAN] ordered the defendant to answer, but he saved the benefit of the demurrer to the hearing.

368

Pheasant v. Pheasant

(Ch. 1670–1672)

Money of a London orphan held by the City is a debt and not a deposit; therefore, if the orphan's husband does not receive it in his lifetime, the debt belongs to the widow.

A London wife cannot be required to elect to receive a sum of money in lieu of dower if she that sum of money is already hers.

1 Chancery Cases 181, 22 E.R. 752

4 July [1670]. Pheasant and others, executors of Walter Pheasant, against Anne Pheasant, the relict of Walter Pheasant, the Mayor and Commonalty of London, and the Chamberlain. The Lord Keeper, Justice Twysden, Justice Wilde.

Walter Pheasant, having taken to wife the defendant Anne, who was an orphan and had her portion in the Chamber of London, after his marriage, took out £40 thereof. And, by his will, he gives his said wife her portion in the Chamber of London, being £2800, and other things to the value of £1000 on conditions she renounce her dower. She accepts this legacy before and after her husband's death.

The bill was to perform the will and to renounce and release her dower. She has a cross-bill for her portion in the Chamber of London against the executors of her husband, the Mayor and Commonalty and the Chamberlain, and she insists that her portion belongs to her in regard the security was unaltered by her husband in his lifetime, and so was as much as if it were a debt due to her by a bond, and she sought to recover her dower besides.

For the executors, it was insisted that the monies in the Chamber of London is not there as a common debt, but vests in the husband by marriage, it being only deposited to remain there until the orphan comes of age, which she attained during the marriage. And it was also insisted that the receiving of £40 out of it is an alteration of the property and owning of the husband's right to the whole and that, however, she was concluded by the acceptance of her legacy in lieu of her dower. And it was said that the Mayor and Chamberlain have only the custody of

[1] *Weymberg v. Touch* (Ch. 1669), see above, Case No. 303.

the child, but not the property of her money, but that is *in custodia legis* until she comes of age, and is only a *depositum*, and not a *debitum* in the meantime. And it would be inconvenient if the property of the portion did not vest in the husband by marriage, for, by the marriage, the woman becomes dowable.

The Lord Keeper [BRIDGEMAN] conceived the money in the Chamber of London is a debt, for the Chamber pays interest for it, and, if so, her acceptance of the matters devised to her will not bar her dower, according to Vernon's Case, 4 Rep.[1] The acceptance of a collateral satisfaction is no bar in a writ of dower. And so he conceived Ann Pheasant is entitled to the money in the Chamber of London, but he said he would consider of it.

And, 30 October 1670, for the executors of the husband, it was insisted that the Mayor and Commonalty have but the custody of the body and goods of the orphan. New Entries, 346.[2] And, so, the property is in the orphan, and the orphan has, in truth, a legal possession, the Chamberlain being in the nature of a servant to the orphan, and possession of the servant is possession of the master. 1 Cro. Jac. 37.[3] So that, by the marriage, this money is the husband's. As, if an infant wife bring money into this court, and marries, and dies, the property is in the infant, and by the marriage becomes the husband's.

But it was answered that was not like the principal case, for, here, the Chamberlain pays interest etc., but no interest is payable for money in court. And the property here is in the infant.

And so all agreed the monies belong to the widow, and not to the executors.

Lord Nottingham, *Prolegomena*, p. 321

Michaelmas [term] 22 Car. II, Ann Pheasant v. Peter Pheasant.

The case was this. A City orphan takes a husband before the portion was received. And he devises the portion to his wife on condition that she does not demand dower. She demands both. The heir obtains an injunction to stay the suit in the Common Bench in dower.

And, on debate, [it was] resolved by BRIDGEMAN, Keeper, TWYSDEN and WILDE that she shall [have] her portion and dower too, and the injunction was dissolved, because the orphan's money in the Chamber of London is a *debitum*, not a *depositum*, so that the property of it is not altered by the marriage until the husband receive it or gain possession of it, but it still remains a chose in action, which accrues to the wife by surviving and which the husband cannot devise, nor annex any condition to, by his will. And, if this money was a *depositum* not a *debitum*, then the orphan at her [full] age could not have [an action of] debt for

---

[1] *Vernon v. Vernon* (1572), 4 Coke Rep. 1, 76 E.R. 845, also 3 Dyer 317, 73 E.R. 718, Benloe 210, 123 E.R. 147, 3 Leonard 28, 74 E.R. 519.

[2] *Bansted's Case* (1568), E. Coke, *Booke of Entries* (1614), 'Habeas Corpus', pl. 5, f. 346.

[3] *Reymund v. Hundred of Oking* (1626), Croke Car. 37, 79 E.R. 636.

her portion, but ought to bring [an action of] trover, and the City would be guilty of a conversion, which would be inconvenient and absurd. And this is not to be compared to the case where money is brought into court, by which no interest is due, for, here, the City has a special interest and property in the money and some profit by it by paying less interest than they make of it.

Objected: The Chamberlain is the orphan's servant, because the property remains in the orphan.

Solution: No, he is the City's servant, for the orphan has no power to refuse him.

[It was] objected to be inconvenient, for, if an orphan marry an infant husband, he shall not receive her portion during her minority, yet his wife shall have dower.

Solution: It is a worse inconvenience that, by stealing an orphan, he shall gain a portion.

Objected: A debt does not vest, because of the folly of the husband not to sue; here, [there is] no possibility to sue.

Solution: *Curiae contra*, for he may sue, though a minor. And, if he receives it, the City is discharged.

And to prove that the property of the portion does not remain in the orphan but is [in] the City, WILDE cited Dr. Ent's Case.[1] The father devises to three sons their orphanage part, and, if they all die before twenty-one, that J.S. shall have it. They all three die. The administrator of the survivor claims it. [It was] resolved on a certificate of Wilde, then the Recorder, that the father can devise this possibility, and [it was] so decreed.

2 Ventris 340, 86 E.R. 475

Peter Phesant *versus* Anne Pheasant, the Lord Mayor of London, and Sir Thomas Player, Chamberlain of London, etc.

The case was this. Anne Hadly (now Pheasant), one of the defendants, being an orphan of London and having an estate of £3000 or £4000 in money in the Court of Orphans there, was married to W. Pheasant, elder brother to the plaintiff. W. Pheasant, before she was at the age of twenty-one years and not having taken out this money, dies, having bequeathed this money *inter alia* to his said wife, provided that she should not claim dower etc. Notwithstanding, she brings [an action of] dower against the now plaintiff, brother and heir to her late husband. Whereupon, he brings this bill in Chancery to make discovery of this estate and to compel her to release her dower or renounce this devise. And, thereupon, he obtains an injunction to stay proceedings in the writ of dower.

The point was whether this money in the Court of Orphans were devisable or no.

[1] Note *Adrian v. Ent* (Ch. 1660), see above, Case Nos. 7, 96.

Serjeant *Goodfellow* argued that it was devisable as a chattel personal in the testator's possession and vested in the husband. The Court of Orphans have but the *custodiam*. Co. Entries 346; 1 Roll. 550.[1] The Chamberlain of London is the officer entrusted and a sole corporation to this purpose, as to take a recognizance, which shall go to his executors, and is the only corporation of that nature in England. His possession is the testator's actual possession. Latch 127.[2] If the servant be robbed, the master shall have the action, as in 1 Cro. 37. This is not a *debitum*, but a *depositum*, as *in custodia in gremio legis* by the custom of London, as if money had been brought into court here by a compulsory order, in which case, it would have vested in the husband. Now, in the Court of Orphans, they compel people to bring in the money or to give security, and they pay no interest, only allow finding money, that is, for the orphan's maintenance, and no more. Seeing the wife is entitled to dower immediately, it were hard that the husband should not have the portion. Debts he shall not have, because of his laches in not bringing an action whereby to reduce them to property. But this cannot be had until the wife's full age. Upon the marriage of orphans, the custom is to appoint the Common Serjeant to treat and take security for the orphan.

Serjeant *Maynard, contra*: This was a chose in action; [an action of] debt lies for it, and it cannot be recovered without an action. Interest is allowed for it according to the custom (though not statute interest) and proportionable to the sum. And the case of Dr. Ent. *versus* Adrian was, by the custom of London, if a man die leaving three sons, his estate shall be equally divided amongst them, and, if either of them die within age, his part shall survive to the other. The father taking notice of this custom, devised that, if any of his sons die within age, his part should not survive, but that it should go to J.S. It was resolved that the father could not thus give the child's portion, because [it was] but a possibility and a thing not vested in himself.

Wilde said that, when he was Recorder [of the City of London], he certified the custom in that case to be that the father might devise.

Curia, viz. Bridgeman, Lord Keeper, Twysden and Wilde assisting: We are clear of opinion that this was a chose in action and not devisable. An [action of] trover and conversion lies not for it if it be refused to be paid. It was the laches of the husband that he did not recover it, for, by the custom, it is to be paid at the full age or marriage of the female orphan. The Chamberlain is not a servant to the orphan, but to the Mayor. If it were purely a *depositum*, it must be paid in specie without interest, but they pay customary interest. And though, whilst the orphans are under age (and unmarried if women), they give them finding money only. Yet, at the end of all, when the orphan comes at full age (or, if a female,

[1] *Bansted's Case* (1568), *ut supra*; 1 Rolle Abr., *Customs de London*, B. 'Le custome touchant Orphans', p. 550.

[2] *Drope v. Thaire* (1626), Latch 126, 82 E.R. 307, also Noy 79, 74 E.R. 1046, Popham 178, 79 E.R. 1274, Benloe 173, 73 E.R. 1034, Paynell K.B. 102.

marries), all is cast up, and the interest is paid. The word '*custodia*' in pleading imports an interest, as in the case of a guardian in socage, etc. the Lord Mayor, etc. have a special interest in it, and, if it be lost or miscarry, they are to answer for it. Let the injunction be dissolved.

Lord Nottingham, *Prolegomena*, p. 218

There was a demurrer on this point, whether the trust of a long lease to attend the inheritance should attend the recovery of dower out of the inheritance for a third part. This depended very long. And, being a doubtful point, it had been much better and cheaper, first, to have ordered the defendant to answer and saved the point of demurrer to the hearing, for so the defendant might have had the benefit of the circumstances on the proof and the demurrer had been sooner dispatched.

Lord Nottingham, *Prolegomena*, p. 233

Hilary [term] 23 Car. II, Pheasant v. Pheasant, by Orlando Bridgeman, Keeper.

Mrs. Pheasant brings a writ of dower in the Common Bench and recovers only a third part of a peppercorn, which was the rent reserved on a long lease appointed to attend the inheritance.

[It was] resolved in Chancery the lease shall attend the dower for a third part of it, because the dower is extracted out of that reversion on which the lease is attendant and because the wife, by her recovery, is in of the best possession of her husband.

But, afterwards, by the importunity of the defendant [in the action at law], it was adjourned.

Monday, 24 July following, it was again debated and urged for the defendant, who demurred: first, that, generally, of a trust there shall be no dower, which was agreed; second, that, where a person comes to have an interest in the reversion by the act of the party, there the lease shall attend it; [it is] otherwise, where the interest in the reversion is gained by an act in law, as the lord by escheat and the like. Now, a tenant in dower comes in by an act in law and, therefore, she shall not mend her dower in Chancery.

The plaintiff denied the difference, and said the lord, by escheat, who lost [the beneficial interest of] his seignory [accruing] by [the] falling [in] of the reversion, should in equity have the benefit of the lease, and so a tenant in dower for the reasons before, and because the seisin of a tenant in dower is *quodammodo* a continuing for the seisin of her husband, for a disseisee may enter upon her after a descent, and it is but reason that a tenant in dower should be aided in equity to set aside a long lease which encumbers her dower as well as a statute. And they denied the case, 37 Eliz., of Upton and Basset, 1 Cro. 445,[1] put by *Beaumond*, for a jointress, after marriage, shall avoid a voluntary lease precedent.

1 *Upton v. Basset* 1595), Croke Eliz. 445, 78 E.R. 685.

And it was adjourned, and a day was appointed for solemn argument, LORD BRIDGEMAN, Keeper, now inclining against the plaintiff.

And, *postea*, it was adjudged against the plaintiff.

3 Chancery Reports 69, 21 E.R. 731

24 July 1671.

The plaintiff is the relict of Judge Pheasant,[1] who had brought a writ of dower of lands and recovered a third part of a peppercorn, the lands being purchased by the judge, and an assignment of a lease for 1000 years made in Queen Elizabeth's time at a peppercorn rent assigned to the trustees. And the bill is to have her dower in equity, setting forth the judgment in dower. But the defendant sets up the lease, which was intended to wait on the inheritance, for that possession never went with it and that the Judge received the profits all along.

To which, the defendant answered that the Judge, by his will, directed the lease should be kept separate from the inheritance to prevent encumbrances or dower or both, as they believed. And he demurred, that she ought not to be relieved.

Whereupon, cases were cited, as, if the inheritance had escheated and that the Chancery ought not to relieve the trust, and Box and Lane and Bennet's Case, and Robinson and Fletcher's Case in 1653, where a wife brought a writ of dower against the heir and a conveyance was set up to a younger brother.[2]

And the court ordered the deed to be given in evidence, but would advise. And, after several arguments before Chief Justice HALE and VAUGHAN, this case was amicably composed; so no judgment was given in the point.

1 Vernon 356, 23 E.R. 520

The plaintiff had by the decree of this court her whole portion restored to her, it having been lodged in the Chamber of London, and the property not altered by her husband. And there was, therefore, the less reason to incline a court of equity to relieve her against the term that prevented her dower. And, in that case, she had not actually recovered dower.

369

Shalmer v. Tresham

(Ch. 1670)

A scrivener does not have a privilege not to disclose communications with a customer.

[1] J. M. Rigg and V. Larminie, 'Phesant, Peter (1584–1649)', *Oxford Dictionary of National Biography*, vol. 44, pp. 8–9.

[2] *Bennet v. Box* (Ch. 1662–1664), see above, Case No. 68; *Robinson v. Fletcher* (1653), 3 Chancery Reports 94, 21 E.R. 739.

2 Chancery Reports 29, 21 E.R. 607

The bill is to discover the deeds of several lands and whether they were not made in trust and whether the debt demanded by the plaintiff were not mentioned in a schedule thereunto annexed.

The defendant pleaded that he was a scrivener by profession, and has taken the accustomed oath that scriveners do before they are made free in London, whereby he is obliged not to discover the secrets of those persons' business that employ him in that trade without their leave and that he was employed by and assisted Sir John Langham in the purchasing of the said lands and the writings concerning the premises he drew, and he has the keeping thereof by the said Sir John's direction, and so he ought not to discover the said writings, contrary to his trust, nor anything relating to this matter.

This court declared that the oath of a scrivener does not oblige from a discovery, more than the oath of any other freeman of London. And, if it had been in the case of a counsellor at law, the said plea had been insufficient in this case. And [the court] overruled the plea, saving he is not to answer to whom he paid the purchase money.

[Reg. Lib. 21 Car. II, f. 560.]

370

Hunton v. Davies

(Ch. 1670–1671)

A suit for purchase money that was brought many years after the transaction, the original parties being dead, will be dismissed as untimely or as the money presumed already paid.

2 Chancery Reports 44, 21 E.R. 611

The bill is for £500, remainder of £2900, which Mr. Hugh Ordley was to pay for the purchase of land to the plaintiff's father, which £500 was decreed to be paid to one Castle in 1637 for the use of the plaintiff, which £500 and interest comes to £1184, and to have the defendants, the purchasers of the land, to pay it.

To which bill, the defendants, the executors of Ordley, pleaded that Mr. Ordley lived in London until 1662 and the plaintiff might have had a remedy against him and it being a debt thirty-three years since and no suit commenced against Ordley in his lifetime nor any until now and the lands enjoyed by others now and the defendants, the executors, have nothing to show for the payment and case and all former parties concerned therein being dead and, therefore, after all this time, the defendants hope this court will not suppose that the said money is unpaid or that the defendants ought to be charged therewith.

And the defendants being executors and strangers to all the matters aforesaid, this court held the plea and demurrer good.

[Reg. Lib. 22 Car. II, f. 386.]

371

Malpas v. Vernon

(Ch. 1670–1671)

Where a purchaser with notice of an encumbrance purchases land without expressly assuming his seller's debt, he is not liable to the creditor beyond the loss of the land.

2 Chancery Reports 45, 21 E.R. 611

A bill of review [was exhibited] to reverse a decree whereby the plaintiff is decreed to pay more money than, by his agreement on his purchase, he was to pay.

This court declared that, without a special agreement at the time of the purchase for the payment of the debt claimed by the defendant, the plaintiff ought not to be obliged by the decree to pay the defendant, no such agreement appearing by the decree or any proof offered at the hearing.

The defendant insisted that, by the proofs, there is an agreement proved, whereby the defendant, amongst other creditors, was to be satisfied his debt.

Now, the point being whether any special agreement was made for the purpose aforesaid and the court had declared no new proofs could be admitted in the cause, this court ordered, by consent, that the cause be heard on the said point of agreement on the old proofs and no other.

Lord Nottingham, *Prolegomena*, p. 209

Hilary [term] 23 Car. II, 7 February. Vernon v. Malpas.

Though the favor of the court be extended to purchasers without notice, yet a purchaser having notice of a former encumbrance is not always subject to it. As, for example, a purchaser has notice of a judgment and yet he buys the land with a resolution to keep a mortgage on foot, which is precedent unto it. Equity will never make him subject to this judgment, though he had notice of it, unless there was a special agreement to pay it and some allowance for it in the purchase, and then he must pay it notwithstanding the mortgage precedent.

[Reg. Lib. 22 Car. II, f. 360.]

372

Earl of Castlehaven v. Underhill

(Ch. 1670–1671)

A bill of review is subject to the defense of laches.

2 Chancery Reports 46, 21 E.R. 612

This is a bill of review to reverse a decree in 12 Car. I [1636–37] wherein the now defendant was plaintiff against the Lady Viscountess of St. Albans, his wife, and others, defendants. The points of error were that the decree was grounded on a bill exhibited by the now defendant against the said Lady St. Albans, his then wife, and was made by consent without any judicial hearing, whereby a settlement and disposition of the said Lady's lands, whereof she had an estate in fee, was made without any fine or recovery levied or suffered or any other legal act done to bar and bind her or her inheritance, which the said plaintiff conceives could not be done, the said Lady being a married woman, and could not in law or equity consent, nor could her trustees, by her consent, charge the inheritance, wherein they had no legal assurance.

The now defendants insist that, 2 Car. I [1626–27], the said Lady St. Albans, after her intermarriage with the now defendant, did settle £300 *per annum*, and several recoveries were suffered, whereby the same would have come to the defendant after the said Lady's death, as an estate in fee, the said Lady dying without issue.

Afterwards, the said Lady and the defendant came to another agreement, *viz.* that the defendant should have £400 *per annum* out of the said Lady's estate to him and his assigns for life and, in consideration thereof, the said defendant agreed to quit and debar himself of and from all claim and interest to any of the rest of the said Lady's estate, real or personal, during their joint lives or after her death. And, in case of failure of payment or the said Lady's death, the defendant was to enter into all the estate for satisfaction. Which said £400 *per annum* was settled by a deed tripartite 14 Car. I [1638–39], and the said agreement and settlement was confirmed by a decree 17 Car. I [1641–42] by the consent of all parties. And the said Lady, by a will, gave away from this defendant all her lands and personal estate, which the defendant had given her a power to do, and she died. And for the non-payment of the said £400 *per annum*, the defendant entered upon the lands liable to the payment thereof. And the defendant hopes the said decree shall not be reversed.

The plaintiff insists that the title in law in the Lady's estate was in trustees before her marriage with the defendant and so agreed to be continued without his intermeddling therewith, he bringing no additional estate to the said Lady, and that there was no fine levied to the trustees or otherwise of her estate of inheritance and that the uses upon the recoveries were with a power of revocation in the Lady alone and that, pursuant to such power, by a deed in 14 Car. I [1638–39], she revoked the same, and settled the same in trust for such persons and their heirs as she, by her will, should appoint and that the said tripartite indenture and decree did not discharge the trust nor take notice of the recoveries and that the said Lady, in 1659, did appoint that her trustees upon the said recoveries shall convey part of her land to the plaintiff Solmes's father and the plaintiff Terrell and the rest to her heir at law and that, in 1650, the said land came first to be charged, which was after the Lady's death and, presently after, there appeared infancies, which was the reason the said decree was not sooner impeached.

This court, being assisted with the judges, taking into consideration the length of time since the decree was made and how long they were resting under it without any complaint and that the heirs have a benefit by the Lady's separate power of disposing, who disposed accordingly by her will, this court, with the judges, declared and are of opinion that the said decree, grounded on the tripartite indenture 14 Car. I [1638–39], was and is a good decree, and ought to be performed. And they dismiss the bill of review.

[Reg. Lib. 22 Car. II, f. 106.]

373

White v. Ewens

(Ch. 1670)

A lease that is to commence after a failure of payment is not the same as a mortgage with a condition subsequent.

The defense of laches applies to suits to redeem mortgages, especially after the time limit of the Statute of Limitation for making an entry has expired at common law.

2 Chancery Reports 49, 21 E.R. 613

This is upon an appeal from a decree, the case being that Dame Anne Brett, relict of Sir Alexander Brett, having a jointure in the manors and lands of Whitstanton and Alexander, her son, having on the marriage with Elizabeth, the daughter of Sir William Kirkham, agreed to settle a £250 *per annum* jointure on the said Elizabeth but, being disabled to do it by reason of Dame Anne's jointure, he being seised only of £120 *per annum* in Whitland and the reversion of Yarkcombe, the said Alexander agreed with the said Dame Anne that his heirs, executors, or administrators should pay yearly after his death to Sir Humphrey Lind and George Brett £250 *per annum* during the said Dame Anne's life if the said Elizabeth should so long live. And, thereupon, the said Dame Anne joined with the said Alexander in a grant of a rent charge of £250 *per annum* out of Whitstanton for the jointure of Elizabeth, and Alexander, 12 Jac. I [1614–15], demised Whitland and Yarkcombe to Lind and Brett, the said trustees, for a hundred years to commence immediately after such time as the heirs, executors, or administrators of Alexander should fail to pay the said £250 *per annum* to the said trustees during the life of the said Elizabeth.

15 Jac. I [1617–18], the said Alexander died. And there being a failure of payment of the £250 by the children, executors, etc. of the said Alexander to the said Elizabeth or to the trustees for the use of the said Dame Anne, the said Dame Anne paid the same out of Whitstanton and, thereby, the said lease of 100 years of Whitland and Yarkcombe did commence. And, thereupon, she entered, and received the profits of Whitland, and the said Dame Anne paid the £250 during the life of the said Elizabeth.

The said Alexander leaving three children, *viz.* Robert, Mary, and Anne, wholly unprovided for and, by agreement, the said Dame Anne was to pay £80 *per annum* for the said children's maintenance from the death of the said Elizabeth, their mother, and that the said Dame Anne and her trustees should assign the said lease of 100 years to the said children when at age, that, 17 Jac. I [1619–20], the said lease was assigned to the children to commence from 1636, that the said Dame Anne paid the said £80 *per annum* maintenance, which, with £1750, she had paid to the said Elizabeth, amounting to more than the value of the said lease of Whitland, whereof she received the profits, until, about 1636, the said Mary, one of the children, being dead and that the defendant Ewens having married Anne, the other daughter, they and the said Robert Brett, the son, held the said premises as joint tenants by virtue of the said lease. But the said Robert Brett receiving more of the profits than his share, the defendant Ewens and his wife sued out a writ of partition in 1654. A moiety was delivered to the defendant Ewens, and judgment was given that the same should be held in severalty. And the defendant Ewens, 12 Car. II [1660–61], for a £132 fine and £20 *per annum*, demised part thereof to the defendant Nurse, who assigned to the defendant Rutland.

The plaintiff White, insisting that Robert Brett acknowledged a judgment to Richard White in 1644, extended the defendants' moiety, and brought an [action of] ejectment, and got a verdict by surprise, since which, the defendant brought an action, and obtained a verdict, whereupon, the plaintiff exhibited his bill, and has stayed the defendants by an injunction. To have an account of the profits received and a lease of 12 Jac. I [1614–15] being twenty years since is contrary to the Limitations[1] and rules both at law and equity.

The plaintiff insists he is now in the place of the said Robert, but in a better condition, his said judgment, under which he claims, being long since extended in the lifetime of the said Richard White and Robert Brett and before any action brought, and, if the said lease be satisfied, the same ought to be set aside. And to take off the length of time, he insists that, by a decree made in the Court of

[1] Stat. 21 Jac. I, c. 16 (*SR*, IV, 1222–1223).

Wards in 1640, the defendants were to account with the said Robert Brett and the plaintiff's father, Richard White, really lent the said money for which the judgment was gotten, and, in 1646, on the extent, had a moiety of Whitland delivered and that, notwithstanding the lease to the three children, the Lady Anne had possession of Whitland until 1637.

The defendants insist that the Lady Anne paid £1750 and £80 *per annum* during the minority of the children, which is more than the value, who looked on herself an absolute owner and disposed of the said lease whereof the said Robert had a moiety, and that this differs from ordinary mortgages, the lease being to commence after a failure of payment by the heirs, executors, or administrators of the said Alexander, and there was no proviso therein, and that the said Lady Anne, in all probability, has paid many hundreds of pounds, and Elizabeth might have lived many years longer. And, though the Lady Anne had paid treble the value, yet she must have been contented with her security, and the said Robert Brett did not think the same worth redeeming. And, though the reversion in fee was extended in 1646, yet the said Robert Brett and the defendant Ewens continued possession until the judgment on the writ of partition and, from thence until 1662, which was twenty years after the plaintiff's judgment, and the Lady Anne was to continue possession until the children attained twenty-one years of age, which was in 1636, when the said demise to them made did commence.

This court, being assisted with the judges, were of opinion and declared themselves fully satisfied that the plaintiff ought not to have any relief against the defendants, but that the bill ought to be dismissed, for that His Lordship [Bridgeman] does take a difference betwixt the lease which is to commence after a failure of payment and a mortgage with a condition subsequent, and the rather in this case, for that the breach was in the failure of payment of £250 *per annum*, which the said Lady was thereby obliged to pay for a young life and so it might have been paid for many years. And, if it had been paid in the casualty for twenty years, the heirs would never have redeemed it. And, therefore, [there is] no reason why the plaintiff should take advantage thereof. And, also, the agreement before mentioned between the said Dame Anne and Kirkham weighed much in this court, to which agreement Robert, the heir, by his enjoying of the premises so assigned, together with the defendant Ewens and his wife, after he came of age, consented, and there was no disturbance during the tenancy in common as to the right, but as to perception of profits only. And the heir permitting the defendant Ewens and his wife to have judgment on the writ of partition was a consent of the whole. And, in this consent, it is not the heir, but a stranger, who seeks to redeem. And no man that puts himself after so long a time into a condition to redeem shall have any relief here. And it is the stronger against the plaintiff that no consideration is proved for the said judgment, which was entered so long since as the year 1640. And, after sixty years, this court will not relieve the plaintiff, but dismiss the bill.

2 Ventris 340, 86 E.R. 474

At a rehearing before My Lord Keeper [BRIDGEMAN], assisted with Justice VAUGHAN and TURNER, concerning the redemption of a mortgage which had been made above forty years since, My Lord Keeper declared that he would not relieve mortgages after twenty years, for that the Statute of 21 Jac., cap. 16, did adjudge it reasonable to limit the time of one's entry to that number of years unless there are such particular circumstances as may vary the ordinary case, as infants, married women, etc. are provided for by the very Statute, though those matters in equity are to be governed by the course of the court, and that it is best to square the rules of equity as near the rules of reason and law as may be.

[Other reports of this case: 1 Eq. Cas. Abr. 313, 21 E.R. 1069.]
[Reg. Lib. 22 Car. II, f. 237.]

374

Boulter v. Chester

(Ch. 1670–1671)

A surety upon a bail bond for an appearance of a defendant in court is only liable for the amount of the ad damnum *in an* ac etiam *bill.*

2 Chancery Reports 55, 21 E.R. 614

The question being whether the plaintiff Boulter, who was a surety for one Ree, should pay any more than the sum of £40, for which he was bail for the appearance of one Roger Ree at the defendant's suit, the *ac etiam* bill being only for £40, whereas the defendant demands £55 for a year's rent for the premises and £10 damages for want of repair of the premises, besides costs, and would fix the same on the plaintiff, the bail.

But the main question being whether the bail ought to answer or pay any more than what was expressed in the writ, which is £40, or whether he ought to answer or pay what might have been recovered in case the said Ree, for whom the plaintiff was bail, had appeared and defended the action, this court conceived that the defendant Stretton ought to have no more than what was expressed in the writ and *ac etiam* bill, for which the plaintiff was only bail, but his costs in the same already taxed at law and by the Master. And [the court] ordered the same accordingly.

[Reg. Lib. 22 Car. II, f. 60.]

375

Hunt v. Jones

(Ch. 1670)

Where the limitations of an estate are void, the estate passes to the executor or the administrator of the estate.

3 Chancery Reports 61, 21 E.R. 728

Trinity [term] or Michaelmas [term] 1670.

The bill was to have a long lease assigned, which came to the plaintiff by virtue of an administration of her former husband. But there were children of the intestate.

And it was referred to the civil law to determine the administration before a decree, for the Statute of Hen. VIII[1] is that administration be granted to the wife or child. And the wife having it, [the court] sent it back to see if the civil law does not proportion the administration.

2 Chancery Reports 56, 21 E.R. 615

The bill is that the defendant Jones, who is the surviving trustee, may assign and convey all his interest and estate in Brockley in the County of Worcester to the plaintiff, the said plaintiff entitling herself thereto as administratrix to Edward Palmer. The plaintiff setting forth by the bill that Edmund, late bishop of Worcester, did by two indentures of 30 & 31 Eliz. [1598] demise the premises to the late queen and her assignee during the several terms and rent therein expressed that the several estates, terms, and interest being come and vested in the said Edward Palmer for the remainder thereof, he, the said Palmer, by a deed in 1652, in consideration of a marriage then to be had between him and the plaintiff Mary, assigns the said premises unto Giles Palmer and the defendant Jones and their executors for the residue of the said terms upon trust to permit Elizabeth Palmer, mother of the said Edward, to enjoy the said premises for life, and then to the said Edward for his life and, after their lives, then to the plaintiff Mary for her life and, after their deceases, then to the heirs male of the body of the said Edward Palmer and the plaintiff Mary and, for default of such issue, then upon trust for the right heirs of the said Edward to their own use, benefit, and dispose, as, by the said deed etc. The said Edward and Elizabeth Palmer being dead, letters of administration were granted to the plaintiff Mary, by virtue whereof, she is well entitled to the said premises and to the trust and benefit thereof for the remainders of the said terms to come. And the defendant Jones, as the surviving trustee, ought to assign to the plaintiff. And the plaintiff insists that all the remainders after her death are void in law and equity.

---

[1] Stat. 21 Hen. VIII, c. 5 (*SR*, III, 285–288).

The defendant Jones insists that the trust extends to the child or children of the said Edward Palmer, and the defendant, Elizabeth Palmer, an infant, being his daughter, she may question him for the same in case he should assign as aforesaid, and prays the court will take care for the infants.

But the plaintiff insisting that, both in the cases of executors and administrators, the point has been frequently adjudged and the limitation to the heirs male or heir general being a void limitation in law where there is no executor, the trust shall come to the administrator, this court declared that, both in law and equity, the benefit of the trust in such case does belong to the executor or administrator. But, the plaintiff Hunt having married the said plaintiff Mary and claiming in right of her, who is administratrix to her former husband, Edward Palmer, the court thought it hard that, by virtue of the said administration, she should carry away the estate to her second husband and thereby strip the infant thereof, from whose father the estate first moved. And it not appearing that the ecclesiastical court, when they granted the administration, took any consideration for a distribution to be made for a provision for her, this court would consider of the case and also of the limitation and consideration of the said deed and deliver their opinion.

This court being assisted with the judges, it appearing that the interest and estate of the terms and the trust and benefit thereof is by the death of the said Edward Palmer and his mother come to the plaintiff Mary for her life and there being but thirty years of the said term to come and, in regard the ecclesiastical court cannot make a distribution of the remainder of the terms, not knowing but that the said Mary may live until the expiration thereof, this court directed the defendant Jones to assign and transfer the premises and all his interest therein etc. in the said terms to the plaintiff or such as they should appoint.

376

Ross v. Ross

(Ch. 1670)

If a tenant in tail agree to convey an interest in land, a court of equity will specifically enforce that agreement. But, if he die before making the conveyance, his issue is not bound by it, unless the issue has accepted and ratified that agreement.

1 Chancery Cases 171, 22 E.R. 747

14 July [1670]. The Lord Keeper, Justices Twysden, Wilde, Rainsford.

The case was this. Francis Ross had issue James, his lawful son, and John, a bastard son, and he devises by his will in writing to his bastard son in tail lands that were held *in capite*, and he suffers copyhold lands to descend on James. James and John agree that John and his heirs should enjoy the copyholds and James and his heirs the devised lands.

This agreement being executed, James had a decree against John to levy a fine and settle it accordingly. John dies in contempt for not doing that which, if he had done, the estate tail had been barred. The defendant, the issue of John, entered into the copyholds, and enjoyed them. And to force him to execute the agreement was the intent of the bill.

Maynard, for the defendant: It is not like the case of Octavian Lumberd,[1] for, by that agreement, the estate tail was made good, which, otherwise, would have been avoided. But a personal agreement or an agreement for other lands will not bind the issue.

It was resolved by the whole court: first, that, if the tenant in tail agree to convey, he is bound by that agreement; second, if he die, his issue is not bound by it; third, that, if the issue do accept of that agreement and enters, as in this case, on the land, it now becomes his own agreement, and shall bind. And so [the court] decreed it against the defendant.

[Other reports of this case: 1 Eq. Cas. Abr. 25, 21 E.R. 846.]

377

Moor v. Morgan

(Ch. 1670)

A court of equity has jurisdiction over foreign debts where the parties thereto are before it.

3 Chancery Reports 53, 21 E.R. 726

Trinity [term] 1670, 22 Car. II.

The bill, [filed by the plaintiff] as executrix to Sir Anthony Morgan, is to have a statute out of the defendant's hands, for £8000, which the defendant kept, being his relict.

The defendant pleads that the statute was entered into in Ireland and the money defeasanced to be paid there and that the statute was there, and being an Irish debt and Sir Anthony dying without issue, the defendant, as his relict, by the custom of Ireland, is entitled to a moiety of it, which custom cannot be determined in this court, as she is advised, and that she had exhibited her bill in Ireland to have the same.

But the plea was overruled.

[1] *Lumbard's Case* (1370), YB Trin. 44 Edw. III, f. 21, pl. 24.

378

Spencer v. Earl Thomond

(Ch. 1670)

Where trustees release to their settlor in breach of the trust and take a covenant from the settlor to save them harmless, the beneficiaries can sue the heir of the settlor without making the trustees co-defendants.

Lord Nottingham, *Prolegomena*, p. 259

Michaelmas [term] 22 Car. II, 1670.

Barnaby, earl of Thomond, conveys land in trust to raise portions for daughters. The trustees release to the earl, and take a covenant from him to save them [harmless], which was in them a breach of trust. The earl receives the profits, and dies. The daughters exhibit their bill against the now earl without making the trustees parties.

[It was] ruled they might do so without making the trustees parties *in odium spoliatoris*, and because the lands remained charged in the hands of the heir.

Yet it was objected that the trustees might have a release from the plaintiffs or show that part of the debt was paid.

379

Jackson v. Jackson

(Ch. 1670)

Where an heir enters on land in the hands of trustees, the heir can be sued without making the trustees parties to the suit.

Fiduciaries of a decedent's estate can make a valid release of the estate before officially entering upon their duties.

Lord Nottingham, *Prolegomena*, p. 260

Michaelmas [term] 22 Car. II, 1670.

Trustees were appointed to receive profits until the heir come to twenty-one [years of age] and a year longer for the raising of portions. The heir enters before twenty, and continues to receive the profits.

[It was] ruled that a bill lay against the heir without making the trustees parties.

Lord Nottingham, *Prolegomena*, p. 333

Michaelmas [term] 22 Car. II.

Though an administrator cannot release before administration, an executor may before probate. Yet, if there be a controversy between a brother and a sister, touching a portion of a dead sister, to whom they are equally entitled to administer, and they agree to divide, and the sister release to her brother, and, afterwards, take administration, though she has nothing to demand at the time of the release, yet she shall be barred in equity, for, in equity, there ought to be a distribution. And [it was] so ruled before, *inter* Morgan v. Maynard.

380

Tall v. Ryland

(Ch. 1670)

A penal bond will not be set aside by a court of equity where the party's damages are unliquidated.

1 Chancery Cases 183, 22 E.R. 753

13 October [1670].

The plaintiff and the defendant were fishmongers, and they had contiguous shops. And differences having been between them, they were made friends, and, by that mediation, the plaintiff was to give, and did give, the defendant a bond of £20 penalty, conditioned to behave himself civilly and like a good neighbor to the defendant, and not to disparage his goods. The plaintiff afterwards asked the defendant's customer, while cheapening a parcel of flounders, why he would buy of the defendant, and he told him those fish stunk, and so the defendant lost that customer. And the defendant, having sued the bond and assigned that for breach, had a verdict.

And to be relieved against that verdict and the penalty of the bond was the prayer of the bill, which alleged that the damage was not considerable nor valuable, and, therefore, the plaintiff ought to be relieved against the verdict for the penalty.

The defendant demurred, for that the bond was not conditioned for the payment of money or the performance of covenants or for any matter for which damages in an action of debt, covenant, or any other action was recoverable, nor was there any way to measure the damages but by the penalty.

And the bond being to preserve amity and neighborly friendship, for the breach of which the plaintiff did submit to pay that penalty, and there can be no trial had to measure the damages for breach of the condition other than the parties have submitted to, His Lordship [Bridgeman] declared that, as this case was, the penalty being but £20, he did not think fit to put the defendant to answer, for that the costs of suit here and at law would exceed the penalty. And so the demurrer was allowed. But His Lordship [Bridgeman] declared this was not to be a precedent in the case of a bond of £100 or the like, and, though the demurrer was allowed, the defendant was to have no costs.

381

Palmer v. Whettenhall

(Ch. 1670)

A court of equity will not decree a rent to be paid personally after a long period of time has passed with no payments or claims made.

1 Chancery Cases 184, 22 E.R. 753

13 October [1670].

The bill was that the plaintiff's brother was seised in fee of a rent of £7 *per annum* and had the same paid him by the owner of the lands, out of which this rent issued, during his life, and that, by his death, this rent descended on the plaintiff as heir and that the owners of the land did pay the rent to the plaintiff until 1641, and there had been several conveyances made of the land in the late troubles, and so no rent was paid since 1641, and that the lands were now come to the defendant. And, so, the bill prayed that he might be decreed to pay the rent and arrears.

The defendant said he did not know any such rent was issuing out of the said lands and that he and those under whom he claims had enjoyed those lands thirty several years under divers purchases without any demand of the rent that he knew of until the bill. And he demurred, for that the bill sought to subject his person, which was not to be liable at law, to pay the rent and arrears and for that, it having been so long unpaid, it was to be presumed the rent was extinguished. And, however, it appearing by the bill that the plaintiff had seisin, he might bring his assize at law and, if that had not been a seisin, it was said that all the relief this court would have given would be but to give seisin.

And, on debate, the demurrer was allowed.

382

Prynne v. Prynne

(Ch. 1670)

A plaintiff cannot have his own bill dismissed where this would defeat a cross-bill.

Lincoln's Inn MS. Hill 125, f. 59v, pl. 3

First day of term, 24 October 1670.

The plaintiff, son of the defendant, pretending a settlement from his father, exhibits a bill to examine witnesses thereto. The father exhibited a cross-bill. And he examined witnesses on his son's bill, who moved to dismiss his bill thereby, indeed, to deprive his father of the proof he had made, some of the witnesses being dead, alleging that he, in his bill, prayed no other relief but to examine his witnesses. And, indeed, he did not in the close pray relief in the premises. And he alleged that his bill was but to examine *in perpetuam rei memoriam*, which may not yet be published.

But, on debate, publication [was] ordered. First, it is not a bill *in perpetuam rei memoriam*, for that is much different from a bill in order to examine to a trial. Second, he moved before for a commission, which was granted on terms of publication to pass this term.

383

Anonymous

(Ch. 1670)

A dismissal for non-prosecution of the case is not a dismissal on the merits and not with prejudice.

Lincoln's Inn MS. Hill 125, f. 59v, pl. 4

24 October 22 Car II.

A dismission for non-prosecution is no bar to a new bill, though enrolled.

384

Squibb and Bradshaw v. Bolton

(Ch. 1670)

Where a court orders the submission of an account to arbitration, the court can review the award, and send it back to the arbitrators with further directions and also send it to a Master of the court for further review.

1 Chancery Cases 186, 22 E.R. 754

25 October [1670]. The Lord Keeper, Justice Wyndham.

The question was if, upon a submission by an order of court by consent to arbitrators and the award to be final and stand decreed, any exceptions lie to such an award as to a report and whether, if it were an unjust award, the court ought to decree it and whether the court should examine the justice of the award and the merits of it, which the Master of the Rolls [Grimston] had taken upon him to do in this cause by ordering the arbitrators to certify the court whether they had considered of certain particulars, which, the party disliking the award, said they had not, which were in issue in the cause.

And upon an appeal from the Master of the Roll's order, it was now ordered that the parties should attend the Master of the Rolls and satisfy him in what he doubted. So, here, the court examined the justice of the award, which, in this cause and the next precedent,[1] the court did think upon circumstances might be done and that, if an unjust award was desired to be confirmed by a decree and the court informed of it, the court ought not to decree it.

Lord Nottingham, *Prolegomena*, p. 308

25 October, Michaelmas [term] 22 Car. II. Boulton v. Bradshaw.

A bill was exhibited to have an account of a co-partnership. And an order was drawn up by consent, that the matter in difference and all other matters should be referred to the award of Mr. Mascall. He awarded £300 to be paid to [Sir William] Boulton.

And yet the award was set aside and [there was a] reference back again to him to review, because he had included in his award shop rent and book debts after the co-partnership was dissolved. He, on review, confirms his first report. Yet [the award] set aside again, and [the court] referred it to a Master upon the whole.

385

Butler v. Coote

(Ch. 1670)

A court of equity will not allow executors to retain their legacies where the decedent's estate is not sufficient to pay all of the legacies, but all of the legacies will be paid proportionably.

3 Chancery Reports 54, 21 E.R. 726

26 October 1670, 22 Car. II.

The plaintiffs, as legatees, came to have an account of the testator's estate, the defendants being executors.

And the defendants submit to the court whether they may not pay their legacies in the first place and then there will be a want assets to pay the plaintiffs.

It was ordered that, after the debts be paid, all legacies are to be paid in proportion with damages so far as the estate will extend. And it is not like the case at common law, where the executors pay their own debts and legacies first or him that first sues his whole legacy before others.

Nelson 142, 21 E.R. 811

The plaintiffs, being legatees, exhibit their bill against the defendants, who were executors, to have an account of the testator's estate and that their legacies might be paid.

---

[1] *Hide v. Petit* (Ch. 1663–1673), see above, Case No. 100.

The defendants submit to the judgment of the court whether they may not retain their own legacies in the first place, and, if so, there will not be sufficient assets to pay the plaintiffs' legacies.

But it was decreed that, after debts are discharged, all legacies shall be paid in proportion so far as the estate will extend. And [it is] not like the case at common law where executors may retain their own legacies or pay him who first gets judgment.

386

Heneage's Case

(Ch. 1670)

The question in this case was whether a trustee who has acted in breach of trust is an executor de son tort.

Lord Nottingham, *Prolegomena*, p. 260

30 October 1670. Sir George Heneage's Case.

This case was brought to me [*Finch*] for my opinion. Trustees for the son permit the father to enter and receive the profits. He does so, and makes his wife executrix, and dies. I was of opinion that the executrix in this case was to be charged on the account to her son and [with] her husband's breach of trust, because, when the father entered having notice of a trust, though it were a breach of trust in the trustees to suffer it, yet withal the land remained charged with the trust in the hands of the father, and the law did create a trust in the father, and the trustee of his own wrong is *quasi* executor of his own wrong.

387

Bush v. Rishley

(Ch. 1670)

The Court of Chancery will not enforce a modus decimandi *to be paid in lieu of tithes in kind.*

1 Chancery Cases 187, 22 E.R. 755

31 October [1670].

The bill was to have a rate tithe settled by a decree against the impropriator and prevent multiplicity of suits.

And, for the plaintiffs, it was prayed that the court would either decree that the plaintiffs should hold their lands under that *modus decimandi*, which, at a trial at law pending this suit, was found by a verdict, or that the court would direct another trial to try the verity of the *modus* and reserve the cause until after the second trial if the court were not satisfied with one verdict, it being insisted that, after such a tithe rate had been ascertained by two verdicts, the court ought to decree an enjoyment of the lands for which the *modus* was payable under that rate tithe and discharge the tithe in kind. And it was compared to the case of copyholders that have their fines and services ascertained by the aid of this court by the directing of trials for that purpose first and after decreeing according to the verdicts on such trials.

But, for the defendant, it was insisted that this court had not at any time decreed a *modus decimandi* and that tithes were payable in kind by common right.

And, though it was insisted for the plaintiffs that it was frequent in the Exchequer to decree a rate tithe, the Lord Keeper [BRIDGEMAN] did not think fit to decree in such a case, but he ordered two depositions to be made use of at law as occasion served. And he dismissed the bill.

[Other copies of this report: 1 Eagle & Younge 482.]

Lord Nottingham, *Prolegomena*, p. 322

Michaelmas [term] 22 Car. II. Bush v. Ridgby.

A *modus decimandi* was refused to be decreed in Chancery, though clearly proved and though the bill prayed to be quitted from a suit and though a verdict for the *modus* had been obtained *pendente lite* but without directions of the court and though both parties offered, on a new trial, to submit to the decree of the court by consent and though the Court of Exchequer always makes such decrees, for, it was said, however, the Court of Exchequer do proceed in such cases, because the parson is *semper debitor domini regis* for tenths or first fruits, yet the constant practice of Chancery is otherwise, because, perhaps, that, anciently, bishops did preside here, but rather because, at best, a *modus*, which extinguishes tithes in kind, though good in law if proved, yet is not good in conscience, and, therefore, a court of conscience will not decree it.

388

Anonymous

(Ch. 1670)

The creditors of a bankrupt judgment debtor cannot take anything that was executed upon before the debtor's bankruptcy.

Lord Nottingham, *Prolegomena*, p. 333

10 November 1670, by Bridgeman, Keeper, with assistance of Wilde and Wyndham.

A decree was pronounced that the plaintiff shall have his wife's marriage portion, which, pending suit, was brought into court. After this, certain creditors of the plaintiff exhibit a new bill, and suggest that commissioners of bankrupts have declared the plaintiff a bankrupt, and pray the money may stay in court.

[It was] resolved this should not hinder execution.

Wyndham cited 4 Car. I, King's Bench, Audley and Halsy's Case,[1] where an act of bankruptcy between an extent and the *liberate* does not impede execution; so on a bankruptcy between a seizure on a *scire facias* and the *venditioni exponas*. 8 Car. I, King's Bench, Lawrence v. Gay.

389

Withers v. Kelsey

(Ch. 1670)

Where a man dies, an unpaid marriage portion in the form of a rent charge goes to his executor and not to his widow.

1 Chancery Cases 189, 22 E.R. 756

16 November [1670].

A factor gives his daughter a £300 portion charged on lands, and dies. The daughter marries, and has a jointure settled on her by her husband, and has no other portion but the £300. The husband dies before any part of the £300 was paid. The plaintiff is the executor of the husband, and he sues the widow and the heir of the lands for the £300.

The question was who should have the £300, whether the executor of the husband or the wife.

For the executor of the husband, it was insisted that he having settled a jointure in consideration of the portion, which jointure the wife enjoyed, that, thereby, in equity, the right of the portion was so vested in him that the executor, and not the wife, ought to enjoy it.

The Lord Keeper [Bridgeman] declared that this £300, being to go out of the rent of the lands and charged upon lands, was not in the nature of a thing in action, but of a rent, and given to the husband by the marriage. And so he decreed for the plaintiff, the executor.

Sed quaere, for a rent belonging to a wife does in case she survives the husband belong to the wife, and so do the arrears that incur during the marriage. 1 Inst. 351.[2]

---

[1] *Audley v. Halsey* (1629), Croke Car. 148, 79 E.R. 731, W. Jones 202, 82 E.R. 107.

[2] E. Coke, *First Institute* (1628), f. 351.

3 Salkeld 65, 91 ER 694

A woman had a portion devised to her. And the payment thereof was charged on certain lands. Afterwards, upon her marriage with T.S., he settled a jointure on her. And he died before he received the portion, having made a will and appointed an executor.

It was adjudged that the executor shall have this money, because it is not in the nature of a chose in action, but in the nature of a rent, for it is charged on lands and it is given to the husband by the intermarriage. And, for that reason, it shall go to his executor, and not to his wife surviving him.

390

Danby v. Read

(Ch. 1670)

A court of equity can order a contracted for interest rate to be reduced to the limit of the statutory usury rate.

Lord Nottingham, *Prolegomena*, p. 286

30 November 1670.

The earl of Kingston, in May 1638, lends Sir Thomas Danby £5000. And Sir Thomas, his son, makes a lease to Francis Pierrepoint for 1000 years to secure the yearly rent of £400, provided that, if, at any time during the term of 1000 years on three months notice first given, the £5000 should be paid, the lease to be void.

It was urged that this was no mortgage, but the purchase of a rent thus secured, for there was no way to compel Sir Thomas Danby or his heirs to redeem or be foreclosed, because they have liberty during the 1000 years.

But the contrary was declared by BRIDGEMAN, Keeper, WILDE, and WYNDHAM, for they held the £400 a year to be plain interest at £8 *per centum*, and, therefore, they reduced it to £300 a year for the future at the rate of £6 *per centum*, and ordered the arrears to be computed at that rate, and gave twelve months time to pay in the £5000 or else the equity of redemption to be barred.

[Later proceedings in this case: Reports *tempore* Finch 226, 23 E.R. 124, 73 Selden Soc. 156.]

391

Low v. Gervis

(Ch. 1670)

Where a purchaser of land that is subject to a mortgage later purchases the mortgage that is secured by his land and more, the mortgage can be redeemed as to the other land.

Lord Nottingham, *Prolegomena*, p. 209

Michaelmas [term] 22 Car. II.

If a purchaser of two acres purchases a mortgage of four acres, this shall protect him only *pro tanto*, for the residue shall be redeemable. But, there, the purchaser was of all by general words.

392

Purefoy v. Bellingham

(Ch. 1670)

A marriage settlement in satisfaction of a jointure without more does not bar dower rights.

An agreement to settle copyhold lands in lieu of a jointure bars dower rights if it be executed.

Where a widow contracts to discharge her rights in copyhold lands, this will not prejudice the heir in tail.

Lord Nottingham, *Prolegomena*, p. 346

Michaelmas [term] 1670, Purefoy and Dame Bellingham, his wife v. Allan Bellingham.

Sir James Bellingham, being seised of some lands in tail and of copyhold lands and other lands in fee simple, on a marriage with Katherine, the daughter of Sir Henry Willoughby, articles that, whereas he had settled some lands in part [satisfaction] of her jointure, he would surrender his copyhold in full [satisfaction] of her jointure, and he gives a bond of £5000 to perform, and he dies without issue. The entailed lands descended to Allan Bellingham, the uncle, as heir male. The fee simple lands and the copyhold [descend] to the sisters and coheirs. The widow enjoys the copyhold nine years without any estate in it. Then, she agrees with the coheirs to divide the personal estate, also to release the bond of £5000, and takes their covenant for the enjoyment of the copyhold, and brings [an action of] dower against the uncle, and recovers a third part of the entailed lands and £2160 damages.

The uncle exhibits a bill in equity.

[It was] resolved: first, the settlement of the lands in part [satisfaction of the] jointure is no bar to dower; second, the settlement of the copyhold lands in full [satisfaction] of the jointure is no bar in law of dower, which is a freehold estate; third, an agreement to settle the copyhold lands in full [satisfaction] of the jointure is a good bar of the dower in equity if it be executed; fourth, as the widow enjoys the copyhold nine years without a title and will not offer to sue for the execution of the articles on marriage but that she may have a pretence to sue the heir male comes to a new agreement with the coheirs to hold the copyhold land by color of a new treaty where she might without such an agreement have enforced the coheirs to surrender by virtue of the marriage articles, the bond and the assets descended, this shall be all one in equity as if she had enjoyed the copyhold by virtue of the marriage articles, for her discharge of the securities or neglect to put them in suit shall not prejudice the heir in tail nor let her into her dower; so she was decreed to release; fifth, on a bill of review, two causes of reversal were assigned: (1) error in law, because the coheirs were not decreed to surrender; (2) new matter since the decree, *viz.* that the coheirs had forfeited the copyhold.

But neither of these causes was allowed, because, the widow having by her own act discharged the means of coercion to surrender, she ought to rest on such remedy as she provided for herself by the covenant, and the inconvenience of a forfeiture must fall on the widow and cannot prejudice the heir in tail.

1660, Allan Bellingham v. Lady Bellingham, and Michaelmas [term] 1670, Purefoy and Dame Bellingham, his wife v. Allan Bellingham.

[Later proceedings in this case: 73 Selden Soc. 129.]

393

Evelyn's Case

(Ch. 1670)

A tenant for life without impeachment of waste cannot be restrained in equity from felling trees if he be in possession, but a tenant in remainder for life without impeachment may be so restrained.

Lord Nottingham, *Prolegomena*, p. 332

1 December 1670, 22 Car. II.

Lady Evelyn was the tenant for life in jointure, remainder to Sir John Evelyn for life without impeachment of waste, remainder to the first, second, third, and so to the tenth son etc. in tail, remainder to George Evelyn in like manner. Lady Evelyn lets to tenants at will. Sir John Evelyn enters by consent of a tenant at will, and cuts down trees.

[It was] resolved: first, the tenant for life without impeachment of waste cannot be restrained in equity from felling trees if he be in possession, but, second, he in remainder for life without impeachment may be restrained, for, though, when a tenant at will does license his entry, he be no trespasser, yet he ought not to prejudice the jointress of her right to the shade and mast. Therefore, an injunction was awarded during the life of Lady Evelyn.

394

Holt v. Holt

(Ch. 1670)

Neither an administrator of a decedent's estate nor his surety are liable to the estate beyond his own bad faith dealings with it.

Where a trustee of a decedent's estate makes a profit from the estate, the profit goes to the beneficiary of the estate.

1 Chancery Cases 190, 22 E.R. 756

7 December [1670]. The Lord Keeper, Justices Twysden, Wilde, Rainsford, Wyndham.

Alexander Holt, a citizen of London, seised and possessed of houses in London and elsewhere, of a public title, and possessed of houses in St. Martins in the Fields by a lease from the Church of Westminster, 18 May 1656, by his will in writing, gave £10,000 to his daughters, being his only children and orphans, to be paid out of his estate real and personal at their age of twenty-one or marriages which first shall happen. And he made Alexander Holt, his nephew, and others, his executors, and he died. The executors proved the will. And the executor, Alexander, and others, as his sureties, in 1658, entered into a recognizance to the Chamberlain of London for the payment of the £10,000, which, by the will, was first to be paid before any others should have any benefit of his lands etc.

By the restoration of the king [in 1660], the lands of the public title reverted to the right owners. And, by, the Fire in London [in 1666], the houses of the testator in London were burnt down, so that it was to be doubted his whole estate would not amount to the £10,000.

And the first question was whether the recognizance should in equity extend any farther than only to make good to the orphans so much as the testator's estate, considering the losses aforesaid and as it now was really worth.

And it was insisted by the counsel of the sureties of the executors that it ought not to be binding any farther in equity, for that, if the Chamber of London had taken the estate of the testator into their hands, it would have been in no better plight than now it is, and the intention of the security was but that the executors should not misemploy or waste the estate, which (as it was declared) they had not done, but were ready to account for what they had already received.

The court, as to that point, were all of one uniform opinion that the recognizance should be made use of no further than to make good the value of the testator's estate over and above the losses by fire and the king's return, and they decreed the same accordingly.

Albeit it was insisted for the orphans that the condition of the recognizance was generally for the payment of the £10,000 (and so it was) and the executor Alexander had thereupon taken upon himself the absolute ownership of the estate and managed it as his own and that, now, a loss had befallen the estate, the orphans ought not to be carried back to the account of the testator's estate, for that, by the recognizance, the orphans' portions were now become debts, nevertheless, for the reasons before, it was decreed as aforesaid.

And the next question was whether the lease held of the Church of Westminster, which had been renewed by the executor, and a fine paid and new houses built thereupon by the executors should be taken to be part of the testator's estate.

For the executors, it was insisted they were not executors in trust for the orphans, but were to pay them out of the estate £10,000 only. And the estate was looked upon at the testator's making his will and really was then and before the said losses of much greater value and a benefit was intended the executor Alexander by the testator.

But the court did unanimously agree that the daughters should have the benefit of the renewed lease, paying the fine and other charges of improving. And so it was decreed accordingly. But this must be understood so far only as to the completing the orphans' £10,000.

But it was agreed by the whole court that, in the case of an executorship in trust, the renewal of such a lease shall go to the benefit of *cestui que trust*.

[Other reports of this case: 1 Eq. Cas. Abr. 85, 21 E.R. 897.]

395

Rawlins v. Rawlins

(Ch. 1670)

A defendant in a suit in equity can plead as res judicata a final judgment at common law, and the plaintiff in equity can reply to such plea.

3 Chancery Reports 54, 21 E.R. 727

8 December 1670, 22 Car. II. Mr. Justice Tyrell.

A bill was to be relieved after an action of trover brought for bonds the plaintiff had cancelled, tried, and a judgment had thereupon, for that the penalties of some were recovered and others were paid, to which, the verdict and judgment were pleaded and allowed. And, 16 January 1670, it was confirmed by the Lord Keeper Bridgeman only the defendants must answer whether they know what the jury gave their verdicts upon, the penalties or the money paid, and no further to proceed if they do not know and consent.

But, afterwards, it was ordered, 13 December 1670, 22 Car. II, by Justice Arthur, that the last order be discharged and the plaintiff may reply.

396

Lambert v. Dunch

(Ch. 1670)

The question in this case was whether depositions in a former case can be used in a subsequent, related case in the absence of mutuality.

Lord Nottingham, *Prolegomena*, p. 315

8 December 1670.

Lambert claims the estate of Dunch by a prior conveyance. Sir Edward Bainton claims it by a second conveyance. The coheirs of Dunch, knowing not of Lambert's conveyance, exhibit a bill against Sir Edward Bainton, supposing his conveyance to be in trust. And they proved it, but, afterwards, let fall their suit. Lambert exhibits a bill for same matter.

I [*Finch*] moved to have the benefit of the former depositions for the trust: first, because it is the same defendant and the same matter of defence, *viz.* trust or no trust; second, because it is usual in Chancery, if a conveyance be made in trust for the payment of debts and one creditor exhibit a bill and prove the trust, another creditor not party to that bill shall have the benefit of those depositions on a new bill exhibited. So, if one devisee prove a will, another devisee, on a new bill, shall have the benefit of those depositions.

And the Clerks, to whom the matter had been referred, certified this to be usual.

But Bridgeman, Keeper, doubted, because the defendant Sir Edward Bainton could not read the former depositions against Lambert. But, as to such witnesses as are dead, it may be more reasonable. At length, on my consent for Lambert that the depositions shall be used against him, it was ordered that those depositions should be used *utraque*. Yet consent does not alter the law.

[Related cases: Lambert v. Bainton (Ch. 1671–1672), see below, Case No. 419.]

397

Gower v. Earl of Sussex

(Ch. 1670)

Growing trees severed from the land by a devise become chattels thereby.

The time for executing a judgment is tolled by the bad faith of the parties.

Lord Nottingham, *Prolegomena*, p. 333

14 December 1670, 22 Car. II, Sir Thomas Gower v. Earl of Sussex.

The earl of Sussex devises all his timber trees that now are or shall be growing during the minority of his son to his wife to pay debts and the land to his son in tail. She marries. A decree is had against her and her husband. And, then, she and her husband go into France, and stay there until her son comes of age, and, shortly after, she dies.

Then, a bill is exhibited against the young earl and the husband and administrator of the countess to have execution of the decree and to have a sale of the timber.

The earl pleads that his mother had only a bare authority, which being not executed during his minority, his timber was free, and he demands judgment.

[It was] resolved: first, that the timber was actually devised to the wife in point of interest and that the wife has more than a bare authority, for the words 'during minority' are only applied to such trees as shall be growing, but the trees then actually timber pass presently in interest; second, trees severed from the land by exception or devise become chattels as much as if they were felled; Coke, lib. 11, Lifford's Case;[1] the exception was not total, which makes the difference; third, it was urged that, if it had been a bare authority, yet, it being a willful fraud in the wife to absent herself until her son came of age, that so the time for the execution of the decree might lapse to her son, he never shall take advantage of this fraud; but, of this point, there was no use; fourth, therefore, the plea was overruled, and an injunction was awarded to stay the felling of the timber unless the money should be brought into court or the vendees give security for it.

398

Burrell v. Ellis

(Ch. c. 1670)

A bona fide *purchaser for value of land cannot be compelled to produce a deed that will impeach his own title.*

Lord Nottingham, *Prolegomena*, p. 207

[Mrs.] Burrell complains in Chancery that her husband was seised of a rent charge of £200 a year after the death of Lydia Ward and he settled this as a jointure upon her marriage for a portion of £1000 received from Sir Thomas Gardiner, her father, with a remainder to her children, that, notwithstanding this, William Ellis [c. 1609–1680], now serjeant at law, has gotten the original deed for the rent charge, without which she could not avow for the rent nor go to law for her jointure. And she prays a discovery.

Ellis pleads that he was a purchaser for a valuable consideration, *viz.* £2400, *bona fide* paid and without notice, and demands judgment if he shall be compelled to deliver or discover deeds against himself. This plea was allowed.

---

[1] *Lifford's Case* (1614), 11 Coke Rep. 46, 77 E.R. 1206, also *sub nom. Stampe v. Clinton*, 1 Rolle Rep. 95, 81 E.R. 354.

And [Mrs.] Burrell appeals to the Lords in Parliament, and, on 4 March 1640 [sic], it was argued before the barons of the House of Peers. And, at length, on 4 March following, the petition was dismissed.[1]

399

Day v. Hester

(Ch. 1670–1671)

A report of a Master in Chancery cannot be grounded on an arbitral award.

Nelson 137, 21 E.R. 809

The bill was to have an account of a partnership, to which the defendant consented upon condition the plaintiff would seal the indenture of partnership and pay £330.

The matter was referred to Sir Justinian Lawin to see the plaintiff seal the indenture and to state the account.

Afterwards, he made his report that the parties had submitted to refer the matters in difference to arbitrators and, if they could not agree, then to an umpire, who, instead of taking care to settle the indenture and the account, did award that the partnership should be dissolved and that the defendant should pay back the £330.

And the Master having grounded his report upon this award of the umpire, the defendant excepted to it as grounded upon an extrajudicial award of things not in difference and contrary to the bill and answer and order of the court, for which reason, he excepted likewise against the award.

And the exceptions were allowed.

400

Westhall v. Carter

(Ch. 1670–1671)

An answer to a bill of revivor cannot raise questions as to the credibility of the evidence already given in the case and then move for a new trial.

Nelson 138, 21 E.R. 810

This was a bill of revivor, where the principal cause was heard and an issue directed to be tried. And, afterwards, one of the plaintiffs died before the trial, yet it went on, and [there was] a verdict against the defendant.

[1] On 11 March 1671: *Lords' Journal*, vol. 12, p. 453.

Now, the plaintiff in the bill of revivor prayed to have all the proceedings revived and the benefit of the verdict.

The defendant, by his answer, sets forth that the plaintiff's witnesses were examined in the first cause twice to the same thing, which was irregular, and that a witness examined in the cause in this court and at the trial swore matters varying from what he had sworn in this court. And so he prayed he might have a new trial.

The plaintiff replied that she was executrix to her husband and was entitled to the bill of revivor, and did demur to so much of the answer as did set forth the pretended irregularity in the examination of the witnesses in the original cause. And as to the variation of the evidence *viva voce* at the trial and what had been deposed here, she insisted that it ought not to be set forth in an answer to a bill of revivor.

And, upon hearing counsel on both sides, the demurrer was allowed.

401

Hanbury v. Walker

(Ch. 1670–1671)

A court of equity will take care of infants, their education, and their estates, and see that the same is preserved and secured by ordering that regular accounts be given.

3 Chancery Reports 58, 21 E.R. 728

Veneris die 22 December, Car. II [1670], *inter Johannem Hanbury, armigerum, et Annam Mariam, infantem, per praedictum Johannem Hanbury, armigerum et proximum amicum, querentes; Theophilum Walker et alios, defendentes.*

The matter, upon the plaintiff's bill and demurrer thereunto put in by the defendant, coming this present day to be argued before the Right Honorable the Lord Keeper of the Great Seal of England [Bridgeman], assisted by Mr. Justice Wilde, in the presence of the counsel learned on both sides, the scope of the plaintiffs' bill being, as grandfather and next friend of the said infant, to call the defendant to account for her personal estate and the rents and profits of her real estate, the said plaintiffs, by their bill, charged the estate real to be about £500 *per annum* and her personal estate to be worth £5000 and that the defendant, Theophilus Walker, who claims to be the guardian to her, the said infant, as great-uncle on the mother's side, is a bachelor that failed in his estate and is become a journeyman to another and is a person disaffected to the discipline of the Church of England and does conceal the plaintiff, the infant, from her said grandfather and his wife and endeavors to instruct her in his own courses to the dislike of that discipline so that the defendant, Walker, is not a fit person to have the education of the said infant or the management of her estate and the infant is in danger to suffer much, both in her estate and education, by the defendant, as she is like to do by Joseph Hawksworth, her former guardian.

Whereupon, the said defendant, for a demurrer, says that he, by the law of the land, has the right, both to the guardianship of the infant during her minority, he being the next of kin by the mother's side, who has no benefit by the death of the said Anna Maria, and that the said John Hanbury having no right, either to the wardship or to the infant's personal estate, he cannot give the defendant a discharge. And, therefore, the defendant conceives he ought not to be compelled to give any account to him of the said infant's estate.

Upon the debate of the matter and hearing what was alleged on either side, His Lordship [BRIDGEMAN] declared that this court ought to take care of infants and their education and of their estates and to see the same preserved and secured for them. And conceiving the plaintiff, the grandfather of the infant, to be a good *prochein ami*, the defendant being charged to be a mean and insolvent person, he does think fit and so order that the defendant Walker shall answer to so much of the plaintiffs' bill as demands an account of the said infant's estate and where the said infant is and how she is bred, without costs. But this is to be without prejudice to the legal interest the defendant has to the custody of the infant and the management of her estate. And the defendant may proceed in the management of the infant's estate for the benefit of the infant as before.

And, 24 February 1670[/71], the defendant having answered and confessed that he had given over his trade and had a salary from another and that the infant's estate was £300 a year, the court ordered him to account yearly, but saw no cause, until a default in him, to make him give security.

Nelson 144, 21 E.R. 811

John Hanbury, next friend of Anna Maria Hanbury, plaintiff, *versus* Theophilum Walker, defendant.

The plaintiff, as grandfather and next friend of the infant Mary Hanbury, exhibited his bill to call the defendant to an account, as well for the personal estate as for the rents and profits of the real estate of the said infant, suggesting that the personal estate was of the value of £5000 and the real estate £500 and that the defendant, who claimed the guardianship at law as great uncle by the mother's side, was a bachelor and that he failed in his estate and became a journeyman to another and that he was a person disaffected to the doctrine and discipline of the established church and did conceal the infant from the plaintiff and his wife and endeavored to instruct her in a separate way from the church, and, therefore, he was not a fit person to educate her or to have the care of her estate.

The defendant demurred, for that, by the law, he has a right to the guardianship of the infant during her minority, he being the next of kin by the mother's side, who can have no benefit by the death of the said infant and that the plaintiff, having no manner of right to the guardianship or to the said infant's estate, cannot give the defendant a discharge. And, therefore, he ought not to be compelled to give any account to him of the said infant's estate.

But it was ordered that the defendant shall answer to so much of the plaintiff's bill as demands an account of the infant's estate and where she is and how she is educated but without costs. And this is to be without prejudice to the legal right of the defendant, both as to the custody of the infant and the management of her estate, but that he may proceed to take care of the said estate for her benefit.

And, afterwards, the defendant having answered, the court ordered him to account yearly, but saw no cause to make him give security until there was a plain and apparent fault in his management of her estate.

402

Mudd v. Warren

(Ch. 1670–1673)

A bill of exchange payable to order is not revocable.

Lord Nottingham, *Prolegomena*, p. 272

Michaelmas [term] 22 Car. II, on a trial at the Guildhall before Hale, Chief Justice.

[It was] ruled: first that the bill of exchange payable for J.S. or his order for the value received is not countermandable; second, if J.S. endorses this bill to be paid to J.D. without saying 'or his order', this is countermandable, because J.D. is only an attorney or receiver of J.S.; third, if he who accepts the bill gives security to J.D. to pay it, the countermand after this comes too late, though J.D. be in a failing condition.

Therefore, the plaintiff was nonsuited on this issue directed out of Chancery.

Lord Nottingham, *Prolegomena*, p. 273

8 April 1673, the Chancellor, Vaughan, and Rainsford. Warren v. Mudd.

Mud being nonsuited, Warren exhibits a suit in equity, because he had paid the money to the assignee of the bill and gave a bill so to do before the countermand came. And he obtained a perpetual injunction.

Mud appeals from the Master of the Rolls [Grimston], because, if the law be for Mud, equity ought to follow the law and equity will cozen nobody and Mud had as much equity not to lose his money by Warren's mispayment as Warren has equity not to pay it twice and the degrees of equity are not material nor is it fit that Warren's note should make the bill irrevocable.

So the injunction was dissolved, and Mud was left to [the common] law, but Warren's bill was retained, and the equity was reserved.

403

Verhorn v. Brewine

(Ch. 1671)

An original bill of discovery lies by an administrator to have a discovery and an account of his intestate's estate.

A nuncupative will that has not been probated in an ecclesiastical court cannot bind an administrator of the decedent's estate.

1 Chancery Cases 192, 22 E.R. 757

18 January [1671].

The plaintiff sued as administrator to have a discovery and an account of the estate of his intestate.

The defendant pleaded that the supposed intestate made a nuncupative will and another person, whom he named in his plea, his executor. And he insisted he was not answerable or accountable to the plaintiff, nor to any other but the executor.

On debate, it was ruled that, before probate of the nuncupative will, which is only to be proved in the ecclesiastical court, it is not pleadable in any court against an administrator. And so the plea was overruled.

404

Barber v. Took

(Ch. 1671)

A mortgage of lands after a devise of the same lands gives the equity of redemption to the devisee unless the mortgagor-devisor intended to revoke the devise by making the mortgage.

1 Chancery Cases 193, 22 E.R. 758

25 January [1671].

Matthew Lindsey was seised in fee of the lands in question, and, by a will in writing, he devises them to the plaintiff [William Barber] in fee. And after[wards], he mortgages those lands to the defendant [William] Took for years, and dies, the defendant Charles Lindsey being his cousin and heir. And the question was who should have the redemption, the plaintiff Barber or the heir.

For the plaintiff, it was insisted that the devise to him, being of the fee and the mortgage after being but a term for years, that was a revocation but *pro tanto*, and not *pro toto*, and the devise did, notwithstanding, pass the reversion and, consequently, the equity of redemption.

And of that opinion was the judge.

But the defendant the heir's counsel insisted that there was an actual revocation of the whole will.

It was directed to be tried whether there was an actual and total revocation.

405

Porter v. Hubbart

(Ch. 1671–1677)

Upon a bill to redeem a mortgage where the mortgagee was in possession, the amount due to the debtor will be abated by the profits of the land received by the mortgagee.

An assignee of a mortgagee cannot be in a better condition than the mortgagee himself, and thus interest is not payable on interest due unless the mortgagor consent.

Civil disturbances and war will excuse the laches in the plaintiff in suing to redeem a mortgage.

3 Chancery Reports 78, 21 E.R. 734

Hilary [term] 1670[/71]. Lord Chancellor, Vaughan, and Rainsford.

A cause was re-heard after almost four years' prosecution after the hearing. And it being touching a redemption of a mortgage, how interest should be abated and an account stated, the case was that the plaintiff's father mortgaged the manor of Alfarthing, in 1636, for £5000, to Dawes, who entered in 1641, no interest being then paid. And he enjoyed it until 1649, and, then, the executor of the mortgagee assigned it to the defendant's father for £7000, part of a debt owing by Dawes, that was a farmer of the Customs.

The defendant's father enjoyed until 1663, and charged the lands with above £5000. And, in 1667, the plaintiff brought a bill to redeem, which was heard in 1669 by Justice RAINSFORD. And a redemption was decreed and interest from 1642 to 1648 to be moderated to £4 *per centum* and profits to be accounted for.

The defendant appealed to the Lord Keeper BRIDGEMAN, who assisted with MORTON, TYRELL, and WILDE, ordered interest to be set against the certain profits from 1641 to 1649, the defendant's father's purchase, but casual profits to be accounted for. And what the interest of the £5000 came to before 1641 was to be taken as principal in 1649 at the assignment, and interest was to be computed from that time for the £5000, and interest then due.

The plaintiff, after four years' proceedings upon this order, appealed to My Lord SHAFTESBURY, *ut supra*, who, upon the hearing declared that no assignee of a mortgage should be in a better condition than the mortgagee. And he ruled interest to be paid but for the first £5000 from the beginning, though precedents were cited, *viz.*: Warder and Sayer, Michaelmas [term] 13 Car. II [1661], by the Master of the Rolls; Hamond and Conningsby, Michaelmas [term] 18 Car. II [1666], by the Lord Chancellor and the Master of the Rolls; Smith and

Pemberton, Easter [term] 17 Car. II [1665], by the Lord Chancellor, as express in the case.[1]

But it is otherwise if the mortgagor came into the assignment. And, as to the abatement of interest, it was alleged that an ordinance about 1653[2] gave a power to abate interest for the troublesome times between 1642 and 1648 as the circumstances required. And precedents were cited, *viz.* Mansell and Jenkins, 22 July, 21 Car., by the Master of the Rolls, upon a mortgage in 1634 and then a redemption decreed and interest mitigated to £4 *per centum* from 1642 to 1648, but, there, both parties were in the king's service, and the lands were sequestered for the mortgagee's delinquency, so that no profit was made of the land; Lord Cobham and Lord Ross, 15 July, and 1 July, 15 Car. II, by the Lord Chancellor Clarendon and the Master of the Rolls, to redeem a mortgage made in December 1642, where it was so mitigated that, there, the mortgagee promised to enter, and agreed so to do, but did not, whereby the lands were sequestered; Lord Cornwallis and Miller, 1668, made upon the precedent of Mansell and Jenkins, and without opposition, being upon an extent and for a tailor's bill; and the Case of the Earl of Derby etc., where interest was quite taken away.[3]

But these were upon the reason that the rents of the lands were lost or but little could be made. But, in this Case of Porter, the lands yielded as much all that time as at any other and the mortgagee was in possession in 1641, so that there was no loss by the land more than taxes.

But Mr. Porter's father was in the king's army, being a Bedchamber man, and was a sufferer in his person. And, therefore, interest was moderated to £6 *per centum* from 1642, not only to 1648, but from thence to £5, and so until this time.

But *quaere* by what power could it be moderated from 1648 to 1651 contrary to the law, and never one precedent in it. *Vide ante.*

But Mr. *Keck* argued that it ought to be but at £6 from 1636, for that, by the Act made 1660 or 1661[4] to settle it at £6, it looked back to all contracts before that time and that it was the constant practice in the Exchequer and that he was overruled in it by the Lord Chief Baron Hale, who drew that Act, and he said that it was the intention of it.

And the Lord Chief Justice VAUGHAN argued for the total taking away the interest between 1642 and 1648, for that most men then buried their money and so made no interest of it.

---

[1] *Sayer v. Glean* (1662), 1 Levinz 54, 83 E.R. 293, 1 Siderfin 27, 82 E.R. 949; *Smith v. Pemberton* (Ch. 1665), see above, Case No. 191.

[2] C. H. Firth and R. S. Rait, *Acts and Ordinances of the Interregnum 1642–1660* (1911), vol. 2, p. 548.

[3] *Earl of Athol v. Earl of Derby* (Ch. 1672–1673), see below, Case No. 498.

[4] Stat. 12 Car. II, c. 13 (*SR*, V, 236–237).

But then a man might have taken it up as occasion served, when as lent upon a mortgage, he could not have it when he would. And these rules being given, an account was directed both of casual and accidental profits from 1641.

Nelson 150, 21 E.R. 813

The plaintiff's father, in the year 1636, mortgaged the manor of Alfarthing to one Dawes for £5000. The mortgagee entered in the year 1641, no interest being paid in those five years, and he enjoyed it until the year 1649. And then he died.

After whose death, his executors assigned the mortgage to the defendant's father, who enjoyed the lands until the year 1663. And he, having charged the same with £5600, died.

In the year 1667, the plaintiff brought a bill to redeem. The cause was heard two years afterwards, and a redemption was decreed, and the interest from 1642 to 1648 [was] to be moderated at £4 percent and the defendant to account for the profits.

From this decree made by the Master of the Rolls [Grimston], the defendant appealed to the Lord Keeper Bridgeman, who, being assisted by Justice Moreton, Tyrrell, and Wilde, ordered the interest to be set against the certain profits, but the defendant [was] to account for the casual profits and that the interest of the £5000 from 1641 to 1649 should be made principal at which time the assignment was made, and interest [was] to be computed for the whole from that time.

The plaintiff acquiesced under this decree four years, and then appealed to the Lord Chancellor Shaftesbury, who upon hearing the cause declared that no assignee of a mortgage, should be in a better condition than the mortgagee himself, and ruled interest to be paid only for the £5000 from the time it was left.

And, as to the abatement of the interest, it was alleged that there was an Ordinance made in the year 1653, which gave power to the court to abate interest in those troublesome times, between the years 1642 and 1648, as the circumstances of the case should require.

But Mr. *Keck* argued that it ought to be at £6 percent from 1636, the time the money was lent, for that the Act made in the year 1660 to settle interest at £6 percent looked back to all contracts made before that time, and that it was the constant practice in the Exchequer to allow that interest, he being overruled in it himself when he insisted on an abatement by the Lord Chief Baron Hale, who drew that Act.

But the Lord Chief Justice Vaughan argued for the total taking away all interest between 1642 and 1648, because most men buried their money in those days and made no interest of it. And the reason was because they might command it as occasion served, which, if lent upon a mortgage, they could not do.

The court directed an account, both of casual and accidental profits, from the year 1641.

Lord Nottingham, *Prolegomena*, p. 288

8 April 1673. Porter v. Hobart.

Endimion Porter[1] mortgaged the manor of Alfarthing in Surrey in 1636 to Sir Abraham Dawes for £5000 who, in 1649, computed the principal and interest at £7000, but does not call Porter to the stating of that account, and, then, he assigns to Hobart in satisfaction of a debt of £7000 owing by Dawes to him.

George Porter exhibits a bill in 1667 against Hobart to redeem, who submits by answer to account so he may have 6 *per centum* for all the £7000.

This cause was thrice heard, first by RAINSFORD, Justice, then by BRIDGEMAN, Keeper, on appeal, then by the EARL OF SHAFTESBURY, Chancellor, wherein they all decreed there should be a redemption notwithstanding the antiquity of the mortgage, partly by reason of the ill times, for it was to no purpose for Porter to redeem during the Troubles, because it would have been sequestered for his delinquency, and partly by reason of the defendant's offer in his answer, which answer nevertheless was not accepted on the terms upon which it was made use of to bind the defendants to account.

Second, RAINSFORD and SHAFTESBURY agreed that interest should not be paid for more than the £5000 and not for the £7000, as the defendant would have it, because the £7000 was made up by interest, and the Chancery would not allow interest upon interest, especially where the mortgagor is not privy to the stating of the account and the assignee did not pay money on the assignment, but only hedged in an old debt, for they held in this case that the assignee could not be in a better condition than the assignor or else it would be in the power of any mortgagee to assign when he pleased and so charge the mortgagor with double interest.

But Lord BRIDGEMAN, Keeper, was of another opinion, because all the £7000 was principal money as to the assignee and because it is good to quicken mortgagors in payment of their debts, which otherwise they would delay at the peril of their creditors if they run no hazard themselves, for single interest after many years delay is scarce half interest, and, which is worst of all, no mortgagee can ever assign his mortgage, though he have never so much need of his money, if the assignee must have no interest for what he pays above the old principal, so that every mortgagee must be forced to enter and be a perpetual bailiff to the mortgagor. And, for these reasons, late precedents have allowed interest on interest, as in 1663, Warder and Sayer's Case etc.

But it was replied that the precedents in Chancery were quite otherwise when the assignment to Hobart was made.

But, then, it being settled the interest should be paid only for the £5000, the next question was after what rate the interest for £5000 should be computed.

[1] R. G. Asch, 'Porter, Endymion (1587–1649)', *Oxford Dictionary of National Biography*, vol. 44, pp. 947–950.

And all agreed that, until 1642, it should be at 8 *per centum*.

But RAINSFORD said that, from 1642 to 1648, it should be at the rate of £4 *per centum* in imitation of the Chancery precedents, which moderate interest during the wars according to discretion ground upon an Act in 1651.[1] And so also it was done in December 1667, Harrison v. Delmahoy,[2] Hale, Chief Baron, and other assistants, and in December 1668, Lord Cornwallis v. Miller, and in June 1669, Mansell v. David Jenkins, both in the king's service, and, in June 1671, Earl of Athol v. Earl of Derby. And, from 1648 until this day, RAINSFORD thought legal interest was to be paid, *viz.* 8 or 6 *per centum prout lex postulata.* BRIDGEMAN, Keeper, would not sink the interest during the wars, but discharged the whole account for the time, and set the profits received against the interest. SHAFTESBURY, Chancellor, took a third course, and allowed 6 *per centum* from 1642 to this day for £5000.

2 Chancery Reports 85, 21 E.R. 623

Porter v. Hubbert.

This bill is to have a redemption of a mortgage made in 1636 by the plaintiff's father to one Abraham Dawes for £5000. And, for the non-payment of the mortgage money, Sir Thomas Dawes, son and heir of the said Abraham Dawes, entered in 1641, and he and his assigns have ever since taken the profits. And the defendant insists that the said Thomas Dawes, in 1649, conveyed the mortgaged premises to Hugh Hubert, the defendant's father, for £7000 and that, in 1641, when Sir Thomas Dawes entered, there was £5000 due on the mortgage besides interest, so he would be charged with £350 *per annum* for mesne profits since that time, and would have £6 *per centum* interest for the £7000 from the time of its appearing on the conveyance.

This cause being first heard by Judge RAINSFORD, who ordered the plaintiffs to redeem and the account for the interest of the £5000 to begin from 1636, the time of lending the money, and, from that to 1642, interest to be paid according to acts then in force, and from 1642 to 1646, interest at £8 and £4 *per centum*.

The cause being heard again by the Lord Keeper BRIDGEMAN, assisted with Judge TYRELL, MORTON, and WILDE, who ordered the plaintiff to pay interest for the £5000 to 1641 at £8 *per centum* and, from 1641 to 1649, the certain profits of the mortgaged premises to go in discharge of the interest until that time, and that, if the remaining interest with the £5000 should in 1649 amount to £7000, then the plaintiff to pay interest for £7000, else only for so much as the principal and interest, according to the statutes in force.

This cause was again reheard by the Lord Chancellor SHAFTESBURY, assisted with Judge VAUGHAN, and Judge RAINSFORD.

[1] C. H. Firth and R. S. Rait, *Acts and Ordinances of the Interregnum 1642–1660* (1911), vol. 2, p. 548.

[2] Note also *Harrison v. Haynes* (Ch. 1667–1668), see above, Case No. 251.

The defendant insisted that setting of the interest against the certain profits from 1641 to 1649, as aforesaid, was a great advantage to the plaintiff, and that, after so long a time, the plaintiff ought not to be permitted to redeem.

This court, nevertheless, was satisfied that the plaintiff ought to redeem. And the matters now in controversy being whether the certain profits of the premises shall go against the interest from 1641 to 1649 or not and whether the plaintiff shall pay interest for any more than the £5000 first lent or not and what interest he shall pay at least during the hard times of war, this court, on hearing precedents, was clear of opinion that the setting the certain profits of the premises against the interest from 1641 to 1649 ought to be discharged. And [the court] decreed the same accordingly.

And, touching that point, for what monies the plaintiff shall pay interest, either for the £5000 only or any greater sum, this court with the judges were of opinion that the plaintiff could not pay interest for any greater sum than only for the £5000, the original mortgages, this court declaring there is no reason to give interest upon interest and that the now defendant ought not to be in any better condition than Sir Abraham Dawes, the first mortgagee.

2 Freeman 30, 22 E.R. 1039

Porter v. Hobbard.

A mortgagee, after money is incurred for interest, assigns over to one that pays him his principal and interest. The question was whether or no this assignee, upon the redemption, should have interest for the interest. And his difference was taken that, when a mortgagee assigns with the consent of the mortgagor to one that pays him the principal and interest, there, the interest and principal are consolidated by the consent of the mortgagor, and, there, upon redemption, the assignee shall have interest for the whole sum that he disburses. And so it is (as it seems) if the mortgagor and mortgagee state their account and come to an agreement to continue the [loan of the] money longer.

But, if a mortgagee assign over without the consent of the mortgagor, there, no interest shall be allowed to the assignee for what he pays for interest, for, if that should be allowed, the scriveners of London would make a trade of assigning every six months and so turn their interest into principal and, by that means, receive interest upon interest.

And this case being cited to the Master of the Rolls [Grimston], he would not allow interest to the assignee for interest that he paid to the mortgagee, it not being done by the consent of the mortgagor.

[Reg. Lib. 24 Car. II, f. 591.]

406

St. Dunstan's Paupers v. Beauchamp

(Ch. 1671)

A decree by charity commissioners can be affirmed in the Court of Chancery even though no exceptions be filed.

1 Chancery Cases 193, 22 E.R. 758

A decree having been made by commissioners upon the Statute of Charitable Uses,[1] those for whom the decree was made brought an original bill, setting forth that the defendant to the decree threatened, when the witnesses were dead, they would except to the decree. And so they prayed that the defendant might show cause why the decree should not be confirmed.

The defendant by answer submitting to the decree, it was decreed by the Lord Keeper [Bridgeman] that the decree of the Commissioners should be confirmed.

Quod nota and *quaere* what is the need of such a bill, for that, when a decree is made by commissioners, the course is to return it into the Petty Bag and then to serve the defendant with a writ of execution, upon which service, the defendant may file exceptions and pray to stay proceedings until they be heard. But, if the defendants do not then except, but submit to the decree, it seems reasonable they should be concluded thereby and not be admitted to exceptions after[wards].

407

Attorney General, ex rel. Cudworth v. Townsend

(Ch. 1671)

A devise or bequest to charitable uses can be enforced by an information in the Court of Chancery brought by or in the name of the Attorney General.

Herne & Duke 115

Richard Risley,[2] seised in fee of a farm in Upton in the County of Huntingdon the 20th of September 1 Mar. [1553], demises the same to James Risley for ninety-six years, paying to him during his life £7 *per annum* and after his decease £6 10s. *per annum, viz.* £3 10s. to the master and fellows of Christ's College in Cambridge for the maintenance of a poor scholar there, 40s. to the minister, constable, and churchwardens of Streatham, and £20 *per annum* to the overseers of the poor of Bingham for the relief of the poor. Richard Risley conveyed

[1] Stat. 43 Eliz. I, c. 4 (*SR*, IV, 968–970).

[2] J. Piele, *Biographical Dictionary of Christ's College* (1910), vol. 1, p. 9.

the inheritance to trustees upon trust that, after the expiration of the lease of 96 years, they should apply all the rents etc. for the relief of a poor scholar in Christ's College and the relief of the poor of Streatham and Bingham. The lease ended in 1649. The scholar and poor had only £6 10s. *per annum* until about 1670.

And upon an information in Chancery by His Majesty's then Attorney General at the relation of the master and fellows of the said College, it was decreed that the whole £30 *per annum* should be paid to the scholar and poor according to their several proportions of the £6 10s. *per annum*.

Note: Where the devisor gives all the estate or the surplusage of his estate to the poor, there, the proper way to have the same applied to charitable uses is by information in Chancery.

Public Record Office C.33/235, f. 391v

31 January 1671.

Attorney General *per relatione* Ralph Cudworth,[1] [Lady] Margaret Professor of Sacred Theology and Master of Christ's College in Cambridge University, *et al.*, informants; William Townsend, gent., Robert Langford, John Chevile, Francis Langford, Henry English, clerk, Peter Becke, Thomas Jefferson, and Walfried Hull, defendants.

Upon the hearing and debating the matter in question between the said parties this present day in the presence of the plaintiff's counsel and the counsel for the defendants English, Jefferson, Beck, and Hull, none appearing for the other defendants, Townsend, the two Langfords, and Chevill, albeit they were duly served with process to hear judgment on this day as by affidavits now read appeared, the end of this suit being to be relieved for charitable uses which were of the gift of Richard Risley to the Master and Fellows of Christ's College in Cambridge for the maintenance of a poor scholar and to the poor of Streatham in the Isle of Ely and the poor of Bingham in the County of Norfolk and by the information exhibited by His Majesty's Attorney General at the relation of the master or keeper of Christ's College aforesaid and of the fellows and scholars of the same college, it is set forth that the said Richard Risley being seised in fee of a farm in Upton in the County of Huntingdon 20 September 1 Mary [1553] demised the same to James Risley for ninety-six years paying to him £7 *per annum* during his life and after his death £3 10s. yearly to the master and fellows of Christ's College for the maintenance of a poor scholar there and £40 to the minister, constable, and church wardens of Streatham and 20s. to the poor of Bingham for the relief of the poor and that the said Richard Risley conveyed the inheritance of the premises to trustees upon trust that after the expiration of the lease of ninety-six years they should apply all the rents for the relief of a poor

[1] D. A. Pailin, 'Cudworth, Ralph (1617–1688)', *Oxford Dictionary of National Biography*, vol. 14, pp. 562–565; J. Piele, *Biographical Dictionary of Christ's College* (1910), vol. 1, pp. 464–467.

scholar in Christ's College aforesaid and the relief of the poor of Streatham and Bingham and that the lease of ninety-six years ended in 1649 and the present trustees let the farm at £30 *per annum* and the £3 10s. and the 40s. and the 20s. *per annum* have been paid ever since the decease of Richard Risley and the whole rent ever since the lease expired ought to have been paid to the scholar and the poor in proportion and that the lands lying in three several fields and in small parcels in every field amongst the lands of the defendant English, who was lord of the manor of Upton, among the glebe lands of the parson and the other defendants' lands and the boundaries are not known. And therefore it was prayed by the information and the replication that the defendants, the trustees, may account for all the rents received since 1649 and that it may be applied according to the intent of the donor and discover the ancient charters and evidences concerning the premises and that a commission may issue to set out and distinguish the lands belonging to the charity from other lands which lie confusedly with them in the said fields and that the moneys in the trustees' hands may go towards the repairs of the housing belonging to the farm aforesaid and that other trustees may be named and the charitable uses preserved and settled and confirmed by the decree of this court.

Whereunto, it was insisted by the counsel for the defendant English that he confesses by answer that he has heard Richard Risley made such lease and feoffment as in the information is set forth and that he died before the expiration of the lease and that James Risley, his executor or assignee, did enjoy the said farm and lands during that lease or very near the end of it and constantly paid the said £6 10s. *per annum* to the use of the scholar in Christ's College in Cambridge and to the poor of Streatham and Bingham and believes that the lease expired about Michaelmas 1649 and that the said farm and lands have been ever since let for £30 *per annum* and conceives that the whole profits of the premises ought to be applied to the charitable uses in the information mentioned and by such proportions as is therein set forth and that he has heard that the deed of trust with the other writings that concerned Mr. Risley's lands were left in the hands of the former tenant of the said farm and were after his death delivered by his wife to an agent sent by the inhabitants of Streatham and says he is lord of the manor of Upton and that the lands belonging to the charity lie intermixed with his and other lands and that the boundaries have been defaced by plowing up the banks and that the same being about one hundred acres do lie in above 160 places and that he is willing that the said lands may be set out by commission and ascertained or that the like number of acres of like value may be set out in lieu thereof in any other part of Upton.

And the defendant Jefferson by his answer confesses that he is tenant of the farm and lands late Mr. Risley's and that the same lie dispersedly and is willing the lands may be set out by commissioners so as he may receive no prejudice.

And the counsel for the defendants Beck and Hull alleged that the defendant Beck by answer says that, as rector of the rectory of Upton, he is seised of divers glebe lands in that parish which lie dispersedly with other lands there and that he is willing a commission should go to set out the lands that were Mr. Risley's or the like quantity of the same value and denies that he has any writings concerning the said lands.

And the defendant Hull says that he is seised of divers lands in Upton which lie dispersedly in the fens of Upton but claims none of the lands given to the charitable uses and is willing a commission should go to set out the said lands so as he may receive no prejudice.

Whereupon and upon reading the answers of the other defendants, William Townsend, Robert and Francis Langford, and John Chevile, who, by their answer, confess they have in their hands several deeds and writings concerning the premises and that the inheritance thereof is in them as surviving trustees and confess the trust and say that all the rent above the £6 10s. *per annum* has been applied to other charitable uses, this court does think fit and so order that a commission do issue to gentlemen in the country to set out and distinguish the lands that were the said Mr. Richard Risley's and given by him to the charitable uses aforesaid from the other lands lying in Upton fields aforesaid and that the rents and profits thereof according to the improved value shall go to the charitable uses expressed in the said deed of trust in proportion to the sums therein expressed. And unless the defendants William Townsend, Robert Langford, and John Chevile shall at the return of process of subpoena to be served on them show cause to the contrary, it is further ordered and decreed that the defendants William Townsend, Robert and Francis Langford, and John Chevile, the present feoffees in trust shall account before Sir Robert Stewart, knight, etc. for the rents and profits of the said farm and lands belonging to the charitable uses aforesaid which they or any of them have received, the said master making all just allowances to them, and what shall be found remaining in their hands upon account shall be paid to the relators to be applied to the charitable uses or for advancement thereof in [the] repair of the premises as the court shall direct and that the said defendants, the trustees, shall produce all the deeds, writings, and evidences concerning the said farm and premises which they or any of them have or has in his or their custody before the said master who is to examine and consider whether the present trustees are fit persons to be continued trustees or not and likewise to consider of other fitting persons to be added to such of them as he shall think fit to continue and report the same to this court. And the said master shall also examine and consider of the decays and ruins that have been suffered in the houses belonging to the charity, and after the master's report, the plaintiffs may move for damages for the money which shall appear due upon the account to be taken by the said master but, before the said defendants shall be admitted to show cause, they shall pay five marks costs to the informants for this days attendance.

408

Williams v. Smith

(Ch. 1671)

When a mortgage is redeemed, all of the securities for the debt must be vacated.

3 Chancery Reports 75, 21 E.R. 733

Hilary [term] 1671.

The bill was to be relieved against several securities gotten from young Mr. Williams presently after he came of age, wherein were cited, in Lord Coventry's time grounded on a precedent in Lord Ellesmere's time, Miller and Carter's Case, where an account was directed to make appear what was paid upon security so gotten; Godscall and Walker,[1] the same; also Walter and Somers, the same.

But, here, Smith had a recognizance and a mortgage and a bond for different sums. And, there appearing no surprise on Williams when the mortgage was made and nothing appearing but that he was a sensible man, the money on the mortgage is decreed with interest. But on the payment thereof, Smith is to assign, and not to enable himself to recover the money on the bond of recognizance by the mortgage.

409

Gains v. Colby

(Ch. 1671)

A final judgment can be enforced by an original bill in equity or by a subpoena scire facias.

Lord Nottingham, *Prolegomena*, p. 197

Hilary [term] 23 Car. II.

A man may exhibit an original bill to have execution of a former decree against those who were bound by that decree or claim in privity under them that were bound. Yet the more common and ordinary way is to take out a subpoena in the nature of a *scire facias*, requiring them, upon service of the decree, to show cause why they should not perform it. So, at common law, a man may either have an original action of debt upon a judgment or a *scire facias*, as he pleases, and the action of debt is the better way when the plaintiff would have better bail.

[1] *Godscall v. Walker* (Ch. 1663), see above, Case No. 101.

410

Pinsent's Case

(Ch. 1671)

In this case, the intent of the testator was that his executors should have the profits of certain lands during life of the wife, not the coheirs.

Where the equities are equal, equity follows the law.

Lord Nottingham, *Prolegomena*, p. 200

22 & 23 Car. II, Hilary [term] 1673 [sic].

John Pinsent, the prothonotary, having lands in Surrey and Oxfordshire and a great personal estate in desperate debts, devised all his lands not worth £300 *per annum* to his wife for life, and £100 *per annum* more to her to be paid by his executors to her out of his moneys, 'and, after my wife's death, I give my lands in Surrey to Edward, my adopted heir, my other grandchildren and coheirs having had large portions'. And then, by a codicil, reciting what he had done for his wife and that she was unwilling to be troubled with receiving the rents, he gives her his house at Comb and £350 *per annum* to be paid by his executors quarterly without taxes in discharge of her former legacy.

[It was] ruled: first, this is a revocation of the devise of the lands to the wife; second, that Edward shall not be let in during her life, but, in the meantime, the lands descend to the coheirs, for it is in effect a devise to a stranger after the wife's death; third, then it was moved that, in equity, the executors ought to receive the profits towards the £350, for the personal estate in good debts will not so come in as to answer quarterly payments without that supply and his will declares his grandchildren and coheirs were well provided for, so he intended not by the codicil to let in the coheirs during the wife's life, but to put the executors in her place to receive the rents and pay her £350 *per annum*.

Lord BRIDGEMAN, Keeper: It is likely this was his true intent. But, if the law, which, in construction of a will, takes in all the parts of it, do not so adjudge it, equity shall not deprive the coheirs of a legal advantage. Therefore, I dismiss it to law, for, in this case, *aequitas sequitur legem*.

[It was] adjudged afterwards in the Common Bench on a special verdict that the executors shall have the profits during life of the wife, not the coheirs, for the intent is apparent.

411

Dakins v. Berisford

(Ch. 1671)

A husband is entitled to receive the payments of an annuity that is payable to his wife.

1 Chancery Cases 194, 22 E.R. 758

6 February [1671]. The Master of the Rolls.

Leases were devised to the defendant by his eldest brother to be sold for several purposes and, amongst others, in trust that the defendant should purchase in his own name an annuity of £80 *per annum* for the life of the plaintiff's wife and pay the same to her and her assigns. The bill was to enforce the payment of his annuity.

The defendant insisted by answer that he had constantly paid the annuity to the plaintiff's wife, from whom the plaintiff lived apart, and that the bill was against her consent and that it was the intent of the donor to be for her only benefit, the will being that he should buy in his own name the annuity in trust for the plaintiff's wife, who is the defendant's mother, and her assigns. And so he insisted that, the plaintiff not inhabiting with her, he ought not to be put to pay the annuity to him.

It appeared by proofs that the cause of the plaintiff's first absenting himself from his wife was for fear of debts and that he had since solicited her by letters to cohabit, but she refused.

The Master of the Rolls [Grimston] declared that, in this case, the husband was the assignee of the wife and that there being no negative words by the will to exclude the husband from the annuity, he could not exclude him. And so he decreed the defendant to pay all the arrears of the annuity since the bill exhibited and the growing annuity for the future to the plaintiff, the husband.

412

Smith v. Stowell

(Ch. 1671)

The Statute of Charitable Uses applies to pre-existing charities, but pre-existing lessees of charities should be neither prejudiced nor benefitted by pre-existing leases that are unfavorable to charities.

1 Chancery Cases 195, 22 E.R. 759

17 February [1671]. The Lord Keeper, Justice Twysden, Justice Morton.

There was a disposition in 1579, which was before the Statute of 43 Eliz., for charitable uses,[1] to a charity. Part of the lands were of a defective title, and the whole disposition was void, being before the Statute. Yet an agreement was made between the parties interested and the trustee for the settling of the use designed so much as was proportionable in value to what the donor had to give. And this was settled accordingly before the Statute, and long leases were let of the ground

[1] Stat. 43 Eliz. I, c. 4 (*SR*, IV, 968–970).

to divers tenants at small rents to build, who had thereby improved that ground that was but £20 *per annum* to £150 *per annum*.

A decree was made by the commissioners for avoiding the tenants' leases, they not being in strictness of law good.

Upon exceptions to that decree, it was declared by the court that, though the charity was precedent to the Statute, yet the Statute subsequent had a retrospect, and would make it a good appointment, that [which] was not so before (but void). And it was declared that, so as the terre tenants be no losers, they ought not to be gainers in the case of a charity. And so it was ordered that, during the terre tenants' leases, there should be an augmentation of £50 *per annum* allowed by them in proportion to the poor.

413

Whitmore v. Crisp

(Ch. 1671)

A bill of discovery against one joint debtor must join all of the joint debtors as co-defendants.

Lord Nottingham, *Prolegomena*, p. 303

1 March 1670[/71].

William Whitmore, a creditor of the late farmers of the Customs, did exhibit a bill against Sir Nicholas Crisp, and prayed a discovery of the real and personal estate.

The defendant demurred, because the rest of the farmers were not made parties and, though, here, the suit was not to have the duty itself, but only to discover assets in order to [aid] a suit at law, where he may sue whom he pleases, yet the demurrer was allowed, for the court of equity must not assist an inequitable suit.

414

Anonymous

(Ch. 1671)

When a mortgage is redeemed, the deceased mortgagee-creditor's executors receive the money, and his heir must execute the re-conveyance.

73 Selden Soc. 204

6 March, 23 Car. II [1671].

Lord Bridgeman, Lord Keeper, declared that, in regard there was no defect of assets, no covenant to repay, no personal security, and the re-conveyance must be by the heir, the money ought to be paid to the heir, unless the constant course of the court had been to the contrary. So His Lordship adhered to his first opinion, as an assistant in Tilly's Case.[1]

But, by this time, [BRIDGEMAN] began to doubt the course of the court. Now this last reason, that the re-conveyance must be by the heir, does not, therefore, conclude he must have the money, for he joins in a conveyance where the land is appointed to be sold by executors, yet has none of the money and, when the mortgagor has once paid the money according to the purport of the defeasance, the estate in law becomes a trust for him, which the heir of the mortgagee is bound to execute.

[Other copies of this report: 3 Swanston 634, 36 E.R. 1002.]

415

North v. Crompton

(Ch. 1671–1672)

The law will not create a trust by implication except in cases of necessity.

1 Chancery Cases 196, 22 E.R. 759

25 March [1671]. The Lord Keeper, Justices Twysden, Wilde, Rainsford, Wyndham.

Katharine Crompton, spinster, seised in fee of the lands in question, by her will in writing the 21st of January 1669[/70], expresses thus:

I ordain and constitute Henry North, Esq. [which is the plaintiff] to be mine executor of this my last will. And I do give all my estate, real and personal, to dispose of for the payment of all my just debts, and, for the performing of all such legacies as I have herein or by the codicil annexed bequeathed unto my executor above-named.

And she gives several legacies in money and amongst others £200 to the defendant [Charles Crompton], her uncle, who is heir at law. And a legacy of £500 being omitted to the plaintiff's sister, it was inserted in a codicil.

Mr. North's bill was to prove this will *per testes*.

Mr. Crompton's bill was to be relieved upon the trust of the devise, as he supposed, after the debts and legacies paid and to discover what the debts were.

These causes came first to be heard 8 February 1670[/71] before the Lord Keeper [BRIDGEMAN] and Baron WYNDHAM, and then these two questions were stirred by the court: first, whether this were a devise of lands in fee; second, whether Mr. North, the plaintiff, Crompton claiming by an implied trust after debts and legacies paid, might not be admitted to aver against that implication.

Of both these points, the court took time to consider.

---

[1] *Tilly v. Egerton* (Ch. 1660), see above, Case No. 4.

3 March 1670[/71], the cause being heard again before the Lord Keeper [BRIDGEMAN] and Mr. Baron WYNDHAM, they declared they were both of opinion that it was a devise of the lands in fee. And, then, they doubted whether a trust be created for the heir of the surplus. And another question they made [was], if a trust, whether an averment did not lie for Mr. North, it being but an implied trust and not within the Statute of Hen. VIII, of wills.[1]

And 25 March 1671, the Lord Keeper [BRIDGEMAN] and the four judges all agreed that a fee passes by the devise. And, as to the implied trust, all conceived there was not any implied trust for the heir for the surplus, for, if there were, the devisee had no benefit and to no purpose was the devise of the £200 to the heir if she had intended the surplus to the heir.

Lord Nottingham, *Prolegomena*, p. 241

Hilary [term] 23 Car. II. Crompton v. North.

Katherine Crompton, intending to marry Mr. Henry North, fell sick, and, by a will, gave him 'all my real and personal estate to dispose of for payments of my debts'. And she gave his sister £500 and her heir at law £200.

[It was] resolved: first, an estate, and that in fee, passed by these words. Second, it was urged that, as to the surplus, the law did imply a trust for the heir and no proof of any contrary intent should be received.

To this, it was said that, as a trust may be averred on a will, so, likewise, an averment may be to answer the implication of a trust. And, here, the circumstances are strong against a trust. Besides, the Chancery will sometimes imply a trust to support an inartificial will, but to imply a trust only to overthrow a perfect will were very strange.

[It was] resolved, by SIR ORLANDO BRIDGEMAN, Keeper, and TWYSDEN, Justice, that no trust should be implied, for it cannot be supposed that Mrs. Crompton intended Mr. North nothing but trouble by her without any benefit. And, regularly, nothing is a trust now but what was a use at common law, nor will the law create a trust by implication but in cases of necessity. Here it can be no trust for the land, because the executor had the power to sell. So the bill was dismissed.

[Other reports of this case: 1 Eq. Cas. Abr. 272, 21 E.R. 1040.]

[1] Stat. 32 Hen. VIII, c. 1 (*SR*, III, 744–746).

416

Newton v. Wigmore

(Ch. 1671)

A prior mortgage cannot be redeemed against a subsequent bona fide *purchaser for value without notice.*

Lord Nottingham, *Prolegomena*, p. 282

Easter [term] 23 Car. II.

Newton in 1647 assigns to Burdet a lease for 1000 years, which, by another deed, was defeasanced as a mortgage. Burdet assigns to Wigmore with notice. Wigmore assigns to Bernard without notice.

[It was] resolved: first, Newton shall have no redemption against Bernard, who comes in without notice of his equity; second, but Wigmore shall be therefore chargeable to make good the value to Newton; third, yet, if at the time of the conveyance to Wigmore, the lands were not worth the redeeming, it shall be otherwise.

And, on this last point, the bill was dismissed without costs.

417

Cutts v. Pickering

(Ch. 1671–1673)

A party's solicitor can be examined as a witness as to the tampering with a will that is in issue.

Nelson 81, 21 E.R. 795

4 May, 23 Car. II [1671].

The defendant claimed an estate by a will for ninety years absolutely, but, after the word 'years', there was an erasure supposed to be written 'if he so long live'. The question was how to find out this fraud and alteration of the will.

And, for that purpose, the plaintiff had exhibited interrogatories to examine Mr. Joshua Baker, the defendant's solicitor, on oath.

And Mr. Baker demurred, for that he knew nothing but as he was solicitor for the defendant and as trusted by him. And he demanded judgment whether he should be examined against his client.

But the demurrer was overruled.

And, upon an appeal to the Lord Keeper [BRIDGEMAN], the order was confirmed.

3 Chancery Reports 66, 21 E.R. 730

4 May 1671, 23 Car. II. Baron Turner.

The defendant claimed an estate by a will for ninety years. And, after the word 'years' was an erasure, where was thought to have been written 'if he so long live'. And the question was to know how to find out this fraud and alteration.

And, for that end, the plaintiffs had exhibited interrogatories to examine Mr. Joseph Baker, the defendant's solicitor, upon.

And Mr. Baker demurred, for that he knew nothing but as he was solicitor for the defendant and as trusted by him. And he demanded judgment whether he should be examined against his client.

And the demurrer coming now to be heard, it was overruled.

And, afterward, the defendant appealed to the Lord Keeper [BRIDGEMAN], who, on the 8th of May, confirmed the order.

Lord Nottingham, *Prolegomena*, p. 317

Easter [term], 24 Car. II.

On the will of Sir John Cutts, the question was whether the erasure of a will, by which a devise to Dorothy Pickering for eighty years if she so long lived was made [to read] for eighty years absolutely, was made in the life of Sir John Cutts or after his death.

Baker, a solicitor for Pickering, was examined.

He demurred, but was ruled to answer: first, because [it was] dubious if a solicitor has any privilege, *quia non definitur in lege quid sit*; second, *quia turpis causa*, and no secrecy is due to the client in crimes; third, and, principally, he ought to answer to his knowledge before he was solicitor.

And, for this reason, Baker was examined upon a trial in the King's Bench, where he proved a duplicate, which Pickering foreswore, and [proved] having viewed the original after Sir John Cutts's death without the erasure, upon which [evidence a] verdict [was given] against Pickering.

1 Ventris 197, 86 E.R. 133

Upon a trial at the bar, one Baker, who had been the solicitor for Pickering, was produced as a witness concerning the erasure of a clause in a will supposed to be done by Pickering.

The court were moved whether he could be examined touching this, because, having been retained as his solicitor, he should by reason of that be obliged to keep his secrets.

But it appearing that Baker had made this discovery to him of which he was now about to give evidence before such time as he had retained him, the court were of opinion that he might be sworn. [It would be] otherwise, if he had been retained as his solicitor before. The same is the law of an attorney or counsel.

3 Keble 2, 84 E.R. 560

Friday, April 26 [1672].

A will in evidence on an issue out of Chancery appeared to be by Sir John Cutts, tenant to him and his heirs of the bishop of Ely for three lives as to one manor on a bargain and sale first made for 99 years if the three lives so long live in trust to such uses and appointments as by Sir John Cutts's last will should be, which was made to enable a devise. By HYDE, Chief Justice.

But the question was upon another manor supposed by the plaintiff to be devised for eighty years to the defendant's wife if she lived so long and that the later words 'if she so long lived' were erased, which the jury believed, and so there was a verdict for the plaintiff.

Lord Nottingham, *Prolegomena*, p. 302

9 October 1673, by the Chancellor and Wilde, Justice.

If a trial be directed by the court in a feigned motion, there, after a verdict given, the parties should resort back to the court, and not enter judgment at law, nor take execution for costs. And they who do otherwise have been made to pay costs for their contempts. But, in special cases and *in odium spoliatoris*, this rule has been dispensed with.

Therefore, in the Case of Pickering, who erased a will, seized the writings, etc., on a verdict against him, Cutts obtained a decree for the will as before the erasure, but [it was] ordered that he should have no costs, which decree was enrolled. Two years after, on debating exceptions to the account, Cutts moved for costs, which motion he had leave to make then by a former order. But it was denied, because the decree of the Keeper, which he had enrolled and indeed could not do otherwise, denied to give costs. But, then, the Chancellor, upon opening the demerits of Pickering, allowed Cutts to enter judgment at law and take his costs there.

418

Pate v. Hatton

(Ch. 1671)

Where a citizen of London makes a devise to a child that is greater than that child's customary share with a devise over if the child die, where the child dies, the child's administrator takes up to the child's customary share, and the devise over passes only what remains of the devise.

1 Chancery Cases 199, 22 E.R. 760

15 May [1671]. Pate against Hatton or Hutton.

A citizen and freeman of London devises to his son a gross sum, which did exceed the customary part, and he devises that, if his son die before he attain twenty-one, that sum go over to another.

The question was if the devise over was good.

And it was adjudged, and so decreed by the Lord Keeper [BRIDGEMAN] that the devise over for so much as was the customary part was void and that, the orphan dying within age, his administrator was entitled to so much as was the customary part, and the surplus of that gross sum was to go to those to whom it was devised over.

419

Lambert v. Bainton

(Ch. 1671–1672)

Where a trustee of a devise to pay debts pays the debts out of his own personal assets, he is a purchaser of the land devised pro tanto and can retain it.

1 Chancery Cases 199, 22 E.R. 760

15 May [1671].

Mr. Dunch, in 1646, had conveyed the lands in question to Sir Edward Bainton in fee in trust to sell all or any part of it for the payment of his debts. Sir Edward Bainton had conveyed his lands to his son, and was dead. Dunch being dead and the plaintiff being entitled to the benefit of the trust after the debts paid, he brought the bill to avoid the conveyance made by Sir Edward Bainton to his son and so have a re-conveyance.

For the defendant, it was insisted that, though it was a trust in Sir Edward, yet Sir Edward had paid the debts to the value of the estate, and was thereby become a purchaser as much as if he had sold the lands to another.

The Lord Keeper [BRIDGEMAN] declared that, if Sir Edward Bainton had paid to the value of the lands, he was a purchaser. But it not appearing what he had paid when he made the settlement more than he received, he referred it to a Master to examine. And he declared that the defendant, as to so much as Sir Edward had then disbursed, should be taken as a purchaser, because Sir Edward might sell all or any part and so the defendant is a purchaser *pro tanto.*

Lord Nottingham, *Prolegomena*, p. 242

Hilary [term] 23 Car. II.

Dunch conveyed to Sir Edward Bainton his real and personal estate for the payment of debts in a schedule. If there be no covenant in the deed on the part of Sir Edward Bainton to pay these debts or to free Dunch, but that Dunch, notwithstanding this deed, received [the profits], then, though there be no express declaration of a trust, yet the law, in this case, shall imply a trust, and shall not suffer this to be construed as a purchase in Sir Edward Bainton.

Nota the conveyance was in 1646 when Bainton was potent and Dunch sequestered. Also *nota* no weight was laid on the words of Dunch that it was a trust, for he could not declare a trust after a conveyance without the concurrence of Sir Edward Bainton.

Lord Nottingham, *Prolegomena*, p. 263

Hilary [term] 23 Car. II. Dunch v. Bainton.

If a trustee for the payment of debts pays debts with his own money near the value of the lands, he shall retain the lands and account for the value of the surplus, and shall not lose the estate, as in the like case of an executor at common law on the payment of debts shall retain the goods etc. Second, if the land so conveyed in trust were charged with a jointure and the trustee pay debts to the value of the land at that time, this is sufficient to entitle him to retain the lands, though the jointure fall in after[wards]. But, if a trustee pay debts by small insensible payments, such as may probably rise and be reimbursed out of the profits, then, he shall not retain, but be decreed to re-convey the land.

Lord Nottingham, *Prolegomena*, p. 267

Dunch conveys land to Bainton for the payment [of debts] in a schedule, and then he declared to all his friends that he had made this conveyance in trust. This declaration had not been sufficient if other circumstances had been wanting, but, there, the deed giving a power to sell all or any part, which was idle if [there was] no trust, and for other reasons, a trust was implied.

[Related cases: Lambert v. Dunch (Ch. 1670), see above, Case No. 396.]

420

Martin v. Douch

(Ch. 1671)

A devise to a person to uses, the uses never being stated, goes to the devisee, and not to the decedent's executors.

1 Chancery Cases 198, 22 E.R. 760

Thomas Martin, clerk, against Douch and Overton.

One Foster devises to the plaintiff in these words:

Item, I give to my cousin Thomas Martin, clerk, late minister of Houghton in Northamptonshire and living thereabouts; I do order £40 to be paid him to be disposed of for certain uses, which I shall in a private note acquaint him with.

And he gave him no note or direction how to dispose of it, but he died, the defendants being his executors. And whether the plaintiff should have the £40 was the question.

The Master of the Rolls [Grimston] was of opinion the plaintiff should have the £40, for that the testator did not intend it should come to his executors, but had by his will given it away from them. And so he decreed the defendant to pay the £40 to the plaintiff.

421

Vanbrough v. Cock

(Ch. 1671)

The judgments of the ecclesiastical courts are as subject to the equity of a court of equity as are judgments in the common law courts.

The question in this case was whether one co-executor of a will who does not act in the administration of the decedent's estate can be charged with the actions of the active co-executor.

1 Chancery Cases 200, 22 E.R. 761

17 May [1671]. William Vanbrough against William Cock and his wife and Peter Drybutter.

About seventeen years since, Cornelius Beard bequeathed to his sister, then in her infancy, £250 to be paid at marriage or twenty-one years, and he made one Andrew Drybutter and the plaintiff executors, and he died, leaving his sister young. Both the executors made probate of the will, but the plaintiff, at the desire of the sister's friends, did forbear to meddle with the testator's estate, and left it wholly to Andrew Drybutter, the other executor, who only did act in it. Andrew dying, he made Elizabeth, his wife, his executrix. She possessed what there was of the first testator's estate, and paid to the defendant Cock's wife, then the wife of one Earl, £100, part of the £250, and the said Elizabeth Drybutter kept all the first testator's books and papers, and that by the desire of the said legatee. And, she dying, she made the defendant Peter Drybutter her executor. The defendant, Cock's wife, libeled in the spiritual court against the plaintiff for her £250, and had a sentence there against him for the whole, hanging this suit. And yet she had by answer confessed £100, part of the £250, to be paid.

The scope of the bill was to be relieved against the spiritual court, setting forth that, by that law, the plaintiff having joined in the probate would be charged with the legacy, though he did not meddle with the estate and that it was against equity to charge one executor with the receipts of another. And the bill charged that the other defendant, Drybutter, had assets, both of Andrew Drybutter and Elizabeth Drybutter's estate, and, if they had not paid as far as they had assets of

Beard's estate, the defendant Drybutter, and not the plaintiff, ought to pay what was unpaid of the £250 legacy.

The defendant Drybutter confessed he had assets of the said Andrew and Elizabeth, his father's and mother's respective estates, and insisted that they had fully administered Beard's estate. And the question was what relief they ought to give the plaintiff against the sentence in the spiritual court.

The Lord Keeper [BRIDGEMAN] declared that the judgments of the ecclesiastical courts were as subject to the equity of this court as judgments in the common law courts. And, howbeit at law, one executor is not liable to the *devastavit* of another, yet, in the ecclesiastical courts and by their law, if an executor prove the will, they will charge him, though he do no further intermeddle to pay the legacies.

(But *quaere* if that be not only where there is a failer of bringing an inventory. Doctor and Student 67.[1])

And the Lord Keeper [BRIDGEMAN] declared the plaintiff is without relief by appeal from the sentence because the Judges Delegate must judge according to that law. And so he inclined to relieve the plaintiff, but he took time to advise.

Doctor and Student, *ut supra*, a law grounded on a presumption, if the presumption be untrue, is not to be held in conscience, for *stabitur praesumptio donec probetur in contrarium.*

[Other reports of this case: 1 Eq. Cas. Abr. 135, 21 E.R. 939.]

422

Rich v. Sydenham

(Ch. 1671)

A confessed judgment that is not grounded on a valuable and honest consideration is not enforceable.

3 Chancery Reports 74, 21 E.R. 733

23 May 1671.

The plaintiff lent Sydenham and Stidulph £200, and they gave him a [confessed] judgment of £1000 to pay £800 within three months after either of their fathers died or they were married. Stidulph's father died, and Sydenham married a co-heir of Porter, who had a good estate, but it was in trustees' names in point of law.

And the plaintiff's bill was to subject that estate to his judgment.

[1] *St. German's Doctor and Student* (Plucknett and Barton, edd., 1974), 91 Selden Soc. 119.

But it was held to be no equitable consideration. And, therefore, his bill was dismissed.

1 Chancery Cases 202, 22 E.R. 762

26 May [1671].

The plaintiff upon the loan of £90 had gotten a bond from the defendant of £1600 for the payment of £800 and a judgment thereupon. The defendant, in the right of his wife, was entitled to certain lands that were estated in other persons in law in trust for her.

The bill was to have those lands subjected to the plaintiff's satisfaction here, inasmuch as the defendant was entitled to the trust in the right of his wife.

But the security being gotten from the defendant when he was drunk, the Lord Keeper [BRIDGEMAN] would not give the plaintiff any relief in equity, not so much as for the principal he had really lent. And so the bill was dismissed.

[Other reports of this case: 1 Eq. Cas. Abr. 88, 21 E.R. 899.]

423

Bovey v. Skipwith

(Ch. 1671)

When a third mortgagee purchases in the first mortgage, the second mortgagee has no equity against the third mortgagee.

Where a trust of a contingent remainder of a lease is void, the interest goes to the holder of the first estate of inheritance unless the reversion and inheritance be conveyed to other trustees.

1 Chancery Cases 201, 22 E.R. 762

25 May [1671].

In 1651, Sir Francis Drake made the plaintiff a security out of the manor and rectory of Waltham upon Thames. Afterwards, in 1656, Drake made the defendant a security for money out of the rectory only, the defendant having no notice then of the plaintiff's security which was for money also. Afterwards, the defendant, hearing of the plaintiff's security, buys in a security precedent to the plaintiff's, which one Beddingfield had both upon the manor and the rectory.

The first question was whether the plaintiff should be admitted to redeem Beddingfield's security without paying off what was due to Skipwith. And it was ruled he should not. *Vide* Marsh and Lee's Case.[1]

The second question was whether, inasmuch as the defendant's security was only out of the rectory and the security he bought in from Beddingfield was of

[1] *March v. Lee* (Ch. 1670), see above, Case No. 363.

both the manor and the rectory, the defendant should make use of Beddingfield's security as to the manor after that, by the profits of the manor and rectory, Beddingfield's debt was satisfied. And whether then the plaintiff should not then be admitted to enjoy the manor, his security being as well of the manor as the rectory, and the defendant to hold only the rectory until he was satisfied.

Wilde and Twysden were of opinion that, after Skipwith had received what was due on Beddingfield's security, he should receive no more profits of the manor, but the plaintiff to be let in to receive them and the defendant only to make use of Beddingfield's security, as to the rectory, to protect his security of the rectory. But it was resolved and ruled that the defendant should hold both the manor and the rectory against the plaintiff until all due to him on both securities was paid him.

Quaere tamen.

Lord Nottingham, *Prolegomena*, p. 208

Easter [term] 23 Car. II.

Sir Francis Drake mortgages the manor and rectory of Walton to Bedingfield, then he borrows £6000 of Sir Ralph Bovy, and secures it by a rent charge out of the manor and rectory. And, after all this, he borrows £700 of Mr. Skipwith, for which he mortgages the rectory only. Then, Mr. Skipwith, coming to discover Sir Ralph Bovy's title, which he knew not of before, buys in Bedingfield's mortgage. Sir Ralph Bovy exhibits his bill, and would fain redeem the mortgage.

[It was] resolved that Skipwith, having equity on his side, *viz.* to be paid his £700, and law too, *viz.* by purchase of Bedingfield's estate, shall not be defeated in Chancery. But Sir Ralph Bovy must either redeem all or none, according to Marsh and Lee's Case. By Orlando Bridgeman, Keeper, and Wilde and Wyndham, an account was directed in order to pay all.

3 Chancery Reports 67, 21 E.R. 731

Easter [term] 1671, 23 Car. II.

The same case as the security upon Drake's estate, *ante*, but Skipwith had but a judgment and it was not extended and, therefore, it could reach but a moiety of what was in the prior encumbrance, and not in Skipwith's security.

But this case was harder, for Skipwith's original title was but to part of the lands, and, then, he bought in precedent encumbrances of all precedent to Bovey, who was before Skipwith. And yet Skipwith must hold all until satisfied all due to him before Bovey came in, by the opinion of the Lord Keeper [Bridgeman], Rainsford, and Wilde, Twysden and Wyndham not concurring.

And the whole bar being of their opinion, the inconvenience and mischief of the case [was] much pressed by Mr. *Keck*, who offered that the first encumbrance should protect what Skipwith had a title to originally against Sir Ralph to satisfy what was due to him. But it was overruled *ut ante* upon the precedent of Marsh and Lee. And, afterwards, Skipwith's original security was recovered at law against him by the heir of Drake so that he had no title to buy the precedent estates.

Lord Nottingham, *Prolegomena*, p. 234

Michaelmas [term] 23 Car. II, King's Bench, on a trial at the bar *per* Hale [C.J.] *et curiam*.

If a long lease or a term in gross be conveyed to trustees on a marriage settlement in trust for the husband for life, remainder to the wife for a jointure, remainder to the heirs of the body of the husband on the body of the wife begotten, this is a void limitation of the trust as to the heirs of the body. And, notwithstanding this, the trust results and rests in the husband, his executors, and administrators.

But, if, at the same time, the reversion and inheritance be conveyed to other trustees on the like trusts as the term was limited, now, the lease is become attendant upon the inheritance, and no trust will result to the husband, nor will the term be disposable by him from the heirs of his own body.

[Related cases: Jennet v. Cooles (1666 × 1667), 1 Siderfin 223, 262, 344, 82 E.R. 1070, 1094, 1147, *sub nom.* Sir Ralph Bovy's Case, 1 Ventris 193, 211, 217, 86 E.R. 131, 142 146, *sub nom.* Jemot v. Cooly, T. Raymond 135, 158, 83 E.R. 73, 84, 1 Levinz 170, 83 E.R. 353, 1 Keble 784, 915, 83 E.R. 1241, 1318, 2 Keble 20, 184, 270, 295, 84 E.R. 13, 115, 168, 184, *sub nom.* Jemott v. Cowley, 1 Williams Saunders 112, 85 E.R. 122, *sub nom.* Cage v. Bovey, Equity Cases Exch. 55; Boeve v. Skipwith (Ch. 1678–1679), 2 Chancery Reports 142, 21 E.R. 640.]

424

Mayor of London v. Slaughter

(Ch. 1671)

The question in this case was whether someone who is not a citizen of London can be required to give security for a London orphan's portion in the London Mayor's Court.

1 Chancery Cases 203, 22 E.R. 762

27 May [1671]. The Mayor and Aldermen of London and Byfield, an infant, against Slaughter, the executor of the plaintiff's father.

The bill was to bring in one that lived out of the jurisdiction of London to come and give security to the City for the orphan's portion, according to the custom of the City.

The defendant, by his answer, offers to do as this court should direct, but being no freeman, he would not be subject to the City orders.

The Recorder [*John Howell*]: This court used to assist the City in such like cases, and, on petition, used to grant subpoenas to persons to appear before the Mayor in his Court. And he cited a precedent 28 February, 3 Jac., Fish and Cole's Case, of a subpoena out of the Subpoena Office.

Maynard, for the defendant: This custom concerns the country as well as the City, and it must be tried by a verdict. And it is inconvenient for country gentlemen to be put to give security to the Orphans Court by recognizance.

The Lord Keeper [BRIDGEMAN] decreed the plaintiffs to try the custom.

[Other reports of this case: 1 Eq. Cas. Abr. 137, 21 E.R. 941.]

425

Lloyd v. Lord Powys

(Ch. 1671)

Where a litigant dies, any court costs payable to him are lost.

Dickens 16, 21 E.R. 172

19 June 1671.

The plaintiff brought his bill against the defendant's father for land, and revived it against the defendant as heir. And, afterwards, the bill was dismissed with costs.

The question was whether the defendant should have the costs expended by his father before the revivor.

And it was ruled he could not, for they died with the person.

Nelson 147, 21 E.R. 812

The plaintiff exhibited a bill against the father of the now defendant, and revived it against the defendant, as his son and heir, which was afterwards dismissed with costs.

And the question was whether the defendant should have the costs expended by his father in the suit before the proceedings were revived.

And it was ruled that he could not, for they were dead with the person.

3 Chancery Reports 65, 21 E.R. 730

19 June 1671.

The plaintiff had brought a bill against the defendant's father for lands, and revived it against the defendant as heir. And, afterwards, [it was] dismissed it with costs. And the question was whether the defendant should have the costs expended by his father before the revivor. And it was ruled he could not, for they were dead with the person.

426

Wright v. Dorset

(Ch. 1671)

If joint tenants or tenants in common are co-plaintiffs and any of them die pending the suit, there is no need for a bill of revivor.

3 Chancery Reports 66, 21 E.R. 730

24 June 1671.

Lord Keeper [Bridgeman] declared that, if joint tenants or tenants in common exhibited a bill and any of them died pending the suit, there need be no revivor.

[Other reports of this case: 1 Eq. Cas. Abr. 1, 21 E.R. 828.]

427

Bennett v. Ecclesfield

(Ch. 1671)

If a prior encumbrancer be not in possession, a court of equity will not help a purchaser to change the possession.

Lord Nottingham, *Prolegomena*, p. 208

Trinity [term] 23 Car. II.

Yet these rules, that no equity shall be against a purchaser and that [he] who purchases a prior encumbrance without notice must be paid all his money or none, are not to be crudely understood, for, first, if a prior encumbrancer be not in possession, but another man, equity shall not help a purchaser to change the possession, and, even in purchases, the value paid and the means by which he became a purchaser are considerable. *Per* Orlando Bridgeman, Keeper.

428

Cranborne and Delmahoy v. Crisp

(Ch. 1671)

In a suit in equity, all joint debtors must be joined as co-defendants.

Lord Nottingham, *Prolegomena*, p. 303

10 July 1671, Trinity [term] 23 Car. II.

Lady Cranborn and Mr. Delmahoy exhibit a bill against Sir Nicholas Crisp and Sir John Jacob, and suggest that Maxwell was bound for the late farmers to the East India Company and that the farmers gave Maxwell a counter-bond to save him harmless, which the plaintiffs, as executors of Maxwell, endeavored to put in suit at law, but were ordered by the Chancery to bring the bond into court, which being done, the bond, whilst it was in Sir Mondford Brampston's custody, happened to have one of the seals torn off, whereby it became a *non factum* at law. Wherefore now, the plaintiffs prayed in equity to be reimbursed the money paid by Maxwell for the farmers of the Customs to the East India Company with damages.

And, at the hearing, it appeared that all the farmers were jointly and severally bound. And, because all were not parties, the bill was dismissed, for, though at law, a man may sue which obligor he pleases, yet no man shall have relief in equity against equity, and it is against equity to charge one obligor without his companions. And, therefore, if a man lose his obligation and exhibit his bill in equity against one obligor, he shall be dismissed. So, if a deed of rent charge be lost, a bill in equity must name all the terre tenants that they may be equally charged in an Assize.

[Later proceedings in this case: Reports *tempore* Finch 105, 23 E.R. 57, 73 Selden Soc. 58.]
[Reg. Lib. 1673/74 A, f. 640.]

429

Myers v. Banks

(Ch. 1671)

The custom of merchants is to be decided by the common law courts and not by the courts of equity.

Lord Nottingham, *Prolegomena*, p. 270

22 July 1671. Lord Bridgeman, Keeper.

Banks buys a parcel of zealots, *viz.* base money, at Leghorn to the value of 24,413 dollars, and consigns them to Miers at Smyrna, and, at the same time, he draws two bills of exchange for 17,000 dollars upon Miers payable to himself by the value received of Bogos. Miers receives the zealots, but protests the bills, and sends back the bills with the protest to Bogos at Leghorn, where Bogos sues Banks. Banks writes still to Miers to satisfy the bills. But, afterwards, Banks, being forced to, agrees with Bogos, comes over into England, and sues Miers at common law for an account of his zealots.

Miers exhibits a bill in equity to stay proceedings, pretending he had answered the proceeds of the zealots to Bogos.

In the debate of this case, it was said: first, that, by the law merchant, a bill of exchange, after it is protested, may still be paid; second, but that he that pays it must have the bill and the protest sent back again to him or else the letters of the first drawer to pay the bill will not serve; third, for else that which Miers pays to Bogos shall not be a sufficient discharge to Banks against Bogos, nor, by consequence, of Miers against Banks.

Qua propter the question being only *de lege mercatoria* and Miers having had the benefit of the Chancery examination of witnesses, the parties were dismissed to the law without a reservation of equity, because, in this case, [*aequitas*] *sequitur legem*.

Lord Nottingham, *Prolegomena*, p. 199

22 July 1671.

If there be a question between a merchant and his factor touching the due execution of the law merchant, this shall be dismissed to law without a reservation of equity, for it is the true interest of trade that, in all such cases, equity should follow the law.

430

Cook v. Delebere

(Ch. 1671)

A case cannot be removed out of the Mayor of London's Court after a final decree and enrollment.

3 Chancery Reports 66, 21 E.R. 730

24 July 1671.

The plaintiff brought a *certiorari* bill. The defendant pleaded a decree in the Mayor's Court and an enrollment, which was said to be only pronuncial. And it was referred to a Master to certify whether it was before the bill.

431

Stuckley v. Cook

(Ch. 1671)

A debt is fully paid where the debtor gives the creditor cash and a bond for the remainder of the debt.

A release of a debt that has been already paid does not have any operation and cannot be consideration for an agreement to give it, the release.

3 Chancery Reports 70, 21 E.R. 732

24 July 1671.

The bill was that the plaintiff bought of the defendant a close for £1100, and paid part, and secured the rest, and the defendant promised the plaintiff's wife that, if she could procure a release of the money from the plaintiff, he would give her £20, and a release was made, but the defendant denied to pay the £20. And the plaintiff had no witness, and to be relieved was the bill.

The defendant demurred that it was no consideration, for that the debt was released by law by the payment and security.

And [it was] allowed. The Lord Keeper [BRIDGEMAN] declared it a *nudum pactum*, for the release was no more [than] by law and conscience ought to have been done.

Nelson 80, 21 E.R. 795

The plaintiff sets forth that the defendant bought cloth of him to the value of £1100, and paid part of the money, and gave security for the rest and that the defendant promised the plaintiff's wife, if she could procure a release from her husband, that he would give her £20 and that he did give a release, but the defendant denied to pay the £20, and the plaintiff had no witness to prove the promise.

The defendant demurred for want of consideration to the promise, because, by payment of part and securing the rest, the debt was released by law.

But the actual release was no more than what by law and conscience ought to be, and, therefore, it was *nudum pactum* and without any consideration to make any such a promise.

432

Barret v. Dunn

(Ch. 1671)

If the intent of the parties was to have a mortgage, the documents signed pursuant thereto will be construed by a court of equity as a mortgage.

Lord Nottingham, *Prolegomena*, p. 282

Trinity 23 Car. II.

No words of a scrivener nor any invention of counsel can make that which was intended as a mortgage to work as an absolute assurance. And, therefore, if it be said that, on failure of payment, the mortgagor shall be barred of all equity of redemption or that he shall release all demands in law or equity, still, the estate is redeemable, and a subpoena lies.

This contrivance was used to prevent [a redemption of] a mortgage. Dun lent £1000 to Barret, and, for it, took an absolute bargain and sale of lands worth much more money. Then Dun re-demises to Barret, rendering £60 *per annum*, and, by a third indenture, covenants with Barret to sell him the land again and that Barret shall purchase when he pleases for £1300.

[It was] resolved by Lord BRIDGEMAN, Keeper, to be a mortgage for £1000 principal and that the £60 a year was interest and the £1300 in the case of repurchase a mere penalty to be set aside in equity.

433

Throckmorton v. West

(Ch. 1671)

Where a merchant's account books that are out of the jurisdiction of the court have been lost, the account can be settled upon the oath of the accountant.

Lord Nottingham, *Prolegomena*, p. 270

1 August 1671.

Philip West, administrator of the goods of Richard Best not administered by John Win, executor of Richard Best, sues Throckmorton at law for an account as factor of Richard Best in the Canaries. Throckmorton exhibits a bill, because he had accounted with Richard Best in 1653 and he was satisfied there remained but £60 due, and so was John Win, the executor, the books of account concerning an old trade in 1647 and an embargo happening in 1653.

The defendant urged that Richard Best died presently after the account and excepted to it before, and [said there were] no proofs that the books were lost by the embargo, but some probable proof they were extant since.

[It was] ordered on appeal that, if Throckmorton make an oath his books are lost, then his oath shall be allowed as proof to discharge himself, and, if the Master of the Rolls had not directed an account, none should have been.

434

Parker v. Sergeant

(Ch. 1671)

A court of equity can give a decree for one co-defendant against another co-defendant.

Lord Nottingham, *Prolegomena*, p. 295

Regularly, there should be no decree between co-defendants. But, if all the matter be so disclosed in the pleadings that the court sees an easy way to settle the whole interest or account without putting the defendants to new suits, it is usually done. In 1652, a decree was made for Sir Nathaniel Hobart against Bell, who were co-defendants at the suit of Sir John Hobart. So a decree was made by ORLANDO BRIDGEMAN, Keeper, for William Sergeant, a co-defendant with Jane Sergeant, at the suit of Parker in 1671.

[Later proceedings in this case: Reports *tempore* Finch 146, 23 E.R. 80, 73 Selden Soc. 48, 87, 241, 79 Selden Soc. 622.]
[Reg. Lib. 1673/74 B, f. 565, 1674/75 B, f. 118.]

435

Jacob's Executors v. Crisp's Executors

(Ch. 1671)

A co-obligor defendant cannot be required to make discovery in a suit for contribution where there could be no contribution received against the plaintiff.

Lord Nottingham, *Prolegomena*, p. 304

Michaelmas [term] 23 Car. II.

The executors of Sir John Jacob, one of the late farmers, exhibit a bill against the heir and the executors of Sir Nicholas Crisp, suggesting that their testators were jointly bound together with the rest of the farmers to A., B., C. in several bonds for money taken up for the service of his late Majesty and that the money given to the farmers by his now Majesty, though £200,000, will not be sufficient to discharge all, so that there must be contribution amongst themselves, and they pray a discovery of assets in order thereto.

The defendants answer that the father and the testator of the plaintiffs received more of the £200,000 than the testator of the defendants and particularly £10,000, which the testator of the defendants should have received without an account, was applied to pay debts wherein the father of the plaintiffs was bound. And, moreover, the plaintiffs in this cause have sworn in another cause at the suit of creditors that they have no assets of the said Sir John Jacob, so that the defendants are liable to be sued without any hopes of contribution from the plaintiff, and, therefore, they conceive they ought not by any discovery in their answer to subject themselves to contribution to him from whom they can receive none.

And, on exceptions taken to the answer, this was allowed by Bridgeman, Keeper.

436

Love v. Oxenden

(Ch. 1671)

A factor or supercargo may charge the principal for wares bought, but not beyond the value of the cargo.

Lord Nottingham, *Prolegomena*, p. 271

Michaelmas [term] 23 Car. II.

Alderman Love[1] and divers others send to the Indies the ship *King Ferdinando* with a stock of £13,300, and they make Christopher Oxendon factor and supercargo. The ship went first to China, as she was appointed, and there made a losing voyage, so that the stock was reduced to £7000 by oppression there. With this stock, the ship comes to Surat, where the President, Sir George Oxendon,[2] had by order from hence provided several goods for re-lading of her, which Christopher buys on the account of the adventurers to the value of several thousand pounds.

[It was] decreed by the EARL OF CLARENDON and affirmed on the review by ORLANDO BRIDGEMAN, Keeper: first, that the factor or supercargo may by his general power charge the principal for wares bought; second, he cannot charge them beyond the value of the cargo; third, though the cargo in the Indies be not of the value of the debt contracted by the factor there, yet, if the product of the goods sent home be sufficient to answer it, the debt must be paid by them.

[Related cases: Smith v. Oxenden (Ch. 1663), see above, Case No. 113.]

437

Knight v. Bee

(Ch. 1671)

The question in this case was whether an administrator of a decedent's estate who was appointed by a bishop, rather than by an archbishop, can collect a debt to the estate where the estate has assets in another diocese.

3 Chancery Reports 71, 21 E.R. 732

12 October 1671.

The plaintiff, as executor or administrator, out of an inferior diocese, came to be relieved for a debt. The defendant pleaded that there was *bona notabilia*, so that the plaintiff could give no discharge and [be] allowed *ex parte*.

But My Lord Keeper [BRIDGEMAN] declared he was not satisfied of the law. But, there being nobody for the plaintiff, he would not defend it.

And the second of November following, it was re-heard before Judge ARCHER, who again allowed it.

---

[1] T. Dickie and A. McConnell, 'Love, William (c. 1620–1689)', *Oxford Dictionary of National Biography*, vol. 34, pp. 505–506.

[2] I. B. Watson, 'Oxenden, Sir George, (1620–1669)', *Oxford Dictionary of National Biography*, vol. 42, pp. 281–282.

438

Purefoy v. Jones

(Ch. 1671)

A court of equity will not order quiet possession of an office in another court of law.

3 Chancery Reports 71, 21 E.R. 732

16 October 1671.

Lord Keeper [BRIDGEMAN] declared he would grant no injunction to quiet possession of an office in another court.

439

Scarborough v. Wilson

(Ch. 1671)

Where a judgment debtor becomes a bankrupt, any proceedings before a Master in Chancery should cease.

In equity, creditors of a common debtor are paid pro rata, *and not by priority.*

Lord Nottingham, *Prolegomena*, p. 333

17 October, 23 Car. II.

A bill was exhibited to account and decree *quod computet.* The defendant is declared a bankrupt. The Master proceeds to take an account and ascertain the sum due to the plaintiff.

[It was] resolved: first, that being declared a bankrupt between the decree *quod computet* and the final report and judgment on this discharges all further [proceeding] of the Master, for, now, the creditors or commissioners ought to be parties to the account; else, the bankrupt, by collusion, may encumber the creditors; second, but it was admitted *per curiam* that a debt ascertained in equity ought to be satisfied in proportion.

440

Hackins v. Blackwell

(Ch. 1671)

Where a defendant has on his side both equity and common law, the court of equity will dismiss the case to the common law court, because, where the equities are equal, equity follows the law.

Lord Nottingham, *Prolegomena*, p. 210

30 October, 23 Car. II.

The defendant pleads himself a purchaser of the father of the plaintiff for a term of 1000 years without notice of any equity in the plaintiff. And, at the hearing, it appeared the defendant had proved himself a purchaser and the plaintiff had not proved notice.

But yet it was insisted on by the plaintiff that the defendant was liable to the plaintiff's equity, notwithstanding his purchase without notice, for the legal estate in the term remained in J.S. in trust for the plaintiff as heir male of his father by virtue of a marriage settlement and in consideration of his mother's portion. *Unde sequitur* that, although [there is] no relief in equity against the purchaser of the legal estate, yet the purchaser of a mere equity shall not be permitted to enjoy against a prior equity, for, as a prior title prevails in law, so prior equity prevails in equity.

This was denied on the other side, for Chancery impeaches no purchaser, whether of a legal or an equitable title. But, if the plaintiff, who has a prior equity, can obtain a legal assignment, he shall avoid a junior purchaser in law, not in equity.

But, afterwards, it appeared that the defendant had the legal estate too. So the plaintiff was dismissed.

441

Foster v. Clapham

(Ch. 1671)

Where the tenants of a manor have gotten a judicial decree settling their fines to the lord of the manor and then the manor is purchased for an abated price that takes into account that decree, the purchaser is estopped to later demand a higher fine from the tenants.

Lord Nottingham, *Prolegomena*, p. 323

4 November 1671, Foster v. Sir Charles Clapham.

A decree was made that the tenants of the manor of Westmoreland should hold their estates on a fine certain, which decree does not bind the heir in tail, who comes in after the lord of the manor. The heir in tail sells to the purchaser, and abates his price for this decree.

[It was] resolved that, now, the purchaser shall be bound, though the land was not, because he takes the land with the allowance for the charge. The like law is *mutatis mutandis* in cases of any other defective encumbrance.

442

Lord Mohun v. Lady Mohun

(Ch. 1671)

The issue in this case was when a jointure will bar dower rights.
A void conditional devise may create a trust.

Lord Nottingham, *Prolegomena*, p. 323

4 November 1671.

[It was] resolved: first, a jointure before marriage without notice of the wife or her friends bars dower; second, a jointure during widowhood after marriage bars dower if it be accepted; third, if a jointure before marriage be only 40s. *per annum*, yet it bars dower if there be notice to and consent of her friends; fourth, the heir shall be relieved in equity against dower on a suggestion that the mother had the writing of the jointure before marriage, for, though detainer of deeds be a good plea to bar dower, yet the plea admits a title of dower, to which the heir in this case shall not be compelled. Therefore, a perpetual injunction was awarded.

Lord Nottingham, *Prolegomena*, p. 242

4 November 1671.

If land be devised to the heir on condition to pay money to the daughters, this condition, though void in law as a condition because it descends on the heir, yet shall make a trust by implication of law.

443

Gale v. Bence

(Ch. 1671)

The custom of merchants is a valid defense to a bill for an account.

Lord Nottingham, *Prolegomena*, p. 271

10 November 1671, Michaelmas [term] 23 Car. II.

Gale exhibits a bill against Bence, and prays an account of the fourteenth part of the cargo of a ship to which he was entitled and which he assigned to the plaintiff in satisfaction of a debt. And he charges Bence and others with the receipt of the whole profits.

The defendants plead the custom of merchants that, if any subscribe to go a fourteenth part or any other part of a cargo and do not pay in their money accordingly, then, the share of him so failing ceases, and goes to such of the partners as shall furnish the same. And [the defendants] aver Monk did not pay his share, but the others did etc.

And this plea was allowed, and the plaintiff was left to reply and take issue on the custom or the payment.

444

Coke v. Turner

(Ch. 1671)

In this case, the pecuniary legacy in issue was given in addition to the specific legacy.

Lord Nottingham, *Prolegomena*, p. 334

11 November 1671, Bridgeman, Keeper, assisted by Hale and Vaughan, chief justices.

'I give to Mrs. Ann Brown a box and what is therein contain as by invoice etc., but, if the particulars shall be disposed of, then, the true proceeds thereof to be paid her with £400 more.'

[It was] ruled the £400 more is a distinct legacy and not a conditional one or in the nature of a penalty if the box were sold, but the box and the value make but one alternative legacy with an addition of £400 more and the word 'but', in this case, shall be taken for 'or', for no reason can be given why £400 should be added to the value of the box and not to the box itself in specie, since the box and the value are equivalent. And the rule is *verba in extremo posita referuntur ad omnia antecedentia.*

445

Underhill v. Jones

(Ch. 1671)

Where a landlord enters for non-payment of the rent, the tenant can redeem the land in a court of equity, but the tenant will not get a reduction of the arrears of the rent due in the amount of the rent that was received by the landlord during his occupancy.

Lord Nottingham, *Prolegomena*, p. 325

23 Car. II, *per curiam.*

A lord enters for non-payment of rent by virtue of a condition to re-enter, and retains.

[It was] resolved: first, [there is] no remedy for the growing rent at law; second, the lessee shall not redeem without allowing for the growing rents in equity.

446

Digby v. Cornwallis

(Ch. 1671–1672)

A beneficiary of a trust of a personal estate can sue the trustees for an account and an execution of the terms of the trust in a court of equity and also sue in the ecclesiastical court for the administrator to produce an inventory of the assets of the estate.

3 Chancery Reports 72, 21 E.R. 732

4 December 1671.

A *cestui que trust* of a personal estate may sue in Chancery to have an account against the executor or administrator, and, at the same time, sue in the Prerogative Court to enforce the executor or administrator to bring in an inventory.

Lord Nottingham, *Prolegomena*, p. 266

1 July 1672.

Sir Kenelm Digby[1] conveys to Hollis and Holman in trust for Charles Cornwallis until his debts and engagements be satisfied, remainder to John Digby in tail, remainder to several others in tail, remainder to the right heirs of John Digby. And there was an express clause in the deed to forbid John Digby to receive the profits, but requiring [the trustees or either of] them to receive and pay.

[It was] resolved that John Digby, having the reversion in the fee and no son, might compel the trustees to execute an estate according to the deed notwithstanding the clause of prohibition and that the trustees were compellable to join in a sale for the payment of debts, notwithstanding the trust for the preservation of contingent remainders, and should be indemnified by the decree of this court against any afterborn issue, because, otherwise, debts would swallow up the whole, and, besides, some of the present remaindermen did consent.

447

Tredcroft v. White

(Ch. 1671)

Upon an account made by a steward, gratuities paid will be allowed on the oral evidence of the steward that he paid them.

3 Chancery Reports 72, 21 E.R. 732

Michaelmas [term] and Hilary [term] 1671.

---

[1] M. Foster, 'Sir Kenelm Digby (1603–1665)', *Oxford Dictionary of National Biography*, vol. 16, pp. 152–158.

[It was] ruled that, for gratuities given by a steward, as in the Marquess of Winchester and Withers's Case, no proof is to be of payment, but it is allowed upon the party's examination that he gave them, and he not to be examined to the particulars nor to whom given. *Quaere.*

And also in this case, part of the decretal order (as it was signed and enrolled) was left out of the entering book in the Register's Office, which directed an allowance to the defendant. And, in respect of the said omission in the order, the Master made no such allowance, but, upon exceptions to the report, the allowance was made.

[Later reports of this case: Reports *tempore* Finch 36, 23 E.R. 20.]

448

Barthrop v. West

(Ch. 1671–1672)

An equity of redemption is assets of a decedent's estate that can be reached by the decedent's creditors.

A voluntary deed of trust can be set aside upon the suit of a creditor.

2 Chancery Reports 62, 21 E.R. 616

The plaintiff's suit is to have the benefit and equity of redemption of leases mortgaged and other trust estates made liable for the payment of his debt, being on a judgment for £2000, and to have a voluntary deed of trust set aside, as against the plaintiff.

This court decreed the plaintiff to have the equity of redemption to be liable and as assets to satisfy his said debt of £2000, and set aside the said voluntary deed of trust, and all trust estate and surplus thereof after preceding debts paid to be assets in equity for the payment of the plaintiff.

[Reg. Lib. 23 Car. II, f. 744.]

449

Hooker v. Arthur

(Ch. 1671–1672)

A court of equity will not take jurisdiction over the amount of damages due upon a breach of contract.

2 Chancery Reports 62, 21 E.R. 616

The defendant having recovered damages for breach of a covenant in a lease at law but the plaintiff insists that there is not so much damages due as the defendant has sworn in his answer, therefore, the plaintiff hopes this court will reimburse him what is overpaid to the defendant.

This court declared they would not try nor ascertain the damages in this court, but ordered the parties to go to law on the covenant.

[Reg. Lib. 23 Car. II, f. 523.]

450

Lady Kemp v. Kemp

(Ch. 1671–1672)

In this case, a marriage settlement was performed by a devise to the widow, and she was not entitled to receive both.

2 Chancery Reports 63, 21 E.R. 617

This is on a case stated, *viz.* that, upon articles of agreement between Sir Robert Kemp and Thomas Steward, the plaintiff's father, upon the marriage of Sir Robert with the plaintiff, it was agreed a £500 marriage portion should be paid unto Sir Robert or his executors, and, in consideration thereof, the said Sir Robert should settle a jointure of £200 *per annum* on the plaintiff, his wife, and, if the said Sir Robert should die before such jointure be settled, then, he was to have lands chargeable with the plaintiff's dower, which should fully recompense the £200. And Sir Robert, by his last will, devised to the plaintiff a rent charge of £200 for her life to be issued out of the manor of Spenishall and lands thereto belonging and of certain farms called Linilts and Mortimore and Ravels and the Frywoods in full satisfaction of the said articles and all dower claimable by the plaintiff. And he also devised the said farms unto the defendant Mary, his grandchild, to have and to hold immediately after the death of the plaintiff, his wife. And, by a subsequent clause in the will, he devised all the lands (not therein before disposed of) to the defendant Thomas Kemp, the father, for life, remainder to Thomas, his son, for life, with a remainder over. And also he gave the plaintiff his coach, horses, plate, and jewels, etc. and one-third part of his clear personal estate. And the plaintiff conceived that she ought by the will to have both the rent charge and the farms for her life by the aforesaid devise, *viz.* where the same are devised to the defendant Mary to have and to hold after the plaintiff's death. So to have the same by the said implicit devise without extinguishment of the said rent charge is the plaintiff's suit.

This court declared they saw no cause to decree both the rent charge of £200 *per annum* and the farms aforesaid to the plaintiff, but the rent charge of £200 *per annum* to the plaintiff only.

451

Boucher v. Anthram

(Ch. 1671)

In this case, the contingent remainder in issue was a perpetuity and was void.

Pollexfen 37, 86 E.R. 504

14 November, 23 Car. II.

Alice Lowman [was] possessed of a personal estate, sufficient to pay all her debts and legacies, which, after her death, came to the hands of her executors by her last will, whereby also she gave £160 to the plaintiff Katherine for her to have the use of it during her life and her children to have it after her decease, but, if Katharine should die, having no child surviving her, the testatrix willed that the £160 should be for the sole benefit of the defendant's wife and her children. And she made the defendant her executor, and died, who proved the will.

The question [was] whether the clause in the will which directs that, for want of issue of Katherine, the £160 shall after her death go for the benefit of the defendant's wife and her children creates any right in them to the £160 on that contingency.

The Lord Keeper [Bridgeman] declared it to be a void limitation and that the defendant's wife and children ought to have no benefit by it. And he decreed the defendant, on security to save him harmless against the children of the plaintiff Katharine, to pay the £160 to the plaintiffs.

2 Chancery Reports 65, 21 E.R. 617

The bill is that Alice Lowman, the plaintiff Katherine's late mother, did in December 1669, by a will, give and dispose unto the plaintiff Katherine a legacy of £160, and she made the plaintiff, who married another of the daughters, executor.

The defendant insists that the testatrix made her will in these words, *viz.*:

> Item, I give unto my daughter, Katherine Boucher, the sum of £160 for her to have the use of it during her life, and her child or children to have it after her decease, but, if she happens to die, leaving no child surviving her, I will that the said £160 shall be to and for the sole benefit and use of my daughter, Elizabeth Antram, and her children.

Which Elizabeth is the defendant's wife, and the defendant is willing to pay the said £160 to the plaintiffs or either of them, he being secured against the title and claim of the surviving child or children of the plaintiff Katherine. And, if she should die leaving no child or children behind her, then against the title of the said Elizabeth and her children.

This court decreed the defendant to pay unto the plaintiff £160 with full interest. But, as to the clause in the will which directs that, for want of issue by the plaintiff Katherine, the said £160 after her decease shall be to and for the benefit and behoof of the defendant's wife and her children, His Lordship [BRIDGEMAN] declared it, being a personalty, is in the nature of a perpetuity and so a void devise, and, therefore, the defendant nor his wife and children ought to have any benefit thereby, but be debarred from the same, and that the said £160 ought to be absolutely vested in and come unto the child or children of the plaintiff Katherine. And he decreed the same accordingly.

[Reg. Lib. 23 Car. II, f. 97.]

452

Barnes v. Gladman

(Ch. 1671)

A court of equity does not strictly regard form where the defect of form will be cured by the judgment.

2 Levinz 19, 83 E.R. 433

[In an action of] debt upon an obligation, conditioned to perform covenants in an indenture of apprenticeship, the defendant pleads performance. The plaintiff replies, and assigns a breach *et hoc etc. unde petit judicium et damna sua sibi adjudicari*. The defendant demurs *quia minus rite conclusit*, for he ought to have said *petit judicium et debitum et damna sua sibi adjudicari*. And so are all the precedents in Coke and Rastell, *Entries*, except two in Coke's *Entries*, and those were after verdict. But this being here specially demurred upon, it was much insisted to be ill for this cause.

But by BRIDGEMAN, Lord Keeper, although it be form, yet it is but unnecessary form, for, by the praying of judgment, all is included, because, when the court gives judgment, of consequence, they give judgment for the debt and damages.

453

Washborn v. Downs

(Ch. 1671)

A fine by a beneficiary of a trust will bar the estate, but not the remainder over to another person.

The question in this case was whether, by a recovery by a beneficiary of a trust, anything can be barred.

1 Chancery Cases 213, 22 E.R. 767

5 December [1671].

The question was whether a recovery by the *cestui que trust* should bar as in a case of an estate at law.

The court held clearly that a fine of a *cestui que trust* will bar the estate, but not the remainder over to another, because a fine will pass or extinguish all right or title which the cognizors have in the land. But it was doubted whether, by a recovery of a *cestui que trust*, anything can be barred, for that, if a tenant in tail at law suffer a recovery, legal exceptions may be taken to it, but, if a recovery may be in equity, all those exceptions are taken away. And, as to the case of Goodrich and Brown, fol. 49,[1] it was said that was without a precedent and the plaintiff in that case did not rely on his decree, but the matter was afterwards compromised. And it was a question in Bathurst's and Emason's Case, and that case was agreed.

The court, in the principal case, took time to advise, and advised the parties to agree.

And, in the debate of this case, it was said that a perpetuity is where if all that have an interest join and yet cannot bar or pass the estate. But, if, by the concurrence of all having the estate tail, it may be barred, it is no perpetuity.

Lord Nottingham, *Prolegomena*, p. 250

In the case of Washborn and Downs, the next point debated was whether a common recovery suffered by a *cestui que trust* in tail be a good bar of an estate tail of trust and of the remainders of the trust.

I [*Finch*] urged it was not, because no *praecipe* did lie of a trust, nor no recompense in value come to it and that a trust was rather a conditional fee than an entail within Westminster II, *utcunque* it could only bind a *cestui que trust* for life, and not the issue, nor the fee. And I compared it to the case of a use at common law before 27 Hen. VIII and after 1 Ric. III,[2] in which case, it had been adjudged that a recovery by a *cestui que use* in tail does not bind the feoffees. 19 Hen. VIII, 13; Brooke, *Feoffment al Uses*, 2.[3] Note *fere per omnes justiciarios et per Fitzherbert, et per optimam opinionem*. And in Graisley's Case of Staffordshire in the time of Henry VIII, he being a *cestui que use* in tail by the advice of Fitzherbert, Serjeant, suffered a recovery; and yet his brother recovered the land in Chancery. Brooke, *Feoffment al Uses*, 48 and 56. Wherefore, if a common recovery did not bar a use

[1] *Goodrick v. Brown* (Ch. 1664), see above, Case No. 151

[2] Stat. 13 Edw. I, Westminster II, c. 1 (*SR*, I, 71–72); Stat. 27 Hen. VIII, c. 10 (*SR*, III, 539–542); Stat. 1 Ric. III, c. 1 (*SR*, II, 477–478).

[3] YB Trin. 19 Hen. VIII, f. 13, pl. 11, Brooke, Abr., *Feffements al uses*, pl. 2 (1527).

with the help of 1 Ric. III, *a fortiori* it would not bar a trust without the help of a statute.

Lord Bridgeman, Keeper, took time to advise with the judges. But, for the present, he inclined against me [Heneage Finch], because cases in equity are to be considered with equity and the times are necessary to be distinguished.

Before 1 Ric. III, trusts and uses were different from what they are now. Time has made a fine to bar a trust. Yet it was once doubted whether it barred a use, for, though Fitzherbert affirmed it [in] 27 Hen. VIII, yet, in Brooke, *Feoffment al Uses*, 7, *non videtur lex*. Time has made a parol declaration of a use void, which was good, and time has made devises of trusts as well as uses good. An entail was sacred before 4 Hen. VII.[1] It is not so now. In Littleton's time, we see how uses were grown frequent. It began to be an opinion that a *cestui que use* might be a juror, which could hardly be maintained in strictness of law. And, therefore, since now trusts are as common as uses, it may be as reasonable to shape them to the common law and to allow a recovery to bar in equity, the rather because the precedent of Brown and Goodricke, in the time of Lord Clarendon, is expressly in point, and because a recovery is now grown a common conveyance and is not to be examined by nice rules, and, especially, because it can be no inconvenience to the subject to allow a recovery to bar a trust. But it may be many ways inconvenient to disallow it, for, if the feoffees do refuse to execute an estate without coercion of the Chancery and therein use all delays by combination with them in the remainders, no *cestui que trust* in tail shall ever dispose of his estate.

Then I [*Finch*] proposed another point. Admitting a recovery by a *cestui que trust* in tail should bar a trust, yet it ought not to bar the trust any otherwise than it would have barred it if the *cestui que trust* in tail had been a tenant in tail in possession. And yet here no recovery by an act executed could have barred the remainders, because Alice, who was tenant for life in jointure, was the true tenant to the *praecipe*. Else, it will be found a much more safe and easy way to bar the entail of a trust than of land.

And, in this point, Lord Bridgeman inclined to me. *Sed adjornatur super totam materiam.*

Lord Nottingham, *Prolegomena*, p. 268

5 December 1671.

Francis Downes, the uncle, and Francis Downes, the nephew, were joint purchasers of the manor of Pitchley in the County of Northampton. And this was in trust for the uncle, who paid the whole purchase money. Afterwards, *viz.* August 15 Car. I [1639], the uncle and nephew join in a deed, wherein it is declared that the nephew shall stand seised of all and singular the lands upon these

[1] Stat. 4 Hen. VII, c. 24 (*SR*, II, 547–548).

trusts, *viz.* in trust for himself for life, the remainder of part to his wife for a jointure, remainder to his son in tail, remainder to his nephew in tail etc.

One question was whether this was a good declaration of trust for the whole or only for a moiety in regard it was not said that the uncle and nephew shall stand seised upon these trusts, but only the nephew, who had but a moiety.

But it was urged by me [*Finch*] that this declaration was good for all: first, because the uncle, who joined in this declaration of trust, was a *cestui que trust* of the whole, and, when he says his nephew shall stand trusted etc., this binds not only the present moiety, but the future possibility of surviving, and, in equity, has put the whole land in another plight; second, the intent was so, for, when the trust comes to be distributed, there, the lands are named, and Pitchley, Isham, etc. are limited to [the wife] for a jointure, but it were absurd to suppose that the jointure did mean but a moiety of what was expressed; third, the deed provides great portions for the daughters, and it were absurd to exempt a moiety from the charge when the rest was covered with a jointure; fourth, the nephew was appointed to execute legal estates; fifth, the deed is with a power of revocation. So, if the nephew die first, [there is a] danger of charging the uncle with more [of the] trust than he has a mind to; if the uncle die first, [there is] no reason to suppose the uncle's moiety is to be left undisposed and a trust to descend, but, rather than this, a moiety is bound in the hands of the survivor by the trusts already declared.

But Lord BRIDGEMAN, Keeper, doubted. Therefore, [it was] adjourned.

Sed tandem finiit per compositionem, and my client Downes had £2000.

454

Atkyns v. Montagu

(Ch. 1671)

The patronage of newly created charitable hospital can be made by a royal charter.

A mastership of a charitable hospital cannot be granted in reversion.

A master of a charitable hospital has a fee simple during his incumbency.

1 Chancery Cases 214, 22 E.R. 768

Sir Robert Atkyns against George Montagu.

There was a trial at bar touching the title of the Master of the Hospital of St. Katharine, which the plaintiff claimed by a grant from the Queen Consort that now is, and the defendant held and enjoyed by two grants, one from Henrietta Maria, the Queen Dowager, another from His Majesty that now is before his marriage.

Upon the evidence, divers points arose.

First, the plaintiff's title was founded upon the charter of Queen Eleanor, Dowager of Henry III (which fee is in Dugdale[1]), who added to the endowment of this Hospital the most part of the possessions, *reservatis nobis et reginis Angliae nobis succedentibus plenam potestatem providendi magistrum etc. volumus etiam quod omnes reginae nobis succedentes jus patronatus habeant etc.*, which was confirmed by the subsequent charters of Edward II, and Edward III.

Second, against the foundation of this title, the defendant's counsel objected that a limitation of the patronage *reginis succedentibus* by the charter is void, for such a desultory kind of inheritance cannot be limited but by an act of Parliament, just as the Duchy of Cornwall was by an act of Parliament, in 11 Edw. III, limited to the king's eldest son for the time being.

But HALE, Chief Justice, and whole court resolved to the contrary, for they took a difference between an advowson *in esse* and the patronage of a hospital newly created. For the land or an advowson, it is true no desultory kind of inheritance can be limited without an act of Parliament, because, then, he who had a right could not always know against whom to bring his action. But, of the patronage of an hospital newly founded, there can be no precedent right, and, therefore, at the very first institution, it may be limited as the king pleases, like the case of a rent *de novo*.

Though the several patents were produced on each side, wherein the Master of the Hospital had been granted in reversion, yet it was resolved by HALE and the whole court that all such grants were void, for the Master of that Hospital, when he is seised in fee in the right of the Hospital and of an estate in fee simple, there can be no reversion to grant. Therefore, this case is not to be compared to the grant of an office in reversion, but it is more like the case of a prebendary or a donative, which cannot be granted in reversion.

Third, then, it was objected by the plaintiff that the defendant's grant from the Queen Dowager was void, because there was a former grant which the Queen Dowager made to one Mr. H. Montagu, who was alive at the time of the grant to the defendant. The defendant showed that the grant to H. Montagu was void, because it was *habendum post mortem* Sir Julius Caesar, and so it was a grant in reversion, which was held a clear answer.

Fourth, it was resolved that, in a patent which grants the mastership of a hospital, the words are not to be so precisely examined as in a patent of land or other office, for, in this case, it is sufficient if there be words of nomination only, because the patentee is not in by the patent alone, but by the original constitution upon the foundation.

Fifth, it was said by HALE that, though, here, the question be touching the interest of a queen dowager in the patronage when there is no queen consort, yet

[1] W. Dugdale, *Monasticon Anglicanum* (1655).

it seemed to him that, if there be a queen dowager and queen consort both at the time of the voidance of the Hospital, the queen dowager shall present.

Sixth, if the dowager's grant be good when there is a queen consort, it is much more so when there is none. And, if there could yet remain a scruple, the king's grant and confirmation clears it, for, if there be no consort nor dowager, doubtless, the king's presentation is good. And this alone is sufficient to support the defendant's title.

The plaintiff replied that the king's presentation in such case was good only by way of a provisional supply until a consort come and then was to cease.

Which all the court denied, for the Master, by his incumbency, gains a fee simple, which cannot be determined by the determination of the plaintiff's interest, as in the case of the Duchy of Cornwall; if the king let the land, the lease is void when the Prince is born. But, if he present to an advowson, the clerk continues.

Wherefore, the plaintiff, seeing the opinion of the court against him, became nonsuited.

2 Keble 808, 84 E.R. 510

In [an action of] ejectment on a lease of Sir Robert Atkins, Master of Saint Katherine's, by a grant of the Queen Katherine the 27th of May 1671, to which the defendant pleaded a grant of the mastership to him in January 1660 by Queen Mary, then dowager, and a grant and confirmation by King Charles II in April 1661 before his marriage with the Queen Katherine. And he traverses *absque hoc* that the plaintiff's lessor is Master. And issue [is taken] thereon.

And, in evidence, it was agreed that this is a corps and an employment that cannot be granted in reversion, being a corporation.

Second, the foundation was at least by the endowment by Eleanor, widow of Edward I, *reservantes nobis et reginis Angliae nobis succedentibus totum jus patronatus*, and, *per curiam*, on 9 Edw. IV, The Chapter of Lincoln's Case; and 14 Edw. IV; and 8 Co. [*blank*], the Case of The Duchy of Cornwall,[1] there may be such a desultory inheritance on the first foundation, albeit not of an advowson in being or of lands or the like.

Third, it was agreed by the court that such a presentation by the king, be it but by a provision, as of a bishopric or of right, yet his incumbent is in for life. Da. 46, Trinity, 2 Jac., this very question was in the Common Bench adjudged between Turner and Gregg, on Fleming's title, which failed only because he could not fully derive it from the crown.

And, afterwards, the plaintiff was nonsuited on the full evidence, hearing the court's opinion.

[1] YB Trin. & Mich. 9 Edw. III, f. 18, pl. 3, and f. 33, pl. 33 (1335); *The Prince's Case* (1606), 8 Coke Rep. 1, 77 E.R. 481.

1 Ventris 149, 86 E.R. 102

The case, as it appeared upon the evidence of a trial at the bar in [an action of] ejectment for part of the lands of the Hospital between the lessee of Sir Robert Atkyns, the queen's solicitor, and George Montagu, Esq., was this.

Eleanor, queen dowager of Henry III, in the year 1273, founded (or at least amply endowed) this Hospital, reserving to herself during her life *et reginis Angliae nobis succedentibus* the nomination of the Master to this Hospital, which was incorporated, and the grants to it were confirmed by the king's letters patents.

In the year 1660, Henrietta Maria, queen mother, granted the mastership of this Hospital to H. Montagu for life. And the king, in the same year, reciting his mother's grant and that the right of it belonged unto her, confirmed it by his letters patents. And he did further by the same letters patents grant unto the said Henrietta Maria the said mastership.

Afterwards, the king married Katherine, the now queen consort. And she granted the mastership to Sir Robert Atkyns for his life.

It was urged on the part of the plaintiff that the right of appointing the Master was only in the queen consort, for Queen Eleanor reserved it to herself and her successors queens of England and a queen of England is not a queen dowager, but a queen consort. And, though land cannot be limited to descend in such manner without an act of Parliament, as is resolved in The Prince's Case in 8 Co.,[1] yet such a desultory inheritance (as this was called) may be created of a thing *de novo*, as a rent may be granted and appointed to cease during the minority of the heir or, upon the first foundation of a church, the patronage may be reserved to A. and, if he presents not within four months, then to B. So, in the book of Edw. III,[2] it was limited that the chapter should present while the deanery was vacant. And to prove that this clause had been construed only to intend the queen consort, a record was shown of a case between Luttishall and Basse, in 4 Edw. III, where Luttishall exhibited a petition to the king, which was entitled 'To our lord the king and his council', which petition was sent into the King's Bench under the Great Seal, in which Luttishall sets forth that Queen Isabel, mother to Edward III, had granted him the mastership of the Hospital for his life and that he was disturbed by Basse. And process was issued out against Basse, who appeared and pleaded a grant from Queen Philippa, wife to Edward III, and a writ came from the king, reciting that the nomination of the Master did belong to Queen Isabel. And so three writs more came after to the same purpose, and expressing that the matter was delayed *ad inestimabile damnum consortis nostrae*. And, in that record, Isabel, though living, is styled *nuper regina*, and Luttishall, that claimed under her, was barred.

---

[1] *The Prince's Case* (1606), 8 Coke Rep. 1, 77 E.R. 481.

[2] YB Trin. & Mich. 9 Edw. III, f. 18, pl. 3, and f. 33, pl. 33 (1335).

On the other side, divers grants were produced during the time that there were no queens by the king, and, sometimes, by a queen dowager during the time that there was a queen consort.

And these points following were agreed by all the court:

First, that an inheritance might be limited in this manner in a thing *de novo*;

Secondly, that this reservation, being to Queen Eleanor and her successors queens of England, did not exclude queens dowager, and extend only to queens consort, for, first, a queen dowager is a queen of England, and (as HALE said) has the prerogative to sue in the Exchequer; second, when once she is so qualified as to have the estate vest in her, it shall continue, though she does not remain in the same capacity, as, where one has a power to limit an estate to his wife, it may very well continue to her after the coverture;

Thirdly, it was much observed and relied upon that Queen Eleanor was an only daughter at the time of the foundation and so it could never be intended to exclude such queens as should succeed her in that capacity;

Fourthly, during such time that there should be no queen, it was held that the king was to constitute the Master, for he is heir to Queen Eleanor. And whereas it was urged for the plaintiff that the king had not a power to dispose of the place, but only by way of provision until such time as a queen should be, so as to commit the care of the power to one, but not the interest of the mastership.

It was clearly resolved that the king might grant it and that the estate of the grantee should continue, though the king's interest devolved upon the succeeding queen. And it was resembled to the Case of the Duchy of Cornwall; if the king, while there is no prince of Wales, makes a lease of lands belonging to that duchy, this shall determine upon the birth of that prince, but, if he presents to a church, the incumbent shall not be removed, as in the case where the king presents to a church by reason of the temporalities of a bishopric, the bishop after[wards] created shall not remove the clerk.

And the Chief Justice said in this case that the interest of the mastership did not properly pass from the king, so as it should have a dependence upon the king's estate, for the king does but nominate, and the Master is entitled as from the first foundation and constitution.

It was further agreed that a thing of this nature could not be granted in reversion, for it is not like an office, but rather as a prebendary or incumbency of a church and the Master, as head of the corporation, with his brethren, has the whole estate in him.

As to the record in 4 Edw. III, it was said and so shown out of Speed's *Chronicles*, produced in court, that, at that time, Queen Isabel was under a great calamity and oppression and what was then determined against her was not so much from the right of the thing as the iniquity of the times; neither has it been heard that one who has been queen of England should be called *nuper regina* in her lifetime, so that the authority was much invalidated from the circumstance of the time.

The plaintiffs, observing the court thus clearly for the defendant's title, were nonsuited.

Note it was not resolved whether, if there had been a queen consort at the time of this grant, it had been good to the defendant. But the judges rather inclined that it should.

T. Jones 176, 84 E.R. 1204

In [an action of] *ejectione firmae* for the house of the Hospital of St. Catherine, which was brought to try whether the said Lord Brunker or Sir Robert Atkins was the rightful Master of the said Hospital, and, to do this, the lease to the plaintiff, on a motion by the defendant, was alleged to be made by the name of the said Lord Brunker, Master, and the brethren and sisters of the said Hospital, for no question can be made but that the house belonged to the said corporation. And, therefore, to confess the lease to be made without the naming of the lessor by his proper name would take away the question intended.

At the trial, on [a plea of] not guilty, the plaintiff made title to his lessor on a grant of the queen consort that now is, bearing date the 27th of August last past, immediately after the death of George Montague, Esq., the last Master of the Hospital. And the defendant made his title by the grant of the said queen consort, 15 Car. II, to which queen he was then solicitor, the said George Montague then being Master by the grant of the present king's mother, then queen dowager, and there being at that time no consort.

The Hospital was founded by Eleanor, queen dowager in the time of Edward I, and by the charter of foundation, the said queen having named the first Master, this clause is added for the appointment of the masters, *reservando nobis et reginis Angliae nobis succedentibus perpetuis futuris temporibus* the nomination etc.

On the evidence at the bar, two points in law were moved and strongly urged by the defendant and his counsel: the first, whether the grant to George Montague by the said queen dowager was good or not, for it was said that such grant was but provisional until there should be a queen consort and a grant made by her.

Curia was to the contrary, for, first, the foundation being by a queen dowager with a reservation *ut supra*, she was properly succeeded by queens dowager. Second, this provisional power was thought by the court to be a conceit invented to answer divers precedents of grants shown by the plaintiff of grants made by queens dowager, as by Isabel in the time of Edward III, and his mother, and others, and the mastership was enjoyed accordingly, and the charter has no footstep of such a provisional power.

The second point was whether the mastership could be granted in reversion, for the defendant's counsel insisted that, though there was no mention of the reversion in the patent, yet it should pass if it be so grantable by law, for the grant of the queen shall be construed as the grants of other subjects. *Quod fuit concessum*.

But, *per curiam*, the mastership is not grantable in reversion, [any] more than a grant to be a parson in the life of the incumbent. And, though the defendant insisted strongly to have these matters found specially, the court would not grant it, because both those points in a trial before Lord Hale for the said mastership between the said Sir Robert Atkins and the said George Montague were moved, and ruled by the court as in the case at bar. And the jury here, being so directed in the matter in law, gave a verdict for the plaintiff. And judgment [was given] accordingly.

3 Salkeld 250, 91 E.R. 806

Eleanor, queen dowager of Henry III, endowed St. Catharine's Hospital near the Tower, reserving to herself *et reginis Angliae nobis succedentibus plenam potestatem* of providing a Master thereof. The queen dowager, in the reign of Charles II, nominated a Master, and, the queen consort taking that nomination to be void, she nominated another.

It was insisted that such a desultory inheritance as this was, *viz. reginis Angliae nobis succedentibus*, could not be good by a charter without an act of Parliament.

But *per curiam*: This is very true if it had been a grant of an advowson *in esse* or of lands, because he who had a right could not always know against whom to bring his action. But of a patronage newly founded, there can be no precedent right. Therefore, it may be limited at pleasure like a rent *de novo*.

Second, it was held that this office of a master could not be granted in reversion and that the right of granting it was in the queen dowager, and not in the queen consort, unless there was no queen dowager.

Skinner 2, 90 E.R. 1

In [an action of] *ejectione firmae* between Lord Brounker and Sir Robert Atkyns for the mastership of the Hospital of St. Catherine's, which is a corporation consisting of the Master, brethren, and sisters, and, in this case, it was said that, where there is a common seal put to a deed, that is title enough of itself without a witness to prove it or that the major part of the college be agreed. And, if it be said that it was put to by the hand of a stranger, that shall be proved on the side that says so.

Sir Robert Atkyns moved that they might declare by the name of Lord Brounker, Master, etc., for that, if they should declare by the name of Master, Brethren, etc. generally and he should confess a lease, entry, and ouster, he should be tricked, for a confession of a lease by the master shall be intended the lawful master.

Wherefore, by consent, they declared by the name of Lord Brounker, Master, etc., and took out a new original.

And Sir Robert Atkyns confessed the lease, entry, and ouster.

And it was said in this case that, where the cause is by an original, it is a favor of the court whether they shall have an imparlance or not. And after[wards], *termino Trinitatis* 35 Car. II, in the King's Bench, an exception was taken by *Pollexfen* for not naming the dean by name, but only generally in the pleading. 1 Inst. 3,[1] and other books were cited. But it seemed to be held well enough, for that upon *non convenit* or *non concessit*, it will so appear well enough.

Skinner 14, 90 E.R. 8

In this case, these things were resolved *per totam curiam*, in the charter of foundation of St. Catherine's Hospital by Eleanor, queen dowager of Henry III, there was this clause, *reservantes nobis et reginis Angliae nobis succedentibus jus advocationis et patronatus etc.* The case depending upon this clause mainly proved this. Henrietta Maria, queen dowager of Charles I, granted the mastership of St. Catherine's to George Montague April 30, 1661. Catharine, queen consort, granted the mastership of St. Catharine's to Sir Robert Atkyns in 1671. George Montague dies in July 1681, and, in August following, the queen grants it to Lord Brounker.

Hereupon, the question was whether the grant of Henrietta Maria, queen dowager, upon the words of the charter of foundation was good to George Montague as a grant or only as a personal appointment to determine when there should be a queen consort, for Sir Robert much insisted that the queen dowager's interest ceased whenever there was a queen consort, which, if so, then the Hospital was not full of Montague at the time of Sir Robert's grant. And so this grant was good. Next, if this point should be against him, he contended that it was a lay hospital and grantable in reversion.

As to the first, the court held clearly that the interest and power of disposing of the Hospital, being vested in a queen consort, does not determine by her becoming a dowager, there being no words in the patent that give such a direction. And, therefore, being general, it shall be for life. And the law will not allow in construction such a desultory kind of inheritance. But, if it had been so specially limited, being a hereditament newly treated, perhaps, it might be otherwise. They held further that she remains a queen after the death of the king, and has always her privilege allowed her in the Exchequer.

But PEMBERTON said, peradventure, a countess ought to be named in a writ *comitissa dotissa*; otherwise, it would be an abatement.

As to the second, they held likewise that it was no office grantable in reversion, though it was admitted a lay hospital, and, although they strongly argued this point might be found specially, the court would not. In this case, the nonsuit against Robert Atkyns in a former trial between him and Montague, the late Master, was given in evidence, though the counsel objected that the Master

---

[1] E. Coke, *First Institute* (1628), f. 3.

comes not in privity and that there was more given in evidence here than in the former trial.

But PEMBERTON, Chief Justice, said that a successor comes in under his predecessor, and is like to an heir and ancestor. Speed's *Chronicle* was given in evidence to prove the death of Isabel, queen dowager to Edward II, and though *Maynard* seemed to oppose it and *Dolbin* said it was done by consent, yet the Chief Justice said he knew not what better proof they could have.

And *Wallop* said that, in the Lord's House, it was admitted by them for good evidence in the Lord Bridgwater's Case.

455

Salmon v. The Hamborough Company

(Ch. 1671)

In this case, the members of a trading company were held to be individually liable for the debts of the company.

1 Chancery Cases 204, 22 E.R. 763

Doctor Salmon against the Hamborough Company, by the name of the Governor, Assistants, and Fellowship of Merchant Adventurers of England, and divers particular members of that Company by name in their natural capacities.

The bill charged that the Company were incorporated *prout per* letters patent, and had power to make by-laws and to assess rates upon cloths, which was the commodity they dealt in, and, by a poll upon every member, to defray the necessary charge of the Company and that the Company had imposed rates accordingly, as namely, 4s. 6d. upon every white cloth exported and divers others and thereby raised £8000 *per annum* towards the support of the common charge of the Company and that they had thereby gotten great credit and borrowed great sums of money by their common seal, and, particularly, the plaintiff lent £2000 upon that security many years since. And the bill did set forth divers advantages they had in trade by being members of this corporation, which others wanted. And the bill did charge that, the Company having no common stock, the plaintiff had no remedy at law for his debt, but did charge that their usage had been to make taxes and levy actions upon the members and their goods to bear the charge of their Company to pay their debts. And he did complain that they now did refuse to execute that power. And he did particularly complain against divers of the members by name that they did refuse to meet and lay taxes and that they did pretend a want of power by their charter to lay such taxes, whereas they had formerly exercised the power and, thereby, gained credit, whereupon the plaintiff lent them £2000, which was for the use and support of the Company's charge. And so it ought to be made good by them, and so he prayed to be relieved.

Easter [term] 1656, this bill was filed, and the Company was served with process, but would not appear, they having nothing by which they may be distrained. But divers particular members, being served in their natural capacities, did appear and demur, for that they were not in that capacity liable to the plaintiff's demands. 10 May 1666, on the argument, the demurrer was allowed. And the bill was dismissed as to them, and that dismission was enrolled.

And, thereupon, a petition of appeal was preferred to the Lords in Parliament, admitting that, in the ordinary course of proceedings in Chancery, that court could not help the plaintiff. But, in causes of this nature, the Lords' House had given special directions to the Chancery to relieve, and it had been accordingly so done. And they produced two precedents against companies in London for that purpose.

And to this petition. The defendants particularly named did put in an answer, plea, and demurrer, and the Company, though several times summoned, did not appear. And upon debate of the matters before the Lords at the bar of the Lords' House 20 January, 1670, this order was made.

> The matter upon the petition of Salmon, Doctor of Physic, exhibited to the Lords Spiritual and Temporal in Parliament assembled against the governors, assistants, and fellowship of the Merchant Adventurers of England, commonly called the Hamburgh Company, and Sir Charles Lloyd, Baronet, Sir Anthony Bateman, Knight, Thomas Smith, Richard Wyan, John Dogget, Henry Colliar, Henry Smith, John Lethieulier, Christopher Pack, George Wytham, and others, members of the said Company, and, upon the answer, plea, and demurrer of the said Rowland Wyan, John Dogget, Henry Collier, and John Lethieulier put in to the said petition (the Governor, Assistants, and Fellowships, though several times summoned, not appearing) being heard at the bar of this House in the presence of counsel learned on both sides, the said petition being on appeal made from a dismission in the High Court of Chancery and the petitioner's bill there, Their Lordships, on reading the said petition, the answer, plea, and demurrer thereto and the said dismission and the charter by which the said Governor and Fellowship are incorporated, and hearing what was alleged on both sides, do order that the dismission for so much as concerns the said Company be and do stand reversed and that the Lord Chancellor or the Lord Keeper of the great seal of England for the time being do retain the said bill and that the said Court of Chancery shall issue forth the usual process of that court, and, if cause be, process of *distringas* thereupon against the said corporation provided the said process be served one month before the return thereof. And, if upon the return of the process, the said corporation shall not file an appearance or shalt appear and not answer, the said bill shall be taken *pro confesso*, and a decree shall thereupon pass. But, in case the said corporation shall appear and answer within the time aforesaid, then the Court of Chancery shall proceed to examine what the plaintiff's just debt is and shall decree the said Company to pay so much money as the same shall appear to

amount unto with reasonable damages. And, in case the corporation shall not pay the sum decreed within ninety days after the service of the said decree upon their Governor, Deputy Governor, Treasurer, Clerk, or Secretary for the time being, then the Lords Spiritual and Temporal do farther order, adjudge, and direct that the Lord Chancellor or Lord Keeper for the time being shall order and decree that the Governor or Deputy Governor and the twenty-four assistants of the said Company or so many of them as by the tenor of their charter do constitute a quorum for the making of leviations upon the trade or members of the said Company for the use of the said Company shall within such time as by the Lord Chancellor or Keeper shall be thought fit make such a leviation upon every member of the said Company as is to be contributory to the public charge as shall be sufficient to satisfy the said sum to be decreed to the plaintiff in that cause and to collect and levy the same, and to pay it over to the plaintiff as the court shall direct. And such a leviation is to be put in writing and signed with the hand of the Governor, Deputy Governor, and assistants of the aforesaid Company for the time being and so many of them as, by the constitution of the said charter do make a quorum, shall not make or return such leviations as aforesaid, the Lord Chancellor or Lord Keeper may issue process of contempt against them as is usual against persons in their natural capacities. And, if, by the said time so to be limited by the said Court of Chancery, the said money so to be assessed shall not be paid, then and from thenceforth, every person of the said Company upon such a leviation shall be made to be liable in his capacity to pay his quota or proportion assessed. And the Lord Chancellor or Lord Keeper is to order or decree that such process shall issue against any such member so refusing or delaying to pay his quota or proportion as is usual against persons charged by the decree of the said court for any duty in their several capacities. And, if the total so returned and filed with the Register shall not amount to so much as shall be sufficient to satisfy the sum decreed with respect had to such person as shall make it appear that they are overcharged or ought not to be charged at all, then the said Lord Chancellor or Lord Keeper for the time being may from time to time order that a new leviation be made and returned into the Registers of the Court of Chancery of such sum as shall be sufficient by way of a supplement for that purpose, to the payment whereof, every individual person is to be bound in such manner as aforesaid.

6 March 1670, the Lord Keeper [BRIDGEMAN], on a motion grounded on the Lords, ordered that the dismission stand reversed and the bill stand revived and that process and other proceedings issue as is thereby directed and the service thereby directed be sufficient.

Accordingly, the Treasurer and Secretary were served with a [writ of] *distringas* against the Company and copies of the Lords' order. The Sheriff returned *nulla bona*. And no appearance is made.

5 July 1671, it was ordered the cause be put into the paper to be heard and notice to be given to the Treasurer, Clerks, and Secretary.

And, now, the 5th of July 1671, none appearing for the defendants, the court decreed the bill to be taken *pro confesso* and the defendants to pay the plaintiff's debt, according to the Lords' order in Parliament.

456

Brainton v. Barker

(Ch. 1671)

A bona fide *purchaser for value will not be required to make a discovery of his title deeds which might defeat his title.*

Lord Nottingham, *Prolegomena*, p. 209

10 December 1671.

The father was tenant for life, with contingent remainders to his first and tenth begotten sons in tail, remainder to his right heirs. The father suffers a recovery, and mortgages to Benedict Hall. He enjoys until 1647, and then he sells to Barker for £4200, who enjoys until 1669.

And then the first son exhibits his bill against Barker to discover his deed.

Barker pleads the recovery, the mortgage to Hall, and his purchase and possession.

The plaintiff replies that he was born before the recovery (whereas the truth was the writ of entry bore *teste* Hilary [term] 15 Car. I [1640], returnable on Easter term following. The son was born the 12th of April but not baptized until 18th of May following).

The defendant rejoins [that] he had no notice of the plaintiff's birth before the recovery at the time of his purchase.

Bridgeman, Keeper, and Hale, Chief Justice, agree: first, that, if the defendant had pleaded himself generally a purchaser without notice, it had been better than specially to have disclosed his title as above; second, that, having pleaded his title specially, it was not necessary to aver want of notice in the plea, for, until the replication, it could not appear that notice of the plaintiff's birth was in any way material; third, that, here, no discovery ought to be made by the defendant in Chancery, for there appears no ill conscience in the defendant, who had reason to presume the title to be good, and that the recovery had barred the contingent remainder by being suffered before the son was born, because, else, the father had forfeited his estate for life and the register book showed the baptism to be long after and Hall had quietly enjoyed for seven years, and, therefore, equity shall not weaken the defense of an honest purchaser. It is true, if the plaintiff proceed at law in [an action of] *ejectione firmae* and endeavor to prove the contents of the deed there, as he may, or, if he bring a writ of detinue for the deed, this court will not stay his suit, and possibly the defendant's plea, being so particular, may help the heir at law. But equity shall not help him against the defendant no more than in Fagg's Case and Sergeant Ellis's Case.[1]

VAUGHAN [held] *contra*, because, in Fagg's Case, the tenant in tail might have docked.

HALE: So here might the father before the son was born, and there is no equity for the issue in tail in the one case more than in the other.

Also by VAUGHAN: Discovery of a deed does not hurt the purchaser directly, but by consequence, which may be said in all cases.

457

Cooper v. Anonymous

(Ch. 1671–1672)

An arbitral award can be set aside by a court of law.

3 Chancery Reports 76, 21 E.R. 733

[There was] a butcher of Croydon, and the plaintiff called him a bankrupt. And a reference was made to arbitrators, who awarded £495 damages upon the plaintiff's bill.

It was ordered that, notwithstanding the award, a trial should be had what the defendant was damnified. And he had a verdict but for £10, and the plaintiff was relieved against the award.

2 Vernon 251, 23 E.R. 763

The Lord Bridgeman did not set aside the award barely because the damages were excessive, but he gave another reason, *viz.* it was agreed it should be referred to indifferent persons, and it appeared one of the referees was the butcher's cousin.

1 Eq. Cas. Abr. 50, 21 E.R. 866

The plaintiff called the defendant, who was a butcher, a bankrupt knave, which being submitted to a reference, the arbitrators gave him £495 to repair his honor, as they called it in the award. And the court thought the damage too excessive, and set aside the award, but directed a trial at law. And the jury gave him £10. The Butcher of Croyden's Case, 3 Chancery Reports 76; [see also] 2 Vernon 251, where it is said that the court had not set aside the award barely for excessive damages, but because it appeared that one of the referees was the butcher's cousin.

[1] *Shirley v. Fagg* (Ch. 1665), see above, Case No. 193; *Burrell v. Ellis* (Ch. c. 1670), see above, Case No. 398.

458

Wilson v. Barton

(Ch. 1671–1672)

A contract to arbitrate can be revoked before the award is made.

A penal bond to enforce the arbitration will be relieved against in a court of equity.

Nelson 148, 21 E.R. 812

The plaintiff, being impropriator of a rectory, sued the defendants in the spiritual court for detaining his tithes. And, thereupon, they obtained a [writ of] prohibition, and the plaintiff declared.

And the case being at issue to be tried at the York Assizes, the parties agreed to refer it [to arbitration], and entered into bonds of £200 penalty to stand to an award. Afterwards, the plaintiff countermanded the reference. And, thereupon, the bond was put in suit against him. And now he exhibited his bill to be relieved against the said bond and penalty.

It was insisted for the defendant that no relief could be had in this cause, because it was a willful breach of the plaintiff, and [it is] not like the case of a failure to pay money on the day, because payment of the money at another day with damages in the meantime makes a recompense for the failure. But, here, the plaintiff, by his willful revocation, has submitted to pay the penalty which he had bound himself to pay.

But *Sir John Churchill* insisted for the plaintiff that this court had relieved in the like cases.

Whereupon, the Master of the Rolls [GRIMSTON] granted an injunction against the penalty, and directed a trial to try what the defendants were damnified by the countermand.

459

Higgins v. Mayor of Southampton

(Ch. 1672)

The requirement of the Statute of Wills that one-third of a testator's land descend to the heir as at common law does not apply to a devise of an annuity payable out of land.

Herne & Duke 119

Nathaniel Mill, by his last will in writing, devised several sums of money, in all amounting to £41, to be paid out of the manor of Wolston to the mayor and the three senior aldermen of Southampton yearly for putting out apprentices, relief of aged persons, etc.

Commissioners upon the Statute of Charitable Uses[1] decree the money.

The exceptant, being owner of that manor, complained of the decree, for that the said manor was held *in capite* and so the said will was void as to a third part thereof.

And upon [a] hearing before the Lord Chancellor BRIDGEMAN, assisted by Mr. Justice WILDE and Mr. Baron WYNDHAM, the decree was confirmed to all the three parts.

Nelson 146, 21 E.R. 812

The plaintiff was heir at law to John Mill, who, in the year 1636, devised £37 *per annum* to charitable uses to be issuing out of his manor of Wolston. And a decree was made for that purpose, to which the plaintiff excepted, for that the manor was held *in capite* and so the testator could charge only two parts in three by his will, which would not amount to £37 *per annum*.

After a long argument and many cases cited, *viz*. Montague's Case in the Court of Wards, and Cro. Car., Ascough's Case,[2] the court was of opinion that the whole was chargeable by the will and that by virtue of the Stat. 43 Eliz., of Charitable Uses, which was an enabling statute, and that the testator had only mistaken the manner of the conveyance, for if he had done it by grant, it had been good for the whole, and being by will, the Statute made it a good appointment for the whole in like manner.

3 Chancery Reports 68, 21 E.R. 731

26 January 1671[/72]. Lord Keeper, Wilde, and Wyndham.

John Mill, whose heir the exceptant had married, in 1636 devised £37 *per annum* to charitable uses to be issuing out of his manor of Wolston, whereupon a decree was made and exceptions, *inter alia*, that the manor was held *in capite* and so but two parts to be charged, which would not satisfy the bequest.

Quaere whether more than two parts of lands held *in capite* may be charged by the Statute 43 Eliz.

And upon a long argument, after several cases cited, as Mountague's in the Court of Wards, one *in tempore Jacobi*, and Aiscough's in Croke 1302, 14 Car. I [1639], and others, the whole court was clear of opinion that the whole were chargeable, for that the Statute is an enabling statute and the testator had only mistaken the conveyance, for had it been by a grant, it had been good, and being by will, they conceived the Statute did make good the act of the devisor.

---

[1] Stat. 43 Eliz. I, c. 4 (*SR*, IV, 968–970).

[2] *Montague's Case* (1619), Ley 63, 80 E.R. 632, Herne & Duke 42; *Ascough's Case* (1639), Croke Car. 526, 79 E.R. 1055, also *sub nom. Ascough v. Phillips*, W. Jones 429, 82 E.R. 225.

Public Record Office C.33/239, f. 36v

14 November 1672.

William Higgins, gent., exceptant; Mayor and Aldermen of Southampton, respondents.

Upon opening of the matter this present day unto this court by Mr. Collins, being of the respondents' counsel, and upon producing of two several orders made in this cause, the one of the 26th of June 23 *Caroli secundi* [1671] whereby it is among other things ordered that the exceptant should pay £37 *per annum* out of the manor or farm of Wolston in the County of Southampton according to the will of Nathaniel Mill with its deduction of his proportion of rates and taxes and the other of the 28th of November then following whereby it is ordered that the said exceptant should at the third general seal after the then Michaelmas term declare to the court whether he would pay the £37 *per annum* with the deduction according to the decree or convey the said manor and premises to the respondents and their successors in trust for the charitable uses aforesaid, this court was now informed by the respondents' counsel that the said exceptant had not made his election or declaration as by the said last order was appointed as appeared by the [. . .] certificate in that behalf now read and that the said exceptant had detained the said yearly payment of £37 for the space of one year and a half ending at Michaelmas last amounting in all to the sum of £55 10s. upon pretense of making deductions out of the same not only for Parliament taxes (which the respondents are willing to allow) but also for chimney money,[1] rates to the poor, repairing of the house, fireboots, and other boots and also had since the making of the said last order made and committed great waste and spoil upon the premises by the cutting down and felling of 140 timber trees and had committed other wastes and spoils upon the premises whereby the same was much impaired and would in a short time not be sufficient to pay the said £37 *per annum* and other incident payments and charges as appeared by the affidavit of Thomas West and John Otteford now also read, it was therefore prayed that the said exceptant might pay the said money so in arrear as aforesaid with deductions of Parliament taxes only and that the exceptant might be restrained from the further felling of timber and committing waste on the premises and might convey the said farm and premises to the respondents which this court thought fit and does order the same accordingly unless the said exceptant upon notice thereof to this court in the Petty Bag office shall on Thursday the 21st of this instant November show unto this court good cause to the contrary and in the meantime the said exceptant is not to commit any waste or spoil upon the said premises in question, Mr. *Phillips*, of counsel with the said exceptant, desiring time to be heard herein.

[1] Stat. 14 Car. II, c. 10 (*SR*, V, 390–393).

Public Record Office C.33/239, f. 163

21 November 1672.

William Higgins, gent., exceptant; Mayor and Aldermen of Southampton, respondents.

Where by an order of the 14th of this instant month for the reasons therein contained, it was ordered that the exceptant should pay the respondents the £55 10s. arrears of the £37 *per annum* therein mentioned with deduction of Parliament taxes only and that the exceptant should be restrained from the further felling of timber and committing wastes on the premises and should convey the farm and premises in question chargeable with the said £37 *per annum* and arrears to the respondents unless cause were shown to the contrary this day and in the meantime the exceptant was not to commit any waste or spoil, upon opening of the matter this present day unto this court by Mr. *Phillipps*, of the exceptant's counsel, in the presence of Mr. *Collins*, being of the respondents' counsel, the said exceptant's counsel offered divers reasons for discharge of the said order and that the exceptant may be at liberty to fell the trees growing on the premises for that by the order of the 28th of November last he having not elected as by that order he was to have done the decree for his payment of the £37 *per annum* is to stand, which he is content to pay so as he may have his proportionable allowance of all taxes, and hopes he shall not be restrained from making the best of the estate or felling the timber thereupon the rather for that his wife is but tenant in tail of the lands, whereto the said respondents' counsel insisted that the exceptant under color of felling trees for the necessary support of the premises does make sale thereof and by that means has already destroyed all the wood and timber on the premises and not left sufficient to keep the premises in repair for the future and therefore the exceptant ought to be restrained from committing of any further wastes or felling any more trees from off the premises the rather for that the said exceptant never yet declared whether he would pay the £37 *per annum* according to the decree made in this cause or convey the manor and premises in question chargeable therewith to the respondents and their successors in trust for the charitable uses in question and therefore it was prayed the said last order may be made absolute and stand confirmed in all points, the said exceptant having used all possible means to elude the decree and avoid the charity, whereupon and on hearing of what was insisted on by the counsel on either side, it is ordered that the said exceptant do forthwith pay unto the said respondents for the arrearages of the said £37 *per annum* unto Michaelmas last the sum of £55 10s. and for damages for the same to this time the 37s. 4d. in all £57 7s. 4d. out of which the respondents are to allow the said exceptant their proportionable part of all Parliament taxes wherewith the whole premises out of which the said £37 *per annum* issues are charged save only chimney money, and the exceptant is to bear the residue and after payment of the same the exceptant may move what he shall think fit touching the injunction granted by the said last order, which is to continue and stand in force [un]til further order. And it is further ordered and decreed that the said yearly payment of £37 *per annum* shall from henceforth forever bear its proportion of all Parliament taxes save only chimney money wherewith the whole premises out of which the same do issue are or shall be charged and of no other rate or taxes whatsoever.

460

Countess of Manchester v. Earl of Burlington

(Ch. 1672)

Notice to a prospective purchaser of land of an unexecuted power of appointment will prevent him from being a bona fide *purchaser without notice.*

Lord Nottingham, *Prolegomena*, p. 211

12 February 1671–72. Countess of Manchester and Carlisle v. Earl of Burlington.

James, earl of Carlisle, the father, [was] tenant for life, remainder to his son for life, remainder to the first, second, and third sons of the son in tail, remainder to the father in fee, with a power in the son to make a jointure. A jointure was accordingly made. Afterwards, *viz.* 11 Car. I [1635–36], for the first settlement was 15 Jac. [1617–18], the father grants the reversion in fee to George, lord Goring. He, in 17 Car. I, *anno* 1641, for £8000, mortgages to the earl of Cork, from whom it descends to the earl of Burlington.

The jointress exhibits a bill against him to produce the deed of 15 Jac.

He pleads the purchase of his father, and avers his father had no notice of the jointure at the time.

And yet [it was] overruled by Baron Wyndham, and [he was] ordered to produce the deed, for, though the earl of Cork purchased without notice of the jointure, yet he had notice of the deed [of] 15 Jac. and the power reserved in it, and, therefore, must take notice of the execution of it at his peril, for a purchaser of land charged with a power, having notice of the power, is bound, though the power be executed after his purchase, and he shall not be protected in equity.

[Later proceedings in this case: 73 Selden Soc. 58.]

461

Codrington v. Codrington

(Ch. 1672)

The question in this case, a suit for the payment of portions, was the proper interpretation of the family settlement in issue.

Lord Nottingham, *Prolegomena*, p. 264

16 February 1671–72, at Essex House.

On the marriage of Jane and Samuel Codrington, the son, a settlement was made whereby, after several uses limited to the father, mother, son, and wife for their lives in several parcels, the same parcels are again limited to trustees for 500 years to secure portions of daughters and until some heir male shall pay unto each daughter etc. And the time of payment is appointed to be at the age of seventeen years of each daughter, which shall be unmarried and unprovided for at the death of her father or, if above the age of seventeen years at the time of the father's death, then, within one year of the father's death. The father, *viz.* Samuel Codrington, the son, having five daughters by Jane, dies. The eldest attains the age of seventeen. The mother, on behalf of herself and the five daughters, sue Thomas Codrington, the uncle and heir male, and also the trustees to enforce a sale of the terms for the raising of present maintenance and portions, upon which [there was] a demurrer.

[It was] resolved by Lord Bridgeman, Keeper: First, if all the lives which preceded the commencement of the terms of 500 years were expired, yet the estate being lodged in trustees until some heir male make default in payment, equity cannot decree a sale, nor take away from the heir male the benefit of laying down the money when he pleases or suffering it to be raised by perception of profits, *quod tamen videtur durus sermo.* Second, *utcunque* there can be no decree to sell before the terms commenced in possession, for, though a certain time be limited for the payment of the portions, yet this must be understood by way of supposition that the terms be then commenced, else the heir male shall be obliged to make bricks without straw or see his estate sold as a reversion and on a great loss while he is under the impossibility of raising the money and, so, that which was intended only as a security for the daughters shall by equity be turned into a penalty upon the heir, *quod foret absurdum.*

462

Summer v. Lloyd

(Ch. 1672)

The question in this case whether a testamentary trust to pay debts comes into existence where the testator dies not having any debts.

Lord Nottingham, *Prolegomena*, p. 265

18 February 1671–72, at the Rolls.

Thomas Lloyd devised part of his lands for the payment of debts, and he lived five years afterwards, and paid all his debts. The trustees sell to Summer or mortgage.

I [*Finch*] urged that the final cause of the trust being [determined and] ceasing by the act of the testator was in equity a determination of the trust and, by consequence, the devisees were trusted by the heir and that there was no difference between a particular trust for raising a portion for a daughter married in the testator's life or for the payment of a special debt afterwards paid by the testator and a general trust.

But it was said the purchaser should enjoy, because he could not know whether debts were unpaid and it was the heir's fault not to exhibit a bill for the reconveyance before sale.

I [*Finch*] replied, the sale being without authority, the purchaser, who took [with] notice of the will, must at his peril take notice of the consequences; else the trustees might be too nimble in their sale.

Accordingly, it was directed. But, afterwards, it fell off, the trust being for the payment of debts and legacies.

463

Tinley v. Church

(Ch. 1672)

An heir of a mortgagor can compel an executor of the deceased mortgagor's estate to redeem the mortgage or to contribute towards the redemption as far as he has assets.

Lord Nottingham, *Prolegomena*, p. 283

Hilary [term] 24 Car. II.

The heir of a mortgagor may compel an executor to redeem it or to contribute towards the redemption as far as he has assets. And the reason of it [*blank*]. To which may be added that the debt of the mortgagor does more nearly concern the executors than the heir, and it was anciently thought to concern the soul. And a court of equity, in case of debts, does not call upon the heir so strictly as it does upon the executor. And, therefore, if a [debt upon a] bond be [unpaid], the executor may be sued in equity; the heir cannot.

464

L'Estrange v. Powle

(Ch. 1672)

A devise to an heir in consideration that he will pay the debts of his father is a trust, not a condition.

Where a devisee to pay the debts of a decedent makes a mortgage, the creditors of the devisor are not necessary parties to a suit to foreclose.

Lord Nottingham, *Prolegomena*, p. 284

Hilary [term] 24 Car. II.

A devise [was made] to the heir in consideration that he will pay the debts of his father.

[It was] ruled: first, it is a trust, not a condition; second, if the devisee mortgage the land, the mortgagee shall have a bill in equity to foreclose the devisee of the redemption if he does not pay within the time prefixed; third, *idque* without making creditors of a devisor parties, because a decree being *res inter alios acta* does not prejudice them. And a decree was pronounced with a *salvo jure* to the creditors.

465

Roscarrick v. Barton

(Ch. 1672)

A suit to redeem a mortgage can be barred by the laches of the plaintiff-debtor.

Lord Nottingham, *Prolegomena*, p. 284

20 February 1671–72.

Charles Roscarrock, in 1637, mortgages to [his stepfather] Greenville. And, in 1638, on his marriage, he settles this land to the use of himself for life, remainder to his wife for life, who was Margaret, remainder to his first, second, and third sons in tail, remainder to Chamond, his brother, in tail. In the year 1652, Serjeant [John] Barton [d. 1684], for £700, purchases Greenville's mortgage, and, in 1656, he obtains a decree against Charles alone to foreclose the equity of redemption, unless £1250 should be paid within fifteen months. In the year 1665, Dorothy, mother of Charles, dies. In the year 1665, Charles dies. In the year 1670, Margaret, wife of Charles, dies. Then, Chamond exhibits his bill against Serjeant Barton to redeem.

His pretenses were: first, that the decree was on a trust and for a further security (but this was not made out); second, that the mortgage was not to be dated from 1637, but from 1652, at which time Serjeant Barton came in with the addition of new sums, from whence it became a new security (but the addition of new sums was not made out); third, because the equity of redemption being entailed on Chamond and he no party to the decree against Charles, the tenant for life, Chamond could not be bound by it.

And to this Justice Wilde inclined.

But Lord Bridgeman, Keeper, Hale, Chief Justice, and Wyndham, Justice, *totis viribus contra*, because here was no color for a redemption: first, because [it was] an old mortgage ever since 1637, not a renewed mortgage in 1652, but [it was] still upon the old foot; second, a mortgage of a redemption is so casual and the creditors being delayed during all their lives, [there is] no reason to let in the debtor to have the benefit of accidents; else, equity shall encourage debtors to trifle; third, the mortgagee was in no fault; fourth, [there is] no cause to make Chamond a party, because the conveyance to Chamond was voluntary, and Charles, from whom the estate moved, was the visible possessor, and it were hard to put the mortgagee to find out the contingent remainder of an equity (true, but here [there was] notice of Chamond's interest at the time of the decree confessed), and, if he had been a party, he could not have been decreed to redeem, because Charles, tenant for life, is likely to have children, and then Chamond's remainder is worth nothing and so he ought not to contribute. So the bill was dismissed.

Yet the plaintiff offered full interest for the £1250 to this day, and proved the land worth £4000.

In the case of Serjeant Barton etc., it was agreed by HALE, Chief Justice, that, if a bill be exhibited against a tenant in tail of an equity of redemption, a decree will foreclose the issue, for this kind of entail being a creature of equity may be finally barred by an act of a court of equity.

In the debate of that case, HALE, Chief Justice, did vehemently inveigh against the growth of the equity of redemption, even to the subversion of the common law and legal contracts, for, whereas, at common law, the estate after a forfeiture is absolute and, before a forfeiture, a fine or feoffment will extinguish a power of redemption, now [this] equity is become a distinct kind of inheritance quite different from an estate in land or a trust, and a fine or feoffment to a stranger will not exclude it, but it will subsist after and become transferable. And men do expect that, in equity, they may delay payment as long as they please. And, if Chancery would redeem mortgages of 100 years standing, no man will pay sooner. And it is the great sore at this day that mortgagees are become bailiffs to mortgagors. Nor let any man say that a bill to foreclose the equity prevents this, for how can Chancery do it unless it be intrinsically just to impose a peremptory day? And, if it be so, why may it not as well be done by the common law, according to the contract of the parties, as here? For these bills are but of late. And he cited 14 Ric. II, in Parliament, where the Parliament refused to allow the redemption of a forfeited mortgage.[1]

Lord BRIDGEMAN, Keeper, accorded, and added that one cause of slow redemptions of mortgages is because men presume they shall never pay more than dead interest, for the old rule of Chancery never allowed interest upon interest, which was reasonable when interest was held sinful or, at best, but permitted. But, now, it is fit to change that rule. Also, he declared he would allow of no redemption after the time for real actions past, and, in some cases, it would be fit to shorten that too.

---

[1] *Changeour v. Knolles* (1390), C. Given-Wilson, *Parliament Rolls*, vol. 7, pp. 134–135.

1 Chancery Cases 217, 22 E.R. 769

21 February [1672]. Chaumond Roscarrick, Esq., against Serjeant Barton. The Lord Keeper, Chief Justice Hale, Justice Wilde, Justice Wyndham.

May 12, 10 Jac. [1612], Charles Roscarrick, on his marriage with Dorothy, his wife, settles the lands in question (*inter alia*) on himself for life, remainder to Dorothy for life, remainder to the heirs male of his own body. He has issue, Charles, his first son, and the plaintiff, his second son, and dies. Dorothy marries with one Greenvil, and they enter on the lands in question as the jointure of Dorothy.

Charles, the son, 15 November 13 Car. I [1637], by a deed, fine, and recovery, for £800, conveys the lands in question to Greenvil and his wife, to the use of Dorothy for life, remainder to the use of Charles and his heirs, until he fail to pay several sums at several days, amounting to £800, and, after default of payment of any sum, to Greenvil and his heirs.

Afterwards, 14 Car. I [1638–39], Charles, on his own marriage, settles the lands in question, *inter alia*, to himself for life, remainder to Margaret, his wife, for life, remainder to his first and other sons in tail, remainder to the plaintiff in tail. In 1650, Greenvil assigns his estate, which was for the security of the £800 and was forfeited to the defendant by the consent of Charles. In 1656, upon a bill exhibited by the defendant in Chancery against Charles, it is decreed Charles shall pay the defendant what is due to him, *viz.* £1250, or the now defendant, plaintiff in that cause, to hold against Charles and all claiming under him. Charles dies without issue male. Dorothy lives until 1668.

Then, the now plaintiff exhibits his bill to redeem, and alleges that the decree against Charles was by consent and that it was agreed between Charles and the defendant that, notwithstanding the decree, it should be still a mortgage in the defendant's hands and be redeemable upon payment of principal and interest. And, however, the plaintiff being no party to that decree and Charles but a tenant for life, that decree could not bind the plaintiff, and, as to the pretense of an agreement between Charles and the defendant, notwithstanding the decree, the estate should remain still a mortgage in the defendant's hands. There was no proof of any such agreement or consent, but he only told Charles he would come to an account.

But there being dealings and accounts between the defendant and Charles, it was declared by the Lord Keeper [Bridgeman], who first heard this cause in July 1671, that general words not particularly applied ought not to shake a decree, for, if they did, there would be no end of suits. But, then, it was insisted for the plaintiff that he, being no party to the decree, was not bound thereby and that he had an equity to redeem and that the mortgage was not to be taken to be more ancient than from the time of the assignment to the defendant, for that an account being then stated with Greenvil and he paid off, there was no account to be precedent to that, and so it could not be taken to be elder than 1650 and that so the plaintiff ought to be admitted to redeem. And the rather, for that the defendant had notice (which was admitted) of the deed of 14 Car. I [1638–39], by which the plaintiff claims before he took the conveyance from Greenvil. And whether the plaintiff should redeem the Lord Keeper doubted, but he took time to consider.

And now, 21 February 1671, this cause was finally heard before the Lord Keeper [BRIDGEMAN], assisted with Chief Justice HALE, Mr. Justice WILDE, and Baron WYNDHAM.

It was insisted for the defendant, the plaintiff was no party to the deed of the mortgage and that the deed of 14 Car. I [1638–39], by which the plaintiff Chaumond claimed, howbeit it was made in consideration of Charles's marriage, was to Chaumond, the plaintiff, purely voluntary, and that, albeit a voluntary conveyance would pass an equity of redemption, yet, in this case, where the plaintiff claims an equity by way of an entail, it ought not to be countenanced in equity, for that the consequence of it would be to make an equity of redemption perpetual. If a mortgagor, after a mortgage made, may make himself a tenant for life of that equity, with remainder in tail, as here, remainder for life, etc., which being but a right of action, a right to a bill in equity ought not to be so entailed, and that this was not such an inheritance as was entailed by the Statute *de Donis*[1] etc. but, being a right of action vested in the father, with a remainder to his first and other sons before Chaumond, there was no need to have made Chaumond defendant to the said decree. And Dorothy, who was the tenant for life, lived until 1668, so that the mortgage was all that time but of a dry reversion. And Margaret, the wife of Charles, who lived until very lately and who had a title of redemption precedent to the plaintiff, did not seek to redeem.

WYNDHAM was of opinion, as this case was, that the plaintiff ought not to be admitted to redeem.

Judge WILDE: There is no fraud in the settlement of 14 Car. I [1638–39], and a decree against a tenant for life will not bind him in the remainder in the case of an estate at law. And he did not see why it should bind in equity, and so he conceived the plaintiff was relievable.

Chief Justice HALE: By the growth of equity on equity, the heart of the common law is eaten out, and legal settlements are destroyed. And he was of opinion there is no color of a decree. In 14 Ric. II, the Parliament would not admit of a redemption. But, now, there is another settled course. As far as the line is given, man will go, and, if a hundred years are given, man will go so far, and we know not whither we shall go. An equity of redemption is transferrable from one to another now, and, yet, at common law, if he that had the equity made a feoffment or levied a fine, he had extinguished his equity at law. And it has gone far enough already, and we will go no further than precedents in the matter of an equity of redemption, which has too much favor already. And he concluded there should

[1] Stat. 13 Edw. I, Westminster II, c. 1 (*SR*, I, 71–72).

be no decree for the plaintiff in respect of the antiquity and, if he will redeem, he must come in time. It is but just to foreclose for not coming in time. It is just to deny a redemption if he come not in time. And a decree to foreclose a tenant in tail shall bind his issue in an equity of redemption, because that is a right set up only in a court of equity and so may be here extinguished. And the estate moved from Charles to the mortgagee, and not from the plaintiff, and Charles was the visible possessor and owner. And it is a great sore that mortgagees are but bailiffs. And the limitation to Chaumond was but voluntary, and so the plaintiff's pretense is not to be supported against a purchaser, for so a mortgagee is. And, here, it is made absolute by the decree. And, if there be divers remainders of the equity, there is no reason to make them all parties.

The Lord Keeper [Bridgeman] concurred with him, and, said he, it goes current that, if a mortgage be twenty years old, the mortgagee shall have no interest on interest. But, herein, he is not satisfied, especially in this case, where the defendant could not get into possession by reason of the estate for life to Dorothy, who lived until 1668. And he was clear of opinion that the plaintiff ought not to be admitted to redeem. And he made a great difference between parties that come to redeem who are no parties to the mortgage and those that are parties to the mortgage. And so the bill was dismissed.

1 Vernon 447, 23 E.R. 577

A tenant for life with a remainder to another in tail was foreclosed. And, after sixteen years time, the remainderman came to redeem. But he was dismissed, for, otherwise, there would be no end of suits.

466

Foyle v. Eyre

(Ch. 1672)

An administrator of a decedent's estate must pay off the decedent's debts, including those debts that are secured by lands which descend to his heir at law.

Lord Nottingham, *Prolegomena*, p. 324

24 Car. II.

[It was] resolved: first, if a father acknowledge a statute and die, leaving assets, the heir may compel the executor to pay these debts in ease of the land; second, if the father purchase land charged with a statute, the heir cannot compel the executor to pay this statute, because the father was never liable in person; third, but, if the father give a bond to the conusee by way of additional security to pay the money due on the statute, the executor ought to pay this bond, and so, by consequence, discharge the statute; fourth, but, if the condition of a bond be special to pay the money due on the statute, if it cannot be raised on the statute, the executor is free.

467

Danvers v. Lee

(Ch. 1672)

A forfeiture for the treason of a trustee does not extend to the beneficial ownership of the trust.

In this case, the ownership of the estate in issue was not in the regicide, and was not forfeited.

Lord Nottingham, *Prolegomena*, p. 235

27 February 1671/72.

Earl Danby made several leases for eighty years to trustees for payment of debts and, afterwards, to such uses as he by deed or will shall appoint. Then, by will, he gives the trust of these leases to Henry Danvers, his nephew, and also the lands themselves. Henry devises the leases to his sister, Ann Lee. She and her sister Elizabeth Danvers come to a decree by consent in 1659 to divide the estate by moieties. The king returns. The Act, 12 Car. II, for pains and penalties,[1] is made. Ann Lee dies. Her daughters, supposing Earl Danby's will void for a third because of a tenure *in capite* and that this third was come to the king by the treason of Sir John Danvers,[2] purchase it of the duke of York, and pretend a third part of the leases attends the forfeiture.

[it was] resolved: first, the leases did attend the inheritance in the earl of Danby until severed by appointment; second, by the devise to Henry, the nephew, they were become leases in gross; third, however, a third part of inheritance not passing by the devise, but being descended upon Sir John Danvers, while the whole interest of the lease was vested in Henry by the appointment of the will, it follows by consequence that the attendancy of the lease as to the third part was absolutely severed; so there was no occasion to debate the operation of the decree of the attendancy on the forfeiture.

In the debate of this, case I [*Heneage Finch*] urged that, where the trust of a long lease does attend the inheritance, it ought likewise to attend the forfeiture. Else, the king shall be every way defrauded, for in Sir George Sonds' Case[3] the trust of a lease was not forfeited for felony, because it attended an inheritance

---

[1] Stat. 12 Car. II, c. 30 (*SR*, V, 288–290).

[2] S. Kelsey, 'Danvers, Sir John (1584/5–1655), politician and regicide', *Oxford Dictionary of National Biography*, vol. 15, pp. 101–103.

[3] *Attorney General v. Sandys* (Ex. 1666–1669), Hardres 405, 488, 145 E.R. 520, 561, 3 Chancery Reports 33, 21 E.R. 720, 2 Freeman 129, 22 E.R. 1106, Nelson 130, 21 E.R.

which was not forfeited, by the opinion of Hale [Chief Baron] *et Curiae Scaccarii*, though, without such attendance, the lease would be forfeited, *viz*. the trust. Hobart 214, 2 Cro. 512, 513.[1] Nor here shall there be a forfeiture, thought it attended an inheritance which was forfeited. So *quacunque via data* the king loses.

468

Anonymous

(Ch. c. 1672)

Where an heir to a seller of land enters the land as a special occupant, the buyer cannot have a decree of specific performance of the land sales contract.

2 Freeman 155, 22 E.R. 1126

A tenant of a frank tenement descendible agrees to sell to B., and B. pays him part of the purchase money. The vendor dies, and his heir enters. The vendee exhibits his bill against him to have his contract executed.

[It was] resolved, by the Lord Keeper BRIDGEMAN and others that the plaintiff shall not be relieved, for the heir is but a special occupant and does not claim under his father. And, therefore, the covenant or agreement of his father shall not oblige him to a conveyance of the land. This was about 1672.

469

Lord Windsor v. Read

(Ch. 1672)

A covenant to make further assurances does not pass to the grantee's grantee.

A covenant to make further assurances is not enforceable by a volunteer.

Lord Nottingham, *Prolegomena*, p. 322

Easter [term] 24 Car. II.

[It was] resolved: first, a bill may be exhibited to compel further assurances in specie, notwithstanding a covenant in the conveyance; second, though the covenant be only for seven years, yet a bill in equity lies after seven years; third, if the covenant be to make further assurances to the feoffee and his heirs, the assignee can have no benefit of the covenant either in law or equity; fourth, if the

808, 1 Siderfin 403, 82 E.R. 1182, Equity Cases Exch. 11, Exch. Repts. *tempore* Car. II, 151.

[1] *Rex v. Daccombe* (Ex. 1618), Hobart 214, 80 E.R. 361, Croke Jac. 512, 79 E.R. 437, also Jenkins 293, 145 E.R. 213, 118 Selden Soc. 475, Exch. Repts. 1604–1648, p. 194.

feoffment be a voluntary conveyance, the covenant is voluntary too, and equity will not enforce further assurances on a deed made without valuable consideration; fifth, if such a feoffee bargain and sell, the purchaser shall not in a better condition.

470

Tirrel v. Lemmings

(Ch. 1672)

A commission to examine witnesses cannot be executed before the date set for the examination.

Lord Nottingham, *Prolegomena*, p. 318

18 April 1672.

A commission was appointed to be executed in Germany [on] 10 September. It was executed in the end of August, because the witness was sick, and, in truth, died before 10 September. And yet it was suppressed, though the party had no other writing to prove a deed.

471

Anonymous

(Ch. 1672)

Where depositions are opened prematurely by a party's clerk in court by mistake and the party is unaware of it but examines other witnesses, the later depositions will be allowed to be used.

Lord Nottingham, *Prolegomena*, p. 318

18 April 1672.

A commission was returned with the examination of the witnesses. And, in the absence of the plaintiff's clerk, [it was] opened before the day of publication. And two new witnesses were examined, but on the former interrogatories. And, afterwards, an affidavit was made of the accidental opening of this commission.

And, because the plaintiff, nor any for him, knew of it or of the former depositions, [it was] ruled that it should stand and the depositions be allowed.

472

Martin, Savage, and Turner's Case

(Ch. 1672)

A conveyance can be set aside on the ground of fraud.

Lord Nottingham, *Prolegomena*, p. 265

25 April 1672, by Lord Bridgeman, Keeper.

Petres purchases lands in Bedfordshire, and conveys them to Sir William Ayloff and Mr. Humphry Weld in trust for such as he shall appoint etc. And, afterwards, he declares the trust for Sir Roger Martin and his heirs, but in trust. This trust was upon a second latent trust, *viz.* to found a college of Jesuits in Essex, which [trust] did not judicially appear. Savage, *alias* Trevor, who was scarce known before to Petres, had learned of Mr. Fulton, whom Petres only trusted, that Martin was to have no benefit nor was to know of the trust until £1200 be raised. And Savage, having been Martin's confessor, which does not judicially appear, applies himself to Martin, conceals the trust from Martin, and said he had used his name in trust for himself, and so obtains a letter from Martin to the trustees to convey to Turner in trust for Savage, which is done.

But all was set aside by a decree, and a reconveyance was ordered with an account of the mesne profits, because of the palpable fraud and *suppressio veri* and *suggestio falsi*.

473

Mico v. Barker

(Ch. 1672)

An infant cannot discharge more than he has received, nor can he allow an account.

Lord Nottingham, *Prolegomena*, p. 266

27 April 1672.

'The residue of my estate, I give to Samuel Mico to be disposed by my executors to his use until he be of age and can give a legal discharge.' Samuel Mico, at seventeen, exhibits a bill to have an account and delivery of his estate.

[It was] resolved that he shall not have it, for an infant cannot discharge more than he receives; therefore, he cannot allow an account. If he might, he might also sue at the age of fourteen.

474

Piggott v. Piggott

(Ch. 1672)

Notice to an agent is notice that will bind the principal.

Lord Nottingham, *Prolegomena*, p. 256

8 May 1672, at the Rolls.

A feoffment was made on a marriage settlement to divers uses, and *inter alia* to the use of the daughters to be begotten, and, if but one, to her and her heirs until £2000 paid or secured. The feoffment proved defective by want of livery. The husband, on the second marriage and for a portion, grants a rent charge out of these lands to [his] second wife for a jointure. And the second wife herself has no notice of the former settlement, nor of any equity arising to the daughter by the first marriage, but, being young, trusted her brother and friends to treat for her in her marriage. And they had express notice of this former settlement.

[It was] adjudged this notice should affect the second wife. And the deed was decreed good against her.

475

Pusy v. Walker

(Ch. 1672)

A receipt by one partner charges the partnership.

Lord Nottingham, *Prolegomena*, p. 272

18 May 1672, Easter [term] 24 Car. II.

Three partners in London trade in company. [It was] adjudged the receipts of one of the partners shall charge the company.

476

Parker v. Dee

(Ch. 1672–1674)

An executor cannot pay a creditor of the estate while litigation is proceeding against the estate.

Lord Nottingham, *Prolegomena*, p. 337

22 May, 24 Car. II.

Parker brings [an action of] debt at law against Dee, executor of Everard, for £700. Dee pleads a special *administravit* and that he has not assets *praeter etc.* which are sufficient to satisfy certain recognizances.

Parker exhibits a bill in equity to discover etc. Dee, pending the bill, acknowledges several judgments for debts on bills and notes to the value of £12,900. Afterwards, he moved for an order to put Parker to make his election, and so fixed him in Chancery.

Dee at the hearing appeared to be both executor and devisee for the payment of debts, and was ordered to account before a Master and to be allowed what he had really paid before the bill was exhibited and all judgments after the bill obtained by coercion of law and not by voluntary confession.

The Master reports the matter *ut supra* and withal that the recognizances pleaded at law were satisfied.

Dee appeals from the Master of the Rolls, who made the first decree, and insists upon it that, for the personal estate, he was not chargeable as a trustee, but only as an executor and so had a power by law to confess judgments and to pay debts in *aequali gradu* according to what priority he please without fraud to be therefore objected against him.

Rainsford, Justice: Since Dee's false plea at law drove Parker into Chancery, where Dee fixed him, and there used many delays to put off the hearing, yet, in the meantime, confessed judgments and, at last, the plea at law is disproved, the falsifying of that plea in equity should avail the plaintiff as much as if it had been falsified at law and so let him in before the subsequent judgments.

Bridgeman, Keeper: Debts paid before the bill must be allowed. Debts paid and judgments acknowledged since the decree of the Master of the Rolls must not be allowed. But of debts between the answer and the first decree *advisari vult*. And he orders a Master to compute these. But, on the trust, the plaintiff must have his proportion with other creditors *in aequali gradu*.

2 Freeman 93, 22 E.R. 1079

An executor pleaded *plene administravit* to an action brought against him, whereupon the plaintiff preferred his bill in this court for discovery of assets, and, whilst the suit was depending in this court, the executor confessed judgment to another person.

This court caused him to pay the whole debt, for that the party should not suffer by an act that was done to defraud him whilst he was proceeding to this court.

2 Vernon 61, 23 E.R. 649

Where creditors come with a bill and make the executor and all the rest of the creditors parties, the executor shall not have the power by the confessing of a judgment or by suffering a judgment to pass by default after the bill be exhibited to prefer one creditor before another. But, there, all the creditors in equal degree shall be paid in proportion.

[Later reports of this case: Repts. *tempore* Finch 123, 23 E.R. 67, 2 Chancery Cases 200, 22 E.R. 910, 3 Swanston 529, 36 E.R. 968, 73 Selden Soc. 83.]

477

Clinton v. Young

(Ch. 1672)

An executor can sue a fellow co-executor only for that which was wrongfully converted out of the decedents' estate.

Lord Nottingham, *Prolegomena*, p. 338

27 June 1672.

One executor demands against another his share in a moiety of the residue.

Curia: This shall be only of such part of the estate which was converted by the executor, for, otherwise, it would change the law of administration and would carry the administration to the next of kin to the executor if he has a right to the residue otherwise than as executor.

478

Shires v. Trotman

(Ch. 1672)

A statute staple or a statute merchant is an encumbrance on all of the debtor's land, and it is not discharged by a foreclosure on only one parcel owned by the debtor.

Lord Nottingham, *Prolegomena*, p. 323

Trinity [term] 24 Car. II.

Trotman had a mortgage of Bucknall from Ewer and several statutes for the performance of covenants etc. Shires purchases the manor of Bainton from Ewer, and is quiet in possession twenty years together. After this, Trotman exhibits a bill against Ewer to foreclose his equity of redemption, and he obtains a decree that Bucknall shall be so held. Then, Trotman, on a pretence that Bucknall was encumbered, extends his statutes on Bainton.

Shires exhibits a bill against Trotman to set aside the statutes against Bainton, because, after the decree between Trotman and Ewer, all Trotman's demands shall be supposed to be satisfied and, though the statutes may be kept on foot to preserve Bucknall from encumbrances, yet not to encumber Bainton etc.

[It was] resolved the value of Bucknall and all Trotman's demands shall be computed and, what Bucknall falls short to satisfy, the statutes shall be let loose to make up.

479

Stokes v. Apreece

(Ch. 1672)

A commission to take a deposition de bene esse *need not be requested on any oath of the necessity thereof.*

Lord Nottingham, *Prolegomena*, p. 219

Trinity [term] 24 Car. II.

It is usual, on the plaintiff's suggestion that he has a sick or aged witness, to pray a commission to examine him *de bene esse* and that without any oath made of the truth of the suggestion or any contempt of the defendant in not answering or delay by praying a commission, because this examination is but provisional in the case of death, for he must be examined again if he live. And, besides, the defendant may join in the commission if he please.

But this is very mischievous, for, unless great caution be used in allowing the examination *de bene esse*, it will be an easy thing to prepare and pre-engage a witness.

480

Ward v. Nosworthy

(Ch. 1672)

Arrears of rent due to a bishop are lost to him when he ceases to be the bishop.

When rent is tendered and refused, it cannot be later recovered in a suit in equity.

Lord Nottingham, *Prolegomena*, p. 324

3 July 1672.

[John] Gawden, bishop of Exeter, makes a lease for three lives to Nosworthy supposed to be voidable. [Seth] Ward,[1] the successor, refuses to accept the rent for some years, and, afterwards, is translated to Salisbury, and, then, he exhibits his bill in equity against Nosworthy for all the arrears.

[It was] resolved: first, the arrears are lost by common law when he departs from his bishopric; second, [there is] no relief in equity, for it is against con-

[1] J. Henry, 'Ward, Seth (1617–1689)', *Oxford Dictionary of National Biography*, vol. 57, pp. 349–352.

science that the bishop, who refused his rent when the tenant would have paid it for confirmation of his lease, should recover it now, when the payment will not avail the tenant.

On another day, *viz.* 9 July 1672, Nosworthy's Case was again debated. And [the court]

held clearly: first, the bishop has no remedy at law after translation, for he can make neither a distraint nor have [an action of] debt for a freehold rent nor can any action of covenant be brought on the reservation in the lease for lives; second, [counsel for the bishop] urged that equity ought to relieve, for, if a rent be reserved to executors, the law bars the heir, yet equity relieves, which the Lord Keeper [BRIDGEMAN] denied, notwithstanding precedents. Besides, the bishop never had any remedy but in equity before his translation from want of a counterpart, and equity will not suffer that equity to be extinguished. But on this point, a case was directed.

2 Chancery Reports 60, 21 E.R. 616

This case is touching a rent of £67 *per annum* reserved on a lease of lands made by John, late bishop of Exeter, to the defendant. And the plaintiff, by his bill, says the defendant never paid the said rent to the plaintiff nor any part thereof during all the time he was bishop of Exeter, which was for six years, whereby a great arrear is incurred and due to the plaintiff from the defendant, for which the plaintiff seeks relief.

The defendant insists that he directly tendered the said rent to the bishop while he was bishop of Exeter. But he refused the same, having an intention to impeach the said defendant's estate. And, now, the plaintiff is translated to another see, and so he ought not in law or equity to demand the said arrears, but ought to be debarred from receiving the same by his refusal, as aforesaid.

His Lordship [BRIDGEMAN] was clear of opinion that, by law, the plaintiff could not recover the said arrears. But how far the plaintiff was relievable in equity was the question. And His Lordship ordered precedents to be produced, where there has been a just duty, but no legal remedy. And he ordered a case to be stated.

It appearing that the plaintiff, while he was bishop of Exeter, would not accept the said rent, His Lordship [BRIDGEMAN], with judges assisting him, were clear of opinion that there was no ground in equity to give the plaintiff any relief, and dismissed the bill.

[Reg. Lib. 23 Car. II, f. 720.]

481

Lightfoot v. Joyce

(Ch. 1672)

The Statute of Limitations can be pleaded to bar the enforcement of a contract obligation but not to discharge the contract obligation.

Lord Nottingham, *Prolegomena*, p. 325

9 July 1672.

If a bill suggests that the defendant sues at law on a bond, whereas, in truth, it is satisfied by a delivery of wares etc., it is no plea to say that the wares were delivered above six years since, for the Statute of Limitations[1] is no bar where the suit is not to recover, but to discharge.

482

Warman v. Seaman

(Ch. 1672)

In this case, the devise in issue did not give the plaintiff any interest in the land in question.

Lord Nottingham, *Prolegomena*, p. 230

9 July 1672.

The trust of a term was devised in these words, 'to Julian for life, then to the issue of the body of Julian, and, for want of such issue, then to Robert Warman for the residue of 100 years'. Julian has issue and dies. The issue die without issue. Robert Warman's heir and executor exhibits a bill against the trustees.

[There was a] demurrer, because plaintiff has no title.

[It was] resolved: first, if these words 'issue of the body' are words of limitation and make an entail, then the remainder is void; second, if they are words of purchase and the issue of the body take as purchaser, then the trust goes to the administrator of that issue, and the plaintiff has no title; third, if the remainder be contingent, that contingency never happened when Julian had issue, though, afterwards, the issue died without issue. So, every way, the was demurrer good.

2 Vernon 24, 23 E.R. 626

[There was an] alienation of a term to one for life and then to her issue. The issue took by purchase. And 'issue' was not taken to be a word of limitation so as to vest the whole term in the mother. And yet 'issue', in legal understanding, is a word of limitation and not of purchase.

1 Stat. 21 Jac. I, c. 16 (*SR*, IV, 1222–1223).

[Later reports of this case: 73 Selden Soc. 197, 217, 248, Pollexfen 112, 86 E.R. 530, 2 Chancery Cases 209, 22 E.R. 914, 1 Freeman 306, 89 E.R. 224, 22 E.R. 1227, Reports *tempore* Finch 279, 23 E.R. 153, 3 Keble 544, 84 E.R. 870.]

483

Chambers v. Greenhill

(Ch. 1672–1673)

A bill of review lies to reverse a final decree where new evidence has been subsequently found which could not have been reasonably found before the decree.

3 Chancery Reports 76, 21 E.R. 734

9 July 1672.

A demurrer was to a bill of review, exhibited on new matter, for that it ought not to be admitted where the matter was of the knowledge of the defendant at the time of the answer and hearing, though there was then no proof of it. But, afterward, the proof came to light. And herein was cited Colt and Colt,[1] where the defendant sets forth deeds that made a title by the answer, but they were lost afterwards, and a decree was against them, but, coming to light afterwards, the bill of review was admitted.

But the Lord Keeper [BRIDGEMAN] said this case was not like the other. And so, in effect, he dismissed the bill, but they have time to produce precedents.

Lord Nottingham, *Prolegomena*, p. 297

9 July 1672.

Sir Thomas Chambers exhibits a bill against Greenhill to review and reverse a decree for £2300 interest to be paid to Greenhill and on new matter discovered, *viz.* clear evidence that the money was tendered in India and refused. And so, he prayed to reverse [the decree] *quoad* damages, and he relied on my Lord Bacon's first rule [that] where new proof comes to light after the decree, which could not possibly have been used at the time of the decree, [such new proof] is admitted to be a ground of review by licence of the court.

But here the Chancellor denied it, and allowed the demurrer, because the fact must needs be known before the decree, though the proof new discovered after, and it were very mischievous to give way [to the view] that every new witness discovered should be a ground of review.

Lord Nottingham, *Prolegomena*, p. 300

19 February 1672[/73], Sir Thomas Chambers v. Greenhill.

---

[1] *Colt v. Colt* (Ch. 1665), see above, Case No. 183.

[It was] resolved: first, an original bill to be relieved against a decree does not lie, though the decree be never so hard, for, then, there would be a decree against a decree, but the defendant should rather be driven to his bill of review; second, error cannot be assigned in a matter of fact which lay in the defendant's knowledge before the decree was pronounced, though the proof of the fact came to his knowledge since, as, where interest was decreed, the defendant in a review would have assigned for error a tender and refusal which was never alleged in the former cause and could not.

But in Colt and Colt's Case in 1665, where a lease and release were alleged but not proved, a bill of review was admitted on new proof discovered.

2 Chancery Reports 66, 21 E.R. 618

A bill of review was brought by the plaintiff to reverse the decree in this cause. The plaintiff would now examine to a matter of tender and refusal, which he could not prove before the hearing, but, since the decree was signed and enrolled, he can prove it.

The court ordered precedents to be searched, which being produced by the plaintiff, His Lordship [Lord Shaftesbury] declared the said precedents seemed of no weight to the plaintiff's purpose. And he dismissed the bill of review.

[Reg. Lib. 24 Car. II, f. 288.]

484

Boys v. Crisp

(Ch. 1672–1673)

The question in this case was whether an executor can have a bill of review to reverse a decree against his testator before it be revived against the executor.

There must be four insufficient answers before a defendant can be committed to prison for contempt for not answering sufficiently.

All contempts between party and party are discharged by a general pardon.

Lord Nottingham, *Prolegomena*, p. 199

10 July 1672.

It was pretended to be the course of the court that an executor can have no bill of review to reverse a decree against his testator until it be revived against the executor.

But it was denied, and said to be most unreasonable for an executor to lie under the danger of a decree until the plaintiff revive, the rather [for] that it was contrary to the rules of law, where an executor may bring a writ of error before a *scire facias* brought against him.

Lord Nottingham, *Prolegomena*, p. 301

19 April 1673, Easter 25 Car. II, by Shaftesbury, Chancellor, and the Master of the Rolls.

There must be four insufficient answers in every case, and so reported, before any man can be committed to the Fleet [Prison] for want of a perfect answer, and, then, he is to remain in custody until [he make] a perfect answer. Second, all contempts between party and party are discharged by the General Pardon.[1]

485

Strickland v. Lock

(Ch. 1672)

Even though a plaintiff had an account as an heir, yet he can have it again in his capacity as an administrator.

3 Chancery Reports 77, 21 E.R. 734

12 July 1672, Master of the Rolls.

The case is that a lease was made in 1642 to trustees in trust to raise several sums and the overplus to go to the heir of the lessor.

The plaintiff's brother, son and heir and nephew of the lessor, exhibited a bill by a guardian in 1663 to have an account of the profits against the lessees, and he dies. And the plaintiff, by a guardian, revives the suit. And the account is settled. And the plaintiff, at nineteen years old, and his guardian take £93 surplus of the profits from the lessees pursuant to the decree.

The plaintiff coming of age takes administration of his brother, and exhibits a bill original without taking notice of the former suit. And the defendant, surviving trustee, pleaded the former decree and payment in bar. And the question was at the arguing whether the plaintiff, having had an account as heir, shall have it again as administrator.

And the plea was overruled.

Nelson 149, 21 E.R. 812

Strickland v. Laske.

A lease was made in the year 1640 to several persons in trust to raise money for several uses etc. and the overplus to be to the heir of the lessor.

The plaintiff, as nephew and heir of the lessor, exhibited his bill by his guardian in the year 1663 to have an account of the profits. And he died. And the now plaintiff, being his brother, revives the suit by his guardian. And the account was settled, and there being £93 surplus in the hands of the defendants, the same was

[1] Stat. 25 Car. II, c. 5 (*SR*, V, 786–791).

decreed to be paid unto him, being then about the age of nineteen years, which money was paid accordingly.

Afterwards, when the now plaintiff came of age, he administered to his brother, and exhibited an original bill against the lessor, without taking notice of the former suit. The defendants pleaded the decree and payment of the £93 in bar of this bill.

But it was overruled, by which it appears that, though the plaintiff had an account as heir, yet he might have it again as administrator.

486

Adderly v. Wise

(Ch. 1672)

The question in this case was whether a bail bond given in a common law action in the Court of Chancery can be defeated by the debtor's voluntarily surrendering himself.

Lord Nottingham, *Prolegomena*, p. 297

24 Car. II.

Adderly, the Cursitor, sues Wise in the Petty Bag in an action of covenant. Goodman gives a bond to the sheriff of £2000 for his appearance, in default of which, the sheriff is amerced, and the bail bond is assigned over to Adderly, who prosecuted Goodman. And, after three years' delay for privilege, Wise desired to stay all proceedings on the bail and to render himself to prison.

I [*Finch*] said it was too late after three years, for other courts do not do it after three terms, unless on special circumstances, which here make against Mr. Wise, he having these last three years entered into several [confessed] judgments, which would now precede us. But, if he would put in good bail to the action according to the course of the court, it would be reasonable. Upon this, the question grew what the course was. I [*Finch*] affirmed that the course of the Petty Bag differed from other courts, for, here, the bail is bound absolutely to pay the condemnation, and not as in the King's Bench or the Common Bench *adjunctive* or that the principal shall render himself to prison.

This, the other side said was unreasonable and against law.

I [*Finch*] replied precedents show the course of the court and that is the law of the court. All courts vary in the manner of bail. The King's Bench takes a recognizance in an uncertain sum; the Common Bench in a certain sum; this court with a different condition, and, reasonably, for none sue here in the Petty Bag but persons privileged, persons who are not to be distracted in their attendance.

And Bridgeman, Keeper, agreed, for, at common law, in an *audita querela*, the bail is to pay the money. But he referred it to an examination of the course.

487

Gibbon v. Buckworth

(Ch. 1672)

An administrator of a decedent's estate may pay any creditor of the estate first.

A chose in action cannot be sequestered.

Lord Nottingham, *Prolegomena*, p. 313

Trinity [term] 24 Car. II.

A partner with Thomas Handra, the master of a ship in a voyage to Guinea, sues his administratrix to a sequestration for want of an answer. And, then, he exhibits a bill against the other merchants, who had seized 19 marks of gold of Handra's and coined them into £535, to have an account of that and other effects of Handra in their hands.

[It was] resolved: first, if these effects were delivered by the consent of the administratrix and before the sequestration, the plaintiff can have no title, for an administrator may pay whom he shall please first; if they were taken by force, still the sequestration is no title, for a mere right of action cannot be sequestered; second, if the plaintiff could be relieved upon the title of the sequestration, yet he must stand in the place of the administratrix, and be liable to account in her place.

488

Wilford v. Ferrars

(Ch. 1672)

Where a trustee invests the trust res in good faith, the trust, and not the trustee, suffers any loss.

If a trustee, pending a suit against him for an account, invests the trust res, *the trustee is liable for any loss.*

Lord Nottingham, *Prolegomena*, p. 326

24 Car. II.

If an executor in trust or trustee for infants lend out the money *bona fide*, which becomes desperate, he shall not make it good; second, if he call in debts on mortgages to lend out on personal security, it is at his own peril; otherwise, it is if the mortgagor pay in the money; third, if he lend out any money pending a suit to call him to account, it is at his own peril.

489

Mason v. Herbert

(Ch. 1672)

An account for a small sum of money can be discharged on the basis of the defendant's own oath.

Lord Nottingham, *Prolegomena*, p. 272

Trinity [term] 24 Car. II.

If an account has been kept several years without any excepting to it, the discharge shall be allowed as well as the charge. Otherwise, the general rule is that the discharge must be proved unless it be for sums under 40s. expended by the defendant, in which case, by the course of the court, the defendant's oath must be taken.

490

Miller v. Higdon

(Ch. 1672)

An account based on a trust will be barred by the plaintiff's laches in suing after a great length of time.

Lord Nottingham, *Prolegomena*, p. 334

15 October 1672.

An extent was assigned in 1642 on trust. But the bill did not charge any profits received on that extent in 1648 nor any further continuance of that trust or demand of any account in twenty-six years until the present bill.

[It was] adjudged the length was a good plea, not by the Statute of Limitations,[1] for the trust was by a deed, but, by the rules of equity, which now limit redemption of mortgages to twenty years unless there be extraordinary circumstances, and for general repose.

491

Cattle v. Stagg

(Ch. 1672)

The title of interrogatories may be amended where it was a mistake of the clerk. Depositions are not amendable.

[1] Stat. 21 Jac. I, c. 16 (*SR*, IV, 1222–1223).

Lord Nottingham, *Prolegomena*, p. 319

24 October 1672.

A commission was taken for the examination of witnesses in a cause between George Cattle, plaintiff, and Thomas Stagg, defendant, as between George, plaintiff, and John, defendant, and all the depositions mentioned John instead of Thomas.

[It was] resolved: first, the title of the interrogatories may be amended as a mistake of the clerk, and so it was done in this case by the Master of the Rolls on a petition; second, but the depositions are not amendable and, therefore, not to be used at the hearing; third, that, therefore, there may be a new examination by an order of court notwithstanding publication, because the former examinations are void; fourth, wherefore, the plaintiff, for expedition, offered to proceed on the bill and answer and replication, because the answer replied to must not be taken for true unless the defendant prove it, but yet it may avail the plaintiff.

492
Strode v. Strode
(Ch. 1672)

Where a father purchases lands in the name of his son in trust for himself or as a joint tenant, the intent of the father determines whether the transaction was intended as an advancement for the son or not.

Lord Nottingham, *Prolegomena*, p. 243

25 October 1672.

In the case between Strode and Strode, the opinion of ORLANDO BRIDGEMAN, Keeper, was: first, that a father may purchase lands in the name of his son in trust for himself; second, that, if his son was a joint purchaser with himself, yet [an] express declaration may make it a trust for the father; third, but yet the sole perception of profits by the father shall not raise a trust for the father, because the father as joint tenant may receive all the profits and yet it may be still intended as an advancement of the son and not a trust; fourth, but, if the purchase be made in the name of the son alone, and not in the name of the father also as a joint purchaser, and the father paid all the money, received all the profits, made all the leases etc., there a trust shall arise to the father by implication, and no advancement shall be intended; fifth, the Earl of Lincoln's Case, *supra* [s.] 10,[1] is not like, for, there, the profits he received were as guardian to his infant daughter; here the son was of full age.

[Later proceedings in this case: 73 Selden Soc. 149, British Library MS. Stowe 406, f. 86.]
[Reg. Lib. 1674/75 B, f. 361.]

[1] *Earl of Lincoln's Case*, Lord Nottingham, *Prolegomena*, p. 242.

493

Anonymous

(Ch. 1672)

An account for a small sum of money can be discharged on the basis of the defendant's own oath.

2 Freeman 136, 22 E.R. 1112

27 October 1672. Lord Bridgeman and the Master of the Rolls.

[Upon an] account before a Master, the party may discharge himself upon his own oath for any sum not exceeding 40s.

494

Pinsell v. Alley

(Ch. 1672)

A court of equity cannot assist a suit in London on a foreign attachment.

Lord Nottingham, *Prolegomena*, p. 335

12 November [1672].

A bill was exhibited to discover fraud in a foreign attachment made for the defendant precedent to a foreign attachment made for the plaintiff and also to discover what subsequent effects of Barrett came to the hands of the defendant to the end they may be liable to the plaintiff's attachment, to whom Barrett had given a note for £600 due on an account stated.

The defendant denied the fraud, and demurred, because Barrett was not bound to discover until after a judgment.

But I [*Finch*] urged another cause of demurrer at the bar, because a court of Chancery ought not to assist a suit in London on a foreign attachment, which was agreed by BRIDGEMAN, Keeper.

495

Weale v. Lower

(Ch. 1672–1689)

A fine can act as an estoppel so that, when a remainder vests, the remainderman can claim an estate as of a descent.

Lord Nottingham, *Prolegomena*, p. 340

Michaelmas term 1672, LORD BRIDGEMAN, Keeper.

On a bill exhibited by Weal *versus* Lower to have further assurance of a lease for 500 years, these points in law were moved in this case. Richard Lower makes a feoffment to these uses, *quoad* two third parts, to the use of himself for life, *quoad* another third part, to the use of himself for the life of Thomas, his son, and, after the death of Thomas, then of that third part to the use of Jane, wife of Thomas, for life, and, as to the two third parts, after the death of Richard and Philadelphia, to the use of Thomas for life and, after the deaths of Richard, Philadelphia, and Thomas, to the use of Jane and such issue male or female as Thomas should beget until such issue be twenty-one and for, default of such issue, to the use of Jane for life and, after the deaths of Richard, Philadelphia, and Jane, all the lands to Thomas and the heirs male of his body, remainder to his right heirs. Thomas has issue a daughter, makes a lease for 500 years to J.S. to commence after the death of Richard, and he levies a fine to J.S. *sur concessit* for 500 years, and he dies. Philadelphia dies, living Richard.

And [it was] resolved by HALE, Chief Justice, and TWYSDEN [Justice]:

First, *quoad* the third part, the remainder to Thomas was not contingent but vested, for, though the last clauses says 'after the deaths of Richard, Philadelphia, and Jane to Thomas and his heirs', yet that ought to be understood distributively, *reddendo singula singulis*, according to all the former clauses, *viz.* as to the third part after the deaths of Thomas and Jane to Thomas and his heirs, and, as to the two third parts after the deaths of Richard and Philadelphia to Thomas and his heirs, on the reason of 5 Coke's reports, Wyndham's Case.[1] The consequence of this first point is that the third part being vested, not contingent, the deed and fine of Thomas did well charge it, and passed an interest for 500 years;

Second, as to the two third parts, the remainder to Thomas was contingent, for, it being to commence after the deaths of Richard and Philadelphia and no estate being limited to Philadelphia, it might so fall out that Richard might have died, living Philadelphia, and, then, the particular estate would have determined, yet the remainder to Thomas should not begin. Therefore, it was contingent. The consequence of this second point was that the deed and fine of Thomas did not convey any estate or present interest for 500 years in the two third parts;

Third, that, nevertheless, this fine did operate by way of conclusion or estoppel against Thomas and his heirs on the two parts, notwithstanding that the same fine did also work by way of an interest on the third part, 3 Coke's reports, Sir George Browne's Case;[2]

Fourth, that, when Philadelphia died in the life[time] of Richard, so that the remainder to Thomas ceased to be contingent by the happening of that death and was now become certain, the fine for 500 years did now bind the daughter

[1] *Wyndham v. Debney* (1589), 5 Coke Rep. 7, 77 E.R. 58, also Moore K.B. 191, 72 E.R. 524.

[2] *Lynch v. Spencer* (1594), 3 Coke Rep. 45, 76 E.R. 742, also Croke Eliz. 513, 78 E.R. 762, Moore K.B. 455, 72 E.R. 691, 2 Anderson 44, 123 E.R. 537.

and heir of Thomas by estoppel, as much as if it had passed by way of an interest or estate.

And the court, on this opinion, decreed old Richard, the grandfather, to make further assurance to the plaintiff, who paid Thomas's debts on this security.

Pollexfen 54, 86 E.R. 509

3 January 1672[/73].

Richard Lower, being seised in fee of lands, 4 June 1652, made a feoffment in fee to Charles Grills, the younger, and Thomas Lower, the elder, as to two third parts, to the use of himself for life without impeachment of waste, as to the other third part, to the use of himself for the life of Thomas Lower, the younger, his son, without impeachment of waste and, after the death of the said Thomas, as to that third part, to the use of Jane, the wife of Thomas, for life and, as to the other two third parts, after the death of Richard and Philadelphia, his wife, to the use of Thomas Lower, the younger, for life and, after the death of Richard, Philadelphia, and Thomas Lower, the younger, to the use of the said Jane and of such issue male or female as the said Thomas shall beget on her, until such issue shall become of the age of twenty-one years, and not otherwise, and, if Thomas shall have no issue by her, then, to the use of Jane for life and, after the death of Richard, Philadelphia, and Jane, all the lands to the use of Thomas Lower, junior, and the heirs male of his body to be begotten on Jane and, for default of such issue, to the heirs of Thomas forever.

Thomas, the younger, has issue a daughter, yet alive, and then he makes a lease of all the lands by deed indented to the said Charles Grills for 500 years to commence after the death of Richard. And, afterwards, he grants by fine to the said Grills for 500 years, and then he and Philadelphia die.

[The question was] whether this be a good lease. The case, in short, is this.

Richard Lower makes a feoffment to the use of himself for life and, after the death of him and Philadelphia, his wife, to the use of Thomas Lower for life and, after the death of Richard, Philadelphia, and Thomas, to the use of Thomas and the heirs male of his body and, for default of such issue, to the use of the heirs of Thomas. Thomas has issue a daughter, and then, by fine and indenture, he grants the land to Grills for 500 years. Thomas dies; then Philadelphia dies, Richard being alive. And whether this lease be good after the death of Richard is the question.

In this case, there are four points, to which I [*Pollexfen*] shall speak briefly, for, though the limitations differ, yet the same questions will be in all of them.

Point 1: Whether the words 'heirs of Thomas', are in this case words of limitation or words of trust.

Point 2: Whether the remainder limited to Thomas and his heirs be a contingent remainder or a remainder vested in Thomas, which is descended to his heir.

Point 3: Admitting that it were a contingent remainder and not actually vested in Thomas, yet whether the same, since the contingency happened, be not vested in the heir of Thomas, if not strictly, yet in the nature of a descent.

Point 4: Admitting that the remainder be not actually vested in Thomas, but were contingent and that, at the time of the lease made, Thomas had no remainder in him and, therefore, no estate is conveyed by his deed and fine, yet whether, if Thomas had been alive, it would not have been good against him by estoppel and so good also against his heir.

First, of the first point, it is a general rule that, where an estate is limited to the ancestor for life and, after, an estate is limited to his right heirs, the word 'heirs' is a word of limitation, and the estate vests in the ancestor. If a man limit an estate to the use of himself for life, remainder in tail, remainder to the right heirs of the tenant for life, the fee vests in the ancestor, and this was never denied in any book. And in our case, if Thomas had survived Philadelphia, there could have been no question but that Thomas would have been a tenant in tail with a remainder in fee, which could never be unless the word 'heirs' had been a word of limitation.

Second, of the second point, first, I [*Pollexfen*] agree that a contingency is when it is uncertain whether the thing will take effect or no. And these uncertainties happen, first, when an estate is limited to a person not *in esse*, as if a lease for life be made, the remainder to the right heirs of J.S., who is alive, this is contingent, because it is uncertain whether J.S. shall ever have an heir. But this is not in our case; here is a person *in esse*, namely, Thomas. Second, when there is a condition precedent or some other accident which ought to happen before that it can take effect, which is uncertain whether it will ever happen or no, as if a lease for life be made and that if A. pay £10, then the remainder to the right heirs of A. or, if A. survive B., then the remainder to the right heirs of B, in these cases, it is uncertain whether the money will be paid or the accident happen. But there is no such thing in our case, for, in our case, it is certain that Richard and Philadelphia will both die. Third, there is another case of a contingent remainder, which is when a remainder is so limited that it is uncertain whether it will continue during the continuance of the particular estate, for, if it cannot vest during the particular estate or immediately when the particular estate determines, it is void.

And then the question in our case will be whether the remainder be so limited that it cannot vest during the particular estate.

Second, I [*Pollexfen*] agree that, if it had been a limitation according to the course of the common law, it had been contingent, for, if a lease had been made to Richard for life and, after the death of Richard and Philadelphia, the remainder to Thomas and his heirs, this would have been a contingent remainder for the particular estate, being only for the life of Richard, and the remainder not to commence until after the death of Richard and Philadelphia, this might determine by the death of Richard before Philadelphia. So it would have been in such a case at common law. And, though it had been by way of a use, yet could not the remainder be preserved without a particular estate.

But, in our case, the question is whether, by implication of law, there be not a use and estate executed in Richard, the feoffor, not only during his own life, which is express, but to Richard and his heirs during the life of Philadelphia. For, if so, then there is no contingency in the remainder, but the remainder vests, and Richard will be seised to him and his heirs during his own life and the life of Philadelphia, remainder to Thomas.

And I [*Pollexfen*] conceive that, by implication of law, such use and estate does arise to Richard. First, if a man make a feoffment in fee and declare no use, the law implies that it is to the use of the feoffor and his heirs. Second, if a man make a feoffment and declare a use for parcel of the estate and declare no use for the residue, by operation of law, the residue shall be to the use of the feoffor and his heirs. And, therefore, if a man make a feoffment to the use of A. for life, remainder to the use of B. in tail, and declare no use over, yet, by operation of law, it shall be to the use of the feoffor and his heirs for the residue.

If a man make a feoffment and declare the use after marriage had between the feoffor and such a woman to be to himself and his wife and the heirs of the feoffor without any declaration to whom the use shall be before the marriage take effect, *per constructionem*, the use shall arise to the feoffor until the contingency happen. So, likewise, if a man make a feoffment to such uses as he shall declare by his last will, by operation of law, it is a qualified fee in the meantime.

The Lord Pagett's Case cited in the Rector of Chedington's Case,[1] was thus. The Lord Pagett covenants to stand seised to the use of Thomas Farmer, who was a stranger, for the life of the covenantor and, after his decease, to the use of J.S. and J.N. for twenty-four years and, after the expiration of the term, to the use of the son of the covenantor in tail, with remainders over; [it was] adjudged that the uses limited to Thomas Farmer, J.S., and J.N. were void. And, there, it had been all one if no use had been limited to them. And [it was] adjudged that the covenantor shall by operation of law have the use and estate to himself until the time that the remainder to his son was to commence.

If a man make a feoffment and depart with all his estate and limit the use to his daughter for life and, after her decease, to his son in tail, remainder to his right heirs, the law creates to the feoffor a use for his life until the future use come *in esse*, and that it is all one when created by law and when by the limitation of the party.

Suppose there had been no use limited to Richard, but it had been that, after the death of Richard and Philadelphia, it shall be to Thomas and his heirs, the

[1] *Lord Paget's Case* (Ex. 1591), 1 Coke Rep. 154, 76 E.R. 346.

law will create a use in the meantime, as in the case of a devise, which is with a use in Shellie's Case.[1]

Then, in this case here, if the limitation of the use had been to the feoffor and his heirs during his own life and the life of Philadelphia, remainder to Thomas, all had been vested and [there would be] no contingent remainder. However, if the law will create a use to the feoffor during the life of Philadelphia, it shall be all one. And, if so, without doubt, the lease is good.

Third, of the third point, first, it is not vested in his heir by purchase, for the word 'heirs', as is aforesaid, is a word of limitation and not of purchase. Second, the heir claims and has it by force of the limitation of his ancestor and as heir to his ancestor and in no other manner and, therefore, in the nature of a descent.

And, in this point, all may be said which is in the argument of Shellie's Case, where the opinion of the judges was that, though the use of the recovery there was never executed in the ancestor, but vested first in the heir, yet it is in the heir in the course and nature of a descent, as is proved by Wood's Case,[2] there cited, where a man covenanted that, when J.S. enfeoffed him of the manor of Dale, he will stand seised of the manor of Sale to the use of the covenantee and his heirs, the covenantee dies, then, J.S. enfeoffs the covenantor, and thereby an estate in the manor of Sale arises to the heir of the covenantee, and he shall have it in the course and nature of a descent, and not by purchase.

A. covenants with B. that his son shall marry the daughter of B. and, if he do not marry her, that then A. and his heirs will stand seised of such land to the use of B. and his heirs until £100 be paid. B. dies; the marriage never takes effect, and the heir of B. shall have the land. And there it is a question whether or no he shall be in ward[ship]. So, in our case, though the heir has not the remainder by descent, yet I [*Pollexfen*] conceive he shall not have it by purchase, but in the course and nature of a descent.

Fourth, of the fourth point, it cannot be denied that, if Thomas had lived after the death of Philadelphia and the remainder had vested in him, that this clause, which, at the beginning, was only good against him by estoppel, would then have been turned into a good estate and term in interest. First, the lease is made by deed indented and by fine, both of very great force in the law to make an estoppel. Second, privies in blood, as the heir; privies in estate, as the feoffee and lessee; privies in law, as the lord by escheat, tenants by the courtesy, tenants in dower, and all others, which come under by act in law or in the post shall be bound by and take advantage of estoppels. So are the words of My Lord Coke and the old books by him cited. And, then, the daughter in this case shall be estopped if she be privy or come in under or in the post or by act in law. And it seems that she is privy in blood, and comes in under or of necessity by act in law.

[1] *Wolfe v. Shelley* (1581), 1 Coke Rep. 88, 76 E.R. 199, 3 Dyer 373, 73 E.R. 838, 1 Anderson 69, 123 E.R. 358, Moore K.B. 136, 72 E.R. 490, Jenkins 249, 145 E.R. 176.

[2] *Wood's Case* (Wards 1560 × 1561), 1 Coke Rep. 99, 76 E.R. 222.

But, as I [*Pollexfen*] conceive, she claims as heir, and can make no title unless she show herself to be the heir of Thomas, and, therefore, she shall be estopped as heir, although the estate never vested in Thomas.

If the eldest son of a tenant in tail levy a fine in the life of his father, the father dies, the eldest son dies without issue, the youngest son is concluded by this fine, for, though the eldest son had nothing at the time of the fine levied, yet, because the youngest must draw his descent from him and as heir to him, therefore, it shall be a bar. But it had been otherwise if the eldest son had died in the life of his father. And, if they are estopped to say *partes finis nihil*, because they make their title and claim as heir to him that levied the fine although he that levied it had no right or title to the estate at the time of the fine levied. So it is in our case.

By what has been said, it plainly appears that the heir in this case comes in as heir, and in the nature of a descent, and, therefore, he must of necessity be privy and claim under his ancestor.

The original act, the purchase and beginning of his title, was in his ancestor. And the execution of everything executory ought to have respect to the original cause and beginning, and shall have relation thereto. And it is great reason that, if he will have an estate as heir to his ancestor, he should be bound by the act of his ancestor, *qui sentit commodum sentire debet et onus*.

And, in this case, there was a purchaser, but this purchaser could not be the heir for the reasons aforesaid, and, if not the heir, then, of necessity, it must be Thomas, the ancestor. And from Thomas came the title to the heir, although more perfect by reason of the contingency which did not happen in the life of Thomas, but afterwards in the time of the heir. And, therefore, it seems that the heir is privy, and comes under the purchase and title of Thomas, and ought, therefore, to be estopped and concluded by the indenture and fine of Thomas. She is the daughter of Thomas, and, therefore, privy in blood. She is heir of Thomas; otherwise, she cannot claim, for she cannot claim by purchase, and, if she cannot have it by purchase, she must of necessity claim it by or in the nature of a descent or under Thomas or by act in law. And one or the other is sufficient.

Thomas, although he had not an estate, yet he had a right to have it if the contingency happen, if Richard survive Philadelphia, and this right, as it seems, is barable, as well as a power of revocation and a limitation of a new use, as in Albany's Case,[1] where a feoffment was made to the use of the feoffor for life, with divers remainders over, provided that, if Penruddock died without issue male, that then the feoffor might revoke and declare new uses. In this case, it was resolved, first, that this power, although contingent, is destroyed by the fine or feoffment of the feoffor, second, that it may be released, third, that, if the power had been reserved to the feoffor and his heirs, that it was an inheritance descendible, and that the release of the ancestor will destroy it. This case was in all re-

[1] *Grendon v. Albany* (1585–1586), 1 Coke Rep. 107, 76 E.R. 246, 4 Leonard 133, 219, 74 E.R. 778, 833.

spects more contingent than ours, for it could not take effect unless Penruddock had died without issue in the lifetime of the feoffor. Ours was but the death of Philadelphia before Richard. In that case, there ought to have been a new declaration of the use; in ours, none, only the happening of the contingency.

But suppose that, in Albany's Case, there had been no revocation and it had been only this, that, if Penruddock die without issue in the life of the feoffor, that then the first uses shall cease and that it shall be to the use of the feoffor and his heirs and then the feoffor levies a fine or makes a feoffment and then the contingency happens; should not this have been a bar? Would not this have been more strong than the other, where, upon a contingency and execution of a power, he might have the estate?

The conclusion is that, if the fine or feoffment of Thomas would have barred or estopped him, it ought to bar and estop his issue, and, then, the lease ought to be good for so much.

But there be some other objections.

Objection 1: That the remainder in fee to the right heirs of Thomas does not distinguish what Thomas, and there are two in the case.

Answer: Thomas, the younger, being last before named in the limitation of the estate tail, and it being to the right heirs of the said Thomas, it shall be intended the last named.

Objection 2: That the fine of Thomas is to Grills, the feoffee.

Answer: I [*Pollexfen*] conceive that will be all one as if it had been to a stranger, admitting the estate which should serve the contingent use were remaining in the feoffees.

First, but suppose there be two feoffees of a contingent use and one accepts a fine *sur concessit* of a stranger for years, this is good by conclusion between them two, but it does not alter the estate of the feoffees, nor impede the rising of the contingent use, but he is seised in privity as he was before, as to the *cestui que use*.

Second, suppose it had fallen out afterwards that the conusor had been the *cestui que use*, as, in this case, it might; I [*Pollexfen*] conceive it would not have hindered the rising of the use, for, although they are estopped, yet in truth the fee simple vests in the feoffee as before, and cannot be divested out of him by acceptance of the fine, and, if it be still in him, it is still subject to the use, as before.

Third, but, if the use do not rise, yet, perhaps, it may be more for the advantage of the feoffee, for he shall then have the land discharged *pro tanto*, and, therefore, if such feoffee make a lease to a stranger, not having notice and for good consideration, how may this lease be avoided and for what? The estate will be executed for the inheritance, but, for the lease, that is not voidable. And it is much like the cases of Bold and Winston, Car. II, and Reignolds and Wood, Car. II.[1]

[1] Perhaps *Bould v. Wynston* (1607), Croke Jac. 168, 79 E.R. 147; *Wood v. Reignold* (1600–1601), Croke Eliz. 764, 854, 78 E.R. 996, 1080.

But all this is upon a supposition that the fee vests in the feoffees until the contingency happen. But the law seems to be to the contrary, and nothing remains in the feoffees, but the use resorts to the feoffor, and remains in him until the contingency happen.

Objection 3: That the two parts limited to Richard for life are not limited to Thomas and his heirs until after the death of Richard, Philadelphia, and Jane and Jane had no estate for life, but is yet alive, and may survive Richard, and, therefore, the contingency, as to those two parts, is not yet happened, for which reason the estate of Thomas is yet in contingency.

Answer: This objection arises upon an over strict and literal construction of the deed. The true sense of the deed is and ought to be taken *reddendo singula singulis* that the estate in the third part which Jane had for life determined by the death of Jane and the estate in the other two parts after the death of Richard and Philadelphia, and not after the death of Jane.

This case was debated by *Sir Francis North*, the King's Solicitor [General], for the defendant, and by Mr. *Pollexfen*, for the plaintiff, before the Lord Chief Justice HALE, to whom it was referred by an order of Chancery, 3 January 1672[/73].

And upon the hearing, the Lord Chief Justice [HALE] was of opinion:

First, that the estate limited to Thomas was a contingent remainder as to two parts, and he took a difference between a contingent remainder by way of a use and a future use or an estate *in futuro* by way of a use, as, if a feoffment be made to the use of A. for life and, after the death of A. and B., to the use of C. in fee, this is a contingent remainder to C. But, if a feoffment be made to the use of C. and his heirs after the death of A. and B., this is no remainder, but a future use, and the feoffee is seised in fee simple, and not of a freehold descendible determinable upon the deaths of A. and B. So, if the limitation of a use be that, after two years or after the death of John at Stiles, it shall be to the use of J.N. in fee, the feoffor has the fee simple remaining in him until this future use come *in esse*;

Second, that this contingent remainder descends to the heir of Thomas, and he shall have it in the course and nature of a descent;

Third, that the fine of Thomas did operate at the beginning by conclusion and passed no interest, yet this estoppel shall bind his heir, and he shall be in the same case with his ancestor;

Fourth, that the estate which comes to the heir upon the happening of the contingency feeds this estoppel and, then, the estate by estoppel becomes an estate in interest, and shall be of the same effect as if the contingency had happened before the fine levied;

Fifth, that, if the fine had been levied by Thomas in fee, this would have barred the estate of the heir, destroyed the contingent use, and have operated to the benefit of the possession as the fine of a disseisee to a stranger, but, being only for years, the fee is vested, and the term is good, being drawn out of the fee;

Sixth, although it do not appear by the case, yet, upon examination, it appears that, by another deed, Philadelphia had an estate for life, and, then, as

My Lord Chief Justice [HALE] said, the use shall not be contingent as to the two parts, but the mentioning that the commencement thereof shall be after the death of Philadelphia is only an expressing when he shall take the profits in possession, and not a contingency.

Objection 1: The first objection, *viz.* what Thomas it should be, was not questioned.

Objection 2: That the fine to the feoffee makes no difference, because my Lord Chief Justice [HALE] held that the estate which preserved the use did not remain in the feoffees, but in the feoffor until the contingency happened.

Objection 3: That the deed shall be construed *reddendo singula singulis* and, therefore, if a lease be made of one acre to A., of another acre to B., and of a third to C. and that, after the death of A., B., and C., it shall remain to E. and his heirs, in this case, E. shall not have a contingent remainder, but the construction shall be relative.

If a feoffment be made to the use of A. for ninety-nine years if he shall live so long and, after his death, to the use of B. in fee, this shall not be contingent, but it shall be presumed that his life will not exceed ninety-nine years, but, otherwise, it would have been if it had been made but for twenty-one years, and so, he said, had it been ruled, and named the case.

As to the third part limited to Jane for life, the Chief Justice [HALE] held that the remainder therein was not contingent, but was vested, because, by the limitation after the deaths of Richard, Philadelphia, and Jane, being construed distributively, it shall be taken that, as to the third part, the estate of Thomas commences in possession after the deaths of Richard and Jane only, for, in this part, Philadelphia had nothing, and, as to the other two parts, where Philadelphia had an estate for life, there, it shall be taken to commence after the death of Richard and Philadelphia.

Objection 4: The counsel of the defendant objected that an estate by estoppel shall not be favored in equity, and said that the jury is not bound to find it, and, if it be found, the court shall judge the lease void.

Answer: The law, as it seems, is so in cases of obligations, covenants, or personal contracts, which cannot be turned into an estate, but, in other cases, where the estate is bound by the conclusion and converted into an interest, although the jury find the matter at large, yet the court shall judge according to the law that the estate is good by reason of the estoppel.

Cartwright made a lease to Warlow for six years, by indenture of a house, in which he had nothing, and, afterwards, he purchases of Rawlins a lease of the said house for twenty-one years upon condition, then Cartwright re-demises to Rawlins for ten years.[1] [It was] adjudged:

---

[1] *Rawlyns v. Somerford* (1587), 4 Coke Rep. 52, 76 E.R. 107, 4 Leonard 116, 74 E.R. 767, Gouldsborough 89, 75 E.R. 1015, Jenkins 254, 145 E.R. 180.

First, that the lease to Warlow for six years was good against Cartwright, by conclusion, but nothing in interest;

Second, that, as soon as Cartwright had purchased his lease for twenty-one years, Warlow's lease for six years became a lease in interest, the reversion in Cartwright;

Third, when Cartwright demised to Rawlins for ten years, Rawlins was bound by the estoppel, and took only a future interest, there being no attornment;

Fourth, that, when the jury has found this matter at large, the court shall adjudge according to the law, and Warlow had a good estate for six years, and Rawlins only an interest *in futuro*.

And Pleadal's Case[1] was there cited to be adjudged that a jury was attainted for not finding a lease, which was good by conclusion. A jury found that the lessor had nothing in the land when he made the lease to the plaintiff, and, afterwards, the lessor entered and ejected him, and, in this case, it was held by Anderson and Periam that this lease was good between the parties and that the jury were bound to find it so or, otherwise, to find the whole matter, and then the court shall adjudge it to be a good estate and interest between them.

Afterwards, forasmuch as My Lord Chief Justice [HALE] had certified the case did contain in it divers considerable points and that he would not have the right of the parties determined by his single opinion, but thought it necessary to have other of the judges joined with him, and, then, the case was again argued by Mr. *Pollexfen* in Chancery, the thirtieth day of January in the twenty-fifth year of King Charles II [1673], before the said Lord Chief Justice [HALE] and before WILDE, WYNDHAM, and ELLIS, called into the Chancery by My Lord Chancellor [COOPER] for his assistance, and they all agreed in opinion that the estate of Thomas was contingent as to two parts but not as to the third part but that the third part was vested in Thomas. And so the counsel of the other side, Serjeant *Maynard* and the Solicitor General [*North*], agreed. And, as to the two parts, that, although it were contingent, yet the fine of Thomas enures by estoppel, and, afterwards, when the remainder comes to his son, that he shall claim in the nature of a descent, and, therefore, shall be bound by the estoppel, and, then, the estoppel was turned into an interest, and the conusee had then an estate in the two parts as well as in the third part.

And accordingly it was decreed.

79 Selden Soc. 591

December 1677.

---

[1] *Pledall v. Pledall* (1567), Croke Eliz. 36, 78 E.R. 302, Moore K.B. 96, 72 E.R. 464.

Upon a bill of review to reverse a decree for further assurance, it was assigned for error that there was no covenant in the original conveyance to the purchaser to make any further assurance.

Yet I [Lord Nottingham] held the decree good and the thing reasonable to be done, though there were no covenant for the doing of it.

2 Freeman 107, 22 E.R. 1089

1689. Lower v. Weale. Lords Commissioners [To Hold the Great Seal]. Upon a bill of review.

The plaintiff's father, tenant in tail, sold his land to the defendant, and made him a conveyance, the defendant taking him then to be tenant in fee. The defendant, afterwards, finding that he was only a tenant in tail, preferred his bill to compel him to levy a fine and make farther assurance. And he had a decree accordingly, having paid his purchase money. And it was decreed that the defendant should enjoy against the vendor and his issue and all claiming under them. The vendor lay in the Fleet [Prison], and would not make farther assurance. And he died in prison.

The plaintiff, being heir in tail, brought his bill of review to reverse the said decree, and assigned for error that he, being heir in tail, ought not to be bound by it.

It was argued by the Attorney General [*Treby*] and Mr. *Finch*, for the defendant, and by Serjeant *Hutchins* and *Sir William Williams*, for the plaintiff.

It was insisted for the defendant that the decree ought not to be reversed, but that the plaintiff, being issue in tail, ought to be bound by it, because the father, in his lifetime, could have barred him by a fine, and it was what in equity he ought to have done, having received his purchase money. And that which carried it farther in this case was that there was a decree and judgment of the court that he ought to have done it.

It was admitted that, if a tenant in tail contracts for the purchase of his estate or makes a conveyance thereof and levies no fine, that no bill will lie against the issue in tail to compel him to convey. But, here, the matter being decreed against him in his lifetime, whether the issue should come in to avoid that decree, it being a decree which ought in justice and conscience to be performed, [was the question].

First objection: The issue in tail claims paramount to the tenant in tail *per formam doni*.

Answer: The issue in tail derives his title through the tenant in tail to convey himself to the estate.

Second objection: This decree is to set aside the Statute *de Donis*.[1]

[1] Stat. 13 Edw. I, Westminster II, c. 1 (*SR*, I, 71–72).

Answer: It is not so much to set aside that Statute as it is to come in aid of the Statute of Fines, which was made to bar entails.[1]

Besides, if this decree should not bind the estate, it would put it into the power of the nocent person to elude the justice of this court, for, if he will lie in prison and be obstinate, the purchaser is cheated of his money.

In many cases, the act or neglect of a tenant in tail shall affect the issue, although no fine be levied, as, in the case of a forfeiture of the double value upon marriage, the estate shall be charged in the hands of the issue, although the party dies.

But to that, it was answered by *Maynard* that is by virtue of an Act of Parliament[2] prior to the Statute *de Donis*, and, then, according to a rule in law, a subsequent statute does not abrogate a precedent statute without express words.

They cited Octavian Lombard's Case,[3] but that differed from this, because the issue in tail there had a benefit by the act of his ancestor, and so was bound by it. Lands devised to a man and the heirs of his body and that the devisee should grant a rent in fee, the devisee grants accordingly, and [it was] adjudged that the issue in tail was bound by it.

But to that, it was answered that the grantee there did not claim under the tenant in tail, but from the devisor. (Brooke, [Abr.], *Feoffment to uses.*)

This court has from time to time enlarged its power to make its decrees effectual. It was held all along until King James's time that the decrees of this court bound only the person, and could not meddle with the sequestering of land, neither did the Court of Exchequer ever do it until of late. But, finding their decrees would be useless in many cases where the person was obstinate, it is now the common practice of both courts.

It was doubted until of late whether a common recovery suffered by a *cestui que trust* in tail should bar the remainderman. In a case between Workman and Downing, the Lord Bridgeman was very doubtful. But that point is since settled in the case of the Lord Chief Justice North, by the opinion of the Lord Nottingham,[4] that it would bar for two reasons, first, because a trust is not within the Statute *de Donis*, second, a trust is a creature of this court and so under the control of it.

For the plaintiff, it was insisted that the issue in tail was entitled, and did claim *per formam doni*, and had an Act of Parliament for his security, which could no way be barred until the Act which gave power to bar by a fine, until the way

[1] Stat. 4 Hen. VII, c. 24 (*SR*, II, 547–548).

[2] Stat. 20 Hen. III, Merton, c. 7 (*SR*, I, 3); Stat. 3 Edw. I, Westminster I, c. 21 (*SR*, I, 32–33).

[3] *Lumbard's Case* (1370), YB Trin. 44 Edw. III, f. 21, pl. 24.

[4] *Lord North v. Williams* (1681), 2 Chancery Cases 63, 22 E.R. 848, *sub nom. North v. Way*, 1 Vernon 13, 23 E.R. 270, *sub nom. North v. Champernoon*, 2 Chancery Cases 78, 22 E.R. 855, 1 Eq. Cas Abr. 255, 21 E.R. 1029, 79 Selden Soc. 888.

of a common recovery was found out, which was taken for a bar because of the supposed recompense.

It is often said here that this court should always be cautious of assuming a legislative power to avoid an act of Parliament. Besides, if it should once be admitted that the issue in tail should be otherwise barred than by a fine or recovery, there would be no stop.

Objection: This is in the case of an honest purchaser, and so the court ought to help as far as they can.

Answer: That may be said in all cases where a man pays money, and every creditor may say as much where his debt is real. And the consequence of that would be to let in all judgments, statutes, and mortgages upon the estate tail.

Curia advisare vult.

2 Vernon 306, 23 E.R. 798

A tenant in tail had sold at a full value, and received the consideration money. And he had covenanted to levy a fine, and was decreed to do it. Yet he dying, though in prison in contempt for not performing the decree, the issue in tail could not be bound by it.

[By Reg. Lib. 1690 B, f. 281, we collect that the original decree was reversed and that the defendant to the bill of review was ordered to redeliver to the plaintiff possession of the premises obtained under the said original decree.]
[Other reports of this case: 1 Eq. Cas. Abr. 266, 21 E.R. 1035.]

496

Basset v. Basset

(Ch. 1672–1673)

A court of equity will not supply a defect in a conveyance for the benefit of a volunteer.

Lord Nottingham, *Prolegomena*, p. 337

11 November, 24 Car. II. Basset v. Lady Martha Basset.

[It was] resolved: first, a devise [by the testator] to his wife of all his real and personal estate for the payment of debts is a fee simple; second, but, when the testator says further that, if his wife die before the debts be paid, the estate shall go to his brother, he paying the debts, and likewise caused those words 'to her and her heirs forever', which the scrivener had added, to be struck out, that, now, on the whole matter, the wife has but an estate for life; third, admitting that she has a fee simple and she makes a voluntary feoffment without livery of seisin, equity will not supply the defect of a voluntary conveyance; fourth, but, when the feoffment is in trust to pay debts and in pursuance of the will, this cannot be looked upon as a conveyance purely voluntary, but the defect of it was decreed to be supplied by new assurances. And a decree of the Master of the Rolls to the contrary was altered by BRIDGEMAN, Keeper, WILDE and WYNDHAM, justices.

Lord Nottingham, *Prolegomena*, p. 338

Hilary [term] 25 Car. II.

The cause of Basset and Basset was again reheard with assistants, HALE, Chief Justice, WILDE and WYNDHAM, and a decree was confirmed that Lady Martha shall make a new assurance. HALE regards not the opinion that she was a tenant for life, but relies on the consideration that the purchaser under the feoffment had paid £3000 [in] debts.

[Later reports of this case: Repts. *tempore* Finch 189, 23 E.R. 104.]

497

O'Bryan v. Countess of Clancarty

(Ch. 1672)

A suit against a single co-obligor will be dismissed for the non-joinder of the other co-obligors.

Lord Nottingham, *Prolegomena*, p. 305

12 November 1672.

Mabella Digby intermarries with O'Bryan by the mediation of the earl of Clancarty, who, to draw on the marriage, enters into a bond of £4000 with two other sureties to make good the jointure. And he dies, having by his will made his countess executrix. And he devised to her several lands for the payment of all debts due in law and conscience.

The countess was sued here in Chancery to discover assets. But the co-obligors and the heir were no parties.

And the bill was dismissed without suffering the plaintiff to proceed for the proportion of the earl of Clancarty, the deceased testator.

498

Earl of Athol v. Earl of Derby

(Ch. 1672–1673)

A writ of execution will not be issued against a member of Parliament during the legislative session and for twenty days thereafter.

As to priority of liens, a final decree in equity is of equal rank with a final judgment at common law.

The alienation of a chattel bona fide, *though* pendente lite, *before the* teste *of the writ of execution, is good and binding.*

1 Chancery Cases 220, 22 E.R. 771

James, earl of Derby, tenant for life, makes a lease for twenty-one years to his wife of the Isle of Man, for a provision for younger children, and he dies. She agrees with the earl of Athol, on the marriage of her younger daughter, the Lady Emilia, to give him a £5000 portion and that he shall have the Isle of Man, valued at £1000 *per annum* for five years to pay it. Charles, the earl of Derby's son, the defendant, opposed this lease, being made by a tenant for life and between a husband and wife. But, by the mediation of certain Lords in Parliament, Earl Charles and his mother came to a new agreement in the year 1660 that she shall have the one moiety of the profits of the Isle and he the other. In 1661, they came to a new agreement, that he should in lieu of the agreement pay his mother £500 *per annum* and, in the close of the deed, he appoints his receiver for the Isle of Man to pay it. All these agreements were made by the countess on behalf of the earl of Athol to enable him to receive the £5000. And, then, the countess dies.

It was decreed by the Master of the Rolls [Grimston], that the earl of Athol shall have his £500 against the earl of Derby and his person to be charged and the earl of Athol shall not be forced to the Isle of Man, which is the place originally charged, for, by the last agreement, he is to pay £500 *per annum* absolutely, and, in lieu of the profits, let the earl of Derby make what he will of them. And the appointment of the receiver to pay it is but directory, and, if the receiver do not pay it, the earl must.

Maynard and other of the plaintiff's counsel held that the court could not by any decree bind the Isle of Man, nor, if they should decree it, could they execute the decree there, it being out of the power of any sheriff. They also held that the letter of attorney being determined by the countess's death, that the court would not have made a decree for the earl, though her administrator is a defendant, unless in the case of a marriage agreement and that it was proved those agreements were made on his behalf. Afterwards, [a writ of] sequestration was awarded against the earl of Derby.

Whereupon, a question arose, what time of privilege a peer has, *viz.* whether twenty or ten days before and after a session of Parliament.

The Lord Keeper [Bridgeman] sent to the Lord Hollis and others to advise in it. And they produced two orders in the House of Lords, whereby it appeared they declared their privilege to commence from the *teste* to the writ of summons for their first coming to Parliament and that, upon every session and prorogation, their privilege is for twenty days after such session. And it is said in the orders that it is a sufficient time for them to come from all parts of the kingdom and to return and they are in those orders desired to take notice of it and of the reason of it.

Those orders are, the one of the 24th of May 1624, the other of the 27th of January 1628, entered into the Journal of the book of the Lords' House. But it is said the Commons never agreed hereto, and, therefore, they think themselves not bound by it.

Note this sequestration was executed accordingly. But the earl of Derby soon after dying and the estate being entailed, the earl of Athol lost the rest of his wife's portion.

2 Levinz 72, 83 E.R. 455

The earl of Athol having a decree against the earl of Derby for £7000, the portion of his wife, who was sister to the earl of Derby, upon a question touching the privilege of peers in Parliament, how long it lasted, the Lord Chancellor, before he would grant a [writ of] sequestration, sent to the Lord Hollis and other lords to be informed in this matter, who, hereupon, sent him two orders of the House of Lords, the one dated the 28th of May 1614, the other the 27th of January 1628, entered in the Journal Book of the House of Lords, by which it appears that they declare their privilege commences from the *teste* of their writ of summons to Parliament and that, upon every session and prorogation, their privilege is for twenty days before and twenty days after each session, which the order says is time enough for them to come from all parts of the realm and to return.

Hereupon, the Lord Chancellor ordered the sequestration to be delivered and executed immediately after the twenty days.

But it is said the Commons never assented to this, but claim forty days after and before each session.

Note the sequestration was executed accordingly, but the earl of Derby died in a small time afterwards and, his estate being entailed, the earl of Athol lost the benefit of the sequestration.

Lord Nottingham, *Prolegomena*, p. 315

July 1673.

The earl of Athol obtains a decree in Chancery for a personal duty, *viz.* a £6000 portion, against Charles, earl of Derby, who dies. Earl William admits service, and appears by the duke of Ormond, his guardian, and, *quoad* the sequestration laid on Derby House in Channon Row, he pleads an entail by Act of Parliament 4 Jac.,[1] which was admitted good. But whether the sequestration should continue on the fee simple lands was not debated.

As to the countess of Derby, administratrix of Earl Charles, I [*Finch*] delivered this opinion: first, that equity would maintain the decree to be in equal rank with a judgment at law, and, therefore, it was to be paid before specialties; second, if Earl Charles bargained and sold all his personal estate before the decree

[1] Stat. 4 Jac. I, c. 3 (*SR*, IV, 1133) (a private act, not printed).

or before the date of the sequestration or the order for it, no revivor of the decree or sequestration against the administratrix would reach it, for, so at common law, the alienation of a chattel *bona fide*, though *pendente lite*, yet, if, before the *teste* of the writ of execution, is good and binding.

499

Rendall v. Long

(Ch. 1667–1672)

A person in contempt of court is entitled to have a copy of the interrogatories upon which he is to be examined before the examination.

Lord Nottingham, *Prolegomena*, p. 219

In the Case of Rendall and Long, who was brought in on a contempt for not bringing back money into court according to a former order, Lord BRIDGEMAN, Keeper, allowed him to have copies of the interrogatories.

I [*Finch*] opposed, and took the difference, where the defendant is to be examined on his title, as when he comes in on a sequestration resisted and where he comes in on an ordinary contempt. In the first case, it is fit he should have a copy of the interrogatories that he may advise with counsel how to answer, because his title is concerned. In the second case, it is not fit he should have any counsel at all because, being to answer a contempt to the king's court, he ought to answer it plainly and directly, without having time to advise with counsel how to shift it off. This was the ancient practice of this court and the [Court of] Star Chamber. And the contrary would be very mischievous.

Yet the Keeper [BRIDGEMAN] held it fit in all cases to have copies of the interrogatories.

But then I conceive it were fit to reform the course of the court in another matter and to appoint all such examinations to be by a Master in Chancery, and not by a common examiner.

500

Earl of Dorset v. Governor of Bridewell Hospital

(Ch. 1672)

A fine and non-claim will not bar a remedy by a commission for charitable uses.

Lord Nottingham, *Prolegomena*, p. 335

25 November 1672, by Shaftesbury, Chancellor. Richard, earl of Dorset, exceptant; Governor of Bridewell, defendant.

If land be given to a corporation to a charitable use, a fine and non-claim bar the entry at law, but will [not] bar the remedy by a commission for charitable uses.

501

Kyman v. Rigby

(Ch. 1672)

Where a plea has been replied to, the only material issue in the case is the matter contained in the plea.

The duress of the principal debtor is a defense for the surety.

Lord Nottingham, *Prolegomena*, p. 298

27 November 1672, by Shaftesbury, Chancellor, and Twysden.

When a plea is allowed and replied to, the defendant has nothing to do at the hearing but prove his plea. And, therefore, if the plaintiff prove all the equity suggested in his bill, yet he shall not be suffered to read, because nothing is material but the truth or falsehood of the plea. So the defendant never examines to the equity suggested in the bill, and, though the defendant do join to the replication, it alters not the case.

Lord Nottingham, *Prolegomena*, p. 335

27 November 1672. Kinion v. Rigby.

A bill on a bond lost of £500 [was exhibited] against a surety. The defendant pleads duress of imprisonment of his uncle, the principal, by the order of Oliver [Cromwell] and his Council.

And [the court] ruled: first, this was duress; second, duress of the uncle shall avoid the bond of the nephew, especially in equity, for a surety cannot have contribution against a principal, if the bond be void against him by duress.

502

Monings v. Lady Monings

(Ch. 1672)

A bill of discovery does not lie to discover a civil forfeiture.

Lord Nottingham, *Prolegomena*, p. 335

5 December 1672.

Land was limited to Lady Monings for life if she so long continued a widow and, afterwards, for raising portions. And he in remainder exhibits a bill against Lady Monings to discover if she be married.

She demurs.

And Wilde, Justice, allowed the demurrer, because the bill tends to enforce a discovery for a forfeiture of her estate, at least for the determination of it by way of limitation. And it is against equity, for the late Act of Parliament,[1] which puts it upon them who claim estates for lives of others to prove their lives in being, had been less needful if the landlord might have forced the tenant to discover in equity. And, besides, no answer can put the defendant in peace, for a new bill of discovery may be exhibited every term.

2 Chancery Reports 68, 21 E.R. 618

The bill is to have the defendant to discover whether she be married since the death of Sir Edmund Monnins, her late husband.

The defendant demurred, for that, in case she was married since the death of her said husband, the same amounts to a forfeiture of her estate and interest in several goods and things devised to her by the will of her said husband to be held and enjoyed by her during such time as she should continue her widowhood, and so she ought not to discover, as aforesaid.

This court held the demurrer good unless the plaintiff produced precedents, which the plaintiff could not. So the bill was dismissed with costs.

[Other reports of this case: 1 Eq. Cas. Abr. 40, 77, 21 E.R. 858, 890.]
[Reg. Lib. 24 Car. II, ff. 85, 178.]

503

Bond v. Bond

(Ch. 1672)

Courts of equity have the jurisdiction to enforce discovery of title deeds.

Lord Nottingham, *Prolegomena*, p. 295

10 December 1672, by Shaftesbury.

A bill was exhibited in Chancery by the heir to discover a particular deed of settlement. The defendant demurs, because the plaintiff had not made an oath of the loss of the deed, as he ought to make when he sues in Chancery to recover money due on a lost bond.

But the demurrer was overruled, for, in the last case, the Chancery is entitled to a jurisdiction which otherwise it could not have. But, in the first case, the Chancery has always power to enforce discovery of deeds, and the plaintiff may as well be compelled to swear the truth of his bill in any case as this.

[1] Stat. 18 & 19 Car. II, c. 11 (*SR*, V, 614–615).

504

Croster v. Wister

(Ch. 1672–1673)

After a final decree has been enrolled and then the plaintiff dies, the plaintiff's executor can sue either a bill of revivor or a subpoena scire facias.

2 Chancery Reports 67, 21 E.R. 618

The defendant insists the plaintiff ought not to have brought a bill of revivor in this case, but to have taken out a subpoena in the nature of a *scire facias* to revive the decree, the same being signed and enrolled in the lifetime of the plaintiff's testator. Therefore, the defendant demurs to the said bill.

The plaintiff insists it is at the plaintiff's election to revive the said decree enrolled and to have execution thereof by a bill or a subpoena in the nature of a *scire facias*. And, as this case is, the whole proceedings could not be revived by a subpoena, in regard several proceedings have been relating to costs since the decree, which proceedings can be only revived by a bill, and, therefore, the most proper course was to revive all things by a bill.

This court held the said bill to be well brought, and held the demurrer insufficient.

[Other reports of this case: 1 Eq. Cas. Abr. 4, 21 E.R. 830.]
[Reg. Lib. 24 Car. II, f. 688.]

505

Stoell v. Botelar

(Ch. 1672–1673)

A writ of supplicavit *of the peace can be issued even though there be no endorsements on the writ.*

2 Chancery Reports 68, 21 E.R. 618

A writ of *supplicavit* of the peace issued against Sir Oliver Botelar upon a petition and articles exhibited by the said Stoell.

The defendant insists, the said writ issuing on a petition and not on a motion in court nor any endorsement made on the back of the writ, as by the form of the Statute[1] is required, and but three of the said articles being sworn to by the articulate [sic], it is irregular.

This court, on reading precedents, notwithstanding the objections aforesaid of Botelar, was fully satisfied that the *supplicavit* was well granted and warranted.

[Reg. Lib. 24 Car. II, f. 390.]

[1] Stat. 34 Edw. III, c. 1 (*SR*, I, 364–365).

506

Warren v. Johnson

(Ch. 1672–1673)

A trust created for the benefit of children does not include after-born children.

2 Chancery Reports 69, 21 E.R. 619

Mary Warren, the plaintiff's grandmother, put £60 into the defendant's hands in trust for the benefit of the children of Mark Warren, her son, who, at that time, had but three children, whereof the plaintiff was one. But now he has six children.

This court is of opinion that the said £60 belonged only to the children of the said Mark Warren, which he had by his then wife at the time when the said money was given, and decreed the same accordingly.

[Reg. Lib. 24 Car. II, f. 543.]

507

Wallop v. Lady Hewett

(Ch. 1672–1673)

In this case, the court held that it was the intent of the testatrix that the gift in the codicil was in addition to the gift in the will.

2 Chancery Reports 70, 21 E.R. 619

The plaintiffs, Henry and John Wallop, seek relief for £400, *viz.* £200 apiece, a legacy given them by the will and codicil of the Lady Crofts.

The case is that the Lady Crofts, by her will, gave the plaintiffs £100 apiece, and, afterwards, by a codicil annexed to her will, she gave the plaintiffs £100 apiece.

The question is whether the said legacies so given be one and the same or distinct and several legacies or what her intention was in reference to the same. And they desire the judgment of the court therein.

This court, with the judges, on reading the said will and codicil, were of opinion and satisfied that the said legacies in the said will and codicil mentioned are not one and the same, but distinct and several legacies of £200. And [the court] decreed the defendants to pay the said plaintiffs £400.

[Reg. Lib. 24 Car. II, f. 218.]

508

Thorne v. Newman

(Ch. 1672–1673)

In this case, a voluntary conveyance was set aside, and a redemption was ordered.

2 Chancery Reports 71, 21 E.R. 619

Nicholas Burnell, father of the defendant Margaret Newman, being seised of the premises in 1652, demised the same to Elizabeth Stone for ninety-nine years at a peppercorn rent with a proviso to be void on the payment of £590. And the said Elizabeth died, and made Elizabeth Wheat her executrix. And Thomas Baker marrying the defendant Margaret Newman, in November 1657, Elizabeth Wheat and the said Nicholas Burnell assigning the premises to Thomas Baker, the said Baker, for £500 borrowed of the plaintiff, assigned to one Minterne in trust for the plaintiff in 1659. And Baker, failing in payment, contracted with the plaintiff for £770 more that he would give his interest in the premises absolutely, without any power of redemption, and Baker and Minterne did join accordingly in 1660.

And the plaintiff insists that the defendant claims [the] premises by a deed dated the 19th of August 1659, whereby it is pretended that, by an indenture made between the said old Burnell of the one part and Thomas Lewis and Bartholomew Pickering of the other part, the said Burnell, in consideration of the natural love and affection to the said Margaret and for the settling and confirming of the premises for the uses therein and for 5s., covenanted to stand seised of the premises to himself for life, remainder to the defendant Margaret for life, then to the wife of the said Thomas Baker, remainder to the heirs of her body, with remainders over. And the said Burnell dying in 1659, the premises were then vested in Margaret, and Baker, in her right, became seised of the freehold thereof, and, thereby, the remainder of the said term of ninety-nine years was drowned and so the assignment to Minterne and the assignment by Baker and Minterne to the plaintiff was void, and, so the plaintiff, a purchaser for £1300, was like to be defeated.

And the plaintiff further insists that, if the said deed were ever sealed, it is with a proviso of revocation to be void on the payment or tender of 12d. to Lewis or Pickering or either of them in the Middle Temple Hall and that Burnell did tender 12d. to Lewis with the intention to make void the said deed. And he declared so to Lewis that he did revoke the said deed and pulled the seal off from it and that a memorandum was endorsed on the backside of the deed that there was 22nd of October 1659 12d. tendered to Lewis to revoke the said deed. But the defendants pretend, because the 12d. was not tendered in the Middle Temple Hall, therefore, the revocation was not legal, and so the said deed is still in force, and the plaintiff's estate drowned.

The defendants admit the case to be as aforesaid, but insist that the said deed of 19 August 1659 was intended for a settlement on the defendant Margaret for a provision for her after the death of the said Baker, her husband, he having not made any jointure, and that the said defendants claim the premises by the said deed, whereby, immediately, upon the death of Burnell, the freehold of the premises vested in Baker in the right of the said Margaret, his wife, and so the plaintiff's estate was drowned, and that Baker was not by the intention of the said deed to sell away the premises for any longer time than his own life without the said Margaret's consent and joining with him in a fine thereof.

And the defendants further insist that the 12d. ought to have been tendered in the Middle Temple Hall, else the deed must be in force and, if any memorandum or declaration were made as aforesaid, the same was done out of a design only to have the said Baker make the said Margaret a jointure.

But the plaintiff insists that he ought to hold the said premises for the residue of the said term for ninety-nine years against the said deed.

This court was satisfied that the plaintiff ought in equity to enjoy the premises against the defendants and that the said deed ought to be set aside as against the plaintiff. But the defendants are to redeem.

The bill being to set aside a pretended voluntary conveyance set on foot by the defendant, which deed is with a power of revocation upon the tender of 12d. and the 12d. was tendered accordingly with the intent to revoke the said deed and the said deed is accordingly cancelled. But the defendants, in respect the 12d. was not tendered at the place appointed, set the said deed up at common law.

And, upon a trial at law, without any defense made by the plaintiff, the defendants were nonsuited. And the plaintiff being a purchaser of the premises, first by a mortgage for £500 and, afterwards, by an absolute assignment for £770 more, the Lord Keeper [Lord Shaftesbury], upon reading the said cancelled deed, saw no cause to alter the Master of the Rolls's decree aforesaid, but he ordered the same to stand confirmed.

[Later reports of this case: Repts. *tempore* Finch 38, 23 E.R. 21, 3 Swanston 603, 36 E.R. 991, 73 Selden Soc. 4.]
[Reg. Lib. 24 Car. II, ff. 8, 371.]

509

Burgh v. Francis

(Ch. 1672–1673)

A defective mortgage deed raises a trust in the mortgagor for the benefit of the mortgagee. Legal or presumptive notice of a prior encumbrance binds as much as actual notice.

Lord Nottingham, *Prolegomena*, p. 257

By Shaftesbury, Chancellor, and Wilde, Justice.

The father makes a feoffment by a mortgage defective by want of livery, and dies. The mortgagee demands the money of the heir, who, on a view of the deed, finds the defect, and refuses payment.

The mortgagee exhibits a bill against the heir and the creditors, and takes out a subpoena returnable 27 January 1670. The creditors of the father sue the heir in [an action of] debt on the bond. The heir pleads nothing by descent except the mortgage lands. So the creditors take judgment presently against the mortgage lands, which relates to the first day of Hilary term, *viz.* before the return of the subpoena but after the service of it.

First, it was debated whether the lands in the hands of the heir were charged with a trust or only with an equity. But that seems not much material, for, be it one or other, notice or no notice is the main question.

Second, it was agreed that all of the creditors who had actual notice of the defects of this mortgage before the judgments obtained should not charge the mortgaged lands, for, though the creditor had equity to be satisfied his debt and committed no fault in obtaining a judgment for his better security, yet, in regard the land was not originally charged with the mortgage, it was not to be suffered that the creditor by bond should supplant or encumber the prior equity of the mortgagee, whereof he had notice.

Third, the greater doubt was touching those creditors who had no actual notice. And it was urged that their judgments ought likewise to be set aside, because legal or presumptive notice binds as much in Chancery as actual notice. Now here was legal and implied notice, because the judgments were obtained *pendente lite* in Chancery, *viz.* after the bill was filed and the subpoena when taken out and served, though before the return of it and, indeed, after the return in point of fact, though, by relation of law, it work before, which, in equity, ought not to prejudice and the subpoena, when returned, relating to the *teste*, which was before the first day of the term, though the return was after.

But of this the court would advise. And it may be of consequence in the example, and is fit to be considered how far innocent persons shall be bound by implied notice.

Lord Nottingham, *Prolegomena*, p. 244

11 December 1672.

A man makes a feoffment in mortgage [that was] defective for want of a livery. It was said that the mortgagee has not only an equity for better assurance, but the law, in respect of the consideration, raises a trust in the mortgagor for the benefit of the mortgagee, as, at common law, a bargain and sale without the word 'heirs' for the consideration's sake did raise a use in fee simple.

1 Peere Williams 279, 24 E.R. 388

Where there was a defective mortgage in fee for £500, it being made by way of a feoffment without a livery, and, after this, the mortgagor confessed a judgment to a third person, nevertheless, the estate being, in equity, specifically bound by the mortgage, it was decreed that the mortgage should be preferred to the judgment, though, at law, the former being in strictness void, the judgment creditor would have taken place.

[Later reports of this case: Repts. *tempore* Finch 28, 23 E.R. 16, 3 Swanston 536, 36 E.R. 971, Nelson 183, 21 E.R. 821, 1 Eq. Cas. Abr. 320, 21 E.R. 1074, 73 Selden Soc. 14, British Library MS. Stowe 406, f. 68.]

510

Anonymous

(Ch. 1672)

Where co-defendants claim a privilege to be sued in another court, all of them must be so entitled.

Lord Nottingham, *Prolegomena*, p. 336

12 December 1672, Shaftesbury, Chancellor, and Judge Atkyns.

If an officer of the Exchequer be a defendant in Chancery alone, he shall have the privilege [of the court]; not so if he is joined with another defendant who has no privilege and yet must of necessity be a party. And on this difference are the book cases.

511

Harrison v. Anonymous

(Ch. 1672)

A conveyance made for the benefit of a third person is different from a conveyance made for one's own benefit.

Lord Nottingham, *Prolegomena*, p. 336

12 December 1672, Shaftesbury, Chancellor.

A tenant in tail of a rent charge grants it to J.S. in fee, from whom [it comes] by mesne assignment to Sir Richard Harrison, who demands the rent with arrears. Jenins, terre tenant of the land and jointress, treats for herself and her son, the heir, and offers to pay the rent, so [long as] her counsel may be satisfied of the title. Counsel say the title is not good unless the issue in tail do corroborate it by a fine, but that, however, the terre tenant ought to pay the rent either to the issue or the grantee. Nevertheless, Sir Richard Harrison obtains a fine from the issue in tail, whose lands in other counties were charged with a like rent if this rent were defeated. And, after the fine was levied, he distrains and avows for the arrears. The fine is pleaded in bar of the avowry, and [the plea] is adjudged in the Common Bench good, because, now, Sir Richard Harrison is in of a new title.

He exhibits a bill in equity to be relieved for these arrears. And the defendant is ordered to answer, and his demurrer is saved to the hearing.

Sir John Churchill cites a case in time of Coventry, Keeper, Poining's Case. A grantee of a rent charge who was to concur in a marriage assurance joins in a fine of the rent charge. Yet [it was] relieved against conusees for the rent and the arrears.

But note a fine levied by a grantee to a special end or to a grantee to the use of another will not be like a fine to the grantee to his own use.

Sed adjornatur.

512

Vandebende v. Levingston

(Ch. 1672)

A bill of review lies to reverse a decree that was less beneficial to the plaintiff than in law it should have been.

Lord Nottingham, *Prolegomena*, p. 261

12 December 1672. Shaftesbury, Chancellor, and Justice Atkyns.

Vandebendten and Levingston come to an agreement touching the fifth part of My Lady Powell's land, then in Levingston's possession. And, until a conveyance was made, Levingston was to answer the profits for such uses as were intended to be limited by the fine so as Levingston stood trustee *prout etc.* Levingston pretends to convey to Skinner, a purchaser without notice. Mr. Skinner, at the hearing, was proved no purchaser.

It was decreed by BRIDGEMAN, Keeper, that both should be charged for what they received, which proved [to be] £1200 from Mr. Skinner [and] nothing from Levingston.

Error was assigned in a bill of review, because Levingston, being the wrongdoer, ought to be liable to the plaintiff for the whole, and not turn the plaintiff on a beggar who comes in by his breach of trust. And, in this case, the plaintiff was admitted to a bill of review to reverse a decree made for him, because it was less beneficial to him than it ought to have been and after enrolment there by the plaintiffs, without which no bill of review would lie.

Wherefore a demurrer to this bill of review was overruled, and Levingston was ordered to answer.

[Later reports of this case: 3 Swanston 625, 36 E.R. 999, 73 Selden Soc. 86.]

513

Earl of Stirling v. Levingston

(Ch. 1672–1673)

Good faith litigation over a doubtful term in a will is not such an attempt to impeach the will as may be forbidden by the terms of the will.

2 Chancery Reports 75, 21 E.R. 620

Sir Peter Vanlore, the elder,[1] being seised in fee of the lands, by a deed, covenanted to stand seised thereof to several uses, under which all parties to the suit claim several parts of the premise. And there being a proviso in the said deed that, if young Sir Peter Vanlore or the issue, whose issues and heir the now plaintiffs are, should attempt to impeach the said settlement, that then the uses to him and them limited by the said deed should be void and that, by the death of several persons, several parts of the premises were accrued to the said plaintiffs, but that, by reason of the said proviso and several ambiguities in the said deed, it was doubtful to what parts the plaintiffs, the heirs general, were entitled unto. So to be protected against the said proviso and to have the partition of the lands is the bill.

His Lordship [Lord Shaftesbury] declared it was most fit that a trial at law be had touching the plaintiff's right and title and that such an action to be brought shall not be taken or construed as a breach of the proviso aforesaid or a forfeiture of the plaintiff's right and title to the premises.

[Reg. Lib. 24 Car. II, ff. 113, 432.]

514

Smith v. Sallet

(Ch. 1672–1673)

A court of equity will not re-consider a common law verdict that settled the fines payable by copyholders.

2 Chancery Reports 76, 21 E.R. 620

The bill is to have an issue directed by this court to try whether the fines of the copyholders due to the lord of the manor were certain or arbitrary.

The defendant insisted that there had been several trials already and verdicts have passed for a fine certain and, particularly, one in ejectment before Mr. Justice Wyndham and another before the Lord Chief Justice Hale upon a special

[1] V. Larminie, 'Vanlore, Sir Peter (c. 1547–1627)', *Oxford Dictionary of National Biography*, vol. 56, pp. 122–123.

issue directed out of the Exchequer, whether the fines were certain at 8d. an acre and 8d. a cottage or not. And a verdict passed on both trials for a fine certain.

This court declared they could not relieve the plaintiff in equity, other than for the preservation of testimony, and dismissed the plaintiff's bill.

[Reg. Lib. 24 Car. II, f. 382.]

515

Lance v. Norman

(Ch. 1672–1673)

A court of equity can order a bond to be vacated on the ground of fraud.

A court of equity can order a husband to pay his wife a separate maintenance.

2 Chancery Reports 79, 21 E.R. 621

The plaintiff Lance's suit is that, the day before the marriage of the plaintiff and his wife, the said plaintiff's wife was persuaded to enter into a recognizance of £2000 without a defeasance to the defendant Norman, being the plaintiff's wife's brother, to which the plaintiff was not privy or consented, which recognizance the plaintiff seeks to have set aside and vacated.

The defendant Norman insists that the plaintiff was a suitor to his sister, designing to gain her estate, but she, not likely to have children, intended the said defendant Norman [to have] part of her estate. And, upon that account, he gave the said recognizance. And, at that time, the said Norman was in the country and had no ways of knowing of it nor had any contrivance in it. But the said plaintiff proving unkind to his wife and having turned her out of doors and parted with her not making any provision for her, this defendant has put the same in suit.

The plaintiff insisted that his said wife voluntarily absented from him and took and conveyed away a great part of his estate and has acted as a most insolent and undutiful wife and entered into the said recognizance without his privity.

This court, being assisted with the judges, was satisfied that the said recognizance was entered into the very day before the marriage without a defeasance or the plaintiff's privity, whereby to defraud the plaintiff. And one witness only deposed the plaintiff's consent to the drawing of the said recognizance, who has an assignment of the same to himself.

The court decreed the said recognizance to be set aside and vacated on the record thereof, and a perpetual injunction is granted against it, and this court proposed, on the said plaintiff's wife's returning back all the estate which she took and conveyed away, that the plaintiff do allow her £20 *per annum*, which was consented to by the plaintiff, for her separate maintenance.

[Other reports of this case: 1 Eq. Cas. Abr. 59, 21 E.R. 872.]
[Reg. Lib. 24 Car. II, f. 233.]

516

Cheeke v. Lord Lisle

(Ch. 1673)

The question in this case was whether a marriage settlement was enforceable where the wife died within a month after the marriage.

Lincoln's Inn MS. Misc. 11, p. 94

The plaintiff married the defendant's daughter, and, before the marriage, there were articles entered into between the plaintiff and the defendant whereby it was agreed that the plaintiff should make a settlement upon his wife, for which time was given by the articles, and the defendant agreed that, upon the plaintiff's making such settlement, to pay the plaintiff a sum of [*blank*] as a portion with the defendant's daughter. The wife died before the settlement was made, and, she being dead without issue and so no occasion for making any settlement, the plaintiff brought his bill to be paid the portion.

1 Freeman 302, 89 E.R. 219, 22 E.R. 1224

Hilary [term] 1673.

Upon the marriage of the plaintiff with the daughter of the defendant, it was agreed by articles under hand and seal that the plaintiff should have £4000 to be paid in this manner, *viz.* £1500 presently and £2500 within six months after he had made a jointure of £800 *per annum*, which, by the articles, he was to do within the space of four years. And it was likewise agreed that, if her husband died before the money be paid, then it was to be paid to the wife. It fell out that she died within a month after she was married, the jointure not being paid according to the articles.

The question was, seeing that the law was against the plaintiff, the jointure not being made and he not being to have the portion until after the jointure made, whether here were any circumstances of weight enough to prevail for a decree to enforce the defendant to pay this money, being in strictness of law not bound to pay it and the wife dying so suddenly after the marriage.

Curia advisare vult.

[Later reports of this case: Repts. *tempore* Finch 98, 23 E.R. 53, 73 Selden Soc. 23, 52, British Library MS. Stowe 406, f. 74.]
[Reg. Lib. 1672 A, ff. 363, 443.]
[Related cases: Cheeke v. Lisle (K.B. 1671), 2 Keble 794, 84 E.R. 502.]

517

Rex v. Foster

(Ch. 1673)

A grant of the crown during pleasure is terminated automatically by the death of the king.

A writ under the signet cannot transfer anything.

1 Freeman 70, 89 E.R. 53

King Charles I, by his letters patent, granted to one Perin the office of under-searcher etc. *durante bene placito nostro*. And since this King [Charles II] was restored, he sends his privy signet to the Lord Treasurer to confirm this Perin in his place. Foster obtains a patent from this king of this place without taking notice of the former patent to Perin. The sole question was whether this second patent was void pursuant to the Stat. 6 Hen. VIII, c. 15.[1]

Winnington, pro defendente, argued that it was not. He admitted that, if this second patent had been granted in the life of the first king without taking notice of the first patent, it had been clearly void. But, here, he held that the first patent was absolutely determined by the death of the king. And, here, he distinguished between the king's politic capacity and his natural capacity. The king's politic capacity never dies, and so there can be no interregnum, as Dyer 165,[2] but his natural capacity may die, and, then, those things which depend upon it die also, as his reason and will and pleasure for these are the proceeds of his natural capacity and person, and die with it. All judges' commissions determine upon the death of the king. 7 Co. 10; 1 Edw. V, 5,[3] because there is a personal confidence that the king has in them. If a man give security to keep the king's peace, if the king die, he must give a new security. 1 Hen. VII, 1.[4] If the grant were during the king's life, it would certainly determine by his death, and then a grant during his will shall not be of longer continuance. 12 Co. 49; 1 Inst. 59; 5 Edw. IV, 8; 5 Edw. IV, 2.[5]

North, pro defendente: The grant does not determine by his death. And he cited 12 Co. 49,[6] if a lease be made *durante bene placito*, it does not determine by his death. And he took a difference between judicial offices and matters of interest or ministerial offices, as this is, for, in judicial offices, if the grant be never so

---

1 Stat. 6 Hen. VIII, c. 15 (*SR*, III, 134).

2 *Anonymous* (1558), 2 Dyer 165, 73 E.R. 359, also 1 Anderson 44, 123 E.R. 344.

3 *Calvin v. Smith* (1608), 7 Coke Rep. 1, 10, 77 E.R. 377, 388; *Worseley v. Gloss* (1483), YB Trin. 1 Edw. V, ff. 4, 5, pl. 10.

4 YB Mich. 1 Hen. VII, f. 2, pl. 1 (1485).

5 *Case of the Justices of Wales* (1608), 12 Coke Rep. 48, 77 E.R. 1328; E. Coke, *First Institute* (1628), f. 59; YB Hil. 5 Edw. IV, f. 8, pl. 1 (1466); YB Pas. 5 Edw. IV, f. 2, pl. 11 and pl. 19 (1465).

6 *Case of the Justices of Wales* (1608), 12 Coke Rep. 48, 77 E.R. 1328.

absolute, it determines by his death, but not so in other things. And this was for the king's advantage, that this should not determine, for the king has his election here to turn him out, and it is not convenient there should be a vacancy in those petty offices. And he cited Moor 176; 2 Inst. 742; Dyer 94.[1]

But it was agreed on all hands that the king's privy signet did but intimate the king's mind, but could transfer no interest.

But the Lord Chancellor [BRIDGEMAN], WYNDHAM, and RAINSFORD inclined that the [first] patent was determined, and the *scire facias* [was] to be quashed without better cause shown.

Lincoln's Inn MS. Misc. 500, f. 214, pl. 1

Hilary term 24 & 25 Car. II (1673).

A *scire facias* was bought against Forster by the king to reverse a patent for the office of one of the Searchers of the Custom House that was granted by Charles I to him *durante bene placito nostro*. And the point was whether it ended by the death of the king who granted it.

And it was held by WILDE, WYNDHAM, and RAYNSFORD, assistants to the Chancellor, that the patent was ended.

518

Dogood v. Robinson

(Ch. 1673)

Where the depositions of witnesses in an action in the Mayor of London's Court are published and then the case is removed into the Court of Chancery, the case can proceed in the Court of Chancery if the parties have not seen the depositions.

Lord Nottingham, *Prolegomena*, p. 320

15 January 1672[/73], Dogood v. Sir John Robinson, by Shaftesbury, Chancellor.

On a *certiorari* bill, the suggestions were proved, and the defendant answered the matter of the bill. But, for a stay of all other proceedings, he pleaded [that], before any writ of *certiorari* was allowed in the Mayor's Court, publication was passed in London.

[It was] ruled: first, the bill should proceed here notwithstanding, because the suggestion of the plaintiff here, who was the defendant below, that he had had witnesses living out of London's jurisdiction was proved, and it did not appear that he had examined any witnesses below; second, yet the plaintiff should be obliged to file an affidavit that neither he nor any for him had seen the depo-

[1] *Anonymous* (1583), Moore K.B. 176, 72 E.R. 514; E. Coke, *Second Institute* (1642), p. 742; *Chasyn v. Lord Sturton* (1553), 1 Dyer 94, 73 E.R. 205.

sitions below; else, the plea should be allowed; *quod videtur* too much of respect to the Mayor's Court.

[Later reports of this case: Repts. *tempore* Finch 224, 23 E.R. 123, 73 Selden Soc. 178.] [Reg. Lib. 1674/75 A, f. 696.]

519

Cholmly v. The Grocers' Company

(Ch. 1673)

The date of a final decree is the day that it was pronounced from the bench in open court.

The priority of the execution of decrees is determined by the dates when they were pronounced.

Lord Nottingham, *Prolegomena*, p. 313

16 January 1672[/73], Shaftesbury, Chancellor.

Cholmly exhibits a bill against the Grocers' Company for a debt due by the Company's seal, and, after many delays, he has a decree *nisi causa*. The Company sets up some of their own members to sue them upon like bonds, and appeared *gratis*, and confessed the bill, and procured the cause to be set down to be heard the same day which was appointed to show cause against the first decree with the intent that the second decree might be as forward as the first.

[It was] ruled: first, the first decree should be a decree of the former term wherein in was pronounced and not of that term wherein it was confirmed on showing cause; second, that a sequestration on the former decree should first be executed before any sequestration issue on the latter decree; third, but, if the plaintiff in the former decree delay the execution or should afterwards come to collude with the Company, then, on motion, the court will consider further.

520

Anonymous

(Ch. 1673)

Creditors of decedent's estates are paid out of trusts proportionably but, out of the personal estate, according to their priority.

Lord Nottingham, *Prolegomena*, p. 338

18 January 1672[/73]. Shaftesbury, Chancellor.

Tandem [it was] ruled that, as at common law, [confessed] judgments acknowledged or payments made after *plene administravit* pleaded do not avail, neither shall they be allowed in equity after that time, though before the bill, but the plaintiff in equity can have no more than his proportion, *viz.* out of the trust, without regard of priority, and, out of the personal estate, according to priority, *viz.* debts on judgments before bonds etc.

521

Godfrey v. Harrison

(Ch. 1673)

A court of equity will refuse to enforce an apparently unjust arbitral award.

Lord Nottingham, *Prolegomena*, p. 309

21 January 1672[/73], Sir Edward Godfrey against Harrison.

After a submission by a rule of court and an award made, exceptions were received. And the court refused to decree the award for the apparent injustice of it, and referred the whole to Sir John Coell as an arbitrator.

522

Kendall v. Hallet

(Ch. 1673)

Where a long lease that attends the inheritance comes to the executors by act of the law because the testator was possessed, if debts be owing, a court of equity will not divest legal assets nor allow the term to attend the inheritance until debts be paid.

A subsequent parol declaration of a trust is sufficient to bind and to disinherit a co-heir.

Lord Nottingham, *Prolegomena*, p. 236

24 January 1672[/73], by Shaftesbury, Chancellor, and Atkyns, Justice.

Hallet purchased a lease for 100 years in the name of Lawrence and the inheritance in the name of Shute, and he dies indebted. His wife and administratrix, who was both plaintiff and defendant in cross-causes, demanded the benefit of this lease as assets in equity.

But it was denied on this difference: first, where a long lease which should attend the inheritance does come to the executors by act of the law because the testator was possessed, there, if debts be owing, equity shall not divest legal assets, nor suffer the term to attend the inheritance until debts be paid; second, but, if the testator was not possessed of the term, but only of the equity of such term, and dies indebted, there, the court will not sever the attendancy of the term on purpose to make assets in equity what the law has not made.

Lord Nottingham, *Prolegomena*, p. 269

24 January 1672[/73].

Lands were purchased by the earl of Bath in the name of Shute and Lawrence in trust for Hallet. The trustees, in the presence of Hallet, do seal a deed declaring several trusts for lives with remainders over. And Hallet's servant is a witness to it. And the deed was found among Hallet's evidences after his death.

Yet, because Hallet was no party to it, nor was any proof made of his directions, nor so much as a recital of it in the deed, [it was] adjudged: first, [there was] no sufficient declaration of a trust; second, Hallet's subsequent declaration by parol was good to bind and disinherit a co-heir.

523

Delves v. Wilbraham

(Ch. 1673)

A purchaser of land with notice of prior encumbrances cannot protect himself against them by purchasing other prior encumbrances.

Notice by one joint tenant binds his companion.

Lord Nottingham, *Prolegomena*, p. 211

25 January 1672[/73]. Shaftesbury, Chancellor.

Hugh Wilbraham makes a conveyance to Peter Brereton, and grants the reversion to Sir H. Delves and Sir Thomas Brereton to the use of himself for life, remainder to Elizabeth, his wife, for a jointure, remainder over. Sir H. Delves seals a counterpart, and accepts [attornment] of Sir Peter Brereton. And, afterwards, *viz.* seven years afterwards, Sir H. Delves and Sir Thomas Delves, his son and heir, purchase a lease of the jointure lands for 500 years and the inheritance in the name of Sir Thomas Delves alone. And to protect their purchase, they buy in their mortgage to Elmes precedent to the jointure.

[It was] ruled: first, the purchaser with notice shall not protect himself by precedent encumbrances; second, here, Sir H. Delves purchases with notice, because he seals the counterpart and accepts attornment; third, notice by one joint tenant affects his companion, as attornment; 2 Co., Rud and Tooker's Case;[1] fourth, here, Elizabeth shall recover the jointure, but she shall redeem the precedent mortgage, and her executors shall hold over.

Quibus auditis, the parties agree in court.

---

1 *Rud v. Tooker* (1594–1601), 2 Coke Rep. 62, 76 E.R. 562, also Croke Eliz. 737, 802, 78 E.R. 969, 1030.

524

Wilson v. Hall

(Ch. 1673)

Co-executors must all sue as co-plaintiffs.

If a matter in abatement is not timely pleaded, it is waived.

Lord Nottingham, *Prolegomena*, p. 200

28 January 1672[/73].

If there be two executors and one only sue, this matter may be pleaded in abatement. But, if the time to plead in abatement be slipped, no advantage can be taken of it afterwards. So in equity, this exception was not regarded at the hearing, because it was not pleaded in abatement.

525

Sadler v. Woodward

(Ch. 1673)

A court cannot give an affirmative decree against a plaintiff.

Lord Nottingham, *Prolegomena*, p. 299

28 January 1672[/73].

No decree can be made against a plaintiff, but only to dismiss his bill with costs. Therefore, where the plaintiff has obtained an injunction to quiet his possession until a hearing, on security given by a recognizance to answer the value received, and, on the hearing, he was dismissed and ordered to account to the defendant for the full value, [it was] resolved: first, the order as to the full value was void, for the court can only dismiss the plaintiff and leave the defendant to the benefit of the recognizance; second, that no costs being given at the hearing, none were fit to be given afterwards, especially not by a new Chancellor, without a rehearing.

526

Goodyer v. Masham

(Ch. 1673)

A suit to perpetuate testimony does not lie to prove a deed of entail against a defendant who is a bona fide purchaser for value.

Lord Nottingham, *Prolegomena*, p. 212

19 February 1672[/73]. Goodyer v. Sir John Masham.

If a bill be exhibited to examine witnessed *in [perpetuam] rei memoriam* to prove a deed of entail, if the defendant pleads himself a purchaser, the court will suffer no further procedure. But, there, the defendant was ordered to sue at law that the plaintiff might have an opportunity to prove his deed at law before his witnesses die. [It was] so ruled in Ashley v. Tregonnel, by Fountaine, Commissioner, 1659, as Mr. *Thomas* says.

527

Allanson v. Daniel and Witcherly

(Ch. 1673)

Tenants of a manor can sue a class action in order to settle the customs of the manor if they are sufficiently responsible for court costs and have a sufficient authority from the other members of the class.

Lord Nottingham, *Prolegomena*, p. 299

19 February 1672[/73].

Three tenants of the manor of Wem exhibit a bill in the names of themselves and of five hundred more for settling the customs of the manor.

[It was] ruled to be good without naming all the tenants as plaintiffs, so as the three tenants, who are named, are responsible for the costs and so as they produce before the Register a sufficient authority to sue in the names of the rest of the tenants, whereby the lord may be secured not to be troubled with more suits of this nature.

[Related cases: Tenants of Wem v. Wicherly (Ex. 1681), Equity Cases Exch. 130.]

528

Archer v. Dawes

(Ch. 1673)

Hearsay or gossip is not sufficient notice to bind a purchaser.

Lord Nottingham, *Prolegomena*, p. 256

Hilary [term] 24 Car. II, by the Keeper and Justice Rainsford.

Archer, on 6 December 1663, makes a parol agreement with Dawes etc. for a sale of land in Ireland, and, on 23 December, Dawes contracts with Mr. Preston of Dublin to sell the same land, and, in January following, makes a conveyance. In April 1665, Archer obtained a decree against Dawes to convey. And, finding afterwards that Preston had a former conveyance, he exhibits a new bill against Dawes to procure a conveyance from Preston, which is so decreed, and, to obtain this, pays Preston money.

[It was] resolved: first, notice of a prior agreement by hearsay and by reading a letter of news is not binding to a purchaser; second, full and perfect notice of a prior agreement by parol executed is not binding neither; third, yet Preston, having taken money to convey, must make good the conveyance according to the meaning of the decree.

529

Holmes v. Atkyns

(Ch. 1673)

If a suit be grounded upon an equitable right that depends on a judgment of a court, a purchaser pendente lite will not be affected with legal and implied notice, but only with actual notice. But a purchase after a final decree gives legal notice.

Lord Nottingham, *Prolegomena*, p. 258

20 February 1672[/73].

The manor of Tufly, held of the Dean and Chapter of Gloucester by a lease, was charged by Colonel Atkins with a provision of £240 *per annum* for his mother and all succeeding leases also. In the year 1661, Colonel Atkins renews the lease, and mortgages it to Sir John Payne, who had then notice of the mother's equity.

A bill is exhibited by Holms, who married the mother, against Colonel Atkins and Sir John Payne demanding the arrears of forty years.

They both, before answer, convey to Colonel Norwood, from whom Sir John Payne received only his mortgage money.

Yet [the court] decreed both to be liable to Holms, because their joining in an act to disable the court to relieve after the notice of the plaintiff's equity by the bill was a fault, especially, when Sir John Payne was in no danger of losing his money, and it looked like a combination, and, though the court, on a new bill, might charge Norwood as coming in *pendente lite*, yet the defendants deserved to be charged.

And the decree was confirmed by the Lord Chancellor.

There seems to be a great difference between a trust and an equity as to a purchaser *pendente lite*. The filing of a bill, nay, the service of a subpoena, seems to be sufficient to bind a purchaser where the suit is for a trust and to be as good as a decree, because it is the act of the court to delay the decree, the right appearing on a fact which proves clear. But, if the suit be on an equity which depends on the judgment of the court, there, the purchaser *pendente lite* shall not be affected with legal and implied notice, but only with actual notice. But a purchase after a decree affects him with legal notice.

530

Clent v. Bridges

(Ch. 1673)

If an executor of a decedent's estate gives a legatee a bond for his or her legacy and has a release, this is a good payment of the legacy.

A remainder after a gift of a chattel is invalid.

Lord Nottingham, *Prolegomena*, p. 339

20 February 1672–73, by Shaftesbury, Chancellor, assisted with Wyndham and Atkins, Justices.

'I give to my daughters £600 apiece to be paid within six months after my decease, and, if either of my daughters die before twenty-one or day of marriage, then I appoint her portion, as far as the law will allow it, to be paid to the grandchildren of my daughter Sutton.'

The executor gives each daughter a bond for her portion, which in law is payment, and, thereupon, has a release. The eldest dies before twenty-one or day of marriage, and devises her estate to her younger sister. The grandchildren exhibit [their bill] against the executor and younger sister, and obtain a decree against the younger sister, but not against the executor, for the last clause was a kind of qualification of the property given by the first clause at six month's end, insomuch that a kind a trust is affixed to the money in the sister's hands, though, if she had spent or given it away in her lifetime, there had been no remedy.

I [*Finch*] urged, for the defendant, that the property of a chattel personal for an hour is perpetual property and that no remainder of a chattel personal could be limited either in law or equity, as was ruled in the case between Dr. Colladon and the Marquis Montgouillan, who married Madame Mayern, that it was strange that the elder sister could grant, release, and forfeit and yet not devise, and it would be yet stranger that, when a gentlewoman received her portion and when she is in full possession of it, this court should put a *noli me tangere* upon it by a construction no way necessary, for all clauses of the will ought to stand together, and, therefore, the portion being limited to be paid at a certain determinate period, the last contingent clause is to have no place unless the contingency happened within six month.

Nihilominus [it was] decreed *ut supra*: first, because the executor has done well and ought to have his costs, which I approve; second, because the elder sister has done ill and had not a power to devise it, which I utterly deny; third, therefore, [there was] a decree against the devisee, but without costs.

But *contra*, 9 December 1673, I [Lord Nottingham] reversed it, and dismissed the plaintiff.

Lord Nottingham, *Prolegomena*, p. 347

9 October 1673.

In the case of Clent and Bridges, [it was] decreed *prout supra*. It came to be a question how the £600 should be divided, whether in thirds or ninths, on the words:

to my daughters Margaret and Hester £600 apiece to be paid etc. and, if either of them die before etc., the portion of her so dying to be equally divided among the survivor [of them], my son Edmund and all the children of my daughter Sutton by both husbands then living.

And the civilians were of opinion that all the children of his daughter Sutton, who were seven in number, should take by way of representation only and so have but one third, because, if the administration was to be granted of the £600, it ought to be so divided and because the new Act for administrations[1] agrees with the civil law and does so distribute it.

But the Chancellor, though this was in the case of a personal legacy wherein the civilians are sometimes advised with, decreed the contrary, that it should be divided into nine parts, for lands so devised would go to all individually and the testator meant so here, but the testator, not knowing who would be then living of Sutton's children, when any of his sons [and daughters] died, could not express his meaning better.

[Later reports of this case: Repts. *tempore* Finch 26, 23 E.R. 14, 73 Selden Soc. 15.]

531

Sherman v. Cox

(Ch. 1673)

No act between a mortgagor and a first mortgagee can foreclose the equity of redemption vested in the second mortgagee.

If a second mortgagee dismisses his own bill of discovery and will not exhibit a bill for a redemption, he will be bound by any foreclosure of a first mortgagee.

Lord Nottingham, *Prolegomena*, p. 287

21 February 1672–73.

Robins mortgages to Patrick in 1650, to Shermar in 1653, to Browning in 1656. Then Browning buys in Patrick's mortgage, and exhibits [his] bill against Robins and Shermar, but he serves not Shermar to the hearing.

[1] Stat. 22 & 23 Car. II, c. 10 (*SR*, V, 719–720).

Shermar, afterwards, exhibits a bill against Robins and Browning to discover encumbrances only, and then he dismisses his own bill without exhibiting a new bill for a redemption. The first cause comes on between Browning and Robins, and a decree is made that Robins shall be foreclosed of the redemption.

Then, the executor of Shermar exhibits a bill in 1669 to redeem.

And it was agreed the conveyance to Shermar, the second mortgagee, did pass the equity of redemption; second, that no act between the mortgagor and the first mortgagee could foreclose the equity of redemption vested in the second mortgagee; third, but, then, it was urged that, when the second mortgagee dismissed his own bill of discovery and would not exhibit a bill for a redemption and no collusion appears or is suggested in obtaining the first decree, now the second shall be bound, because he has surceased his time, else the first mortgagee should be a perpetual bailiff and never sure of his title, because *nescit* how many mesne estates or mortgages have been made. And the Case of Roscarrock and Barton[1] was cited.

And, to this, the court inclined.

On the other side, it was objected that then every second mortgagee may be cozened by a colorable payment of interest to blind him until a decree pass between the mortgagor and the first mortgagee, and that without any collusion.

And *sic pendet.*

Nelson 71, 21 E.R. 792

One Robins mortgaged his estate in August 1650 to Smith for 99 years and, in November following, to Partridge for forty years and, four years afterwards, to the plaintiff, Sherman's husband, for a term of years to secure the payment of £1500, and, last of all, to one Browning, who bought in the two first mortgages.

In the year 1664, the plaintiff Sherman exhibited his bill against Robins, the mortgagor, and against Browning to set forth and discover their title and that the plaintiff might redeem. The defendants put in their answer, but there was no farther proceedings in that cause.

Two years afterwards, Browning exhibited his bill against Robins alone that he would pay the money or that he might be foreclosed of the equity of redemption, which was decreed accordingly, and an account stated of what was due for principal and interest, and a time was set to pay the money or be foreclosed. The money was not paid at the time.

After Robins was foreclosed, the defendant Cox bought Browning's title, and, two years afterwards, the plaintiff Sherman brought a new bill against Cox to redeem, who pleaded his purchase and the equity of redemption foreclosed.

[1] *Roscarrick v. Barton* (Ch. 1672), see above, Case No. 465.

And the question was whether Browning should have made the now plaintiff Sherman a party to his bill as well as Robins, which he had not done, and, therefore, should he now be let in to redeem.

The Lord Keeper FINCH declared the case was to be judged by the circumstances and by comparing the mischiefs on both sides and so to choose the least; that it would be very mischievous to the mortgagee to make everyone who had any interest parties to his bill, for, if so, then, every mortgagee would be in the nature of a bailiff or a steward and his business would never be done, for there might be several mortgagees. It is true he would be helped at last, having his principal, interest, and costs, though he might be at some trouble and pains in getting it. But, if the plaintiff should not be relieved, his loss would be irreparable. Therefore, he thought trouble and pains [were] less than ruin and total loss. And so he overruled the plea, but he declared that the account stated by the decree should bind, unless some collusion was proved.

And he declared he would consider of some method to make men take care to redeem their mortgages by ordering that interest upon interest should be allowed or by taking away the rule that mortgagees should answer for what they might receive without their willful default or by ordering that the account of a mortgagee upon oath should bind, unless disproved by two witnesses.

[Later reports of this case: 3 Chancery Reports 83, 21 E.R. 736, 2 Freeman 13, 22 E.R. 1026, Repts. *tempore* Finch 406, 23 E.R. 221, 73 Selden Soc. 76, 281.]

532

Bawdes v. Browning

(Ch. 1673)

An account stated between a merchant and his factor does nor bind the merchant's creditors.

A court of equity can order a discovery, accounting, and relief against the administrator of a deceased merchant's estate in favor of a creditor.

Lord Nottingham, *Prolegomena*, p. 272

24 February 1672[/73].

Browning was indebted to Sir Thomas Bawdes in £3000 by bond, who brought an action of debt against the administratrix. She pleads fully administered and that she had no assets *ultra* £140. Sir Thomas Bawdes prays judgment of that and of the residue *cum acciderit*, and then exhibits a bill in equity against the administratrix and one Mr. Jacob Lynn, suggesting that Lynn was an apprentice, factor, and sometime partner with the intestate, and sent divers false accounts from Malaga, and was greatly indebted to the intestate, but the administratrix combined with him and would not sue, lest the money, when recovered, should be assets. And so he prays a discovery of the books and an account and relief.

Lynn pleads that he sent the intestate several accounts, *viz.* in 1663, 1666, and 1668, and the intestate lived until 1671 and never took any exceptions to those accounts, so that, by the custom of merchants, these accounts, after so long an acquiescence, amounted to accounts stated, and any creditor might as well sue the defendant as the plaintiff.

But, because it was suggested that the dealings between the intestate and Lynn continued until 1671, therefore, no regard was had to the acquiescence on the former accounts, nor were they allowed as stated accounts. But the defendant was ordered to answer that so an account might be taken between him and the co-defendant administratrix, whereof the plaintiff should have the benefit.

533

Bland v. Wytham

(Ch. 1673)

The question in this case was whether a writ of sequestration survives the death of the party sequestered.

Lord Nottingham, *Prolegomena*, p. 314

4 March 1672/73.

Bland had a decree against Wytham for £5000 and a sequestration. Henry Wytham, the son, pretends a title by a voluntary conveyance pending the suit, offers to appear and be examined, and gives security for the rents, which was accepted and ordered. Then, Mr. Wytham, the father, dies.

[It was] resolved: first, that, though Henry had made himself *quasi* a party in court by the examination and security, yet now, a new title was accrued to him as heir, which would not be bound unless the decree was revived against him and also the executor, who might have assets, which was so done, and a subpoena in the nature of a *scire facias* [issued] against both.

Then, it was urged that, the demand and decree being only for a personal duty, there could be no sequestration of land for it against the father, at best no continuation of it against the heir, for a sequestration only imitates the [writ of] *levari facias* at common law, which was the only way of charging land and ceased by the death of the party. It cannot pretend to imitate the [writ of] extent brought in by Westminster II,[1] which takes only a moiety.

On the other side, it was said that there was a difference between an original sequestration against the heir on a [bill of] revivor and a continuance of a former sequestration against the father and a difference between an heir in tail and an

[1] Stat. 13 Edw. I, Westminster II, c. 18 (*SR*, I, 82).

heir in fee and a difference between a purchaser without notice and an heir, who, *pendente lite*, comes in by a voluntary conveyance. In the latter cases, sequestration has always gone; else, the justice of Chancery would fail and all the proceedings become illusory. Nay, a man might borrow money to buy land, and, being sued in Chancery for the money, when the bond is lost, by a voluntary conveyance to the heir, defeat the remedy. Sequestration imitates not the common law, nor the Statute of Westminster II, for, though it be like an extent and an injunction for possession be like a [writ of] *liberate*, yet it covers the whole and reaches copyhold lands, which are not extendible, and it is a special remedy warranted by the course of the court.

Curia inclined accordingly, but referred to precedents.

[Later reports of this case: Repts. *tempore* Finch 126, 23 E.R. 69, 3 Swanston 276, 36 E.R. 862, 73 Selden Soc. 3, 113, British Library MS. Stowe 406, f. 69, 1 Chancery Cases 241, 22 E.R. 781.]

534

Lord Cavendish v. Anonymous

(Ch. 1673)

Bonds given to pay illegal gambling debts are enforceable where they have been assigned over to third persons for a valuable consideration.

Lord Nottingham, *Prolegomena*, p. 340

Easter [term] 25 Car. II, [Shaftesbury], Chancellor, and Hale, Chief Justice.

Earl Meath wins £500 at play from the Lord Cavendish. And, about a year after, he procures the Lord Cavendish to enter into bonds to several shopkeepers to whom Earl Meath stood indebted for wares and [Earl Meath] is bound with him as surety, and he has a counter-bond to save him harmless. The shopkeepers sue their bonds. And Earl Meath sues his counter-bond.

For the counter-security, the Lord Cavendish exhibits [his] bill, and prays to be released, paying only the principal, because the debt grew from play. But it could not be against the interest and charges or any further than against the penalties, for the debt was now in another degree by the security given to the shopkeepers and it were mischievous to trace debts to their original after their coming to a second or third hand.

535

Hockly v. Hockly

(Ch. 1673)

Specific performance of a covenant will not be granted where, if the covenant had been performed, it might still have been defeated by a common recovery.

Lord Nottingham, *Prolegomena*, p. 342

Easter [term] 25 Car. II.

John Hockly covenants to surrender a copyhold to the use of himself and Ann, his wife, and the heirs of the body of the said John on the body of Ann (to which kind of entail, if it had been executed, a daughter would have been inheritable), remainder to his own right heirs. Afterwards, he makes a surrender to make the use of himself and his wife for life, remainder to the heirs male of his body on her body begotten, remainder to the use of his last will. Ann dies, having issue Elizabeth. John takes a second wife, has issue, John, and devises the copyhold to him, and dies.

The daughter by the first marriage exhibits a bill to have the land decreed in specie according to the meaning of the covenant on the first marriage.

But [it was] dismissed, for, where the covenant, if it had been performed, might yet have been defeated by a common recovery, there, the performance is no ground for a decree. He, who had *potestatem disponendi*, had otherwise disposed it.

Note, if he had been actually a tenant in tail, no disposition without a recovery would have been supported in equity. *Secus* of a bare covenant to entail. In the first case, the Statute *De Donis*[1] works, not in the second.

536

Alanson v. Johnson

(Ch. 1673)

A court of equity will not grant relief against a judgment at common law for damages in an action of dower, even though the widow was acting in bad faith.

Lord Nottingham, *Prolegomena*, p. 342

Easter [term] 25 Car. II, Chancellor [Shaftesbury] and Thurland.

A bill was exhibited to be relieved against damages recovered in [an action of] dower after a judgment by default. And, for equity, it suggests that the husband devised the land away from the coheirs, and so breaks the descent, that the

[1] Stat. 13 Edw. I, Westminster II, c. 1 (*SR*, I, 71–72).

wife knew of this will and, by consequence, [that] the coheirs were not terre tenants, and yet, she brings [an action of] dower against them, and, after the usual proclamations *ad ostium ecclesiae*, gets a judgment by default without any other notice.

But, nevertheless, relief was denied, because the proceedings were legal and dower is favored. *Nota quia* mischievous, and it may be an occasion of fraud.

537

Weedon v. Donnington Paupers

(Ch. 1673)

A charitable trust can be defeated by a sale of land to a bona fide purchaser without notice.

Lord Nottingham, *Prolegomena*, p. 343

Easter [term] 25 Car. II.

A purchaser with notice of a charitable use sells to one who has no notice. [It was] resolved the second purchaser is free.

538

Young v. Cooke

(Ch. 1673)

A court of equity can grant relief against an excessive arbitral award.

3 Chancery Reports 82, 21 E.R. 735

9 April 1673. Lord Chancellor Ashley and Justice Atkyns.

Upon a demurrer to a bill to be relieved against an award bond for excessive damages given, it was ordered that the defendant should answer, but the benefit of the demurrer saved to the hearing, upon which, the cases of Morgan *contra* Pindar, and Cooper *contra* the butcher of Croydon, were cited.[1]

Lord Nottingham, *Prolegomena*, p. 309

28 June 1673. Young v. Cock.

A wharf was sold with a covenant to remove a lime house and stables in six months. The covenant being broken, a voluntary submission was made to arbitrators without a rule of court.

The arbitrators awarded for the plaintiff in covenant £100, which was refused as unreasonable, then [it] fell to £80, which was also refused, the thing not

[1] *Morgan v. Pindar* (1633 × 1634), 3 Chancery Reports 75, 21 E.R. 733; *Cooper v. Anonymous* (Ch. 1671–1672), see above, Case No. 547.

deserving £20, and at last [they] awarded £340, when the submission bond was but £400.

Curia: Try the damage in [an action of] covenant notwithstanding the award.

539

Earl of Holland v. Garrett

(Ch. 1673)

Where a plaintiff has seized the defendant's accounts and papers, he cannot afterwards sue to have an account, because the defendant has lost or may have lost his evidence by the plaintiff's bad faith dealings.

Lord Nottingham, *Prolegomena*, p. 274

22 April 1673, Lord Chancellor, Atkyns and Turner assisting.

If the plaintiff who demands an account has seized any papers or vouchers of the defendant, though he deliver them back again on oath, yet he shall be foreclosed from demanding any account in equity, for the defendant having been disarmed shall never be forced to enter the lists again without any other means to defend himself than such which shall depend on the integrity of his adversary and the truth of his oath. [It was] so ruled between Moor, defendant, against Lady Bucock in the time of Bridgeman, Keeper.

[Later proceedings in this case: 73 Selden Soc. 97.]

540

Richardson v. Westland

(Ch. 1673)

To take a bond to secure a payment is to receive the payment.

Lord Nottingham, *Prolegomena*, p. 340

2 May 1673.

Westland recovers £250 from Richardson at law, and, for his speedier remedy, he attaches £130 of Richardson's in the hands of Blacket, and he has a judgment and execution against Blacket, but received nothing. Then, he released Blacket out of execution, and took new security from him, but did not acknowledge satisfaction on the record.

Hereupon, Westland is sued by Richardson to discount what is overpaid by Blacket, and [it was] adjudged he should so do, though he had received nothing from Blacket by actual payment, but, having discharged Blacket against Richardson, it shall be accounted as a payment for Richardson in equity.

Yet it was prayed for Westland that he might assign his securities from Blacket to Richardson and not be paid in equity by fiction. Nevertheless [it was] decreed *ut supra*.

In the same case, it was held that, if a parcel of rubies be attached and appraised at £46, and, afterwards, in time of war, be sent into Holland and there sold for £126, yet no more shall be discounted than £46, because the merchant, having made no insurance here, ran the hazard of losing all there, and, therefore, the improvement of this adventure shall not avail the debtor.

541

Clayton v. Bedel

(Ch. 1673)

A consent decree that is beneficial to an infant binds the infant when he attains his full age.

Lord Nottingham, *Prolegomena*, p. 343

14 May, *per* Shaftesbury, Chancellor, and Wyndham.

An infant, *viz.* Edward Bedel, exhibits a bill by his guardian against the executors of his father to bring them to an account for the personal estate and to enforce them to lay out the surplus in the purchase of land. The surplus is computed at £18,000, and the manor of Woodrising in Norfolk was by all the friends of the infant held a convenient purchase of £25,000.

But, for the securing of the £7000, which was to be borrowed to complete the purchase money, it was decreed: first, that the overplus land should be settled as a security for the £7000 borrowed; second, because that was too close a security, the profits of the manor of Woodrising should be received by Gabriel and the profits of the infant's paternal estate in Huntingdonshire should be received by Philips during the minority and applied to the paying off the money borrowed, deducting £500 a year for maintenance.

Upon this, Mr. Ravenscroft lends £3000; Mr. Rushout £1000; and Clayton and Morris £3000. Gabriel and Philips suffer the infant to receive all the profits until full age, and then the infant enters upon Woodrising. Ravenscroft and Rushout are unpaid.

Clayton exhibits his bill against all. And, because his security is in the last place, he prays relief.

[It was] resolved: first, this decree, being without fraud and for the infant's good, shall bind him at full age, and the rather because he then entered on the purchased land and so consented to the decree in a manner; second, it should bind him for the profits of the paternal estate, *quod nota*; third, that the overplus land shall be held discharged of the infant's equity of redemption; fourth, that the overplus land shall be sold, and the infant join in the sale; fifth, that what the money raised by sale fell short of satisfying the debts to Ravenscroft, Rushout, and Clayton should be supplied by the profits taken during minority; sixth, that the infant, having at his full age released the account of profits, must stand charged with and be in the place of the accountants.

542

Williams v. Wentworth

(Ch. 1673)

A decree of foreclosure ends any right of redemption claimed by a person claiming an entail in the land.

Lord Nottingham, *Prolegomena*, p. 290

26 May 1673.

A bill was exhibited to foreclose the equity of redemption. The defendant [Sir John Williams] makes a title to part of the mortgaged land by an entail.

Yet [it was] decreed for the plaintiff, and all equity of redemption was barred, leaving the defendant, who was the heir of the mortgagor, to make what he could of his title at law to the part whereof he claimed by entail; the rather because the plaintiff in equity had once recovered the whole at law on a trust, where no entail was pretended.

543

Bell v. Hemmings

(Ch. 1673)

A written contract cannot be altered by other agreements that were not in writing.

Lord Nottingham, *Prolegomena*, p. 310

2 June 1673.

A marriage agreement was put in writing, *viz.* a £400 portion was to be paid and three years' diet to be given, and, on the other side, a jointure was to be settled. Yet after the marriage, the husband sued the aunt, who gave his wife her portion, on this further pretence, that there was another part of the agreement, *viz.* to convey houses, make over her trade of salt, and make the portion worth £1000, which part of the agreement was left out of the articles by consent [so] that it might be concealed, but it was intended and agreed to be performed. And it was now so prayed by the bill.

[It was] resolved: first, parol agreements are not to be considered after articles under hand and seal; second, the suggestion that part of the agreement was left out by consent, though punctually proved, was not regarded by reason of the ill consequence if such averments were to be received and that witnesses would have the power to enlarge agreements under hand and seal.

So the bill was dismissed, but without costs.

544

Beringer v. Beringer

(Ch. 1673)

In this case, the court of equity ordered a contract for a third-party beneficiary to be specifically performed, even though the decree was for money only and the time of payment had not accrued.

Lord Nottingham, *Prolegomena*, p. 344

16 June, Trinity [term] 25 Car. II.

The father, being aged and intending to make a provision for his daughter by a farm called Mildridge Farm, acquaints his son with his intention, who persuades his father and promises, if he will let the farm descend, he will pay his sister £1000 within three years after his death and interest for it and diet in the meantime. The father agrees, and makes his son executor, and he dies. The farm descends. The son refuses to perform.

[He was] decreed to pay the money at three years' end and to account for the interest, though the bill were exhibited before the time and though it concerned only a sum of money, which, in due time, might be recovered at law in [an action of] *assumpsit.*

545

Kilby v. Norris

(Ch. 1673)

Payment to a person who is not an agent of the creditor to receive it is not a proper payment.
A court of equity can abate interest payable in a case of hardship.

Lord Nottingham, *Prolegomena*, p. 344

16 June 1673, Kilby v. Sir Edward Norris.

Kilby borrows money of Smith, for which he gives security to Sir Francis Norris, who keeps the bond. Then, Kilby offers to pay it in to Smith, who desires him to put it out again for Sir Francis. Kilby does so, and lends the money to Fox, and takes a recognizance for it in the name of Sir Francis.

Yet Kilby was decreed to pay the money again to Sir Edward, executor to Sir Francis, because Smith was no clear agent for Sir Francis to receive the money, not having the bond and, also, because Smith did not accept of Fox's security in discharge of the bond, unless a mortgage were also given, which was never done.

But yet, half interest was abated, because the case was hard, as they who paid Yarway, the scrivener, without the bond, were abated all the interest and Kilby had the benefit of Fox's recognizance.

546

Sivier v. Parker

(Ch. 1673)

At the suit of legatees, a court of equity can order an executor to put up security to faithfully execute a decedent's will.

Lord Nottingham, *Prolegomena*, p. 344

16 June, Trinity [term] 25 Car. II, 1673.

The legatees sued the executor to put in security, because he prodigally wasted the estate of the testator and his own estate.

And it was decreed he should do so within a fortnight or bring the legacies into court, and the court would see them put out at interest according to the will.

547

Thorold v. Wray

(Ch. 1673)

The question in this case was whether a debt by a lunatic's estate payable to the administrator is valid and enforceable.

Lord Nottingham, *Prolegomena*, p. 344

23 June 1673, at Exeter House.

An account was taken before Sir John Coell of the estate of Sir Bethel Wray, a lunatic, the custody of whose person was committed to Mr. Cooper with an allowance of £400 a year and of his estate to Mr. Thorold.

This account was taken by the direction of the Chancery, and contested by the Lord Fanshawe, to whom the custody of the estate was to be transferred, he having married the mother of the next infant heir. And, after several references, the account was stated, and the lunatic's estate was made indebted to Thorold for £1100, which (though it were a considerable estate) happened so to be by reason that Thorold had paid off a statute with his own proper money, which encumbered the estate. So a decree was made that the lunatic's estate should be charged with it.

Thorold dying and the lunatic dying, the administratrix of Thorold revives the decree against the infant heir. But she was put to his original bill, that so the account might be reexamined and all the equity of her pretensions, for the court had no power to make the lunatic run into debt. But the decree was allowed to be formal enough without a bill, answer, or pleadings, because the nature of this case bears no other proceedings but a petition and orders.

And, therefore, [the court] ordered now, if, after an original bill be exhibited, the defendant stand on the privilege of Parliament, the former decree is to proceed.

Quod mirum, because, [in the Court of Wards, it was the practice] that the way to settle accounts was on an information exhibited to deliver an account and so to proceed orderly to a decree.

548

Wheeler v. Young

(Ch. 1673)

The executor of a guardian can sue for an account of the ward's estate.

Lord Nottingham, *Prolegomena*, p. 345

26 June 1673.

A guardian of a lunatic passes an account in the ordinary form, whereby the lunatic is made indebted to his guardian £800. The guardian dies. His executor sues the bailiff of the manor for an account of the profits received whilst the guardian lived.

He demurs, because the account might be demanded by the new guardian or the king, whose Attorney General was no party, and also the former account of £800 might be reexamined; so the defendant was in danger of accounting twice.

[It was] overruled, and [he was] ordered to answer.

549

Howard v. Howard

(Ch. 1673)

Where a woman secretly conveys her property to trustees and then marries a husband who was not aware of the secret trust, the trust will be set aside as fraudulent.

Lord Nottingham, *Prolegomena*, p. 345

28 June 1673, Shaftesbury, Chancellor, and Ellis, Justice.

The Lady Baker treated with Sir Philip Howard about a marriage, but she told him she should have nothing to do with that estate which her former husband left her. Hereupon, the treaty broke off, which she renews again. She undertakes to be worth £10,000 to him, and she marries without her father's consent, pretending it could be best for Sir Philip, lest her father should hold him to hard terms. After the marriage, she procures her father to give her £3000 to clear Sir Philip's estate, which was to be settled in jointure, and prevails with him to seal articles touching her jointure as if nothing had been done already. They live quietly for two or three years, during which time, Sir Philip received the rents of her first jointure, and joined in acquittances etc. Afterwards, they separate, and she sets up a deed concealed, by which all her estate had been conveyed away to trustees two years before her marriage, calls in the old acquittances, and gives new ones in her own name etc.

Sir Philip Howard exhibits a bill to set aside the deed as fraudulent.

And the court decreed against it [the deed], though it was said to be a common practice amongst widows.

2 Chancery Reports 81, 21 E.R. 622

Howard v. Hooker.

The bill is to set aside a deed made by the plaintiff Elizabeth in February 1666, before her marriage with the plaintiff, Sir Philip Howard, and that the plaintiff, Sir Philip, in the right of his said wife, might have all her benefit and interest in or to the estate of Sir John Baker, her former husband, and receive the rents and profits of the premises.

The case being that Sir John Baker, the father, being seised in fee of lands by two deeds tripartite of lease and release made between himself of the one part, Sir Robert Newton, deceased, of the second, and Sir John Baker, the son, and Dame Elizabeth, the plaintiff, and sole daughter of Sir Robert Newton of the third part, in consideration of a marriage between the plaintiff, Dame Elizabeth, and Sir John Baker, the son, and a £4000 portion, conveyed the same to Sir Robert Newton and his heirs, part of which lands were for the said Dame Elizabeth's jointure. And Sir John Baker, the father, and Dame Mary, his wife, being dead, Sir John, the son, sold part of the premises for the payment of debts, part whereof was the jointure of Dame Elizabeth and in consideration of the said Dame Elizabeth's joining in such sale and parting with her jointure, Sir John, her husband, in lieu thereof and of £1500 to be paid to Dame Elizabeth for a jointure house, limited the premises unsold to the said Dame Elizabeth and the defendants for 400 years upon trust, by sale thereof to pay the said Dame Elizabeth the said £1500 and also the rents and profits of the whole until sale, and the residue of the said premises remaining unsold to Dame Elizabeth during her life and, after[wards], to wait on the inheritance. And, in 1658, the inheritance was conveyed to Sir Robert Newton and his heirs. And he, by a will, devised the same to the said Dame Elizabeth for life, remainder to the first son of the plaintiff, Sir Philip, and Dame Elizabeth. So the plaintiff being entitled to the £1500 and the term of 400 years after the trusts performed and so ought, in the right of the said Dame Elizabeth, his lady, to continue in the possession of the premises and receive the rents and profits thereof, which the defendants refused to do, pretending the term of 400 years is limited to them upon other trusts, and, in particular, that the plaintiff Dame Elizabeth, before her marriage to the plaintiff, Sir Philip, by her deed of the 9th of February 1666, assigned to the defendants all monies then due or to be payable to her by virtue of the deed in trust for her benefit and to be at her disposing during the joint lives of her and the said Sir Philip, whether she married or continued sole, and that she should have a power, by a writing under her hand and seal, to dispose thereof for the benefit of her daughter by her former husband, and that she has disposed thereof accordingly, which said deed, the plaintiff insists is fraudulent or with a power of revocation and never mentioned to Sir Philip and that Sir Philip, after his marriage, settled £500 *per annum* on the said Dame Elizabeth for her jointure, which he would not have done if he had known or understood the said Dame Elizabeth had made such a deed or disposition, as aforesaid, of her former husband's estate and, since their marriage, she desired leave of Sir Philip that she might receive the rents and profits of the said lands of her former husband without mentioning the said deed. And, therefore, the same ought to be set aside.

The defendants do insist the said Dame Elizabeth, before her marriage with the said Philip, did declare to him that whoever did marry her should have no benefit of any estate that she had by her former husband and that Sir Philip did agree to bar himself thereof and take no benefit thereby and that, Sir Robert Newton looking upon the estate as settled on his grandchildren, as aforesaid, and had given his personal estate and £700 *per annum* to the plaintiffs and their sons and the said Sir Philip, in all the lifetime of the said Sir Robert Newton, never pretended a right to the said estate or intermeddled therewith, that there is no reason to set aside the said deed of the ninth of February aforesaid.

This court, being assisted with the judges, on reading the said deed, it not appearing unto this court that the said Sir Philip had any notice of the said deed of the 9th of February 1666 until after the death of the said Sir Robert Newton, which was several years after the marriage, nor was privy nor consented to the making of any such deed, but having an intimation that Dame Elizabeth intended to dispose of her interest in her former husband's estate from such husband as she should marry, broke off the treaty of marriage, which was afterwards brought on again by some friends of the said Dame Elizabeth, and that the said Sir Philip was induced to marry the said Dame Elizabeth upon the hopes and confidence of having the interest she had in the estate of the said Sir John Baker, her former husband, without which he would never have married her, and that the said Sir Philip never knew of the said deed of the 9th of February 1666, but the same was a fraud upon Sir Philip, and that, therefore, no use ought to be made thereof, [the court] decreed the said deed of the 9th of February 1666 be absolutely set aside and no use to be made thereof against the said Sir Philip or any claiming under him.

[Other reports of this case: 1 Eq. Cas. Abr. 59, 21 E.R. 872.]
[Reg. Lib. 24 Car. II, f. 587.]

550

Cary v. Williams

(Ch. 1673)

The Statute of Limitations does not apply to accounts among tenants in common.

Lord Nottingham, *Prolegomena*, p. 345

1 July 1673, Cary v. Sir John Williams.

A bill was exhibited by a tenant in common to call his companion to account for the profits received. He pleads the Statute of Limitations.[1] But was overruled, for no [action of] account lies at law and the law raises a mutual trust between them.

551

Levingston's Case

(Ch. 1673)

In a suit for a partition of land, all of the court costs can be taxed against a single party, where that party was very vexatious.

Lord Nottingham, *Prolegomena*, p. 303

2 July 1673, Lord Chancellor.

Where a trial in ejectment was directed by the Chancery in order to ascertain the proportion of twenty tenants in common for a partition to be had in Chancery, judgment was entered and execution was taken against Levingston only for £300 costs, which the Chancellor, on debate, allowed, because Levingston had been very vexatious and greatly misdemeaned himself in the cause.

---

[1] Stat. 21 Jac. I, c. 16 (*SR*, IV, 1222–1223).

552

Duke of Buckingham v. Earl of Shaftesbury

(Ch. 1673)

In this case, a court of equity ordered a trustee who was appointed to pay the settlor's debts to make a release to the other co-trustees in regard to a particular transaction.

Lord Nottingham, *Prolegomena*, p. 266

5 July 1673.

The duke of Buckingham conveys all his estate to the Chancellor, Treasurer, and other great men to pay debts by sale etc. and with a power to make leases. Afterwards, the duke, in his own name and the names of the trustees, makes a lease for forty years of York House at a £1560 rent, with a covenant that, on payment of £30,000 more, they will convey all their estate and interest to Campion, the lessee for forty years. This lease was sealed by the duke and the Lord Treasurer and some others, but not by the Lord Chancellor. The duke and Campion, who had made several underleases to tenants on contracts for new building, exhibit their bill against the Lord Chancellor and all the trustees to enforce them to seal the lease and transfer the trust.

And this cause being heard by the Master of the Rolls [Grimston], Wilde, Justice, and Baron Littleton, it was resolved: first, that, though some of the creditors were made parties to the bill, yet it was not of necessity, because they were no parties to the conveyance, though mentioned in a schedule; second, that the Chancellor should not be compelled to seal the lease, because of the covenants contained in it to convey the inheritance, which was hard, for the covenants could not oblige him, when no inheritance was in him, especially as Campion, the covenantee, was a plaintiff in equity to enforce a transferring of the inheritance; third, the Chancellor should not be obliged to transfer his estate to new trustees and be put to rely upon a decree in Chancery for his indemnity, but should release or assign to the old trustees at the plaintiff's election, which seems hard after a trust accepted, and is not *unum pondus et una mensura*, for I [Finch] was decreed in 1656 to execute a trust for the earl of Dirlton,[1] which I had never accepted, but disclaimed by answer and under hand and seal.

And it is hard to assign a material difference in point of consequence to the trustee between immediate transferring the trust to J.S. and relinquishing to the co-trustees to the intent they may transfer it.

However, it was ordered that the Chancellor should empower the co-trustees by letter of attorney to make use of his name in suing for the arrears, for that cause of action, which was vested in all the trustees, could not be altered by a

[1] *Duchess of Hamilton v. Countess of Dirlton* (1654), 1 Chancery Reports 165, 21 E.R. 539.

release of one co-trustee to the other, but must be prosecuted as it ought to have been if no release had been made.

553

Isaak's Case

(Ch. 1673)

The lower clerks of the Court of Chancery cannot enroll a decree after six months without a motion and order of the court, but this rule does not apply to the Master of the Rolls.

Lord Nottingham, *Prolegomena*, p. 301

7 July 1673.

The printed rule that no decree shall be enrolled after six months without first moving the court was first made in 1652 by the late Commissioners, and continued by My Lord Clarendon. But the same was only intended to bind inferior clerks, whose irregularities may be fit to be examined by the Masters, and it does not bind the Master of the Rolls, who remains trusted as before with the power of enrollment as he sees cause. And he is not to be restrained from enrolling any decrees after the six months, unless there were a particular order in the case to stay the enrollment, for the proceedings of the Master of the Rolls cannot be referred to any inferior Master to examine or judge of.

And accordingly it was held in the Case of Isaak etc., 7 July 1673, at the last seal by SHAFTESBURY, Chancellor, and GRIMSTON, Master of the Rolls, where the enrollment after six months, which had been trifled out by reference, was allowed to stand, being made by the direction of the Master of the Rolls without any motion in court.

554

Morgan v. Butler

(Ch. 1673)

There can be no second bill of review in the same case.

Lord Nottingham, *Prolegomena*, p. 302

7 July 1673, Lady Morgan v. Sir James Butler.

Lady Morgan brings a bill of review to reverse a decree made for Mrs. Moore, devisee and executrix of Sir Anthony Morgan, which was affirmed. Then, she brings a second bill of review on the pretence of new matter discovered since the first bill of review was dismissed.

But it was rejected, for, by the course of the court, new matter may be a ground for the first bill of review and, if it might be so also for the second, bills of review would be infinite.

555

Mole v. Franklyn

(Ch. 1673)

The rights of a junior creditor cannot be defeated by a sale of the land securing his debt by the joint act of the mortgagor and a senior mortgagee.

Lord Nottingham, *Prolegomena*, p. 290

9 July 1673.

The mortgagee for 99 years, together with the mortgagor, for £300 paid to the mortgagee, which was the principal and interest then due, join in an assurance to Franklyn for 99 years without any proviso for a redemption.

It was urged that, now, Franklyn was become a purchaser discharged of all equity of redemption, because the mortgagor, in whom the equity was [vested] and who only had a power to discharge it, joined in the assurance.

But it was decreed [to be] a mortgage transferred in the hands of Franklyn, and not a purchase, for the joining of the mortgagor might be necessary for reducing the principal and interest to a stated debt and the leaving out a condition of redemption might be a blind to protect the estate, and yet the equity remains. But, if it had been a purchase, some part of the money would have been paid to the mortgagor, or there would have been some covenant on his part, which there was not. And, besides, it is not usual to purchase from a mortgagee and a mortgagor no more than the first mortgagee for years had. Also, Franklyn was a brother to the wife of mortgagor, which made all suspicious. Therefore, [it was] decreed *ut supra* that the plaintiff, being a puisne creditor of the mortgagor, should redeem.

[Later proceedings in this case: Repts. *tempore* Finch 51, 23 E.R 27, 73 Selden Soc. 88.]

556

Culpeper v. Austin

(Ch. 1673)

Lis pendens *is legal notice to all subsequent purchasers after a bill be exhibited so as to bind the purchasers to the result of the litigation.*

Lord Nottingham, *Prolegomena*, p. 259

12 July 1673.

H. Culpepper, trustee of Sir Thomas Culpepper to sell land for the payment of debts, was sued by the heir to reconvey, because the trust was performed. And, *pendente lite*, [Culpepper] conveys to Sir Robert Austin.

[It was] resolved: first, *lis pendens* was legal notice to all purchasers; second, if the trustee has not raised enough to pay debts, he may sell, and a purchaser may safely buy notwithstanding the *lis pendens*; third, the Master's report that the trustee has raised enough to pay the debts without a sale does not conclude the purchaser; fourth, a decree against the trustee and all claiming under him since the bill was exhibited had bound the purchaser, nor could he have had relief on any cross-bill without proof of collusion; fifth, the making the purchaser a party to the suit after the account ended did let him in to except to the account, and so hindered the enrolment of the decree pronounced against the trustee and lost the land.

[Later proceedings in this case: 2 Chancery Cases 115, 221, 22 E.R. 873, 919, 1 Eq. Cas. Abr. 272, 21 E.R. 1040, 73 Selden Soc. 443.]

557

Lewis v. Lewis

(Ch. 1673)

In this case, the remainder that was in issue was superseded and revoked by a later gift.

Lord Nottingham, *Prolegomena*, p. 347

25 July 1673.

Dr. William Lewys, Master of St. Cross,[1] makes a lease to Turner for three lives, *viz.* his wife, Alice, his eldest son, Theodore, and one Fielder, but in trust for himself. And, in 1666, by his will in writing, he devises to Alice, whom he made executrix, for life, remainder to Theodore, to be disposed as the Doctor by deed or will shall appoint. In 1667, the Doctor, by a deed, declares the trust to himself for life, remainder to Alice for life, remainder to such as the Doctor, by deed or will, should appoint, and, in default thereof, to his executors. And he dies without making any other will. Alice enters, and claims the whole as executrix.

Theodore sues in equity, and prays a decree for the remainder after her death.

Judge Atkyns thought fit to decree it so.

But the Chancellor, after advice with Wyndham and two others, decreed the contrary, and gave the lease to the executrix, for the declaration in 1667 revoked the will in 1666 as to Theodore, so that, without a new publication, he could not claim by the will, for all the parol discourses proved in favor of Theo-

[1] S. Wright, 'Lewis, William (1591/2–1667)', *Oxford Dictionary of National Biography*, vol. 33, pp. 662–663.

dore were before the declaration which revoked the will and the making Theodore *cestui que vie* was not material.

2 Chancery Reports 77, 21 E.R. 621

A trust of a term was devised to J.S. and then to J.D. to be disposed of as the testator should appoint by his will or writing. He makes a writing, and declares it to himself for life, and, after[wards], to such persons as he should by a will or deed appoint and, for default of that, to his executors, and he made no other will or deed; the executor shall have it.

This is on a case stated, *viz.* that the Lord St. John and his trustees demised a lease on the premises for ninety-nine years unto the defendant Turner, if the plaintiff Alice, then wife of Dr. William Lewis, and Theodore Lewis, son of the said Dr. Lewis, and on Fielder or either of them should so long live. This lease was made at the nomination of and in trust for the said Dr. Lewis. After[wards], in July 1666, the Doctor made his will, and, as to the premises, he devised them to the said Alice for life and, after her death, then to the said Theodore Lewis to be disposed of as the said Doctor shall appoint them by his will in writing or deed. And, of his will, he made the said Alice his executrix. In March 1667 by a declaration in writing, to which the said Doctor and the defendant Turner are parties and executed by them both, the trust of the premises was thus declared, *viz.* for the said Doctor for life, afterwards, for such person or persons as the said Doctor, by his will or deed, should appoint, and, in default, then, for the executors or administrators of the said Doctor. In July 1667, the Doctor died without making any other will or deed or other appointment for the disposing of the premises. Alice, by virtue of the said will and deed, entered and possessed the premises.

It appears also in the case some proof was offered touching a parol declaration of the said Dr. Lewis's intention, that his son Theodore should have the benefit of the said lease. But that being by parol against a declaration in writing, the court conceived it not material in the case. And it is also in the case that the said Theodore claims so much of the term as should be behind at the death of the said Alice and that the said Alice claims the whole term as executrix to the said Dr. Lewis.

The court, at the first hearing, was assisted with Mr. Justice Atkyns, who inclined to be of opinion for the said Theodore and that the said defendant Turner, the trustee, ought to execute the trust for him.

But His Lordship [Lord Shaftesbury] differing in opinion and having since advised upon the case with Mr. Justice Wyndham and several other of the judges, who were all clear of opinion that, according to the declaration in writing, the plaintiff Alice, the executrix, is well entitled to the benefit of the said lease.

This court, therefore, does decree that Turner, the trustee, do execute the trust and convey and assign the said lease and the remainder of the term therein to the plaintiff Alice or to whom she shall appoint.

[Reg. Lib. 24 Car. II, f. 664.]

558

Anonymous

(Ch. 1673)

A devise to surviving siblings does not include a deceased sibling's issue.

1 Freeman 301, 89 E.R. 219, 22 E.R. 1223

Michaelmas [term] 1673.

A. has three daughters, and he devises them £300 apiece to be paid at the age of twenty-one years or day of marriage, which should first happen, and, if either of them should die before the said times, then her portion was to be equally divided between the survivors. The eldest marries, and has her portion, and dies, leaving issue. The youngest dies before she either is married or attains the said age of twenty-one. The second survives.

The question was whether the second, surviving, should have all the portion of the youngest or whether the children of the eldest should have a share.

[It was] resolved by ELLIS, WYNDHAM, and Lord Chancellor [LORD SHAFTESBURY] that the second sister should have the whole, and, though it was objected that the words 'equally to be divided' did imply that they should be sharers, yet that is to be understood *reddendo singula singulis* in case two of them had survived.

559

Bowman v. Trim

(Ch. 1673)

To take a bond to secure a payment is to receive the payment. Such a bond taken by an administrator of a decedent's estate is an asset of the estate.

Proof made of a plea of plene administravit *is binding in a suit in equity.*

Lord Nottingham, *Prolegomena*, p. 348

10 October 1673.

Campian is indebted to the estate of Rogers, his partner. Rogers is indebted to Bowman, and he dies. The executrix of Rogers takes a bond from Campian to pay what is due to Rogers's estate. And he has a promise from Bowman to pay what Campian should have paid if Campian fail. The executrix sues Bowman on the promise, and has a verdict for £271.

Bowman exhibits a bill against the executrix to have the money recovered against him on the promise discounted out of the money due to him from the estate of Rogers, supposing that the money recovered came in lieu of what Campian should have paid to Rogers's estate, and, therefore, ought to be assets in equity, the rather because the executrix to Bowman's suit at law pleaded fully administered and was now married to Trim, an insolvent person.

But the bill was dismissed, for, first, when the executrix took the bond from Campian, that was all one as a payment by Campian, and was in law as assets received by the executrix, whether Campian ever paid the money or no; second, the money recovered on the promise was not recovered as executrix, nor could she declare upon it as executrix; so it could not be assets at law; third, [there is] no reason to make it assets in equity to help a plaintiff to make a stoppage or recoup, which is not allowed in equity; fourth, if the executrix can prove [the plea of] fully administered at law, [there is] no reason to charge her in equity.

560

Smith v. Hanbury

(Ch. 1673)

The widow of a mortgagee in fee has a dower right in the land at common law.

The money received by a doweress of a mortgagee in fee in possession does not go to discharge the debt of the mortgagor.

Lord Nottingham, *Prolegomena*, p. 349

16 October 1673, by Judge Ellis.

A mortgagee in fee takes a wife, and dies. The wife recovers dower against the heir of the mortgagee. Then, the heir of the mortgagor sues for a redemption, and an account is decreed. But the plaintiff refused to allow on account the profits which were recovered and received by the tenant in dower, because, in equity, there ought to be no dower of an estate in mortgage.

This is generally true. But, here, the heir of the mortgagee had no pretence either in law or in equity to bar dower, though the heir of the mortgagor might have had a bill to stay the suit. Therefore, his negligence, though an infant, shall not be prejudicial to the mortgagee, but he shall be allowed the dower in an account, and the mortgagor left to his remedy in equity against the executrix of the tenant in dower.

Nelson 70, 21 E.R. 792

The plaintiff brought the equity of redemption of a mortgage in.

And, upon an account directed to be taken of the profits under the mortgage, it was decreed that the Master should examine whether the wife of the mortgagee recovered her dower out of the lands, it being a mortgage in fee and her husband died seised and what satisfaction was made for her dower.

And the Master certified that the wife had recovered her dower and that it was set out by the sheriff.

And the question was whether it should go towards satisfaction of the mortgage.

And it was ruled it should not.

3 Chancery Reports 82, 21 E.R. 735

16 October 1673. Justice Ellis.

The plaintiff bought the equity of redemption of a mortgage in fee. And, upon an account directed of profits taken under the mortgage, by an order on a hearing, 26 November 1670, it was also ordered that the Master examine whether the wife of the mortgagee did recover dower out of the premises and what satisfaction was made for that dower and certify how he finds the same.

The Master stated the matter specially that the wife recovered dower and it was paid, the sheriff having set it out.

And, then, the question was whether this should go to discharge the mortgage. And she having recovered by law and received it without opposition of the mortgagor or his heirs, it was ruled that it should not go towards a discharge of the mortgage, though the heir of the mortgagee did not prevent her dower.

And it was said that the heir of the mortgagor might recover it of the doweress. But *quaere* whether the Statute[1] bars it or not.

But note, in this case, she was a party to the bill, but not brought to the hearing.

561

Needham v. Leicester

(Ch. 1673–1674)

Money in trust to raise marriage portions if the beneficiary marry with consent is payable to an unmarried beneficiary at the age of majority if security be given to marry only with consent.

Lord Nottingham, *Prolegomena*, p. 349

16 October 1673. Mary and Elizabeth Needham, daughters of Lord Viscount Kilmurrey v. Sir Peter Leicester and others, trustees.

[1] Note Stat. 4 Will. & Mar., c. 16, s. 4 (*SR*, VI, 405).

A conveyance is made to trustees for thirty-one years for raising portions for daughters of £1500 apiece to be paid at their marriages with the consent of the trustees or the major part of them and, in the interim, to have a maintenance with a proviso that, when they marry or the portions be raised, then the yearly maintenance to cease and they to have the interest of their portions for their maintenance, provided also that she who marries without consent in writing shall have only £100 and the residue of her portion to be employed for the use of younger children. The portions are raised. The daughters are thirty years old and unmarried, and exhibit a bill to have their portions, intending to buy annuities.

And it was urged: first, if any daughter die unmarried, her portion shall go to her executors, which was agreed, and it had been so decreed in this very case in Chester after the death of a sister; second, that this proviso was only *in terrorem*, the conveyance being made in December 1652, when the daughters were very young, and not intended to last after they were so far advanced in years, but this was denied by Judge Ellis, who held the restraint to continue, and so it was formerly held by Orlando Bridgeman, Keeper, who offered to decree for a plaintiff on a security given not to marry without consent; third, it being now moved again and pressed hard for the plaintiff, at last, it fell off, because the younger children in the remainder of the portions were not parties.

Afterwards, on 1 May 1674, I [Lord Nottingham] decreed for the plaintiffs on a security *prout*.

562

Doyly v. Persall

(Ch. 1673)

A trust created before marriage for the sole benefit of a wife cannot be touched by her husband or anyone claiming under him.

A trust created after the marriage by the husband for his wife is voluntary and fraudulent against purchasers.

1 Chancery Cases 225, 22 E.R. 773

25 October [1673]. Doyly v. Perfull.

The wife having assigned her term in trust for herself before marriage and, then, the husband without joining with the trustees does mortgage the trust. And the husband being dead, the mortgagee, being the plaintiff, exhibits his bill to have the lands conveyed to him or that they should redeem.

And the court dismissed the plaintiff's bill, for, since Queen Elizabeth's time, it has been the constant course of this court to set aside and frustrate all encumbrances and acts of the husband upon the trust in the wife's term and that he shall neither charge nor grant it away. And it is the common way of proceeding for the jointures of women to convey a term in trust for them upon marriage that it may be out of the power and reach of the husband. Neither shall he forfeit it by outlawry or felony if, for jointure or in pursuance of articles of marriage or being the wife's term, it is assigned before in trust, as here, or if, on other good consideration, it be assigned. But, if it be an assignment after marriage by the husband in trust for the wife, this is voluntary and fraudulent against purchasers. And this was the great Exchequer Chamber Case.[1]

2 Freeman 138, 22 E.R. 1113

The wife assigned her term in trust for herself before marriage, and then the husband, without joining the trustees, mortgaged the trust. The husband being dead, the mortgagee exhibited his bill to have the land either conveyed to him or that they should redeem.

The court dismissed the plaintiff's bill, for, since Queen Elizabeth's time, it has been the constant practice of this court to set aside and frustrate all encumbrances and acts of the husband upon the trust of the wife's term and that he shall neither charge nor grant it away. And it is the common way of providing jointures, for a woman to convey a term in trust for her upon marriage that it may be out of the power and reach of the husband. Neither shall he forfeit it by outlawry or felony if, for a jointure or in pursuance of articles of marriage or being the wife's term, it is assigned before in trust or if, on other good consideration, it be assigned. 1 Inst. 351.[2] But if it be an assignment after marriage by the husband in trust for the wife, that is voluntary and fraudulent against a purchaser. And thus was the great Exchequer Chamber Case.

[Other reports of this case: 1 Eq. Cas. Abr. 57, 21 E.R. 871, 73 Selden Soc. 29.]

563

Tilney v. Price

(Ch. 1673)

The question in this case was whether a debtor, suggesting the bankruptcy of his creditor, can demand security for repayment before paying his debt in case the creditor be adjudicated a bankrupt.

Lord Nottingham, *Prolegomena*, p. 350

27 October 1673.

[1] Perhaps *Attorney General v. Sandys* (Ex. 1666–1669), Hardres 405, 488, 145 E.R. 520, 561, 2 Freeman 129, 22 E.R. 1106, 3 Chancery Reports 33, 21 E.R. 720, Nelson 130, 21 E.R. 808, 1 Siderfin 403, 82 E.R. 1182, Equity Cases Exch. 11, Exch. Repts. *tempore* Car. II, 151.

[2] E. Coke, *First Institute* (1628), f. 351.

A man is sued at law for a debt, and he exhibits a bill in equity, suggesting that he knew of a secret act of bankruptcy committed by the plaintiff at law and, therefore, cannot safely pay him his debt without security to save him harmless against the commission of bankruptcy which may issue. And he had relief.

Mirum, quia videtur, if a bankrupt recovers a debt without collusion, this may be safely paid. *Secus* of a voluntary payment. Also this is a way to scandalize any man, unless the plaintiff offer to swear to his bill.

564

Dethick v. Banks

(Ch. 1673–1674)

A freeman of London can make an inter vivos *assignment of a partnership to a son.*

2 Chancery Reports 92, 21 E.R. 625

A freeman of London did assign over an adventure to the defendant, his son, against which the plaintiff complains, and insists it is contrary to the custom of London and tends to defeat the plaintiff's wife of a full third part of the personal estate.

This court, with the judges, held the disposition to be good, and could not relieve the plaintiff.

[Later proceedings in this case: Repts. *tempore* Finch 16, 23 E.R. 9, 73 Selden Soc. 18, 19.]
[Reg. Lib. 25 Car. II, f. 143.]

565

Harmer v. Brooke

(Ch. 1673–1674)

In this case, the court of equity enforced specifically the terms of a marriage settlement against the obligor's estate.

2 Chancery Reports 92, 21 E.R. 625

The bill is to have an execution of a marriage agreement. The plaintiff, Harmer, with the encouragement of Thomas Hamling, was to marry the plaintiff Elizabeth, the only daughter and heir of the said Thomas Hamling, the plaintiff, Harmer, being a man of a great trade. And, in consideration thereof, the said Thomas Hamling was to pay to the plaintiff Harmer £500 at Christmas following and to settle on the plaintiff and his heirs a house in Sussex and, at his death, to give to the plaintiff Elizabeth, his daughter, all his estate, real and personal, except £400, which he intended to the defendant, his brother's son. Whereupon, the plaintiff, Harmer, married the said Elizabeth. But, now, the said Thomas Hamling, the plaintiff's father, refuses to perform his agreement and promise aforesaid, the plaintiff marrying without his consent and liking, as is pretended. And he died without performance thereof. And he made a will, and the defendant his executor, which will, the plaintiff insists was voluntary and ought in equity to be set aside, the plaintiff being disinherited thereby. And to have the said marriage agreement performed is the plaintiff's bill.

The defendant insists that the said marriage was had by surprise and without the consent of the said Thomas, the father, and that he did never approve of it, but, when he was told of it, he was in a great passion, and said his daughter was undone, and then he made his will in these words, *viz.*:

I give and bequeath unto Elizabeth, my only daughter, lately married against my consent and good liking to Francis Harmer, the sum of £20, over and above the sum of £500 which I intend to pay her myself in full for her portion.

And the said Thomas, the father, being afterwards moved to alter his said will, declared he would not alter the same and that he would not be a precedent to disobedient children. And the defendant claims the said estate, real and personal, by virtue of the said will.

This court ordered it to be tried at law whether Thomas, the father, did agree to give the plaintiff Francis Harmer with the said Elizabeth any other or further estate, real or personal, at any time over and besides the said £500.

A verdict passed for the plaintiff that Thomas, the father, did agree to give the plaintiff Francis Harmer with the said Elizabeth a further estate, real and personal, besides the £500.

This court was satisfied there was such a marriage agreement and that the same ought to be made good, and decreed accordingly.

[Reg. Lib. 25 Car. II, f. 648.]

566

Tregonwell v. Lawrence

(Ch. 1673–1674)

A court of equity can enjoin a life tenant from committing waste.

2 Chancery Reports 94, 21 E.R. 626

The bill is to restrain the defendant, being a tenant for life, from plowing up or converting into tillage pasture ground to the damage of the plaintiff's inheritance.

The defendant insisted that the said land was very full of bushes and furze and that the plowing and burnbeating was an improvement of it.

The plaintiff insisted that the lands are sheeps strete or sheeps slight, the surface or soil being so thin, that, if the same be plowed up two years together, the lands will yield no profit in many years after.

This court, on reading an order 20th February 25 Car. II [1673] and a certificate of referees, does decree that a perpetual injunction be awarded to restrain the defendant from plowing up or burnbeating of the said lands above two years.

73 Selden Soc. 58

The burnbeating of pasture in Dorsetshire was allowed for two years upon a country certificate. But it was restrained after, as tending to waste by decree.

[Reg. Lib. 25 Car. II, f. 582.]

567

Sutton v. Jewke

(Ch. 1673–1674)

A condition to marry with consent is valid and enforceable.

2 Chancery Reports 95, 21 E.R. 626

£1500 was to be put out at interest for the use and benefit of the plaintiff Anne, and, then, the said £1500 and the proceed thereof were to be paid her at her age of twenty-one or marriage, but, if the plaintiff Anne should marry without the consent of the defendant Jewke and his wife, being her father and mother, or one of them or the survivor of them, then, £500 part of the said £1500 was to be paid to such person as the defendant Jewke's wife, by a writing under her hand and without her husband, should appoint.

The said defendant Jewke's wife died in 1668 without making any appointment, so that the plaintiff Anne is thereupon become entitled to the whole £1500 and the proceeds thereof. The plaintiff Anne married in 1671, and this suit is to be relieved for the £1500 and interest.

The defendant Jewke insists that Mary, his wife, died in 1670, but, before her death, in 1696, by a deed parol, directed that, in case the plaintiff Anne married without the consent of her, the said Mary, or the defendant Jewke, her husband, then £500 part of the said £1500 was to be paid to her and the defendant or the survivor of them and that the said deed was made upon mature deliberation to keep the said plaintiff in due obedience and that, the plaintiff Sutton having in a clandestine manner married with the plaintiff Anne without the defendant Jewke's privity or consent and after he had forbidden his daughter to marry with him on the forfeiture of his blessing or what otherwise she might expect from him, the said defendant Jewke, by means thereof and by being administrator to his late wife, became entitled to £500 part of the said £1500.

So the chief point now controverted is whether the plaintiff Anne be entitled to the whole £1500 or whether she had not forfeited £500 thereof by her marriage without her father's consent and privity and contrary to his direction and advice.

His Lordship was fully satisfied that the plaintiff's said marriage was without the defendant's privity and against his consent and that, therefore, the plaintiff Anne cannot have the said £500, but he decreed the defendant to have the same with interest from the plaintiff's marriage.

[Reg. Lib. 25 Car. II, f. 178.]
[Later proceedings in this case: 73 Selden Soc. 49.]

Index of Names of Persons and Places

[These references are to case numbers, not page numbers.]

Subject Index

[These references are to case numbers, not page numbers.]